THE CASSELL FOOD DICTIONARY

THE CASSELL FOOD DICTIONARY

Sonia Allison

CASSELL

Cassell Publishers Limited
Villiers House, 41/47 Strand, London WC2N 5JE, England

First published 1990

British Library Cataloguing in Publication Data
Allison, Sonia
The Cassell food dictionary
1. Food
I. Title
641.3
ISBN 0-304-31875-2

Database processing and typesetting by Media Conversion Ltd, Ruislip
Printed and bound in Great Britain by Mackays of Chatham PLC

Contents

The dictionary is dedicated to my husband, Norman, for his devoted research and for being my most trusted and dearest friend.

List of Illustrations

Preface

Do you know what to do with a bath chap, how to handle a prickly pear, or coddle an egg? Is caproic acid related to the goat, aji-no-moto a make of car, Ayrshire roll a Highland game? Is teisen lap something to sit on, dolcelatte an Alpine resort and stickjaw a medical phenomenon? *The Cassell Food Dictionary*, with its six thousand and more entries, will give you the answers to these and countless other food and cooking queries that crop up time and time again, especially now when we are bombarded with exotic foods from far and wide and confronted with culinary terms and idioms that were unheard of even a decade ago.

One of my friends, hearing of my venture into the world of definitions, claimed my sole purpose for even considering a book of this magnitude was to help crossword buffs find solutions to 9 Across or 24 Down. Wrong. The dictionary was written as a means of self-defence, a way of helping me to sort out cooking queries with speed, to satisfy my own curiosity without wading through endless books to find a simple answer to a basic question, and then to pass on my findings to others in as concise a way as possible.

It all started in a supermarket. There was I, in the South of France, examining some spindly green asparagus, when this Englishman came over and asked me how to cook it. I explained at length, he listened intently, then toddled off, to surprise his wife in their self-catering apartment. Nearer home, in Watford to be precise, the same thing happened but this time it was over virgin olive oil, passion fruit, pumpkin, kumquats, pheasant and fromage frais. Clusters of us formed discussion groups and there, in one of the aisles of Sainsbury or Waitrose or Tesco or Gateway, this dictionary was conceived.

Friends, family and even colleagues had questions of their own and turned to me for answers. Not great intellectual diatribes, you understand, but easy-to-follow definitions for the likes of you and me — ordinary cooks with a bit of knowledge who wanted basic information without boredom.

Research and writing the dictionary meant two and a half years of hard, unswerving graft. It took over my life, and my husband's. We lived on microwave meals and fish and chips day after day. We spent hours in libraries, months travelling to authenticate information and more hours than I can even remember going over facts and Latin names to minimize mistakes.

For me, it was a culinary crash course like no other and I am greatly indebted to the powers that be at Cassell for taking the dictionary on board and giving me the opportunity to share my experiences with those of you out there who are foodies in the broadest sense of the word.

Especial thanks to my publisher, Steve Cook, for his cheerfulness, encouragement, support and good humour. I am also grateful to Alison Leach, the copy-editor, for her courage in the face of unpredictable problems, spelling mistakes, idiosyncratic terminology (sometimes) and all the hassles which inevitably arise when tackling any kind of specialist reference book.

Sonia Allison
Watford 1990

Guide to the Use of the Dictionary

The main body of the work functions in the same way as any other dictionary, with entries appearing in alphabetical order. Each entry is defined and any variant terms are listed. On occasion the reader is referred to another entry for a full definition.

For ease of use and maximum clarity of text, other cross-references have been separated to form an Index, which appears after the main A-Z entries.

An additional point of entry is provided by the Thematic Index, which follows.

Thematic Index

Most of the headwords which are defined in the Dictionary of Food are listed here under subject headings. The thematic index, therefore, enables you to follow a particular food theme with the minimum of difficulty. For example, if you have a particular penchant for nuts you will find under this subject heading an alphabetical list of all headwords which pertain to that area of cuisine in the Dictionary.

An additional list groups headwords which relate to a particular national or regional cuisine.

Acids and Alkalis
Acetic Acid, Acids, Alegar, Alkalis, Alkaloid, Baking Powder, Baking Soda, Bicarbonate of Soda, Butyric Acid, Capric Acid, Caproic Acid, Caprylic Acid, Cider Vinegar, Citric Acid, Cream of Tartar, Hydrochloric Acid, Lactic Acid, Lemon Juice, Malic Acid, Malt Vinegar, Nicotinic Acid, Oleic Acid, Oxalic Acid, Palmitic Acid, Quinine, Rice Vinegar, Salicylic Acid, Stearic Acid, Tarragon Vinegar, Tartaric Acid, Vinegar, White Distilled Vinegar, Wine Vinegar

Additives
Additive, Aji-no-moto, Anti-oxidant, Artificial Sweeteners, Azo Dyes, Bleaching Agents, Caramel, Carmine, Chlorine, Cochineal, E Numbers, Emulsifiers, Food Colourings, Monosodium Glutamate, Potassium Bromate, Preservative, Stabilizers, Tartrazine, Thickeners

American Cooking Terms
All-purpose Flour, Alpino, Bacon Strip, Biscuit, Broiler, Broiling, Brunch, Candy, Catsup, Charqui, Chevron, Chips, Cold Cuts, Confectioner's Sugar, Cook Out, Corn Syrup, Cornstarch, Cotto, Deli, Donut, Doughboys, Drawn Butter, Dressing, Eggplant, Endive, Filé Powder, Filet Mignon, Fish Sticks, Flapjack, Fortune Cookie, Frank, French Fries, Frizzes, Frost (to), Fruit Streusel, Fryer, Graham Cracker, Graham Flour, Gumbo Filé, Half-and-Half, Hard Sauce, Heavy Cream, Hickory, Hot Biscuit, Indian Corn, Indian Rice, Jelly, Jelly Roll, Jerked Beef, Lebanon Bologna, Light Corn Syrup, Light Cream, Link Sausages, Molasses, Muffins, Mush, Pit, Planked, Popovers, Relish, Scallion, Shake, Shortening, Shuck, Skillet, Squab, Submarine, Summer Sausage, Sunny Side Up, Tangelo, Variety Meats, Vienna Sausage, Wiener

Bacon and Ham
Ayrshire Cure, Ayrshire Gigot, Ayrshire Roll, Back Bacon, Bacon, Bacon Butt, Bacon Collar, Bacon Fore Slipper, Bacon Forehock, Bacon Hock (Small), Bacon Rasher, Baconer, Canadian-style Bacon, Corner Gammon, Cumberland Ham, Dunmow Flitch, Gammon, Gammon Hock, Gammon Slipper, Gammon Steaks, Green Bacon, Griskin, Ham, Honey-roast Ham, Jambon Cuit de Prague, Jambon de Paris, Jambon Persillé, Long Back Bacon, Middle Bacon, Middle Gammon, Mild Cure Bacon, Old-Smokey Ham, Oyster Bacon, Pale Bacon, Plain Bacon, Prague Ham, Quick Cure (of Bacon), Rasher, Smithfield Ham, Smoked Bacon, Spencer, Streaky Bacon, Suffolk Ham, Sweet Cure Bacon, Tender Cure Bacon, Throughcut Bacon, Ulster Roll, Virginia Ham, Virginia-style Ham, Westphalian Ham, Whole Gammon, Wiltshire Cure (of Bacon)

Batters
Austrian 'Pancakes', Baked Batter Pudding, Batters, Beignets, Coating Batter, Crêpes, Dropped Scones, Flapjack Scones, French Fritters or Puffs, Fritter Batter, Fritters, Galette, Griddle Cakes, Pancakes, Pouring Batter, Pfannkuchen, Salzburger Nockerln, Scotch Pancakes, Waffles, Yorkshire Pudding

Biscuits

Abernethy Biscuits, Almond Macaroons, Amaretti, Bath Oliver Biscuits, Biscotte, Biscuits, Bourbon Biscuits, Brandy Snaps, Bretzels, Cats' Tongues, Coconut Pyramids, Cornish Fairings, Crackers, Cream Crackers, Crispbread, Digestive Biscuits, Flapjack, Florentines, Garibaldi Biscuits, Ginger Nuts, Ginger Snaps, Grasmere Shortbread, Ischler Biscuits, Janhagel, Jumbles, Ladyfingers, Langues de Chat, Macaroons, Melting Moments, Napoleon Biscuits, Oatcakes, Petticoat Tails, Pretzels, Ratafias, Refrigerator Biscuits, Sablé Biscuits, Salt Sticks, Saltine Biscuits, Sand Biscuits, Savoy Biscuits, Scottish Shortbread, Sedgemoor Easter 'Cakes', Shortbread, Shortbread Biscuits, Shrewsbury Biscuits, Shrewsbury Eastertide Biscuits, Sponge Finger Biscuits, Spritz Biscuits, Tuiles, Wafer Biscuits, Wafers

Breads and Yeasted Goods

Anadama Bread, Bagels, Baguette, Baker's Yeast, Bap Loaves, Bap Rolls, Bara Brith, Barrel Bread, Batch Loaves, Bath Buns, Bienenstich, Black Bread, Bloomer Loaf, Boston Brown Bread, Bread, Breadcrumbs, Breadstuffs, Bridge Rolls, Brioche Loaf, Brioches, Brown Bread, Bun Loaf, Buns, Challah, Chapatis, Chelsea Buns, Cob, Coburg Loaf, Coffee Cake, Cookie, Corn Bread, Cornish Saffron Cake, Cornish Splits, Cottage Loaf, Croissants, Crumbs, Crumpets, Damper, Dough, Doughnuts, Dried Yeast, Enriched Bread, Farmhouse Loaf, French Bread, French Stick, French Toast, Fruit Bread, Germ Bread, Graham Rusks, Granary Bread, Grissini, Gugelhupf, Hamburger Buns, Hot Cross Buns, Hotel Rolls, Irish Soda Bread, Italian Bread Sticks, Johnnycake, Lardy Cake, Limpa Bread, Linseed Bread, Loaf, Malt Bread, Melba Toast, Milk Bread, Milk Loaf, Mohnkuchen, Muffins, Naan, Pain Perdu, Pandoro, Paratha, Pikelets, Pitta Bread, Pizza, Pizza Base, Poor Knights of Windsor, Pumpernickel, Ring Doughnuts, Rolls, Rum Babas, Rusks, Rye Loaf, Saffransbröd, Sally Lunn, Savarin, Sippet, Soda Bread, Sour Dough, Split Tin Loaf, Streusel Cake, Swiss Buns, Teabread, Toast, Vienna Bread, White Bread, Yeast, Yeasted Goods

Cakes

Almond Slice, American Fudge Cake, Angel Food Cake, Apple Cake, Applesauce Cake, Bakewell Tart, Baklava, Banbury Cakes, Bannock, Barm Brack, Battenberg Cake, Birthday Cake, Black Forest Cherry Cake, Boston Cream Pie, Bûche de Noël, Butterfly Cakes, Cake Mixes, Cakes, Carrot Cake, Cheesecake, Cherry Cake, Chiffon Cake, Chilled Cheesecake, Chocolate Cake, Chocolate Log, Christening Cake, Christmas Cake, Coffee Kisses, College Cake, Cornish Heavy Cake, Cornish Sly Cakes, Coventry Cakes, Creamed Cakes, Croquembouche, Cup Cakes, Cut-and-come-again Cake, Dacquoise, Devil's Food Cake, Dobostorte, Dough Cake, Dresdener Christollen, Dripping Cake, Dundee Cake, Eccles Cakes, Fadge, Fairy Cakes, Farl, Fatless Sponge, Fortunés, Frangipane Tart, Fruit Cake, Fudge Cake, Gâteau, Gâteau Saint-Honoré, Genoese Cake, Gingerbread, Gypsy's Arm, Heavy Cake, Iced Fancies, Irish Potato Cakes, Jalousie, Jam Tart, Lady Baltimore Cake, Lancashire Parkin, Lardy Cake, Lekach, Linzertorte, Madeira Cake, Madeleines, Maids of Honour, Malakofftorte, Manju, Melted Cakes, Norfolk Apple Cake, Nusstorte, Pain d'Épice, Panforte, Pannetone, Paradise Cake, Paris-Brest, Parkin, Pitcaithly Bannock, Plain Cakes, Plava, Pound Cake, Quatre-quarts Cake, Queen Cakes, Quick-mix Cakes, Rich Cakes, Rock Cakes, Ruladă de Nuci, Sachertorte, Saffron Cake, Sand Cake, Seed Cake, Simnel Cake, Singin' Hinnies, Sly Cakes, Soda Cake, Spice Bread, Sponge Cake, Sponge Flan, Sponge Sandwich, Stollen, Strawberry Shortcake, Swiss Roll, Teisen Lap, Torte, Twelfth Night Cake, Upside-down Cake, Vacherin, Victoria Sandwich, Wedding Cake,

Welsh Cakes, Whisked Cakes, Yorkshire Parkin, Yorkshire Spice Bread, Yule Log

Cheese

Abbeydale, Achiote, Ädelost, Akureyri, Allgäu Emmental, Alp Cheese, Altaiski, Altenburger, American, American Blue, American Pasteurized, Anari, Añejo, Annatto, Appenzell, Applewood, Aralar, Argentinian Quartirolo, Asadero, Asiago, Ayrshire Cream, Azietão, Baby Bel, Baker's, Bandal, Barbarossa, Barie, Bashan, Bavariablu, Beaufort, Bel Paese, Bellelay, Berg, Biarom, Billinge, Black Crowdie, Blanco, Blarney, Bleu d'Auvergne, Blue, Blue Cheshire, Blue Tendale Cheese, Blue Vinny, Blue Wensleydale, Boerenkaas, Bonbel, Bondail, Bondon, Boulette, Boursin, Braid Cheese, Brandza de Burdouf, Brat, Braudost, Bresse Bleu, Brick, Brie, Brie de Coulommiers, Brie de Meaux, Brie de Melun, Brillat-Savarin, Brin d'Amour, Briquette, Broccio, Brood, Brousse-du-Rôve, Brynza, Buost, Burgos, Burmeister, Burrini, Butterkäse, Buttermilk Quark, Cabécou, Caboc, Cabrales, Cabreiro, Cachet, Caciocavallo, Caciofiore, Caciotta, Caerphilly, Caillebotte, Caithness, Camargue, Cambridge Cheese, Camembert, Camembert de Normandie, Camosun, Canadian Cheddar, Canestrato, Cantal, Cantalon, Caprice des Dieux, Carré-de-Bray, Carré-de-l'Est, Cassette, Castelo Branco, Castle Cheese, Cebrero, Cendré, Certosa, Chabichou, Chambarand, Chamberat, Chambourcy, Chantelle, Charnwood, Charolais, Charouce, Chateaubriand Cheese, Cheddar, Cheddar 'n' Scotch, Cheedham, Cheese, Cheese Dye, Cheese Layer Cake, Cheese Production, Cheese Spread, Cheshire, Cheviot, Chèvre, Chevru, Chezzarella Cheese, Chhana, Cincho, Coeur, Colbi, Colby, Colwick, Comté, 'Cooked' Cheese, Coon, Cornhusker, Cornish Pepper, Cornish Yarg, Cotherstone, Cotswold, Cottage Cheese, Coulommiers, Cream Cheese, Crema Bel Paese, Cremet Nantais, Creole, Crescenza, Crottin de Chavignol, Crowdie, Crowley, Cuajada, Cumin Gouda, Curd Cheese, Curworthy, Dacca, Dalia, Danbo, Danish Blue, Danish Blue Brie, Danish Blue Crème, Danish Mellow Blue, Dauphin, Delice de Saint-Cyr, Demi-Camembert, Demi-Sel, Derby, Dessertnyī-Belyī, Devon Garland, Dobrogea, Dolcelatte, Dorobouski, Dorset Blue Vinny, Double Cream Cheese, Double Gloucester, Dry Jack, Dunlop, Duo, Echourgnac, Edam, Edamer, Edelpilzkäse, Ein Gedi, Elbo, Elmo Cheese, Emek, Emmental, Enchilado, Entrammes, Eskdale, Esrom, Estonski, Évora, Excelsior, Explorateur, Farmers', Farmhouse English Cheddar, Fermier, Feta, Fin de Siècle, Fiore Sardo, Fjordland, Fleur de Maquis, Fondu au Marc, Fontainebleau, Fontal, Fontina, Formagelle, Formaggio, Fourme d'Ambert, Fourme de Cantal, Fourme de Laguiole, Frais, French Fondu, Fresh Cheese, Friese Kanterkaas, Frisch, Fromage, Fromage Affiné, Fromage Blanc, Fromage de Bruxelles, Fromage Fort, Fromage Frais, Fromage-de-Trappiste, Fromez, Frühstückskäse, Full-fat Soft Cheese, Fynbo, Gad, Galic, Galil, Gálit, Gammelost, Gamonedo, Gapron, Gaucho, Geheimrats, Gerardmer, Gérômé, Gérômé Anise, Getmesost, Gien, Gigha, Gilboa, Gilead, Gjetost, Glärnerkäse, Goats' Milk, Golan, Gold 'n' Rich, Gomolya, Gorgonzola, Gornoaltaysky, Gouda, Gournay, Goya, Graçay, Gradaost, Grana, Grape Cheese, Graviera, Graz, Grazalema, Green Cheese, Grevé, Grièges, Gruth Dhu, Gruyère, Gush Halav, Güssing, Hajdú, Haloumi, Hand, Harduf, Harz, Havarti, Haymaking Cheese, Herkimer, Herrgårdsost, Herve, Highland Choice, Highland Herbs, High-moisture Jack, Hokkaido, Homolky, Howgate, Hramsa, Huntsman, Hushållsost, Idiazábal, Ilha, Incanestrato, Irish Swiss Cheese, Islay, Jarlsberg, Jbane, Jochburg, Juhla, Juustoleipä, Kaggost, Kanter, Kartano, Käse, Kaseri, Kashkaval, Kefalotir, Kefalotiri, Kernhem, Kesti, Killarney, Knaost, Kol-Bee, Kopanisti, Kostromskoī, Kräutekäse, Kreivi, Kryddost, Kwark,

Labna, Ladies' Cheese, Laguiole, Lancashire, Langskaill, Latviiski, Laughing Cow, Le Moine, Leiden, Leipajuusto, Liederkranz, Limburger, Liptauer Cheese Spread, Liptó, Livarot, Loaf Cheese, Lorraine, Lothian, Low-fat Quark, Low-fat Soft Cheese, Luostari, Lymeswold, Maasdam, Macquée, Mahón, Maigrelet, Mainz, Málaga, Mamsell Babette, Manchego, Manoori, Manur, Maredsous, Maribo, Marienhofer, Maroilles, Mascarpone, Mature Gouda, Mecklenburg, Medium-fat Quark, Medium-fat Soft Cheese, Melbury, Mesost, Mi-Chèvre, Mimolette, Minas, Minnesota Slim, Mischling, Mizithra, Molbo, Monastery, Mondseer, Monsieur, Montasio, Monterey Jack, Montrachet, Moravský Bochnik, Morón, Morven, Moskovski, Motal, Mountain Cheese, Mousetrap, Mozzarella, Mozzarella Affumicata, Munnajuusto, Munster, Münster, Mycella Blue, Mysost, Mysuost, Na'ama, Nagelkaas, Neufchâtel, New Cheese, Niolo, Niva, Nokkel, Norbo, Norwegian Whey, Nutcracker, Odalsost, Oelenberg, Oka, Old Heidelberg, Olenda, Olmützer, Olomouc, Orkney, Óvár, Ovoli, Oxford, Pannarone, Parenyica, Parmesan, Parmigiano Reggiano, Pasiego Prensado, Pasiego Sin Prensar, Pasta Filata, Pata de Mulo, Patagras, Peat-smoked, Pecorino, Pelardon, Peneteleu, Pepato, Petit-Suisse, Petrus Cheese, Philadelphia Cream Cheese, à la Pie, Pilz, Pindos, Pineapple Cheese, Pinzgauer Bier, Pipo Crème, Plateau, Plattekaas, Pont-l'Evêque, Port-Salut, Pot Cheese, Pourly, Pour-on Cheese, Prästost, Prato, Pressed Cheese, Processed Cheese, Provolone, Provolone Affumicata, Pultost, Pur Chèvre, Pyrénées, Quark, Quartirolo, Quesillos, Quesucos, Rabaçal, Raclette, Ramost, Rat, Reblochon, Red Cheshire, Red Leicester, Reino, Remoudou, Requeijão, Ribbon Cheese, Ricotta, Ridder, Robiola, Romadur, Romano, Roncal, Roquefort, Roulé, Royalp, Rutland, Saanen, Sage Derby, Sage Lancashire, Saint-Albray, Saint-Chevrier, Saint-Paulin, Salers, Saloio, Samsø, San Simón, Sapsago, Sauermilchkäase, Sbrinz, 'Scalded' Cheese, Schabzieger, Schafmilch, Schlosskäse, Schmelz, Schnitt, Schwyzerkäse, Serra, Sherwood, Shropshire Blue, Siciliano, Silba, Single Gloucester, Sirene, Skimmed Milk Quark, Skimmed Milk Soft Cheese, Skyros, Small Gouda, Smallholder, Smoked Cheese, Snir, Soft Cheeses, Soft Paste Cheese, Somerset Cider Cheddar, Sour Milk Cheese, Speisequark, Steinbuscher, Stepnoĭ, Steppe, Stilton, Stracchino, String, Surati Panir, Sveciaost, Swaledale, Swiss, Tal Ha'Emek, Taleggio, Tartare, Teleme, Teleme Jack, Tête de Moine, Tetilla, Tillamook, Tilsit, Toggenburger, Tomer, Tomme au Raisin, Tomme de Savoie, Tourrée-de-l'Aubier, Trappist, Trappiste de Chambarand, Tybo, Urbasa, Urdâ, Vacherin Fribourgeois, Vacherin Mont d'Or, Valençay, Västerbotten, Vermont, Villalón, Warszawski, Washed-rind Cheeses, Weisslacker, Wensleydale, Wexford, White Cheshire, White Lymeswold Cheese, White Stilton, York, Yunnan, Zakoussotchnyĭ, Ziegen, Zsendice

Coffee

Arabica Coffee Bean, Armenia, Blue Mountain Coffee, Brazilian Coffee, Brazilian Santos, Café Brulot, Cafe Liègeoise, Caffeine, Camp Coffee, Cappuccino, Coffee, Coffee Bean, Coffee Essence, Coffee Bags, Colombian Coffee, Cona Coffee, Continental Roast, Decaffeinated Coffee, Drip Coffee, Espresso, Ethiopian Harrar, Filter Coffee, French Coffee, German Coffee, Green Coffee Bean, Harrar, Instant Coffee, Irish Coffee, Italian Coffee, Jamaica Blue Mountain Coffee, Java Coffee, Jug Coffee, Kahve, Kenya Coffee, Kilimanjaro, Liberica, Manizales, Medellin, Mocha, Peaberry, Percolated Coffee, Robusta, Russian Coffee, Santos, Turkish Coffee, Vacuum-Method Coffee, Viennese Coffee, Vintage Colombian, White Coffee

Confectionery
Acid Drop, Almond Paste, Barley Sugar, Boiled Sweet, Brittle, Bull's Eye, Burfi, Candied Fruits, Candied Peel, Candy Floss, Caramels, Chewing Gum, Chocolate Truffles, Chocolate Vermicelli, Chopped Mixed Peel, Citron Peel, Coconut Ice, Comfit, Crystallized Flower Petals, Divinity, Dolly Mixture, Dragées, Drop, Edinburgh Rock, Everton Toffee, Fondant, Friandises, Fudge, Gajjar Halwa, Glacé Cherries, Glacé Fruits, Gobstopper, Gum, Gum Acacia, Gum Arabic, Gum Drop, Halva, Honeycomb, Humbug, Hundreds and Thousands, Jellies, Jelly Baby, Jelly Bean, Jordan Almond, Jubes, Liquorice, Lokum, Lollypop, Loukoum, Lozenge, Maraschino Cherry, Marshmallow, Marzipan, Milk Chocolate, Nougat, Nut Brittle, Pastilles, Peppermint Cream, Petits Fours, Pontefract Cake, Praline, Rock, Silver Balls, Spanish, Spun Sugar, Stickjaw, Sugared Almond, Sugarplum, Sweetmeat, Toffee, Toffee Apple, Torrone, Treacle Toffee, Truffles, Turkish Delight, Turron

Convenience Foods
Baked Beans, Canned Foods, Convenience Foods, Fast Food, Junk Food, Ready-meals, TV Dinner

Dairy Products — Cream
Aerosol Cream, Clotted Cream, Clouted Cream, Coffee Cream, Cream, Crème Fraîche, Double Cream, Extended-Life Cream, Extra-thick Double Cream, Freezing Cream, Frozen Cream, Half Cream, Light Cream, Long Life Cream, Mock Cream, Single Cream, Soured Cream, Spoonable Cream, Sterilized Cream, Ultra-Heat Treated Cream, Whey Cream, Whipped Cream, Whipping Cream

Dairy Products — Milk
Ayran, Beestings, Butterfat, Buttermilk, Casein, Chal, Channel Islands Milk, Colostrum, Condensed Milk, Culture, Cultured Buttermilk, Curd, Curds and Whey, Dahi, Dairy, Dried Milk, Drinking Yogurt, Evaporated Milk, Felisowka, Filbunke, 'Filled' Milk, Frozen Yogurt, Fruit Yogurt, Fruit-flavoured Yogurt, Full-cream Milk, Goat, Homogenized Milk, Jodda, Kefir, Kern Milk, Koumiss, Lactalbumin, Lactoglobulin, Lactose, Lassi, Leben, Leben Raid, Live Yogurt, Mast, Matzoon, Metchnikoff, Milk, Milk Shake, Milk Sugar, Nut Yogurt, Pasteurization, Pasteurized Milk, Piima, Rennet, Rennin, Semi-skimmed Milk, Set Yogurt, Skimmed Milk, Skyr, Smetana, Soured Milk, Starter, Sterilized Milk, Tako, Ultra-Heat Treated Milk, Untreated Milk, Villi, Whey, Yaout, Yiaourti, Yogurt, Zabady

Drinks (selected)
Absinthe, Alcohol, Ale, Angostura Aromatic Bitters, Aperitif, Beer, Bitters, Brandy, Bubbly, Calvados, Champagne, Cider, Cognac, Crème de Cassis, Crème de Menthe, Fortified Wine, Fruit Brandies, Gay-Lussac, Gin, Ginger Ale, Ginger Beer, GL, Kir, Kirsch, Kümmel, Lager, Lemonade, Liqueurs, Madeira, Maraschino, Marsala, Perry, Pimms, Port, Punch, Ratafia, Rum, Schnapps, Sherry, Spirit, Stout, Vermouth, Vodka, Whisky, White Beer, Wine

Eggs
Albumen, Baked Eggs, Boiled Eggs, Boiled Eggs in a Glass, Coddled Eggs, Decorated Eggs, Duck Eggs, Egg, Egg Cup, Egg Flip, Egg Shell, Egg Sizes, Egg Storage, Egg White, Egg Yolk, Eggnog, Eggs Florentine, Flip Iron, Free-range Eggs, French Meringue Mixture, Freshness of Eggs, Fried Eggs, Goose Eggs, Guinea Fowl Eggs, Gulls' Eggs, Italian Meringue Mixture, Meringue, Oeufs en Cocotte, Oeufs Mollets, Oeufs sur le Plat, Omelette, Pickled Eggs, Plain Omelette, Plovers' Eggs, Poached Eggs, Prairie Oyster, Quails' Eggs, Royal Custard, Scotch Eggs, Scrambled Eggs, Shirred Eggs, Soufflé Omelette, Swiss Meringue Mixture, Turkey Eggs, Ukraine Eggs

English Cooking Terms
Acidify (to), Acidulate (to), Adulterate (to), Aerate (to), Aroma, Astringent, Bake (to), Bake Blind (to), Barbecue (to), Bard (to), Barrel, Baste (to),

Beard (to), Beat (to), Bind (to), Blanch (to), Blend (to), Boil (to), Bone (to), Braise (to), Brine (to), Brown (to), Brush (to), Brush-Fry (to), Butchery, Button, Can (to), Candy (to), Canned, Caramelize (to), Carbonate (to), Carve (to), Casserole (to), Cate, Cater (to), Chill (to), Chine (to), Chop (to), Churn (to), Clarify (to), Clear (to), Coagulate (to), Coat (to), Coddle (to), Coller (to), Collop (to), Colour (to), Combine (to), Confection, Conserve, Consistency, Cool (to), Core (to), Cover, Cream (to), Crimp (to), Crumble (to), Crust, Cube (to), Curdle (to), Cure (to), Cut (to), Cut and Fold (to), Cut in (to), Daub (to), Decant (to), Decanter, Decoct (to), Decorate (to), Deep-Fry (to), Defrost (to), Deglaze (to), Density, Desiccate (to), Dice (to), Dilute (to), Dip (to), Disjoint (to), Dissolve (to), Done, Drain (to), Draw (to), Dredge (to), Dress (to), Dry, Dry-fry (to), Dunk (to), Dust (to), Effervesce (to), Egg (to), Egg Wash, Extract (to), Farce (to), Farinaceous, Fatty, Fillet (to), Filling, Filter (to), Finger, Fish Stock, Fizz, Flake (to), Flash, Flavour, Fleshy, Flour (to), Flute, Fold (to), Fortify (to), Frizzle (to), Froth, Fry (to), Garnish, Gel (to), Gild (to), Glaze (to), Granulate (to), Grate (to), Gravy Browning, Grease, Grill (to), Grind (to), Gut (to), Hard, Hard-Boil (to), Hash (to), Heat (to), Ice (to), Incise (to), Infuse (to), Interlarding, Joints, Jug (to), Kipper (to), Knead (to), Knock down (to), Lace (to), Lard (to), Leaven, Leftovers, Liaise (to), Light, Line (to), Liquidize (to), Liquor, Macerate (to), Marbled, Marinate (to), Mash (to), Mask (to), Melt (to), Mince (to), Mix (to), Moisten (to), Mould (to), Mull (to), Natives, Overdo (to), Parboil (to), Pare (to), Peel (to), Pepper (to), Pickle (to), Pip (to), Pipe (to), Pit (to), Plain, Ploat (to), Pluck (to), Poach (to), Pod (to), Pot (to), Pot-Roast (to), Pound (to), Pre-cook (to), Preheat (to), Preserve (to), Press (to), Pressure Cooking, Prove (to), Purée, Raise (to), Rancid, Rare, Rasp (to), Raw, Reconstitute (to), Reduce (to), Refresh (to), Render (to), Rice (to), Rich, Rind (to), Roast (to), Roll (to), Rub in (to), Scald (to), Score (to), Scramble (to), Scum, Sear (to), Season (to), Seethe (to), Separate (to), Set (to), Sew (to), Shallow-Fry (to), Sharp, Shell (to), Shirr (to), Shorten (to), Shred (to), Sieve (to), Sift (to), Simmer (to), Singe (to), Skewer (to), Skim (to), Skin (to), Slake, Sliver, Smoke (to), Soak (to), Soft-Boil (to), Soften (to), Soufflé, Souse (to), Spit-Roast (to), Sprinkle (to), Steam (to), Steep (to), Stew (to), Still, Stir (to), Stone (to), Store (to), Strain (to), Stud (to), Stuff (to), Sweat (to), Sweet, Sweeten (to), Sweet-Sour, Swirl (to), Tammy, Taste (to), Tenderize (to), Tepid, Thicken (to), Tinned, Toast (to), Top and Tail (to), Toss (to), Trim (to), Truss (to), Turn (to), Turn out (to), Underdone, Unleavened, Warm (to), Well-done, Well-hung, Whip (to), Whisk (to), Work (to), Yeasty

Fats and Oils

Almond Oil, Arachis Oil, Blubber, Butter, Butter Pats, Cacao Butter, Cholesterol, Clarified Butter, Cocoa Butter, Coconut Oil, Concentrated Butter, Cooking Fat, Corn Oil, Cottage Butters, Cottonseed Oil, Dairy Spreads, Deep Fat, Dripping, Essential Oil, Fats and Oils, Fish Oil, Ghee, Groundnut Oil, HDL, Lactic Butter, Lard, LDL, Leaf Fat, Leaf Lard, Margarine, Monosaturated Fatty Acids, Mustard Oil, Oil, Olive Oil, Palm Kernel Oil, Palm Oil, Peanut Oil, Polyunsaturated Fatty Acids, Rapeseed Oil, Refined Oils, Safflower Oil, Saturated Fatty Acids, Savoury Butters, Schmaltz, Sesame Oil, Shea Butter, Shortening, Solidified Cooking Oil, Soy Bean Oil, Suet, Sunflower Oil, Sweetcream Butter, Vanaspati, Virgin Oil, Walnut Oil, Whale Oil

Fish — American Atlantic

Albacore, Alewife, American Plaice, Atlantic Croaker, Atlantic Thread Herring, Black Halibut, Black Sea Bass, Bluefish, Boston Bluefish, Butterfish, Canadian Plaice, Capelin, Crevalle Jack, Cusk, Gaspereau, George's Bank Flounder, Greenland Halibut, Gurnard, Little Tunny, Northern Fluke, Ocean Perch, Pompano, Red Porgy, Red Snapper,

Robalo, Sand Dab, Scrod, Sea Robin, Sheepshead, Silver Hake, Silverside Fish, Snapper, Snook, Spiny Dogfish, Striped Bass, Summer Flounder, Tusk, Winter Flounder, Yellowtail Flounder

Fish — American Freshwater
Arctic Char, Bluegill, Char, Cisco, Dorado, Freshwater Drum, Inconnu, Lake Bass, Lake Herring, Lake Trout, Lake Whitefish

Fish — European Atlantic
Aberdeen Fillet, Angel Fish, Angler-Fish, Arbroath Fillet, Arbroath Smokies, Atlantic Cod, Atlantic Mackerel, Atlantic Salmon, Bannock Fluke, Bass, Beluga Sturgeon, Bismarck Herrings, Black Drum, Bloater, Bluefin Tuna, Bonito, Brill, Brisling, Brit, Catfish, Chicken Halibut, Chicken Turbot, Clipfish, Coalfish, Cod, Codling, Coley, Croaker, Dab, Dogfish, Dover Sole, Drum, Eel, Elver, Farmed Salmon, Finnan Haddock, Flounder, Flying Fish, Garfish, Gizzard Shad, Glasgow Pale, Golden Fillets, Gravlax, Grilse, Gurnard, Haddock, Hake, Halibut, Hammerhead Shark, Herring, Huss, Kipper, Kipper Fillets, Kippered Herring, Lemon Sole, Ling, Long Flounder, Longnose, Lumpfish, Mackerel, Mako Shark, Matjes, Megrim, Monkfish, Needlefish, Norway Haddock, Parr, Pilchard, Plaice, Pole Dab, Pollack, Pollock, Porbeagle Shark, Rainbow Smelt, Red Herring, Red Salmon, Red Sea Bream, Redfish, River Trout, Rock Eel, Rock Salmon, Rollmop, Saithe, Salmon Dace, Samlet, Sand Smelt, Sand Sole, Sardine, Scup, Sea Bream, Sea Cat, Sea Drum, Sea-Wolf, Shad, Shark, Sild, Silver Smelt, Skate, Smelt, Smoked Cod, Smoked Cod's Roe, Smoked Eel, Smoked Fillets, Smoked Haddock, Smoked Mackerel, Smoked Salmon, Smoked Sprats, Smokies, Smolt, Sole, Soused Herrings, Soused Mackerel, Spanish Ling, Sparling, Spitchcock, Sprat, Stockfish, Sturgeon, Swedish Anchovies, Swordfish, Tai, Tope, Torbay Sole, Tuna, Tunny, Turbot, Whiting, Witch Sole, Wolf-Fish

Fish — European Freshwater
Barbel, Brown Trout, Burbot, Carp, Chub, Conger Eel, Dace, Freshwater Bream, Grayling, Gudgeon, Jackfish, Loach, Perch, Pickerel, Pike, Pike-Perch, Pink Trout, Pullan, Rainbow Trout, Roach, Salmon Trout, Sea Trout, Trout, Vendace, Vendace Roe, Windermere Char, Zander

Fish — Mediterranean
Anchovy, Barracuda, Dentex, Dolphin Fish, Dory, Grey Gurnard, Grey Mullet, Grey Mullet Roe, Grouper, Gurnard, Kilkis, Moray Eel, Red Gurnard, Red Mullet, Scorpion Fish, Spur Dog, Striped Mullet, Tarama, Tub Gurnard

Fish — Pacific
Alaska Black Cod, Alaska Pollock, Black Cod, Chinook Salmon, Chum Salmon, Coho Salmon, Lingcod, Pacific Cod, Pacific Dogfish, Pacific Halibut, Pacific Mackerel, Pacific Thread Herring, Pink Salmon, Rock Sole, Rockfish, Roughback, Sockeye Salmon, Walleye Pollock

Fish — Shellfish
Abalone, Alaska Dungeness Crab, Awabi, Barnacle, Bay Scallop, Beard, Bivalve, Blue Crab, Bluepoint, Brown Shrimp, Butter Clam, Clam, Cockle, Coconut Crab, Common Crab, Common Prawn, Conch, Coral, Crawfish, Crayfish, Crustacean, Deepwater Shrimp, Dressed Crab, Dublin Bay Prawn, Dungeness Crab, Earshell, Edible Crab, European Flat Oyster, Gasteropod, Geoduck, Goose-necked Barnacle, Hard Clam, Hardshell Clam, Horse Clam, Japanese Oyster, King Crab, King Prawn, Limpet, Little-neck Clam, Lobster, Market Crab, Mollusc, Mussel, Muttonfish, Natives, Norway Lobster, Ormer, Oyster, Pacific Oyster, Paua, Periwinkle, Pink Shrimp, Pipi, Portuguese Oyster, Prawn, Quahog, Queen Scallop, Scallop, Scampi, Sea Ear, Shellfish, Shrimp, Smoked Oyster, Snail, Soft-shelled Crab, Spider Crab, Spiny Lobster, Spot Prawn, Surf Clam, Whelk, Winkle

Flavours and Essences
Almond Essence, Coffee Essence, Essence, Essential Oil, Grenadine, Lemon Essence, Orange Essence, Orgeat, Peppermint, Peppermint Oil, Rose Hip Syrup, Rose Oil, Rose Water, Sarsparilla, Tonka Bean, Vanilla Bean, Vanilla Pod

Foods for Festivals
Ackara, Basler-Leckerli, Birthday Cake, Black Bun, Botvinia, Brandy Butter, Brandy Sauce, Bûche de Noël, Christening Cake, Christmas Cake, Christmas Pudding, Coventry God Cakes, Dresdener Christollen, Easter Biscuits, Easter Eggs, Figgy Pudding, Galette, Hot Cross Buns, Julskinka, Kaha Bath, Kiri Bath, Knishes, Lebkuchen, Lekach, Macque Choux, Michaelmas Goose, Mince Pies, Mincemeat, Parkin, Paskha, Pecan Pie, Pepparkakor, Plava, Plum Pudding, Pumpkin Pie, Rum Butter, Rum Sauce, Saffransbröd, Scots Black Bun, Sedgemoor Easter 'Cakes', Selkirk Bannock, Semlor, Shrewsbury Eastertide Biscuits, Shrove Tuesday Buns, Simnel Cake, Speculaas, Stollen, Succotash, Tirggel, Twelfth Night Cake, Wedding Breakfast, Wedding Cake, Yule Log

Freezing
Deep-Freeze, Fast-Freeze (to), Freeze (to), Freezer-Burn

French Cooking Terms
à la, Abats, à l'Africaine, Agneau, Aiguillettes, à l'Ail, Alcoöl, à l'Algérienne, à l'Allemande, Allumettes, à l'Alsacienne, Amandine, à l'Amiral, à l'Andalouse, à l'Angevine, à l'Anglaise, à l'Antiboise, à l'Anversoise, à l'Archiduc, à l'Ardennaise, à l'Argenteuil, à l'Ariégeoise, à l'Arlésienne, à l'Arpajonnaise, Assiette Anglaise, au (aux), à l'Autrichienne, Ballon, Ballotine de Volaille, à la Basquaise, à la Batelière, à la Bayonnaise, Belle Vue, à la Belle-Dijonnaise, à la Benoiton, à la Bergère, à la Berrichonne, Beurre, au Beurre, à la Biarrotte, Bifteck Haché, à la Bigoudenne, Blanc (Blanche), Blé Noir, au Bleu, à la Bohémienne, Bonne Bouche, à la Bonne-Femme, à la Bordelaise, Bouchées, à la Boulangère, Boulettes, Bouquet Garni, à la Bourgeoise, à la Bourguignonne, à la Brabançonne, à la Bragance, à la Bressane, à la Bretonne, Bretzel, Brochette, Brûler, Brunoise, à la Bruxelloise, Canapé, à la Cancalaise, à la Canotière, Cardinale, Carte, à la Carte, à la Catalane, à la Cauchoise, à la Cévenole, à la Chablisienne, Chambré, aux Champignons, Charcuterie, à la Chasseur, à la Châtelaine, en Chemise, Chemiser, Chiffonade, à la Chilienne, à la Chinonaise, Choucroûte, Cocottes, à la Colbert, Compôte, Concasser, à la Concorde, Confiture d'Oranges, Consommé, à la Conti, Contre-Filet, Coque, en Coquille, Coquilles Saint-Jacques, Cordon Bleu, Cornichon, Coulis, Court-Bouillon, Couverture, à la Crapaudine, à la Crécy, Crème Anglaise, Crème à l'Anglaise, Crème Chantilly, Crème Fleurette, Crème Pâtisserie, Crème Pâtissière, à la Créole, Crêpes, Croustades, en Croute, Croûtons, Crudités, Cuisine, Cuisine Minceur, Cuit, à la Cultivateur, à la Cussy, Dartois, à la Daumont, à la Deauvillaise, Dégorger, Dégraisser, Dégustation, Demi-tasse, à la Diable, à la Dieppoise, Digestif, à la Dijonnaise, Doria, à la Dubarry, à la Duchesse, à la Duse, Duxelles, Échauder, à l'Écossaise, en, Entrée, Entremets, Esaü, Escargot, à l'Espagnole, Estouffade, à l'Estragon, Étouffat, à l'Étouffée, Étuver, à la Façon de, Farci, Faux-Filet, à la Favorite, à la Fermière, Feuilletage, Filet Mignon, à la Financière, Fines Herbes, à la Flamande, Flamber, Flan, à la Fleuriste, Fondue, Fouetter, au Four, à la Française, Frangipane, Frapper, Fricassée, Friture, Frivolités, Fruits de Mer, Fumer, Fumet, Galantine, Galette, Garnir, Garniture, Gelée, en Gelée, Genoese, à la Génoise, Gigot, Glace, Glace de Viande, Goujon, Goûter, au Grand-Duc, à la Grand-Mère, Gratin, à la Grecque, Grenadins, à la Grenobloise, Grenouilles, Grillade, Hacher, Haute

Cuisine, à la Hollandaise, Homard, à la Hongroise, à l'Hôtelière, à la Hussarde, à l'Impériale, à l'Indienne, à l'Italienne, à la Jardinière, Judic, Julienne, Jus, au Jus, Jus Lié, à la Jussière, Laitier, Langouste, Langoustines, à la Languedocienne, Liaison, à la Liègeoise, à la Ligurienne, à la Limousine, à la Livornaise, à la Lyonnaise, Macédoine, Macédoine de Fruits, à la Mâconnaise, Madère, à la Madrilène, au Maigre, à la Maillot, à la Maintenon, de la Maison, Maître d'Hôtel, à la Maltaise, à la Maraîchère, au Maréchal, à la Marie-Louise, à la Marinière, Marmelade, à la Marocaine, Marrons, Marrons Glacés, à la Marseillaise, à la Mascotte, à la Masséna, Matelote, Medaillons, à la Médici, à la Mentonnaise, Meunière, à la Mexicaine, à la Milanaise, Mimosa, à la Mirabeau, Mirepoix, à la Mode de, à la Moderne, à la Montmorency, Montpensier, à la Mousquetaire, Mousse, Mousseline, à la Nantaise, à la Nantua, à la Napolitaine, à la Narbonnaise, au Naturel, à la Niçoise, Noisette, Nonpareils, Nouilles, Nouvelle Cuisine, Oeufs à la Coque, Oeufs Brouillés, Oeufs Frites, Oeufs Pochés, à l'Opéra, à l'Orientale, à l'Orléanaise, Panaché (Panachée), Paner, Panetière, en Papillote, à la Parisienne, Parmentier, à la Parmesane, Pastille, Pâte, Pâté, Pâté Maison, Pâtisserie, Pâtissière, Paupiettes, Paysanne, à la Paysanne, à la Périgourdine, Persillade, Petit Déjeuner, au Petit-Duc, Petit-Lait, Pièce de Résistance, à la Piémontaise, Piquant (Piquante), à Point, à la Poivrade, au Poivre, à la Polonaise, à la Portugaise, Potage, à la Princesse, à la Printanière, Prix Fixe, à la Provençale, Quatre-Épices, à la Rachel, Ragoût, Rechauffé (Rechauffée), Réduire, à la Réforme, à la Reine, Relevé, Repas, à la Richelieu, Ris de Veau, Rissole, au Riz, Rognons Blancs, à la Romaine, à la Royale, à la Russe, Saignant, à la Saint-Germain, Salpicon, à la Sarde, Sarrasin, Saucisse, Saucisson, Saumure, Saur (Saure), Sauter, à la Savoyarde, Sec (Sèche), à la Soissonaise, Sommelier, à la Soubise, à la Souvaroff, à la Strasbourgeoise, Suprême, à la Talleyrand, Terrine, Timbale, à la Tivoli, à la Toscane, à la Toulousaine, à la Tourangelle, à la Tsarine, Turban, à la Tyrolienne, Véronique, à la Victoria, à la Viennoise, au Vin, Vin Ordinaire, Vin-aigre, à la Viroflay, à la Waleska, à la Zingara, Zwieback

Fruit — Berry
Alpine Strawberry, Barberry, Berry, Bilberry, Blackberry, Blackcurrant, Blueberry, Bounceberry, Boysenberry, Bramble, Cloudberry, Cowberry, Cranberry, Craneberry, Crowberry, Dewberry, Elderberry, Gooseberry, Huckleberry, Japanese Wineberry, Juneberry, Ligonberry, Lingonberry, Loganberry, Mountain Cranberry, Mulberry, Olallieberry, Raspberry, Redcurrant, Rose Hip, Rowanberry, Serviceberry, Strawberry, Tayberry, Whitecurrant, Whortleberry, Wild Strawberry, Wineberry, Wood Strawberry, Worcesterberry, Youngberry

Fruit — Citrus
Bitter Orange, Blood Orange, Calamondin Orange, China Orange, Citrange, Citron, Citrus, Clementine, Cumquat, Grapefruit, Jaffa, Kumquat, Lemon, Lime, Mandarin, Mineola, Naartje, Navel, Orange, Ortanique, Panama Orange, Pith, Pomelo, Pummelo, Satsuma, Seville Orange, Shaddock, Shamouti, Sweet Orange, Tangelo, Tangerine, Texas Red, Topaz, Ugli, Valencia

Fruit — Dried
Currants, Dried Apple Rings, Dried Apricots, Dried Bananas, Dried Fruit, Hunza Apricots, Muscatel Raisins, Prunes, Raisins, Semi-dried Dates, Sultanas

Fruit — Exotic
Achee, Akee, Alligator Pear, Apple Banana, Asian Pear, Atemoya, Avocado, Babaco, Banana, Barbados Cherry, Bladder Cherry, Brazilian Cherry, Brazilian Guava, Breadfruit, Bromeliad, Bullock's Heart, Cape Gooseberry, Carambola, Ceriman,

Cherimoya, Chiku, Chinese Cherry, Chinese Gooseberry, Chinese Lantern, Custard Apple, Custard Banana, Dragon's Eye, Durian, Feijoa, Golden Passion Fruit, Granadilla, Green Sapote, Grenadilla, Guava, Hairy Lychee, Hog Plum, Indian Date, Indian Fig, Jackfruit, Jamaica Plum, Jamberry, Jambos, Japanese Medlar, Japanese Pear, Jujube, Kaki, Kiwano, Kiwi Fruit, Lady's Fingers, Langsat, Lichee, Longan, Loquat, Lychee, Mammee, Mango, Mangosteen, Mediterranean Medlar, Monstera, Naseberry, Nashi, Neeseberry, Orange Passion Fruit, Otaheite-Apple, Papain, Papaya, Passion Fruit, Pawpaw, Persimmon, Pineapple, Pineapple Guava, Plantain, Pomegranate, Prickly Custard Apple, Prickly Pear, Purple Passion Fruit, Rambutan, Rose Apple, Sapodilla, Sapote, Scaly Custard Apple, Sharon Fruit, Sour Sop, Star Apple, Star Fruit, Sugar Apple, Surinam Cherry, Sweet Granadilla, Sweet Sop, Tamarillo, Tamarind, Tomarillo, Tomatillo, Tree Tomato, Yellow Passion Fruit

Fruit — Firm
Apple, Azarole, Cooking Apple, Crab Apple, Dessert Apple, Medlar, Naples Medlar, Pear, Quince

Fruit — Seeded
Cantaloupe Melon, Carob, Cassaba, Charentais Melon, Fig, Galia Melon, Grapes, Green Fig, Honeydew Melon, Locust Bean, Melon, Muscat Grape, Musk Melon, Netted Melon, Ogen Melon, Pineapple Melon, Watermelon, Winter Melon

Fruit — Stoned
Apricot, Black Olive, Cherry, Damson, Date, Gage, Golden Gage, Green Olive, Greengage, Mirabelle, Morello Cherry, Nectarine, Olive, Peach, Plum, Sloe, Stuffed Olive

Game
Agami, Barnacle Goose, Blackcock, Brent Goose, Buck Venison, Bustard, Button Quail, Canvasback, Capercailzie, Corncrake, Deer, Doe Venison, Game, Gamecock, Gamey, Grouse, Guinea Fowl, Hare, Hazel Hen, Humbles, Landrail, Leveret, Mallard, Moorfowl, Ortolan, Partridge, Pheasant, Pigeon, Plover, Ptarmigan, Quail, Rabbit, Red Grouse, Reindeer Meat, Roe Buck, Snipe, Squab, Teal, Thrush, Tinamou, Trumpeter, Venison, Wigeon, Wild Boar, Wild Duck, Wood Grouse, Wood Pigeon, Woodcock

Grains and Flour
American Long-grain Rice, Arrowroot, Atta, Barley, Barley Flakes, Barley Flour, Basmati Rice, Beechwheat, Bessan, Bran, Bread Flour, Breakfast Cereals, Brown Flour, Brown Rice, Brown Self-raising Flour, Buckwheat, Buckwheat Flour, Bulgur, Cake Flours, Cake Mixes, Cargo Rice, Carolina Rice, Cassava Root, Cereal, Corn, Cornflakes, Cornflour, Cornmeal, Couscous, Cracked Wheat, Crushed Oats, Durum Wheat, Ear, Einkorn, Endosperm, Farina, Farinose, Flaked Rice, Flour, Germ, Gluten, Go-Han, Graham Flour, Grain, Grits, Groats, Ground Rice, Gruel, Hard Flour, Hard Wheat, Hominy, Hominy Grits, Household Flour, Husk, Japanese Millet, Japonica Rice, Jumbo Oats, Kasha, Kibbled Wheat, Long-grain Brown Rice, Low-starch Flour, Maize, Maize Meal, Malt, Malted Brown Flour, Maranta, Masa Harina, Meal, Millet, Muesli, Oat Flakes, Oat Flour, Oaten, Oatmeal, Oats, Paddy Rice, Parboiled Rice, Parched Corn, Patna Rice, Pearl Barley, Pearl Sago, Pinole, Plain Flour, Polenta, Polished Rice, Popcorn, Porridge Oats, Proprietary Flours, Quinoa, Ragi, Regular-milled White Rice, Rice, Rice Flakes, Rice Flour, Risotto Rice, Rolled Oats, Roller-milled Flour, Rye, Rye Flakes, Rye Flour, Sago, Saracen Corn, Scottish Oatmeal, Self-raising Flour, Semolina, Short-grain Brown Rice, Short-grain Rice, Shredded Wheat, Soft Flour, Soft Wheat, Sorghum, Soy Flour, Spike, Stoneground Flour, Strong Plain Flour, Tapioca, Teff, Toasted Buckwheat, Triticale, Unbleached White Flour, Wheat, Wheat Flakes, Wheat Flour, Wheaten,

Wheatgerm, Wheatmeal Flour, White Flour, Whole Grain Wheat, Wholemeal Flour, Wholewheat Flour, Wild Rice

Herbs and Spices

Abelmosk, Ajowan, Alexander, Allspice, Angelica, Angostura Aromatic Bitters, Anise, Aniseed, Apple Mint, Asafoetida, Basil, Bay Leaves, Bee Balm, Bergamot, Black Mustard, Black Pepper, Borage, Bouquet Garni, Bowles Mint, Camomile, Capers, Caraway Seeds, Cardamom, Cassia, Cayenne Pepper, Celery Salt, Celery Seeds, Chamomile, Chervil, Chilli Powder, Chinese Five Spice, Chinese Parsley, Chive, Cicely, Cinnamon, Clary, Clear Eye, Cloves, Coca, Continental Mustard, Coriander, Costmary, Cress, Crushed Chillies, Cumin Seeds, Curry Leaves, Curry Powder, Dandelion, Dill, Dry Mustard, Eau-de-Cologne Mint, Faggot, Fennel Seeds, Fenugreek, Filé Powder, Five Spice Powder, Flat Parsley, French Sorrel, Galangal, Garam Masala, Garlic, Garlic Clove, Garlic Powder, Garlic Salt, Gentian, Geraniums, Ginger, Grains of Paradise, Green Peppercorns, Gumbo Filé, Haldi, Herbal, Herbes de Provence, Herbs, Horseradish, Hyssop, Indian Cress, Jalapeno Peppers, Jamaica Pepper, Jasmine, Jesuit's Cress, Juniper Berries, Knotted Marjoram, Laos Powder, Lemon Balm, Lemon Grass, Lemon Thyme, Lemon Verbena, Lovage, Mace, Madagascan Green Peppercorns, Marigold, Marjoram, Melilot, Melissa, Methi, Mignonette Pepper, Mint, Mixed Herbs, Mixed Spice, Mugwort, Mustard, Mustard and Cress, Mustard Seeds, Myrtle, Nasturtium, Nutmeg, Oregano, Pansy, Paprika, Parsley, Patience, Pennyroyal, Pepper, Peppermint, Pickling Spice, Poppy Seeds, Pot Marjoram, Potherb, Prepared Mustard, Quatre-Épices, Red Pepper, Root Ginger, Rosemary, Rue, Saffron, Sage, Salad Burnet, Sambal Manis, Sambal Oelek, Sassafras, Savory, Screwpine Leaves, Serai Powder, Sesame Seeds, Shallot, Sorrel, Spearmint, Spices, Star Anise, Summer Savory, Sweet Basil, Sweet Cicely, Sweet Marjoram, Szechuan Peppercorns, Tamarind Pulp, Tandoori Spice Mix, Tansy, Tarragon, Thyme, Tisane, Turmeric, Vanilla, Watercress, White Mustard, White Pepper, Wild Marjoram, Winter Savory, Woodruff, Wormwood, Yarrow

Ices

Bombes, Brown Bread Ice Cream, Cassata, Cone, Cornet, Coupes, Granita, Ice Cream, Ice Cream Soda, Ice Cream Sundae, Ice Lolly, Iceblock, Ices, Kulfi, Lolly, Neapolitan Ice Cream, Parfait, Sherbets, Sorbet, Sundae, Tortoni, Tutti-Frutti, Water Ice

Icings and Fillings

American Frosting, Australian Fondant Icing, Boiled Frosting, Butter Cream, Confectioner's Custard, Crème Beurre, Crème Chantilly, Crème Pâtisserie, Crème Pâtissière, Custard Cream, Fondant Icing, Frosting, Fudge Icing, Glacé Icing, Icing, Marzipan, Pastry Cream, Piping, Pithiviers Cream, Plastic Icing, Royal Icing, Seven-minute Frosting, Transparent Icing, Water Icing

Jams and Preserves

Chow-Chow Preserve, Chunky Peanut Butter, Confiture d'Oranges, Fruit Butter, Fruit Cheese, Fruit Jelly Preserve, Honey, Honeycomb, Jam, Lemon Curd, Marmalade, Mincemeat, Peanut Butter, Rowanberry Jelly

Meat

Aberdeen Angus Beef, Alligator, Baron of Beef, Bear, Bed of Beef, Beef, Beef Olives, Belly of Pork, Belly Slices of Pork, Best End Neck of Lamb, Best End Neck of Veal, Biltong, Blade of Lamb, Blade of Pork, Boneless Breast of Lamb, Boneless Loin and Belly of Pork, Boneless Rolled Lamb, Bosum of Beef, Breast of Lamb, Breast of Veal, Brisket of Beef, Butterfly Chop, Calf, Camel, Caribou, Chateaubriand, Chine of Beef, Chipped Beef, Chop, Chuck and Blade Beef Steak, Chump Chops of Lamb, Chump of Pork, Clod of Beef, Collagen, Collop, Connective Tissue, Crackling, Crown Roast of Lamb,

Cutlet, Cutlet of Lamb, Cutlet of Veal, Double Loin of Pork, Double Loin Steaks of Pork, Elastin, Entrecôte Beef Steak, Escalope, Extractives, Fat Mouse, Feather Beef Steak, Fillet Beef Steak, Fillet of Beef, Fillet of Lamb, Fillet of Pork, Fillet of Veal, Fine Chine of Beef, Fine End and Loin of Lamb, First Cutting of Beef, Flank of Lamb, Flank of Veal, Flash-fry Beef Steak, Fore Rib of Beef, Foreleg of Beef, Forequarter of Meat, Foreshank, Gambrel, Gigot Lamb Chops, Gigot of Lamb, Goat, Gristle, Guard of Honour, Gullet of Beef, Half a Leg, Hand and Spring of Pork, Hand of Pork, Hanging Meat, Haunch, Hedgehog, Heuk Bone of Beef, Hindleg of Beef, Hip Bone of Beef, Hock of Meat, Hock of Pork, Hog, Horsemeat, Hough of Beef, Jerked Meat, Joint, Jowl, Kid, Knuckle, Knuckle of Lamb, Knuckle of Pork, Knuckle of Veal, Lamb, Lamb Riblets, Lap of Lamb, Lardon, Lean Cubes of Lamb, Leg Chops of Lamb, Leg of Beef, Leg of Lamb, Leg of Mutton Cut, Leg of Pork, Leg of Veal, Leg Steaks of Lamb, Loin of Lamb, Loin of Pork, Loin of Pork Chop, Loin of Veal, Loin or Single Loin of Lamb, Loin Steaks of Lamb, Lyre of Beef, Meat, Meat Loaf, Meat Texture, Medium Beef Steak, Middle Neck of Lamb, Mince, Mince of Lamb, Minute Beef Steak, Moose, Muktuk, Mutton, Neck End of Pork, Neck of Beef, Noisettes of Lamb or Pork, Nutria, Opossum, Ox, Oyster of Veal, Paca, Pemmican, Picata, Pie Veal, Pig, Pin Bone of Beef, Plate of Beef, à Point, Pope's Eye of Beef, Pork, Pork Chop, Pork Crackling, Porker, Porterhouse Steak, Possum, Potted Meat, Quarter of Meat, Raccoon, Rack of Lamb, Rare Beef Steak, Red Meat, Reindeer Meat, Rib Roast of Beef, Rolled Pork and Shoulder, Rump, Rump Steak, Rump Top, Saddle, Saddle of Lamb, Salt Pork, Scrag, Scrag of Lamb, Shank, Shank of Lamb, Shin of Beef, Shoulder of Beef, Shoulder of Lamb, Shoulder of Pork, Shoulder of Veal, Shoulder Steaks of Pork, Side of Meat, Silverside of Beef, Single Loin of Pork, Sirloin of Beef, Sirloin Steak, Skink of Beef, Skirt of Beef, Sloat of Beef, Sowbelly, Spare Rib of Pork, Spareribs of Pork, Spaul of Beef, Squirrel, Standing Ribs of Beef, Steak, Steak Bone of Beef, Steak Piece of Beef, Sucking Pigs, T-Bone Steak, Tender Meat, Tenderloin of Pork, Thick Flank of Beef, Thick Ribs of Beef, Thin Flank of Beef, Thin Ribs of Beef, Top Rib of Beef, Top Rump, Topside Leg Steaks of Pork, Topside of Beef, Tournedos, Veal, Veal Chops, Veal Riblets, Vein of Beef, Whale, White Meat, Wiener Schnitzel, Wing Rib of Beef

Nuts

Acajou, Almond Nibs, Almond Oil, Almonds, Arachis Oil, Babassu, Beech Nuts, Betel Nuts, Bitter Almonds, Blanched Almonds, Brazil Nuts, Butternuts, Candlenuts, Cashew Nuts, Chestnuts, Cobnuts, Coconut, Coconut Milk, Coconut Oil, Coconut Water, Creamed Coconut, Desiccated Coconut, Dried Chestnuts, Filberts, Ginkgo Nuts, Green Walnuts, Ground Almonds, Groundnut Oil, Groundnuts, Hazelnuts, Hickory Nuts, Indian Nuts, Kemiri Nuts, Kernel, Macadamia Nuts, Monkey Nuts, Nut Meal, Nuts, Nutty, Paradise Nut, Peanuts, Pecan Nuts, Pignolias, Pine Nuts, Piñon, Pistachio Nuts, Sapucaya Nut, Shanghai Nuts, Shea Nuts, Spanish Chestnut, Split Almonds, Sweet Almonds, Sweet Chestnut, Walnut Oil, Walnuts

Offal

Amourettes, Animelles, Blanket Tripe, Blood, Bone Marrow, Brains, Caecum, Calf's Head, Calf's Tongue, Calves' Brains, Calves' Feet, Calves' Liver, Caul, Chap, Chaudin, Chickens' Feet, Chickens' Livers, Chitterlings, Colon, Cow-heel, Dressed Tripe, Ducks' Feet, Fries, Giblets, Gizzard, Heart, Honeycomb Tripe, Humbles, Intestines, Kangaroo Tail, Kidney Fat, Kidneys, Lambs' Brains, Lambs' Fry, Lambs' Kidneys, Lambs' Liver, Lambs' Tongues, Lights, Liver, Lungs, Marrow Bones, Milt, Mountain Oysters, Neck Bone, Offal, Ox Brains, Ox Cheek, Ox Kidney, Ox Liver, Ox Tongue, Oxtail, Pettitoes, Pigs' Ears, Pig's Fry, Pig's Head, Pigs' Kidneys, Pigs' Liver, Pigs' Trotters, Pluck, Poche, Prairie

Oysters, Pressed Ox Tongue, Sac, Spleen, Sweetbreads, Testicles, Thick Seam Tripe, Tongue, Tripe, Trotters, Turkey Livers, Udder

Pasta

Acini, Agnolotti, Anellini, Angel's Hair, Anolini, Ave Maria, Bavette, Bean Thread Noodles, Bow-shaped Pasta, Bucatini, Buckwheat Noodles, Buckwheat Spaghetti, Butterfly-shaped Pasta, Cannelloni, Cannolicchi, Capelli d'Angelo, Capellini, Cappaletti, Cellophane Noodles, Cha-Soba, Conch Shells, Conchiglie, Conchigliette, al Dente, Ditali, Ditalini, Dried Pasta, Egg Noodles, Egg Pasta, Elbow Macaroni, Farfalle, Farfallini, Farfel, Fettucine, Fresh Pasta, Fusilli, Gemelli, Hokkien Mee Noodles, Lasagne, Lasagne Verdi, Lasagnette, Lingue di Passero, Linguine, Lokshen, Lumache, Macaroni, Maccheroncini, Maccheroni, Mafalda, Maniche, Manti, Mee Noodles, Mein Noodles, Noodles, Nüdeln, Orrecchiette, Orzo, Paglia e Fieno, Pansotti, Panzerotti, Pappardelle, Pasta, Pasta all'Uovo, Pasta Secca, Pasta Twists, Pastine, Paternostri, Pazlache, Penne, Penne Rigate, Pennette, Perciatelli, Pierogi, Pizzoccheri, Quadrucci, Ravioli, Raviolini, Rice Noodles, Rice Vermicelli, Rigatoni, Rotelle, Rotine, Ruote, Ruotini, Soba Noodles, Somen Noodles, Spaghetti, Spaghettini, Spätzel, Stellette, Tagliarini, Tagliatelle, Tagliatelle Verdi, Tagliolini, Tortelli, Tortellini, Tortiglione, Transparent Noodles, Trenette, Tubetti, Udon Noodles, Verdi, Vermicelli, Vermicellini, Wholewheat Lasagne, Wholewheat Pasta, Ziti, Ziti Mezze, Zitoni

Pastry and Pies

Almond Slice, Apple Strudel, Bakewell Tart, Barquettes, Biscuit-crust Pastry, Bridie, Cheese Pastry, Cheese Straws, Chess Pie, Chiffon Pie, Choux Pastry, Cream Buns, Cream Horns, Cream Puffs, Cream Slices, Crumb Crust, Curd Cheese Pastry, Danish Pastry, Devonshire Squab Pie, Double-crust Pie, Éclairs, Filo, Flaky Pastry, Flan Pastry, Fleurons, Fork-mix Shortcrust Pastry, Fruit Pie, Fruit Turnovers, Gougères, Hamantaschen, Hot-water Crust Pastry, Jam Puffs, Jam Turnovers, Key Lime Pie, Knishes, Lemon Meringue Pie, Meat Pie, Melktert, Melton Mowbray Pie, Milk Tart, Mille Feuilles, Mince Pies, Noodle Pastry, Oggy, Oil Pastry, Pastries, Pastry, Pastry Case, Pasty, Pâte, Pâte Brisée, Pâte Sucrée, Patty, Phyllo, Pie, Piecrust, Pork Pie, Puff Pastry, Puffs, Pumpkin Pie, Raised Pie, Rétes, Rough Puff Pastry, Shoo Fly Pie, Shortcrust Pastry, Star-Gazey Pie, Steak and Kidney Pie, Strudel Pastry, Suet-crust Pastry, Sweet-crust Pastry, Tart, Tartlet, Treacle Tart, Turnover, Veal and Ham Pie, Vol-au-Vents, Wonton Wrappers, Yorkshire Cheesecake

Pickles

Chutney, Cornichon, Dill Pickles, Gherkins, Mustard Pickle, Pearl Onions, Piccalilli, Pickle (to), Pickled Cucumber, Pickled Eggs, Pickling Spice, Relish, Sour Cucumber, Sweet Pickle, Vegetable Pickles

Poultry

Ailerons, Bantam, Barbary Duck, Boiling Fowl, Broiler, Capon, Chicken, Cock, Cockerel, Cockscomb, Corn-fed Chicken, Crop, Drumstick, Duck, Duckling, Fowl, Fresh Chicken, Frozen Chicken, Fryer, Gallinaceous, Goose, Gosling, Green Goose, Greylag Goose, Hen, Michaelmas Goose, Oven-ready Chicken, Parson's Nose, Pinion, Pope's Nose, Poulet Noir, Poultry, Poussin, Pullet, Spatchcock, Spring Chicken, Turkey, Turkey Cock, Wing, Wishbone

Puddings and Desserts

Ambrosia, Apple Amber Pudding, Apple Charlotte, Apple Crumble, Apple Dumplings, Apple Fritters, Baked Alaska, Baked Apples, Baked Bananas, Baked Egg Custard, Bakewell Puddings, Baklava, Banana Fritters, Banana Split, Bananas Foster, Beresford Pudding, Black Cap Pudding, Blancmange, Boodles' Orange Fool, Bread and Butter Pudding, Bread Pudding, Brown Betty,

Burnt Cream, Cabinet Pudding, Cambridge Burnt Cream, Canary Pudding, Caramel Cream, Caramelized Oranges, Cassata alla Siciliana, Castle Puddings, Charlotte Russe, Chiffon Pie, Christmas Pudding, Clafouti, Clootie Dumpling, Cobbler Pudding, Coeur à la Crème, College Pudding, Compôte, Condé, Cream Caramel, Crema Catalana, Crème Brûlée, Crème Caramel, Crème Moulée, Crème Renversée, Devonshire Junket, Double-crust Pie, Dulce de Leche, Eve's Pudding, Figgy Pudding, Floating Islands, Flummery, Fool, French Flan, Fresh Fruit Salad, Friar's Omelette, Fruit Batter Pudding, Fruit Crumble, Fruit Fritters, Fruit Salad, Fruit Snow, Fruit Sponge Pudding, Frumenty, Gulab Jamon, Honeycomb Mould, Indian Pudding, Jalebi, Jam Roly-Poly, Jelly Cubes, Junket, Keşkül, Kissel, Knickerbocker Glory, Kugel, Lemon Meringue Pie, Lemon Soufflé, Milanese Soufflé, Milk Jelly, Milk Pudding, Mince Pies, Mont Blanc, Mousse, Norwegian Omelette, Packet Jelly, Pandowdy, Parfait, Peach Melba, Pineapple Fritters, Plum Duff, Plum Pudding, Port Wine Jelly, Posset, Prince Albert Pudding, Profiteroles, Queen of Puddings, Ras Gulas, Rice Pudding, Roly-Poly Pudding, Rote Grütze, Sponge Pudding, Spotted Dick, Steamed Pudding, Suet Pudding, Summer Pudding, Sussex Pond Pudding, Syllabub, Syrup Roly-Poly, Tipsy Cake, Trifle, Upside-down Pudding, Whim Wham, Zabaglione, Zuppa Inglese *See also* Ices

Salads

Aemono, Blue Cheese Dressing, Caesar Salad, Chef's Salad, Coleslaw Salad, Crab Louis, Curry Mayonnaise, Egg Salad, Ensalada de Arroz, Fruit Salad, Garlic Dressing, Green Goddess Dressing, Green Salad, Horiatiki, Mayonnaise, Mechouia, Melitzanos Salata, Mixed Salad, Potato Salad, Russian Salad, Salad Cream, Salad Dressings, Salade Niçoise, Salade Tiède, Salads, Slaw, Sunomono, Tabbouleh Salad, Thousand Island Dressing, Vinaigrette Dressing, Waldorf Salad, West Coast Salad

Sauces

Aillade, Aïoli Sauce, Allemande Sauce, Amandine Butter, Anchovy Butter, Anchovy Sauce, Andalouse Mayonnaise, Apple Sauce, Aurore Sauce, Avgolemono Sauce, Bagna Cauda, Barbecue Sauce, Bavaroise Sauce, Béarnaise Sauce, Béchamel Sauce, Bercy Butter, Bercy Sauce, Beurre Blanc, Beurre Manié, Beurre Monté, Beurre Noir, Beurre Noisette, Beurres Composés, Bigarade Sauce, Black Butter and Caper Sauce, Black Butter Sauce, Blender Mayonnaise, Blue Cheese Dressing, Bolognese Sauce, Bordelaise Sauce, Bourguignonne Sauce, Brandy Butter, Brandy Sauce, Bread Sauce, Brown Butter Sauce, Brown Sauce, Burgundy Sauce, Caboul Sauce, Caper Sauce, Chantilly Mayonnaise, Chasseur Sauce, Chaud-Froid Sauce, Cheese Sauce, Chilli Sauce, Chocolate Fudge Sauce, Chocolate Sauce, Choron Sauce, Coating Sauce, Cocktail Sauce, Colbert Butter, Cold Cucumber Sauce, Cornflour Sauce, Cranberry Sauce, Crème à l'Anglaise, Crème Chantilly, Cucumber Sauce, Cumberland Rum Butter, Cumberland Sauce (Cold), Cumberland Sauce (Hot), Curry Butter, Curry Mayonnaise, Curry Sauce, Custard, Custard Sauce, Demi-glace Sauce, Devil Butter, Diane Sauce, Doria Sauce, Drawn Butter Sauce, Dutch Sauce, Epicurienne Sauce, Espagnole Sauce, Estragon Sauce, French Dressing, Garlic Butter, Garlic Dressing, Gooseberry Sauce, Gravlaxsås, Gravy, Green Dressing, Green Mayonnaise, Gribiche Sauce, Grilling Sauce, Guaymas Sauce, Hard Sauce, Harissa, Hoi Sin Sauce, Hollandaise Sauce, Horseradish Sauce, Hungarian Butter, Hungarian Sauce, Hunter's Sauce, Jam Sauce, Kecap Manis, Ketchup, Kneaded Butter, Lea and Perrins, Lemon Butter Sauce, Louis Sauce, Lyonnaise Sauce, Madeira Sauce, Maître d'Hôtel Butter, Maltese Sauce, Marchand de Vin Sauce, Marinade, Marmalade Sauce,

Maximilian Sauce, Mayonnaise, Melba Sauce, Meunière Butter Sauce, Mint Sauce, Mock Hollandaise, Mole, Mornay Sauce, Mounted Butter, Mousquetaire Sauce, Mousseline Sauce, Mushroom Ketchup, Mushroom Sauce, Mustard Butter, Mustard Pickle Sauce, Mustard Sauce, Neapolitan Sauce, Newburg Sauce, Normandy Sauce, Onion Sauce, Orange Sauce, Oxford Sauce, Oyster Sauce, Panada, Paprika Butter, Parsley Sauce, Pepper Sauce, Périgueux Sauce, Pesto, Piquant Sauce, Piri-piri, Pizzaiola Sauce, Plum Sauce, Poivrade Sauce, Portugaise Sauce, Pouring Sauce, Prawn Cocktail Sauce, Ravigote Dressing, Ravigote Sauce, Red Bean Sauce, Reform Sauce, Rémoulade Sauce, Robert Sauce, Roux, Rum Butter, Rum Sauce, Sabayon Sauce, Salad Cream, Salad Dressings, Salsa alla Pizzaiola, Salsa Verde, Sauce Verte, Sauces, Scandinavian Sweet Mustard Sauce, Skorthalia, Smitane Sauce, Soubise Sauce, Sour Cream Sauce, Soy Sauce, Spanish Sauce, Suprême Sauce, Swedish Sauce, Sweet-Sour Sauce, Tabasco Sauce, Tartare Sauce, Thousand Island Dressing, Tomato Sauce, Velouté Sauce, Vinaigrette Dressing, Weinschaum Sauce, White Butter Sauce, White Sauce, Worcestershire Sauce, Zabaglione Sauce

Sausages and Cold Meats

Aberdeen Sausage, Alpino, Andouille, Andouillette, Ardennes Ham, Banger, Bayonne Ham, Beef Sausages, Beer Sausage, Belfast Ham, Bierschinken Sausage, Black Forest Ham, Black Pudding, Blood Sausage, Blutwurst, Bockwurst, Boerewors, Boiling Ring, Bologna, Boudin Blanc, Boudin Noir, Bradenham Ham, Bratwurst, Brawn, Bresaola, Brühwurst, Bully Beef, Bundnerfleisch, Cabanos, Casing, Cervelas, Cervelat, Charcuterie, Chinese Sausages, Chipolata Sausages, Chipped Beef, Chorizo, Cold Cuts, Cooked Sausages, Coppa, Corned Beef, Cotechino, Cotto, Cumberland Ham, Cumberland Sausage, Extrawurst, Fleischwurst, Frankfurters, Fresh Sausages, Frizzes, Fromage de Tête, German Salami, Goetborg, Goettinger, Gothaer, Gutsleberwurst, Gyulai, Ham Sausage, Head Cheese, Hot Dog, Hunter's Sausage, Jagdwurst, Jambon Blanc, Jambon Cuit de Prague, Jambon d'Ardennes, Jambon de Paris, Jambon Persillé, Játernice, Jelita, Jésus, Jewish Salami, Kabanos, Kalbsleberwurst, Kassler, Katenrauchwurst, Katenspeck, Kielbasa, Kiszka Kaszanka, Knackwurst, Kochwurst, Krakauer, Kräuterleberwurst, Lachsschinken, Landjäger Sausage, Laxschinken, Lebanon Bologna, Leberkäse, Leberwurst, Linquisa, Liver Sausage, Longazina, Lonza, Loukanika, Luganeghe, Luncheon Meat, Merguez, Mettwurst, Morcilla, Mortadella, Oxford Sausages, Pancetta, Pastrami, Pepper Salami, Pepperone, Pfälzer Leberwurst, Pinkel, Plockwurst, Polony, Pork Sausages, Prague Ham, Preserved Sausages, Prosciutto, Prosciutto Crudo, Prosciutto di Montagna, Regensburger, Rosette, Rostbratwurst, Salami, Salsiccia, Salt Beef, Saucisse Sèche, Saucisson Sec au Poivre, Saucisson Sec aux Herbes, Saucisson Sec d'Arles, Saucisson Sec de Ménage, Saucisson Sec de Montagne, Sausage Meat, Sausages, Saveloy, Scalded Sausages, Schinkenwurst, Schlackwurst, Schwarzwurst, Smithfield Ham, Soppressate, Sopressa, Spam, Speck, Suffolk Ham, Sülzwurst, Summer Sausage, Tasso, Teewurst, Thüringer Rotwurst, Toulouse Sausage, Vienna Sausage, Virginia Ham, Weisswurst, Westphalian Ham, White Pudding, Wiener, Wurst, York Ham, Zampone, Zungenwurst

Soups

Avgolemono Soupa, Avocado Soup, Bisque, Borsch, Borshchok, Bortsch de Fasole, Botvinia, Bouillabaisse, Bouillon, Brodo di Manzo, Broth, Brown Onion Soup, Caldo Verde, Chowder, Clear Soup, Cock-a-Leekie Soup, Consommé, Cream Soup, Crème Agnès Sorel, Erwenten Soep, Fish Soup, Fruit Soup, Garbure, Gazpacho, Gildeneh Yoich, Goulash Soup,

Griessnockerlsuppe, Gulyás le Leves, Hot and Sour Soup, Kangaroo Tail Soup, Leberknödelsuppe, Legume Soups, Manhattan Clam Chowder, Minestrone, Miso-Shiru, Mock Turtle Soup, Mulligatawny Soup, New England Clam Chowder, Oxtail Soup, Pepper Pot Soup, Petite Marmite, Potage, Pot-au-Feu, Potée, Pottage, Purée, Risengrød, Scotch Broth, Shark's Fin Soup, Shchi, Shiromono, Solianka, Soup, Soupe Germou, Stracciatella, Thick Soup, Vichyssoise, Westfälische Bohensuppe, Zuppa Pavese

Sugar Products
Barbados Sugar, Beet Sugar, Black Treacle, Brown Sugar, Cane, Caramel, Caster Sugar, Cinnamon Sugar, Coffee Sugar, Confectioner's Sugar, Corn Syrup, Cube Sugar, Dark Sugar, Demerara Sugar, Dextrose, Foot Sugar, Fructose, Fruit Syrups, Glucose, Golden Syrup, Granulated Sugar, Icing Sugar, Invert Sugar, Jaggery, Jam Sugar, Light Corn Syrup, Light Muscovado Sugar, Loaf Sugar, Lump Sugar, Maltose, Maple Sugar, Maple Syrup, Molasses Sugar, Muscovado Sugar, Palm Sugar, Panocha, Pieces Sugar, Preserving Sugar, Saccharose, Sucrose, Sugar, Sugar Cane, Sugar Syrup, Sugarloaf, Syrup, Treacle, Vanilla Sugar, White Sugar

Tea
Assam, Black Tea, Bohea, Breakfast Blend, Broken Orange Pekoe, Caravan Tea, Ceylon Tea, Cha, Chamomile Tea, Congou, Darjeeling, Dimbula, Dust, Earl Grey, Fannings, Formosa Oolong Tea, Green Tea, Gunpowder, Herbal Tea, Jasmine Tea, Keemun, Kenya Tea, Lapsang Souchong, Maté, Oolong, Orange Pekoe, Pekoe, Russian Tea, Souchong, Tannin, Tea, Tea-bag

Utensils
Aluminium Saucepan, Attelette, Bain-Marie, Baking Sheet, Baking Tray, Baller, Basins, Beater, Blancmange Mould, Blender, Bombe Mould, Border Mould, Bread Saw, Broach, Bun Tins, Can Opener, Canelle Knife, Cannikin, Carafe, Carborundum Stone, Casserole Dish, Casserolette, Charlotte Mould, Chessel, Chicken Brick, Chinois, Chip Basket, Chopping Board, Chopsticks, Churn, Cocottes, Coffee Grinder, Colander, Cooker, Cook's Knife, Cooling Jug, Copper Pans, Corer, Coupe Dish, Couscousière, Creamer, Crêpe Pan, Crock Pot, Cruet, Cutters, Dariole Moulds, Daubière, Deep-Fryer, Digester, Dipper, Double Boiler, Double Saucepan, Dredger, Earthenware, Egg Poacher, Egg Pricker, Egg Separator, Egg Slicer, Egg Wedger, Enamel Saucepan, Fish Kettle, Fish Slice, Flan Ring, Flour Dredger, Food Processor, Food Safe, Forcing Bag, Freezer Knife, Fryer, Frying Basket, Frying Pan, Game Pie Mould, Garlic Press, Girdle, Grater, Griddle, Gridiron, Grill, Grill Pan, Haybox, Hob, Hydrometer, Icing Bag, Infuser, Jelly Bag, Jelly Mould, Juice Extractor, Knife Sharpener, Ladle, Larding Needle, Lemon Squeezer, Lemon Zester, Liquidizer, Mandoline, Marmite Dish, Measuring Cup, Measuring Jug, Meat Cleaver, Meat Safe, Melon Baller, Mill, Mincer, Mixer, Mortar, Mould, Needles, Nozzle, Omelette Pan, Oven, Palette Knife, Pan, Pancake Pan, Pasta-making Machines, Pastry Board, Pastry Cutters, Patty Tins, Peeler, Pestle, Pestle and Mortar, Pie Dish, Piping Bag, Popper, Pot, Potato Masher, Potato Peeler, Poultry Shears, Pressure Cooker, Ramekin, Refrigerator, Ring Mould, Rolling Pin, Roman Pot, Römertopf, Rotary Beater, Rotisserie, Saccharometer, Salad Shaker, Salamander, Saté Sticks, Sauce Spoon, Sauceboat, Saucepan, Sausage Machine, Sauté Pan, Saw, Sawknife, Scales, Scissors, Serrated Knife, Sieve, Sifter, Sink Tidy, Skewer, Slip, Soda Siphon, Soufflé Dish, Spatula, Spit, Spurtle, Stainless Steel Saucepan, Steamer, Steel, Strainer, Sugar Thermometer, Terrine Dish, Thermostat, Tin, Tongs, Trencher, Tureen, Vegetable Parer, Waffle Iron, Whisk, Wok, Zester

Vegetables — Fruits
Aubergine, Bamiya, Beef Tomato, Bell Pepper, Bindi, Brinjal, Candle Fruit, Capsicum, Cherry Tomato, Chilli, Cow-cumber, Cucumber, Eggplant, Gombo, Green Tomatoes, Ladies' Fingers, Okra, Pea Aubergines, Pimiento, Red Peppers, Spanish Pepper, Sweet Pepper, Tomato

Vegetables — Fungi
Bay Bolete, Beefsteak Fungus, Blewit, Brown Fungus, Button Mushroom, Cep, Cèpe, Chanterelle, Chinese Mushrooms, Cloud Ear Fungus, Common Mushroom, Cultivated Mushroom, Cup Mushroom, Dried Mushroom, Fairy Ring Mushroom, Field Mushroom, Flat Mushroom, Fungus, Giant Puffball, Grisette, Honey Fungus, Horn of Plenty, Horse Mushroom, Ink Cap, Jew's Ear, Matsutake, Morel, Mushroom, Oyster Mushroom, Paddy Straw Mushroom, Parasol Mushroom, Penny Bun, Poor Man's Beef Steak, Porcini, Puffball, Saffron Milk Cap, St George's Mushroom, Shaggy Cap, Shaggy Parasol, Shiitake, Steinpilz, Straw Mushroom, Truffle, Umbrella Mushroom, Wood Blewit, Wood Ear

Vegetables — Leaves
Arvi Leaf, Bamboo Leaves, Batavia Endive, Belgian Endive, Betel Leaf, Borecole, Brassica, Broccoli, Brussels Sprout, Cabbage, Cabbage Lettuce, Cabbage Palm, Calabrese, Callaloo, Cauliflower, Chicory, Chinese Cabbage, Chinese Leaves, Chinese Spinach, Cole, Collard, Corn Salad, Cos Lettuce, Couve Tronchuda, Curly Endive, Curly Kale, Dandelion, Dasheen Leaf, Escarole, Florentine, Frisée, Green Vegetables, Greens, Heart of Palm, Hop, Iceberg Lettuce, Kail, Kale, Knol-Kohl, Kohlrabi, Lamb's Lettuce, Lamb's Quarters, Leaf Beet, Lettuce, Mâche, Nasturtium, Nopales, Oak Leaf Lettuce, Pak-Choi, Palm Heart, Patra, Pe-Tsai, Portugal Cabbage, Purslane, Radicchio, Rape, Rocket, Romaine Lettuce, Romanesco, Savoy, Sea Kale Beet, Spinach, Spinach Beet, Spring Greens, Succory, Swiss Chard, Vine Leaves, Watercress, Webb's Wonderful Lettuce, White Cabbage, Witloof

Vegetables — Onions
Allium, Chinese Chive, Chinese Leek, Chinese Onion, Green Onion, Kuchai, Leek, Onion, Rocambole, Salad Onion, Scallion, Spanish Onion, Spring Onion

Vegetables — Pods and Seeds
Adzuki Bean, Arhar, Asparagus Bean, Bean, Ben Tree, Bengal Gram, Black Bean, Blackeye Bean, Borlotti Bean, Broad Bean, Butter Bean, Cannellini Bean, Channa, Chickpea, Chinese Pea, Chori, Corn-on-the-Cob, Drumstick Pod, Dwarf Green Bean, Egyptian Bean, Fava Bean, Fazolia Bean, Feijao Bean, Field Bean, Flageolet Bean, French Bean, Frijoles Negros, Ful Medames, Garbanzo, Golden Gram, Great Northern Bean, Green Gram, Haricot Bean, Horse Bean, Hyacinth Bean, Kidney Bean, Lablab Bean, Legume, Leguminous, Lentil, Lima Bean, Lobia, Madagascar Bean, Mange-Tout, Marrowfat Pea, Mexican Black Bean, Mung Bean, Mushy Peas, Navy Bean, Pea, Petits Pois, Pigeon Pea, Pinto Bean, Processed Peas, Pulse, Rarhar, Red Gram, Red Kidney Bean, Rosecoco Bean, Runner Bean, Sieva Bean, Snap Bean, Snow Pea, Soya Bean, Split Pea, Sugar Pea, Susumber, Sweetcorn, Tuware, Val, Wax Bean, Yard-long Bean, Yellow Split Pea

Vegetables — Roots and Tubers
Beet, Beetroot, Black Salsify, Carnauba, Carrot, Cassava, Celeriac, Chinese Artichoke, Chorogi, Chufa, Coco, Cologassi, Crosnes, Daikon, Dasheen, Eddo, Jacket, Jerusalem Artichoke, Kumara, Lotus, Manioc, Mooli, Neep, Oyster Plant, Parsnip, Poi, Potato, Pratie, Radish, Rampion, Rettich, Root Vegetable, Rutabaga, Salsify, Scorzonera, Spud, Sugar Beet, Swede, Sweet Potato, Tannia, Taro, Tattie, Tiger Nut, Tuber, Turnip, Wax Palm, White Radish, Winter Radish, Yam, Yautia, Yuca

Vegetables — Sea Vegetables
Alaria, Arame, Brown Ribweed, Carrageen, Dulse, Finger Kombu, Green Laver, Hijiki, Irish Moss, Kelp, Kombu, Laver, Mekabu, Murlins, Nori, Pearl Moss, Sea Girdle, Sea Lettuce, Sea Oak, Sea Vegetable, Seaweed, Sloke, Tangle, Wakame, Wing Kelp

Vegetables — Squashes
Balsam Apple, Bitter Gourd, Bitter Melon, Bottle Gourd, Butternut Squash, Calabash, Calabaza, Chayote, Chinese Bitter Melon, Chow-Chow, Christophene, Courgette, Crookneck Squash, Cymling, Doodhi, Fuzzy Melon, Gourd, Hubbard Squash, Karela, Marrow, Mirliton, Parwal, Pattypan Squash, Pepo, Pumpkin, Round Gourd, Scalloped Squash, Spaghetti Fruit, Spaghetti Marrow, Squash, Squash Melon, Tinda, Tindori, Turban Squash, Turk's Cap Squash, Vegetable Marrow, Vegetable Pear, Yellow Squash, Zucchini

Vegetables — Stalks and Shoots
Alfalfa, Asparagus, Bamboo Shoots, Bean Sprouts, Celery, Florence Fennel, Glasswort, Pokeweed, Rhubarb, Samphire, Seakale, Sparrowgrass, Spear, Sprue, Sweet Anise

Vegetables — Thistles
Cardoon, Choke, Globe Artichoke, Nettle

Vitamins
Aneurin, Ascorbic Acid, Biotin, Cholecalciferol, Cyanocobalamin, Folic Acid, Menaquione, Niacin, Nicotinamide, Nicotinic Acid, Pantothenic Acid, Pyridoxine, Retinol, Riboflavin, Thiamine, Tocopherol, Vitamin A, Vitamin B Complex, Vitamin B_1, Vitamin B_2, Vitamin B_3, Vitamin B_5, Vitamin B_6, Vitamin B_{12}, Vitamin C, Vitamin D, Vitamin E, Vitamin K, Vitamins

Argentina
Arequipe, Asado, Cajeta de Celaya, Chimichurri, Dulce de Leche, Manjar Blanco, Matambre, Natillas Piuranas, Parrillada

Australia
Australian Fondant Icing, Kangaroo Tail Soup, Lamingtons, Pavlova

Austria
Apfelstrudel, Backhendl, Blue Trout, Emperor's Omelette, Forelle Blau, Griessnockerlsuppe, Gugelhupf, Kaiserschmarren, Kalbshaxen, Leberknödelsuppe, Linz Cake, Linzertorte, Obers, Palatschinken, Sachertorte, Salzburger Nockerln, Schlag Obers, Tafelspitz, Wiener Schnitzel, Wiener Schnitzel Holstein, Zwiebelrostbraten

Belgium
Anguilles au Vert, Carbonade of Beef, Carbonnade à la Flamande, Chicorées au Jambon, Gauffres, Moules Marinières, Oiseaux sans Têtes, Tarte au Riz, Tomates Farcies, Waterzooi

Bolivia
Guiso de Repollo, Pollo Rebozado, Repollo Relleno

Brazil
Acarje, Carne Ensopada, Churrasco a Gaucho, Cozido, Doce de Leite, Feijoada Completa, Picadinho

Britain
Afternoon Tea, Almond Macaroons, Almond Paste, Angels on Horseback, Apple Crumble, Arbroath Smokies, Aspic Jelly, Baked Apples, Baked Batter Pudding, Bangers and Mash, Bannock, Bara Brith, Bath Chap, Beef Olives, Black Bun, Black Pudding, Black Treacle, Blancmange, Blind Scouse, Blood Sausage, Boar's Head, Boiled Beef and Carrots, Boodles' Orange Fool, Brawn, Brose, Brown Bread Ice Cream, Bubble and Squeak, Buck Rarebit, Cauliflower Cheese, Chip Butty, Civet, Clootie Dumpling, Cock-a-Leekie Soup, Confectioner's Custard, Corned Beef, Cornish Fairings, Cornish Heavy Cake, Cornish Pasty, Cornish Saffron Cake, Cornish Sly Cakes, Cornish Splits, Cottage Pie, Cream Tea, Cullen Skink, Devonshire Junket, Devonshire Squab Pie, Dropped Scones, Eccles Cakes, Egg Salad, Fadge, Faggots, Fish and Chips,

Fish Fingers, Fish Soup, Fishcakes, Flapjack, Floating Islands, Flummery, Fool, Forfar Bridies, Frumenty, Game Pie, Grasmere Shortbread, Haggis, Haricot Lamb, Hash, Haslet, Hodge-Podge, Hotch-Potch, Jam Roly-Poly, Jellied Eels, Jelly Cubes, Jersey Wonders, Jugged Hare, Junket, Kedgeree, Knickerbocker Glory, Lancashire Hot-Pot, Lancashire Parkin, Lardy Cake, Laver, Love in Disguise, Macaroni Cheese, Maids of Honour, Marzipan, Mashed Potatoes, Meat Pie, Melton Mowbray Pie, Mixed Grill, Mulligatawny Soup, Mushy Peas, Oatcakes, Oxford John, Packet Jelly, Partan Bree, Pease Pudding, Petticoat Tails, Ploughman's Lunch, Poor Man's Goose, Pork Pie, Potted Hough, Potted Shrimps, Prawn Cocktail, Raised Pie, Roast Beef, Roly-Poly Pudding, Russian Fish Pie, Salmagundi, Salmis, Sausage Rolls, Scone, Scone Round, Scotch Broth, Scotch Eggs, Scotch Pancakes, Scotch Woodcock, Scots Black Bun, Scottish Shortbread, Scrambled Eggs, Scrapple, Sea Pie, Shepherd's Pie, Shortbread, Shortbread Biscuits, Simnel Cake, Smoked Oyster, Smokies, Soused Herrings, Soused Mackerel, Spotted Dick, Squab Pie, Star-Gazey Pie, Steak and Kidney Pie, Steak and Kidney Pudding, Syllabub, Syrup Roly-Poly, Toad-in-the-Hole, Tripe and Onions, Veal and Ham Pie, Welsh Rarebit, Whim Wham, Wimpy, Yorkshire Parkin, Yorkshire Pudding, Yorkshire Spice Bread

Bulgaria
Agneshka Kebab, Chopkebab, Guvetch, Kebabchés, Shoppe Kebab, Shopska, Stomna Kebab, Tarator

Burma
Ame Hnat, Blachan, Chetha Si Biyan, Ghaw-Be-Thot, Mohingha, Panthe Kaukswe, Wetha See Pyan

Canada
Acadian Blueberry Grunt, Alberta Oranges, Bakeapples, Bonavista Bay Cod's Tongues, Boundary Bay Crab Bouchées, Chuckwagon Stew, Cloudberry, Cretons, Fiddleheads, Flipper Pie, Habitant Pea Soup, Maple Syrup Pie, Ogopogo Apple Dumplings, Okanagan Savoury Tomatoes, Pain au Sucre, Pile o'Bones Turkey, Roasted Cheese Canapés, Rose Hip Catsup, Saanich Fruit Plate, Saltspring Lamb, Solomon Grundy, Sweetgrass Buffalo and Beer Pie, Tourtière, West Coast Halibut Royal

Caribbean
Accra, Achiote Seeds, Ackra Fritters, Acra Lamori, Aji-Li-Mojili, Butifarrón Sabroso, Callaloo Soup, Caribbean Banana Bread, Carne Mechada, Chochon Rouci, Conkies, Coo-Coo, Crab Backs, Créole Christmas Cake, Floats, Gâteau Noir, Jan Coude Mai Marge, Jug-Jug, Kallaloo, Le Colombo, Mountain Chickens, Paimi, Pain Fig Banane, Pastelillos, Pelau, Pepper Pot Soup, Pigeon Pea, Pouile Dudon, Sancoche, Sofrito, Soupe Germou, Stamp and Go, Tostones

Chile
Caldillo de Congrio, Caznela de Cordero

China
Bird's-Nest Soup, Cantonese Cooking, Chinese Egg Roll, Chinese Steaming, Chop Suey, Chow Mein, Crabmeat and Sweetcorn Soup, Dim Sum, Egg Roll, Eggs Foo Yung, Fried Rice, Fukien Cooking, Honan Cooking, Hot and Sour Soup, Mandarin Cooking, Mongolian Fire Pot, Pancake Roll, Peking Cooking, Peking Duck, Prawn Crackers, Red Cooking, Rice Wine, Shanghai Cooking, Shark's Fin Soup, Spring Roll, Stir-Fry, Suan La Tang, Sweet and Sour Prawns, Sweet-and-Sour Pork, Szechuan Cooking, Tahu, Tangerine Peel, Wontons

Colombia
Ajiaco, Sancocho, Sopa de Almejas

Czechoslovakia
Knedlíky, Palačinky

Denmark
Aeblekage, Aebleskiver, Aeggekage, Bondepige med Slør, Brunede Kartofler, Caramelized Potatoes,

Iceland
Blódmör, Hákarl, Hangikjöt, Hardfiskur, Head Cheese, Lifrarpylsa, Pickled Testicles, Riklingur, Skyr, Whale Blubber

India
Achar, Amchar, Barfi, Basmati Rice, Bessan, Bhaji, Bhel Puri, Bhuna, Biriyani, Bombay Duck, Burfi, Chapatis, Chutney, Curries, Dahi, Dhal, Dhansak, Gajjar Halwa, Ghee, Gulab Jamon, Idli, Jalebi, Kababs, Koftes, Korma, Kulfi, Lassi, Masala Dosa, Naan, Paan, Pakoras, Paneer, Papadum, Paratha, Pilau, Poppadom, Pulao, Puris, Raita, Ras Gulas, Rogan Josh, Sambals, Samosas, Tandoori, Tikka, Varak, Vindaloo Curry

Indonesia
Acar, Gado-Gado, Gulé, Ketan, Ketjap Sauce, Krupuk, Nasi Goreng, Rijst-Tafel, Saté, Selamatan, Seroendeng

International
Beef Wellington, Egg Mayonnaise, Grilled Grapefruit, Hamburgers, Lobster Mayonnaise, Pepper Steak, Steak au Poivre, Steak Diane, Steak Tartare

Ireland
Barm Brack, Boxty, Champ, Colcannon, Dublin Coddle, Irish Coffee, Irish Stew, Stirabout

Italy
all'Amatriciana, Amaretti, Antipasti, Arance Caramellate, Bollito, Bollito Misto, Brodo di Manzo, Calzone, Cappuccino, Caramelized Oranges, Cassata alla Siciliana, Chicken Cacciatora, Chicken Marengo, Espresso, Fonduta, Frittata, Fritto Misto di Mare, Gnocchi, Granita, Grissini, Lasagne Pasticciate, Minestrone, Osso Bucco, Pannetone, Peperonata, Piccata, Pizza, Pizza Base, Polenta, Pollo alla Cacciatora, Pollo alla Marengo, Risi e Bisi, Risotto, Risotto alla Milanese, Saltimbocca, Scaloppine, Scaloppine Milanese, Spaghetti alla Carbonara, Spaghetti all'Amatriciana, Stracciatella, Stufato, Vitello Tonnato, Zabaglione, Zuppa Inglese, Zuppa Pavese *See also* Pasta

Japan
Aemono, Agemono, Bean Curd, Cha-Soba, Daikon, Dango, Dashi, Donabe, Glutinous Rice, Go-Han, Gohanmono, Kinoko, Manju, Menrui, Mirin, Miso, Miso-Shiru, Mountain Hollyhock, Mushimono, Nabemono, Nimono, Nori-Make, Okashi, Onigiri, Sake, Sashimi, Shiromono, Soba Noodles, Somen Noodles, Soy Bean Curd, Sukiyaki, Sunomono, Sushi, Tempura, Teriyaki, Tofu, Tsukemono, Udon Noodles, Wasebi, Yakimono, Yakitori

Jewish and Israeli
Bagels, Blintzes, Challah, Charoset, Cholent, Cholla, Chopped Egg and Onion, Chopped Herring, Chopped Liver, Farfel, Felafel, Gefilte Fish, Gildeneh Yoich, Hamantaschen, Holishkes, Hummus, Jewish Chicken Soup, Kishka, Knaidlech, Knishes, Kosher, Kreplach, Kugel, Lekach, Lokshen, Matzo, Passover Bread, Petcha, Pirogen, Plava, Potato Latkes, Salt Beef, Schav, Schmaltz, Stuffed Derma, Tzimmes

Korea
Bulgogi Wa Sanjeog Gui, Gaji Jijim, Gochu Jeon, Gogi Jeon-Gol, Oi Gimchi, Yang-Baechu Gimchi, Yang-Hoe

Malaysia
Acar, Ayam Kichup, Gulai, Ikan Berinti, Kelepa Sayur, Laksa Asam, Otak-Otak, Sambal Goreng Sotong, Satay

Malta
Timpana

Mexico
Albondigas, Avocado Soup, Buñuelos, Burritos, Cabrito Asado, Ceviche, Chilaquiles, Chiles Rellenos, Chilli con Carne, Chimichangas, Corn Chips, Empanadas, Empanaditas, Enchiladas, Frijoles Refritos, Guacamole, Masa Harina, Mole, Mole Poblana de Guajalote, Nachos, Picadillo,

à la
(au, aux)
French term meaning in the style of or after the manner of, for example, *à la Bourgeoise*. The definition of such phrases is to be found under the main word in the phrase, that is, under *Bourgeoise* in the above example.

ABALONE
A single-shelled mollusc (*Haliotis* species) found in the Pacific. The shell can exceed 15 cm/6 inches in length and is shaped rather like an ear. The edible part is the 'foot', which is lean and may be eaten raw or fried. This mollusc, in its various species, is very popular in Japan.

ABATS
French term for offal, giblets and head of an animal.

ABATTOIR
See *Slaughterhouse*.

ABBEYDALE
An English, semi-soft and extra high-protein cows' milk cheese which contains chopped chives and onions. It has reduced fat and salt levels.

ABELMOSK
A bushy plant (*Hibiscus moschatus*) of the hollyhock family with musky seeds which are used to flavour coffee. It is native to tropical Asia and the East Indies.

ABERDEEN ANGUS BEEF
Breed of black and hornless beef cattle, originating in Scotland and highly prized for the quality of their meat.

ABERDEEN FILLET
Smoked haddock from the north-east coast of Scotland.

ABERDEEN SAUSAGE
A Scottish sausage, based on mutton.

ABERNETHY BISCUITS
Originated in the town of Abernethy in Scotland. Caraway seeds are always used for flavouring.

ABSINTHE
A dry liqueur, green in colour, produced from spirit flavoured with oil of wormwood and additional herbs and spices. Because of the dangerous nature of oil of wormwood, absinthe, in its original form, is either limited or prohibited in many European countries. Modern substitutes are the aniseed-flavoured drinks which, like absinthe, turn cloudy when diluted with water. Absinthe was invented during the 18th century.

AC
Abbreviation of *Appellation Contrôlée*.

ACADIAN BLUEBERRY GRUNT
A speciality of Nova Scotia in Canada, consisting of stewed blueberries topped with spoonfuls of scone mixture. The saucepan is covered and left over a gentle heat until the scone topping is cooked. The grunt is served from the saucepan with cream.

ACAJOU
See *Cashew Nuts*.

ACAR
(Achar, Atjar)
Indonesian mixed-pickle salad consisting of shredded cabbage, carrots, cauliflower and other vegetables which have been partially boiled in a spicy vinegar mixture tinted yellow with turmeric and left for about a week before they are eaten.

ACARJE
Brazilian fritters made from a blackeyed bean and dried shrimp mixture, usually fried in palm oil

and served as a cocktail savoury or appetizer with a spicy shrimp sauce.

ACCRA
Trinidadian yeasted and fried doughnuts made from salt cod. The traditional flavourings are garlic and chillies and the *accra* are eaten hot with floats.

ACESULPHAME-K
A modern sugar substitute used in Britain.

ACETIC ACID
Pure acid of vinegar, made up of equal parts of carbon and oxygen and 5% hydrogen.

ACHAR
(Aachar, Achard)
Indian pickles and relishes which accompany curries and other dishes.

ACHEE
See *Akee*.

ACHIOTE
(Achuete)
Spanish term for annatto.

ACHIOTE SEEDS
(Annatto Seeds)
The seeds of the annatto tree (*Bixa orellana*) which grows in the Caribbean. They are heated slowly with cooking oil or lard until the mixture turns bright orange in colour. It is used to add colour to foods.

ACID DROP
Hard boiled sweet, sharpened with tartaric acid.

ACIDIFY (TO)
(Acidulate)
To add acid to a food or mixture of foods. The acid can be vinegar, acetic acid or lemon or lime juice.

ACIDS
Chemical compounds with a sour taste. Direct opposite of alkalis. Many acids are used in cooking, pickling and preserving. Can be in powder form (cream of tartar) or liquid form (lemon juice). All acids tend to corrode metals such as iron or aluminium; therefore enamel, glass, earthenware, plastic and stainless steel kitchen utensils are more satisfactory.

ACIDULATE (TO)
See *Acidify*.

ACIDULATED WATER
Water to which lemon juice or vinegar has been added; about 5 ml/1 teaspoon to every 300 ml/½ pint.

ACINI
(Acini de Pepe)
Very small pasta shapes, about the size of peppercorns, used in soup.

ACKARA
A Gambian dish served seven days after the birth of a child, at the naming ceremony. It consists of soaked white beans ground finely, then worked to a stiff paste with water. The mixture is shaped into balls, deep-fried and served with a sauce made from tomatoes, onions, peppers, garlic and chilli.

ACKRA FRITTERS
(Akkra Fritters)
Jamaican fritters made from mashed blackeye beans and chillies and served as appetizers.

ACRA LAMORI
Fish cakes from St Lucia in the Caribbean, made from a basis of salt cod shaped into small cakes and fried.

ADDITIVE
A substance (or substances) added to foods as a preservative, also used to enhance the taste and smell. Some are now considered harmful and, it appears, responsible for certain allergies.

ÄDELOST
A factory-produced, Swedish blue cheese made from cows' milk.

ADOBO
The national dish of the Philippines, a piquant pork, poultry or fish stew containing pepper, soy sauce, garlic, vinegar and sometimes coconut milk.

ADULTERATE (TO)
To reduce the quality of a food or drink product, usually by adding inferior ingredients.

ADZUKI BEAN
(Aduki Bean)
A vegetable (*Phaseolus angularis*) native to the Far East and widely cultivated in China and Japan. It is a legume which grows on a bush and may be cooked whole as a vegetable. More usually, however, the bean is extracted from its pod and either dried to be used as a pulse or ground into powder and used as flour. The very small, hard, dried browny-red bean is a slightly flattened oval shape with a distinctive, tiny white stripe on one side. It features extensively in Japanese and Chinese cookery and is also used in those countries to treat mild kidney disorders. It is a good source of protein but must be boiled briskly for the first 15 minutes of cooking to destroy harmful toxins found in the outer skin which can prove very dangerous to the human body. The adzuki bean is suitable for sprouting.

AEBLEKAGE
Although the literal English translation is apple cake, this Danish speciality is a dessert, made from layers of sweetened apple purée and butter-fried breadcrumbs with sugar. It is prepared in individual glass dishes and each portion is topped with whipped cream and either red-coloured jam or grated chocolate.

AEBLESKIVER
A form of doughnut with an apple filling, cooked in a special cast-iron pan with seven indentations. This Danish speciality is non-yeasted and light-textured.

AEGGEKAGE
Danish egg cake which is very similar to an omelette. It is left unfolded, topped with bacon rashers and cut into wedges for serving.

AEMONO
Beautifully presented Japanese salad with a dressing made from *miso, tofu* or egg yolk, vinegar and seasonings.

AERATE (TO)
To introduce air into a mixture mechanically or chemically. Mechanical aeration is achieved by such processes as rubbing fat into flour; creaming together fat and sugar; whisking eggs and sugar; whipping cream. Chemical aeration is the result of using raising agents such as baking powder or yeast.

AERATED WATERS
See *Soda Water* and *Mineral Waters*.

AEROSOL CREAM
Ultra-heat treated (UHT) dairy cream in an aerosol can. It contains about 5% sugar, emulsifier E471, stabilizer E407 and propellant nitrous oxide. It is basically designed as a topping to be squirted on to drinks and desserts. It should never be used as a cake filling or decoration because it collapses rapidly on standing.

à l'AFRICAINE
French term for an African-style garnish composed of aubergines, tomatoes, mushrooms and potatoes.

AFTERNOON TEA
A typically English institution. The popularity of this mid-afternoon refreshment was at its height in the middle of the last century; the fashion, according to some

authorities, was started by Anna, wife of the 7th Duke of Bedford, in order to stave off hunger pangs between lunch and tea. In addition to tea, sandwiches, bread and butter, scones, small cakes and biscuits are all eaten for afternoon tea.

AFTERS
A British colloquial term for the pudding course at the end of a meal.

AGAMI
(Trumpeter)
A popular game bird (*Guiana agami*) in South America, used for soups, stews and braised dishes.

AGAR-AGAR
A gelatine derived from seaweed, widely used in Oriental cookery and by vegetarians. Dishes made with agar-agar stay firm and set without refrigeration — a major advantage in hot and humid climates.

AGEMONO
A general Japanese term for the coating of batter or crumbs covering food which is to be deep-fried.

AGNEAU
French term for lamb.

AGNESHKA KEBAB
Called 'butcher-style' casserole, a Bulgarian speciality made from lamb, kidneys, sweetbreads, onions, chillies, herbs, lemon juice, wine and seasonings cooked in the oven and thickened with milk and beaten eggs. The usual accompaniment is rice.

AGNOLOTTI
(Pazlache)
Oblongs or rounds of pasta stuffed with meat or a ricotta cheese and spinach mixture, which are similar in size and character to ravioli. They are served with meat or tomato sauces or coated with melted butter.

AIGRETTE
An Anglo-French savoury cocktail fritter containing cheese and based on choux pastry.

AIGUILLETTES
French term for long thin strips or slices of meat, poultry, game or fish.

à l'AIL
French term for any food flavoured with garlic.

AILERONS
Fillets cut from the breast of chicken, including a small piece of wing bone.

AILLADE
A French mayonnaise sauce, flavoured with garlic and walnuts. It is usually served with Mediterranean fish dishes.

AÏOLI SAUCE
A southern European sauce based on mayonnaise, copiously flavoured with peeled and crushed garlic. It can be served with freshwater fish, dishes made from salt cod, tomato salads and boiled beef. There is an alternative version made from breadcrumbs, milk, garlic, egg yolks, olive oil, seasonings and lemon juice.

AIR-DRIED
Food, such as Parma ham, that is placed in curing sheds and dried naturally by air currents entering the sheds through built-in openings.

AJIACO
A thick Colombian soup made from chicken, vegetables including sweetcorn, stock, sausages and milk. Sliced hard-boiled eggs and tablespoonfuls of cream are added to each serving.

AJI-LI-MOJILI
A sour garlic sauce from Puerto Rico, served with barbecued pork.

AJI-NO-MOTO

(Monosodium Glutamate, MSG)
Derived from Japanese seaweed, sugar beet pulp and the gluten from wheat. Its function is to intensify the flavour of protein foods, making them more appetizing. Whether it can cause allergic reactions, known as the Chinese restaurant syndrome, including queasiness, cardiac palpitation, dizziness and even migraine, is now open to debate.

AJOWAN

A member of the parsley, caraway and cumin family, an Oriental seed which has a similar flavour to thyme. It is widely used in lentil dishes, especially in India. Ajowan is considered to be good for the digestion and ajowan water is said to have a calming effect on troubled stomachs.

AKEE

(Achee, Ackee)
The fruit of the evergreen tree *Blighia sapida*, native to West Africa, which was introduced to the West Indies by Captain Bligh. The tree can often be cropped twice a year, making the fresh fruit available for much of the year. The fruit is about the same size as a peach, must only be eaten when ripe and has a skin that hardens and turns from yellow to red as it matures. When fully ripe, the skin splits and reveals three poisonous black seeds surrounded by milky-white flesh. Only the flesh is edible; it may be eaten raw and has the kind of delicate flavour associated with an avocado. When cooked, it is used in savoury dishes and, in Jamaica, it is popularly served with boiled and salted cod. Canned akee is exported from Jamaica.

AKUREYRI

A factory-produced, Icelandic blue cheese made from cows' milk.

AL DENTE

Firm and chewy. A term to describe the way Italians like their freshly cooked pasta to be: still with a bit of bite to it and *not* overcooked.

ALARIA

A sea vegetable (*Alaria esculenta*) of the brown algae group of plants found in the coastal waters of the North Atlantic. It is a leafy vegetable, similar to Japanese wakame. Alaria has a number of local names and is called murlins in Ireland, brown ribweed in England and wing kelp in North America.

ALASKA BLACK COD

See *Black Cod*.

ALASKA DUNGENESS CRAB

See *Dungeness Crab*.

ALASKA POLLOCK

See *Walleye Pollock*.

ALBACORE

A small member (*Thunnus alalunga*) of the tuna family with a streamlined shape and a maximum length of about 1 metre/39 inches. The back of the fish is blue, gradually changing to silver-grey on the sides and belly. Albacore is caught in warm seas worldwide and the main season is late autumn. The flesh is not so heavy as that of the larger tuna and the fish may be baked or grilled.

ALBERTA ORANGES

A Canadian term for rose hips in Alberta because they are so rich in Vitamin C.

ALBONDIGAS

Mexican meat balls containing olives, chilli powder, eggs, spices, herbs, onions and bread which are simmered in stock with garlic and tomatoes.

ALBUMEN

A water-soluble protein found in egg white, milk and animal blood. It coagulates on heating.

ALCOHOL
Intoxicating liquid which is colourless, volatile and inflammable. It is formed by the activity of enzymes secreted by living micro-organisms known as yeast cells.

ALCOÖL
French term for alcohol.

ALE
The old English word for beer, which, before the introduction of hops, was flavoured with herbs and therefore left no bitter after-taste. It is an excellent base for full-flavoured soups, stews and casseroles and is available as pale, bitter, mild, etc. The alcoholic content ranges from 3.5–10° proof (2–5.5 GL).

ALEGAR
Vinegar made from ale; also sour ale.

ALEWIFE
A member (*Alosa pseudoharengus*) of the herring family with a similar streamlined shape but with a deeper belly. It is caught at an average length of 25–30 cm/10–12 inches. Its back is coloured greeny-grey, shading to silver on the sides and belly. It lives mainly in the sea, but spawns in the fresh water of rivers. The principal landing season is May to July when most of the fish are taken from rivers and estuaries around the North American coast between Nova Scotia and North Carolina. The flesh is oily and the fish may be baked, fried or grilled.

ALEXANDER
A perennial herb (*Smyrnium olusatrum*) native to the Mediterranean but also found in other parts of Europe, including Britain, with a flavour that is reminiscent of celery. The herb, once eaten as a vegetable, is now rarely used; celery tends to be the more readily available substitute.

ALFALFA
A vegetable (*Medicago sativa*) native to the Mediterranean region and grown in many parts of the world, mainly as animal feed. It is a legume and the seeds have become popular for sprouting. The fine, almost hair-like shoots have a mild flavour and may be eaten on their own or in salads.

à l'ALGÉRIENNE
French term for a garnish of tomatoes, peppers and/or potato croquettes.

ALKALIS
Chemical compounds with an acrid taste which form salts when combined with acids. The most widely known alkalis in domestic use are washing soda, bicarbonate of soda and ammonia.

ALKALOID
Organic compound containing nitrogen which reacts chemically in the same way as an alkali.

à l'ALLEMANDE
French term for a German-style garnish of both noodles and mashed potatoes.

ALLEMANDE SAUCE
A rich version of suprême sauce to which extra egg yolks and more double cream are added. It can be served with poached white fish dishes, vegetables and roast or boiled chicken or veal.

ALLGÄU EMMENTAL
A Bavarian Alp cheese produced from cows' milk in the Allgäu area of southern Germany. It closely resembles Swiss Emmental, with a pleasantly mild and nutty flavour. The cheese is a warm yellow, interspersed with cherry-sized holes and the rind is a deep beige colour.

ALLIGATOR
Popular with Acadians (or Cajuns) in the Louisiana Bayou area of North America, alligator meat is

considered a rare treat and luxury, enjoyed once a year when hunting is permitted. The meat is said to be delicious and that from the tail as white and as sweet as crabmeat.

ALLIGATOR PEAR
See *Avocado*.

ALLIUM
Any of a large genus of plants belonging to the lily family including chives, garlic, leeks, onions and shallots.

ALL-PURPOSE FLOUR
North American term for plain white flour, usually blended from hard and soft flours.

ALLSPICE
(Jamaica Pepper, Pimento)
Native to the West Indies, Mexico and South America, allspice is the round, pea-sized and unripe fruit of an evergreen tree (*Pimenta dioica*) belonging to the myrtle family. Known in the trade as pimento (not to be confused with pimiento, which is a type of red pepper), the berries are picked while green and dried in the sun for about a week until they turn dark red. Allspice tastes and smells like a blend of cinnamon, nutmeg and cloves, hence its name. The whole berries are used in pickles, chutney, beef stews and pot roasts; ground allspice can be added to apple dishes, tomato sauce, fruit cakes and gingerbreads, milk puddings and marinades.

ALLUMETTES
French term for matchstick-sized strips of deep-fried potatoes.

ALMOND ESSENCE
Pure, natural almond essence is made by distilling almond oil; however, a synthetic essence is most commonly used in baking, desserts and confectionery; it is very strong and should be added sparingly.

ALMOND MACAROONS
See *Macaroons*.

ALMOND NIBS
Evenly chopped blanched almonds available in packets. Their purpose is chiefly decorative and they are often used, plain or toasted, to coat the sides of gateaux and sweet soufflés.

ALMOND OIL
An oil extracted from both sweet and bitter almonds and used principally by the cosmetic industry.

ALMOND PASTE
(Marzipan)
Made from a base of sugar, ground almonds and usually egg white. It is pliable and capable of being moulded into varied shapes. It can also be coloured.

ALMOND SLICE
A popular British cake comprising oblongs of pastry with an almond topping, generally decorated with flaked or halved blanched almonds.

ALMONDS
See *Bitter Almonds* and *Sweet Almonds*.

ALP CHEESE
See *Berg*.

ALPINE STRAWBERRY
A small fruit with a delicate flavour, from a cultivated plant (*Fragaria vesca semperflorens*) related to the wood or wild strawberry, grown both commercially and in gardens in Europe. It has a longer fruiting season than the larger hybrid kinds of strawberry and can be easily raised from seed.

ALPINO
A North American term for salami.

à l'ALSACIENNE
French term meaning in the manner of Alsace, indicating the inclusion of sauerkraut and/or potatoes in a specific dish.

ALTAISKI
(Altaysky)
Factory-produced cows' milk cheese from the USSR which resembles Emmental.

ALTENBURGER
An East German cheese which is made from unpasteurized goats' milk or a mixture of cows' and goats' milk. It has a strong and pungent taste and is often flavoured with caraway. This warm yellow-coloured cheese is interspersed with a sprinkling of irregular-shaped holes.

ALUMINIUM FOIL
(Foil)
A protective, waterproof wrapping made from paper-thin sheets of aluminium which may be folded, bent or twisted.

ALUMINIUM SAUCEPAN
Available in a wide range of shapes and sizes, it is light to handle, conducts heat well, is relatively inexpensive and can be obtained with a non-stick interior coating. When required for use on an electric cooker, the base should be thick, flat and slightly grooved.

AMANDINE
French term for any sweet or savoury dish prepared with almonds.

AMANDINE BUTTER
Softened, whipped butter to which ground almonds are added. It is shaped into a 2.5 cm/1 inch diameter roll, wrapped and refrigerated until hard, then cut into rounds of about 5 mm/¼ inch in thickness. These are used to garnish grilled fish or chicken.

AMARETTI
(Amoretti)
Small Italian meringue-like biscuits, containing nuts. They are usually served with coffee at the end of a meal. Although they are very sweet, the word in English means 'little bitters'!

all'AMATRICIANA
(alla Matriciana)
The Italian term for dishes containing a tomato sauce flavoured with chopped onions and salt pork or bacon. The sauce is served with pasta (*spaghetti all' Amatriciana*, for example), meat or poultry dishes.

AMBROSIA
A classic dessert made from thin slices of peeled oranges layered with sliced bananas, fresh pineapple pieces, desiccated coconut and caster or sifted icing sugar.

AMCHAR
(Amchoor)
Dried mango powder, used in India as a cooking additive.

AME HNAT
A Burmese braised beef dish containing fried onions, garlic, ginger, chilli powder, lemon peel and seasonings, garnished with fried onions.

AMERICAN
General term to describe North American Cheddar-type cheeses made from cows' milk.

AMERICAN BLUE
A North American blue-veined cheese made from cows' milk, said to resemble French Roquefort.

AMERICAN FROSTING
A snow-white, North American cake icing which is crisp on the outside and soft inside. It is made from a hot sugar syrup combined with beaten egg whites. It is flavoured with essence and can also be used as a cake filling.

AMERICAN FUDGE CAKE
See *Fudge Cake*.

AMERICAN LONG-GRAIN RICE
See *Regular-milled White Rice*.

AMERICAN PASTEURIZED
Identical to processed cheese, sold in square slices in packets.

AMERICAN PLAICE
(Canadian Plaice, Sand Dab)
A flatfish (*Hippoglossoides platessoides*) of the plaice family which can be up to 60 cm/24 inches or more in length in North American Atlantic waters but only about half this size on the European side. It is particularly popular in Canada where it is also called Canadian plaice or sand dab. It has a typical plaice shape but the markings on the upper side are less well-defined. It is caught all year round and the fish may be poached, steamed, baked, fried or grilled.

AMINO ACIDS
The twenty-two constituents of protein. Proteins are of two types: complete proteins, which contain all the amino acids essential to the body for growth and repair, found in foods such as fish, meat, poultry, cheese, eggs and milk, and incomplete proteins, which lack one or more of the essential amino acids, found in pulses and cereals. The body requires ten essential amino acids for efficient biological action.

à l'AMIRAL
French term for an admiral's garnish (usually for large fish) composed of truffles, mussels, lobster, oysters and crayfish.

AMMONIA
A powerful, strong-smelling gas which, when diluted with water, is used as a cleaning and/or bleaching agent in the home (household ammonia). It is also found occasionally as carbonate of ammonia in certain raising agents.

AMMONIUM CARBONATE
See *Salt of Hartshorn*.

AMOURETTES
The marrow from beef bones which is poached and served as a garnish, often with brains.

ANADAMA BREAD
A traditional North American yeasted loaf, containing polenta and molasses or sometimes black treacle.

ANADROMOUS
A term used to describe fish, such as salmon, which spend time at sea but swim up river to spawn.

ANALEPTIC
A restorative diet of easily digested foods such as beef tea, milk puddings and sweet and savoury jellies.

ANARI
A soft, white ewes' milk cheese, produced in Cyprus. It is identical to Greek Mizithra and eaten for dessert with sugar or honey.

ANCHOVY
A round-bodied fish (*Engraulis encrasicolus*), found in warm sea water. It measures up to 20 cm/8 inches in length and has a dark blue-black back with silvery sides and belly. It is caught mainly in the Mediterranean and the Bay of Biscay from January to September. It is a fish with a very distinctive flavour and oily flesh, and may be fried or grilled. Commercially, it is very important as it is used in many prepared forms and is sold preserved in cans and jars, salted, dried, as a pâté and an essence. The flavour survives almost any treatment and adds distinction to many dishes. Among its relatives are the anchovy caught in the Pacific (*Engraulis mordax*) and the one caught off the North American Atlantic coast (*Anchoa hepsetus*).

ANCHOVY BUTTER
Softened, whipped butter to which lemon juice and either chopped canned anchovies or anchovy essence are added. It is shaped into a 2.5 cm/1 inch diameter roll, wrapped and refrigerated until hard, then cut into rounds of about 5 mm/¼ inch in thickness. These are used to garnish grilled fish and steaks.

ANCHOVY SAUCE
A white sauce flavoured with bottled anchovy essence and lemon juice. It can be served with a variety of fish dishes, hard-boiled eggs and roast veal.

à l'ANDALOUSE
French term for food cooked or garnished in Andalusian style. The ingredients generally comprise tomatoes, red peppers, rice and sometimes aubergines.

ANDALOUSE MAYONNAISE
A mayonnaise flavoured with tomato purée and finely chopped canned pimientos. It can be served with cold roast veal and poultry, also hard-boiled eggs.

ANDOUILLE
A French speciality sausage, usually made from chitterlings, tripe, fat, seasonings and spices packed into a pig's large intestine and sold ready-cooked. It is served cold in slices as an *hors d'oeuvre*.

ANDOUILLETTE
A French speciality sausage, closely resembling *andouille*, and consisting of chitterlings, tripe, fat, seasonings and spices packed into a pig's small intestine. It is generally heated and served with mustard.

AÑEJO
Mexico's favourite cheese, made from cows' or goats' milk. It is well-matured with a strong, salty flavour and firm but crumbly texture.

ANELLINI
Very small rings of pasta, generally served in soup.

ANEURIN
See *Vitamin* B_1.

ANGEL FISH
(Angel Shark)
A member (*Squatina squatina*) of one of the shark families, with a slightly flattened body, large pectoral fins and an elongated tail. It lives on the sea floor and the colour of the back varies from grey to sandy-yellow while the underside is white. It can measure up to 2 metres/6½ feet in length. It is caught in the Mediterranean and Atlantic all year round. The flesh is lean and white and may be poached, grilled, fried or baked. An American relation (*Squatina dumerili*) is caught off the Atlantic coast of North America.

ANGEL FOOD CAKE
A North American speciality, this is a fairly complex cake to make and requires a large number of egg whites. It is very light in texture, almost white in colour, dry and completely fatless (recipes for authentic angel food cake can be found in North American cookbooks). A version of angel food cake, which is sold in Britain, is often pink and white with mock cream in the middle.

ANGELICA
Native to the northern hemisphere, angelica (*Angelica archangelica*) is said to be named after an angel who came to earth during a plague and recommended it as a cure. Introduced in Britain in the 16th century, the herb is a tall, biennial plant with large light-green leaves and sturdy stems. All parts may be used and the stems are often candied and sold for decorating cakes and desserts. When dried, the leaves may be added to pot-pourri or made into a tisane. The aroma is similar to juniper berries and angelica is also added to gin for flavouring.

ANGEL'S HAIR
(Capelli d'Angelo, Vermicellini)
Very fine lengths of pasta, the thinnest of all noodles, which are said to be as fine as angel's hair. They are available dried in packets, woven together in round nests. Angel's hair is generally added to clear soups.

ANGELS ON HORSEBACK
A traditional British savoury course at a formal dinner, also a cocktail snack. Smoked or raw oysters, wrapped in half rashers of streaky bacon, are speared on to cocktail sticks and grilled. They are served hot.

à l'ANGEVINE
French term for food prepared in the style of Anjou, generally denoting the addition of the regional wine.

à l'ANGLAISE
French term meaning 'English style' and applied particularly to fried fish which has been coated with egg and crumbs, and poached, boiled or steamed fish and poultry which is subsequently coated with melted butter.

ANGLER-FISH
See *Monkfish*.

ANGOSTURA AROMATIC BITTERS
(Angostura)
Proprietary aromatic bitters, first produced in 1824 from a mixture of herbs and spices in a rum base. Originally made by Dr J.G.B. Siegert as a medicinal preparation in the town of Angostura (later renamed Ciudad Bolivar) in Venezuela, it is now produced in Trinidad in the West Indies. Once prescribed as a treatment for loss of appetite, it is currently used for many mixed drinks and also as a food flavouring.

ANGUILLES AU VERT
A Belgian stew containing green eels and thickened with egg yolks, which is served hot or cold. It is one of Belgium's national dishes, although it originated in Antwerp.

ANIMELLES
The French term for the testicles of the male ox.

ANISE
An aromatic herb of the *Pimpinella* family and a native of eastern Mediterranean countries. The oil extracted from the herb is used as a flavouring in confectionery and also in some alcoholic drinks.

ANISEED
The fruit of a small annual plant (*Pimpinella anisum*) belonging to the parsley family and grown mainly in Spain, North Africa and Turkey. The seeds are oval and dark grey-brown with a mild and pleasant liquorice flavour and are often sprinkled on top of bread, buns and rolls. They are also used in the manufacture of some confectionery. In the 9th century, Charlemagne ordered aniseed to be grown on royal farms.

ANNATTO
Hard red seeds (like grape pips) from the Oriental annatto tree (*Bixa orellana*). The seeds are used in the Orient and South America for colouring; when soaked in water, they produce an amber-coloured liquid. The nearest equivalent can be made from paprika and a dash of turmeric blended with water. Annatto is also used as a cheese dye.

ANOLINI
Half-moon-shaped *ravioli* with a meat or cheese filling.

à l'ANTIBOISE
French term for the style of cooking in Antibes, in the south of France, denoting the use of tomatoes, garlic, cheese and sometimes sardines.

ANTICUCHOS
Peruvian kebabs made from pieces of vinegar-marinated ox heart threaded on to skewers and brushed with a hot local sauce after grilling. They are treated as a snack and eaten both formally and informally.

ANTI-OXIDANT
In simple terms, a food preservative, used to prevent fats from turning rancid and fruits from

discolouring. It may be nothing more complicated than vitamin C (ascorbic acid).

ANTIPASTI
The Italian term for *hors d'oeuvre*, although in Italy appetizers do not often include a large variety of small savouries. Typical *antipasti* include Parma ham with melon or fresh figs, cold meats and sausages with olives, bean salads, pasta dishes and soups. When a mixed *antipasti* does appear, it usually consists of an arrangement of sliced salami, green and black olives, hard-boiled eggs, sardines or anchovies, mushrooms, pickled peppers and beans.

à l'ANVERSOISE
French term meaning in the style of Antwerp (Anvers) in Belgium, denoting a garnish of hop shoots in cream.

APERITIF
A French term for a drink taken before a meal as a stimulant to the appetite, for example, sherry, vermouth, champagne or champagne mixes such as Buck's Fizz.

APFELSTRUDEL
See *Apple Strudel*.

APOLLINARIS
See *Mineral Waters*.

APPELLATION CONTRÔLÉE
A government certification for French goods such as wine and cheese, which guarantees that the product originates from the area stated on the label and has been manufactured in the traditional way and reaches the area's standards of production.

APPENZELL
(Appenzeller)
A Swiss cheese from the canton of Appenzell dating back to the 12th century. Now also produced in Saint-Gall and Thurgau, the cheese is made from cows' milk and has a characteristic, full-cream taste with a certain degree of fruitiness. The pale, creamy-coloured texture contains a scattering of pea-sized holes. It is a tender, semi-hard cheese which is easy to slice. The rind is yellow-brown and the cheese is matured in a secret blend of herbs which is responsible for its unique flavour.

APPLE
The fruit of a deciduous tree (*Malus* species) of the same family as the rose, probably native to the region of ancient Persia and growing wild and in cultivated species throughout temperate parts of the world. Over thousands of years the apple has developed in numerous varieties which may be classified loosely into three main kinds: the wild crab apple, the cultivated dessert apple and the cooking apple. The thin, usually shiny skin ranges from pale yellows and greens to dark red in colour. The flesh is firm and generally a creamy colour, sometimes with tinges of green or pink, and at the centre of the fruit there is a core of small seeds enclosed in scaly pockets. The taste of an apple ranges from the acidic flavour of the wild apple to the relative sweetness of recent hybrids. The apple is bred in many shapes, sizes and skin colours consistent with the soil and climate of the country of origin. All varieties of apple have many culinary applications and apple juice may be drunk as it is or used in the making of cider or apple brandy.

APPLE AMBER PUDDING
A British speciality, made from a shortcrust pastry case filled with sweetened and flavoured apple purée which is then topped with meringue and baked.

APPLE BANANA
The fruit of a large herb (*Musa* species), cultivated in tropical regions. It is quite small. It is very sweet with a flavour reminiscent of pineapple and apple.

APPLE CAKE
See *Norfolk Apple Cake*.

APPLE CHARLOTTE
Some say this pudding was called after Charlotte de Medici, daughter-in-law of the Prince of Condé, others that it was named after Charlotte, the wife of George III. The pudding simply consists of layers of buttered breadcrumbs and thickly stewed apples, lightly sweetened, topped with a final layer of crumbs, then dotted with butter and baked until golden brown and crisp. Sometimes fingers of bread and butter are used instead of crumbs.

APPLE CRUMBLE
See *Fruit Crumble*.

APPLE DUMPLINGS
A typically British pudding, made from peeled and cored apples which are packed with a sweet filling. They are then enclosed in pieces of shortcrust pastry, placed on a buttered baking tray, brushed with beaten egg and baked. Apple dumplings are served with cream or custard.

APPLE FRITTERS
See *Fruit Fritters*.

APPLE JUICE
A naturally sweet drink made from the juice of apples. It is golden-coloured and non-alcoholic.

APPLE MINT
(Bowles Mint)
A herb of the mint family (*Mentha rotundifolia*) with fleshy, round leaves which have a woolly texture. They are suitable for adding to fruit cups or punches and drinks such as Pimms.

APPLE SAUCE
A thick and lightly sweetened sauce made from apples. It can be served with roast goose, duck or pork.

APPLE STRUDEL
(Apfelstrudel)
An Austrian and Hungarian speciality made by covering thin strudel pastry with melted butter or margarine, breadcrumbs, chopped almonds, thinly sliced apples, sugar, raisins and cinnamon. It is then rolled up, transferred carefully to a baking tray and cooked. When removed from the oven, it is dusted thickly with sifted icing sugar, left until lukewarm, cut into portions and served, sometimes accompanied by *obers*, the Austrian term for whipped cream.

APPLESAUCE CAKE
A North American speciality cake containing mixed dried fruits, sometimes nuts and apple sauce. It is baked in a large spring-clip tin.

APPLEWOOD
A British Cheddar cheese which is smoked over apple wood.

APRICOT
The fruit of a deciduous tree (*Prunus armeniaca*) native to China and cultivated around the world in warm and temperate zones. Although basically a globular fruit, there are many variations in the shape and apricots sometimes have flat sides or bases or pointed ends. The indentation running down one side may be well-defined or only noticeable close to the stalk. The size can be 4–7.5 cm/1½–3 inches in diameter and the skin colour varies from pale greeny-yellow to a deep orange. Often there is darker shading on the skin and mottling on the side facing the sun. The sweet, juicy flesh may be white, yellow or orange, depending on the type, and there is always a central stone. Apricots can be divided into two main categories: the free-stone variety, where the flesh does not stick to the stone, and the cling variety, where it does. In some varieties, the kernel of the stone is edible, and may be used in cooking and in the making of a liqueur called

eau de noyaux. The apricot is very rich in vitamin A. It may be eaten raw or used in preserves, desserts and many cooked dishes. It is a favourite with pastrycooks for use in pies, flans and tarts. When ripe the fruit does not travel well but this disadvantage is more than compensated for by its excellence in dried form.

ARABICA COFFEE BEAN
Type of coffee bean from which the finest, most delicately flavoured coffee is made. Jamaica Blue Mountain coffee is one of the best examples of this variety. Although the names of the country and region or exporting town are shown prominently on the label of any coffee, the best varieties will also indicate which bean was used. The original *arabica* tree came from Africa, probably from Ethiopia, and today all American trees are varieties of this type. From Africa to the Far East, the *arabica* bean is grown in a number of countries which also produce coffee from the other main type: the *robusta* bean. The caffeine content of the *arabica* bean is lower that that of the other kinds.

ARACHIS OIL
French term for groundnut or peanut oil.

ARALAR
See *Idiazábal*.

ARAME
A sea vegetable (*Eisenia bicylis*) of the brown algae group of plants, found in quantity in Japanese coastal waters. When dried, the long, narrow fronds or 'leaves' are cut into thin strips to facilitate cooking. It is widely used in many Oriental dishes and the mild and relatively sweet flavour of this sea plant also renders it acceptable to Western tastes.

ARANCE CARAMELLATE
An Italian dessert of oranges coated with thick syrup and decorated with strips of caramelized orange peel.

ARBROATH FILLET
(Arbroath Smokies)
Scottish smoked haddock.

ARBROATH SMOKIES
See *Arbroath Fillet*.

à l'ARCHIDUC
French term meaning in the style of the archduke, usually denoting food coated with a rich white sauce flavoured with paprika.

ARCTIC CHAR
(Char)
A group of round-bodied fish (*Salvelinus* species) belonging to the salmon and trout family. Various species are found in Arctic waters around Scandinavia, Siberia, Alaska, Greenland and Iceland and also in lakes and rivers in both North America and Europe. The British freshwater species is called Windermere char. The seawater varieties can be up to 1 metre/39 inches in length; freshwater char only reach about half the size. The average weight is 1–3 kg/2½–6¼ lb. The back of the seawater species is blue or green with yellowish spotted sides. The freshwater kinds are more variable in colour and with lighter, brighter spots. Arctic char are caught all year round. The flesh is oily, varying from pink to white depending on environment, and the fish may be poached, baked or fried. When lightly smoked, it is similar to smoked salmon.

à l'ARDENNAISE
French term meaning in the style of the Ardennes, in southern Belgium, denoting the inclusion of juniper berries, especially in game dishes.

ARDENNES HAM
(Jambon d'Ardennes)
Cured and air-dried ham (*jambon d'Ardennes*) from the Ardennes area of Belgium.

AREQUIPE
See *Dulce de Leche*.

à l'ARGENTEUIL
French term for any food garnished with asparagus, for which the area of Argenteuil is famous.

ARGENTINIAN QUARTIROLO
An Argentinian cows' milk cheese which could be likened to Italian Mozzarella.

ARHAR
(Rarhar)
Indian name for pigeon pea.

à l'ARIÉGEOISE
French term meaning in the style of Ariège in south-west France, denoting a dish containing salt pork, kidney beans, cabbage and potatoes.

à l'ARLÉSIENNE
French term meaning in the style of Arles in southern France, denoting the use of tomatoes, onions, garlic, rice and sometimes olives.

ARMENIA
One of the finest types of Colombian coffee beans.

AROMA
Fragrance, perfume or bouquet from food and drink.

à l'ARPAJONNAISE
French term meaning in the style of Arpajon in the Île-de-France, denoting the inclusion of haricot beans.

ARROWROOT
An edible starch made from the pith of roots and stems of any plants of the *Maranta* family. The plants originated in South America and now grow in the West Indies, Bermuda and the East Indies. The roots are turned into a fine, white powder which is used extensively in cooking as a thickening agent. Arrowroot may be substituted for cornflour and, because it contains no gluten, it makes cakes and biscuits fine and light-textured. As glazes thickened with arrowroot remain clear and unclouded, they are ideal to use on fruit flans. A standard proportion is 10 ml/2 teaspoons of arrowroot to 150 ml/¼ pint of water.

ÄRTER MED FLÄSK
A Swedish split pea and pork soup, traditionally served every Thursday during the winter. It is thick and filling and must be considered Sweden's national soup.

ARTIFICIAL SWEETENERS
(Sweeteners, Sugar Substitutes)
Substances other than sugar and saccharin which are used to sweeten food. Latest sweeteners permitted in Britain include aspartame, acesulphame-K, thaumatin and xylitol.

ARVI LEAF
See *Dasheen Leaf*.

ASADERO
Its name meaning 'good for roasting', this is a Mexican cooking cheese of the *pasta filata* variety. It is made from cows' milk.

ASADO
An outdoor Argentinian meal, usually cooked on a barbecue and consisting of assorted meats, sausages and offal.

ASADOS
A spit-roast from Uruguay.

ASAFOETIDA
Used in very small quantities, asafoetida (*Ferula asafoetida*) gives a pleasant onion flavour to some Indian vegetarian dishes and is available dried in powder form. It is pale yellow in colour and is the product of a resinous sap coming

from a vile-smelling perennial plant which grows wild in Iran, Afghanistan and parts of India.

ASCORBIC ACID
See *Vitamin C*.

ASIAGO
A cows' milk cheese from northern Italy which is hard and full-flavoured. It resembles Parmesan and is used as a dessert cheese. Asiago can also be grated for cooking and sprinkling.

ASIAN PEAR
(Japanese Pear)
The fruit of trees (*Pyrus pyrofolia* and *P. ussuriensis*) native to Japan and grown for centuries in the East. New varieties have been developed and are now widely cultivated in both Japan and New Zealand. The fruit resembles an apple in shape and size with golden-coloured skin and white, juicy, crisp flesh which tastes like pear. Although Asian pears have firmer flesh than most Western ones, they too may be eaten raw as a dessert fruit or cooked. The Japanese name for the best-known kind of Asian pear is *nashi*.

ASPARAGUS
A perennial plant (*Asparagus officinalis*), which is a member of the lily family. It is native to northern temperate zones of Europe and Russia but is now widely cultivated in both Europe and North America. Asparagus is harvested when very young because the stalk develops a woody texture and the buds open out too much as the vegetable matures. The asparagus spear should be picked when it is 13–20 cm/5–8 inches from ground level to tip and comprises a stalk with a head of tightly closed, immature buds. The thickness of the stalk may vary from type to type and country to country and the different varieties may be coloured white or tinged with green or purple. This delicately flavoured vegetable may be steamed or gently boiled and eaten on its own with melted butter or with Hollandaise sauce. When cold, it is generally served with French dressing. Older stems may be used in soups or cooked dishes. Asparagus should not be used in dishes containing red wine because the sulphur in the vegetable spoils the flavour of the wine. Many years ago, the name asparagus was corrupted to 'sparrowgrass' and today it is still referred to as 'grass' in some British markets.

ASPARAGUS BEAN
See *Yard-long Bean*.

ASPARTAME
A modern sugar substitute used in Britain.

ASPIC JELLY
A savoury jelly which is well-flavoured and light gold in colour. It is used for pouring into raised pies, making elaborate and highly decorated moulded savoury dishes, and coating traditional buffet foods such as whole cooked salmons, hams and turkeys. It is also one of the components of a *chaud-froid* sauce. It can either be made traditionally from cleared stock or from aspic jelly crystals sold in packets.

ASSAM
One of the basic types of tea plant grown in northern India, producing a leaf which is among the strongest-flavoured of all. Unblended, the tea is often used to make the first cup of the day and is also used in blends of tea with names like Breakfast Blend or English Breakfast Tea. Assam teas keep well and suit most kinds of water.

ASSIETTE ANGLAISE
(Assiette à l'Anglaise)
French term for a plate of assorted cold meats including roast beef, ham and tongue.

ASSIETTE DE CHARCUTERIE
French term for a plate of assorted sliced *saucissons*.

ASTRINGENT
Having a binding or contracting effect. In vegetables, fruits and tea, the astringent property comes from tannin. Lemon juice is the astringent most commonly used in cooking.

ATEMOYA
The fruit of a tree (*Anona* species) of the custard apple family. It is one of the hybrids developed from the cherimoya and the sweet sop to improve cropping. It is being increasingly grown in many parts of the world both for its quality and because it will fruit in climates not suitable for the true cherimoya.
As with most of the custard apple family, the fruit can be as small as an apple or as large as a melon. The general appearance is rather scaly and like a large, green, unopened fir cone. The flesh, which is of a thick, custardy consistency, is studded with inedible seeds and is usually eaten raw when the fruit is fully ripe and the skin has darkened.
Commercially, the atemoya is often sold under the generic name of custard apple.

ATLANTIC COD
See *Cod*.

ATLANTIC CROAKER
A round-bodied seawater fish (*Micropogonias undulatus*) which is one of the group called 'drum' or 'croaker' in North America because of its ability to make drumming or croaking noises with its air bladder. The size varies from 25–50 cm/10–19 inches in length and the weight is between 200 g–1 kg/7 oz–2¼ lb. The back and sides are a greyish colour with diagonal spotted bars. The colour lightens to a whitish shade on the belly. It is caught off the eastern coast of North America all year round. The flesh is lean and delicate and the fish may be poached, baked, fried or grilled.

ATLANTIC MACKEREL
See *Mackerel*.

ATLANTIC SALMON
One of the most highly prized fish in the world, wild salmon (*Salmo salar*) is renowned for its delicate pink flesh and its mild but distinctive flavour. Scottish salmon is reputed to be the finest but other excellent species can also be fished from rivers in northern Europe and North America. A sea fish in type, a salmon returns to freshwater rivers to spawn. When fully grown, it can weigh 4–18 kg/9–40 lb. Its body is covered with bright, silvery blue scales which shimmer. Fresh wild salmon should have red gills and a firm body. Salmon may be cooked in a variety of ways, such as steaming, poaching, grilling and baking, and served hot or cold.

ATLANTIC THREAD HERRING
(Thread Herring)
A member (*Opisthonema oglinum*) of the herring family, its distinctive feature is a long, thread-like ray at the end of the dorsal fin. The length is about 15 cm/6 inches and the weight about 75 g/3 oz. The thin body has a light bluish-green back, shading to a silvery underside. It is caught in the coastal waters of the Gulf of Mexico and the south-east of North America and is found in salt, brackish and fresh waters. It has oily flesh and may be fried or grilled but is important commercially for canning. A close relative called the Pacific thread herring is found on the west coast of North America.

ATTA
An Asian wholemeal flour, used for making Indian unleavened breads such as chapati.

ATTELETTE
A small skewer with an ornamental head, often made of silver or silver plate, which is used for holding garnishes and decorations in place

on elaborate dishes for the formal buffet table, such as whole salmon in aspic, cold roast turkey and so on.

au (aux)
See *À la*.

AUBERGINE
(Eggplant)
The fruit of a plant (*Solanum melongena*) of the same family as the tomato. Originally from tropical Asia, it is now cultivated in the Mediterranean region and in parts of North America. The modern varieties range from the original eggshape to globular or elongated and slightly waisted specimens. The size varies widely but is mainly 7.5–10 cm/3–4 inches in diameter and 15–20 cm/6–8 inches in length. The tender skin is usually a glossy purply-black but may be green, yellow or white. The flesh is pale creamy-green and firm-textured when raw, but tends to be wet and pulpy when cooked. It is peppered with small edible seeds which are slightly darker than the colour of the flesh. Aubergine may be sliced and grilled or fried as a vegetable, or used in savoury recipes, one of the most popular of which is Greek *moussaka*.

AURORE SAUCE
A velouté sauce made with fish stock, then flavoured and lightly coloured with tomato purée. It can be served with all fish dishes.

AUSTRALIAN FONDANT ICING
See *Plastic Icing*.

AUSTRIAN 'PANCAKES'
(Salzburg Nockerln)
Confusingly described in English as pancakes, these individual soufflé omelettes from Salzburg in Austria are baked in threes on a large dish. They are sometimes served with cream, first flavoured with crushed strawberries and sweetened with sugar. The alternative accompaniment is a jam sauce.

AUTOMAT
(Food Dispenser)
The trade name of a brand of coin-operated food dispenser situated in North American cafeterias. Similar machines are found worldwide.

à l'AUTRICHIENNE
French term meaning in the Austrian style, denoting the inclusion of soured cream, paprika, onions and sometimes fennel.

AVE MARIA
(Cannolicchi)
Short and fairly thick tubes of pasta, used in soup such as *minestrone*.

AVGOLEMONO SAUCE
An egg (*avgo*) and lemon (*lemono*) sauce which is typically Greek. It is a white coating sauce with the addition of beaten egg and lemon juice and is served with meat and vegetable dishes.

AVGOLEMONO SOUPA
The national soup of Greece, made from chicken stock, rice, eggs, lemon juice and seasoning.

AVOCADO
(Alligator Pear)
The fruit of a related group of trees (*Persea gratissima/americana*) which originated mainly in Central and South America and belong to the same family as the bay tree. Different varieties flourish in tropical or semi-tropical climates and offer a wide choice throughout the year. Depending on the country of origin, the skin can be bright green and smooth, purple and smooth, or purple and rough. Some may even have a golden tinge when ripe. Most avocados are of a characteristic pear shape and size, although some varieties are almost circular. All have a large, central, inedible stone and the flesh ranges from off-white to greeny-yellow. The avocado has a mild, distinctive flavour which differs very little between varieties and the fully ripe

fruit has the texture of butter. Ripe avocados will bruise if handled roughly but the darker, bruised portion is still edible. The flesh can be eaten raw as a savoury with dressing, or plain as part of a mixed salad, either with fruits or vegetables. Its delicate flavour can enhance many cooked dishes if not masked by stronger-tasting foods.

AVOCADO SOUP
See *Sopa de Aguacate*.

AWABI
Japanese for abalone.

AYAM KICHUP
A Malaysian chicken and soy sauce dish.

AYRAN
A Lebanese drink similar to Indian *lassi*.

AYRSHIRE CREAM
A Scottish cows' milk cheese which is rich, smooth and creamy.

AYRSHIRE CURE
A Scottish cure for bacon, similar to the Wiltshire cure used in England. In Scotland the bacon is often stripped of skin and fat, then rolled.

AYRSHIRE GIGOT
A Scottish gammon cut which is boned, rolled and tied.

AYRSHIRE ROLL
A Scottish bacon joint, from the middle or throughcut with the rind removed.

AZAROLE
(Mediterranean Medlar, Naples Medlar)
The fruit of a deciduous shrub (*Crataegus azarolus*) related to the hawthorn and found mainly in the countries bordering the western Mediterranean. It resembles a small apple and the skin colour can vary from white to red, depending on variety. It is very popular in Italy, where some of the largest and best varieties are cultivated. The flesh has an apple-like flavour; the fruit may be eaten raw but is generally used in preserves.

AZIETÃO
A Portuguese cream cheese produced near Setúbal from ewes' milk. It is soft and mild, coated with a yellow rind.

AZO DYES
Food colourings, produced synthetically from coal tar chemicals, which are believed to cause or aggravate certain allergies.

BABACO
A hybrid of the pawpaw (*Carica* species), originally from Ecuador and commercially produced in New Zealand. The fruit looks rather like a straight-sided marrow with five longitudinal panels, each of which has a central groove, so that when the babaco is sliced across the middle, the cut ends are star-shaped. The colour of the skin changes from green to yellow as it ripens and the whole fruit, including the skin, is edible. There is a layer of soft flesh under the skin and the centre is lightly packed and pulpy. The unique flavour is a mixture of strawberry, peach, guava and redcurrant: a mixed fruit salad in itself. The babaco may be eaten on its own or used in both sweet and savoury dishes.

BABASSU
A tall palm (*Orbignija speciosa* or *Orbignija martiana*) native to north-east Brazil, with hard-shelled nuts which yield a valuable oil.

BABI LEMAK
A Singaporean pork stew containing coconut milk, onions, dried fish paste (blachan) and assorted herbs and spices.

BABY BEL
French version of Dutch Edam cheese, made from pasteurized cows' milk.

BACALAO
The Spanish term for dried and salted cod, which is used in omelettes, added to casseroles and eaten boiled, accompanied by potatoes and olive oil mixed with garlic.

BACALHAU
Dried and salted cod, the national dish of Portugal. It is frequently boiled after soaking and served coated with melted butter and crushed garlic. The traditional garnish for *bacalhau* consists of sliced onions, black olives and wedges of hard-boiled egg. Sometimes the fish is mashed and casseroled with potatoes, garlic, oil and onions.

BACK BACON
A cut from the top of the pig, near the shoulders, which is divided into bacon rashers or chops for frying and grilling. The cut can also be left as a whole joint and boiled.

BACKHENDL
Austrian version of fried chicken. Coated with flour, beaten egg and breadcrumbs, it is usually fried in lard or oil. It is garnished with lemon and parsley and served with boiled potatoes and sometimes a salad.

BACON
Pork flesh, mostly boned, which has been cured with salt, sugar and spices as a means of preservation. Unsmoked bacon is also known regionally as green, plain or pale; smoked bacon does not have alternative names.

BACON BUTT
A joint cut from the prime forehock which is lean and fleshy. It is suitable for boiling.

BACON COLLAR
A cut of bacon near the head of the pig, recommended for boiling and braising. It may also be cut into rashers for grilling and frying. It tends to be a salty joint and needs the same treatment as smoked bacon.

BACON FORE SLIPPER
A joint cut from the prime forehock. It is best suited to boiling.

BACON FOREHOCK
A joint from near the head of the pig and just above the front legs. It can be boiled as a joint, diced and used in stews and casseroles or minced for an assortment of pâtés and terrines. Sometimes the joint is divided into three portions: small hock, fore slipper and butt.

BACON HOCK (SMALL)
A joint cut from the prime forehock, most suitable for mincing.

BACON RASHER
(Rasher)
British term used for a slice of bacon.

BACON STRIP
North American term for a bacon rasher.

BACONER
A pig bred specifically for bacon and usually slaughtered at 6 months. The body is generally long, fairly slim, and with a broad and rounded rear. The head tends to be small.

BAGASSE
The residue of sugar cane and grapes after the liquid (juice) has been extracted.

BAGELS
Jewish bread rolls, shaped into rings, which are boiled briefly before

being baked. They are served halved and buttered, sometimes spread with cream cheese and filled with smoked salmon or lox.

BAGNA CAUDA
An Italian mixture of melted butter and oil, flavoured with chopped anchovies, garlic, basil and seasoning. It is served hot as a dip for pieces of raw and cooked vegetables.

BAGUETTE
A long, thin, crusty French loaf.

BAIN-MARIE
A pan filled with hot water in which a pot or a number of pots and pans containing sauces, stocks, soups and stews may stand over the heat. To quote the famous chef Ude, 'You put all your stewpans into the water, and keep that water always very hot, but it must not boil. The effect of this is to keep every dish warm without altering either the quantity or quality. If you keep your sauce, or broth, or soup, by the fireside, the soup reduces and becomes too strong, and the sauce thickens as well as reduces.'

BAISER
A French word meaning a kiss, used in both France and Germany to describe two meringue halves sandwiched together with whipped cream.

BAKE
A North American social gathering at which baked food is served, for example, a clam bake.

BAKE (TO)
To cook in an oven by radiation coming from the metal oven lining and convection currents from the hot air circulating around the foods. Baked foods are usually crisp with a brown surface.

BAKE BLIND (TO)
This term generally refers to a pastry case or cases lining a sandwich tin, flan ring on a baking tray, or bun tins, baked without a filling. To prevent the pastry from rising as it bakes, the pastry is 'weighed down' with a lining of greaseproof paper and white dried beans. Alternatively, foil is used to line the pastry, which also retards rising. It is essential that the lining paper or foil be high enough to cover the sides of the pastry to prevent any unevenness.

BAKEAPPLES
Canadian term for cloudberries, found in parts of Canada and Scandinavia.

BAKED ALASKA
(Norwegian Omelette, Omelette Soufflé Surprise)
A popular sweet consisting of sponge cake topped with ice cream and sometimes fruit, then covered completely with meringue. It is then cooked quickly in a very hot oven to brown the meringue, at the same time keeping the ice cream solid. Occasionally it is flamed with alcohol on serving.

BAKED APPLES
A British dessert of cored and stuffed apples which are baked in the oven.

BAKED BANANAS
Peeled and halved bananas, baked with lemon juice, rum, brown sugar and butter, usually served with whipped cream or ice cream.

BAKED BATTER PUDDING
A thin batter of the kind used for Yorkshire pudding, which is baked in the oven. It is either left plain or contains sweet or savoury additions such as fruit or meat.

BAKED BEANS
Cooked haricot beans in a tomato sauce, widely available canned.

BAKED EGG CUSTARD
A milk pudding, cooked slowly in the oven, made from milk, eggs, sugar and flavouring. Traditionally, the top

is sprinkled with grated nutmeg before cooking. It may be eaten hot or cold.

BAKED EGGS
There are two methods of baking eggs: in a small ramekin or cocotte dish that is large enough to hold one or two eggs (*oeufs en cocotte*), or in a shallow heatproof plate (*oeufs sur le plat*). Either container should be well-greased. The eggs in the cocotte dish should be topped with flakes of butter or margarine, placed in a second shallow dish of hot water and cooked in a moderate oven for 10 minutes or until the whites are just set and the yolks creamy. The eggs in the plate are coated with melted butter, then baked in a hot oven for about 5–6 minutes.

BAKEHOUSE
A place where breads and cakes are baked.

BAKER'S
A North American cheese made from skimmed cows' milk or skimmed milk powder. It is like a soft version of cottage cheese and used commercially by bakers for cheesecakes and other items.

BAKER'S YEAST
Suitable for use in baking as a raising agent. This yeast (*Saccharemyces cerevisias*) should be beige in colour (brown patches denote staleness), and break easily and cleanly. It is available from bakeries and health food shops.

BAKERY
A place where bread and cakes are baked and frequently sold.

BAKEWELL PUDDINGS
Made exclusively in Bakewell, Derbyshire, to a secret recipe, these are the original puddings from which the more familiar Bakewell tarts have been adapted. The baked puddings consist of puff pastry cases filled with jam and an almond mixture. They are available in various sizes and may be eaten warm or cold.

BAKEWELL TART
A British speciality for afternoon tea from Derbyshire. A tart made from shortcrust pastry is filled with jam and a mixture made from ground almonds, cake crumbs, lemon, butter, sugar and egg. It is baked until golden, covered with icing, and served cold in wedges.

BAKING POWDER
Powder used instead of yeast as a raising agent in baked goods such as scones and cakes. Baking powder usually comprises two parts acid (cream of tartar) to one part alkali (bicarbonate of soda). Ground rice is frequently added to home-made mixtures to prevent lumps from forming.

BAKING SHEET
See *Baking Tray*.

BAKING SODA
Alkali which acts as a raising agent in baked goods when combined with either cream of tartar, soured milk, buttermilk or vinegar.

BAKING TRAY
(Baking Sheet)
A flat metal sheet, commonly made of pressed steel, which may be square with a shallow rim on one or more sides, or circular with a rim all round. It serves as a firm base for small containers such as patty tins and is ideal for baking biscuits and scones. The circular version is suitable for pizzas, tea cakes and other round items.

BAKLAVA
A Greek cake, served as a dessert, made from layers of filo (phyllo) pastry filled with a mixture of ground almonds, breadcrumbs, sugar, spice and butter. It is baked until golden, coated with hot syrup and left for 24 hours before being cut into squares for serving.

BALLER
See *Melon Baller*.

BALLON
French term for a joint of meat, usually lamb, which has been boned and rolled into a ball.

BALLOTINE DE VOLAILLE
French term for boned and pâté-stuffed poultry which is coated with aspic jelly and served cold in slices.

BALSAM APPLE
(Balsam Pear)
See *Bitter Gourd*.

BAMBOO LEAVES
Used in some Chinese recipes to wrap food prior to cooking.

BAMBOO SHOOTS
Young shoots of tropical and sub-tropical grasses (*Bambusa, Arundinaria* and *Dendrocalamus* genera), which are very large and woody. Not all shoots are edible and some are poisonous before they are boiled. The shoots are harvested when they have just appeared at ground level and are still delicately flavoured and tender. Bamboo shoots are widely used in Chinese and Japanese cooking, either fresh, canned or dried.

BAMIYA
See *Okra*.

BAMYE
A Turkish stew of minced lamb, okra, tomato, onion and green pepper, flavoured with lemon juice and seasonings. Traditionally it is served with *pilav*.

BANANA
The fruit of a large herb (*Musa sapientum*), originating in the Far East, but now grown in other warm and hot regions throughout the world and an important food item in many countries. One of the first fruits to be cultivated by man, the present-day banana is the result of careful selection and cross-breeding over many years. Although there are numerous edible varieties, the commercially grown banana is elongated and slightly curved, with an inedible yellow skin which may be speckled or flecked with brown when ripe. The length can be 7.5– 23 cm/3–9 inches. Bananas grow in large clusters and are picked when full-sized but slightly unripe. The clusters are divided into 'hands' of about 12 bananas each for packing and transporting. Because the banana has no specific fruiting season, it is available throughout the year. The flesh is creamy-white to yellow when ripe and is smooth, sweet and flavourful. In addition to being eaten raw, the banana may be baked or fried or used with other ingredients. Commercially dried bananas are available and in some countries the dried fruit is ground into flour. The varieties of banana that are cooked as a vegetable are known as plantain.

BANANA FRITTERS
See *Fruit Fritters*.

BANANA SPLIT
A peeled and split banana sandwiched together with vanilla ice cream and topped with whipped cream and chopped nuts.

BANANAS FOSTER
A speciality of New Orleans in the USA, consisting of fried bananas which are then spiced, sweetened, flamed with rum and served accompanied by whipped cream.

BANBURY CAKES
Dating back to the early part of the 17th century with origins in Oxfordshire. They comprise flattish ovals of puff pastry with a filling of dried fruit, spice, sugar, butter, flour and sometimes rum. They are glazed with egg white and caster sugar towards the end of baking, then returned to the oven for 2–4 minutes to set the glaze.

BANDAL
Rich Indian cream cheese made from buffaloes' or cows' milk. It can be eaten fresh, or smoked over a wood fire.

BANGER
Colloquial British term for a fried sausage.

BANGERS AND MASH
A British colloquial term for a meal of sausages and mashed potatoes.

BANNOCK
(Pitcaithley Bannock)
A Scottish speciality which closely resembles shortbread but contains chopped mixed peel and almonds.

BANNOCK FLUKE
See *Turbot*.

BANQUET
A luxurious meal, composed of many courses, prepared for a large gathering of people. It is usually a formal occasion.

BANTAM
Small variety of domestic fowl.

BAP LOAVES
Fairly flat Scottish loaves, usually white, which are heavily dusted with flour.

BAP ROLLS
Smaller versions of bap loaves.

BARA BRITH
A heavily fruited Welsh loaf, usually made from a yeasted dough.

BARBADOS CHERRY
(Brazilian Cherry)
The fruit of a tree (*Malpighia glabra*) native to Brazil but better known in the West Indies where it is grown mainly in Barbados and Jamaica as a garden fruit tree. It has also been introduced to parts of Australia. The fruit looks like a large, vertically scalloped cherry and the bright red skin darkens almost to black when very ripe. The flesh surrounding the single seed is juicy and sweet and may be eaten raw when very ripe or used in jams or preserves.

BARBADOS SUGAR
Brown sugar exported from Barbados.

BARBAROSSA
A fairly new Bavarian cows' milk cheese with a semi-soft and creamy texture. It is mild, dotted with small holes, and is warm yellow in colour.

BARBARY DUCK
Originally from South America, this variety of bird now comes from southern and south-eastern France. It is fleshy, full-flavoured and comparatively lean. The Barbary duck is sometimes found in Britain and limited quantities of the cooked and smoked bird are being produced in Wales.

BARBECUE (TO)
(Barbeque)
This term originally meant to cook a whole trussed animal over direct heat. The word appears to be derived from the French *barbe à queue*, meaning 'beard to tail'. It is a method of cooking which dates back to the Old Testament. It is essentially an outdoor style of cooking and is best carried out on barbecue equipment. However, the modern grill and oven rotisseries are a good way of barbecueing foods indoors.

BARBECUE SAUCE
(Grilling Sauce)
A spicy cold sauce, used for brushing over foods which are being barbecued or grilled. It usually comprises onion, vinegar, Worcestershire sauce, Tabasco sauce, herbs, spices, sometimes wine and a little sugar.

BARBEL
A freshwater fish (*Barbus barbus*) related to the carp family. It can measure up to 45 cm/18 inches in length and it is caught in some

European rivers. It is not considered a fine fish for eating but, if suitably flavoured, it may be poached, baked or grilled.

BARBERRY
The fruit of a bush (*Berberis species)*, with both evergreen and deciduous varieties, growing in many countries in Europe and Asia. It is often grown as a garden plant both for decoration and its fruit. The small, elongated berry grows in clusters, is mainly red in colour and, in most species, contains a few small seeds. The barberry is seldom sweet enough to eat raw but it is suitable for preserves. Some species of barberry bush act as a host to a wheat disease and are often eliminated from farming regions.

BARD (TO)
A technique whereby delicate parts of meat or poultry are protected from drying-out by a thin covering of bacon fat, held in place with string and removed before serving.

BARFI
See *Burfi*.

BARIE
Sold in triangular-shaped boxes, this Israeli cheese produced from cows' milk loosely resembles Brie.

BARLEY
The oldest cultivated cereal, barley (*Hordeum vulgare*) still exists in its original form on the shores of the Red and Caspian Seas. Because it contains less gluten than wheat, it is unsuitable for bread-making, but has other culinary applications and is often used as a thickener in soups, stews, casseroles and hot-pots. Malt, made from barley, is widely used in brewing and distilling, and barley water — simply made by cooking barley in water — is said to be of benefit to the kidneys and bladder. Barley is an important crop in Britain and barley flakes make a nourishing breakfast cereal which closely resembles porridge. Barley flakes are often one of the constituents of muesli.

BARLEY FLAKES
See *Barley*.

BARLEY FLOUR
Milled from barley, the flour gives an attractive taste to bread but should be combined with wheat flour in the ratio of one-third to two-thirds.

BARLEY SUGAR
Originally made from the decoction of barley, hence its name. Barley sugar is a popular sweet made from a water and sugar syrup. It is clear and glossy, very brittle and its preparation requires a certain amount of skill.

BARLEY WATER
A drink made from the water in which barley was cooked.

BARM BRACK
An Irish fruit loaf which is generally yeasted. It sometimes includes caraway seeds and is eaten at Christmas.

BARNACLE
(Goose-necked Barnacle)
Crustacean (*Pollicipes cornucopia*) which lives on rocky coasts on both sides of the Atlantic. It has a tubular, dark-skinned body with a hoof-like foot at one end. The barnacle is considered a delicacy in Spain, Portugal and parts of South America. It may be eaten raw but is usually boiled and eaten when cold. The edible part is extracted from the tough skin which, along with the foot, is then discarded.

BARNACLE GOOSE
See *Brent Goose*.

BARON OF BEEF
A large joint for roasting, consisting of both the sirloins which are left uncut along the backbone. It is often served at banquets in London's Guildhall.

BARQUETTES
Small, boat-shaped pastry cases usually containing an assortment of sweet or savoury fillings.

BARRACOUTA
(Snoek)
A large, deep-sea fish (*Thyristes atun*) caught in the South Pacific and Indian Oceans.

BARRACUDA
A slender, round-bodied deep-sea fish (*Sphyraena* species) which resembles a freshwater pike in appearance and ferocity. The average weight in the shops is about 2.5 kg/5½ lb. Back colours vary from bronze to black, shading to silvery-white on the underside. The various species are found in the warmer waters of the Atlantic, Pacific and Caribbean and are caught when they come inshore. The flesh is mainly lean and firm-textured and in the USA, where it is a popular game fish, it is often cut into steaks and barbecued.

BARRAMUNDA
(Lungfish)
A general name given to various Australian freshwater fish.

BARREL
A liquid measure of approximately 164.5 litres/36 gallons.

BARREL BREAD
(Crinkled Musket, Lodger's or Landlady's Loaf, Pistol, Piston, Rasp)
A cylindrical loaf baked in a ridged tin. The tin leaves indentations on the loaf which make it easy to cut into even slices.

BARYA A JAGNJETINOM
A Yugoslavian lamb and okra casserole from Serbia.

BASHAN
An Israeli smoked cheese made from a mixture of ewes' and goats' milk. It is shaped like a loaf and covered with a glossy red rind. It has a tangy and sharpish flavour and is said to resemble Italian Provolone cheese.

BASIL
(Sweet Basil)
A herb native to India and Iran, basil (*Ocimum basilicum*) is now grown all over Europe. Related to the mint family and also known as sweet basil, it has long slender leaves of up to 2.5 cm/1 inch in length, and tender stems. It is bright green, but turns pale brown when dried. It is extensively used in Italian cooking because its sweet, mild and pungent flavour goes well with tomato dishes. In France, basil is regarded as the 'royal herb' and makes an interesting addition to dishes containing lamb, eggs, bacon and green beans. Its name comes from the Greek word for 'king' and its origins are ancient. Hindus plant it round their homes and places of worship to ensure happiness and, if an Italian gentleman approaches a lady with a sprig of basil in his hair, it proves his matrimonial intentions are honourable.

BASINS
Bowl-shaped utensils of assorted sizes used for mixing, storing and steaming puddings and so on. They can be made of earthenware, metal, heat-resistant glass or rigid plastic.

BASLER-LECKERLI
Swiss-style biscuits, flavoured with cinnamon and containing mixed peel, almonds, hazelnuts and kirsch. They are a Christmas speciality and baked in ornately carved wooden moulds, depicting traditional scenes.

BASMATI RICE
A superior type of Indian white rice which is long-grained and slender. It is traditionally served with curries and comes from the area of the Himalayas.

à la BASQUAISE
French term meaning in the style of the Pays Basque in south-west France, denoting a garnish of *cèpes* or food cooked with tomatoes, peppers, ham and garlic.

BASS
(Salmon Dace, Sea Bass)
A round-bodied, saltwater fish (*Dicentrarchus labrax*), similar in shape to the salmon, which can reach a length of 80 cm–1 metre/24–39 inches. The overall colour is silver with a grey or blue tinge on the back becoming yellowish or white on the belly. Bass is caught most of the year, except April and May, and lives in saltwater lakes and the lower reaches of some rivers; also waters off the North European coasts and in the Mediterranean. The flesh is firm, lean and white and the fish may be poached, steamed, baked, fried, grilled or barbecued. Although there are fish in North American waters with 'bass' in their names, they are, at best, only distantly related.

BASTE (TO)
To keep roasted meat or poultry moist by spooning over pan juices while it is cooking. This tends to reduce evaporation and therefore shrinkage, lessens the risk of scorching and improves the final flavour.

BATAVIA ENDIVE
(Escarole)
Variety of endive which has much broader leaves than the curly endive, although they do have the typically ragged edges. It is used in the same way as curly endive.

BATCH LOAVES
The loaves are baked close together on a baking tray so that the dough touches and, after baking, they are split apart, revealing soft sides with crusts top and bottom. They are popular in Scotland.

à la BATELIÈRE
French term meaning in boatman's style, denoting a garnish for fish to include fried eggs, mushrooms, small onions and sometimes crayfish. The term also describes small tartlet shells with a fairly rich fish filling.

BATH BUNS
Dating back to the 18th century these buns, as their name suggests, originated in Bath. They are made from a white yeast dough containing chopped mixed peel, sugar and sultanas. Spoonfuls of the mixture are placed on baking trays, the tops are brushed with egg and sprinkled with crushed cube sugar before baking.

BATH CHAP
An English speciality from the West Country, comprising half the lower part of a pig's cheek (the chap) including the jaw bone, half the tongue and snout. It is pickled, boiled, boned, coated with breadcrumbs and served cold in slices or sometimes sliced and fried.

BATH OLIVER BISCUITS
Invented during the 18th century by a Dr Oliver of Bath. They are large flat biscuits, pale in colour and very dry. They are usually unsweetened and team well with full-flavoured cheeses.

BATTENBERG CAKE
An oblong cake made from strips of pink and natural-coloured sponge which are first baked in shallow, oblong Swiss roll tins. The strips are held together with jam and the cake is completely covered with almond paste. When the cake is cut, the slices have a chequered appearance.

BATTERS
The word batter comes from the French word *battre*, meaning to beat. Most batters are made from a mixture of brown or white flour, eggs and a liquid such as milk,

water, a combination of milk and cream or water and milk, or sometimes beer. The proportions vary according to the type of batter and its subsequent use. Sweet batters sometimes contain sugar, while savoury batters used for puddings and fritters rarely do. If the batter is of the yeasted variety, a small amount of sugar is added to quicken the action of the yeast.

BAVARIABLU
A rich German cheese made from Alpine cows' milk. It is lightly dotted with blue and contains 70% butterfat. It is a light creamy yellow in colour and mild and soft in texture.

BAVARIAN CREAM
See *Crème Bavaroise*.

BAVAROIS
See *Crème Bavaroise*.

BAVAROISE SAUCE
A Hollandaise sauce, flavoured with grated horseradish. It can be served with trout, herring, mackerel and roast beef.

BAVETTE
Long, thin strips of pasta which sometimes contain egg and are available fresh or dried.

BAY BOLETE
An edible mushroom (*Boletus badius*) with a smooth, brown, bun-shaped cap, slightly sticky when young, and a short, slender stem. It flourishes in coniferous woods during summer and autumn when most other fungi have disappeared. Bay bolete is closely related to the cep or penny bun.

BAY LEAVES
A herb native to the Mediterranean area but also grown in Mexico and throughout Europe. The elongated leaves come from the evergreen sweet bay or laurel tree (*Laurus nobilis*) and are 2.5–5 cm/1–2 inches in length. The fresh leaves are bright green, but lose colour when dried. Their flavour is distinctive and pungent and they are used in stews, hot pots, casseroles, pickles, marinades and chutneys. They are among the world's oldest herbs and were used in the form of wreaths by the Greeks and Romans to crown heroes.

BAY SALT
See *Sea Salt*.

BAY SCALLOP
A small bivalve shellfish (*Argopecten irradians*) of the scallop family with a maximum shell size of 7.5 cm/3 inches. It is the popular scallop of the North American Atlantic coast and the colour can vary from off-white to black. As with the larger scallops, the muscle controlling the shell is the main edible part; it is lean and rich and may be poached, baked, shallow-fried or grilled.

à la BAYONNAISE
French term meaning in the style of Bayonne in south-west France, denoting the inclusion of Bayonne ham.

BAYONNE HAM
A French speciality ham (*jambon de Bayonne*) from the Basque region which is cured with salt, saltpetre, sugar, seasonings and flavourings, sometimes including red wine. It is dried for 4–6 months and has a superior, lightly salted taste. The ham is generally left on the bone.

BEAN
The name given to any seed or pod of the legume family, dried or fresh, which is not a pea or lentil. The term was originally used to describe the European broad bean until other kinds were introduced, mainly from North America.

BEAN CURD
See *Tofu*.

BEAN SPROUTS
Sprouting beans have had their place in Oriental cuisine for centuries and are becoming more widely used in the Western world. The sprouts are available in shops but can be grown at home from the beans themselves in suitably damp conditions. The sprouts are ready for eating when they are 1–5 cm/½–2 inches in length, depending on the type of bean. The mung bean is the most popular of all the sprouting beans and its shoots may be eaten raw or cooked. Other beans suitable for sprouting include soya, lentils and aduki. Peas and alfalfa seeds may be used in the same way and also various grains such as wheat and rye. Mustard and cress are also sprouting seeds.

BEAN THREAD NOODLES
See *Cellophane Noodles*.

BEAR
All bears are edible and bear steaks, which taste like strongly flavoured beef, are a luxury food in Lapland and parts of the USSR. Scarcity and the consequent price have made this meat an exclusive rarity.

BEARD
The gills of an oyster; the fibrous threads on mussels, with which they attach themselves to rocks and stones.

BEARD (TO)
To remove the beard of shellfish such as mussels.

BÉARNAISE SAUCE
The history of this classic sauce is uncertain: either it comes from the Béarnaise region of France or it has no regional associations but was created by a chef near Paris towards the middle of the last century. It is Hollandaise sauce, flavoured with shallot or onion, vinegar, dry white wine, tarragon and parsley. It can be served with grilled steak, poached fish and poached eggs.

BEAT (TO)
To break up or bind ingredients together with a wooden spoon or whisk; also, to pound a piece of meat with a mallet or rolling pin to tenderize the fibres and/or make the meat the correct thickness for a specific dish such as veal escalopes which should be very thin.

BEATER
A general term covering anything from a fork to a whisk, rotary beater, an attachment to an electric mixer, hand-held electric beater or a more elaborate electric food processor. It is used to mix two or more ingredients together, for example, butter and sugar; to blend together two parts of one ingredient, such as the white and yolk of an egg; to change the state of an ingredient, as in turning egg white into foam.

BEAUFORT
A superior French Gruyère cheese which is higher in fat than other varieties and made from cows' milk in the mountain area of Beaufort in Savoie. It is a fine-flavoured cheese with a smooth and creamy texture, devoid of holes.

BÉCHAMEL SAUCE
A classic French sauce, said to be named after Louis de Béchameil who created it while he was employed as maitre d'hôtel in the court of Louis XIV. It is made in exactly the same way as white sauce but the milk is first infused with onion, carrot, celery, parsley, mace or nutmeg, cloves and peppercorns and then strained. It can be served with grilled, baked, poached or steamed fish, grilled chicken, hard-boiled eggs and cooked vegetables such as cauliflower or broccoli. It can also form the basis of fillings for vol-au-vent cases.

BÊCHE DE MER
(Sea Cucumber, Trepang)
Large sea slug found in the waters off the northern coasts of Australia. It is mainly sold dried, either whole or in segments, and is considered a delicacy in China. Related species live in other parts of the world but are of poorer culinary quality.

BED OF BEEF
Term used in the Midlands in Britain for a beef cut also known as thick flank of beef and top rump.

BEE BALM
See *Bergamot*.

BEECH NUTS
Small nuts (*Fagus sylvatica* in Europe and *F. grandifolia* in North America) which are edible when roasted and taste like a cross between hazelnut and chestnut. Beech nuts also yield a top quality oil.

BEECHWHEAT
See *Buckwheat*.

BEEF
The meat of mature cattle, primarily bulls and cows. The flesh is muscular and the cuts used for slow cooking are usually more fatty than the prime cuts used for grilling, frying and barbecuing. The meat is dark red when fresh, turning brown when stale.

BEEF BOURGUIGNONNE
See *Boeuf Bourguignonne*.

BEEF OLIVES
A cut of meat for stuffing, rolling and stewing, comprising thin slices of beef taken from the sirloin or silverside; also the British term for a classic beef dish, made all over Europe under different names.

BEEF SAUSAGES
British sausages containing beef, cereal and seasonings, which are either fried or grilled.

BEEF STROGANOV
(Beef Strogonoff)
An extravagant Russian dish, created for Count Stroganoff during the 19th century, consisting of strips of tender beef fried with chopped onions and mushrooms, then quickly simmered in soured cream. It is flavoured with gherkins, sometimes tomato purée and sherry or wine, seasoning to taste and a squeeze of lemon juice and is traditionally served on a bed of rice.

BEEF TEA
An old-fashioned, invalid drink made from simmering beef in water.

BEEF TOMATO
An extra large variety of tomato.

BEEF WELLINGTON
(Beef en Croute, Boeuf en Croute)
A pre-roasted and cooled fillet of beef, spread with liver pâté and a cooked mushroom mixture, which is then encased in puff pastry, glazed with egg and baked. It is sliced for serving.

BEEFSTEAK FUNGUS
(Poor Man's Beef Steak)
A bright red, edible fungus (*Fistulina hepatica*) which grows on trees. It is shaped rather like a tongue and is eaten as a mushroom when mature.

BEER
Popular as a drink and also used in a number of savoury dishes, beer is the alcoholic liquid produced by the fermenting of malted grain. Variations are found around the world, but the ingredients used by the main beer-producing countries are malted barley, water, hops and sometimes sugar. The alcoholic content ranges from 3.5–10° proof (2–5.5 GL). Beer is the generic term for ale, stout and lager.

BEER SAUSAGE
A German scalded sausage (*bierwurst*) which is said to go well with beer. It is a large, smooth, mottled oval sausage, light pink in

colour. It is made from a well-spiced mixture of chopped beef and pork and contains mustard seeds. It is excellent for slicing and may be eaten cold or cut in pieces and used in hot dishes.

BEESTINGS
The first milk a cow gives after calving. It is thick and golden, and also contains sufficient albumen to set like a custard when baked without the addition of eggs. It is still used in rural areas.

BEET
General term for any of the various plants (*Beta* species) with thick, long-stalked leaves and a swollen root. The root is treated in three ways: as a vegetable, source of sugar and animal feed. Beetroot, spinach beet and Swiss chard are examples of the species.

BEET SUGAR
Sugar produced from beets.

BEETROOT
A root vegetable (*Beta vulgaris*) which is a member of the beet family. It is native to the Mediterranean region and has been cultivated for many centuries to achieve the sweet juiciness of the modern varieties. The root shape may be globular, cylindrical or conical; the colour of the skin is dark purply-red and the foliage above ground is green. When young, both the root and the greenery are tender but the root becomes hard and fibrous with maturity. Beetroot is usually baked or boiled whole and unpeeled as it loses its red juices if the skin is pierced. It may be eaten hot or cold as a vegetable on its own, as part of a salad or used in soups and savoury dishes.

BEIGNETS
Much appreciated in France and North America, these are light and golden fritters made from a type of choux pastry batter. Spoonfuls of the mixture are fried in deep fat or oil, well-drained and sprinkled with icing sugar. They are traditionally eaten warm.

BEL PAESE
The literal meaning of the name of this whole cows' milk cheese is 'beautiful country'. It is made in Lombardy, in the north of Italy, and has a fairly mild and delicate flavour. It takes 6–8 weeks to ripen (mature), has a soft and creamy texture, and may be used in cooking or as a dessert cheese. It is covered with a bright yellow, shiny rind.

BELFAST HAM
Produced mainly in western Scotland, a dry salted ham smoked over peat.

BELGIAN ENDIVE
See *Chicory*.

BELL PEPPER
See *Sweet Pepper*.

BELLE VUE
French term for a beautiful-looking dish of food.

à la BELLE-DIJONNAISE
French term describing a dish with blackcurrants for which Dijon is famous.

BELLELAY
See *Tête de Moine*.

BELLY OF PORK
Literally meat from the belly of the pig, this cut is long, slender and streaked with lines of flesh and fat like streaky bacon. It is often sliced and either fried, grilled or used in pâtés and terrines. The thick end can be stuffed and roasted and belly of pork is sometimes salted and boiled.

BELLY SLICES OF PORK
A new and leaner British cut of meat in long and narrow steaks for grilling or frying.

BELUGA STURGEON
A member (*Acipenser huso*) of the sturgeon family of fish and renowned for the quality of the caviar it produces. It is also one of the largest in the family and is caught in the Black and Caspian Seas and the rivers which flow into them.

BEN TREE
(Ben Oil Tree)
See *Drumstick Pod*.

BENGAL GRAM
See *Chickpea*.

à la BENOITON
French term for a red wine sauce served with fish, flavoured with onions or shallots.

BERCY BUTTER
Softened, whipped butter, flavoured with wine, shallots and parsley. It is shaped into a 2.5 cm/1 inch diameter roll, wrapped and refrigerated until hard, then cut into rounds of about 5mm/¼ inch in thickness. These are used to garnish grilled steaks and lamb chops.

BERCY SAUCE
A velouté sauce made with equal amounts of fish stock and dry white wine, and flavoured with shallots and chopped parsley. It is either based on a roux or thickened at the end with beurre manié (kneaded butter).

BERESFORD PUDDING
An old English steamed pudding, made from a Victoria sandwich mixture flavoured with grated orange peel. Sometimes 25 g/1 oz of white breadcrumbs are substituted for 25g/1 oz of the flour.

BERG
(Alp Cheese, Alpenkäse, Alpine Cheese, Mountain Cheese)
A hard mountain cheese with good keeping qualities. It is made from whole cows' milk, has a high fat content and small holes. It closely resembles Emmental but is a smaller cheese and produced almost exclusively in Germany's High Alps (Allgäu). It has a relatively mild, nutty flavour and is pale yellow in colour.

BERGAMOT
(Bee Balm)
A herb native to North America, it also grows in Britain and other parts of Europe. Bergamot (*Monarda didyma*) is also known as 'bee balm' because bees are attracted to its fragrance and the nectar from its blossom. North American Oswego Indians made the scarlet flowers into a drink and the herb is now used primarily in the form of a sleep-inducing tisane.

à la BERGÈRE
French term meaning in the style of the shepherdess, denoting a garnish of fried mushrooms and straw chips. The term is also used to describe a dish of poultry cooked with mushrooms, ham and onions and garnished with straw chips.

BERNARD L'HERMITE
See *Hermit Crab*.

à la BERRICHONNE
French term for a garnish of cabbage, bacon, onion and chestnut for large joints of meat.

BERRY
Any small fruit with pulpy flesh enclosing a seed or seeds.

BESSAN
Chick pea flour, originally from India.

BEST END NECK OF LAMB
A cut of lamb from between the shoulder and loin which is known by this name in London and the South-East, the West Country and Wales. It consists of a joint with 6–7 bones which the butcher will chine by separating the backbone from the ribs. The best end may then be cut downwards into 6–7 cutlets for

frying or grilling; left as a whole piece and roasted; or boned, stuffed and roasted. Two best end necks are often joined together to make a Guard of Honour and Crown Roast.

BEST END NECK OF VEAL
This cut is converted into chops or cutlets for grilling, frying, stewing or braising.

BETEL LEAF
Leaf of a vine (*Piper betle*) widely used in India as the outer wrapping of *paan* (*pan*), considered to be an aid to the digestion.

BETEL NUTS
The sharp-tasting seeds of the betel palm (*Piper betle*), a climbing pepper. The nuts and leaves of the palm are chewed with lime, especially by South-East Asians, in order to stimulate the flow of saliva.

BEURRE
French term for butter.

au BEURRE
French term for food cooked in butter, or coated with melted butter after cooking.

BEURRE BLANC
A classic French sauce which originated in the Loire Valley and is very popular in France and Belgium. It is made from a concentrated mixture of white vinegar, white wine and shallots, into which small pieces of very cold butter are gradually beaten over a low heat. The resulting sauce is quite warm and just thick enough to coat the back of a spoon and is served with fish dishes and vegetables.

BEURRE MANIÉ
A French term for a mixture of softened butter and flour which is added, in small pieces, to meat, poultry or fish stock at the end of cooking time in order to thicken it.

BEURRE MONTÉ
(Mounted Butter)
Much used in *nouvelle cuisine*, this sauce is very similar to *beurre blanc* but is made with butter and a slightly thickened stock instead of wine, wine vinegar, shallots and seasonings.

BEURRE NOIR
See *Black Butter Sauce*.

BEURRE NOISETTE
See *Black Butter Sauce*.

BEURRES COMPOSÉS
Made from well-creamed butter with the addition of such items as finely chopped anchovies, ground almonds, lemon juice, chopped parsley, chopped chives, curry powder or crushed garlic. Obviously the butter should be flavoured so that it complements the food; for example, mustard goes well with gammon steaks, curry is piquant with shellfish, parsley suits white fish and chicken. The butter is formed into a sausage shape of 2.5 cm/1 inch in diameter, wrapped in foil or cling film and refrigerated until hard. Slices of about 5 mm/¼ inch in thickness are then placed on top of hot foods such as cooked steaks, chops, fish cutlets and vegetables to add flavour and moisture. Some flavoured savoury butters are available in supermarkets.

BEYENDI
A smooth, pale and light-textured aubergine purée from Turkey made from a basic white sauce mixture; sometimes Swiss cheese is included.

BHAJI
Spicy fritters or fried vegetable dishes served as a starter or side-dish to an Indian meal.

BHEL PURI
A northern Indian snack made from puffed rice, peanuts and lentils flavoured with chopped onion and coriander which is served in small dishes with a spicy sauce.

BHUNA
A dry curry from southern India.

BIAROM
A German cheese produced in Bavaria from semi-skimmed milk, which resembles Esrom.

à la BIARROTTE
French term meaning in the style of Biarritz, denoting a garnish of *cèpes* and potato cakes.

BIBER DOLMASI
A Turkish speciality of sweet peppers stuffed with onions, raisins, pine nuts, rice, seasonings and chopped parsley or dill. They are baked in the oven, then served lightly chilled.

BICARBONATE OF SODA
Combined with cream of tartar, the foundation of baking powder. Bicarbonate of soda is an alkali, often used with acids, such as soured milk or buttermilk, to make scones and cakes rise. A pinch of bicarbonate of soda added to the cooking water helps green vegetables to stay a good colour, but this practice should be avoided as it destroys vitamin C.

BIENENSTICH
A German and Austrian version of almond slices made with yeasted pastry and an almond topping. Sometimes called bee stings in Britain.

BIERSCHINKEN SAUSAGE
A literal translation of the name of this German scalded sausage is 'beer-ham'. It is similar to beer sausage but coarser, and there are chunky pieces of ham to be found in an otherwise smooth texture. It is well-spiced, flavoured with garlic and easy to slice.

BIFF À LA LINDSTRÖM
Swedish meat cakes made from raw minced beef, mashed potatoes, cream, chopped beetroot, chopped onion, capers and seasoning which are fried with sliced onions.

BIFTECK HACHÉ
Formal French term for hamburger or beefburger.

BIGARADE SAUCE
An Espagnole sauce, flavoured with orange. It can be served with duck and goose.

BIGOS
The national dish of Poland, a hearty stew of cabbage, sauerkraut, coarsely chopped lean pork and gammon, Polish sausage, chopped onions, lard, tomato purée, paprika, garlic, dried mushrooms and seasonings. It is cooked 2–3 days before eating, reheated and accompanied by rye bread.

à la BIGOUDENNE
French term meaning in the style of Bigouden in Brittany, north-west France, denoting baked slices of unpeeled potatoes.

BILBERRY
See *Blueberry*.

BILLINGE
A Swedish cows' milk cheese which is mild yet mellow, almost white, and peppered with holes. It is factory-produced.

BILTONG
A dried meat used in South Africa which has a shelf-life of 10 years.

BIND (TO)
To make a dry mixture hold together by the addition of a small amount of liquid.

BINDI
See *Okra*.

BIOTIN
A member of the B group of water-soluble vitamins, biotin protects skin, hair, the nervous system and bone marrow. It is found chiefly in offal, eggs, brewer's yeast, oats, wheatgerm, bran, brown bread and fish. Lack of biotin may result in eczema, depression, weariness,

falling hair and loss of appetite. In a normal balanced diet, deficiency of biotin is unusual, but may be caused through an excessive intake of raw egg white and courses of certain types of antibiotic.

BIRD'S-NEST SOUP
A Chinese speciality made from the edible nests of southern Asian swifts, a composition of seaweed and saliva, combined with chicken stock, chicken, ham, seasonings, egg whites and cornflour. The bird's nests give the soup a slightly gelatinous consistency.

BIRIYANI
(Biriani)
A central Indian dish, introduced by the Moguls about 300 years ago, this is a dry, Basmati rice-based combination containing pieces of fried meat, seafood or chicken, saffron, onion, herbs, spices and water. It is mounded on to a plate and garnished with fried onion rings, wedges of tomato and hard-boiled egg slices. A *biriyani* is a complete meal in itself, usually accompanied by a dish of curried vegetables to add moisture.

BIRTHDAY CAKE
The base can be either a rich fruit cake, a Victoria sandwich or a fatless sponge. The cake is iced and decorated according to taste. Particularly for children, the cake mixture is often baked in special tins shaped like animals or numerals. Candles are a traditional feature.

BISCOTTE
A type of dry and crumbly rusk.

BISCUIT
(Hot Biscuit)
North American term for the British scone.

BISCUIT-CRUST PASTRY
See *Flan Pastry*.

BISCUITS
These are made from a pastry-type dough, generally fairly thin and crisp, sweet or savoury, and in virtually any shape: round, square, triangular, oblong and in rings. The average diameter of a circular biscuit is 6–10 cm/2½–4 inches. All biscuits, once cold after baking, should be stored in airtight containers. They should never be put in the same container as a cake because they would soon lose their characteristic crispness. The word is also used in North America to describe what are known in Britain as scones.

BISMARCK HERRINGS
A German speciality of fresh boned herrings, marinated overnight in vinegar with herbs and spices.

BISQUE
A traditional French speciality, a puréed shellfish soup thickened with cream and/or egg yolks. The fish makes the soup pale pink in colour.

BISTRO
A type of old-established small French café or restaurant.

BITOCHKI
(Bitok)
Russian-style meat balls made from a well-seasoned hamburger mixture. They are shaped into fairly small balls, then fried and served with a piquant white sauce, enriched with soured cream.

BITOK
French term for a type of Russian meat or poultry loaf served with soured cream.

BITTER ALMONDS
Resembling sweet almonds in shape, these almonds owe their bitterness to the presence of benzaldehyde, which is toxic if consumed in quantity. Bitter almonds are sometimes used as a flavouring in very small quantities.

BITTER GOURD
A vegetable (*Momordica charantia*) native to Asia and widely used in Indian and Chinese cooking. It grows in a variety of shapes, sizes and colours but all kinds have seeded flesh which tends to be bitter in flavour. In India, a popular bitter gourd is the *karela* which is rather like a crisp courgette in appearance and taste. Other names for types of bitter gourds are balsam apple, balsam pear, kerela, kerala, bitter melon and Chinese bitter melon. In Europe, the bitter gourd family are mainly available canned, but they can sometimes be bought fresh in shops specializing in Asian foods.

BITTER MELON
See *Bitter Gourd*.

BITTER ORANGE
See *Seville Orange*.

BITTERBALLEN
Dutch appetizers, served hot, made from a ham and white sauce base, stiffened with gelatine. The mixture is shaped into balls, coated with egg and crumbs and fried.

BITTERS
Concentrated alcohols with a bitter and pungent taste. Some are based on fruit; others, known as aromatic bitters, are made from medicinal compounds with a preponderance of herbs and spices. Bitters are used in cocktails and mixed drinks.

BIVALVE
A shellfish, such as the oyster, with a hinged double shell.

BLACHAN
(Blacan, Kapi, Terasi)
An Oriental dried paste made from salted and fermented prawns or shrimps sold in small blocks. It has a powerful smell but lends a delicate and subtle taste to many dishes from the Pacific area.

BLACK BEAN
(Black Kidney Bean, Mexican Black Bean)
A vegetable (*Phaseolus vulgaris*) native to South America and widely cultivated in Latin America and the Far East. It grows as a legume and the mature bean is extracted from the pod and dried to be used as a pulse. It is a medium-sized, kidney-shaped bean with a shiny black skin and white flesh. It has a distinctive taste, suggestive of meat or mushroom, and is suitable for most savoury dishes, particularly casseroles and soups. The black bean can be used instead of the red kidney bean and similarly must be boiled briskly for the first 15 minutes of cooking time to destroy harmful toxins found in the outer skin which can prove very dangerous to the human body. Another name for this bean is *frijoles negros*, and it is used extensively in the cooking of Latin America.

BLACK BREAD
A generic term for various dark and heavy Continental breads made from rye and wholemeal flours.

BLACK BUN
See *Scots Black Bun*.

BLACK BUTTER AND CAPER SAUCE
Clarified butter, heated slowly until it turns deep brown, then flavoured with vinegar and chopped capers and poured over poached skate or brains.

BLACK BUTTER SAUCE
Clarified butter, heated slowly until it turns deep brown, then flavoured with vinegar and poured over cooked vegetables, steamed white fish dishes and poached eggs. The French term is *beurre noir* or *beurre noisette*.

BLACK CAP PUDDING
A steamed pudding made from a Yorkshire pudding-type batter which is poured into a greased basin,

base-lined with currants. It is covered, steamed, turned out on to a plate and served with a sauce of jam or golden syrup which has been thinned slightly with a little water, then heated until hot.

BLACK COD
(Blue Cod, Alaska Black Cod)
A round-bodied fish (*Anoplopoma fimbria*) caught in the North Pacific all year round. It is grey-black to black on the back, becoming paler on the underbelly. The average weight is 2.5 kg/ 5½ lb and the length is about 60 cm/24 inches. In spite of its name, it is not a member of the cod family and is an oily fish with rich, white flaky flesh. It is sold fresh, smoked, frozen and salted.

BLACK CROWDIE
(Gruth Dhu)
Scottish Crowdie cheese which has been combined with cream and coated with oatmeal and crushed black pepper.

BLACK DRUM
See *Sea Drum*.

BLACK FOREST CHERRY CAKE
Originally from the Black Forest region of Germany, this is a chocolate layer cake filled with cherries and cream and laced with kirsch. It is usually covered with extra cream and decorated with chocolate (vermicelli or grated) and glacé cherries.

BLACK FOREST HAM
A superior, air-dried ham from southern Germany with a strong and smoky flavour, usually served with potato salad.

BLACK HALIBUT
See *Greenland Halibut*.

BLACK MUSTARD
The seed has a stronger flavour than the paler varieties and is widely used in Indian cookery.

BLACK OLIVE
See *Olive*.

BLACK PEPPER
The berries are picked from vines (*Piper nigrum*) before they are fully ripe and are then dried, cleaned and ready for use. When ground, they become a mixture of black and white particles, because of their dark brown hulls and light kernels. Black pepper has a characteristic, pungent taste and is a popular additive to savoury dishes, especially those containing red meat and offal. It is also used as a condiment.

BLACK PUDDING
(Blood Sausage)
A British cooked blood sausage, produced from the blood of sheep, pig or ox or sometimes a mixture of these. The sausage is thickened with cereal, seasoned, flavoured with onions and enriched with small pieces of fat. The texture is smooth and the sausage is generally heated in water or fried. The traditional accompaniments to black pudding are creamed potatoes and either parsnips or swedes.

BLACK SALSIFY
See *Scorzonera*.

BLACK SEA BASS
A deep-bodied, seawater fish (*Centropristes striatus*) which lives on the bottom of the sea. The colour of the back varies from grey to blackish, becoming paler on the underside and the average weight of black sea bass in the shops is 500 g– 2 kg/18 oz–4½ lb. The dorsal (back) fin is sharp enough to cause injury and should be removed with care. It is caught all along the North Atlantic coast of the USA from Florida to Boston, both as a game fish and commercially. The flesh is lean, firm, white and delicate and the fish may be poached, fried or baked.

BLACK TEA

One of the three main types of tea produced from the original green leaves. The green leaves are left to wither and partially dry out and then they are broken up by a rolling process and left to ferment, when they turn a copper colour. The fermented leaves are treated in a hot-air chamber where they turn dark brown and, finally, they are graded. Black tea is graded by size of leaf or leaf particle, rather than by quality: there are the leaf grades, such as Orange Pekoe and Pekoe, and the broken grades, such as Broken Orange Pekoe, Fannings and Dust. The final quality depends on the blending and is reflected in the selling price. Almost all tea used in Europe and North America is black tea.

BLACK TREACLE

(Treacle)

A syrupy by-product of sugar which is brownish-black in colour, rich in iron and contains invert sugar to prevent crystallization. The flavour is strong and unmistakable. Available in cans or jars, treacle has an almost indefinite shelf-life and is used in baking and confectionery.

BLACKBERRY

(Bramble)

The fruit of a climbing plant (*Rubus* species) which has grown in its wild state for many centuries in parts of the northern hemisphere with moderate climates. The plant was introduced to Australia and elsewhere by settlers and travellers. Although widely cultivated, the wild plant varieties often produce the finest fruit. The berry is generally of a conical or oval shape up to 2.5 cm/1 inch long and consists of a cluster of tiny, single-seeded globules on a central core. The skin colour ranges from green to red to black as the fruit ripens and all three stages are found on any one plant for most of the early autumn season, with the largest and sweetest being the earliest to mature. The blackberry is a good source of vitamin B1 and calcium, and as far back as the mid-18th century was considered to be helpful in cases of sore throats, coughs and colds. It is an excellent fruit to eat on its own, in fruit salads and in many cooked dishes and preserves.

BLACKCOCK

(Black Grouse (Male))

The male black grouse, in season from the end of August to the middle of December but at its best during September and October. It should be drawn and trussed as for chicken and roasted for approximately 1 hour.

BLACKCURRANT

The fruit of a bush (*Ribes nigrum*) native to cooler, moister parts of Europe and northern Asia and cultivated in Britain and France. It is a small, almost black, round and juicy seeded berry which grows in clusters on the bush. It has a small calyx (the remnant of the original flower) at the opposite side to the small thin stalk on which it grows. The fruit does not ripen uniformly and there are often currants at all stages of maturity in any one cluster. Even when ripe the blackcurrant is seldom pleasant to eat raw but it has many culinary applications and may be used in preserves, drinks and cooked dishes. It is a rich source of vitamin C.

BLACKEYE BEAN

(Black-eyed Bean, Blackeyed Bean, Blackeyed Pea)

A vegetable (*Vigna unguiculata*) probably native to Africa, also cultivated in North America and Asia, and a legume which can be cooked when young as a vegetable in its pod. However, in much of the mature crop the bean is extracted and dried to be used as a pulse, either whole or split. It is a smallish, kidney-shaped bean, pale cream in colour with a distinctive 'black eye' situated to one side, consisting of a dark and oval mark with a light central 'pupil'. The blackeye bean has a pleasant flavour which blends well with other ingredients. It is used in many dishes round the world and is also suitable for sprouting. It must be boiled briskly for the first 15 minutes of cooking time to destroy harmful toxins found in the outer skin which can prove very dangerous to the human body. The blackeye bean is also sold under the names *chori* or *lobia* (*lobya*), particularly in shops specializing in Asian foods. In North America it is known as black-eyed Suzie.

BLADDER CHERRY
See *Chinese Lantern*.

BLADE OF LAMB
A joint cut from a shoulder of lamb, suitable for roasting, mincing or dicing for stews, braised dishes, casseroles and kebabs.

BLADE OF PORK
A cut of pork from the neck end of the pig which is finely flavoured and tender. It is recommended for roasting and may be boned and rolled or left on the bone. Blade meat may also be used in stews, braised dishes and casseroles.

BLANC (BLANCHE)
French term for anything white from wine to chicken breast.

BLANCH (TO)
To immerse foods in hot or boiling water, or to boil foods in water for a few minutes; a technique which is used to loosen tomato and almond skins; to preserve colour, texture, flavour and nutritional value of foods before home deep-freezing; to keep certain foods white, such as sweetbreads and rabbit; to reduce saltiness of foods such as kippers, smoked haddock and bacon; to destroy bacteria.

BLANCHED ALMONDS
Shelled almonds from which the skins have been removed.

BLANCMANGE
A British pudding with a French name, this is a sweetened mixture of cornflour or blancmange powder (flavoured and coloured cornflour) cooked with milk and sugar. It is poured into a mould or moulds and left until cold and set.

BLANCMANGE MOULD
See *Mould*.

BLANCMANGE POWDER
See *Blancmange*.

BLANCO
A South American cows' milk cheese which resembles Ricotta.

BLANKET TRIPE
Considered the finest variety of tripe, this comes from the smooth, first stomach of an ox, known as blanket or plain.

BLANQUETTE DE VEAU
A French white stew of veal, thickened at the end of cooking with double cream and egg yolks and flavoured with lemon juice. It is served with rice or boiled potatoes. Chicken or turkey may be used instead of the veal.

BLARNEY
(Irish Swiss Cheese)
An Irish cows' milk cheese which is either red- or cream-skinned and mild in flavour. It is firm, pale-coloured and peppered with fairly large holes.

BLÉ NOIR
(Sarrasin)
French term for buckwheat flour, used for Breton *galettes* and other types of *crêpes* or pancakes.

BLEACHING AGENTS
Used to make flour turn white, rather than stay a natural pale beige colour. They include potassium bromate and chlorine.

BLEND (TO)
(Slake)
To mix a starchy ingredient, such as flour or cornflour, to a smooth consistency with a small amount of liquid.

BLENDER
(Liquidizer)
A leak-proof goblet with rotating cutting blades set in the base, sitting on a motorized unit which drives the blades. It works by electricity and is fitted with a lid. Blenders are available as individual units or as an attachment to a food mixer and can be used to purée, liquidize, chop, mince, grate and grind both liquid and solid ingredients.

BLENDER MAYONNAISE
Whole eggs, not just the yolks, are used for this form of mayonnaise, which is quickly made in a blender goblet or food processor.

au BLEU
French term for method of cooking freshly caught and cleaned trout in fish stock containing vinegar, which results in the skin developing a blue tinge. This method is also practised in Austria. The term is also used to describe very rare steak and some varieties of cheese.

BLEU D'AUVERGNE
A blue-veined, cows' milk cheese produced in the Massif Central region of France. It is soft in texture, fairly pale in colour, and has a sharpish flavour.

BLEWIT
An edible mushroom (*Tricholoma saevum*) with a pale brown cap and a short stem which has a blueish, ink-stained appearance. It grows in both open and wooded sites, frequently in circles of grass which are darker green than the surrounding turf. The blewit is often still available in the autumn when most edible wild mushrooms are scarce. It should be thoroughly cooked to eliminate a possibly harmful substance.

BLIND SCOUSE
A meatless and economical hot-pot from Lancashire, which evolved during times of austerity. It is based on mixed vegetables with plentiful amounts of potatoes. The scouse often contains mushrooms and is sometimes enriched with beef stock.

BLINTZES
Related to Russian *blinis*, Jewish pancakes folded like envelopes around a sweetened cream cheese filling. They are then fried in butter, sprinkled with cinnamon and served with soured cream and sometimes jam.

BLINY
(Blini)
Russian yeasted pancakes made from a mixture of buckwheat and plain white flour. They are eaten hot with caviar, with soured cream or with creamed butter mixed with chopped hard-boiled eggs.

BLOATER
Whole, gutted herring or mackerel which is first brined, then threaded on to rods and wood-smoked.

BLÓDMÖR
An Icelandic blood sausage which owes much to Scottish haggis. Equal amounts of blood and salted water are mixed with barley or oatmeal. The mixture is packed into small bags, made from sheep's intestines, and boiled for several hours. A variation called *lifrarpylsa* is made, substituting sheep's liver for blood.

BLOOD
Animal blood is widely used in the production of Britain's black pudding, France's *boudin* (black sausage) and other French *charcuterie*.

BLOOD ORANGE
A variety of sweet orange with a reddish skin and red and orange flesh. It may be sharper in taste than the normal orange.

BLOOD SAUSAGE
See *Black Pudding*.

BLOOM
The velvety appearance of some fruits such as plums or peaches; also, the white marks on stale chocolate.

BLOOMER LOAF
About 23 cm/9 inches long and tapered at the ends, it is generally made with white flour and the top is characterized by six diagonal slashes.

BLOOMY
An adjective to describe edible cheese rinds which are covered with soft white bloom.

BLØTKAKE
A Norwegian sponge cake, layered with cream and sometimes coated with marzipan.

BLUBBER
The fat of large marine mammals, particularly the whale.

BLUE
A general term to describe fairly soft cheeses which are marbled with veins of completely harmless greenish-blue mould. These are usually made from cows' milk.

BLUE CHEESE DRESSING
Either French or vinaigrette dressing flavoured with crumbled blue cheese. It can be served with green, mixed, tomato and egg salads.

BLUE CHESHIRE
A blue-veined version of English Cheshire cheese which is difficult to find and rather expensive. It has a rich and distinguished flavour.

BLUE CRAB
One of the most popular crabs (*Callinectes sapidus*) caught along the coast of the USA from Maryland to Florida and in the Gulf of Mexico; also, in relatively recent years, the blue crab has been introduced to the eastern Mediterranean. The maximum body width can be up to 20 cm/8 inches but the crab is caught and eaten from about 7.5 cm/3 inches upwards in various graded sizes. The blue colour of the claws is the distinguishing feature of this crab, in addition to the excellence of the meat, both white and brown. The meat may be boiled, steamed or fried and also used in made-up dishes. When small, and after shedding its shell, this is the crab sold as 'soft-shelled'.

BLUE MOULD
Blue patches (*penicillium*) which appear on stale foods.

BLUE MOUNTAIN COFFEE
(Jamaica Blue Mountain Coffee)
A top-quality coffee produced in Jamaica from *arabica* beans in relatively small quantities, commanding a very high price.

BLUE RIBBON
See *Cordon Bleu*.

BLUE TENDALE CHEESE
A British blue cheese made from skimmed cows' milk. It contains half the fat of a traditional blue cheese, such as Stilton.

BLUE TROUT
See *Forelle Blau*.

BLUE VINNY
(Dorset Blue Vinney)
An ancient British cheese, exclusive to Dorset, and now difficult to find. It is a blue-veined cheese made from semi-skimmed cows' milk with a firm texture and fairly strong flavour.

BLUE WENSLEYDALE
A blue-veined version of Wensleydale with an exquisite flavour. Sadly, this is now hard to find since its production is limited to one or two farms.

BLUEBERRY
(Bilberry, Blaeberry, Whortleberry) The fruit of shrubs (*Vaccinium* species), both deciduous and evergreen, native to many temperate parts of North America, Europe and eastern Asia and intensively cultivated in eastern parts of Canada and the USA. It also grows wild in suitable conditions. The berry is spherical, grows in clusters, has a calyx (the remnants of the original flower) and is 5 mm–1 cm/ ¼–½ inch in diameter, depending on the type and whether wild or cultivated. The skin is blue or blue-black in colour and usually has a noticeable pale bloom. The flesh is sweet, juicy and non-acidic in taste and the whole fruit may be eaten raw or used in cooked dishes.

BLUEFIN TUNA
See *Tuna*.

BLUEFISH
A deep-water sea fish (*Pomatomus saltarix*) which approaches coasts during the summer months. The average length of the whole fish in the shops is 45–60 cm/18–24 inches and the average weight is 1–3 kg/2¼–6½ lb. The back is greyish or greenish-blue in colour and the underside is silver. It is found all year round in the Mediterranean and in the Atlantic on the North American side from the Caribbean to the Canadian border, but on the European side only as far north as Spain and Portugal. The flesh is oily and the fish is best poached, baked or grilled. Bluefish is noted for its ferocity towards other fish and for its fighting power as a game fish.

BLUEGILL
A favourite fish with freshwater fishermen, the bluegill (*Lepomis macrochirus*) is found in lakes and streams in North America from the Gulf of Mexico as far north as Canada. It is also farmed in the USA and Japan. The average weight is 250–450 g/9 oz–1 lb. The general colour is bluish with darker gill covers (hence the name), and some have orangey undersides. The flesh is firm and moist and the fish may be fried or partially poached, skinned and then fried in batter.

BLUEPOINT
One of the best-known North American oysters. It is found on the coast of Long Island.

BLUTWURST
A German version of black pudding, this is a cooked sausage made from pork, pig's blood, pieces of fat and seasonings. It is thickened with cereal and sometimes flavoured with onion. The sausage is generally well-spiced and is cut into thickish slices and fried. The traditional German accompaniments are creamed potatoes and stewed apples.

BOAR'S HEAD
A traditional British dish, once served on festive occasions. A modern substitute is a whole roasted pig's head, ornately glazed and decorated.

BOBOTIE
A traditional South African dish made from minced beef mixed with bread soaked in milk, raisins, almonds, vinegar, chopped onions, seasonings and a small amount of sugar. It is topped with an egg and milk mixture and baked.

BOCKWURST
A German scalded sausage which closely resembles the frankfurter but is slightly plumper and more spicy. To prevent splitting, bockwurst should be placed in

water which has just boiled and left to stand away from the heat for about 5 minutes, and should be well-drained before serving.

BOERENKAAS
Dutch term for traditional farmhouse cheese.

BOEREWORS
A heavily spiced South African sausage, usually made from a combination of beef and pork.

BOEUF BOURGUIGNONNE
A superior French beef stew in which the cooking liquid is red burgundy. Shallots and button mushrooms are usually added to the mixture, which should be lightly flavoured with garlic. It is served with boiled potatoes.

BOHEA
A black tea leaf produced in the mountains of the province of Fukien (Fujian) in south-east China.

à la BOHÉMIENNE
French term meaning in Bohemian style, denoting a garnish of tomatoes, rice, fried onions and sometimes also red peppers and paprika.

BOIL (TO)
To cook in a liquid registering a temperature of 100°C/212°F. When water boils, bubbles rise to the surface and a considerable amount of steam is given off. Boiling is used to tenderize food and sometimes to reduce stock, sauces and gravies by evaporation. In general, the pan in which food is boiled is kept covered with a lid.

BOILED BEEF AND CARROTS
Traditional British dish comprising boiled beef served in slices and accompanied by cooked carrots and sometimes dumplings.

BOILED EGGS
Eggs which are cooked in gently boiling water for a specific time: 3½–4 minutes for soft-boiled, 6 minutes for *oeufs mollets* and 10 minutes for hard-boiled. If the water is cold initially, these cooking times apply after the water has come to the boil. To prevent the shells from cracking, the rounded ends of the eggs should be punctured with a pin, needle or special egg-puncturing implement to release air. Alternatively, vinegar or salt may be added to the cooking water. For the yolks to be in a central position, the egg or eggs should be stirred gently round in the water during boiling. To prevent a dark ring forming round the yolk of a hard-boiled egg, it is important not to exceed the above cooking time. Eggs should be removed from the refrigerator at least 30 minutes before boiling. For large eggs such as British grade 1, a little extra cooking time should be allowed; for small eggs such as British grades 5, 6 and 7, a little less. To facilitate shelling, hard-boiled eggs should be tapped gently to crack the shells, then plunged into cold water. They keep for about 4 days under refrigeration but should be put into a plastic bag or well-covered basin.

BOILED EGGS IN A GLASS
A North American and north European custom. Soft-boiled eggs are broken into a glass or dish and eaten with a spoon. Sometimes the eggs are seasoned with salt and pepper and enriched with butter. Bread, rusks or toast are the traditional accompaniments.

BOILED FROSTING
A North American cake icing made from very hot syrup, beaten egg whites and flavouring.

BOILED SWEET
A hard sweet made from boiled sugar and frequently flavoured and coloured.

BOILING FOWL
Older hen birds which have had one or two laying seasons. They are

well-flavoured birds but tend to be a bit tough and stringy and need long, slow cooking, such as boiling or casseroling, to tenderize the flesh. They weigh 2.25–3 kg/5–6½ lb.

BOILING RING
Sausage coiled into a ring and generally heated in water.

BOLLITO
An Italian word meaning 'boiled', frequently applied to boiled beef.

BOLLITO MISTO
An Italian speciality consisting of a variety of meats (beef, veal and chicken, for example) boiled together with vegetables, herbs, spices and seasonings. The liquid is served as soup with *pastini*; the meats as a main course with potatoes and horseradish.

BOLOGNA
A popular sausage which is a relation of the frankfurter. It is made from a mixture of pork and beef, and is scalded and smoked. Sometimes bologna is coloured deep pink.

BOLOGNESE SAUCE
An Italian sauce consisting of minced meat flavoured with onion, tomatoes, sometimes garlic, sometimes bacon, herbs, spices and a little sugar. It is eaten with *spaghetti*.

BOMBAY DUCK
Raw fish which is cured, dried and salted. It has a very strong flavour and is generally served with Indian-style dishes. It is available from speciality shops and has no connection whatsoever with duck.

BOMBE MOULD
A round or cylindrical mould designed for making elaborate ice cream bombes.

BOMBES
Frozen ice creams which are artistically moulded in conical bombe moulds. They are generally composed of two different ice creams; one is used to line the mould while the other, frequently containing glacé fruits, liqueurs and nuts, fills the centre.

BONAVISTA BAY COD'S TONGUES
A speciality of Newfoundland, consisting of washed and dried cod's tongues, coated with egg and flour and then fried. Four or five are allowed per person.

BONBEL
A factory-produced French cheese, almost identical to Saint-Paulin. It is made from cows' milk.

BONDAIL
A barrel-shaped French cream cheese from Normandy. It is produced from cows' milk and flavoured with garlic.

BONDEPIGE MED SLØR
A traditional Danish dessert and a national favourite, this is very similar to Danish apple cake but the layers consist of crumbled Danish rye bread, sweetened apple purée and melted red-coloured jam. The topping is whipped cream and more jam.

BONDON
(Bondard, Bonde)
Shaped like a cider barrel (hence its name), a French cream cheese produced in Normandy from cows' milk. It is manufactured in a wide variety of sizes.

BONE (TO)
To remove bones from meat, game, poultry and fish.

BONE MARROW
A great delicacy, found in the large leg bones of cattle. It was served in Britain as early as the 16th century and is used in certain dishes of the French classic repertoire. Because it is rich in fat, it disintegrates if overcooked; therefore, marrow taken from split bones should be

sliced fairly thickly and gently steamed on a covered plate over a saucepan of hot water. Marrow is often used as a topping for *canapés*, or is treated like dripping and spread on hot toast.

BONELESS BREAST OF LAMB
A new and leaner British cut of meat, suitable for roasting.

BONELESS LOIN AND BELLY OF PORK
A new and leaner British pork joint, suitable for roasting.

BONELESS ROLLED LAMB
A new and leaner British lamb joint, suitable for roasting.

BONITO
A small member (*Sarda sarda*) of the tuna family with a streamlined shape and a maximum length seldom exceeding 70 cm/27 inches. The colour of its back is blue, shading to silver-grey on the sides and belly. It is caught in warm seas worldwide and the principal landing season is late autumn. The flesh is not as heavy as that of the larger tuna and the fish is best baked or grilled. As with other types of tuna, the light flesh is less oily than the dark.

BONITO FLAKES
Dried fish flakes widely used in Japanese cooking, especially in stock.

BONNE BOUCHE
French term for a mouthful of tasty food; for example, a savoury canapé.

à la BONNE-FEMME
French term literally meaning good woman and descriptive of any dish cooked with mushrooms, potatoes, onions and sometimes fried bacon. It is especially applicable to chicken.

BOODLES' ORANGE FOOL
Named after the famous London club which was established in the 18th century, this is similar to a syllabub but made with orange juice instead of alcohol.

BORAGE
The origins of this annual herb (*Borago officinalis*) are unknown, but it was very highly regarded by the Greeks and Romans. The leaves are greyish-green, pointed and long; the flowers are cornflower blue and were often preserved or candied in the 18th and 19th centuries. The leaves, with a mild cucumber flavour, are traditionally added to fruit cups, punches and Pimms.

à la BORDELAISE
French term meaning in the style of Bordeaux, denoting the use of Bordeaux wine in cooking; also food served with Bordelaise sauce or garnished with fried *cèpes*.

BORDELAISE SAUCE
An Espagnole sauce, flavoured with red wine, shallots, thyme, tarragon, parsley and lemon juice. It can be served with meat grills, fried sweetbreads and grilled kidneys.

BORDER MOULD
See *Ring Mould*.

BORECOLE
See *Kale*.

BÖREK
Turkish puff pastry pasties filled with meat or cheese.

BORGRÁCS GULYÁS
A Hungarian beef stew containing fried onions, green peppers, tomatoes, garlic, stock, caraway seeds, and pasta. It is never thickened and always served in deep plates.

BORJUPAPRIKÁS
Similar to the Hungarian *paprikás csirke* but made with veal.

BORLOTTI BEAN
(Rose Cocoa Bean, Rosecoco Bean)
Italian name for a dried, kidney-shaped bean (*Phaseolus vulgaris*) native to South America which is pink-skinned with brownish mottling. When used in cooking, the beans must be boiled briskly for the first 15 minutes of cooking time to destroy toxins found in the outer skin which can prove very dangerous to the human body. Borlotti beans are also available ready-cooked in cans.

BORSCH
(Borshch, Bortsch)
A Russian beetroot, beef and mixed vegetable soup, traditionally accompanied by soured cream. For a vegetarian version, the beef is omitted.

BORSHCHOK
(Borshchchok, Bortschchok)
A clear Russian beetroot soup, sometimes containing woodcock or pigeon. It is generally served with *croûtons*.

BORTSCH DE FASOLE
A Romanian soup made from haricot beans, raw beetroot, onions, celery, spinach, tomatoes, vinegar, oil and seasonings.

BOSANSKE CUFTE
Yugoslavian meatballs, a speciality of Bosnia-Herzegovina, named after the Arab word *cufte*, meaning any meat which is minced or chopped. They are made from beef or lamb, flour, egg and seasonings and are baked in the oven. The meatballs are then coated with an egg and yogurt sauce flavoured with caraway seeds and reheated.

BOSANSKI LONAC
Named after the deep earthenware casserole, the *lonac*, in which it is cooked, this is a popular Yugoslavian speciality from Bosnia-Herzegovina consisting of diced pork, lamb and beef casseroled with vegetables, garlic, a calf's foot, wine, water, vinegar and seasonings.

BOSTON BAKED BEANS
A speciality from Boston in the USA consisting of white beans, salt pork, mustard, sugar or treacle and salt simmered together for many hours; sometimes an onion stuck with cloves is added. The cooked beans are eaten with heavy brown bread.

BOSTON BLUEFISH
North American term for coley.

BOSTON BROWN BREAD
A heavy, steamed, North American bread containing white and brown flours, polenta or semolina and treacle. It is usually eaten with Boston baked beans.

BOSTON CREAM PIE
A North American sandwich cake filled with a thick layer of confectioner's custard and coated with chocolate icing.

BOSUM OF BEEF
Term used in the Midlands in Britain for clod of beef.

BOTERKOEK
Renowned Dutch butter cake, which closely resembles Scottish shortbread.

BOTTLE GOURD
See *Doodhi*.

BOTULISM
A dangerous and insidious form of food poisoning caused by the action of *Bacillus botulinus* on some canned and preserved foods. There are no outward signs of decay, hence the danger.

BOTVINIA
A Russian summer soup made from spinach, sorrel, beetroot tops, pickled beetroot juice, vinegar, white wine, pickled cucumber, shrimps, horseradish, sturgeon, crushed ice, herbs and seasonings.

Originally from Poland, the soup is popular in the Ukraine where it is served on important occasions and celebrations.

BOUCHÉES
French term for 'mouthfuls' (the literal translation) of savoury food eaten at a cocktail party; usually miniature vol-au-vents or tiny choux puffs, filled with a creamed chicken or fish mixture.

BOUDIN
A Créole sausage mixture from Louisiana in the USA. It is made from a base of pork liver, cooked pork, rice, spring onions and seasonings.

BOUDIN BLANC
White, cased sausage from France, made from the light flesh of pork and poultry. The meat is finely minced, then mixed with chopped pork fat, cream, breadcrumbs, egg and seasonings. It is heated slowly in boiling water, then lightly fried and eaten while still very hot.

BOUDIN NOIR
French blood sausage made from pig's blood, cream, onions, pork fat and seasonings.

BOUILLABAISSE
A strongly flavoured classic Mediterranean fish soup, containing locally caught fish, together with saffron and other herbs, tomatoes, olive oil, potatoes and white wine. The soup is ladled into bowls over slices of French bread and served piping hot.

BOUILLON
A clear French soup based on meat.

BOUILLON CUBE
See *Stock Cube*.

à la BOULANGÈRE
French term meaning in the style of a baker's wife, referring to meat or poultry braised or baked with sliced onions, potatoes and stock. A thickened sauce is made with the pan juices.

BOULETTE
Hand-formed in assorted shapes, these fresh little cheeses from Belgium are usually made from cows' milk. They are generally flavoured with herbs and are relatively strong in taste.

BOULETTES
French term for rissoles. Traditionally, round or square pockets of thin, puff or shortcrust pastry with a cooked meat or poultry filling are dipped in egg, coated with crumbs and fried.

BOULETTES CREOLE
Spicy minced beef balls from the Gambia which are simmered with onions, green peppers, tomatoes, oil, garlic and chilli, ginger and stock.

BOUNCEBERRY
See *Cranberry*.

BOUNDARY BAY CRAB BOUCHÉES
Small puffs, eaten as appetizers, from British Columbia in Canada, made from choux pastry flavoured with cheese. The filling consists of crabmeat, green onions, celery, caraway seeds and mayonnaise.

BOUQUET GARNI
French term for a small bunch of herbs, either tied together or enclosed in a muslin bag, used to flavour soups, stews, braised dishes, casseroles and stocks. The herbs usually consist of bay, thyme, marjoram and parsley.

BOURBON BISCUITS
Chocolate biscuits, about 7.5 cm/3 inches in length, which are sandwiched together in pairs with chocolate cream.

BOUREKAKIA
Greek pasties made from filo (phyllo) pastry filled with cheese, poultry, vegetables or meat. They are either fried or baked and eaten hot or cold.

à la BOURGEOISE
French term meaning in the style of the middle classes, referring to stews and braised dishes of meat with onions, carrots and bacon.

à la BOURGUIGNONNE
French term meaning in the style of Burgundy and referring to meat cooked in red Burgundy with shallots, mushrooms and usually bacon.

BOURGUIGNONNE SAUCE
A French sauce based on red burgundy, flavoured with shallots or onion, parsley, thyme, bay leaf, mushrooms and seasonings. It is thickened with beurre manié and can be served with grills and roasts of beef.

BOURRIDE
A French fish stew with *aioli*, served on or with toast.

BOURSIN
Brand name of a thick, pasteurized cream cheese from France. It is flavoured with herbs, pepper and garlic, and made from cows' milk.

BOVRIL
A brand name for a thick and dark brown paste which is an extract of beef. It can be used as a spread, a flavouring in soups, stews, gravies and sauces, or diluted with water to make a drink.

BOWLES MINT
See *Apple Mint*.

BOW-SHAPED PASTA
See *Farfalle*.

BOXTY
Irish potato cakes made from both cooked and raw potatoes mixed with flour, baking powder, fat and seasonings. They are baked, split and buttered.

BOYSENBERRY
The fruit of a trailing shrub (*Rubus* species), the precise origins of which are obscure, finally developed in California in the 1930s by a man called Boysen. It is probably a hybrid of blackberry, loganberry and raspberry. Although it has been introduced to other countries, it is still in the USA that major production exists and elsewhere only the canned variety can usually be bought. The shape is oval and the fruit consists of a cluster of little globules on a small, fleshy stem. It is one of the larger fruits in its family and can be up to 5 cm/2 inches in length. The colour is red, becoming darker as it ripens. The flesh is juicy with a tangy sweetness and with fewer seeds than its ancestors. It may be used, either fresh or canned, in any dishes suited to the loganberry or blackberry.

à la BRABANÇONNE
French term meaning in the style of Brabant in Belgium, denoting the inclusion or garnish of Brussels sprouts, whole or in purée form, hops or chicory.

BRADENHAM HAM
An English speciality ham from the West Country which dates back just over 200 years. It is brined for a minimum of 4 weeks, then steeped in a 'treacle' bath made from dark sugars, salt and saltpetre and left for another 4 weeks to mature. It is subsequently smoked for several days over applewood and oak, and the resulting ham has an intensely black skin and a mild yet distinctive flavour.

BRAEIVLEIS
(Braii)
The South African term for barbecue.

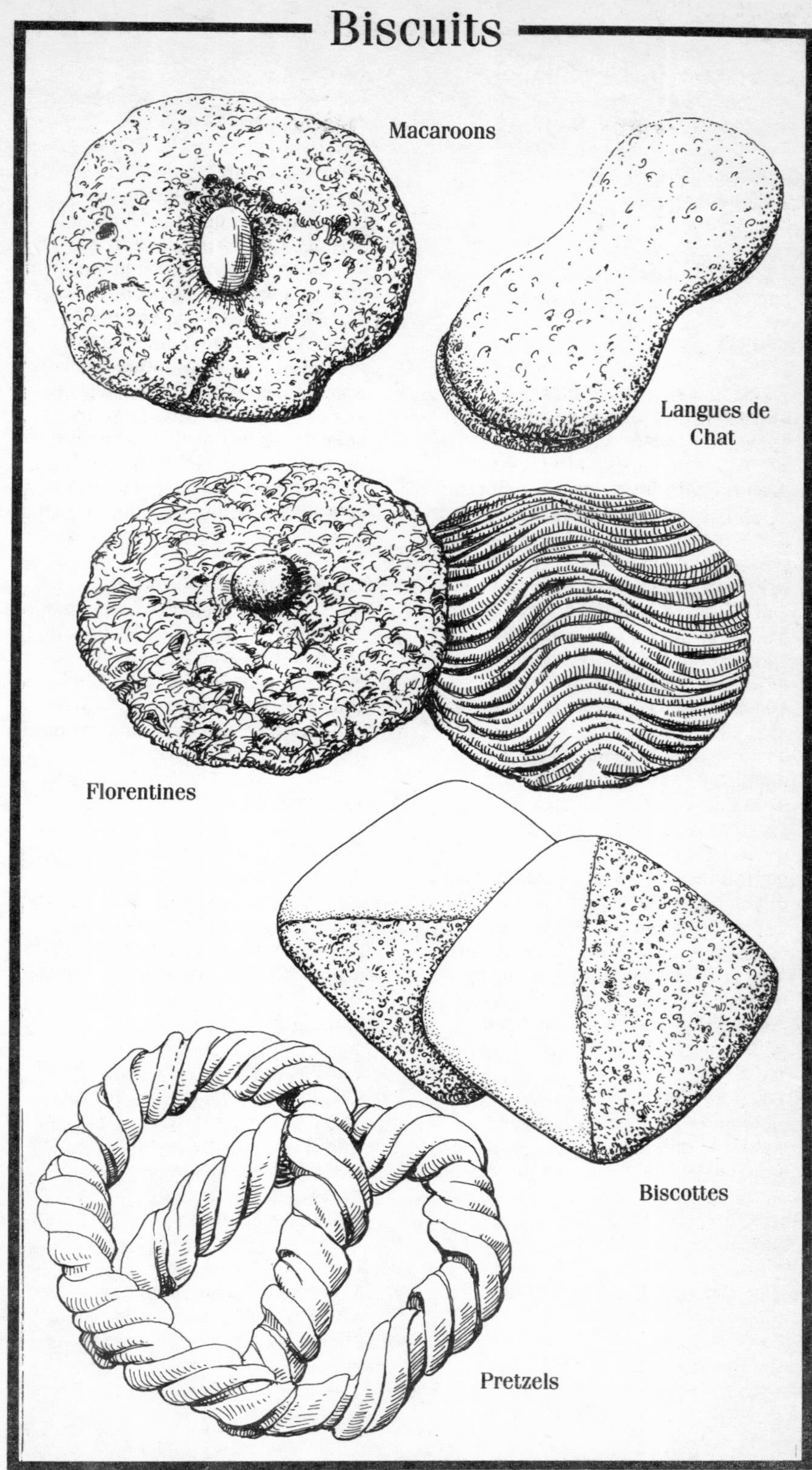
Biscuits
Macaroons
Langues de
Chat
Florentines
Biscottes
Pretzels

à la BRAGANCE
French term meaning in the style of the Braganza area of Portugal, denoting a garnish of stuffed tomatoes (sometimes with Hollandaise sauce) and potato croquettes.

BRAID CHEESE
See *String*.

BRAINS
Unlike other members of the offal family, brains are not highly nutritious and tend to be rather fatty. They are, however, considered a delicacy and are relatively easy to digest. Brains deteriorate rapidly, so should always be bought when very fresh and used within 24 hours of purchase. A set of two calves' brains (said to be the best) or two ox brains will serve two people; a set of lambs' brains, being smaller, will serve only one person. Fresh, top-quality brains are pinkish-grey in colour and glossy. The outside membrane is moist and unwrinkled, giving the brains a plump appearance; the membrane should peel away easily from the meat but will sink into the crevices if the brains are stale. Brains are generally soaked for 1–2 hours in salted water to dislodge the blood, before the outer membrane and arteries are removed with a sharp, pointed knife. The brains are then ready for cooking, usually by poaching in salted water to which lemon juice or vinegar has been added.

BRAISE (TO)
To simmer partly on top of the cooker and then to finish cooking in the oven. Braised meat or poultry is usually cooked on a bed of assorted vegetables, the liquid from which may be thickened in the same way as gravy. When in the oven, the dish must be covered to prevent dryness.

BRAMBLE
See *Blackberry*.

BRAN
The hard outer casing or husk which surrounds grains of cereal such as wheat and maize. When milling white flour, the bran layer is removed; some is used in the preparation of certain breakfast cereals, while a proportion is used for animal feed. Bran, also found in brown flour products, brown rice and so on, adds roughage or fibre to the diet which is valuable in the prevention of constipation and is now said also to avert illnesses such as diverticulitis, varicose veins, haemorrhoids and hiatus hernia. Bran constitutes about 13% of the grain and is an excellent source of cellulose, calcium, phosphorus and iron.

BRANDADE DE MORUE
A French dish from Provence, made from a purée of cooked, dried salt cod mixed with olive oil, milk, usually garlic, lemon juice and seasonings. The mixture is stirred constantly over a medium heat until light in consistency and pale in colour. It is best served lukewarm with fried bread.

BRANDY
Spirit distilled from wine, most commonly the grape wines. Brandy is a warm golden-amber in colour and has a high alcohol content, 70° proof (40° GL). It is used worldwide as a drink, in cooking and for flaming (*flambé*).

BRANDY BUTTER
A solid sauce made from butter, sugar, brandy and spice. It is traditionally served with hot mince pies or Christmas puddings and melts over the food, providing flavour and moisture.

BRANDY SAUCE
A sweetened white sauce flavoured with brandy. It can be served with Christmas pudding or mince pies.

BRANDY SNAPS
Lacy in appearance, ginger-flavoured and rolled biscuits which are hollow in the centre. They are usually filled with whipped cream and occasionally chocolate-coated.

BRANDZA DE BURDOUF
Romanian ewes' milk cheese eaten at the end of Lent. It is stronger than ordinary Brandza (commonly known as Brynza), fairly soft, spreadable in consistency, and matured in a *burduf*, which is a special bag made from leather. Sometimes the cheese is left to ripen in rings of fir bark and becomes very slightly tinged with the palest green. The taste is distinctively piney.

BRASSERIE
French term for a brewery; also, a café, restaurant or beer garden.

BRASSICA
Any of a large genus (*Brassica*) of the mustard family of temperate zone plants that include many important vegetables and crop plants, including cabbage, turnip, mustard and rape.

BRAT
Swiss grilling cheese made from cows' milk.

BRATWURST
(Rostbratwurst)
A German sausage, made from veal or pork, which is fried or grilled. It is beige in colour and can be coarse or fine in texture.

BRAUDOST
An Icelandic cows' milk cheese which resembles Edam.

BRAWN
A cold meat loaf containing pieces of meat in a savoury jelly. The best brawn is generally made from a boiled calf's head; a pig's head gives equally good results but is less readily available.

BRAZIL NUTS
These nuts grow on a very tall tree (*Bertholletia excelsa*) and are named after their country of origin (where they are rarely eaten!). Found in Paraguay as well as Brazil, the nuts are clustered inside large, coconut-like shells. The nuts are wedge-shaped with three sharp edges and a tough, dark brown shell which houses a fleshy white kernel, rich in oil. A highly popular dessert nut, Brazils reached Europe in the 17th century and were very popular in the Victorian era. They remain a widely used nut in both sweet and savoury dishes and are also used in confectionery.

BRAZILIAN CHERRY
See *Barbados Cherry*.

BRAZILIAN COFFEE
Brazil is the world's largest producer of coffee, accounting for over one-quarter of total exports. Although the coffee is all of the *arabica* type bean, the methods of growing and gathering, plus the relatively unreliable weather, mean that the quality is variable. The combination of reasonable price and mild flavour makes Brazilian coffee suitable for blending with stronger-flavoured beans from other countries. The most popular type of bean is called Santos or Brazilian Santos.

BRAZILIAN GUAVA
See *Feijoa*.

BRAZILIAN SANTOS
See *Santos*.

BREAD
Bread is a staple food in many countries of the world and bread-making dates back to the time of the Old Testament. The original breads made by the Hebrews, Ancient Chinese and Egyptians were unleavened; later, the Egyptians discovered how to use yeast to leaven or raise bread and, as early as 200 BC, the Romans established

bakeries for making leavened bread. Wheat flour in its various forms is used to make most commercially available bread but other cereals are also used.

BREAD AND BUTTER PUDDING

Very popular in Britain, this is a dessert made from slices of white bread and butter, sugar, currants, eggs and milk and baked until golden-brown.

BREAD FLOUR

(Strong Flour)

A strong, plain flour which is rich in gluten, enabling yeasted goods to rise well and hold their shape.

BREAD PUDDING

A baked pudding made from bread which is soaked in milk, beaten until smooth, then mixed with dried fruit, sugar, jam or marmalade, flour, eggs, spices and butter or margarine. It is eaten hot with custard or served cold, cut into squares and eaten as cake.

BREAD SAUCE

A thick sauce made from breadcrumbs, milk, onion, herbs, spices and seasonings. It is traditionally served in Britain with poultry.

BREAD SAW

(Sawknife, Serrated Knife)

A bread knife with a serrated edge.

BREADCRUMBS

(Crumbs)

Crumbled or grated bread, made either from fresh or left-over bread which has been dried out in a cool oven.

BREADFRUIT

(Breadnut)

Fruit of a tropical tree (*Atrocarpus communis*) native to South-East Asia and the Pacific islands and widely cultivated in lowland, humid regions. It is round with a thick, rough, green skin which becomes tinged with yellow as the fruit ripens. The weight can be 1–3 kg/2–6 lb or even more, and the diameter 10–15 cm/4–6 inches. Most varieties are seedless and the flesh is pale yellow, pulpy and sweet. Although the flesh of the breadfruit may be used in dessert dishes, it is more often cooked as a vegetable. If baked when not too ripe, the result is reminiscent of fresh bread. Varieties which contain seeds are called breadnut and the seeds, which are about 2.5 cm/1 inch long, may be roasted or boiled and eaten as nuts.

BREADSTUFFS

Cereal products to include bread and buns.

BREAKFAST

The first meal of the day which literally breaks the fast of the night.

BREAKFAST BLEND

(Breakfast Tea, English Breakfast Tea)

Term used by blenders to indicate a strong, full-bodied black tea considered suitable for the first cup of the day. Originally blended from strong teas from China, it is now more usually a mixture of Assam and Ceylon types.

BREAKFAST CEREALS

Made from rice, wheat, oats, maize and other cereals, sometimes puffed, flavoured, sugar-coated or left plain, these are served straight from the packet with hot or cold milk and sugar. Cereals based on bran add a relatively high proportion of fibre to the diet and are recommended for those suffering from constipation. Hot cereals such as porridge, cooked barley flakes and millet are also eaten for breakfast.

BREAST OF LAMB

A long, thin cut of fairly fat meat which is usually boned-out in readiness for braising or stuffing and roasting. It comes from the underside of the lamb (the equivalent of belly in other animals) and is economically priced. It is known as breast in London and the South-East, the Midlands, the West Country and Wales.

BREAST OF VEAL
A bony, forequarter cut of veal for stewing, braising or casseroling. It may also be boned, rolled and roasted.

BREDIE
South African meat and vegetable stew.

BRENT GOOSE
(Barnacle Goose)
Any of several small dark geese (genus *Branta*, especially *Branta bernicla*) that breed in the Arctic and migrate to the south.

BRESAOLA
Air-dried beef from Italy, now more generally available in Britain, served in wafer-thin slices as an *hors d'oeuvre*.

à la BRESSANE
French term meaning in the style of Bresse, in eastern France, particularly denoting a cream of pumpkin soup containing small pasta or croûtons.

BRESSE BLEU
(Bleu de Bresse)
A post-Second World War French cheese which resembles Gorgonzola. It is made from pasteurized cows' milk and has a rich and semi-soft texture, woven with blue threads.

à la BRETONNE
French term meaning in the style of Brittany, in north-west France, referring to any hearty dish of braised or stewed lamb containing haricot beans. It also refers to strips of fried leeks, celery, onions and mushrooms mixed with velouté sauce and served with fish.

BRETZEL
French term for pretzel.

BRETZELS
See *Pretzels*.

BRICK
A North American cheese made from cows' milk. Originally created by a Swiss in Wisconsin, the cheese has been likened to Münster, Limburger, Cheddar, Saint-Paulin and Tilsit. It is brick- or loaf-shaped, creamy-yellow in colour and interspersed with irregular holes. It is a medium-soft cheese with an appealing pungency and slightly sweet after-taste. The rind is an orange-brown and, because the cheese is easy to slice, it is often used in sandwiches.

BRIDGE ROLLS
Finger-length, soft rolls which taper at both ends. They are generally split, filled and sandwiched back together, though smaller ones are often halved, topped attractively with savoury fillings and served as appetizers or at functions such as weddings and christenings. They were originally served at bridge parties, hence their name.

BRIDIE
A Scottish and North Country term for a meat pasty.

BRIE
(Brie Laitier)
A French cows' milk cheese which dates back to the 13th century, Brie is a flattish, circular cheese which is usually sold in wedges; either pre-packed in boxes or cut from a large Brie at a cheese counter. It has a velvety, white and edible skin encasing a cream-coloured cheese with a fruity, well-balanced and piquant flavour, usually fairly mild. It is a smooth and paste-like cheese which should be eaten while still firm; runny Brie smelling of ammonia indicates an over-ripe and deteriorating cheese. If the centre is hard, this means the cheese is

under-ripe and will tend to be bland and tasteless. Brie is now produced in many other countries besides France and is sometimes flavoured with pepper, mushrooms and herbs. Blue-veined versions are also becoming more generally available. In general, Brie needs 6–8 weeks to reach full maturity.

BRIE DE COULOMMIERS
(Coulommiers)
A milder and smaller version of traditional Brie.

BRIE DE MEAUX
Said to be the best of its kind, this type of Brie is produced in the Île-de-France from unpasteurized cows' milk. It is large, round, fairly thin and marked *fermier*.

BRIE DE MELUN
A strong and potent Brie made from unpasteurized cows' milk. The rind is orange-red streaked with white. Brie de Melun is said to be the original cheese from which other Bries have been developed.

BRIK
A large Turkish pasty made from very thin pastry with a filling of raw egg, vegetables and tuna which is deep-fried and served hot.

BRILL
A flatfish (*Scophthalmus rhombus*) caught in the shallow waters of the North Atlantic and Mediterranean during most of the year, but at its best in autumn and winter. The upper side is freckled grey or brown and the average length of the whole fish as seen in the shops is 30–40 cm/12–16 inches. The flesh is firm and the fish may be poached, steamed, baked, fried or grilled.

BRILLAT-SAVARIN
A French triple cream cheese made from cows' milk in the Normandy region. It is named after the famous 19th-century epicure and is rich, creamy and looks something like Brie.

BRIN D'AMOUR
(Fleur de Maquis)
A French goats' milk cheese produced in Corsica. It is flavoured with herbs and the grey rind is encrusted with savory and rosemary. It is matured for 3 months and shaped into shallow squares. The flavour is distinctively herby and the texture fairly soft.

BRINE (TO)
To soak food in a salt and water solution. The length of time depends on the recipe, as does the strength of the solution.

BRINJAL
Term used in India and parts of Africa for aubergine.

BRIOCHE LOAF
A large *brioche* which is sliced like a loaf.

BRIOCHES
French speciality rolls, made from a rich yeasted batter containing eggs and butter. They are usually baked in individual fluted tins and resemble cottage loaves in appearance. The texture is light and spongy and the colour golden.

BRIQUETTE
See *Neufchâtel*.

BRISKET OF BEEF
A coarse, well-flavoured and fairly fatty cut of beef from the underside of the animal. It is sometimes sold on the bone but is more generally boned and rolled. Brisket can be salted and boiled or left unsalted and then boiled. Other suitable methods of cooking include braising and slow-roasting.

BRISLING
(Swedish Anchovies)
Sprat, canned in oil.

BRIT
North American term for young herring or mackerel.

BRITTLE
A sweet made with caramelized sugar and nuts, such as peanuts.

BROACH
A spit for roasting meat.

BROAD BEAN
(Fava Bean)
The seed of a dwarf or climbing plant (*Vicia faba*) which is the oldest known podded vegetable in Europe. Native to Asia and/or Europe, its origins are uncertain. The bean was cultivated in the Old World for thousands of years and introduced to Britain about the time of the Roman occupation. It grows as a long green pod containing pale green, oval-shaped beans which are best eaten when very young as a boiled vegetable. The broad bean is available in fresh, dried or canned forms; the dried bean is cream or pale-brown coloured.

BROCCIO
(Brocciu Cheese)
A French ewes' or goats' milk curd cheese, produced in Corsica. It is rather like German Quark or Italian Ricotta.

BROCCOLI
(Sprouting Broccoli)
A vegetable (*Brassica oleracea*, var. *botrytis*) which is a member of the cabbage family and very closely related to the cauliflower. It was probably first developed in Italy and was introduced to Britain during the early part of the 18th century as a result of the increasing popularity of the cauliflower itself. Broccoli consists of long green stalks with branching shoots which end in small tight clusters of immature flowers. The clusters may be green or purple in colour and most of the surrounding green leaves of the broccoli are usually removed before it reaches the shops. It is one of the best-tasting members of the cabbage family and may be eaten raw, boiled or steamed, or used in vegetable salads and cooked dishes. One of the finest forms of green broccoli was developed in Italy and is called calabrese.

BROCHETTE
French term for skewer.

BRODO DI MANZO
A clear Italian beef broth, usually containing *pastini*.

BROILER
North American term for a young chicken weighing about 1.25 kg/ 2½ pounds.

BROILING
North American term to describe grilling. In Victorian times in Britain, broiling and grilling were synonymous.

BROKEN ORANGE PEKOE
One of the larger broken grades of black tea leaf which is sorted after processing and before blending.

BROMELIAD
Any member of the Bromeliaceae family, chiefly tropical American plants including the pineapple.

BROOD
A Belgian cheese with a Flemish name meaning loaf cheese. It is similar to Dutch Edam, but has a yellow, waxed coat and is rectangular in shape. It is made from cows' milk.

BROSE
A Scottish dish which is similar to a thin porridge and is eaten with butter, cream or milk.

BROTH
Thin soup made from meat, poultry or vegetable stock, sometimes with the addition of rice or pearl barley.

BROUSSE-DU-RÔVE
A French ewes' milk curd cheese, farm-produced in Provence. It resembles German Quark or Italian Ricotta.

BROWN
An adjective to describe foods that are partially or wholly untreated, unrefined or unpolished; examples are brown sugars, brown rice and brown flours.

BROWN (TO)
To bake, grill or roast in the oven so that the food turns a golden-brown colour.

BROWN BETTY
A North American pudding, made from layers of sugar, breadcrumbs, spices, butter, grated lemon peel and sliced apples, baked until brown and served hot with cream.

BROWN BREAD
A general term for breads made from brown flour such as wholewheat and wholemeal.

BROWN BREAD ICE CREAM
Old-fashioned British ice cream containing fresh brown breadcrumbs and usually flavoured with vanilla.

BROWN BUTTER SAUCE
Clarified butter, heated slowly until it turns light brown, then poured over hot asparagus, broccoli, celery hearts, chicory or brains.

BROWN FLOUR
See *Wheatmeal Flour*.

BROWN FUNGUS
See *Cloud Ear Fungus*.

BROWN ONION SOUP
(French Onion Soup)
A fairly thin soup made from a basis of fried onions. Traditionally, it should be ladled into bowls, topped with thick slices of French bread and sprinkled heavily with cheese; the bowls are then placed in a very hot oven or under the grill until the cheese melts and browns.

BROWN RIBWEED
See *Alaria*.

BROWN RICE
Unprocessed rice (*Oryza sativa*), from India and North America. It is a natural and nutritious rice from which only the husk has been removed; the bran layer is intact.

BROWN SAUCE
English term for Espagnole sauce.

BROWN SELF-RAISING FLOUR
Usually refers to wholemeal, wholewheat or wheatmeal flours containing controlled amounts of raising agent, added during production.

BROWN SHRIMP
See *Shrimp*.

BROWN SUGAR
Unrefined or partly refined sugars which are brown in colour, such as demerara, muscovado and molasses. Brown sugar may be light or dark, coarse or fine.

BROWN TROUT
(River Trout)
The name of the river trout found in its natural state in some remoter parts of Britain. Rivers are re-stocked annually and the fish is sold during the game fishing season, from April to October.

BRÜHWURST
See *Scalded Sausages*.

BRÛLER
French term for 'to burn' or 'to caramelize', hence the dish *crème brulée*.

BRUNA BÖNOR
A popular Swedish dish, consisting of soaked brown beans simmered in water until tender. Salt, vinegar and dark brown sugar are then added to give the beans their characteristic tan colour and flavour and they are eaten with fried pork dishes.

BRUNCH
North American term now also used in Britain. A combination of

breakfast and lunch which can be eaten any time from mid-morning until early afternoon.

BRUNEDE KARTOFLER
A Danish speciality consisting of new potatoes which are fried in butter and sugar until a deep gold colour. They are known in English as caramelized potatoes.

BRUNOISE
French term for any food which is cut into small dice or cubes; also a garnish of diced vegetables.

BRUNSWICK STEW
A famous North American stew made from chicken and/or squirrels, mixed vegetables, garlic, seasonings, tomatoes, sweetcorn, broad beans and sometimes okra.

BRUSH (TO)
To cover or coat foods, before or after cooking, with milk, beaten egg, oil, melted fat, melted jam or syrup, glaze or thin icing, using a nylon or bristle pastry brush.

BRUSH-FRY (TO)
To fry in a heavy, smooth-based pan first lightly brushed with melted fat or oil. This method of frying is one used for pancakes and similar mixtures.

BRUSSELS SPROUT
A vegetable (*Brassica oleracea*, var. *gemmifera*) which is a member of the cabbage family, developed from the wild cabbage in Belgium in the 13th century or earlier, when it was widely grown in the countryside around Brussels. It was introduced to Britain in the early part of the 19th century and is now cultivated over much of Europe and in North America. Brussels sprouts grow as a number of small, individual, tight clusters of green leaves, resembling miniature cabbages, distributed evenly on a long stalk. On each stalk, the sprouts mature from the base upwards; the topmost sprout is similar to a small, open cabbage and is picked and sold separately from the main crop as 'greens' or sprout tops. As a general rule, the smaller and tighter the sprout, the better, since it deteriorates rapidly when too mature. Brussels sprouts may be boiled or steamed and eaten with meat and poultry or used in savoury dishes.

à la BRUXELLOISE
French term meaning in the style of Brussels in Belgium, referring to a garnish of Brussels sprouts and braised chicory, usually for large joints of meat.

BRYNZA
(Brînză, Bryndza, Brandza)
A Balkan and Central European ewes' and goats' milk cheese which is almost pure white and ranges in texture from firm to soft. It is a factory-produced cheese, made from the milk of mountain animals, and inclined to be salty since it is cut into blocks and packed with salt. It is similar to Feta when firm; when soft and creamy, it is used to make the Hungarian speciality, Liptauer spread.

BUBBLE AND SQUEAK
So called because the mixture splutters and squeaks as it cooks. A combination of leftover cold mashed potatoes and chopped cabbage is pan-fried in lard or dripping to form a crisp shallow cake. It is stirred frequently while frying so that the crusty bits from the underneath are distributed throughout the mixture. Sometimes pieces of cold roast meat are also added. Bubble and squeak is a British speciality and used to be considered a 'Monday' dish, made from the leftovers of Sunday lunch.

BUBBLY
A British colloquial term for champagne.

BUCATINI
(Perciatelli, Perciatelloni)
A thick type of *spaghetti*.

BÛCHE DE NOËL
The traditional Christmas cake of France, this is a rolled cake (Swiss roll) decorated to resemble a log of a tree, usually coated with chocolate butter cream or whipped cream flavoured with chocolate that is ridged with a fork to give the impression of bark. It is dusted with icing sugar for a snow-like effect.

BUCK RAREBIT
Welsh Rarebit topped with a poached egg.

BUCK VENISON
See *Venison*.

BUCKWHEAT
(Beechwheat, Saracen Corn)
The fruit of a plant (*Fagopyrum esculentum*) belonging to the dock family and native to the USSR (where it is known as kasha). Buckwheat is regarded as a cereal and its three-cornered grains are much used in the USSR as a cooked accompaniment to traditional beetroot and cabbage soups, a stuffing for fish and poultry, and a side dish to accompany stews. The husks are generally removed during production and the grains are sometimes toasted. The flavour of buckwheat is pleasantly nutty and it makes an excellent winter 'porridge'. Buckwheat is now grown in Japan, North America, France, Germany and parts of eastern Europe. In Japan, buckwheat is used to produce a kind of light brown spaghetti.

BUCKWHEAT FLOUR
Brownish flour made from buckwheat and used in Russian yeasted *blinis* and other pancakes such as the Breton-type *crêpes* or *galettes*. Buckwheat pancakes are also popular in North America.

BUCKWHEAT NOODLES
Japanese flat noodles made from buckwheat flour instead of wheat flour. They should be treated in exactly the same way as European noodles.

BUCKWHEAT SPAGHETTI
Japanese *spaghetti* made from buckwheat flour instead of wheat flour. They should be treated in exactly the same way as European *spaghetti*.

BUFFET
A 'help-yourself' meal, formal or informal, consisting of large tables laid out with hot and/or cold foods and drinks. It is said that the Beefeaters of the Tower of London are so called from a corruption of the word 'buffeters', or attendants at a buffet.

BULGOGI WA SANJEOG GUI
A Korean dish, consisting of slices of beef which are marinated in a mixture of onions, garlic, ginger, soy sauce, sugar, sesame oil, rice wine and seasonings, then grilled or barbecued.

BULGUR
(Bulgar, Burghul)
One of the Middle East's most popular cereals, this is made from kibbled or cracked wheat, first hulled and parboiled. It requires minimal cooking and is used both in made-up dishes and as an accompaniment to meat and fish.

BULLOCK'S HEART
See *Custard Apple*.

BULL'S EYE
Old-fashioned, peppermint-flavoured, long-lasting boiled sweet which was usually round and black with white stripes.

BULLY BEEF
British colloquial term for corned beef.

BUN LOAF
Fairly sweet and light yeasted loaf which resembles a bun in flavour and texture. It is eaten sliced and spread with butter at teatime in Britain.

BUN TINS
See *Patty Tins*.

BUNDNERFLEISCH
Salted and air-dried beef from Switzerland, served thinly sliced and eaten *après ski* with plenty of brown bread and butter.

BUNS
Miniature loaves, made from yeasted dough, usually sweet and frequently containing dried fruit. The shape can vary from round to elongated.

BUÑUELOS
Mexican biscuit fritters which are light and puffy. They are sprinkled with icing sugar and cinnamon and eaten, freshly fried, with coffee or hot chocolate.

BUOST
A low-fat, cows' milk cheese from Sweden which is firm, slightly pungent and rather like Tilsit.

BURBOT
A round-bodied north European freshwater relative (*Lota lota*) of the cod family. It has lean flesh and the fish can be poached, steamed, baked, fried or grilled. The North American burbot (*Lota maculosa*) is found in the Great Lakes and other northern waters.

BURFI
(Barfi)
Indian confectionery resembling fudge, made from a combination of sugar syrup and ground almonds or pistachio nuts, often decorated with silver leaf. *Burfi* is served cut into squares after a meal or with afternoon tea.

BURGONYA
See *Krumpli*.

BURGOS
A Spanish curd cheese made from ewes' milk. It is produced in Burgos, is very mild and often eaten with sugar for dessert.

BURGUNDY SAUCE
English term for Bourguignonne sauce.

BURMEISTER
A North American cheese, factory-produced in Wisconsin from cows' milk. It is another version of Brick cheese.

BURNT CREAM
(Cambridge Burnt Cream)
Associated with Trinity College, Cambridge, since the 19th century, this is the British version of *crème brûlée*.

BURRINI
A small, south Italian cheese which resembles a large pear in shape and size. It is moulded by hand round a central core of butter and, when cut, the slices reveal a ring of cheese surrounding a round of butter. It is left to ripen for a few weeks only, has a fairly mild taste and is made from cows' milk. Burrini cheese is wax-coated for export in order to prolong its keeping qualities.

BURRITOS
A Mexican-style dish made from rolled pancakes filled with *chilli con carne* which are arranged in a dish, coated with cheese sauce and reheated in a fairly hot oven. The traditional accompaniments are a salad of lettuce, thin onion slices or chopped onion, and extra grated cheese for sprinkling over the top of each serving.

BUSTARD
Any of a family (*Otididae*) of large Eurasian, African and Australian game birds. They build nests on the ground, have a slow, stately walk and are powerful birds, capable of swift flight.

BUTCHERY
The preparation of meat for sale.

BUTIFARRÓN SABROSO
Caribbean minced beef meat loaf containing bread, chillies, peppers,

onion, coriander, oregano, salt pork and ham. It is cooked in a *caldero*, or heavy frying pan.

BUTTER
A concentrated and rich fat, churned from pasteurized cream, which contains small amounts of lactose, minerals and water. It owes its characteristic and individual flavour to its own particular fatty acid known as butyric acid. It is available as sweetcream, lactic, salted or unsalted and the colour and flavour may vary according to the type of cattle, season of the year, method of manufacture and amount of salt added. Well-wrapped butter may be deep-frozen for 2–3 months.

BUTTER BEAN
A vegetable (*Phaseolus lunatus* and *P. limensis*) native to Central and South America and widely cultivated around the world in warm climates; Madagascar has become a major producer. In the countries where it is grown, the leguminous butter bean is often eaten as a fresh vegetable when removed from the pod. For export purposes, the bean is dried and used as a pulse. The name 'butter bean' is derived from its pale, buttery colour although some kinds are a very pale shade of green. All types have the kidney shape which is typical of most beans of American origin. The Madagascar is the largest butter bean, the sieva the smallest. Butter beans have a good texture and flavour and are suited to many savoury dishes. In the USA butter beans are generally called lima beans and are an ingredient in the traditional dish called succotash, originally a native Indian speciality. All varieties of butter bean must be boiled briskly for the first 15 minutes of cooking time to destroy harmful toxins found in the outer skin which can prove very dangerous to the human body. Ready-cooked beans are sold in cans.

BUTTER CLAM
Either of two (*Saxidomus* species) large, edible, delicately-flavoured clams of the Pacific coast of North America.

BUTTER CREAM
Traditionally made with butter and an equal amount of icing and/or caster sugar, this is a sweet, rich cake cream which is often flavoured and coloured. It is used both for filling and covering layered cakes. Economical versions contain margarine instead of butter, and sometimes half the quantity of fat to sugar, with the addition of milk, alcohol or coffee to ensure that the consistency is smooth and creamy.

BUTTER PATS
See *Pat*.

BUTTERFAT
Natural fat found in milk and the main constituent of butter.

BUTTERFISH
(Atlantic Butterfish)
A thin, deep-bodied seawater fish (*Peprilus tricanthus*, formerly *Poronotus tricanthus*) with a small head and mouth and a blunt snout. Its average length is 15–23 cm/6–9 inches and its back is bluish in colour, shading to a silvery underside. The weight can vary from 90–200 g/3½–7 oz. It is caught all year round, but mostly between May and November, on the Atlantic coast of the USA and as far north as Newfoundland; there is also a close relative in the Gulf of Mexico. The flesh is white, oily, tender and flaky and the fish may be baked or fried.

BUTTERFLY CAKES
Small sponge cakes from which the tops are removed, cut in half and replaced as wings, held in place with cream or butter cream. These cakes were very popular in Britain between the First and Second World Wars.

BUTTERFLY CHOP
A double chop, cut through until almost separated, then opened out and flattened so that the two halves look like butterfly wings. It is then grilled or fried.

BUTTERFLY CUT
Large prawns, double chops or thick pieces of steak are cut through until almost separated. The food is then opened out and flattened so that the two halves look like butterfly wings.

BUTTERFLY-SHAPED PASTA
See *Farfalle*.

BUTTERKÄSE
See *Ladies' Cheese*.

BUTTERMILK
Residual liquid left after butter-making which contains a small amount of fat. It is a delicious drink when well-chilled and was once widely favoured for making scones, soda bread and certain cakes. Buttermilk made from raw cream thickens on its own due to bacterial activity and does not require a culture.

BUTTERMILK QUARK
(Buttermilchquark)
This version of Quark is made from a mixture of buttermilk and skimmed milk.

BUTTERNUT SQUASH
A vegetable (*Cucurbita maxima*) of the squash family native to North America. It is one of the winter squash group which matures slowly and is usually eaten in the winter months. The shape is rather like a thick-skinned, elongated pear or a marrow with a bulbous end. The skin is smooth and pale gold in colour and the orange flesh contains a central core of flat seeds. The texture of the flesh is smooth and the flavour is rather nutty and slightly sweet. The butternut squash is often small enough to be cooked whole; it is then halved and deseeded. The flesh is delicious as a vegetable on its own or used in savoury dishes.

BUTTERNUTS
Native to North America, these are the edible oily nuts of a tree of the walnut family (*Juglans cinerea*).

BUTTERY
Having the qualities, consistency and appearance of butter; containing or spread with butter; a storeroom for alcoholic drinks; a type of restaurant, serving light foods and snacks.

BUTTON
Something that is round and small like a button, such as a whole baby (button) mushroom.

BUTTON MUSHROOM
See *Common Mushroom*.

BUTTON QUAIL
Any of various small birds (family *Turnicidae*) from the warmer parts of Africa, Europe and Asia. These ground-living birds resemble quails but are related to cranes and bustards.

BUTTY
British colloquial word for sandwich.

BUTYRIC ACID
Acid found in butter and responsible for its characteristic flavour.

CABANOS
Small, flavoursome German smoked sausages similar to *landjäger* sausages, made from medium-coarse chopped pork seasoned with garlic and spices.

CABBAGE
A vegetable (*Brassica oleracea*, var. *capitata*), the main descendant of the wild or sea cabbage, native to Europe and now cultivated in several forms in both the old and new worlds. Popular in Europe for centuries, it was introduced to Britain at least 2,000 years ago, possibly by the Romans, and the word cabbage comes from the Latin word *caput* which means head. The vegetable consists of a short thick stalk and a large, globular, multi-layered leafy head in green, red or white. The green cabbage may be densely packed with a firm heart or be more open with little or no heart (leafy cabbage); white cabbage is tightly packed and red cabbage slightly less so. Green varieties may be eaten raw but are usually boiled. White cabbage is particularly suitable for eating raw, shredded in salads such as coleslaw. Red cabbage is best for pickling and cooking as a sweet-sour side dish for pork and goose.

CABBAGE LETTUCE
One of the main types of commercially produced lettuce, this grows as a ball-shaped, loose cluster of wide leaves on a short stem or stalk.

CABBAGE PALM
(Heart of Palm, Palm Heart)
Palm tree (*Sabal palmetto*) with buds which resemble the heads of cabbage and are eaten as a vegetable known as palm hearts. Palm hearts are grown in tropical and sub-tropical regions around the world. Outside the producer countries they are available canned.

CABÉCOU
(Cabicou)
A small, French ewes' or goats' milk cheese produced on farms in Aquitaine. It is fairly forceful in flavour.

CABINET PUDDING
An old-fashioned British steamed pudding, made from sponge cake or fingers, milk, eggs, glacé cherries and sugar, sometimes flavoured with brandy or vanilla.

CABOC
A Scottish double cream cheese made from cows' milk. It has a very mild flavour and smooth texture and is coated with fine oatmeal. Caboc dates back to the 15th century.

CABOUL SAUCE
Mayonnaise flavoured with curry powder, which can be served with cold poultry, cold lamb and hard-boiled eggs.

CABRALES
(Cabraliego)
A Spanish, blue-veined cheese made principally from cows' milk and matured in Asturian mountain caves, sometimes wrapped in leaves from local trees. The flavour is relatively strong and the texture smooth and creamy. The aroma of Cabrales is distinctive.

CABREIRO
A Portuguese cheese made from a mixture of goats' and ewes' milk and either eaten young and fresh or matured in brine for up to 3 months. It is white and fairly piquant.

CABRITO ASADO
Roast baby kid from Mexico, flavoured with garlic and chilli powder.

CACAO
Cocoa tree or its edible seeds.

CACAO BEAN
(Cacao)
Seed of the cocoa tree.

CACAO BUTTER
See *Cocoa Butter*.

CACHET
(Fromage Fort)
A French mountain farm cheese from Provence. It is made from ewes' milk and is white, creamy and mild when fresh. It is also very soft.

CACIOCAVALLO
An Italian cheese from Sicily, similar to Provolone.

CACIOFIORE
An Italian ewes' or goats' milk cheese, coloured yellow with saffron. It is very creamy and soft.

CACIOTTA
An Italian farm cheese made from cows', ewes' or goats' milk. The cheeses are usually small and left to mature up to 2 weeks. Factory-produced versions are very mild and made from pasteurized cows' milk.

CAECUM
(Sac, Poche)
Medium-sized intestine, used in sausage-making.

CAERPHILLY
(New Cheese)
Almost 200 years old, Caerphilly started life in Wales and was called New Cheese because it matured in less than two weeks. Based on cows' milk (traditionally unpasteurized), Caerphilly is now made almost exclusively in England and is a moist, mild, slightly acidic and almost white cheese which crumbles easily. It is pleasant both as a cooking and dessert cheese and makes an excellent substitute for Greek Feta. It is also easy to digest.

CAESAR SALAD
A traditional North American salad which originated in Mexico in the 1920s. It is made from pieces of crisp lettuce, garlic-flavoured *croûtons* and anchovies, tossed with a raw egg, seasoning to taste and grated Parmesan cheese.

CAFÉ
French term for an informal eating place, sometimes self-service, selling assorted drinks and snacks.

CAFÉ BRULOT
Spicy, hot black coffee, flamed with brandy.

CAFE LIÈGEOISE
Iced coffee served in a glass with ice cream and whipped cream.

CAFFEINE
A stimulating ingredient, mainly of coffee and tea, which may produce extra activity, mental agility, insomnia or palpitation, depending on the metabolism of the individual. If taken in moderation, most people experience little or no side effects. The caffeine content of coffee (1.1–2.3%) is about half that of tea, but as much more coffee is used per cup, perhaps three or four times the quantity by dry weight of tea, it is more stimulating.

CAILLEBOTTE
A French white, curd-type cheese made from cows', ewes' or goats' milk, depending on the area of production. Its name comes from *caille*, meaning curdled milk. It is rich and creamy in texture and should be soft to the touch. The fresh cheese is usually packed into little wickerwork baskets or earthenware pots.

CAITHNESS
A Scottish cream cheese with a fairly mild flavour and creamy spreadable consistency. It is a pale yellow colour and sometimes enclosed in a tartan-patterned wrapper. It is made from cows' milk.

CAJETA DE CELAYA
See *Dulce de Leche*.

CAKE FLOURS
Widely used in North America, these are specially treated, pure white flours which are soft, starchy

and fine. They make light-textured cakes but have minimal nutritional value.

CAKE MIXES
Manufactured packet mixes to which milk, eggs and sometimes fat are added by the purchaser. They require minimal preparation and are light and fluffy-textured.

CAKES
Baked or fried mixtures, amalgamated in an assortment of ways, and generally made from a basis of flour, fat, eggs and sugar. A raising agent is frequently added, as are flavourings. There are a vast number of cakes produced internationally, closely reflecting the tastes of different countries.

CALABASH
See *Doodhi*.

CALABAZA
(Calabaza Pumpkin)
A member of the squash family, popular in the West Indies and exported to Britain. It is usually sold in sections as it tends to be large and the orange flesh is generally used in savoury dishes.

CALABRESE
A superior variety of broccoli, first developed in Italy, with green bud clusters (curds) comprising a main central head and side shoots with smaller heads.

CALAMARES EN SU TINTA
Stuffed, fried squid served in a sauce containing ink from the ink bags. It is a Spanish speciality and the name of the dish means 'squid in their own ink'.

CALAMONDIN ORANGE
(China Orange, Panama Orange)
The fruit of a tree (*Citrus mitis*) probably originating in the Far East and widely grown in Europe and North America as a houseplant or an ornamental tree in the garden. It is a small fruit, a cross between a kumquat and a lime, not exceeding 4 cm/1½ inches in diameter, with a spherical shape and a shiny golden-red skin. The flesh has a sharp flavour similar to a lime and both the skin and the flesh may be used in preserves and pickles.

CALCIUM
An inorganic element, classified as a mineral, necessary for the healthy and proper development of bones and teeth, for satisfactory muscle control and for normal clotting of blood. Bones and teeth are primarily made up of both calcium and phosphorus; consequently it is important that the proportion of calcium to phosphorus is properly balanced in the diet. Milk, cheese, sardines and some green vegetables are good sources of calcium, while phosphorus-rich foods are cheese, oatmeal, liver, kidney, eggs, milk and, to a lesser extent, cabbage, potatoes and oranges. Normal, healthy adults need about 1 part calcium to 1.5 parts of phosphorus. Pregnant and nursing mothers require calcium and phosphorus in equal parts; so do young, growing children. Calcium also works in conjunction with vitamins C and D.

CALDEIRADA DE PEIXE
A Portuguese fish stew similar to the French *bouillabaisse* but subject to regional variations. In the south, it is based on shellfish; in Lisbon, boiled potatoes, white fish and clams are included; in the north, eel is an important ingredient.

CALDILLO DE CONGRIO
Chilean fish soup made from the congrio, a fish found in local waters.

CALDO VERDE
A Portuguese potato and cabbage soup, a national speciality.

CALF
The young of a number of animals but, in food terms, the young of a domestic cow.

CALF'S HEAD
The head of a calf, which may be boiled and used for brawn, or boned after cooking and added to pies.

CALF'S TONGUE
A finely flavoured tongue which weighs a maximum of 900 g/ 2 pounds, enough for two servings. It is generally served freshly boiled and skinned, accompanied by a suitable brown sauce such as Madeira. The tongues may also be salted in the same way as ox tongue, boiled and skinned, and four or more pushed well down into a cake tin, covered with a plate and weighed down with a brick or heavy stone; any gaps should be filled with aspic jelly. The tongues should be turned out when firm and may then be sliced and served with salad.

CALIPASH
(Calipee)
A fatty, gelatinous, dull-green edible substance, found inside the upper shell of a turtle.

CALLALOO
(Chinese Spinach)
A spinach-like vegetable (*Aramanthus* species) used in the traditional pepperpot soup of Jamaica. This is not, however, the same vegetable as used in the callaloo soup of the eastern region of the Caribbean which is made from dasheen leaves.

CALLALOO SOUP
(Calaloo, Callau, Callilu, Kallaloo)
A famous Créole soup found in the Caribbean, made from dasheen leaves, okra, crabmeat, salt pork, water, onions, garlic and sometimes coconut.

CALORIE
See *Large Calorie*.

CALORIFIC VALUE
See *Kilocalorific Value*.

CALTROPS
See *Chinese Water Chestnuts*.

CALVADOS
French apple brandy, produced in Normandy and named after the town of Calvados, the centre of the French apple-growing region. It is made from double-distilled apple wine and matured in oak casks. Calvados is a feature of Norman cuisine and is often used in conjunction with cider. It is especially good with chicken and veal. It is 70° proof (40° GL).

CALVES' BRAINS
The most delicate of the brain family, though not readily available. A set of two brains will serve two people.

CALVES' FEET
Very hard to find on the domestic market, these must be ordered from the butcher in advance. Calves' feet are used to make aspic and nourishing calves' foot jelly, traditionally fed to invalids, and also added to dishes where a gelatinous texture is required, such as brawn.

CALVES' KIDNEYS
Lighter in colour than ox kidneys, these may be used for the same purposes. They are delicately flavoured, tender and respond well to grilling and frying; one kidney is generally sufficient for two servings.

CALVES' LIVER
The most exclusive of all liver, this is difficult to find in shops in Britain and is very expensive when available. It is a high-protein, golden-brown liver which is smooth, creamy and delicate in flavour but, unlike ox liver, a poor source of iron. Many classic Italian recipes call for calves' liver and it is often lightly fried in butter with fresh sage and Marsala.

CALZONE
A large, baked turnover from Italy made from yeasted white bread dough. It usually contains cheese

and ham and resembles *pizza* without the tomatoes. Sometimes the *calzone* is shaped into small turnovers which are baked or fried.

CAMARGUE
A ewes' milk cheese produced in the Camargue, in France. It is flavoured with fresh thyme and bay, and is rich, soft and creamy.

CAMBRIDGE BURNT CREAM
See *Burnt Cream*.

CAMBRIDGE CHEESE
See *York*.

CAMEL
Young camels are sometimes killed for food in desert regions and the hump is considered a delicacy.

CAMEMBERT
One of France's most renowned cheeses, this came into being at the beginning of the 18th century and a hundred years later was heavily promoted by Madame Marie Harel, a farmer's wife from the village of Camembert in Normandy. In fact, some reference books give her credit for 'inventing' the cheese. Now in worldwide production, Camembert is generally made from fresh cows' milk and sold in 225–250g/8–9oz rounds, packed into boxes. The best is still the traditional Normandy Camembert made from unpasteurized milk and, as a guarantee of authenticity, its label should include the term *fermier* and/or *lait cru* and the mark of the AC classification. The best Camemberts have a white rind flecked with red and should be plump and resilient without signs of a sinking middle. No smell of ammonia should be apparent, nor should the centre be runny, as these factors indicate old age and deterioration. The colour of the cheese itself should be creamy yellow.

CAMEMBERT DE NORMANDIE
The traditional Norman cheese, made from unpasteurized cows' milk and its label marked with the words *fermier* and/or *lait cru*, together with the AC classification.

CAMOMILE
See *Chamomile*.

CAMOSUN
A North American Cheddar-type cheese made from cows' milk. It originated in Washington and was first produced in the early 1930s to use up surplus milk supplies. It is a fairly soft and mild cheese which is left to mature for 4–12 weeks.

CAMP COFFEE
(Camp Coffee Essence)
A coffee and chicory concentrate first made towards the end of the 19th century by the firm of R. Patersons and Sons of Glasgow. It was the pre-eminent brand of instant coffee until the arrival of the soluble granules and powders of more recent years.

CAMPDEN TABLET
A tablet containing potassium metabisulphate used in wine-making to purify and sterilize.

CAN (TO)
To preserve in a tin.

CAN OPENER
An implement for removing the tops from cans of food. In its simplest form it is a short pointed cutter which is operated manually by a levering movement. It can also be a handle-driven cutting wheel which may be either free-standing or wall-mounted and manually or electrically operated.

CANADIAN CHEDDAR
Strong and fine-flavoured mature Cheddar cheese made from unpasteurized cows' milk. One of the best known brands is Black Diamond.

CANADIAN PLAICE
See *American Plaice*.

CANADIAN-STYLE BACON
A term used to describe quick-cured bacon which owes its particular flavour, colour, mildness and texture to the ingredients contained in the curing solution.

CANAPÉ
French term for a small biscuit or piece of toast on which savoury toppings are decoratively arranged. Canapés are served with pre-meal drinks or at cocktail parties.

CANARD À L'ORANGE
A classic French dish, consisting of roast duck served with a sauce flavoured and sweetened with orange juice and shredded orange peel, red wine, redcurrant jelly and sherry or brandy. The dish is garnished with slices of fresh orange and sprigs of watercress.

CANARY PUDDING
An old-fashioned British steamed pudding, made from a Victoria sandwich cake mixture, usually flavoured with finely grated lemon peel. It is generally accompanied by cream or custard.

à la CANCALAISE
French term meaning in the style of Cancale in Brittany, north-west France, referring to a white fish sauce made from a base of white wine with mussels, shrimps or prawns and oysters.

CANDIED FRUITS
(Glacé Fruits)
A traditional French speciality in which pieces of fruits are treated with a heavy sugar solution for varying lengths of time. Candied fruits are now made worldwide and are characteristically very sweet, slightly transparent and highly decorative by virtue of shape and colour.

CANDIED PEEL
Made from the peel of oranges, lemons, limes and sometimes citrons. The peel is first treated with brine, steeped in a heavy sugar solution and then dried. Some peels are finely chopped and without a crystalline sugar coating. Larger segments of peel — usually mixed and comprising one or two pieces of each type of fruit — are available at Christmas in boxes and are generally coated with a heavy layer of hardish sugar. This should be removed from the peel before use. For maximum freshness, all peel should be stored in airtight containers.

CANDLE FRUIT
A North African variety of aubergine, shaped like a miniature banana with very smooth, ivory-coloured skin. The flesh is pale cream in colour and dotted with tiny seeds. Once cut and exposed to air, the candle fruit discolours rapidly, turning light brown.

CANDLENUTS
(Kemiri Nuts)
Shaped like hazelnuts, these Oriental nuts grow on candleberry trees and are much used as a thickening agent in Malay cooking. They are both oily and waxy, white-fleshed and delicate. Macadamia nuts make a good substitute.

CANDY
North American term for sweets and chocolates.

CANDY (TO)
To cook in sugar syrup; to encrust or coat with sugar; to become crystallized into sugar. The origin of the word candy may have come from the Latin *candidus*, meaning 'glittering white', or may have originated from the word *khand*, the Sanskrit for sugar cane.

CANDY FLOSS
A form of spun sugar.

CANE
See *Sugar Cane*.

CANELLE KNIFE
A vegetable knife with a small cut in the blade which is used for paring the skin of citrus fruit into even, narrow strips. It can also be used on cucumber to produce a serrated effect.

CANESTRATO
(Incanestrato, Pecorino, Pecorino Canestrato, Siciliano)
An Italian cheese produced in Sicily, traditionally from ewes' milk. It is matured in a wicker basket which leaves a pattern on the outside surface. It has a distinctive flavour and the texture is punctuated with small holes.

CANNED
Term to denote food preserved in a tin.

CANNED FOODS
Preserved foods which have a long shelf life, provided the cans are undented and have no bulges. Most canned foods are of very high quality and modern methods of processing ensure flavour and nutrient retention; only occasionally are the colours of canned foods adversely affected. In general terms, canning is a relatively simple procedure. Food is automatically packed into cans, liquid is added if necessary and the cans are sealed. They are then sterilized and rapidly cooled.

CANNELLINI BEAN
(Fazolia Bean)
An oval or kidney-shaped white bean (*Phaseolus vulgaris*), first grown in South America and now cultivated in Italy where it is very popular. It has a firm texture and may be substituted for the slightly smaller, closely related haricot bean in savoury dishes.

CANNELLONI
Large hollow tubes or pipes of pasta which are cooked, stuffed and finished off in the oven with a suitable sauce.

CANNIKIN
A small drinking vessel or can.

CANNOLICCHI
See *Ave Maria*.

à la CANOTIÈRE
French term meaning in a boatman's style, referring particularly to freshwater fish (carp, for example) cooked with shallots, mushrooms and sometimes white wine.

CANTAL
(Fourme de Cantal, Fourme de Salers, Salers)
One of France's oldest cheeses, if not the oldest, Cantal goes back about 2000 years and is similar to top-quality English Cheddar with a warm, mellow flavour and firm, golden-yellow paste. It is allowed to mature for 3–6 months, is made from cows' milk and has a grey rind with a powdery surface. It is a large cheese (up to 49 kg/110 lb) and not often available outside France.

CANTALON
A small version of French Cantal.

CANTALOUPE MELON
A type of melon (*Cucumis* species) developed in central Italy and grown in several varieties including the French Charentais and the Israeli Ogen. All these melons are sweet and fragrant and excellent to eat on their own. In the USA, this name also includes melons better known in Europe as musk or netted melons.

CANTONESE COOKING
Stir-frying, steaming and sweet-and-sour dishes come from this south-eastern region of China. The seasonings are delicate, the ingredients perfectly fresh and there is a wide choice of dishes. Canton is famous for *dim sum*, both sweet and

Bread and Yeasted Goods
Lardy Cake
Bara Brith
Soda Bread
Brioches
Bath Bun

savoury, which are presented in small bamboo baskets. Tea accompanies Cantonese food.

CANVASBACK

A North American wild duck (*Aythya valisineria*) which lives on a diet of wild celery shoots, giving the flesh a characteristic flavour.

CAPE GOOSEBERRY

The fruit of a plant (*Physalis peruviana*) of the tomato family, originally from South America, but now cultivated in other warm parts of the world. The name seems to have become popular from the time when the fruit was first widely grown in South Africa. The edible part is a cherry-sized berry which is yellowish when fully ripe and enclosed in a multi-part, parchment-like husk. The berry has an agreeable flavour and may be eaten raw or used in making preserves. As with all the varieties of the tomato family, the flavour and sweetness are at their best when the fruit is fully ripe.

CAPELIN

(Capelan (in Quebec), Caplin (in Newfoundland))

A herring-like fish (*Mallotus villosus*) of the same family as the smelt. It can reach up to 23 cm/ 9 inches in length. The back is transparent olive to bottle-green in colour, the sides silvery and the underside white. It is a fish of the cold high seas, coming inshore to spawn on the coasts of Iceland, Greenland and the North American coast as far south as Maine, where the main catches are in June and July. The flesh is lean to medium-oily and the fish may be poached, steamed, fried or grilled.

CAPELLI D'ANGELO

See *Angel's Hair*.

CAPELLINI

Slim *spaghetti*, said to resemble the fine hair after which they are named.

CAPER SAUCE

A white sauce flavoured with chopped capers and vinegar. It can be served with grilled herring and mackerel, poached skate and roast lamb.

CAPERCAILZIE

(Capercaillie, Woodgrouse)

A large game bird (*Tetrao urogallus*), common to Scotland and Sweden, in season from late August to early December. This comparatively rare bird is about the size of a turkey and is cooked in the same way.

CAPERS

The flower buds of a small Mediterranean bush (*Capparis spinosa*) which are picked and pickled before the flowers blossom. The plants grow in a rambling fashion like blackberries, against and through walls, and prefer sheltered spots. They seem to require minimal nourishment for survival. Capers vary in size but are rarely bigger than peas. When pickled (the way in which they are always used) they have a wide number of culinary applications, including sauces and some salad dressings.

CAPON

A neutered cock bird which is larger and plumper than other roasting chickens. It is popular at Christmas and Easter and often substituted for turkey.

CAPPALETTI

Little tricorn-shaped 'hats' of pasta, with a stuffing.

CAPPUCCINO

Coffee made by the *espresso* machine method with the addition of hot, foaming milk. Sugar may be added, together with spices such as cinnamon and nutmeg. Without a machine, this coffee may be imitated by the combination of hot, strong coffee and milk which has just been brought to the boil.

CAPRIC ACID
See *Caprylic Acid*.

CAPRICE DES DIEUX
A boxed, double cream cheese from the Champagne area of France. It is oval in shape, soft, mild and produced from cows' milk.

CAPROIC ACID
See *Caprylic Acid*.

CAPRYLIC ACID
Acid found in goats' milk and its derivative products, all of which have a distinctive taste and smell. It is also found in coconut oil and in butter made from cows' milk. Capric acid and caproic acid are two other fatty acids found in these products. Their names all come from the Latin word *caper*, meaning goat.

CAPSICUM
See *Sweet Pepper*.

CARAFE
A bulbous glass container with a narrow neck used for serving wine or water at table. It should not be corked or stoppered.

CARAMBOLA
(Star Fruit)
The fruit of a small evergreen tree (*Averrhoa carambola*) native to South-East Asia but now grown in the warmer regions of Asia from India eastwards, and also in parts of Australia and South America. It is shaped rather like a small banana but with five deep clefts running lengthwise so that a slice cut across the fruit has the appearance of a five-pointed star. The colour is an almost translucent yellow and the skin is thin and edible. The yellow flesh has an acidy-sweet taste when fully ripe. The decorative star-shaped slices are often used in fruit salads. The fruit can also be used in jams and preserves such as chutney.

CARAMEL
A brown colouring and flavouring agent made from sugar or glucose which has been heated or chemically treated. Also, a chewy caramel-flavoured toffee.

CARAMEL CREAM
See *Crème Caramel*.

CARAMELIZE (TO)
To change sugar or mixtures with high sugar contents into caramel by applying heat until the substance turns brown.

CARAMELIZED ORANGES
See *Arance Caramellate*.

CARAMELIZED POTATOES
See *Brunede Kartofler*.

CARAMELS
Hard, chewy sweets which were originally made in Spain in Medieval times from cane sugar. Any dish flavoured with browned sugar syrup, or topped with a coating of sugar and then browned, is generally referred to as caramel; caramel cream or crème caramel, for example.

CARAVAN TEA
(China Caravan Tea, Russian Caravan Tea)
Blends of black China teas which are similar to the teas which used to be sent overland by camel, usually to Russia. These blends are particularly suitable for serving with Eastern foods.

CARAWAY SEEDS
Native to Europe and widely grown in the Netherlands, caraway (*Carum carvi*) is a biennial plant. The seeds are brownish, hard, fairly short, curved and tapered at both ends with a pleasant, slightly sharp flavour with a sweet undertone. They are the principal flavouring in rye bread and are also used in other baked goods, sauerkraut, goulash, cheese

spreads and seed cake. Caraway seeds are the basis of kümmel liqueur.

CARBOHYDRATES
Composed of starches and sugars and classified as energy foods. Eaten in excess, carbohydrates turn into fat and can cause an increase in weight, encourage dental decay and aggravate skin conditions such as acne. Carbohydrate foods include bread, biscuits, buns, cakes, cereals and any product made with flour and cornflour, such as pies and puddings; also sweets, chocolates, fruits, jam, syrup, treacle and sugar. Carbohydrates are made up of carbon, hydrogen and oxygen. In theory, half the daily calorie intake should come from carbohydrate foods, but this may vary from person to person, especially if medically approved diets are involved. Carbohydrate foods are divided in three groups: monosaccharides or simple sugars; disaccharides composed of two simple sugars; and polysaccharides which are termed complex or compound sugars, derived from the breakdown of starchy foods.

CARBON
One of the elements found in proteins and carbohydrates.

CARBON DIOXIDE
A harmless gas produced by the chemical interaction of, for example, flour mixed with liquid, eggs and a raising agent in a cake or loaf. The gas expands on heating and, in turn, pushes up the gluten strands in the flour, forcing the cake or loaf to rise in the oven and hold its shape.

CARBONADE OF BEEF
See *Carbonnade à la Flamande*.

CARBONATE (TO)
To impregnate with carbon dioxide; to aerate.

CARBONATED WATER
See *Soda Water, Soda Siphon* and *Mineral Waters*.

CARBONNADE À LA FLAMANDE
A Belgian stew made from beef cooked with onions, garlic and dark beer which is thickened with slices of bread spread with French mustard.

CARBORUNDUM STONE
See *Knife Sharpener*.

CARDAMOM
(Cardamon, Cardamum)
Native to Asia and South America, cardamom is the dried fruit of a plant (*Elettaria cardamomum*) belonging to the ginger family. The pods are cream-coloured and the seeds inside are brownish-black. The spice is bitter-sweet, very aromatic and has a slightly lemony aftertaste. Ground cardamom is widely used in Scandinavian, Eastern and Indian dishes and is also one of the ingredients in curry powder. The seeds are sometimes used whole in pickling spice and marinades.

CARDINALE
French term for food which is pinky-red in colour, similar to the red robes worn by cardinals. There is also a Sauce Cardinale, based on lobster and truffles, which is served with fish.

CARDOON
A vegetable native to Mediterranean countries, a member (*Cynara cardunculus*) of the thistle family and related to the globe artichoke. It grows as a cluster of prickly, fibrous stalks with fleshy roots which are topped with thistle-like leaves. Its general appearance is not unlike a large head of celery. It is cultivated, particularly in France and Italy, as an autumn vegetable and is usually blanched to reduce the natural bitterness. Although a relatively uncommon vegetable outside the

regions of production, cardoon has been popular in Italy since Roman times. The stalks may be boiled and eaten as a vegetable and the roots, leaves and even the flower buds have various culinary uses in certain French and Italian dishes.

CARÊME, ANTONIN

One of the greatest chefs of all time and originator of the classic French repertoire of cooking, *La Grande Cuisine*.

CARGO RICE

Paddy rice which has had its cellulose husks removed. The resulting grains are rich in bran, vitamins and trace elements.

CARIBBEAN BANANA BREAD

See *Pain Fig Banane*.

CARIBOU

See *Moose*.

CARMINE

See *Cochineal*.

CARNAUBA

(Wax Palm)

A fan-leaved palm (*Copernicia cerifera*) native to Brazil with a starchy, edible root. It is also the palm from which carnauba wax is produced.

CARNE ENSOPADA

A Brazilian pot roast of beef cooked with bacon, ham, garlic, onions, seasoning and margarine.

CARNE MECHADA

A stuffed beef roll from the Dominican Republic and Cuba. It is gently boiled and served sliced with the puréed liquid in which it was cooked.

CAROB

The fruit of an evergreen tree or shrub (*Ceratonia siliqua*) of the pea family native to the eastern Mediterranean region and now both cultivated and found growing wild in most of the Mediterranean area. It is a pod averaging 20 cm/8 inches in length and up to 2.5 cm/1 inch across its flattened width, containing a number of dark and hard inedible seeds. When ripe, the pods are brown in colour with a leathery skin and the inner pulp, surrounding the seeds, is very sweet. The pod is a popular sweetmeat in some countries under the name 'locust bean'. Its culinary uses are limited, but ground carob pod is now much appreciated as a substitute for both chocolate and cocoa powder in drinks, desserts and confectionery.

CAROB POWDER

(Carob Flour, St John's Bread)

Powder or flour milled from the pulp of a pod which grows on a Mediterranean evergreen tree (*Ceratonia siliqua*), related to the pea family. Carob is free of caffeine and lower in calories than cocoa powder for which it is often substituted both as a cake additive and drink. It is also higher in natural sugar, fibre and iron than cocoa powder and should be used in exactly the same proportions.

CAROLINA RICE

(Medium-grain Rice)

A round, fairly short-grain rice which originally came from South Carolina in the USA. It is used in milk puddings and sometimes to make Italian-style *risotto*. It is a type of rice popular in China and Japan where its stickiness makes it easy to eat with chopsticks.

CARP

(Common Carp)

A freshwater fish (*Cyprinus carpio*) which, with its close relatives, is found worldwide in ponds and lakes. It has an olive to bronze back, with golden sides shading to a yellowy-white on the underside. The size in the shops is usually 30–60 cm/1–2 feet in length and 1.5–2.5 kg/ 3½–5½ lb in weight. In Asia, where carp is very highly regarded and has been the preferred fish for thousands of years, it is widely farmed and this practice is now extending to Europe and North America. The flesh is medium-oily and the fish may be steamed, poached, fried or baked.

CARPETBAG STEAK
So named because of its shape, this is a North American speciality made from a thick steak in which a pocket is cut and then filled as tightly as possible with raw oysters. The steak is grilled and served sliced.

CARRAGEEN
(Carragheen, Irish Moss, Pearl Moss)
A sea vegetable (*Chondrus crispus*) of the red algae group of plants, found in coastal waters on both sides of the North Atlantic. It is eaten after being dried, and is said to be a protection against disorders of the lungs and the digestive system. A by-product of carrageen is a food additive, produced mainly in North America, where it is used as a gelling and emulsifying agent.

CARRÉ-DE-BRAY
Sold on rush mats, a small, square, French cheese made in Normandy from cows' milk. It is soft, creamy, and rich.

CARRÉ-DE-L'EST
A small French cheese, closely related to Camembert, made in Lorraine and Champagne from cows' milk. The name means 'square of the East' and the cheese itself is square-shaped with a smooth white rind enclosing a fairly soft, mild paste. It is less firm than Camembert, and is rather salty. The flavour acquires greater depth as the cheese matures.

CARROT
A root vegetable (*Daucus carota sativa*) which has been developed from the ancient native wild European carrot and is now grown all over the world. Although found wild in Britain, the first cultivated variety was introduced by the Flemish around the time of Elizabeth I. The shape of the carrot root is generally conical and elongated but some varieties are shorter and rounder. The colour of most kinds is a distinctive orange and the root is topped above ground by a plume of green leaves. In the reigns of James I and Charles I, when quality carrots were still a novelty, these feathery leaves were used to decorate ladies' hats and banqueting tables. The carrot is best eaten young as it becomes woody and less flavoursome with age and it is often most delicious when eaten raw as its taste alters when cooked and becomes fairly bland. Carrots may be boiled, steamed or roasted and served with meat, fish and poultry dishes or used in soups, stews and casseroles.

CARROT CAKE
(Paradise Cake, Passion Cake)
A North American cake containing grated raw carrots, oil instead of fat and crushed pineapple. It generally has a top icing based on cream cheese. Sometimes chopped nuts are also added to the cake mixture before it is baked in a square or oblong tin.

CARTE
French term for menu. To eat *à la carte* means to choose individual items from a restaurant menu.

à la CARTE
See *Carte*.

CARVE (TO)
To cut slices of flesh from cooked meat, poultry or game with a sharp carving knife. To make the task of carving easier, it is advisable to leave the item to stand for 5–10 minutes after cooking. This gives the flesh a chance to firm up and prevents the slices from being crumbly and jagged.

CASEIN
One of the three main proteins found in milk and, in conjunction with calcium, responsible for giving milk its white colour.

CASHEW NUTS
The fruit of the pear cashew tree (*Anacardium occidentale*), cultivated in tropical countries but native to South America and grown profusely in India. Cashew nuts were introduced to Europe in the 16th century when members of the Portuguese navy brought them home from the Indian colonies and called them *caju* (which subsequently was translated into cashew). The curvaceous cashews have a distinctively mild, delicate, slightly sweet flavour and are used in sweet and savoury dishes. They are always exported without their shells since these contain a natural chemical which can cause skin eruptions.

CASING
Usually refers to the cleansed gut (intestine) of an animal which is filled with meat mixtures to form sausages.

CASSABA
The variety of melon (*Cucumis melo inodorus*) from which winter melons, such as honeydew, have been developed.

CASSAREEP
The thickened, spiced juice of the rootstock of a bitter variety of cassava, used in West Indian cooking as a condiment.

CASSATA
(Neapolitan Ice Cream)
An Italian speciality made from a minimum of three ice creams of different flavours and colours which are frozen together in layers. At least one of the ice creams is mixed with chopped glacé fruits and nuts. Cassata is made in either an oblong or a basin-shaped mould. It is turned out for serving and cut into slices or wedges.

CASSATA ALLA SICILIANA
A multi-layered, Sicilian chocolate cake which is soaked in liqueur, filled with ricotta cheese and decorated with glacé fruits and nuts.

CASSAVA
(Manioc, Yuca)
A vegetable (*Manihot* species) which is the fleshy tuber of a plant native to South America and now widely cultivated in tropical countries. It grows as a cylindrical and swollen root, tapering at the end and it may grow up to 30 cm/12 inches in length and 4–7.5 cm/1½–3 inches in diameter.
There are many varieties but two main types: sweet and bitter. Some bitter varieties are extremely poisonous if eaten raw and therefore *must* be cooked. It is mainly the sweet varieties which are available in Britain and these are not as dangerous, but it is still wise to cook them. Cassava is high in starch and low in protein but it is a versatile vegetable and may be used in many dishes, both sweet and savoury. The best-known use of cassava, outside the areas where it grows, is in the form of tapioca.

CASSEROLE (TO)
To cook a selection of ingredients, such as meat or poultry, vegetables and liquid, in a tightly covered dish. The contents are usually served straight from the dish.

CASSEROLE DISH
(Casserole)
Fairly heavy earthenware, glass or enamel dish with a tightly fitting lid, designed for oven-cooked stews, hot-pots and so on. The original casserole dishes were made of copper. Modern casseroles can be used as serving dishes and flameproof ones can be used over direct heat on top of the cooker or hob.

CASSEROLETTE
Any container in which individual portions of food can be heated

and/or served. Examples include small glass, metal or porcelain dishes, pastry cases and even cup-sized baskets made from fried potatoes. Casserolettes are used for *hors d'oeuvre*, desserts and so on.

CASSETTE
Belgian soft cheese which is pale, creamy and seasoned with salt and pepper. A type of Boulette, it is hand-shaped into rectangles, wrapped in leaves (traditionally walnut) and sold in small baskets made of willow. It is produced from cows' milk.

CASSIA
This spice (*Cinnamomum cassia*) is a close relation to cinnamon.

CASSOULET
A robust casserole from the Languedoc area of France, containing layers of haricot beans, fresh and smoked pork, smoked sausages, a split pig's trotter, onions and carrots. It is cooked slowly in the oven and develops a characteristic top crust. The *cassoulet* made in Castelnaudary is claimed to be the best.

CASTELO BRANCO
Named after the city in central Portugal where it is produced, a sheeps' milk cheese which is smooth, white and comparatively tangy when left to mature for 3–4 weeks. If eaten fresh, the flavour has greater delicacy.

CASTER SUGAR
(Castor Sugar)
Very fine crystals of refined white sugar which dissolve rapidly in water, widely used in cake-making and as a sweetening agent.

CASTLE CHEESE
See *Schlosskäse*.

CASTLE PUDDINGS
Small puddings made from a Victoria sandwich cake mixture, flavoured with vanilla essence and grated lemon peel. They are baked or steamed in dariole moulds and served with jam sauce.

CATADROMOUS
A term used to describe fish which descend to lower parts of rivers or to the sea to spawn.

à la CATALANE
French term meaning in the style of Catalonia in north-east Spain, denoting the inclusion of tomatoes and sometimes rice.

CATE
An old-fashioned term to describe dainty or choice food.

CATER (TO)
To provide food, at home or in restaurants, for large or small groups.

CATFISH
(Atlantic Catfish, Wolf-fish, Sea Cat)
A blunt-headed, carrot-shaped, seawater fish (*Anarhichas lupus*) with a dorsal (back) fin extending from behind the head to the tail. The catfish is greenish-grey in colour, marked with mottled darker stripes. The length may exceed 1 metre/39 inches and the weight ranges from 1–10 kg/2–22 lb. It is caught all year, but mainly in the summer months, in the North Atlantic from France to Greenland and on the north-eastern coast of North America. The flesh is white and medium-oily and may be poached, steamed, baked, fried or grilled. Because of its ferocity, it is also called wolf-fish.

CATS' TONGUES
See *Langues de Chat*.

CATSUP
North American term for ketchup.

CAUCASIAN PILAF
A Russian chopped lamb, onion and rice *pilaf* which is fried in lard, then simmered in stock and flavoured with bay leaves and seasonings.

à la CAUCHOISE
French term meaning in the style of Normandy in northern France, denoting meat, usually veal, cooked with apples, cream and Calvados.

CAUL
The fatty membrane which covers the intestines of animals and is semi-transparent and woven with fat. Pork caul is considered the best and, before aluminium foil was available, was used to protect joints of meat while roasting. Caul is sometimes used as an outer skin for sausages.

CAULIFLOWER
A vegetable (*Brassica oleracea botrytis*) which is a member of the cabbage family. Native to either the eastern Mediterranean or Asia, cauliflower has been cultivated in Spain and Italy since the Middle Ages and subsequently has been widely grown in Europe and North America. Although introduced to Britain in the late 16th century, it was not generally cultivated until nearly 200 years later. Cauliflower consists of a sturdy stalk topped by a closely-packed, fleshy white head of immature flowers fringed with green leaves. A good cauliflower should have a creamy-white head with a firm, tightly packed texture; size is immaterial. Cauliflower may be eaten raw, boiled or steamed, used in vegetable salads or in cooked dishes.

CAULIFLOWER CHEESE
A British speciality consisting of cooked cauliflower coated with cheese sauce, sprinkled with extra grated cheese and browned under the grill. It is served hot as a main course or vegetable accompaniment.

CAVIAR
The prepared roe of the female sturgeon, which can vary in colour from black to grey. Because of the price of genuine caviar, the roe of other fish such as lumpfish and salmon are similarly treated and have gained acceptance in their own right, with colours varying from black to pink. Caviar has been enjoyed as a luxury food since it was popularised in France in the middle of the 18th century and was also a great favourite with the Tsars of Russia. Traditionally, it is served lightly chilled in small glass dishes and accompanied with chopped hard-boiled egg, chopped onion and soured cream. It should be served with toast and a silver spoon with which to eat it.

ÇAY
The Turkish word for tea, the national drink of Turkey. The strong tea is served in glasses, without milk and is heavily sweetened.

CAYENNE PEPPER
Made from very hot and pungent peppers of the capsicum family (*Capsicum frutescens*) which grow in North America and West Africa. Available ground, the pepper is very fiery and ranges in colour from dull orange to dark red. It should be used cautiously in cheese, fish and devilled dishes, curries, marinades and some sauces.

CAZNELA DE CORDERO
A Chilean lamb and vegetable stew, containing pumpkin and thickened by the addition of beaten eggs.

CEBRERO
A Spanish mountain cheese produced from cows' milk. It is full- and distinctively flavoured with a firm texture.

CELERIAC
(Turnip-root Celery)
A root vegetable (*Apium graveolens* var. *rapaceum*) which is a variety of celery with a round, swollen root and inedible stalks. Although known in Roman times it was used only for medicinal purposes in its early, bitter-tasting forms. It was later developed to produce the modern variety. It has long been popular in

mainland Europe but was not introduced to Britain until the 18th century. Celeriac is an unattractive-looking vegetable and appears in the shops as a knobbly, wrinkled and brown-skinned ball, covered with roots. The fibrous skin needs to be thickly peeled to remove the root ends. Celeriac is at its best before it fully matures and smaller roots are preferable, 7.5–13 cm/3–5 inches in diameter. The flesh is firm and cream-coloured, tasting rather like a celery-flavoured potato. Celeriac is sometimes grated and eaten raw but is usually boiled, steamed or fried or used in savoury dishes.

CELERY

A vegetable (*Apium graveolens* var. *dulce*) native to many countries in its wild state. It was used by the Greeks and Romans in its early bitter-tasting forms for medicinal purposes. Modern varieties are mainly the result of cross-cultivation improvements carried out in Italy in the 17th century; celery began to be widely cultivated in Britain in the 18th century and subsequently around the world. It grows as a cluster of stalks or stems, closely packed at the base to form a heart, opening out into separate stems with leafy tops and fibrous ridges running up and down the outside of each stem. The natural colour of stems and leaves is green but celery is often blanched while growing to become creamy-white to pale green up to the leafy fronds. Celery is crisp, juicy and sweet or bitter-sweet and is at its best when fairly young. It may be eaten raw, as a cooked vegetable or as a flavouring in savoury dishes. The green leaves may be used in similar ways when young and also as a garnish. In Continental Europe, bundles of thin green celery are sold for use as a herb.

CELERY SALT

Made from a mixture of table salt and a strong-flavoured variety of celery which has been dehydrated and ground.

CELERY SEEDS

Seeds of a plant (*Apium graveolens*) native to southern Europe but now widely cultivated in India and France. Small and light brown, the seeds have a distinct celery flavour and are used in soups, sauces, salads such as coleslaw, pickles, egg dishes, cheese dishes and stuffings.

CELLOPHANE NOODLES

(Bean Thread Noodles, Transparent Noodles)

Fine pasta strands, similar to vermicellini, eaten in China and Japan. They are made from mung bean flour or seaweed and are almost transparent, hence the name 'cellophane'. They are sold dried and used in stir-fry dishes and soups. They can be deep-fried straight from the packet to make crispy noodles.

CELLULOSE

The indigestible matter derived from carbohydrate or cereal foods. It is found in the cell walls of plants, including fruits, vegetables and grains. Although it has minimal nutritional value, it adds bulk to the diet and activates the large intestine, thus preventing constipation. Cellulose is a polysaccharide.

CENDRÉ

General term to describe small French cheeses in assorted shapes which have been matured in wood ash. They have a relatively forceful flavour and are produced from cows' milk.

CEP

(Cèpe)

An edible mushroom (*Boletus edulis*) with a cap which is smooth and brown on top and white to greeny-yellow underneath. The thick, bulbous stem is white when young, becoming pale brown in maturity. It grows in or near woods and is both abundant and popular during the autumn season. The cep can grow to a considerable size and a height of 30 cm/12 inches and a weight of over 900 g/2 lb is not uncommon. It has many culinary applications and may replace the common or cultivated mushroom in most recipes. The cep can be bought dried and is sometimes found in packet soups. When young, it is also known as the penny bun because of its resemblance to a baked brown bun.

CÈPE
See *Cep*.

CEPHALOPOD
Marine animal, such as octopus, squid and cuttlefish, with legs and tentacles growing from the head.

CEREAL
Originating from the name of Ceres, the Greek goddess of harvesting, the word cereal applies to edible grains such as wheat, rice, barley, maize and oats. Cereal, in one form or another, constitutes the staple diet of most people throughout the world.

CERIMAN
(Monstera)
The fruit of an evergreen tree (*Monstera deliciosa*) native to Central America and found occasionally in gardens or greenhouses in other suitable warm regions. It looks rather like a cross between a corn-on-the-cob and an elongated pineapple. It averages about 23 cm/9 inches long and 5 cm/2 inches in diameter at its widest point. The scaly skin is green. The scales, which give it a pineapple-like appearance, break away from the white, pulpy flesh when the fruit is fully ripe and only then is the flesh itself edible. It may be squeezed to provide juice for a drink or used in desserts. The flavour is reminiscent of a mixture of pineapple and banana.

CERTOSA
(Certosino, if small*)*
A mild and creamy Italian cows' milk cheese, and a member of the Stracchino family. It can be small or relatively large, depending on type.

CERVELAS
A French version of the saveloy sausage.

CERVELAT
A German preserved sausage, made from finely minced beef and pork. It is lightly smoked, mildly seasoned and contains no garlic. It can be either ultra-smooth in texture or very slightly speckled with fat. The colour of the sausage is pink but the outside turns golden-yellow when smoked. Cervelat is excellent in sandwiches or for a cold buffet.

CEVAPCICI
Yugoslavian grilled minced meat balls, a Serbian speciality.

à la CÉVENOLE
French term meaning in the style of Cévennes in southern France, denoting the use of chestnuts and mushrooms.

CEVICHE
(Seviche, Cebiche)
Originally from Peru, raw white fish, cut into cubes and marinated in a mixture of lime juice, lemon juice, garlic, onions, chillies and seasonings. The acid 'cooks' the fish and it is served with sweetcorn and pieces of boiled sweet potato. *Ceviche* is also popular in Mexico.

CEYLON TEA
Black tea produced in Sri Lanka, once known as Ceylon. Sri Lanka is one of the largest tea producers in the world and the varieties grown at high altitudes include some of

the best in the world. Ceylon teas tend to have a strong but delicate flavour and may be purchased unblended or mixed with other teas.

CHA
(Char)
Still used colloquially in Britain, the word cha comes from the English pronunciation of the Chinese word *chai*, used in the region of Canton for the drink known as tea. It was replaced over the years by the word *t'e*, used in the neighbouring region of Amoy, and from this came the word tea, now used in the English-speaking world. In other languages the name for tea is derived from either of the Chinese words, depending on which area the original imports came from.

CHA GIO
A Vietnamese speciality, rice paper rolls containing pork, fish, vegetables and noodles, which are deep-fried and served hot.

CHABICHOU
(Cabichou, Cabrichiu, Chabi)
A French goats' milk cheese from Poitou. It is shaped like a small, stubby cone and has a pronounced, goat-like flavour. The colour is white and the texture fairly firm.

à la CHABLISIENNE
French term meaning in the style of Chablis, south-east of Paris, referring to food cooked in the famous dry white wine of the same name; also a sauce made with a base of Chablis and served with fish.

CHAKCHOUKA
A North African vegetable stew reminiscent of *ratatouille* and containing the same vegetables.

CHAL
Central Asian fermented camels' milk with a strong taste and smell.

CHALLAH
(Challa)
Jewish Sabbath bread made from a yeasted dough containing eggs. The loaf is generally shaped like a plait and sprinkled with poppy seeds.

CHAMBARAND
(Trappiste de Chambarand)
A fairly small, French monastery cheese made from cows' milk. The rind is a light pinky-orange and the cheese itself is delicate, creamy and flexible.

CHAMBERAT
French cows' milk cheese similar to Saint-Paulin.

CHAMBOURCY
Brand name of a mild, French cream cheese. It is produced commercially from cows' milk.

CHAMBRÉ
French term to describe red wine or cheese which has been allowed to reach room temperature before it is served.

CHAMOMILE
(Camomile)
An annual herb (*Anthemis nobilis*) which has been grown in Britain since pre-Roman times. Its flowers and leaves are used medicinally and camomile tea is a popular tisane as it is considered to have a beneficial effect on nervous stomachs and rheumatism.

CHAMOMILE TEA
(Camomile Tea)
A soothing herbal tea made from the flowers of the chamomile plant. Different varieties of the plant are used in different countries to make similar drinks. In Britain, the plant is sometimes called Roman Camomile.

CHAMP
A creamed potato dish from Ireland containing chopped spring onions. A well is made in each portion which is filled with melted butter and

mouthfuls of the potato mixture are dipped into the butter. Chives, chopped leek or parsley are sometimes used instead of spring onions.

CHAMPAGNE
Featured in sauces and fruit desserts by top chefs in exclusive restaurants, champagne is a naturally sparkling white wine from the areas in France around Reims, Epernay and Châlons-sur-Marne. It can be dry to sweet and the name 'Champagne' is strictly controlled by law in France and applies only to wine made by the champagne method (*Méthode Champenoise*). It is considered a luxury drink.

aux CHAMPIGNONS
French term for any dish cooked or garnished with mushooms; also food coated with a mushroom sauce.

CHANNA
(Chana)
See *Chickpea*.

CHANNEL ISLANDS MILK
(Jersey Milk, Devon Milk)
Milk from Jersey, Guernsey and South Devon cows which is richer than other milks with a very creamy flavour and colour, containing a legal minimum of 4% butterfat. In Britain the foil tops of the bottles are gold and a distinct cream-line is visible. The breed of cow is Channel Island and herds are found throughout the British Isles. The milk is pasteurized.

CHANTELLE
Produced in the USA and Canada, a cows' milk cheese similar to Bel Paese.

CHANTERELLE
An edible mushroom (*Cantharellus cibarius*) which has a very distinctive rich yellow colour and an odour similar to that of an apricot. When young it has a small, circular, flat cap but this develops an upturned wavy edge and a deep hollow in the centre. The chanterelle is found in clusters in woods during the autumn and is seldom disfigured by insects. The flavour is excellent, making this fungus a favourite in many French dishes. It is available dried, canned or fresh.

CHANTILLY MAYONNAISE
Mayonnaise to which whipped cream is added. It can be served with cold cooked poultry, hard-boiled eggs, avocados, cold cooked globe artichokes and asparagus.

CHAP
Lower part of a pig's cheek.

CHAPATIS
(Chapathis, Chapattis)
Indian unleavened bread made from a wholewheat flour dough shaped into thin rounds and dry-fried in a heavy-based pan or on a griddle.

CHAR
See *Arctic Char*.

CHARCOAL
The carbon residue left after fierce heat has been applied to animal or vegetable matter. Charcoal is used as a barbecuing fuel and charcoal biscuits, sold mainly in health food shops, are said to aid digestion and prevent flatulence.

CHARCUTERIE
French term for pork products, cooked and ready-prepared, which can be anything from ham to assorted sausages. They are sold in a shop of the same name.

CHARENTAIS MELON
A variety of cantaloupe melon noted for its sweet and juicy orange flesh. The skin is greeny-yellow in colour and grooved to give a wide-panelled effect. It is excellent eaten on its own.

CHARLOTTE
A traditional French hot fruit pudding which moved across to Britain in the 18th century. The

derivation of the name is rather uncertain: some say it was invented for Charlotte de Medici, wife of the son of the Prince of Condé; others that it was named after Charlotte, the wife of George III. It consists of layers of either fingers of bread and butter or buttered fresh breadcrumbs, a little sugar and sweetened stewed apples baked with the minimum of liquid. It is served with cream.

CHARLOTTE MOULD
A straight-sided, round mould used for making fruit charlottes and the classic *Charlotte Russe*. Ordinary round cake tins are almost identical to charlotte moulds and may be used instead.

CHARLOTTE RUSSE
With a name meaning 'Russian charlotte', this dessert comprises a layer of jelly, usually decorated, set in the base of a round tin lined with sponge finger biscuits. It is then filled with a rich custard mixture made from milk and/or cream, egg yolks, gelatine, flavouring and whipped cream. When firm and set, the charlotte is unmoulded and either left plain or decorated with extra cream.

CHARNWOOD
British Cheddar cheese which is smoked and coated with paprika.

CHAROLAIS
(Charollies)
A French cheese made from either goats' or cows' milk, or a combination of the two. It is shaped like a small cylinder with a greyish-blue rind and is a hard cheese with a forthright flavour. When eaten fresh with minimal maturation, Charolais is soft and creamy.

CHAROSET
(Charoseth)
A Jewish Passover condiment containing chopped apples, walnuts, wine and cinnamon.

CHAROUCE
A French cows' milk cheese produced in the province of Champagne. It is relatively small with a creamy flavour and rich, white texture.

CHARQUI
North American term for sun-dried and smoked strips of beef or venison.

CHA-SOBA
Japanese buckwheat noodles to which powdered green tea has been added, giving them a distinctive colour and aroma.

à la CHASSEUR
French term for anything cooked in hunter's style, denoting the inclusion of onions or shallots, fried sliced mushrooms, tomatoes, white wine and brandy.

CHASSEUR SAUCE
An Espagnole sauce, flavoured with extra fried onions, fried mushrooms, tomate purée, white wine, sometimes brandy and chopped parsley. It can be served with grilled and roast meat and some entrées.

CHATEAUBRIAND
A double steak cut from the thickest part of beef fillet. It generally serves two people and is grilled.

CHATEAUBRIAND CHEESE
A French triple cream cheese from Normandy, made from cows' milk.

à la CHÂTELAINE
French term for food garnished with artichoke hearts, chestnuts and puréed onions in a cream sauce.

CHAUD-FROID SAUCE
Made from equal amounts of hot Béchamel sauce and cold (but still liquid) aspic jelly. When cold and beginning to thicken, it is used to coat whole skinned salmon, salmon trout, portions of chicken or turkey, and whole gammon, particularly for cold buffets.

CHAUDIN
See *Colon*.

CHAYOTE
(Cho-cho, Choko, Chow-chow, Christophene, Mirliton, Vegetable Pear)
A vegetable (*Sechium edule*) of the squash family native to Central America and now cultivated around the world in tropical and semi-tropical regions. It grows as the fruit of a trailing vine and looks rather like a ridged pear with a thick and sometimes prickly skin which may be white or green. The different varieties range in weight from about 175 g/6 oz to over 900 g/2 lb, but all are best when not too mature. The flesh is crisp and light green in colour and each fruit contains a large, cream-coloured edible seed. The flavour is delicate and very mild and a cross between vegetable marrow and radish. Chayote may be cooked as a vegetable on its own or used in dishes suitable for courgettes.

CHEDDAR
Originally English, this cheese is now made worldwide from Japan to Eastern Europe. It is a full-fat cheese (48% butterfat) produced from cows' milk and weighs between 5 kg/11 lb and 27 kg/60 lb. It dates back to the early 16th century and can be mild to mature in flavour, depending on how long it has been left to ripen; usually from 5 months to a year (although it is ready to eat after 3 months). It is a firm-textured cheese which is smooth and non-crumbly, a warm yellow in colour and with a flavour that is rich, mellow and pleasing, both as a dessert and cooking cheese.

CHEDDAR 'N' SCOTCH
A Scottish Cheddar cheese, blended with 10-year-old single malt whisky.

CHEEDHAM
An Australian cows' milk cheese with similarities to both Cheddar and Edam.

CHEESE
A high-protein food and an excellent source of calcium, phosphorus and vitamins A and D. When made from whole milk, cheese contains approximately one-third protein, one-third fat and one-third water. Dating back to pre-Biblical times when cheese was a staple food, made almost exclusively from the milk of ewes and cows, it has always been appreciated as much for its nutritional value as for its piquancy. Today, there are thousands of cheeses marketed worldwide; some are simple, others less so, but all are concentrated, condensed and solid forms of milk, and can be stored for a much longer time than milk itself.

CHEESE DYE
See *Annatto*.

CHEESE FONDUE
A Swiss speciality made from Emmental and Gruyère cheeses melted in a *caquelon* (a wide-based pot with a short handle on one side) with garlic, wine, a little cornflour and Kirsch liqueur. It is eaten by spearing cubes of crusty bread on to long-handled fondue forks, then swirling them in the cheese mixture. The cheese-coated bread is eaten straight from the dish and traditionally washed down with Kirsch.

CHEESE LAYER CAKE
An exotic North American cows' milk cheese made from three layers of cheese. One layer is flavoured with pistachio, another with pink champagne and the third is white Cheddar. The cheese is coated with almonds.

CHEESE PASTRY
Pastry, usually shortcrust, with cheese and seasonings added to the mixture, generally used for savoury snacks and dishes. In

England's North Country, cheese pastry is sometimes the basis for apple pie.

CHEESE PRODUCTION
Cheese is made from different types of milk, soured or ripened by a starter which is usually a culture of lactic acid bacteria. This has the effect of turning some of the lactose naturally found in milk into lactic acid; the development of acid is carefully controlled throughout the cheese-making process to ensure a good-quality end-product. The milk is then coagulated or thickened by the addition of rennet and the resultant mixture is subsequently cut up to enable the whey to separate from the curd. To remove further excess whey, the curd is scalded and coagulates again. When the curd has settled, more drainage of whey occurs, after which the curd is milled or broken up. Salt is added both to act as a preservative and to bring out the flavour, and the curd is then pressed into moulds for the required length of time to make whole cheeses. After they have been turned out of the moulds, the final ripening process takes place in a special room which is maintained at the correct temperature and humidity level. Particular flavour development and texture of any given cheese is due to the action of bacteria and enzymes present in the cheese during ripening.

CHEESE SAUCE
A white sauce flavoured with grated Cheddar or Swiss cheese, a little mustard and a small amount of cayenne pepper. It can be served with egg dishes, boiled bacon, ham, fish, poultry and vegetables.

CHEESE SPREAD
A general term for a soft, sometimes processed, cheese which is used for spreading on bread, toast or biscuits.

CHEESE STRAWS
Savoury cheese biscuits made from cheese pastry cut into narrow, finger-length sticks and baked. They are sometimes threaded through a ring of baked pastry to resemble bales of hay, hence the name.

CHEESECAKE
Made from either cream, curd or sieved cottage cheese, eggs, sugar, butter or cream, sometimes lemon, vanilla and a small amount of cornflour. The mixture is usually cooked on top of a base of crushed biscuits in a spring-clip tin but occasionally it is baked inside a pastry case. The cake originates from Central Europe.

CHEF
A senior cook in restaurants.

CHEF'S SALAD
A large North American salad, often a combination of seasonal fruits, vegetables, ham and Swiss cheese. There are many variations on this theme and some chef's salads contain cottage cheese, poultry and eggs.

CHELSEA BUNS
An 18th-century favourite with George III and his wife, Charlotte, these buns are still very popular in Britain and are usually reserved for the tea-table. They are made from a fairly rich, white yeasted dough which is rolled out, brushed with butter and sprinkled with currants and sugar. The dough is then rolled up like a Swiss roll, cut into slices and baked. The buns have a characteristic pinwheel appearance.

en CHEMISE
French term for food which has been wrapped prior to cooking. This can apply to potatoes in their own skins or food covered with pastry, egg and crumbs, vine leaves and even batter.

CHEMISER
French term meaning to coat the inside of a mould with aspic or sweet gelatine mixture.

CHERIMOYA
(Cherimoyer)
The fruit of a tree (*Anona cherimolia*), originally from Peru, but now cultivated in many tropical parts of the world. It is considered to be the finest of the custard apples and, as with all members of this family, the fruit can be as small as an apple or as large as a melon. The general appearance is rather scaly and like a large, green, unopened fir cone. The flesh is white, studded with black seeds and with the texture of thick, sweet custard. It may be eaten raw or used with other ingredients in dessert dishes.

CHERRY
The fruit of a tree (*Prunus* species) of the rose family, related to the plum. It is native to the Middle East, where it has been cultivated for hundreds of years, though many varieties are now grown worldwide in countries with temperate climates. The shape varies from globular to oval to heart-shaped and the fruit can be 1–2.5 cm/½–1 inch long. Both the skin and flesh colour may range from pale yellow to red and almost blackish-red; the thin, shiny skin surrounds juicy flesh with a central stone. There are three main types of cherry: the sweet, the sour and the varieties in-between. When fully ripe, the sweet varieties are best eaten as they are; the other kinds may be incorporated in a wide range of cooked dishes, both sweet and savoury. The blanched and peeled kernels from cherry stones may be used for culinary purposes. Some kinds of cherries are used in the production of exclusive liqueurs and brandies.

CHERRY CAKE
A popular, rich fruit cake containing glacé cherries. It is flavoured with lemon or vanilla.

CHERRY TOMATO
Perfectly rounded and very small type of tomato.

CHERVIL
A herb (*Anthriscus cerefolium*) native to Asia but now grown in all temperate zones of the world, chervil is related to the carrot family. The small green leaves are slightly pungent with a mild parsley flavour and well-suited to soups, salads, some sauces, chicken dishes and egg dishes.

CHESHIRE
Britain's oldest cheese, the production of Cheshire goes back to pre-Roman times when the northern part of the country was inhabited by Celtic tribes. It has a slightly salty taste, crumbles readily and the flavour is mellow, well-rounded, yet fresh at the same time. Its unique character is due to the rich salt deposits in the soil of the Cheshire Plain, in Cheshire itself or Shropshire where the cattle graze. It is a full-fat cheese (48% butterfat) made from cows' milk and allowed to mature for 4–8 weeks. Some farmhouse varieties are left for up to 15 months and are superbly flavoured. Cheshire stands up well as a dessert or cooking cheese and there are two varieties: White Cheshire, which is white or cream-coloured, and Red Cheshire, which is coloured orange with the dye annatto.

CHESS PIE
A pie from North America, said to have come originally from England, which consists of a pastry case filled with a mixture of walnuts or pecans, fruit juice or sherry, butter, sugar, eggs and cream.

CHESSEL
A vat or mould used in cheesemaking.

CHESTNUTS
More starchy and floury than most other nuts and lower in protein and fat, chestnuts are the edible fruit of the sweet chestnut tree (*Castanea sativa*), native to the Mediterranean and a member of the oak and beech

family. The best quality nuts come from Spain and France and must be shelled and skinned before use. Dried chestnuts are becoming more readily available; these should be soaked overnight before use.

CHETHA SI BIYAN
A mild Burmese chicken stew containing onions, garlic, turmeric, fresh ginger, salt, lemon and fresh coriander.

CHEVIOT
A British Cheddar cheese, flavoured with chopped chives.

CHÈVRE
(Pur Chèvre)
A general French term to describe all cheeses made only from goats' milk with a minimum butterfat content of 45%. They have a distinctive flavour and may be mild, salty, strong, very soft or fairly firm. All are white and creamy in texture and are left to mature from 2 weeks to 6 months.

CHEVRON
North American term for a young goat.

CHEVRU
A French cows' milk cheese from the Île-de-France. It has a warm, characterful flavour and is similar to Brie de Coulommiers cheese.

CHEWING GUM
Made from chicle, a gummy substance from the milky sap of the sapodilla tree.

CHEZZARELLA
A soft-textured North American cheese made from Cheddar and Mozzarella cheeses. It has a marbled effect.

CHHANA
(Chauna)
A sour cows' milk cheese from India.

CHICKEN
The common domestic fowl (*Gallus gallus*).

CHICKEN À LA KING
A North American dish of diced cooked chicken in a rich white sauce with fried chopped onions, green peppers, mushrooms and pimientos. It is flavoured with sherry and served with rice.

CHICKEN BRICK
(Römertopf, Roman Pot)
A porous, earthenware casserole with lid in the traditional brick-red terracotta colour. It is oblong in shape and specially designed to hold a whole chicken which then cooks in its own natural juices. No additional fat is necessary and all the flavours are retained. Every time the brick is used, it must be soaked in water for approximately 15 minutes before it is put in the oven. This method of cooking chicken appeals to slimmers and those on a low-fat diet, and is based on a traditional technique which dates back to Roman times. The German brand name for the brick is *Römertopf*.

CHICKEN CACCIATORA
See *Pollo alla Cacciatora*.

CHICKEN HALIBUT
A small halibut.

CHICKEN KIEV
A classic Russian dish, this is made from flattened chicken breasts stuffed with garlic butter. The breasts are coated with egg and breadcrumbs, then fried until crisp and golden. When cut, the melted butter from the centre pours out of the chicken, creating a sauce.

CHICKEN MARENGO
See *Pollo alla Marengo*.

CHICKEN MARYLAND
A traditional dish from North America of chicken portions, coated in egg and breadcrumbs, which are deep-fried in oil. They are served with corn fritters, gravy and fried bananas.

CHICKEN PAPRIKA
See *Paprikás Csirke*.

CHICKEN PIRI-PIRI
Portuguese charcoal-grilled chicken, basted before and during cooking with a combination of piri-piri sauce, olive oil, garlic, tomato puree, Worcestershire sauce and salt.

CHICKEN TETRAZZINI
A North American speciality of cooked chicken pieces in a *velouté* sauce which are spooned over cooked *spaghetti*, sprinkled with crumbs and Parmesan cheese, and browned under the grill. It is traditionally served with broccoli and sometimes a little dry sherry is added to the sauce.

CHICKEN TURBOT
A young turbot, often sold whole.

CHICKENS' FEET
Occasionally sold with roasting chickens and boiling fowl, these may be added to soups or used to make stock. They enhance flavour, increase protein content and also lightly set the liquid in which they are cooked. Chickens' feet need scaling prior to cooking and should therefore be blanched in boiling water, then the scales can be carefully removed with a knife.

CHICKENS' LIVERS
Widely available fresh or frozen, chickens' livers are excellent in *pâtés*, terrines, meat loaves, stews, casseroles and braised dishes. They are relatively small with a delicate flavour and the colour can vary from deep beige to a reddish-brown.

CHICKPEA
(Bengal Gram, Chana, Channa, Chick Pea, Garbanzo, Garbanzo Pea)
A vegetable (*Cicer arietinum*) native to Asia and widely cultivated from the Mediterranean region to the Far East. The chickpea is a legume which contains only two or three seeds in each pod and, although the seeds can be shelled from the pod and cooked as a fresh vegetable, the main use is as a dried pulse. The colour of the dried chickpea is light brown and it looks more like a small, knobbly nut than a pea or bean, with different kinds varying in size and colour. Being both nutritious and flavourful, it is used in many basic dishes in southern Europe, North Africa, the Middle East and India.

CHICORÉES AU JAMBON
A Belgian speciality consisting of cooked heads of chicory wrapped in ham, reheated in cheese sauce and usually served with boiled potatoes.

CHICORY
(Belgian Endive, Succory, Witloof)
A vegetable (*Cichorium intybus*) which is a member of the daisy family, originally from the Far East and found growing wild for centuries in Europe where it was used for medicinal purposes. Modern cultivation methods have reduced the bitterness of the natural plant and improved the size and quality of chicory. It is harvested when still at the shoot or bud stage and comprises a tight and elongated cluster of leaves about 10 cm/ 4 inches long. The colour of the leaves of most varieties of chicory is creamy-white with pale greeny-yellow edges and tips; the natural colour is blanched out by the growing and harvesting methods. Chicory may be eaten raw in salads, cooked as a vegetable or used in savoury dishes. The dried and ground roasted root of one variety is used as a coffee additive.

CHIFFON CAKE
A North American cake which is light-textured and moist. It is closely related to angel cake but enriched with oil.

CHIFFON PIE
A North American speciality consisting of a baked pastry case filled with a fruity mousse mixture

which is lightened by the addition of beaten egg whites, set with gelatine and decorated with cream and/or fruit.

CHIFFONADE
French term for a garnish for clear soups made from fine shreds of lettuce or sorrel.

CHIKU
(Chico, Chikku)
See *Sapodilla*.

CHILAQUILES
A Mexican speciality made from strips of corn *tortilla* which are fried until crisp, then reheated with tomato sauce. Sometimes cold cooked meat is added and the dish is garnished with grated cheese, chopped chillies and chopped onions.

CHILES RELLENOS
Mexican stuffed peppers, sometimes served with walnut sauce.

à la CHILIENNE
French term meaning in the style of Chile, denoting the use of rice and red peppers.

CHILL (TO)
To make prepared food, or ingredients cold, but not frozen, by placing them in a refrigerator or cold larder.

CHILLED CHEESECAKE
A refrigerated cheesecake which is set with gelatine and never baked. It is characteristically smooth and creamy.

CHILLI
(Chili)
A vegetable (*Capsicum frutescens*) which is the smallest of the capsicum family and has a strong and fiery flavour. Chillies grow in several shapes and sizes but most resemble cones or are long and tapering. The colour can be red, green or yellow and the inner core of seeds is the hottest part of the vegetable. Chilli is used mainly for flavouring and should be added cautiously as it can make dishes unbearably hot if used in excess. The actual taste of chilli varies with type and is used in many ethnic dishes to achieve a specific flavour, particularly in Mexico and India.

CHILLI CON CARNE
More 'Tex-Mex' than pure Mexican, a dish of stewed minced or chopped meat, simmered with onions, garlic, tomatoes, chilli powder, red kidney beans, spices, sometimes chopped chillies for extra heat, water and seasonings. *Chilli con carne* is served with refried beans, *tortillas*, white rice and salad.

CHILLI POWDER
(Chilli Seasoning)
A spice blend made from a base of chilli pepper to which red pepper, ground cumin, oregano and garlic powder are added. The colour is reddish-burgundy and the spice is used for *chilli con carne* and other Mexican-style dishes.

CHILLI SAUCE
A hot and peppery orange ketchup widely used as an additive and accompaniment to Chinese and other Oriental cuisines.

CHIMICHANGAS
A speciality of the state of Sonora in Mexico, fried stuffed *tacos* made from flour *tortillas*. When fried, they puff like flaky pastry. The filling is usually based on minced beef. Traditional accompaniments are shredded lettuce, grated cheese, sliced radishes and chopped spring onions.

CHIMICHURRI
An Argentinian sauce for grilled, roasted and barbecued meat and poultry, made from oil, vinegar, garlic, chopped onions, cayenne pepper and other seasonings.

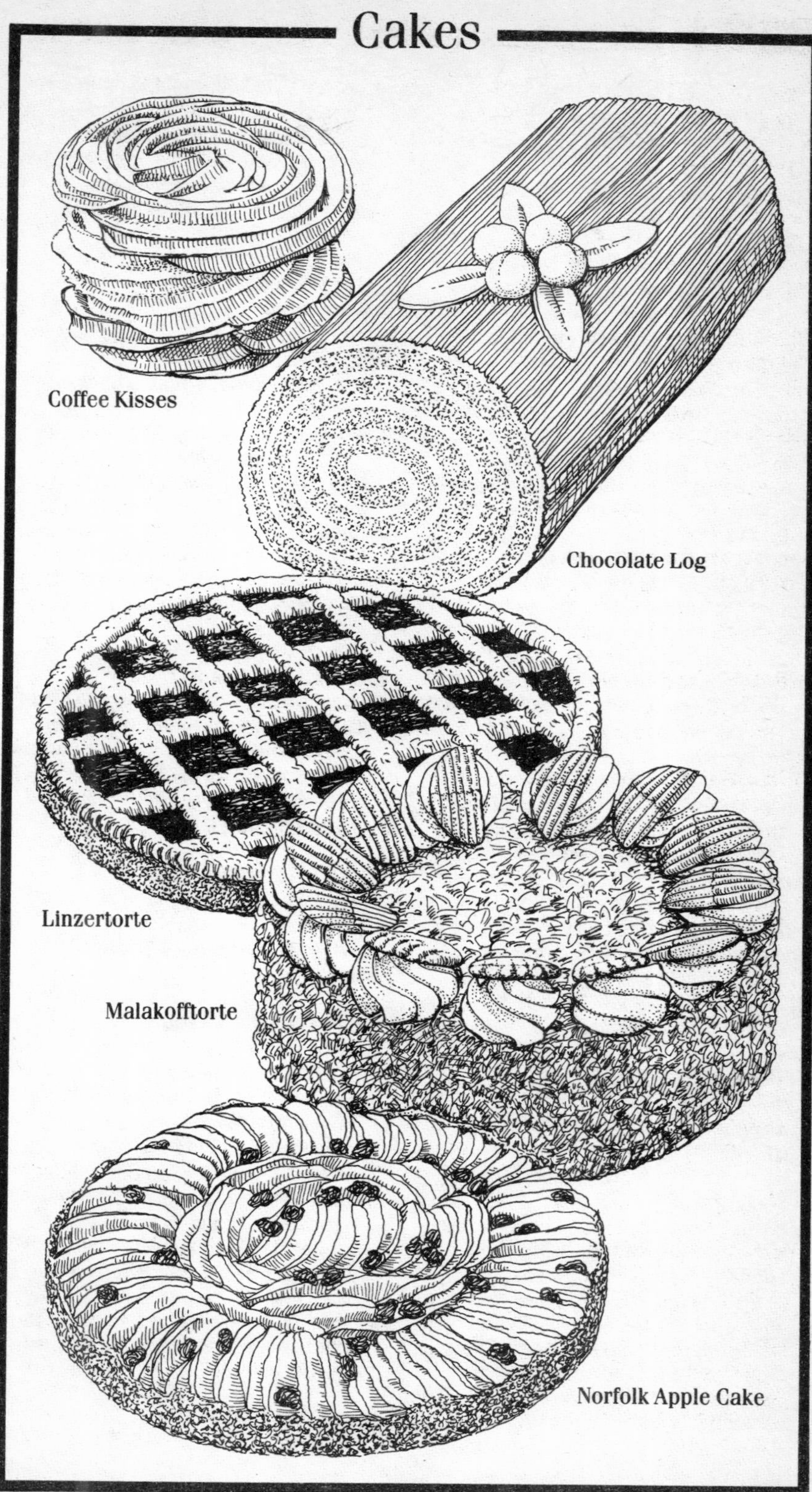
Cakes
Coffee Kisses
Chocolate Log
Linzertorte
Malakofftorte
Norfolk Apple Cake

CHINA
An all-embracing term for crockery.

CHINA ORANGE
See *Calamondin Orange*.

CHINE (TO)
A method of treating the bones in a best end neck of lamb. The butcher cuts along the backbone between the ribs so that the rib chops or cutlets are easier to carve when cooked. The term also means to cut through the backbone of a carcass.

CHINE OF BEEF
Term used in the Midlands in Britain to describe fore rib of beef.

CHINESE ARTICHOKE
(Chorogi, Japanese Artichoke)
A root vegetable (*Stachys sieboldii*) native to the Far East and introduced to Europe from Peking in the latter part of the 19th century. In France this vegetable is called *crosnes* (pronounced 'crone') after the place where it was first grown in the West. The Chinese artichoke is now cultivated on both sides of the Atlantic and grows as a pale, short and tapering tuber with well-defined concentric segments, looking rather like a fat caterpillar or maggot. The flavour is delicate and the Chinese artichoke may be boiled or fried.

CHINESE BITTER MELON
See *Bitter Gourd*.

CHINESE CABBAGE
(Chinese Leaves, Pe-tsai)
A vegetable of the cabbage family (*Brassica pekinensis*) native to China and cultivated in many parts of the world. It is almost cylindrical in shape and comprises long, veined leaves which are tightly bunched. The leaves are a pale green, lighter at the base, and their spines are almost white. It is more delicately flavoured than most of the cabbage family and the texture is crisp and crunchy. The taste makes it particularly suitable for salads and it may also be cooked as a vegetable or used in savoury dishes. The Chinese name is *pe-tsai*; this vegetable should not be confused with its very close relative *pak-choi*, which is sometimes also called Chinese leaves.

CHINESE CHERRY
See *Lychee*.

CHINESE CHIVE
(Chinese Onion, Chinese Leek, Kuchai, Kuichai)
A vegetable (*Allium tuberosum*) of the onion family native to China and found both wild and cultivated in the Far East. It is much larger than the European varieties of chive and both its leaves and flowering stems are used for flavouring. The taste can vary from that of strong garlic to mild Spanish onion.

CHINESE EGG ROLL
(Egg Roll, Pancake Roll, Spring Roll)
Thin egg pastry pieces filled with chopped vegetables, meat or poultry and shellfish, formed into individual rolls and deep-fried until golden-brown.

CHINESE FIVE SPICE
See *Five Spice Powder*.

CHINESE GOOSEBERRY
See *Kiwi Fruit*.

CHINESE LANTERN
(Bladder Cherry)
The fruit of a plant (*Physalis alkekengi*) of the tomato family, closely related to the cape gooseberry and mainly grown in Asia from the Caspian Sea region to China. The edible berry, which is yellowish when fully ripe, is enclosed in a multi-part, parchment-like husk. This husk is more brightly coloured than those of other members of the family but the fruit is not as pleasant to eat. The calyx is inedible.

CHINESE LEAVES
See *Chinese Cabbage* and *Pak-Choi*.

CHINESE LEEK
See *Chinese Chive*.

CHINESE MUSHROOMS
Available dried from Oriental food shops, these are costly whole mushrooms from China. There is no substitute for their strong and distinctive flavour.

CHINESE ONION
See *Chinese Chive*.

CHINESE PARSLEY
See *Coriander*.

CHINESE PEA
See *Mange-Tout*.

CHINESE SAUSAGES
Heavily spiced and made from cubes of pork, pork fat and sometimes liver, these are generally cut into pieces and added to stir-fried dishes. Chinese sausages are available from Chinese food shops.

CHINESE SPINACH
See *Callaloo*.

CHINESE STEAMING
Carried out in multi-tiered steamers, the metal ones having perforated bases and the bamboo ones, lattice-work bases. Close-fitting lids prevent the steam from escaping.

CHINESE WATER CHESTNUTS
(Caltrops, Water Caltrops, Water Chestnuts)
The crunchy tubers of any of several Asian sedges (especially *Eleocharis tuberosa*), widely used in Oriental cooking.

CHINOIS
A conical metal strainer which resembles a Chinese coolie's hat.

à la CHINONAISE
French term meaning in the style of Chinon in the Loire valley, denoting a garnish of potatoes and cabbage filled with sausage.

CHINOOK SALMON
The largest member (*Oncorhynchus tshawytscha*) of the Pacific salmon family, caught from Alaska to California. It varies from dark green to slate-colour on the back, shading to silver sides and undersides, with numerous small black spots on the tail fin. The weight can be 4–22 kg/9–50 lb. The main fishing season is March to October. The flesh is very oily and flaky and the fish may be poached, steamed, baked, fried or grilled.

CHIP BASKET
See *Frying Basket*.

CHIP BUTTY
British colloquial term for a sandwich containing chips.

CHIPOLATA SAUSAGES
Small British pork or beef sausages used for frying or grilling.

CHIPPED BEEF
(Charqui, Jerked Beef)
Very thin slices of dried and smoked beef.

CHIPPY
(Chippie)
A British colloquial term for a fish and chip shop.

CHIPS
(Potato Chips)
Squared-off lengths of potato, deep-fried in fat or oil. Also North American term for potato crisps.

CHITTERLINGS
The small intestines of any animal, most commonly of the pig. Chitterlings are generally sold ready-cooked, jellied and pressed, and are usually fried in hot fat with onion and bacon.

CHIVE
A sturdy perennial with small mauve flowers (*Allium schoenoprasum*) which grows worldwide. Related to the onion family, it has a faintly similar taste and, when chopped, is

used as a garnish and flavouring for cold sauces and dressings. It also goes well with egg dishes but is rarely used in recipes which require prolonged cooking.

CHLORINE
(Chlorine Dioxide)
See *Bleaching Agents*.

CHŁODNIK LITEWSKI
A Polish chilled summer soup which is made from a mixture of vegetables including beetroot and thinly sliced cucumber, milk, lemon juice, chopped dill, chopped chives and soured cream. It is served with quarters of hard-boiled egg.

CHLOROPHYLL
Green colouring matter found in plant life.

CHOCHON ROUCI
A pork stew from St Lucia in the Caribbean known as 'family pork stew', containing onions, leeks, celery, cabbage, tomatoes, garlic, carrots and cucumber, well-seasoned with herbs and spices.

CHOCOLATE
It appears to take its name from two Aztec words: *schoco* meaning noisy (which has been corrupted into cocoa) and *catté* meaning water. This would indicate that the Aztecs drank a type of bitter chocolate long before the idea of block chocolate, as is known today, came into being. Chocolate is made from cocoa butter derived from cocoa beans, and was introduced to Europe in the middle of the 16th century.

CHOCOLATE CAKE
A general term to describe any cake containing chocolate or cocoa powder.

CHOCOLATE CHIP COOKIES
(Maryland Cookies)
Dating from just before the Second World War, North American biscuits containing chocolate dots and sometimes chopped nuts. They are traditionally flavoured with vanilla.

CHOCOLATE FUDGE SAUCE
A thick sauce, which resembles melted chocolate fudge, which can be served hot over ice cream and ice cream sundaes. It contains melted chocolate and/or cocoa powder, brown sugar, butter or margarine, vanilla essence and sometimes milk.

CHOCOLATE LOG
A Swiss roll coated with chocolate butter cream and ridged with a fork to emulate tree bark. See also *Bûche de Noël* and Yule Log.

CHOCOLATE SAUCE
A white sauce flavoured with melted chocolate or cocoa powder and served hot with baked or steamed puddings; also, a sauce based on chocolate melted with sugar, butter or margarine and vanilla essence, and used cold for *profiteroles* or hot with ice cream.

CHOCOLATE TRUFFLES
See *Truffles*.

CHOCOLATE VERMICELLI
Short, fine strands of chocolate or chocolate substitute, used for decoration of cakes, desserts and sweetmeats.

CHOKE
The central, hairy and inedible part of a globe artichoke which, in a mature plant, becomes the flower head.

CHOLECALCIFEROL
See *Vitamin D*.

CHOLENT
(Scholet, Shalet, Sholent, Sholet)
A Jewish speciality for the Sabbath, this is a brisket, bean, barley and vegetable casserole which is baked very slowly for 24 hours. It is put into the oven before the onset of the Sabbath and removed for the midday meal.

CHOLESTEROL
A fatty substance produced and recycled in the liver and 'topped-up' by the diet. Though essential to life, and found in every body cell, excessive amounts in the bloodstream can cause furring-up of the arteries, leading to heart disease and strokes. There are two kinds of cholesterol, often known by their initials: HDL or high-density lipoproteins and LDL or low-density lipoproteins. LDL is associated with animal fats found in meat, dairy products and eggs and is the type of cholesterol that clings to artery walls, leading to blockages. HDL is found in monosaturated oils such as rapeseed, grapeseed, olive and fish oils and encourages the liver to rid the body of the more harmful LDL.

CHOLLA
(Cholla Plait)
A very rich Jewish bread made from a yeasted dough.

CHOP
Small slice of meat, often including a piece of rib bone. It is usually grilled, fried or baked.

CHOP (TO)
To divide food into large, medium or small pieces (hence the terms coarsely or finely chopped) with the aid of a sharp knife and chopping board. An effective system is to hold the tip of the knife in the left hand and move the handle backwards and forwards, with a semi-circular up-and-down motion of the right hand, keeping the blade as close to the food as possible (reversed for left-handed people).

CHOP SUEY
An Americanized version of a Chinese dish made from shredded meat or chicken, strips of mushroom, bamboo shoots and onions with bean sprouts and seasonings. It is served with soy sauce and rice.

CHOPKEBAB
A Bulgarian speciality featuring cubes of lamb and peeled marrow which are threaded on to skewers and marinated in tomato juice before being seasoned and grilled.

CHOPPED EGG AND ONION
A Jewish appetizer made from chopped hard-boiled eggs, chopped onion, melted chicken fat and seasonings.

CHOPPED HERRING
A Jewish Sabbath sweet-sour appetizer made from specially salted herring fillets which are chopped and mixed with soaked white bread, grated sour apple, chopped onion, vinegar, chopped hard-boiled egg white and seasoning. The mixture is arranged on lettuce leaves and garnished with sieved hard-boiled egg yolk.

CHOPPED LIVER
A Jewish Sabbath appetizer made from chopped cooked liver, chopped onions, chopped hard-boiled egg yolks, seasonings and melted chicken fat. The mixture is spooned on to lettuce leaves and garnished with chopped hard-boiled egg white.

CHOPPED MIXED PEEL
(Cut Mixed Peel)
Chopped citrus fruit peel, very evenly cut, usually mixed with sugar, glucose syrup and preservatives. The peel is added to Christmas cake, Christmas pudding and other baked goods.

CHOPPING BOARD
Traditionally wooden, a flat board used for chopping and cutting a variety of foods. No wooden board should ever be left to soak in water as it will warp. After washing, it should be wiped with a cloth and left to stand upright to dry thoroughly; if put away while still damp, it could become misshapen. Chopping boards can be round, oblong or square.

CHOPSTICKS
A pair of sticks, made of wood, plastic or ivory, used mainly in the Far East and Indonesia as implements for eating food.

CHORI
See *Blackeye Bean*.

CHORIZO
A salami-type sausage from Spain, made throughout the country and subject to regional variations. Colourful in appearance, it is often a scalded sausage, produced from pork, pieces of fat, garlic and paprika. The sausage is generally dried, sometimes also cold-smoked. In Spain, it is served as an appetizer (*tapa*) or with chick peas as a main course.

CHOROGI
See *Chinese Artichoke*.

CHORON SAUCE
A Béarnaise sauce, coloured and flavoured with tomato purée. It can be served with steaks and roasts of beef, poached salmon and baked eggs.

CHOUCROÛTE
French term for sauerkraut, particularly popular in the Alsace area.

CHOUX PASTRY
Pastry containing flour, salt, water, butter or margarine and eggs which is made like a thick sauce in a saucepan, then spooned or piped on to trays before baking. Choux pastry has many culinary applications, in both sweet and savoury dishes.

CHOW MEIN
A North American version of a Chinese dish, this is very similar to chop suey but is served with noodles, usually fried. Sometimes it also contains celery and green pepper.

CHOW-CHOW
(Cho-cho, Choko)
See *Chayote*.

CHOW-CHOW PRESERVE
A Chinese preserve of ginger, fruits and peel in heavy syrup; a relish of chopped mixed vegetables in a mustard pickle sauce.

CHOWDER
A traditional North American soup, made from a potato and bacon mixture and usually containing fish. New England clam chowder is a famous, milk-based soup; Manhattan clam chowder is tomato-based.

CHRISTENING CAKE
Made from a densely-fruited, rich cake mixture baked in either a round or square tin. The top and sides are traditionally covered with almond paste and then a smooth layer of royal or fondant icing. Piping is generally blue or pink and appropriate decorations are added. Sometimes a creamed cake, such as a Madeira type, is used instead of a fruited one.

CHRISTMAS CAKE
Typically British and at least three centuries old, a rich, heavy and moist cake packed with dried fruits and nuts. Originally, Christmas cake contained an abundance of 'plumbs' (raisins), alcohol and butter and was covered with almond paste. Christmas cakes are now coated with almond paste and royal icing and decorated with seasonal ornaments.

CHRISTMAS PUDDING
A traditionally British pudding containing dried fruits, sugar, suet, breadcrumbs, flour, spices and either milk or beer for mixing. It is steamed or boiled for several hours some weeks before Christmas, then put away to mature. It is reheated for 2–3 hours before serving on Christmas Day.

CHRISTOPHENE
See *Chayote*.

CHROMIUM
Mineral required by the body for the normal metabolism of sugar, often lacking in diabetics and those who rely heavily on refined foods. Chromium is found in brewer's yeast, wheatgerm, nuts, whole grains, fish, liver and sea vegetables.

CHUB
A freshwater fish (*Leuciscus cephalus*) which is a relative of the carp. Although it may grow to a length of 30 cm/12 inches and weigh up to 3.5 kg/8 lb, it is usually caught for sport rather than food because of the abundance of small bones and the muddy flavour of the flesh.

CHUCK AND BLADE BEEF STEAK
A cut of beef found between the fore rib and neck. It is good quality meat but is fairly tough and recommended for stewing, braising and casseroling.

CHUCKWAGON STEW
A speciality of Alberta in Canada made from strips of beef fried in fat, then cooked with water, herbs, potatoes, carrots, apples, small onions and seasonings, and thickened with cornflour.

CHUFA
Spanish name for tiger nut.

CHUM SALMON
A member (*Oncorhynchus keta*) of the Pacific salmon family which is caught in Alaska, Canada and the state of Washington in the USA. The back is a metallic dark blue, shading to silver on the underside and the average weight when caught is 4 kg/9 lb. The main fishing season is July to November. The flesh is pink and less oily than other Pacific salmon and the fish may be poached, steamed, baked, fried or grilled.

CHUMP CHOPS OF LAMB
Large chops cut from a joint situated between the leg and loin of lamb. They are characterized by small round central bones and are fleshy and succulent. Chump chops are usually grilled or fried and are known by this name in London and the South-East, the West Country, Wales and Scotland.

CHUMP OF PORK
Situated towards the rump end of the pig, chump of pork is recommended for roasting and may be boned and rolled or left on the bone. It is often divided into chops and grilled or fried.

CHUNKY PEANUT BUTTER
Commercial term for smooth peanut butter mixed with coarsely chopped peanuts for added texture.

CHUPE DE CAMARONES
A thick soup from Peru containing prawns, fried onions, garlic, tomatoes, peppers, potatoes, peas, sweetcorn, eggs, cream, parsley or coriander and seasonings.

CHURN
A container used in butter-making in which milk or cream is agitated to separate the oily globules from the watery whey.

CHURN (TO)
To agitate milk or cream in a churn in order to separate the oily globules from the watery whey, and produce butter.

CHURRASCO A GAUCHO
A Brazilian barbecue, usually featuring beef or poultry.

CHURROS
Spanish fritters which are eaten for breakfast, sprinkled with, or dipped in, fine sugar.

CHUTNEY
(Chutnee, Sweet Pickle)
A sweet-and-sour condiment which appears to have originated in India in the middle of the 19th century. Westernized chutney is made primarily from apples, onions, garlic, vinegar, sugar and spices.

Tomatoes and other fruits, such as rhubarb and gooseberries, are sometimes used instead of apples and dried fruits are often included. Oriental chutneys contain more exotic fruit, the best known being mango.

CICELY
See *Sweet Cicely*.

CIDER
(Cyder)
An alcoholic drink made from fermented apple juice (apple wine). It is widely produced in southern England and northern France and used as a drink and for cooking in both countries. It can be dry, medium or sweet and alcoholic strength varies with the brand.

CIDER VINEGAR
A strong vinegar made from cider with an acetic acid content of 50–60%.

CINCHO
A Venezuelan ewes' milk cheese that closely resembles Spanish Villalón.

CINNAMON
A spice native to the Far East, cinnamon is made from the dried bark of an evergreen tree (*Cinnamomum zeylanicum*) belonging to the laurel family and is available ground or in sticks (made from quills of rolled bark). Extensively used, cinnamon is said to be the world's most important spice and its sweet, spicy and pungent flavour is pleasing in baked goods, stewed fruits, marinades, curries and hot winter punches.

CINNAMON SUGAR
Caster sugar flavoured with ground cinnamon. It is dark beige in colour. It can be sprinkled on buttered toast and is widely used in central and northern Europe for baking.

CIOPPINO
A mixed seafood stew from the West Coast of the USA, containing garlic, onions, tomatoes, green peppers, wine, oil and seasonings. It is said to be related to the French *bouillabaisse*.

CISCO
See *Lake Herring*.

CITRANGE
The fruit of a tree of the citrus family, this is a hybrid of the sweet orange and was developed in North America at the turn of the century. Several varieties of the fruit exist, with sharp-tasting flesh which can be used in the same ways as sweet oranges. The main advantage of the citrange is that it is the hardiest of the orange trees and can be grown in cooler climates than other members of this family.

CITRIC ACID
Water-soluble acid found in citrus fruits, gooseberries, raspberries and other plants. It has a slightly acid taste and is used for making lemonade and in commercially produced boiled sweets.

CITRON
The fruit of an evergreen tree (*Citrus medica*) native to the Far East and one of the first of the citrus family to be introduced to the Middle East and Mediterranean regions. The general appearance of the citron is rather like an over-sized lemon covered with small nodules. The average length is 18–20 cm/7–8 inches and it is about 13 cm/5 inches in diameter. The fragrant skin and pith is particularly thick, leaving little space for the rather sour-tasting flesh. The thick skin is widely used commercially as candied peel.

CITRON PEEL
The sugar-preserved peel of the citron.

CITRUS
Trees and fruit of various species of the citrus family which grow in tropical and semi-tropical regions; oranges, grapefruit, lemons and tangerines are the main types. Cross-breeding has produced varieties such as the ugli and mineola, which have been developed to give combinations of the best characteristics of both parents. The trees or bushes in this family are evergreen and the fruits have yellow to red skins when ripe, pith of varying thickness and flesh which is both pulpy and juicy.

CIVET
A British dark brown game stew made from rabbit or hare.

CLAFOUTI
A French dessert comprising black cherries baked in a thick, creamy batter until golden-brown. Clafouti is traditionally eaten at harvest time, sprinkled with sugar and served warm with cream.

CLAM
A bivalve shellfish which is found in various species around the world. Gathering of clams is usually controlled in each locality to ensure good quality and freedom from pollution. The flesh is lean and may be eaten raw, poached, steamed, baked or fried and is also used in many made-up dishes. Among the popular species are the geoduck, horse, little-neck, quahog and surf clams.

CLAM BAKE
See *Bake*.

CLARIFIED BUTTER
Melted butter from which the milky solids have been removed, leaving behind pure fat.

CLARIFY (TO)
(To Clear)
To remove impurities from fats, stocks and jellies by passing the melted or liquid ingredients through filter paper or a piece of fine cloth such as muslin. This process renders the ingredients clear and non-cloudy.

CLARY
(Clear Eye)
Any of several plants of the genus *Salvia* which belong to the mint family and are also closely related to sage.

CLEAR (TO)
See *Clarify (to)*.

CLEAR EYE
See *Clary*.

CLEAR SOUP
A thin soup, such as *consommé*, with an unclouded appearance.

CLEMENTINE
A cultivated version of the tangerine and one of the many citrus varieties developed to produce finer fruit. The clementine is a larger member of the group with a slightly smoother, shinier skin than the mandarin and is often seedless.

CLIPFISH
(Klipfish)
Norwegian smoked cod.

CLOD OF BEEF
(Clod and Sticking of Beef)
A cut of beef found between the neck of the animal and the shin, this tough and coarse meat requires long, slow cooking such as stewing, braising and casseroling. It is often minced and used in recipes requiring fresh minced beef. Clod is known by this name in London and the South-East, the West Country and Wales.

CLOOT
Scottish term to describe a large square of cotton or linen in which a variety of puddings are boiled.

CLOOTIE DUMPLING
(Cloutie Dumpling)
A Scottish spiced pudding, boiled in a cloth and served with custard. It contains dried fruit, sugar, suet,

flour, breadcrumbs and milk. It is sometimes eaten as cake.

CLOTTED CREAM
(Clouted Cream)
A very thick pasteurized cream which is golden-yellow in colour and has a legal minimum butterfat content of 48%. It originated in Britain's West Country, and originally was made by leaving pans of milk all day to heat slowly by the fireside, cooling them through the night, then removing the thick layer of cream from the top the following morning. Today the process is mechanized and clotted cream is readily available throughout Britain. It is a slightly grainy cream that spreads easily. It is eaten with scones and jam as part of the traditional 'cream tea' or spooned over strawberries. It does not whip but may be frozen for up to 1 month.

CLOUD EAR FUNGUS
(Wood Ear, Wood Fungus, Tree Fungus, Brown Fungus)
An edible fungus (*Auricularia polytricha*) grown in China on oak trees and available dried in pieces which are small, black and brittle. The pieces expand to about five times their original size when soaked, changing colour and eventually looking rather like brown ears. The fungus is used in dishes for its texture, as well as its mild and delicate flavour.

CLOUDBERRY
The fruit of a creeping plant (*Rubus chamaemorus*) of the same family as the blackberry, native to and growing wild in northern parts of Europe and North America. It is seldom cultivated. It looks rather like a round, deep-golden blackberry in appearance and size with a sweet taste resembling a mixture of honey and baked apple. The fruit may be eaten raw or used in any dishes suited to blackberries. Although relatively rare, a luxury liqueur is produced from the berries in limited quantities.

CLOUTED CREAM
An old-fashioned term to describe clotted cream, thought by Britain's Milk Marketing Board to be named after the appearance of the cream; crinkled and uneven like 'clout', meaning a patch of wrinkled leather.

CLOVES
Native to Indonesia, cloves now come mainly from Zanzibar and Madagascar and are the dried, unopened, dark brown buds of an evergreen tree (*Eugenia aromatica*), resembling small nails or tacks. The word clove comes from the French *clou* meaning nail, and the flavour of the spice is strong, sweet, very aromatic and unmistakable. Whole cloves are used to stud ham and also to flavour pickles, chutneys, marinades, stews, stock, strong soups and hot punches. Ground cloves are added to Christmas cakes and mince pies, rich fruit cakes and gingerbreads.

CLUB SANDWICH
A North American speciality, consisting of a sandwich made from two slices of toast with a filling of lettuce, mayonnaise, sliced chicken, sliced tomatoes and cooked bacon rashers. The garnish is chutney, pickles or olives.

COAGULATE (TO)
To congeal or thicken, as applied, for example, to fats when cooling, eggs when scrambling and jellies when setting.

COALFISH
See *Coley*.

COAT (TO)
To cover pieces of cooked or uncooked food with batter, egg, breadcrumbs or flour; to cover foods with sauce or melted butter or margarine; to mask flans with glaze.

COATING BATTER
A fairly thick batter, capable of clinging to and coating foods such as fish prior to frying. It is made from flour, seasoning, egg and milk.

COATING SAUCE
Either a brown or white sauce used to cover foods to improve both their appearance and overall flavour. The usual proportion is 25 g/1 oz thickening agent to every 300 ml/½ pint milk or other liquid.

COB
A round white or brown loaf, baked on a greased baking tray. The brown version sometimes has a criss-cross pattern on the top.

COBALT
A mineral which is part of vitamin B12, vital for the formation of red blood cells. It is found in meat, dairy foods, eggs and fortified yeast extracts. Strict vegetarians or vegans may risk being deficient in it but this can be rectified by vitamin supplements.

COBBLER PUDDING
A cold, stewed fruit mixture, topped with round scones, brushed with egg and baked until brown.

COBNUTS
See *Hazelnuts*.

COBURG LOAF
A round loaf with a cross cut in the top.

COCA
A herb from an American shrub (*Erythroxylaceae coca*). An extract is obtained from its leaves which is used in cola.

COCA-COLA
A brand of cola, drunk worldwide.

COCHINEAL
(Carmine)
A dark red food colouring made from the dried bodies of certain insects which live in Mexican and Brazilian cactus plants. It is now mostly produced synthetically.

COCIDO A LA MADRILEÑA
A slowly cooked Spanish stew which contains meat, fowl, vegetables, sausage and chickpeas and is closely related to the Jewish *cholent*.

COCK
The adult male of the domestic fowl (*Gallus gallus*); also a woodcock and the male of various aquatic animals, such as fish or lobster.

COCK-A-LEEKIE SOUP
A Scottish leek and chicken soup containing rice.

COCKEREL
A male chicken used for roasting.

COCKLE
A bivalve shellfish, with an almost circular shell, and ribs radiating from the hinge. The shell colour can range from dirty white to brown and the size can be 2.5–10 cm/1–4 inches in diameter. Cockles can be harvested all year round but are best during the summer months and poorest at the beginning of the year. The European species can be found from northern Norway to the Baltic and Mediterranean and on the West African coast. The Japanese kinds are abundant in most of the shallow coastal waters. The North American varieties are found from Greenland southwards to the Caribbean. Cockles can be eaten raw, or cooked in their shells and may be poached, baked or fried.

COCKSCOMB
Decorative crest, usually red, on the top of a cockerel's head.

COCKTAIL
A combination drink based on one or more types of alcohol plus fruit juices, cream and so on; also, an appetizer served at the beginning of a meal, such as prawn cocktail; a mixture of chopped fruits.

COCKTAIL SAUCE
(Prawn Cocktail Sauce)
A mayonnaise flavoured with tomato purée, horseradish sauce, Worcestershire sauce and Tabasco. It can be served with prawns, crab and lobster.

COCKTAIL STICK
A small, pointed stick made from wood, metal or plastic, which is used to serve small pieces of food at parties and to spear cherries and other garnishes for cocktails.

COCO
(Coco-yam)
See *Taro*.

COCOA
A popular British bedtime drink made from cocoa powder, sugar and milk.

COCOA BEAN
A tropical bean, originally from South America, which grows on trees (*Theobroma cocos*) belonging to the cocoa family, Sterculiaceae. The trees bear fleshy yellow pods containing many beans (or seeds). The dried beans are used to make cocoa powder, cocoa butter and chocolate.

COCOA BUTTER
A fatty substance obtained from the cocoa bean.

COCOA POWDER
A powder prepared from ground roasted cocoa beans from which some of the fat has been removed.

COCONUT
This versatile nut is the fruit of a tropical palm (*Cocus nucifera*), native to Malaysia. The fibrous outer covering is made into coconut matting, the flesh is eaten fresh or dried and the milk makes a mild, sweet and cooling drink. As well as its many culinary uses, coconut oil is used in the manufacture of soaps, cosmetics, animal feed and some margarines. Though imported, coconut is inexpensive in Britain and the freshly grated flesh is excellent in curry and other Oriental dishes.

COCONUT CRAB
A large, edible, burrowing land crab (*Birgus latro*), widely distributed throughout the islands of the tropical Indian and Pacific Oceans.

COCONUT ICE
An old-fashioned British sweet made from milk or water, coconut and sugar. It is usually coloured pink and white.

COCONUT MILK
Made by soaking grated or desiccated coconut in water and straining the liquid, coconut milk is an important ingredient in some Oriental and Indian dishes.

COCONUT OIL
A delicately-flavoured oil extracted from the coconut. This is widely used in Asian cooking and also in the manufacture of some margarines, salad cream, mayonnaise, cooking fats and cooking oils. It solidifies at low temperatures and is highly saturated; not recommended for those on a low-cholesterol diet.

COCONUT PYRAMIDS
Pyramid-shaped biscuits based on desiccated coconut, eggs and sugar.

COCONUT WATER
The liquid found naturally inside coconuts.

COCOTTES
French term for large or small lidded casseroles. The term is also given to dishes such as *œufs en cocotte*.

COD
A cold-water fish (*Gadus morhua*) from northern areas of the Atlantic and Pacific oceans with a greyish-green scaly skin. Regarded by some authorities as the 'King of the Seas', cod is a large fish (up to 40 kg/90 lb) with flesh that is lean,

white, easy to digest and characterized by large flakes. Because of its size, it is usually sold pre-cut and is available as steaks and fillets for steaming, poaching, grilling, frying, baking, barbecuing and microwaving. It is excellent in dishes such as pies, flans and fish cakes. It is at its best from October to January, though it is caught and eaten all year round. About 20 kinds of fish are related to cod, including haddock and coley. In North America it is called Atlantic or Pacific Cod depending on the ocean of origin.

CODDLE (TO)
To soft-cook eggs in water without boiling.

CODDLED EGGS
Basically soft-cooked eggs which are not allowed to boil. The eggs, at room temperature, are lowered into a pan of boiling water. The pan is immediately removed from the source of heat and covered. Large eggs should be left in the water for 8–9 minutes; medium-sized eggs, 7–8; small eggs, 5½–6. This is a gentle method of treating eggs and even if they are left in the water for a little longer than specified, there is minimal risk of overcooking.

CODLING
A young cod.

COEUR
See *Neufchâtel*.

COEUR À LA CRÈME
A French dessert, made from curd or cream cheese which has been allowed to drain in a perforated heart-shaped mould, lined with muslin. It is turned out on to a dish and usually eaten with soft summer fruits and sugar.

COFFEE
Drink made from the roasted and ground beans of evergreen trees of the *coffea* family. Most commercially produced coffees are a blend of two or more kinds of bean. Coffee beans were probably first eaten in Abyssinia (Ethiopia), as a food with medicinal properties and later made into a drink. The origins of the first uses of coffee are obscure and several legends exist. All, however, centre on events and people in Ethiopia or nearby Yemen. The name itself is probably derived from an Arabic word for wine; this seems a reasonable assumption as the Moslem Arabs were able to substitute coffee as a stimulating beverage in place of prohibited wine. Originally coffee was a closely guarded monopoly of the Arabian producers, who exported treated, edible beans but not plants or fertile seeds.

COFFEE BEAN
Fruit of an evergreen tree of the *coffea* family native to Africa. When ripe, the outer casings are removed, revealing a matching pair of greyish-green kernels or beans. These are oval, slightly flattened and indented on their facing sides. When dried, these hard beans will keep almost indefinitely but the distinctive aroma and flavour of coffee is only released when they are roasted. Since the 17th century, coffee has been cultivated in the world's tropical regions in over 50 countries, with Brazil being by far the major exporter. There are more than 60 kinds of coffee tree but only a few have beans which are suitable for human consumption. The two main types are called *arabica* and *robusta* but the coffee itself is usually named after the country or region of production, or the town from which it is exported.

COFFEE CAKE
A light-textured North American cake, usually served while still warm with coffee but not necessarily containing coffee itself. In Britain it would be described as a plain cake.

COFFEE CREAM
See *Light Cream*.

COFFEE ESSENCE
See *Camp Coffee*.

COFFEE GRINDER
An implement used to grind whole coffee beans to a suitable fineness for coffee-making. Manual versions are usually made with a cast-iron grinding mechanism and most have a simple adjustment to regulate the fineness of the grinding. Electric versions speed up the process.

COFFEE KISSES
Small, meringue-type cakes containing ground hazelnuts or toasted almonds. They are generally sandwiched together in pairs with coffee butter cream.

COFFEE SUGAR
(Brown Coffee Sugar)
Small and irregular-shaped crystals of brown sugar.

COFFEE-BAGS
Similar to tea-bags, finely perforated bags containing ground coffee. One bag per cup is the usual recommended allowance.

COGNAC
A fine brandy from France produced in a limited region centred on the town of Cognac, just north of Bordeaux. It is a double-distilled spirit and accepted as the finest brandy in the world. It is 70° proof (40° GL) and the name 'Cognac' is protected by law; brandies produced outside the designated area may not use the name. Because of its high cost and quality, it should be used sparingly in exclusive dishes such as *pâté de foie gras*, creamy fish *bisques*, a limited number of desserts and confectionery such as chocolate truffles.

COHO SALMON
A member (*Oncorhynchus kisutch*) of the Pacific salmon family which is caught on the west coast of America from Alaska to Calfornia. The back is a metallic silvery-blue, shading to silver on the sides and underside. The average weight is 2–4.5 kg/4½–10 lb. The main season is June to November. The flesh is oily and pink or red (second only to sockeye salmon in intensity of colour) and the fish may be poached, steamed, baked, fried or grilled.

COKE
A colloquial term for Coca-Cola.

COLA
A reddish-brown, non-alcoholic drink made from a blend of essences and flavours to which water and sugar are added. The sweetness and aeration vary slightly in different countries to take account of national preferences.

COLA BEANS
(Cola Nuts, Kola Nuts)
African beans, the extract from which contains caffeine and other stimulants. The extract is red and used in the preparation of cola drinks.

COLA NUTS
See *Cola Beans*.

COLANDER
A perforated and usually bowl-shaped utensil for draining foods. The most practical are those with handles.

à la COLBERT
French term to describe a clear soup containing small pieces of mixed vegetables and poached eggs; also a classic sole dish.

COLBERT BUTTER
Named after Monsieur Colbert, who was a prime minister in Louix XIV's reign. It is softened, whipped butter to which parsley, lemon juice, tarragon and meat extract (such as Bovril) are added. It is shaped into a 2.5 cm/1 inch diameter roll, wrapped and refrigerated until hard,

then cut into rounds of about 5 mm/¼ inch in thickness. These are used to garnish grilled fish, steaks and thick slices of rare roast beef.

COLBI

(Kol-bee)

An Israeli cows' milk cheese which resembles Dutch Gouda.

COLBY

A North American cheese from Colby, in Wisconsin. It is mild to mellow in flavour and made from whole cows' milk, needing 1–3 months to ripen (mature). Colby is a popular, all-purpose cheese which resembles Cheddar, though it is slightly softer in consistency and more open in texture. Colby is deep yellowy-orange in colour and generally cylindrical and is either waxed, or divided into pieces and vacuum-packed.

COLCANNON

(Kolcannon)

An Irish dish, very similar to bubble and squeak, flavoured with chopped onions. Each portion is topped with grilled bacon rashers.

COLD COLLATION

A meal comprising a selection of cold dishes. Often the meal is light and allowed on fast days instead of lunch or supper. One Victorian reference describes it as 'signifiying merely a collection of cold foods'.

COLD CUCUMBER SAUCE

Mayonnaise to which chopped cucumber, chopped chives and parsley are added. It can be served with cold fish dishes.

COLD CUTS

A North American term for a selection of cold meats, usually bought from a delicatessen counter. The range could include roast beef, ham, corned beef, tongue and salami.

COLD TABLE

See *Open Table*.

COLD-SMOKING

A technique whereby foods are lightly smoked at approximately 50°C/85°F. It is a slow process used for salmon which is eaten raw, kippers which are poached or grilled, and gammon which is boiled or baked. Some sausages are also cold-smoked.

COLE

(Colewort)

Term applied to members of the cabbage family such as broccoli, Brussels sprouts, cabbage and cauliflower.

COLESLAW SALAD

(Slaw)

Finely shredded white (Dutch) cabbage combined with French dressing, soured cream, yogurt, mayonnaise or salad cream; sometimes a mixture of dressings is used such as yogurt with mayonnaise. Grated carrots and onions may be included, depending on personal taste.

COLEY

(Saithe, Coalfish, Pollock, Boston Bluefish)

A fish (*Pollachius virens*) of the cod family which is easily distinguished from other members by its darker colour, which varies from greenish-brown to charcoal. The interior of the mouth is also darkly coloured. It is as small as 10 cm/ 4 inches long when caught young, but can be 60–90 cm/2–3 feet when fully grown and may weigh as much as 6.75 kg/15 lb. It is caught in coastal waters on both sides of the North Atlantic all year round, with heavier catches in the winter months on the European side and in the summer months off Canada. The flesh is lean and darker than cod but lightens when cooked. The fish may be poached, steamed, baked or fried. Coley has a bewildering number of names, regionally, locally and depending on size when caught.

COLLAGEN
A fairly soft type of connective tissue in meat which becomes gelatinous and edible when cooked. It is an excellent source of protein.

COLLARD
(Collard Greens)
Term used for the green leaves of certain members of the cabbage family with a loosely-formed head, kale for example. The edible leaves of many root vegetables are also sold under this name.

COLLEGE CAKE
An old-fashioned, spiced fruit cake which contains caraway seeds.

COLLEGE PUDDING
An old-fashioned British steamed suet pudding containing mixed dried fruit, mixed chopped peel and spices.

COLLER (TO)
To give body to a mixture by adding dissolved gelatine.

COLLOP
A small slice of meat, usually thin and sometimes referred to as escalope; also a minced beef stew, generally from Scotland.

COLLOP (TO)
To cut meat or vegetables into small slices.

COLOGASSI
(Kolocassi)
A vegetable tuber (*Colocasia* species) which is cultivated in the Mediterranean region. It grows as a swollen root or corm which can weigh up to 1.75 kg/4 lb, sometimes with smaller corms attached. The shape of the main corm is roughly triangular but the smaller ones are irregular both in shape and size. The rough skin is light brown in colour and the flesh is white. The flavour is bland and the starchy flesh may be boiled or fried as a vegetable on its own or used in savoury dishes. Cologassi and similar tuberous species are known variously as dasheen, taro, coco and eddo, depending on type and region, and all should be boiled or baked to eliminate possible harmful chemicals. In most kinds the green leaves, often large, are also edible when cooked.

COLOMBIAN COFFEE
Colombia, the world's second largest coffee exporter after Brazil, is the leading grower of good quality *arabica* beans. The most popular kinds include Medellin, Armenia and Manizales. The finest of all is called Vintage Colombian and is among the best coffee in the world for flavour and aroma.

COLON
(Chaudin)
The large intestine, used in sausage-making.

COLOSTRUM
See *Beestings*.

COLOUR (TO)
To give colour to foods by the addition of food colourings, caramel, gravy browning, tea, coffee, chocolate, some herbs such as saffron, tomatoes, soft fruits and so on.

COLWICK
An English soft cheese, made from cows' milk. It is white, creamy-textured and smooth, with a mild, acidic tang.

COMBINE (TO)
To mix ingredients together.

COMFIT
(Confit, Confite)
A small sweetmeat. The word comfit is an old-fashioned one, derived from the French word *confit* which means confected or prepared. This in turn can be traced back to the Latin *conficere*.

ÇÖMLEK KEBABI
A Turkish lamb and mixed vegetable casserole, traditionally served with boiled potatoes or *pilav*.

COMMIS
A junior chef in a restaurant.

COMMON CRAB
(Edible Crab)
A member (*Cancer pagurus*) of the family of crustaceans and the only crab regularly caught for human consumption in British coastal waters and found from Norway to Spain, though rarely in the Mediterranean. The fan-shaped upper shell can be over 20 cm/8 inches at its widest span and on each side of the mouth there is a large claw with four legs ranged behind it round the shell. The colour of the shell, which is shed at regular intervals to allow for growth, is a mottled brown. It is caught all year round with heaviest catches in the summer months. The meat is lean and the crab, after being killed, is boiled whole. When cold, the edible meat is removed from the shell and used as required.

COMMON MUSHROOM
(Cultivated Mushroom)
A mushroom (*Agaricus bisporus*) which has been cultivated for hundreds of years and is now available all year round. It has a cap which is white on top and brown underneath. It is the mushroom used in almost every British recipe which does not specify a variety. The common mushroom is sold in three categories. The button mushroom is the youngest, picked before the head has opened to reveal the brown underside. The next stage is the cup mushroom, when the head has half opened and the brown underside is visible. When mature and fully open it is called a flat mushroom. The flavour of the common mushroom is mild and pleasant but somewhat bland when compared to the wild varieties.

COMMON PRAWN
See *Prawn*.

COMMON ROOM FOOD
Food served to students at their school or college.

COMPÔTE
French term for stewed fruit, usually served cold.

COMTÉ
A French version of Gruyère cheese, produced from cows' milk in Franche-Comté. It has a long history, is widely respected, and is used both for cooking and as a dessert cheese.

CONA COFFEE
See *Vacuum-method Coffee*.

CONCASSER
French term meaning to chop up coarsely. It is most commonly applied to tomatoes, which are usually first skinned and deseeded.

CONCENTRATED BUTTER
Sporadically available in Britain, economically priced concentrated butter is similar to solidified clarified butter and is almost entirely free of water. It is recommended for shallow-frying, basting and cake-making, when only three-quarters of the weight shown in the recipe should be used. To balance the absence of water, a little extra milk or egg should be added to cake mixtures. Concentrated butter should not be used for shortbread.

CONCH
A large, boneless sea snail with a spirally coiled shell. It is found in the Gulf of Mexico and the Atlantic in the region of Florida and is an important part of the diet for the islanders in the Caribbean. Conch can also be found along the Pacific coast of Central America. The flesh is generally tough and needs tenderising by pounding or marinating.

CONCH SHELLS
See *Conchiglie*.

CONCHIGLIE
Seashell-shaped pasta which may be plain or patterned (ridged). A literal translation of the Italian name is 'conch shell'.

CONCHIGLIETTE
Small pasta shells used in soup.

à la CONCORDE
French term referring to a garnish of mashed potatoes, peas and carrots.

CONDÉ
A classic French dessert, made from a thick and very creamy rice pudding mixture, topped with canned or poached fruit and glazed with melted jam. It is usually served well chilled in glass dessert dishes, decorated with whipped cream.

CONDENSED MILK
(Sweetened Condensed Milk)
The milk is treated in much the same way as evaporated milk, but is then sweetened with approximately 40% sugar, which acts as a preserving agent. The thick, very sweet and creamy milk is canned but not necessarily sterilized. It may be used in tea, coffee and hot chocolate straight from the can, but should not be given to babies without medical advice. When diluted as directed, condensed milk may be used in cooking and can also be used undiluted as a spread on bread or toast. There is now a skimmed-milk version.

CONDIMENT
A flavour enhancer such as salt and pepper.

CONE
See *Cornet*.

CONFECTION
A sweetmeat or rich and fancy dish.

CONFECTIONER'S CUSTARD
(Crème Pâtisserie, Crème Pâtissière, Custard Cream, Pastry Cream)
A fairly thick, golden filling for cakes, flans and pastries (cream buns and éclairs, for example) made from an egg custard sauce thickened with flour. It is usually flavoured with vanilla and used cold.

CONFECTIONER'S SUGAR
North American term for icing sugar.

CONFITURE D'ORANGES
French term for orange marmalade.

CONGER EEL
A marine eel (*Conger conger*) which differs from the common eel in that the dorsal (back) fin starts much nearer the head. The long, scaleless, serpentine body is also much larger. The back colour varies with the habitat of the eel, but is generally brown to dark slate lightening to a silvery underside. The male is sold at about 1 metre/39 inches and the female at 1.5–2 metres/5–6½ feet long. The European species is caught, during spring to autumn, from Iceland to the Mediterranean and various close relatives are found on rocky coasts in other parts of the world and are popular in South American and Japanese cookery. The flesh is oily, rather coarse but well-flavoured, and the fish may be poached, baked or fried. In Britain the conger eel is usually sold in cutlets.

CONGOU
General name for the principal black teas of China which are exported to the West. Congous from northern China were once widely used in the Breakfast Blends popular in the West, but are now being replaced by Assam. One of the finest of the northern Chinese Congous is called Keemun. Congous from southern China are high-quality teas with a lighter flavour and not as well known outside the Far East.

CONKIES
(Paimi)
A sweet or savoury cornmeal and coconut mixture from the Caribbean which is wrapped in plantain or banana leaves and steamed.

CONNECTIVE TISSUE
Another term for gristle (cartilage) which is found round muscle fibres in meat. It looks like a fine, silvery and glistening coating on the outside of a piece of meat or, when the meat is cut, shows up as a distinct white-coloured line. When cooked, the cartilage or gristle becomes gelatinous in behaviour and appearance and loses its whiteness. It is an excellent source of protein.

CONSERVE
A fruit and sugar preserve which includes jam, marmalade and fruit jelly such as quince.

CONSISTENCY
A term used to describe the density of a mixture. This can be thick or thin, heavy or light, stiff-dropping or soft-dropping (for cakes), smooth or lumpy, slack or firm, runny or solid, syrupy or jam-like, buttery or milky, etc.

CONSOMMÉ
French term for a clear soup based on meat, poultry, fish or vegetable stock.

à la CONTI
French term for a garnish of boiled bacon and lentil purée for joints of meat.

CONTINENTAL BREAKFAST
A light breakfast consisting of fruit juice or a piece of fruit, rolls or croissants, bread, toast, butter, jam, marmalade and tea, coffee or chocolate.

CONTINENTAL MUSTARD
See *Prepared Mustard*.

CONTINENTAL ROAST
Term used by coffee blenders to indicate a strongly flavoured, well-roasted blend reflecting the tastes of Continental Europeans. It is often drunk black after dinner, or for breakfast with milk.

CONTRE-FILET
See *Faux-Filet*.

CONVENIENCE FOODS
Time-saving foods or meals which require minimal preparation and cooking. They are available frozen, chilled, canned, in packets or in boil-in-the-bag sachets. Many are designed for microwave cooking.

COO-COO
(Cou Cou)
A Caribbean side-dish for fish which is a speciality of Barbados. It is made from cornmeal, okra and water and resembles thick mashed potatoes. Sometimes breadfruit is used instead of cornmeal and the *coo-coo* is generally served with boiled or fried flying fish.

COOK (A)
Someone who prepares food for eating.

COOK (TO)
To make food edible, often by subjecting it to heat.

COOK OUT
North American term to describe a meal cooked outdoors; also the meal itself.

COOKBOOK
(Cookery Book)
A book of instructions on preparing food.

'COOKED' CHEESE
A hard and fairly dry cheese, made by cooking the curds in the whey before draining.

COOKED SAUSAGES
See *Kochwurst*.

COOKER
An apparatus or appliance for cooking food, typically consisting of an oven, hot plates or rings, a grill and sometimes a rotisserie. Cookers can be operated by gas, electricity or solid fuel. In a modern fitted kitchen the hot plates or rings are often set into a separate unit, known as a hob.

COOKERY
The art or practice of cooking.

COOK-GENERAL
Someone who works for a family as cook/housekeeper; some cleaning duties are involved.

COOKIE
(Cooky)
North American term for a biscuit; also Scottish term for a plain bun.

COOKING APPLE
See *Apple*.

COOKING FAT
Usually a white, bland and unsalted fat made from refined vegetable oils. Some are lightened or whipped-up in texture, making them easier to rub into dry ingredients or cream with sugar. Most cooking fats may also be used for frying.

COOK'S KNIFE
The sturdiest of kitchen knives with the heavy steel blade often continuing into the handle for extra strength. The cutting edge of the blade is straight nearest to the handle but then curves gently to meet the back edge of the blade in a point; this shape is useful for cutting and when chopping with a rocking motion. The handle should be almost as heavy as the blade since this gives a good balance to the knife and makes it easier to use.

COOL (TO)
To reduce the temperature of hot food either by leaving it to cool in the kitchen or (to hasten the operation) by standing the container in a sink filled with cold water. Sometimes, ice cubes may be added to the water as well. If ingredients are suitable, they may be cooled under cold running water or refrigerated.

COOLGARDIE SAFE
An Australian container in which food is kept cool by the controlled evaporation of water.

COOLING JUG
A jug that keeps drinks cool by means of ice fully enclosed in an inner compartment, thus avoiding dilution of the drink with melting ice.

COON
A strong, North American Cheddar made from cows' milk.

COPPA
(Sopressa)
In Italy, this refers to a salted pork sausage from Corsica, which is always dried and smoked with herbs and served cut into thin slices. In France, *coppa* usually refers to a large sausage containing pieces of shoulder pork and pork fat, cut from a pig which has been fed on chestnuts. In appearance the *coppa* is distinctly marbled.

COPPER
A mineral which, in small amounts, is necessary in the diet so that iron can function efficiently and prevent anaemia.

COPPER PANS
Expensive and requiring frequent cleaning and polishing, these are used more by professional chefs than domestically. They are excellent conductors of heat. The inside of the pans is generally lined with a layer of tin to stop the copper coming into direct contact with the food. This is especially important if the latter contains an acid which could cause a poisonous reaction.

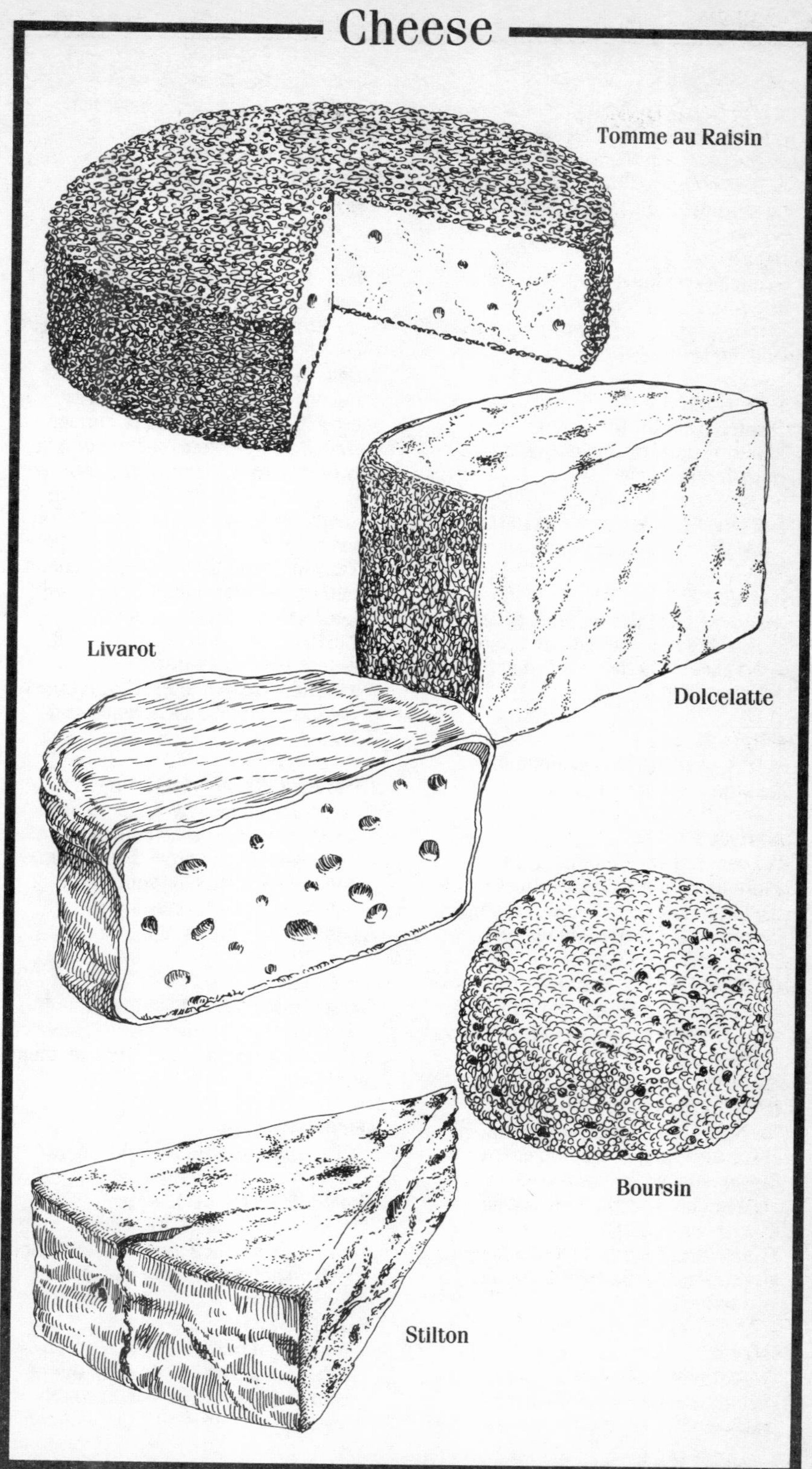

Cheese
Tomme au Raisin
Livarot
Dolcelatte
Boursin
Stilton

COQ AU VIN
A classic French chicken stew containing dry red wine, onions, garlic, bacon, mushrooms, herbs and seasonings. The stew should be accompanied by boiled potatoes.

COQUE
French term for a scallop or other sea-shell; also a yeasted *brioche*-type cake containing citron and made for Easter.

en COQUILLE
French term for food cooked in scallop shells or in shell-shaped, heat-resistant dishes.

COQUILLES SAINT-JACQUES
French term for scallops.

CORAL
The ovaries of the lobster, which turn red when cooked and are often the basis of a sauce served with lobster dishes.

CORDIAL
A fruit syrup or a non-alcoholic sweetened fruit drink.

CORDON BLEU
A French term meaning 'blue ribbon', which refers to a distinctive and fine class of cooking, very much based on French *haute cuisine*.

CORDON BLEU COOK
Someone who has been trained in top-class cookery and in the style of *Cordon Bleu*.

CORE (TO)
To remove the centre of fruit such as apples, pears or quinces, by means of a sharp, thin knife or patent corer without otherwise cutting or damaging the rest of the fruit. If fruit is quartered before coring, the cores can be cut away afterwards.

CORER
(Vegetable Parer)
An implement comprising a wooden handle with a curved blade for removing the cores or centres of fruit and vegetables; one version has a cutting ring at the tip.

CORIANDER
(Chinese Parsley)
Fresh coriander (*Coriandrum sativum*) looks like unwrinkled leaves of vivid green parsley and is much used in eastern Mediterranean, Asian and Japanese cookery. It is now available in Britain and its unusual but subtle flavour is growing in popularity, especially when added to curries. Dried, ripe seeds of coriander are exported from North Africa, the Balkans and South America. The seeds are relatively small and range in colour from white to dark yellow. They are available whole or ground and the flavour resembles grated lemon peel mixed with sage. Coriander is used in curry powder and mixed pickling spice. When ground, it also makes a pleasing flavouring for cakes, breads and biscuits.

CORKSCREW GREENS
A term used in New England, in the USA, for edible ferns known as 'fiddleheads' because they resemble the top of a fiddle or violin.

CORN
See *Maize*.

CORN BREAD
Popular North American bread made with cornmeal, which is deep yellow in colour.

CORN CHIPS
See *Tortilla Chips*.

CORN FRITTERS
North American fritters containing sweetcorn which are deep-fried and served hot with chicken Maryland.

CORN OIL
An extract of maize (corn) and a light, golden and delicately-flavoured oil which can be used for frying, salad dressings, mayonnaise

and in baking. It is high in polyunsaturated fatty acids and therefore recommended for those on a low-cholesterol diet.

CORN SALAD
See *Lamb's Lettuce*.

CORN SYRUP
(Light Corn Syrup, Light Syrup)
A syrup containing sugar compounds (maltose and dextrose, for example) obtained by partial hydrolysis of maize meal. It is also a North American term for golden syrup.

CORNCRAKE
(Landrail)
A small migratory game bird (*Crex crex*) which returns to Britain from Africa in May, although it is not ready to eat until September. It nests in long grass and is noted for its somewhat harsh and grating nocturnal noises. Corncrake is roasted and served with bread sauce.

CORNED BEEF
(Bully Beef)
Brisket, or sometimes silverside, of beef which is left to soak for 8–12 days in a solution of salt, bicarbonate of soda, sugar and saltpetre (sodium nitrate); it is then rinsed and boiled. The saltpetre turns the meat a characteristic red colour. Canned corned beef is prepared in the same way but is pressed, packed into tins and then sterilized at a high temperature.

CORNED BEEF HASH
A North American speciality consisting of coarsely mashed potatoes, chopped corned beef and onions formed into a thick cake and then fried. Each portion is usually topped with a poached egg and accompanied by toast and chilli sauce.

CORNER GAMMON
A small, triangular-shaped joint which is lean and economical. It should be boiled and can be eaten hot or cold.

CORNET
(Cone)
Cone-shaped wafer in which scoops of ice cream are placed.

CORN-FED CHICKEN
Chicken with yellow-coloured flesh, due to a diet of maize grains.

CORNFLAKES
One of the world's most popular breakfast cereals, made from crispened and toasted flakes of maize (corn).

CORNFLOUR
The pure starch of maize (corn), which is gluten-free and very finely milled, widely used in Britain since the time John Polson first discovered the way to extract it from maize kernels in the middle of the 19th century. It is the basis of blancmange powder and used as a thickener in gravies, sauces, stews and casseroles. When mixed with wheat flour, it produces a 'softer' flour which makes lighter than usual cakes and biscuits, and shortbreads with a soft crumb. Cornflour has minimal nutritional value.

CORNFLOUR SAUCE
A white sauce made by combining cornflour and milk, then heating it until boiling. A little butter or margarine is sometimes added at the end of the cooking time to enrich the flavour and improve the gloss. The sauce may be seasoned with salt and pepper; or sweetened with sugar. It can be made either as a thin or pouring sauce to add moisture to dry foods, or a thicker or coating sauce to cover foods and improve their appearance.

CORNHUSKER
A mild, Cheddar-related North American cheese shaped into blocks and waxed. It is produced in the Mid-West and is made from cows' milk.

CORNICHON
French term for gherkin.

CORNISH FAIRINGS
Crisp and spicy biscuits sweetened with brown sugar and syrup. They are enriched with butter and are a much appreciated 'export' from England's West Country.

CORNISH HEAVY CAKE
(Heavy Cake)
A flaky pastry cake based on lard and containing currants.

CORNISH PASTY
A speciality of the British West Country, originating in Cornwall, this is a pastry turnover with a fluted seam across the top. With its filling of meat and vegetables, it is considered a complete and convenient meal, ideal for taking to work and eating at lunch time.

CORNISH PEPPER
An English farmhouse cream cheese, produced in Cornwall from cows' milk. It is coated with cracked black peppercorns.

CORNISH SAFFRON CAKE
(Saffron Cake)
A fruited yeast cake flavoured with saffron. It is generally baked in a deep, round cake tin, then cut in slices when cold and spread with butter or margarine.

CORNISH SLY CAKES
(Sly Cakes)
Flaky pastry cakes from Cornwall, consisting of two layers of pastry sandwiched together with currants, chopped mixed peel, spice and sugar. The layers are rolled together until the currants just peep through 'slyly', then the pastry is cut into fancy shapes and arranged on baking trays. The tops are dusted with caster sugar before baking.

CORNISH SPLITS
Plain, round yeasted buns, generally split open and filled with clotted cream and jam.

CORNISH YARG
A creamy, English farmhouse cheese produced in Cornwall from cows' milk. It has a distinctive and fairly mild flavour. The cheese is generally covered with nettles.

CORNMEAL
Made from North American yellow or white maize (corn), *Zea mays*, this is a fine or coarse meal which can be yellow or cream-coloured, depending on the variety of corn. There is no difference in nutritional value between the two types and cornmeal is widely used in North America to make assorted breads. Sometimes some of the fibre is removed during processing.

CORN-ON-THE-COB
(Corncob)
A term for an ear of sweetcorn (maize) which is usually boiled and eaten with melted butter.

CORNSTARCH
North American term for cornflour.

COS LETTUCE
One of the main types of commercially grown lettuce, this is elongated and crisp with centre leaves which are lighter in colour and more tender than the tougher, outer leaves. The flavour and texture make it very suitable for green salads. Cos lettuce is also known as romaine in North America.

COSTMARY
A herb (*Chrysanthemum majus*) of the daisy and dandelion family which resembles tansy and is occasionally used in cooking.

COTECHINO
An Italian cooking sausage made from pork, pork fat and pork skin, mixed with white wine, spices and seasonings. It is a fresh sausage and should be eaten fairly soon after purchase. One sausage will serve 3–4 people and the casing is usually punctured before

simmering. It is generally served with polenta or lentils.

COTHERSTONE

A British cheese from Yorkshire made from unpasteurized cows' milk. It is white, loose-textured and has a clean, fresh flavour.

COTSWOLD

A British cows' milk cheese from Leicestershire. It is basically Double Gloucester flavoured with chopped chives and onions.

COTTAGE BUTTERS

Fresh butters produced in the traditional dairy farming areas of Britain: Devon, Cornwall and Wales. Welsh butter is the saltiest of the three and Devon butter particularly creamy. They are usually shaped into 250-g/9-oz rolls and wrapped in parchment.

COTTAGE CHEESE

A milky-tasting and low-fat soft cheese, very popular on both sides of the Atlantic. It is produced from pasteurized cows' milk or reconstituted skimmed milk powder to which small amounts of rennet may be added. The milk is then inoculated with a special culture (starter) and the final result is a loose-textured and mild cheese, made up of small white curds which are seasoned with salt. Sometimes, cottage cheese is enriched with single cream. There is also a very low-fat version.

COTTAGE LOAF

A round loaf with a knob on top, generally made from a white yeasted dough. It is baked on a greased baking tray and sometimes has a lop-sided appearance.

COTTAGE PIE

A typically British dish made from cooked minced beef and gravy, topped with a thick layer of creamed potatoes, then reheated and browned in the oven.

COTTO

A North American salami, made from pork and peppercorns.

COTTONSEED OIL

Made from the oily extract of cottonseeds and used fairly extensively by fish-canning industries.

COULIBIAC

(Koulibiak)

French term for a Russian fish pie filled with salmon, butter, rice and cream. Sometimes chopped hard-boiled eggs are added.

COULIS

French term for a thick purée of fruit or vegetables.

COULOMMIERS

See *Brie de Coulommiers*.

COUNTRY CAPTAIN

A North American chicken stew, based on an East Indian recipe, containing green pepper, onion, garlic, stock, curry powder, herbs, seasonings, raisins, tomatoes and almonds.

COUPE DISH

A small, goblet-shaped glass dish in which some cold desserts are served.

COUPES

There are a great number of classic coupes, all consisting of individual dishes of ice cream festooned with sauces, fresh and/or glacé fruits, nuts, whipped cream, crystallized flower petals and chopped jelly. Their classic names are similar to those used for cocktails in the 1920s.

COURGETTE

(Zucchini)

A vegetable (*Cucurbita pepo*) which is a small variety of the marrow family with a dark green skin. The flesh is crisp and watery and there is a central core of edible seeds. It usually has a milder, sweeter flavour than larger types of marrow, is best at about 10 cm/4 inches long and may be eaten raw or steamed, boiled, baked or fried. The terms *courgette* (French) and *zucchini* (Italian) are used interchangeably for these varieties of small marrow as there is no English equivalent.

COURSE
A part of a meal such as the main course or dessert course.

COURT-BOUILLON
French term for a well-flavoured fish stock, often containing wine, which is used both for poaching fish and for making classic fish sauces.

COUSCOUS
A North African cereal traditionally served with a lamb stew containing chick peas. It is made, basically, from semolina which is rubbed between dampened hands to form the tiniest of dumplings, about the size of seed pearls. Although still made by hand in its countries of origin, couscous is now available ready-prepared and packeted.

COUSCOUSIÈRE
An open steamer, used for cooking *couscous* over a pan of stew.

COUVE TRONCHUDA
See *Portugal Cabbage*.

COUVERTURE
French term for specially prepared chocolate used mainly by the catering trade for coating, icing or decorating confectionery.

COVENTRY CAKES
Jam-filled and sugar-glazed puff pastry triangles which are baked in a hot oven until golden and crisp. They originated in Coventry in Warwickshire.

COVENTRY GOD CAKES
Made in the same way as Coventry cakes but filled with mincemeat and traditionally eaten at Christmas.

COVER
Place setting for a person at table; a lid.

COVER CHARGE
An entrance or service charge made by a restaurant or night club in addition to the charge for food and drink.

COWBERRY
(Mountain Cranberry)
The fruit of a member (*Vaccinium vitisidaea*) of the cranberry family which grows wild in north-western America, northern Europe and in parts of north-east Asia.

COW-CUMBER
The name by which the cucumber was known until the 19th century. The term may still be found in old cookery and reference books.

COW-HEEL
Part of the foot of the cow or ox which is very gelatinous when cooked. Because of its size, a piece of cow-heel may be substituted for a whole calf's foot.

COZIDO
A Brazilian meat stew, similar to Portugal's *cozido à Portuguesa* or 'boiled dinner'.

COZIDO À PORTUGUESA
The literal translation is 'Portuguese boiled dinner'. This hearty meat stew, made from brisket, bacon knuckle, chicken, sausage, yams, mixed vegetables, cabbage, haricot beans and rice, is one of Portugal's national dishes. Some of the liquor is served separately as soup; the remainder is treated as gravy and poured over the meat and vegetables.

CRAB
See *Common Crab* and other individual entries.

CRAB APPLE
See *Apple*.

CRAB AU GRATIN
A typical dish from Louisiana in the USA, this is made from a *roux*-based white sauce to which soured cream, crabmeat and seasonings are added. It is transferred to a dish, topped with grated cheese and browned under a hot grill.

CRAB BACKS
A hot crab dish from the Caribbean made from crabmeat mixed with fried onions and tomatoes, Worcestershire sauce, vinegar and seasonings. The mixture is put into cleaned crab shells, dusted with breadcrumbs, dabbed with butter and browned in the oven.

CRAB BISQUE
A milky soup from Louisiana in the USA which is made from a *roux* base and usually contains fried onions, crabmeat, creamed sweetcorn, Tabasco, Worcestershire sauce and seasonings.

CRAB LOUIS
A famous Californian salad consisting of a bed of lettuce topped with crabmeat, then coated with Louis sauce, a mayonnaise resembling Thousand Island Dressing in flavour. The salad is garnished with wedges of hard-boiled egg and black olives.

CRABMEAT AND SWEETCORN SOUP
A Chinese soup which owes its unique texture and flavour to the canned cream-style sweetcorn. Crabmeat and spring onions are the other main ingredients. The delicate flavour is further enhanced by the addition of fresh ginger, sesame oil, soy sauce and sherry. When the soup is bubbling and hot, egg beaten with a little oil is added which forms lacy threads, giving the soup its characteristic appearance.

CRACKED WHEAT
See *Kibbled Wheat*.

CRACKERS
Fairly thin and almost flaky biscuits which are generally unsweetened. Sometimes they are flavoured with savoury items such as cheese or sesame seeds.

CRACKLING
See *Pork Crackling*.

CRANBERRY
(Bounceberry, Craneberry)
The fruit of an evergreen shrub (*Vaccinium* species) of the heather family, with various related species growing in suitably cool, marshy regions in Asia, North America and northern Europe. The size of the berry varies with the species and the cultivated North American kind (*V. macrocarpum*) is the largest, with a diameter of 1–2 cm/½–¾ inch. The colour when ripe is a bright wine-red and the quality in North America is judged by how well the berry bounces on a hard surface, hence its alternative name. Although too sharp and acid-tasting to be eaten raw, the cranberry can be used in many sweet and savoury dishes. It travels well and is sold fresh and frozen; also as canned and bottled sauce, juice and jelly. An autumn and winter fruit, the cranberry features in the festival of Thanksgiving, celebrated in the USA and Canada.

CRANBERRY SAUCE
A vivid red, sweet-sour sauce made from cranberries, water and sugar. It can be served with poultry, duck, goose and game.

CRANEBERRY
An old-fashioned English term for the fruit now know as the cranberry. The name is said to be a corruption of two words, crane and berry; crane because the pink cranberry blossom looks like the heads of cranes, and also because the cranes themselves greedily feast on berries.

à la CRAPAUDINE
French term for spatchcock, referring to chicken which is split down the centre, opened out and grilled flat.

CRAWFISH
(Spiny Lobster)
A seawater crustacean (*Palinurus* species) which looks like a lobster without claws. The colour is basically brown but with local variations, as the crawfish is found in temperate to warm seas in both hemispheres. The European crawfish is found in the Mediterranean and adjoining Atlantic waters as far north as the south-west coast of England. The flesh is lean and may be poached, baked, fried or grilled. The crawfish is also called spiny lobster and sometimes crayfish, but should not be confused with the small, clawed, freshwater crayfish which are so popular in Scandinavia.

CRAYFISH
A freshwater crustacean (*Astacus* species) which resembles a lobster but in most species is much smaller. It is found in rivers and lakes in many parts of the world and is particularly popular in Scandinavia where summer crayfish parties are one of the highlights of the year. The flesh is lean and may be boiled, steamed or fried or used in made-up dishes such as soups. In some countries, the USA in particular, the term crayfish is often used for all similar crustaceans both fresh and saltwater, with and without claws.

CREAM
(Dairy Cream, Real Dairy Cream)
Fat of the milk (butterfat) combined with water and a decreased proportion of the other milk constituents. By its very nature, cream is richer than milk with a much higher proportion of butterfat. It contains appreciable amounts of vitamin A, calcium, vitamins of the B group and protein, so it is nourishing as well as enjoyable. Single cream yields approximately 54 kilocalories per 25 ml/1 fl oz and double, 128 kilocalories.

CREAM (TO)
To beat an ingredient until it takes on the consistency of whipped cream; in cake-making to beat sugar and fat until light in colour and texture and the consistency of whipped cream.

CREAM BUNS
(Cream Puffs)
Irregular-shaped round buns made from choux pastry. When baked and cold, they are split and filled with sweetened whipped cream or confectioner's custard and the tops are either dusted with sifted icing sugar or coated with chocolate or coffee glacé icing.

CREAM CARAMEL
See *Crème Caramel*.

CREAM CHEESE
A soft and creamy-coloured cheese, made from the cream of cows' milk. It has a butterfat content averaging between 45% and 65%.

CREAM CRACKERS
Light, puffy and unsweetened biscuits made from flour, water and a little fat. They are usually eaten with butter and cheese at the end of a meal. Cream crackers are often served as a snack, either plain with mid-morning tea or coffee or sandwiched together in pairs with sweet or savoury fillings.

CREAM HORNS
Strips of puff pastry which have been wound round conical metal moulds and baked until golden-brown. The moulds are then removed and the cold pastries are filled with jam and whipped cream.

CREAM OF TARTAR
In chemical terms, cream of tartar is an acid, potassium tartrate. It occurs naturally on the inside of wine bottles in the form of a

crystalline substance referred to as crust. Also, used as a raising agent in cooking and often combined with bicarbonate of soda in the ratio of two to one.

CREAM PUFFS
See *Cream Buns*.

CREAM SLICES
See *Mille Feuilles*.

CREAM SODA
A soft drink which is carbonated, flavoured with vanilla and sweetened with sugar and/or substitute.

CREAM SOUP
Usually made from puréed vegetables, which have been enriched by cream.

CREAM TEA
Peculiar to Britain, cream teas are a speciality of the West Country and Channel Islands and generally consist of tea served with scones, thick cream and jam.

CREAMED CAKES
(Rich Cakes)
These are classed as rich cakes because the proportion of fat and sugar to flour is high and the allowance of eggs is one to every 50 g/2 oz of flour. As the ratio of fat, sugar and eggs to flour increases and more air is incorporated into the mixture, there is an automatic decrease in the amount of raising agent needed; thus many of the recipes for large creamed cakes require plain flour (instead of self-raising) with varying amounts of baking powder or, in some cases, none at all. It is the air, forced into the mixture during creaming, and the eggs which act as raising agents, lightening and 'lifting' the cakes as they bake. Creamed mixtures are used to make rich fruit cakes, Madeira-type cakes and Victoria sandwiches.

CREAMED COCONUT
Made from the coconut kernel, this is a popular additive in the Orient and is frequently thinned down with water to make coconut milk. It is available in blocks from supermarkets and Oriental grocers.

CREAMER
A can or pan for separating cream from milk.

à la CRÉCY
French term for any dish containing or garnished with carrots.

CREMA BEL PAESE
A processed version of Bel Paese cheese.

CREMA CATALANA
The Spanish version of *crème brûlée*.

CRÈME À L'ANGLAISE
(Crème Anglaise)
French term for custard sauce.

CRÈME AGNÈS SOREL
A French cream of chicken soup garnished with mushroom slices and tongue strips. The term *Agnès Sorel* is also used for a garnish of chopped fried mushrooms, small rounds of tongue and chicken mousse or rich *pâté*.

CRÈME BAVAROISE
(Bavarois)
A French dessert based on a mixture of jellied custard and whipped cream set in a mould, with additions and flavourings, according to taste.

CRÈME BEURRE
A rich French butter cream made by combining hot sugar syrup with egg yolks, allowing it to cool, then whisking the mixture into well-creamed butter. It has an excellent flavour, consistency and appearance. It may be used for icing and filling cakes.

CRÈME BRÛLÉE
Popular French dessert made from thick, rich egg custard baked slowly in individual dishes. The mixture is then chilled, sprinkled with sugar and caramelized under the grill before serving.

CRÈME CARAMEL
(Caramel Cream, Cream Caramel, French Flan)
Egg custard baked in a large dish or individual dishes containing a base layer of caramel. When chilled and turned out, the caramel flows down the side of the custard.

CRÈME CHANTILLY
French term for sweetened, whipped cream.

CRÈME DE CASSIS
A low-alcohol French liqueur made from blackcurrants. This dark-red, fairly sweet drink dates back to the 16th century and was originally produced by monks in Dijon. It is mixed with white wine to create the popular cocktail, Kir.

CRÈME DE MENTHE
A bright green or colourless sweet liqueur, strongly flavoured with peppermint or mint. It is fairly strong, about 52° proof (30° GL).

CRÈME FLEURETTE
French term for unsweetened, whipped cream.

CRÈME FRAÎCHE
Cultured thick cream with a delicate trace of sourness. It originated in France where, as in other parts of Europe and in the USA, it is used extensively in cooking. The *crème* is a stable product which can be brought to the boil without separating. It is available from some supermarkets and speciality shops and keeps fresh for about 2 weeks under refrigeration. It makes a good accompaniment to berry fruits and fruit salads. It is similar to soured cream.

CRÈME MOULÉE
French term for a baked egg custard which is served cold, either unmoulded or left in its dish.

CRÈME PÂTISSERIE
See *Confectioner's Custard*.

CRÈME PÂTISSIÈRE
(Crème Pâtisserie)
French term for confectioner's custard.

CRÈME RENVERSÉE
French term for *crème caramel* which has been unmoulded or 'reversed' on to a dish.

CREMET NANTAIS
A soft, white, unsalted cream cheese from Brittany in France. It is produced from cows' milk.

CREOLE
A North American cheese, made in Louisiana from cows' milk. It is produced like cottage cheese, but is unique in that it comprises one piece of curd in a pool of double cream. It is much appreciated in New Orleans.

à la CRÉOLE
French term for food containing rice and sometimes also tomatoes and peppers.

CRÉOLE CHRISTMAS CAKE
(Gâteau Noir)
A dark and rich cake from the Caribbean, brimming with dried fruits and alcohol including rum, brandy, port and cherry or orange liqueur. It is eaten at Christmas in Trinidad.

CRÊPE PAN
See *Pancake Pan*.

CRÊPERIES
French restaurants which specialize in pancakes.

CRÊPES
French term for pancakes, which are traditionally very thin and quite

large. They are made from white flour and may be rolled or folded with sweet or savoury fillings.

CRÊPES SUZETTE

French dessert consisting of pancakes, folded into triangles, which are simmered in a buttery orange sauce and flamed with brandy.

CRÉPINETTE

A French croquette which is wrapped in bacon, then grilled or fried. Also a fairly flat, small sausage.

CRESCENZA

A North Italian cows' milk cheese which is a type of Stracchino.

CRESS

A native herb (*Lepidium sativum*) of Iran which grows profusely almost everywhere. Its tiny leaves have a delicate flavour and, in Britain, it is usually grown with mustard (*Sinapis alba*), the seeds from which sprout small, green leaves of a similar size to cress. When both are grown together, the greenery is known as mustard and cress. It is used in salads and sandwiches and as a garnish.

CRETONS

Pork crackling. Also a pork dish from Quebec in Canada, usually served between slices of bread and butter. It consists of bacon crackling simmered with pork, onions, spices and seasonings until very soft. It is thickened with breadcrumbs and filled into dishes to set. It is related to French *rillettes*.

CREVALLE JACK

(Crevalle, Jack, Common Jack)

A deep-bodied seawater fish (*Caranx* species) which is found in tropical and sub-tropical waters around the world. The colour of the back is generally a bluish-green, lightening to a silvery underside which may have mottled yellow patches. There is a dark spot behind the eye on the edge of the gill cover. The average length is 30–50 cm/12–19 inches and the weight 1–3 kg/2¼–6½ lb. The flesh is oily and the fish may be baked, fried or grilled.

CRIMP (TO)

To score the skin of a large fish, to ensure even cooking and heat penetration; to pinch up the edges of a double-crust sweet or savoury pie both to decorate and seal; to run the prongs of a fork down an unpeeled cucumber so that, when sliced, there will be tiny flutes around the edge.

CRISPBREAD

A high-fibre, often whole-grain biscuit made from crushed rye or wheat. It is unsweetened, crisp, light brown in colour and frequently used as part of a calorie-controlled diet.

CRISPS

(Potato Crisps)

Wafer-thin slices of potato, deep-fried and either left plain or salted and flavoured. They are sold in packets, though some top hotels and restaurants make their own. Crisps are generally eaten as a snack.

CROAKER

A term to describe those fish which have the ability to make croaking noises through their air bladders. They are classed with similar fish which make drumming noises by similar methods (drum fish) and, between the two types, represent over 200 species caught in temperate and tropical waters. A typical example is the Atlantic croaker.

CROCK POT

A deep, round stoneware vessel with a removable inner bowl and a heating element that is used to cook food very slowly.

CROCKERY

Plates, dishes, cups and so on in which food and drink are served.

CROISSANTS
Traditional French and Belgian crescent-shaped breakfast rolls, made in the same way as puff pastry but with white yeasted dough. They are characteristically light, flaky and best served warm.

CROMESQUIS
A cork-shaped French croquette, wrapped in bacon, dipped in a coating of fritter batter and deep-fried.

CROOKNECK SQUASH
(Yellow Squash)
A vegetable (*Cucurbita* species) of the squash family native to America. It has a rough, yellow skin and an elongated shape, swollen at the end, with a curved, narrow neck. It is usually cooked and used as a vegetable on its own.

CROP
The pouch in a bird's gullet.

CROQUE MONSIEUR
(Croque M'Sieu)
A very popular French savoury consisting of sandwiches made from thinly sliced white bread with a filling of ham and Gruyère cheese. Each decrusted sandwich is cut into squares or triangles, dipped in egg and fried until golden. *Croque Monsieur* should be eaten while still very hot.

CROQUEMBOUCHE
An elaborate French cake, traditionally served at weddings. It is a tall pyramid of small, cream-filled choux pastry buns coated with caramel. It may be decorated with extra cream and glacé fruits. It has a combined soft and crisp texture, and a rough translation of the name is 'crisp in the mouth'.

CROQUETTE
A French speciality consisting of either minced cooked meat, poultry, fish or offal combined with mashed potatoes and/or breadcrumbs, herbs, seasonings, sometimes onions, then bound together with egg or stock. The mixture is usually shaped into 7.5-cm/3-inch 'corks' for meat and offal, rounds for fish mixtures, ovals for poultry and balls for vegetables. The *croquettes* are coated with beaten egg and breadcrumbs, and fried in deep fat until golden brown and crisp. They are eaten hot.

CROSNES
French name for the Chinese artichoke.

CROTTIN DE CHAVIGNOL
A French goats' milk cheese, produced by farmers in the Berry region. It is a very small cheese with a piquant flavour and hard texture.

CROUSTADES
French term for cases for holding pieces of cooked meat, poultry, offal, fish, game or vegetables in a savoury sauce. They are made in various sizes from hollowed-out pieces of bread, which are deep-fried until golden, or from baked pastry cases.

en CROUTE
French term used to describe meat or fish encased in pastry and then baked.

CROÛTONS
French term for small dice of toast or fried bread, added to soups or sometimes used as a topping or garnish.

CROWBERRY
The fruit of a shrub (*Empetrum nigrum*) which grows wild in some hilly regions of northern Europe. The skin is black and the fruit may be used as a substitute for the cranberry in cooked dishes.

CROWDIE
A type of Scottish cottage cheese, made from skimmed and unpasteurized cows' milk curdled by the addition of rennet. It usually has some cream mixed in with it and

should be eaten freshly-made. The flavour is mild. It is used to make Black Crowdie cheese.

CROWLEY
Somewhat similar to Colby, a North American cheese from Vermont. It is made from cows' milk, with a loose texture and a robust flavour.

CROWN ROAST OF LAMB
A lamb joint comprising two best end necks of chined meat, joined in such a way that the bones curve outwards and form a traditional crown. Stuffing may be put in the centre of the crown before roasting. Cutlet frills should be placed over the top of each bone before serving.

CRUDITÉS
French term for a selection of prepared, raw vegetables served with cold sauces, mayonnaise or well-seasoned soured cream. *Crudités* are usually served with apéritifs before a meal.

CRUET
Made up of matching containers for salt, pepper and mustard which are placed on the table and passed round. Generally speaking, the salt pot has one central hole and the pepper pot has several (although there may be variations from country to country); the mustard pot is either lidded or open and is presented with its own tiny spoon.

CRULLERS
A North American speciality, made from strips of pastry fried in deep hot fat or oil. They are drained thoroughly and eaten warm, dusted with icing sugar. The pastry is enriched with butter, eggs and sugar.

CRUMB CRUST
Term for a pie case made from crushed biscuits combined with melted butter or margarine and sugar. The mixture is usually pressed evenly over base and sides of dish or tin and is frequently used for cheesecake.

CRUMBLE (TO)
To rub a dry ingredient between fingers to reduce it to small, crumbly pieces. Also a fruit dessert topped with a crumbly mixture of flour, fat and sugar.

CRUMBS
See *Breadcrumbs*.

CRUMPETS
Round, fairly flat 'cakes' made from a yeasted batter and cooked in rings on greased griddles. They have a honeycomb texture giving their top surfaces a pitted appearance, caused by the action of yeast and heat. Crumpets are usually served freshly toasted and buttered.

CRUSHED CHILLIES
A commercial preparation made from dried and crushed chillies. It is quite hot and recommended for curries and Mexican-style dishes.

CRUSHED OATS
Crushed oats are groats which have been broken down.

CRUST
Outer, golden-brown covering on a loaf of bread; pie with a pastry topping.

CRUSTACEAN
Any one of a large class of mainly aquatic animals with a hard external skeleton (shell) encasing a soft body. Lobster, prawn and crab belong to this category.

CRYSTALLIZED FLOWER PETALS
Red rose, yellow primrose or mauve violet petals which are sugar-coated and used for decorative purposes.

CSIPETKE
Tiny but fairly heavy Hungarian 'dumplings' made by cooking pieces of egg noodle dough in water until *al*

dente. When drained, they are tossed in lard and served with *gulyás, pörkölt, tokány* or *paprikás*.

CUAJADA
A soft and creamy Venezuelan cows' milk cheese, frequently wrapped in banana leaves.

CUBE (TO)
To cut any food into small, square-shaped pieces resembling dice. Also a lump of sugar.

CUBE SUGAR
(Loaf Sugar, Lump Sugar, Sugar Cubes, Sugar Lumps)
White or brown sugar crystals compressed into blocks, cut into cubes and used for sweetening drinks such as tea or coffee.

CUCUMBER
A vegetable (*Cucumis sativus*) which is a member of the marrow family and native to Asia. It has been grown in India for over 3,000 years and was introduced to China some 2,000 years ago. It was also cultivated by the Greeks and is mentioned in the Bible. It was first grown in Britain in the 14th century, then went out of fashion and was re-introduced during the reign of Henry VIII. It became more popular over the next 100 years and, until the 19th century, was called 'cow-cumber'. The cucumber is the fruit of a creeping plant and the Western salad variety is tubular in shape, usually narrowing to a short 'handle' at the stem end. The skin of most kinds is thin, green or yellowy-green, may be smooth or rough and is generally ridged lengthwise. The flesh is very pale green in colour; crisp, refreshing, but very watery. There is a soft central core which may have edible seeds. Different varieties vary in length from a stubby 10 cm/4 inches to well over 30 cm/12 inches with a diameter of about 4 cm/1½ inches. Some types of cucumber are suitable for use in pickles but most are best eaten raw in a salad or on their own. They may also be cooked and used in some recipes.

CUCUMBER SAUCE
English term for the classic French Doria sauce.

CUISINE
French term for a manner or style of preparing food; also the food prepared.

CUISINE MINCEUR
French term for an elegant style of low-calorie French dishes for slimmers, created by the well-known chef Michel Guérard.

CUIT
French term for cooked, used to describe grilled rump, sirloin or fillet steak which is cooked through, known in Britain as well-done.

CULLEN SKINK
A Scottish dish made from a mixture of cooked and flaked Finnan haddock, boiled onions and mashed potatoes, butter, seasonings and milk, garnished with chopped parsley.

CULTIVATED MUSHROOM
See *Common Mushroom*.

à la CULTIVATEUR
French term meaning in farmer's style, denoting a dish cooked with mixed vegetables and pork or bacon.

CULTURE
(Ferment)
A group of bacteria specially developed to inoculate milk for the purpose of producing cheese and cultured milk products.

CULTURED BUTTERMILK
A processed buttermilk, sold in sealed cartons, made from skimmed milk to which an appropriate culture has been added. It makes a wholesome and refreshing drink and is sometimes available with added flavourings and sugar.

CUMBERLAND HAM
Traditional English ham from Cumberland, made from the back leg of a fairly large pig. It is preserved by being rubbed regularly and for a specific length of time with salt, saltpetre and dark sugar; this draws moisture out of the meat and the briny, liquid preserve is then reabsorbed into the ham via the skin. The ham is allowed to dry off in a shed, then further dried by being suspended from a rafter in a special ham loft for an average of 3 months. It acquires a strong and distinctive taste after maturation and is either boiled or baked before serving. The usual accompaniment is Cumberland sauce.

CUMBERLAND RUM BUTTER
The same as rum butter but flavoured with nutmeg.

CUMBERLAND SAUCE (COLD)
A piquant sauce made from red wine flavoured with orange, lemon, redcurrant jelly, onion, spices and seasoning. It is heated, strained and cooled before serving with cold meats, game and brawn.

CUMBERLAND SAUCE (HOT)
A piquant sauce made from a basis of port, thickened with cornflour and flavoured with orange, lemon, redcurrant jelly, mustard, cayenne pepper and other herbs and spices. It can be served with game, roast pork and offal.

CUMBERLAND SAUSAGE
An English sausage from Cumberland, made from coarsely ground pork, well seasoned with pepper and nutmeg. It is not linked in the usual way but consists of a long length of sausage which is shaped into a coil, cut into pieces and sold by weight. It can contain as much as 98% pork, but recipes vary according to different butchers and cereal is often added. Cumberland sausage may be fried or baked.

CUMIN GOUDA
A young Dutch Gouda cheese to which cumin seeds have been added.

CUMIN SEEDS
(Cummin)
Native to Egypt, cumin (*Cuminum cyminum*) also grows in Mediterranean countries, Iran and India. The seeds are the small, dried fruit of an annual plant of the parsley family and rarely reach more than 5 mm/¼ inch in length. Golden-brown in colour, the seeds have a flavour which resembles caraway. They are used either whole or ground in Mexican-style dishes, curries, sauerkraut, beef dishes and savoury cheese spreads.

CUMQUAT
See *Kumquat*.

CUP CAKES
Originally cooked in cups, nowadays these small golden-brown cakes are usually baked in individual bun tins or paper cake cases. They are sweet, light and flavoured according to taste.

CUP MUSHROOM
See *Common Mushroom*.

CURD
The thick casein-rich part of soured or cultured milk which separates from the whey. It is either used as food or turned into cheese.

CURD CHEESE
(Lactic Curd Cheese, Soft Cheese)
A soft white cheese, with a low or medium fat content, formed by the action of lactic acid on the protein called casein in milk. A starter culture is mixed with cows' milk and the milk coagulates when the required degree of acidity has been reached. It is a pleasant eating cheese and frequently used for making cheesecake.

CURD CHEESE PASTRY
A Central European pastry made from equal quantities of curd cheese, butter or firm margarine and plain flour. When baked, it is golden, puffy and finely-flavoured and may be used instead of flaky pastry for sweet or savoury dishes.

CURDLE (TO)
To cause a mixture to separate into curds and whey (junket or cheese, for example) by the addition of an ingredient known to have a curdling effect, such as rennet; to cause a creamed mixture of sugar and fat to separate by adding eggs too quickly; to cause some sauces to separate by allowing them to boil after eggs have been added; to overcook a Hollandaise sauce until it separates; to add oil too quickly to a mayonnaise mixture, which causes it to separate.

CURDS AND WHEY
A term to describe soured milk or junket which separates into solids and liquid.

CURE (TO)
To treat meat, poultry and game by salting and/or smoking, which are reliable methods of preservation. Parma ham, for example, is salted and air-dried but unsmoked; the Westphalian and Ardennes hams are salted and smoked. The curing process may be mild or strong.

CURLY ENDIVE
See *Endive*.

CURLY KALE
See *Kale*.

CURRANTS
Dried grapes of the small black Corinth seedless variety, originally from Greece and now cultivated in other areas such as California. Currants have a tart taste compared with raisins and sultanas and may be used in baking and cooking where excessive sweetness is not required from the fruit.

CURRIES
Oriental or Indian dishes made from meat, poultry, fish or vegetables flavoured with curry powder and other hot or aromatic Oriental spices and herbs. Curries can be mild or fiery, depending on type, and are generally accompanied by rice, chutneys and *sambals*.

CURRY BUTTER
Softened, whipped butter to which curry powder, cayenne pepper, ginger and lemon juice are added. It is shaped into a 2.5 cm/1 inch diameter roll, wrapped and refrigerated until hard, then cut into rounds of about 5 mm/¼ inch in thickness. These are used to garnish grilled chicken, grilled meats and grilled lobster halves.

CURRY LEAVES
Small and green, curry leaves grow on trees (*Murraya koenigii*) native to Asia and are a popular addition to curries. With a mild but distinctive taste and aroma, the leaves are easy to find in the Orient where they grow profusely and are mostly used fresh. In the West they are sold dried, either as leaves or ground to a powder. Easily crumbled in the fingers, curry leaves may be used to flavour marinades, savoury rice dishes and chicken stews.

CURRY MAYONNAISE
English term for caboul sauce.

CURRY POWDER
A blend of spices, the formula for which varies according to the manufacturer. Although originating from India, curry powder as sold in the West is not used by Indian cooks, who prefer to make up their own blends from personally chosen herbs and spices. However, a good selection of commercial curry powders is available; these may be mild, medium, hot or very hot.

CURRY SAUCE
A fairly hot, Anglo-Indian sauce made from fried vegetables, tomato

purée, curry powder, herbs, spices and stock or water. It is thickened with flour or cornflour and sometimes flavoured with apple, coconut and raisins. It can be served with meat, poultry, eggs and fish.

CURWORTHY
An English farmhouse cheese, prepared from a West Country recipe which dates back three centuries. It is made from unpasteurized cows' milk, is left to mature for 6 weeks, and is relatively hard with a distinctive flavour.

CUSK
North American term for the tusk.

à la CUSSY
French term for a garnish of large mushrooms, chestnuts, cock's kidneys and truffles, usually used for steaks and roast chicken.

CUSTARD
A typically British sauce made from milk, sugar and packeted custard powder. It can be used for exactly the same dishes as custard sauce.

CUSTARD APPLE
(Bullock's Heart)
The fruit of a tree (*Anona reticulata*), native to Central America, but now cultivated in many tropical parts of the world. As with most of the fruit in this family, the size and colour vary. The yellow-to-brown skin, with its fir-cone-like pattern, darkens as it ripens, sometimes turning black. The sweet flesh is creamy-coloured, studded with black seeds, and of a thick custard-like consistency. It is scooped out of the open skin and eaten raw or used with other ingredients. Related species of the custard apple family include the cherimoya, sweet sop, sour sop and atemoya. The fruits have seeds in the flesh but they are loosely embedded and easily removed. As the skin of the species is delicate, they are only available in cans in many parts of the world.

CUSTARD BANANA
The fruit of a tree (*Asimina tribola*) native to south-eastern North America, of the same family as the custard apple, and seldom exported. It is an elongated, cylindrically shaped berry with a thin skin which is browny-black when the fruit is fully ripe and fit to eat. The average length is about 10 cm/4 inches. The seed-studded flesh, pale yellow and tasting like bananas crushed in custard, is best eaten on its own. Sometimes called pawpaw locally, it should not be confused with the more widely known fruit of that name (*Carica papaya*).

CUSTARD CREAM
See *Confectioner's Custard*.

CUSTARD POWDER
A yellow powder, based on cornflour, created by Bird's in the mid-19th century. It becomes custard when boiled with milk and sugar and is one of Britain's most popular sauces.

CUSTARD SAUCE
A heated sauce made from milk, eggs and sugar, sometimes flavoured with essence such as vanilla or grated citrus rind. It should never be allowed to boil but merely warmed over hot water until it thickens sufficiently to coat the back of a spoon. If overcooked, it quickly turns into scrambled eggs. It can be served, warm or cold, with fruit pies, flans, tarts, baked or steamed puddings, soufflés or canned and fresh fruit. It is the traditional topping in Britain for a trifle.

CUT (TO)
To use a knife or scissors to divide food into pieces.

CUT AND FOLD (TO)
To add dry ingredients to a thick, foamy mixture of whisked eggs and sugar by sprinkling them on top and gently working them in using a spatula or metal spoon.

CUT IN (TO)
To add butter, margarine or fat to dry ingredients and cut it into the mixture with a knife until all the little pieces are well-coated with the dry ingredients. This often precedes rubbing-in with finger-tips. See Rub-in (to).

CUT-AND-COME-AGAIN CAKE
Usually a fairly plain cake, sometimes containing dried fruit, to which the family help themselves whenever they fancy a piece of home-made cake, hence the name.

CUTLET
Usually refers to a piece of meat with bone, such as a chop.

CUTLET FRILL
See *Frill*.

CUTLET OF LAMB
Term used in the Midlands in Britain for best end neck of lamb.

CUTLET OF VEAL
An average-size chop cut from the neck end of the loin of the animal and containing a curved bone. It is suitable for frying, grilling or stewing.

CUTTERS
(Pastry Cutters)
Assorted-sized hollow outlines of rings, oblongs, ovals and squares, either fluted or plain, made from metal or plastic and used to cut pastry, biscuit, scone and yeasted mixtures, almond paste and so on. Other available shapes include hearts, diamonds, spades, clubs, gingerbread men, toys and numbers.

CUTTLEFISH
A member (*Sepia officinalis*) of the cephalopod group of molluscs (which includes the squid family), the cuttlefish has an oval body with an internal shell or bone. It has two long tentacles and eight 'arms' which sprout from the head. It can reach up to 25 cm/10 inches in length and has variable colouring. This cuttlefish is caught in the Mediterranean and on the Atlantic coasts of western Europe and Africa. The flesh is lean and may be poached, steamed, baked or fried.

CYANOCOBALAMIN
See *Vitamin B_{12}*.

CYMLING
See *Pattypan Squash*.

DAB
A flatfish (*Limanda limanda*) caught in the inshore waters of north-west Europe as far as the White Sea to the north, and France to the south. The main season is the autumn. The average size is 25 cm/10 inches and the upper side is mainly brown with greenish spots. The flesh is white and lean and dabs may be baked, fried and grilled. This fish is more popular on the mainland of Europe than in Britain.

DACCA
An Indian cheese made from cows' or buffaloes' milk or a blend of both. It is ripened for 2–3 weeks in wicker baskets and then smoked.

DACE
A freshwater fish (*Leuciscus leuciscus*) which resembles a small haddock in shape. It has a silvery body and the flesh, which contains many bones, is lean. Dace may be steamed or fried.

DACQUOISE
A layered cake made from meringue containing toasted and coarsely ground hazelnuts or walnuts. The layers are sandwiched together with whipped cream and

berry fruits such as raspberries or sliced strawberries. The top is covered with more cream and fruit and the cake is cut into wedges for serving.

DAHI
The Indian name for yogurt.

DAIKON
(Mooli, Rettich, White Radish)
Variety of radish (*Raphanus sativus*) widely used in Oriental cooking. It originated in Japan, but is now generally available in the West. Daikon is a tapering tuber of up to 30 cm/12 inches in length and 7.5 cm/3 inches across at the widest part. The thin skin and crisp flesh are white and the flavour is less pungent than that of the smaller red-skinned radishes. It can be eaten raw in salads as well as in many cooked Oriental dishes.

DAIRY
Of or concerned with the production of milk or milk products.

DAIRY PRODUCTS
General term for milk products such as butter, cream and cheese.

DAIRY SPREADS
Mixtures of buttermilk and oil, or cream and oil. Most taste of butter and can be spread straight from the refrigerator.

DALIA
Romanian cows' milk cheese which is a version of Kashkaval.

DAMPER
Unleavened bread from Australia and New Zealand, made from flour and water and frequently baked in the ashes of a fire or barbecue.

DAMSON
A species of plum which is the fruit of a tree (*Prunus damascena*) of the rose family. It is believed that the damson was first cultivated in the Middle East, probably Syria, and it is now widely grown in gardens as well as on a commercial basis. It is oval in shape and about 2.5 cm/1 inch in length. The skin is tough, blue-black and sometimes has a delicate bloom. The flesh is yellowish-green and there is a central oval stone. The damson is too sharp in flavour to eat raw but it is very suitable for preserves and cooked dishes.

DANBO
A firm Danish cheese, made from cows' milk and allowed to mature for about 5 months. It is flattish and square, the colour is creamy and the texture is firm and interspersed with a sprinkling of regularly-shaped holes. Mild-flavoured Danbo frequently contains caraway seeds and its deep cream-coloured rind is covered with a coating of red or yellow wax.

DANDELION
A plant (*Taraxacum officinale*) which grows wild all over Europe and Scandinavia. The leaves can be used in salads or as a vegetable and the root can be cleaned, dried and roasted and made into a natural coffee substitute without caffeine.

DANGO
A Japanese dumpling.

DANISH BLUE
(Danablu)
A 20th-century cheese, this is produced from cows' milk in 3 kg/6½ lb pieces. It is a whitish, crumbly cheese, streaked with distinct blue veins. The flavour is quite sharp and often salty.

DANISH BLUE BRIE
An imitation of French Brie cheese, this Danish version is threaded with blue veins and covered with a soft, white, edible crust.

DANISH BLUE CRÈME
A fairly new dessert cheese from Denmark, shaped like an ingot. It comprises layers of Danish Blue,

interspersed with cream cheese. It is both mild and piquant at the same time, and is produced from cows' milk.

DANISH MELLOW BLUE
A cheese almost identical to Danish Blue but somewhat more mellow and creamy-textured. It is produced from cows' milk.

DANISH PASTRY
A yeasted version of puff pastry which is used to make Danish pastries.

DANSK LEVERPOSTEJ
Danish liver pâté made from calf's liver, flour, cream, egg, onion, butter and seasonings. It is very rich and is either served warm with boiled potatoes or cut into slices when cold and used as a topping for open sandwiches.

DANSKA WIENERBRØD
The literal English translation is Danish Vienna Bread. These are the internationally known Danish pastries, made from a yeasted, buttery pastry and shaped into pinwheels or snails, crescents, stars and cockscombs. They are Denmark's best known speciality.

DARIOLE MOULDS
Small, bucket-shaped moulds used for making such dishes as caramel creams, madeleines and castle puddings.

DARJEELING
One of the finest of black Indian teas. It is grown high in the foothills of the Himalayas and has a very distinctive flavour. As an unblended tea it is highly regarded and supply seldom matches demand; the USSR is a major importer of this very expensive tea. It may be drunk after dinner as an alternative to coffee and makes a good accompaniment to Indian food.

DARK SUGAR
General term for brown sugar.

DARTOIS
French term for a piece of sweet or savoury puff pastry baked with a filling enclosed; also a meat garnish of celery, carrots, turnips and potatoes.

DASHEEN
A vegetable tuber (*Colocasia* species) native to Africa and widely cultivated in tropical and sub-tropical regions. It grows as a cluster of swollen roots with light brown skins and white flesh. The flavour is bland and the starchy flesh may be cooked as a vegetable on its own or used in savoury dishes. Dasheen and similar tuberous species are known variously as taro, eddo, coco and cologassi, depending on type and region, and all should be boiled or baked to eliminate possible harmful chemicals. In most kinds the green leaves, often large, are also edible when cooked.

DASHEEN LEAF
(Arvi Leaf)
The green leaf of a tropical and sub-tropical tuber known as dasheen (*Colocasia* species). It resembles a Japanese fan in appearance and is one of the main ingredients in the callaloo soup or stew of the eastern Caribbean. It should not be confused with the spinach-like callaloo vegetable (*Aramanthus* species) which is used in the traditional pepperpot soup of Jamaica.

DASHI
A Japanese stock made from kelp (seaweed) and bonito flakes.

DATE
The fruit of an evergreen tree (*Phoenix dactylifera*) native to the Middle East, now cultivated along the North African coast and as far east as India, with some cultivation in parts of North America. The date is an elongated fruit and averages about 4 cm/1½ inches in length. The skin colour on the tree is yellowish but by the time it is sold,

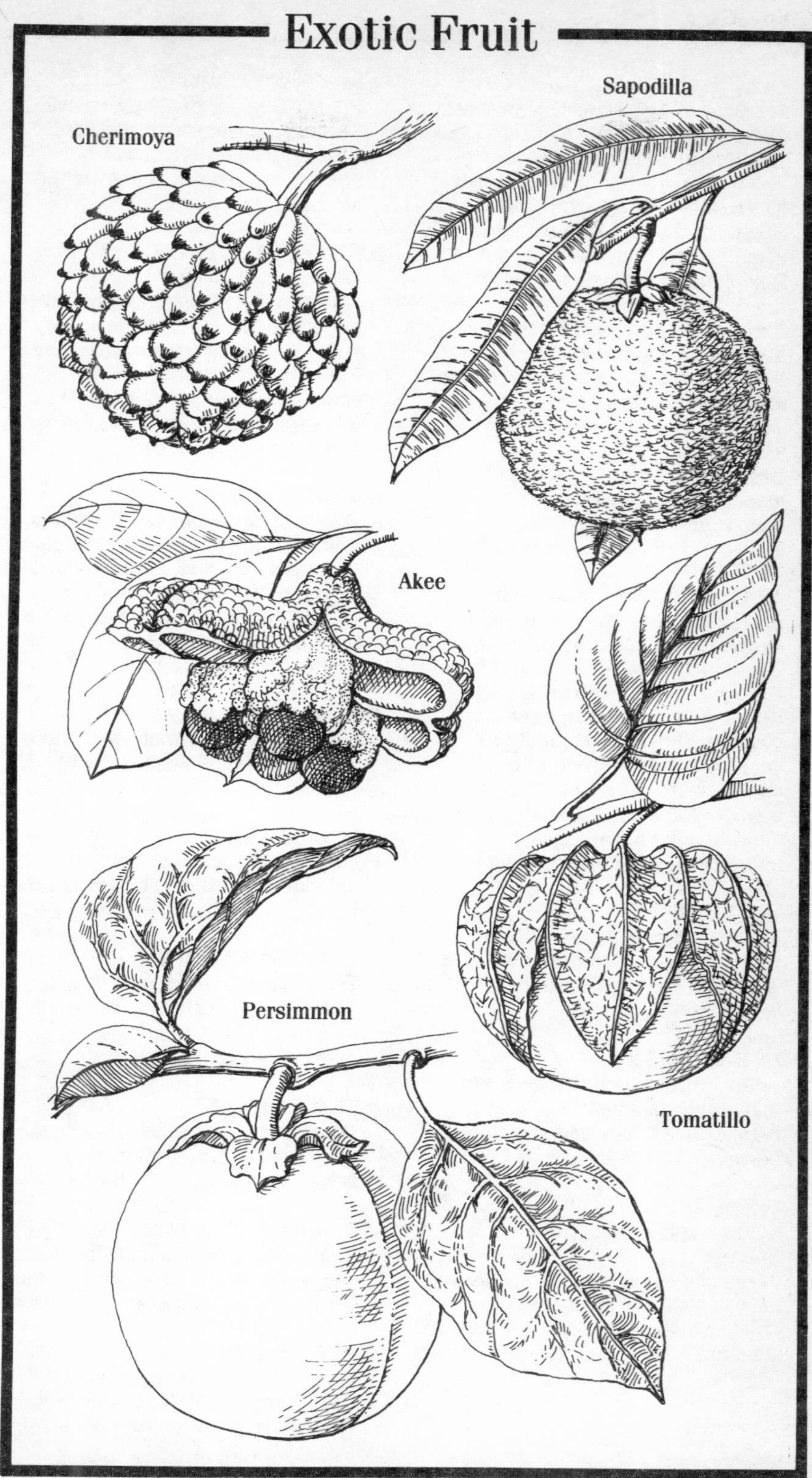
Exotic Fruit
Cherimoya
Sapodilla
Akee
Persimmon
Tomatillo

either fresh or dried, it is brown. The flesh is also brown, very sweet and contains a single elongated and slender stone. Fresh dates may be eaten with or without the thin skin which slides easily away from the ripe flesh. Exported dates are usually dried or semi-dried, but the fresh kinds are becoming more readily available in many countries. It is worth noting that fresh dates are sometimes frozen after picking to ensure freshness on delivery and should not be re-frozen.

DAUB (TO)
To make incisions in meat and insert strips of bacon to add flavour and moisture.

DAUBE
A rich, French-style casserole (subject to regional variations) made with meat, wine, garlic, root vegetables, onions and seasonings. The meat is usually marinated in the wine and vegetables before cooking. The mixture should be cooked in a *daubière*, a lidded earthenware pot which gives its name to the dish. The traditional accompaniments are boiled potatoes or some form of pasta.

DAUBIÈRE
An earthenware, heat-resistant, lidded casserole, traditionally used in France for cooking *daubes*, a type of stew.

à la DAUMONT
French term meaning a garnish for fish to include mushrooms, soft roes, crayfish tails and sometimes *quenelles* of fish as well.

DAUPHIN
A cows' milk cheese from Flanders, in France. It is flavoured with herbs and spices and formed into assorted shapes that include shields, hearts, crescents and fish. Dauphin resembles Maroilles cheese.

à la DEAUVILLAISE
French term meaning in the style of Deauville in Normandy, particularly applied to sole which has been poached with cream and chopped onions.

DECAFFEINATED COFFEE
Coffee which has had approximately 97% of the caffeine removed. This takes place at the green bean stage, before roasting. It is a suitable drink for coffee-lovers with a caffeine intolerance, as most of the flavour and aroma are retained.

DECANT (TO)
To pour liquid from one container to another. In general use it means to transfer a liquid, usually wine, from a bottle to a decanter (or second bottle), taking great care to trap any sediment in the first bottle.

DECANTER
A crystal or glass container with a stopper which is used for alcoholic drinks.

DECOCT (TO)
To extract essence by boiling; to boil down in order to concentrate a liquid.

DECOMPOSITION
The process of food going rotten, showing visible signs of decay and usually emitting an unpleasant odour.

DECORATE (TO)
To make attractive; to enhance the appearance of a sweet dish by adding decorative trimmings.

DECORATED EGGS
A highly ornamental and traditional way of treating eggs in the Ukraine. They are an Easter speciality.

DEEP FAT
Sufficient very hot fat or oil in a cooking utensil to cover the food being deep-fried. The utensil itself

must be deep enough to prevent the fat or oil from bubbling over the side and causing accidents.

DEEP-DISH PIZZA
A North American-style pizza with a deep layer of filling on top of a fairly thin base of dough.

DEEP-FREEZE
A cabinet in which food is frozen and stored at very low temperatures.

DEEP-FRY (TO)
To cook food in a large, deep-frying pan, half filled with melted fat or oil. For most deep-frying, the fat or oil should be heated until the bubbling stops and a faint haze rises from the surface. The thermometer at this stage should register 190°C/375°F. To test without a thermometer, a small cube of bread should be dropped carefully into the pan. If the temperature is correct, the cube should sink to the bottom, rise to the top immediately and turn pale gold in 50 seconds. If the cube becomes dark and the fat or oil begins to smoke, overheating is indicated. Food should be added gradually to the deep-fryer, as too much at any one time will lower the temperature of the fat or oil unnecessarily and will result in pale, greasy-looking food which may be raw in the middle.

DEEP-FRYER
See *Fryer*.

DEEPWATER SHRIMP
See *Shrimp*.

DEER
See *Venison*.

DEFROST (TO)
To thaw from a frozen state.

DEGLAZE (TO)
To remove a joint of cooked meat from a roasting tin, pour off the fat and then add a little water to the coagulated meat juices left behind in the tin. This liquid is then gently heated and continuously stirred, resulting in a fairly concentrated meat extract which, in French cooking, is frequently the basis of *demi-glace* and other rich brown sauces.

DÉGORGER
French term meaning to cleanse or remove unwanted matter from food and drink.

DÉGRAISSER
French term to describe the removal of grease and scum as it rises to the top of a boiling liquid such as stock.

DÉGUSTATION
French term to describe the tasting of food and drink; also relishing a special food such as caviar.

DEHYDRATE (TO)
To remove moisture from foodstuffs. This usually results in long-lasting products which may then be reconstituted with water. Commercial examples are dried vegetable flakes, instant coffee, skimmed milk powder, dried pulses, potato powder and desiccated coconut.

DELI
North American term for delicatessen.

DELICATESSEN
A loose translation from the German is 'delicacies for eating'. Delicatessen foods are generally pre-cooked and savoury and can range from smoked salmon and potato salad to pickles and assorted meats.

DELICATESSEN COUNTER
The part of a supermarket selling delicatessen.

DELICATESSEN SHOP
A shop selling delicatessen.

DELICE DE SAINT-CYR
Produced in small French factories in Île-de-France, this is a rich and tasty triple cream cheese made from cows' milk.

DEMERARA SUGAR
A light brown sugar, originally from Demerara in British Guiana, with coarse and granular crystals. It is not recommended for baking delicate cakes but may be used in some desserts, to sweeten breakfast cereals, grapefruit halves and drinks such as tea or coffee. Some varieties are unrefined.

DEMERSAL
Term used to describe fish which live on or near the sea bed. They are often caught as a mixture of species in the same net.

DEMI-CAMEMBERT
(Half Camembert)
Term used to describe half a round Camembert cheese, packed in a semi-circular box.

DEMI-GLACE SAUCE
(Demi-Glaze)
An Espagnole sauce, flavoured with jellied meat juices (left over from roasting) or meat extract such as Bovril, and dry sherry. Alternatively, it may be made from meat juices and beef stock, reduced by boiling until glossy and thick enough to coat the back of a spoon. It can be served with beef and game dishes.

DEMI-SEL
A fresh country cheese from France which is just over a hundred years old and was first produced in the Pays de Bray. It is moist, white, salted (without being too salty) and mild with the merest hint of sourness. It is one of France's best curd-type cheeses, contains 40% butterfat and is made from pasteurized cows' milk.

DEMI-TASSE
French term meaning half a cup and referring especially to small cups of coffee served at the end of a meal.

DENSITY
In scientific terms, this refers to the mass per unit volume of a substance, expressed in grams per cubic foot, or grammes per cubic centimetre. While food technologists may use density in this way, ordinary cooks in the kitchen use the term to refer to the thickness or thinness of a liquid, or whether it is clear or opaque.

DENTEX
A group of Mediterranean fish (*Dentex* species) of the same family as the sea bream. The back varies in colour from a metallic blue to red or rosy shades. The length can be up to 1 metre/39 inches and the maximum weight in the shops could be 13.5 kg/ 30 lb. The flesh is firm and the fish may be baked or grilled.

DERBY
A factory-produced English cheese which is pale yellow in colour, with a flaky texture. It is generally mild and made from cows' milk.

DESICCATE (TO)
See *Dehydrate (to)*.

DESICCATED COCONUT
Dried and finely shredded coconut used in cakes, savoury dishes and for decoration.

DESSERT APPLE
See *Apple*.

DESSERT COURSE
A popular term for the sweet course served at the end of a meal in Britain; also, fresh fruit and nuts served as the last course at a banquet.

DESSERTNYÏ-BELYÏ
(Desertny Bely)
A young and fresh-tasting cows' milk cheese, factory-produced in the USSR. It has a white and velvety rind and is matured for a week to 10 days.

DESSERTS
Sweet dishes served at the end of a meal, such as soufflés, pancakes, fritters, puddings, pies, ices, charlottes, mousses and jellies.

DEVIL BUTTER
Softened, whipped butter to which continental mustard, Worcestershire sauce, Tabasco, cayenne pepper and wine vinegar are added. It is shaped into a 2.5 cm/1 inch diameter roll, wrapped and refrigerated until hard, then cut into rounds of about 5 mm/¼ inch in thickness. These are used to garnish fried or grilled fish, grilled gammon steaks and chops, boiled bacon and grilled kidneys or liver.

DEVIL'S FOOD CAKE
A rich and sweet North American chocolate cake which is dark brown and moist.

DEVON GARLAND
An English farmhouse cheese, produced in North Devon from cows' milk. It is laced with fresh herbs and has a delicate flavour.

DEVONSHIRE JUNKET
A type of junket made in the West Country of England, topped with clotted cream and sprinkled with grated nutmeg.

DEVONSHIRE SQUAB PIE
A deep-dish pie from the West Country of England filled with a mixture of lamb, apples, onions, seasonings and water which is covered with pastry and baked.

DEWBERRY
A fruit closely related to the blackberry. In its various kinds (genus *Rubus*), it is native to both Europe and North America and has been cultivated and cross-bred to improve quality and yield. It is probably one of the parents of the loganberry. It differs from the other members of the blackberry family in that it grows on a more trailing type of plant, the fruit is less plentiful but larger and juicier, and it also ripens earlier. The dewberry may be eaten on its own or used in cooked dishes suited to the blackberry.

DEXTRAL
See *Flatfish*.

DEXTRIN
A polysaccharide or complex carbohydrate visible as the brown part of a starchy food after heat has been applied to it. Toast is an excellent example.

DEXTROSE
See *Glucose*.

DHAL
The Indian name for lentils and also the term for a lentil-based dish.

DHANSAK
Brought to India from Persia by the Parsees, a mild lamb and vegetable dish containing lentils and spices, topped with fried onion rings. Sometimes chicken is used instead of lamb.

à la DIABLE
French term meaning devilled, referring to any food which has been strongly seasoned with condiments such as Worcestershire sauce, mustard, vinegar, Tabasco or cayenne pepper.

DIANE SAUCE
A poivrade sauce, enriched with cream. It can be served with steaks.

DICE (TO)
To cut into small cubes.

à la DIEPPOISE
French term meaning in the style of Dieppe in northern France, referring to any dish containing shrimps, coated with a shrimp sauce or garnished with shrimps.

DIET (THE)
The food and drink habitually taken by an individual, family or larger group.

DIET (TO)
To follow an eating regime for slimming, to increase weight, or for medical or health reasons.

DIETARY FIBRE
This term refers to edible fibre, the most important coming from cereals.

DIETETICS
The study and application of the principles of nutrition.

DIETITIAN
(Dietician)
A specialist in food, nutrition and dietetics.

DIGESTER
The original word for pressure cooker. The technique of pressure-cooking was invented in the latter part of the 17th century by a French physician called Denis Papin.

DIGESTIF
French term for a drink taken at the end of a large meal to aid digestion. It can be a fortified wine (port), spirit (brandy) or a liqueur based on herbs, mint or fruit.

DIGESTION
Process whereby various enzymes and digestive juices from the mouth, liver, gall bladder, stomach, pancreas, duodenum and small and large intestine break down food taken in by the body, the nutrients from which then carry out their work via the bloodstream.

DIGESTIVE BISCUITS
Lightly-sweetened biscuits, usually made with wholemeal flour and very crumbly. They are frequently served with butter and cheese at the end of a meal, and were once considered to be the traditional biscuits to accompany mid-morning tea and coffee. Crushed digestive biscuits are used as a base for some cheesecakes.

à la DIJONNAISE
French term meaning in the style of Dijon in eastern France, denoting the inclusion of mustard; also blackcurrants or a liqueur such as *crème de cassis*.

DILL
(Dill Weed)
This herb (*Anethum graveolens*) is widely grown all over Europe and is popular in Scandinavia, northern and eastern Europe and parts of the Balkans. The name comes from the Norse *dilla*, meaning to lull, as at one time it was thought to induce sleep. Fresh dill is a bright green, feathery herb which is also known as dill weed. Related to the parsley family and with a mild taste of caraway, bunches of dill are often used for pickling and as a garnish. Chopped dill is used to flavour soups, sauces, dressings, fish and veal dishes and some salads. Dill seeds, small and light brown, have a similar flavour to fresh dill and are available whole or ground.

DILL PICKLES
Small cucumbers (or large gherkins) pickled in white vinegar with garlic, spices, salt and either dill seed or dill weed. They are particularly popular in North America and with Jewish people.

DILUTE (TO)
To weaken, by adding one liquid to another such as water to vinegar.

DIM SUM
Chinese steamed and deep-fried snacks, in the form of sweet or savoury dumplings served in baskets.

DIMBULA
An unblended black Ceylon tea leaf grown in the hills of Sri Lanka. It is mellow and smooth and is one of the island's finest teas.

DINNER
The main meal of the day, usually eaten in the evening. The term is

sometimes used colloquially in Britain for a midday meal. In the home, dinner usually consists of a minimum of two courses. In restaurants, it can be a formal meal of several courses or a banquet.

DIOSMERÉLT
A Hungarian dessert made from freshly cooked egg noodles tossed with lard, finely chopped walnuts and sugar.

DIP (TO)
To immerse, for example, a piece of bread into milk or the yolk of a soft-boiled egg; fish into batter; a little finger into a lukewarm liquid to test for heat. Dip also refers to a soft mixture, usually savoury, scooped up on pieces of raw vegetables, crisps, biscuits and baby sausages and eaten with drinks.

DIPPER
A large ladle with an especially long handle.

DIRTY RICE
A Creole dish from Louisiana in the USA, this is a mixture of fried onions, celery, peppers, garlic and minced beef cooked with long-grain rice, stock and seasonings. The name refers to the colour of the dish.

DISACCHARIDE
Carbohydrate composed of two simple sugars.

DISJOINT (TO)
To divide poultry and game into pieces by cutting at the joints.

DISSOLVE (TO)
To mix a dry ingredient with a liquid until clarity is reached. Often the application of heat is necessary for this process.

DISTIL (TO)
To manufacture products such as alcohol and vinegar by evaporation and condensation.

DITALI
Thimble-sized tubes of pasta.

DITALINI
Small versions of *ditali*, used in soup.

DIVINITY
A North American sweetmeat, a type of fudge, made with egg whites, sugar and nuts.

DJUVEČ
A national dish of Yugoslavia, *djuveč* is a meat, vegetable and rice casserole. The vegetables used are tomatoes, aubergines, peppers, courgettes, celery and onions and sometimes garlic is added for flavour.

DJUVEČ OD PRAZILUKA
A leek, chilli, tomato and rice casserole from Macedonia in Yugoslavia.

DOBOSTORTE
(Dobostorta)
Hungary's national cake, this multi-layered confection is filled with chocolate cream and topped with a 'lid' of caramel, divided into segments before it hardens. The sides are also covered with chocolate cream.

DOBROGEA
See *Peneteleu*.

DOCE DE LEITE
Brazilian term for *Dulce de Leche*.

DODINE
A French term to describe boned poultry, often duck, stuffed with *pâté*, then simmered in wine and served with deglazed pan juices.

DOE VENISON
See *Venison*.

DOGFISH
(Huss, Rock Eel, Rock Salmon)
A cartilaginous (non-bony), round-bodied, torpedo-shaped fish (*Scyliorhinus canicula*) and a

member of one of the shark families. It can be up to 1 metre/39 inches long and has a brown back with spots. It is caught in the seas around western Europe all year round. The flesh is white and medium-oily and the fish may be poached or baked. Dogfish is perhaps best known as a standard item in British fried fish shops where it is also called huss, rock eel and rock salmon.

DOLCELATTE
Meaning sweet milk, a blue-veined Italian cheese made from cows' milk. Factory-produced, the cheese is creamy, soft and relatively mild.

DOLLY MIXTURE
Brightly coloured small sweets, usually square.

DOLMATHES
(Dolmades, Dolmas)
Greek stuffed vine leaves which generally contain a filling of fried onions, rice, water, currants, pine nuts, parsley and seasonings. They are simmered in water and lemon juice and served cold as an appetizer. *Dolmathes* sometimes contain minced beef or veal instead of currants and nuts.

DOLPHIN FISH
(Dorado)
A seawater fish (*Coryphaena* species) found in warm waters worldwide and particularly popular in Mediterranean countries. The colours are bright and metallic, silvery and golden. The average weight in the shops is 1–7.25 kg/ 2–16 lb. The flesh is very tender and the fish may be poached, baked, fried or grilled.

DOM YAM GUNG
Spicy Thai prawn soup containing a generous selection of herbs and sharpened with citrus.

DOMATES DOLMASI
A Turkish speciality of tomatoes stuffed with a mixture of onions, raisins, pine nuts, rice, seasonings and chopped parsley or dill. They are baked in the oven, then served lightly chilled.

DONABE
A Japanese earthenware casserole used for *nabemono* or one-pot meals.

DONE
Sufficiently cooked.

DÖNER KEBAB
See *Döner Kebapi*.

DÖNER KEBAPI
(Döner Kebab)
A huge, layered Turkish kebab, cooked on an upright spit revolving close to a source of strong heat. It is a restaurant speciality and made from thin rounds of lamb, a minced lamb mixture and layers of fat, closely packed together on the spit. It is carved from top to bottom when the outside edges are cooked, resulting in small shavings of well-cooked meats.

DONUT
North American term for doughnut.

DOODHI
(Dudi, Doodi)
A vegetable (*Lagenaria siceraria*) of the squash family. The origins of this plant are obscure but evidence shows that it was known in both North Africa and North America over 5,000 years ago. It is grown widely in tropical countries and eaten only when young as it matures into the inedible calabash or bottle gourd which has a hard shell and is used for making culinary implements and musical instruments. The doodhi grows in many shapes and sizes, with both smooth or ridged skins, coloured light green to creamy-yellow. The flesh is pale, seeded and marrow-like, and the doodhi may be cooked whole or stuffed, baked or boiled.

DORADO
A freshwater fish caught in South American rivers. Dorado is also an alternative name for the seawater dolphin fish.

DORIA
French term for any dish or sauce containing cucumber.

DORIA SAUCE
Béchamel sauce, enriched with double cream and flavoured with cooked chopped cucumber and a very little nutmeg. It can be served with all fish dishes.

DOROBOUSKI
(Dorogoboukski, Dorogobuzhsky)
A cows' milk cheese from the USSR, with a strong flavour and aroma. It is left to mature for about 6 weeks. It has an orange-red rind and is sold in small squares.

DORSET BLUE VINNY
See *Blue Vinny*.

DORY
(John Dory)
A seawater fish (*Zeus taber*) with a length of 50–60 cm/19–24 inches for the female, but only 40–45 cm/16–18 inches for the male. It is a sandy-beige colour tinged with yellow and blue, and has a narrow body, flattened from side to side. The head takes up nearly half the total size and on each side of the body, just behind the gill cover, is a large black spot ringed with yellow which is called 'St Peter's thumbprint'. It is caught, mainly in the summer months, in the Mediterranean and the Bay of Biscay and, with reducing frequency, as far north as Norway. The flesh is white and finely flavoured and the fish may be poached, steamed, baked or fried. The dory is not a common fish in Britain and much of the catch is sold to the restaurant trade.

DOUBLE BOILER
See *Double Saucepan*.

DOUBLE CREAM
This thick and very rich cream is the one used primarily for whipping. It is pasteurized and has a legal minimum butterfat content of 55%. To prevent curdling and overbeating, 15 ml/1 tablespoon milk should be added to every 150 ml/¼ pint of refrigerated cream before whipping.

DOUBLE CREAM CHEESE
A soft, very rich, deep cream-coloured cheese, made from the cream of cows' milk. It is best eaten fresh as a sandwich filling or dessert cheese.

DOUBLE DECKER
A large sandwich made from three slices of bread and two fillings, originating in North America.

DOUBLE GLOUCESTER
A vivid orange-coloured English cheese produced in creameries and dyed with annatto. It has a buttery, open texture and a creamy, full flavour which is often described as rich and mellow. It is an excellent dessert and cooking cheese. The word 'Double' refers to the large size of the cheese, and 'Gloucester' because it was originally made only from the milk of the Gloucester black cattle.

DOUBLE LOIN OF PORK
Alternative term used in the east of Scotland for a loin of pork chop.

DOUBLE LOIN STEAKS OF PORK
A new and leaner British cut of meat which is divided into steaks for grilling or frying.

DOUBLE SAUCEPAN
(Double Boiler)
A two-part saucepan, designed to cook food without the application of direct heat or moisture. The lower part is filled with water which is heated sufficiently to cook the contents of the upper section.

DOUBLE-CRUST PIE
A pie with a pastry base and lid.

DOUGH
Pliable flour mixture usually containing yeast, liquid and sometimes fat and sugar.

DOUGH CAKE
Originally from Lincolnshire, it is made from white bread dough containing mixed dried fruit, chopped mixed peel, spices, sugar, eggs and butter. It is baked in a deep round cake tin or oblong loaf tin.

DOUGHBOYS
North American term for dumplings.

DOUGHNUTS
Rings or rounds of yeast dough, sometimes filled with jam, which are deep-fried, drained and rolled in caster sugar and cinnamon.

DOVER SOLE
(Sole)
This is the finest flatfish (*Solea solea*) of the sole family. The size may be up to 50 cm/19 inches and the upper side is muddy greyish-brown. It is caught all year round off the coasts of north-west Europe, particularly the North Sea, the Bay of Biscay and also in the Mediterranean. The flesh is white, lean and fine and the fish may be poached, steamed, baked, fried or grilled. The fish is said to look like the sole of a shoe or sandal, hence the name. The term Dover sole became popular in Britain because that was where supplies for south-east England were landed.

DRAGÉES
French term for sugared almonds. Also silver balls and small chocolate drops.

DRAGON'S EYE
See *Longan*.

DRAIN (TO)
To allow a liquid to fall away from any food which has been moistened either by washing or cooking; for example, water from vegetables and fat or oil from chips or other fried food.

DRAW (TO)
To clean the insides of poultry or game birds by removing the entrails (stomach, intestines, lungs, etc.).

DRAWN BUTTER
North American term for clarified butter.

DRAWN BUTTER SAUCE
An old English sauce, similar to white sauce, made from a roux of butter and flour but with water replacing the milk. It was traditionally served with vegetables or, when flavoured with lemon juice, with steamed or poached fish.

DREDGE (TO)
To sprinkle or dust with flour or sugar using a perforated dredger or traditional sugar-sifter.

DREDGER
(Sifter)
Can-shaped utensil for sifting small quantities of flour or sugar. It may or may not have a handle and has either a mesh base or perforated lid. For flour, the dredger may have further refinements such as extra mesh screens for fineness and aeration, or an oscillating device to allow sifting without shaking. For large quantities, a sieve is more practical.

DRESDENER CHRISTOLLEN
A variation of *stollen*, this is a yeasted and fruited Christmas cake from Dresden in East Germany.

DRESS (TO)
To add dressing to a salad; to garnish a dish.

DRESSED CRAB
Cooked crab which is removed from the shell and separated into light and dark meat. It is then prepared and seasoned, and replaced in the

shell ready for eating. The traditional garnishes are chopped hard-boiled egg and parsley; the accompaniments are mayonnaise and salad.

DRESSED TRIPE

Tripe which has been bleached and partially cooked by the butcher.

DRESSING

North American term for stuffing or forcemeat.

DRIED APPLE RINGS

Made from rounds of peeled and cored apples. Sometimes sulphur is used as a preservative, making the rings a very pale creamy colour.

DRIED APRICOTS

Produced from fruit grown in all five inhabited continents of the world, they have a particularly enticing fragrance and may be eaten as they are, stewed with water and sugar, or used in cooking. They have one of the highest dietary fibre contents of any food.

DRIED BANANAS

Dried when fully ripe as whole bananas or pieces. They have a distinctive taste, chewy texture and are brown in colour.

DRIED CHESTNUTS

See *Chestnuts*.

DRIED FRUIT

Dried fruits are those from which most of the moisture has been evaporated, leaving pieces of fruit which have a high concentration of sugar, important minerals, fibre and some vitamins, although a measure of the water-soluble vitamins B and C will be lost in the drying process. The fruits most commonly dried are apples (usually in rings), pear halves (unpeeled), apricots and peaches (stoned), figs, bananas, dates, plums (prunes) and, of course, the grape family, from which come raisins, sultanas and currants. It takes approximately 4.5 kg/10 lb of fresh fruit to produce 450 g/1 lb of dried, which accounts for its high calorific and nutritional value. All dried fruits should be kept in containers with tight-fitting lids and stored in cool, dry and dark conditions. Unless pre-washed, the fruit should be washed thoroughly before use and well dried by rubbing gently in a clean teatowel.
Sometimes raisins, sultanas and currants taste better if they are plumped up before cooking; this can easily be done by soaking the fruit for 10–15 minutes in the cooking liquid recommended in the recipe.
When chopping dried fruit, a little flour sprinkled on the blade of the knife will help to prevent sticking.
Larger pieces of fruit, such as apricots and pears, are best cut to the required size with kitchen scissors dipped in and out of hot water.

DRIED MILK

A granule or powder made from whole or skimmed milk. When 'low-fat' is shown on a tin or packet, this indicates that the powder has been made from skimmed milk and is high in protein and vitamins but low in fat. Before drying, the milk is homogenized and then completely dehydrated, either by being sprayed into a current of hot air or passed in a thin layer over heated rollers. The resulting product keeps almost indefinitely in sealed, airtight containers. Once reconstituted, it should be treated as fresh milk. It is not suitable as a baby food.

DRIED MUSHROOM

Available in Britain, this type of mushroom is imported from Mediterranean, Middle Eastern and Far Eastern countries. It is highly flavoured, lightweight and used in stews, some soups and northern European speciality dishes.

DRIED PASTA

(Pasta Secca)
Factory-produced dried pasta which is hard and fairly brittle. Generally

available in packets and boxes, it should be cooked for the length of time stipulated by the makers — no longer or both the texture and flavour will be impaired.

DRIED YEAST
Available in small tins or sachets, which, once opened, should be stored in an airtight container where the yeast will keep for up to four months. Because it is concentrated, 15 g/½ oz of dried yeast is equivalent to 25 g/1 oz of fresh yeast. Dried yeast must be reconstituted before use with warm liquid and a little sugar. The mixture should be allowed to stand for 10–15 minutes, until it becomes foamy; it is then ready for use. There is a newer, easy-mix dried yeast now available.

DRINK (A)
An alcoholic or non-alcoholic liquid for drinking.

DRINK (TO)
To take in liquid refreshment.

DRINKING CHOCOLATE
Made from a ready-prepared mixture of cocoa powder and sugar which is generally combined with milk to make a hot or cold drink. In some countries, the drink is made by melting block chocolate slowly in milk, or milk and water mixed.

DRINKING WATER
Water which is safe for humans to drink.

DRINKING YOGURT
A blend of low-fat yogurt and fruit juice combined to make a healthy drink. In general, the product contains no artificial colour, flavouring or preservatives.

DRIP COFFEE
See *Filter Coffee*.

DRIPPING
This British term once meant the fat which melted during cooking and dripped off a roast joint. Now it tends to refer to any kind of melted and strained meat fat, including bacon.

DRIPPING CAKE
An old-fashioned favourite, this is a spicy fruit cake containing beef dripping (fat) instead of butter or margarine.

DROP
A small round sweet or lozenge, sometimes medicated.

DROPPED SCONES
(Flapjack Scones, Scotch Pancakes)
Small, fairly flat cakes cooked in a greased frying pan or griddle until golden on both sides. They are made from a thick batter mixture, similar to a coating batter but containing a raising agent. They are served warm with butter and either jam or honey.

DRUM
A term to describe those fish which have the ability to make drumming noises through their air bladders. They are classed with fish which make croaking noises by similar methods (croaker fish). Between them, the two types include over 200 species caught in temperate and tropical waters. A typical example is the sea drum.

DRUMSTICK
The part of a chicken's leg between the thigh and foot.

DRUMSTICK POD
(Ben Oil Tree, Ben Tree, Susumber)
A vegetable which is the seed pod of a tree (*Moringa oleifera*) native to India and now also grown in the Caribbean region, Africa and the southern USA. The drumstick looks like a straight, ridged cucumber, pointed at both ends, 38 cm/15 inches or more in length, but as thin as a young runner bean. The green skin is thin but tough, and the sticky flesh is pale green with regularly spaced and edible creamy-coloured seeds. The taste is rather peppery and the under-ripe

pod may be eaten raw or cooked. The pod is added to curry dishes in India, where other parts of the tree are also used in cooking.

DRY

Any alcohol which is dry (as opposed to sweet) because of a low sugar content; also to remove moisture from food; without liquid or moisture.

DRY (TO)

To remove surplus moisture from foods, such as fruit, vegetables, fish and meat.

DRY JACK

See *Monterey Jack*.

DRY MUSTARD

A well-known and frequently used condiment and additive in Britain, made from yellow mustard seeds. It has many culinary applications, whether used in powder form or mixed to a paste with water, milk, vinegar or lemon juice.

DRY-FRY (TO)

To fry food in a frying pan without fat or oil. This method is suitable for bacon and sausages as the fat from both runs, making additional fat unnecessary. Non-stick pans require no fat and are therefore ideally suited to dry-frying.

à la DUBARRY

French term for any dish containing cauliflower or garnished with it. Madame Dubarry was a mistress of Louis XV.

DUBLIN BAY PRAWN

A seawater crustacean (*Nephrops norvegicus*) of the lobster family; not really a prawn at all. It is caught up to 25 cm/10 inches long, excluding the claws, and the jointed body shell is pink or orangey-fawn. It is harvested from Iceland to the Mediterranean as far as the east coast of Italy all year round but is most abundant during the summer months. The shelled tail meat is known in Britain as 'scampi', which is the plural of the Italian name (*scampo*) for this crustacean. The more correct English name is Norway lobster, but because of landings from the Irish Sea at Dublin the name Dublin Bay prawn became general. The tail meat may be poached, baked, fried or grilled.

DUBLIN CODDLE

An Irish casserole of onions, bacon rashers, potatoes, pork sausages and water which is traditionally served with soda bread.

à la DUCHESSE

French term meaning in the style of the duchess, usually referring to potato purée mixed with egg yolks, then piped into assorted shapes and browned in the oven.

DUCK

Edible swimming birds (family *Anatidae*) which have webbed feet and a broad flat beak.

DUCK EGGS

Large, rich and beautifully-flavoured eggs with almost translucent shells of the palest turquoise colour. Ducks, unfortunately, often lay their eggs in unclean and polluted areas, so the eggs are in danger of absorbing bacteria through their porous shells. Therefore, they must be hard-boiled if eaten plain (never lightly cooked) or used in cakes, custards, soufflés and omelettes.

DUCKLING

Usually a young duck.

DUCKS' FEET

Regarded as a delicacy, these are frequently used in Chinese cooking.

DULCE DE LECHE

(Arequipe, Cajeta de Celaya, Manjar Blanco, Natillas Piuranas)
Caramelized milk, a Latin American speciality which is eaten as a dessert. It is made by heating a mixture of milk and sugar very

slowly and gently. An easy way to make *dulce de leche* is to boil an unopened can of condensed milk for 2 hours or until it caramelizes. It is served cut in slices.

DULSE
A sea vegetable (*Rhodymenia palmata*) of the red algae group of plants, found in coastal waters on both sides of the North Atlantic. It is eaten dried, either raw or cooked. It has a high mineral content, more protein than most sea vegetables and, until the end of the 19th century, was eaten for its supposed health-enhancing properties in both north-west Europe and north-east America.

DUMPLINGS
Small dough balls, usually made from a mixture of flour, seasonings, suet (or other fats) and water, cooked in water, soup or stock, or simmered in meat stews.

DUN DUN
(Dundu)
An African speciality made from slices of yam or sweet potato dipped in flour and egg, deep-fried and served hot with omelettes.

DUNDEE CAKE
Originally from Dundee in Scotland, a fruit cake containing chopped mixed peel and traditionally topped with rings of blanched and halved almonds before baking.

DUNGENESS CRAB
(Market Crab)
A member (*Cancer magister*) of the family of crustaceans and the most popular crab caught off the shores of the North Pacific from Alaska to California. The average weight is 1 kg/2¼ lb, and the legs are often as large and meaty as the claws. It is harvested all year round, with the heaviest catches in the summer months in the Alaska area. The meat is lean, white and flaky and the crab, after being killed, is boiled whole and usually frozen. It is sold whole, sectioned or as prepacked meat.

DUNK (TO)
To dip biscuits into hot drinks.

DUNLOP
A mild, fine-flavoured, Cheddar-type cheese produced in Scottish creameries. It is named after the Ayrshire village where it originated and is said to date back to the time of Charles II. It is produced from cows' milk.

DUNMOW FLITCH
An old English custom which involved the presentation of a flitch (side) of bacon, by the Dunmow monastery in Essex, to the married couple who, for 12 months and a day, neither quarrelled nor wished themselves single! Apparently only eight people were winners between the 13th and 18th centuries.

DUO
A North American pasteurized and processed Emmental cheese with a mousse-type filling made from walnuts, herbs, spices, salami or smoked salmon and black pepper.

DURIAN
The fruit of a tree (*Durio zibethinus*) native to Malaysia and cultivated in other tropical areas of South-East Asia and in parts of East Africa. It is of a generally oval shape and may weigh up to 4.5 kg/10 lb. The skin is very thick and spiky and, when ripe, is a dirty yellow. The flesh, divided into four sections, is a yellowy pulp and contains up to six brown, inedible seeds. This fruit has a taste that is said to be so delicious as to defy a precise description but there is no dispute over the intrusive, offensive and putrid smell. (The Dutch name for durian translates as 'stink-fruit'.) When ripe it does not keep and is either split open and eaten as it is, or used with other ingredients in both sweet and

savoury dishes. The durian fruits in mid-summer and mid-winter and is available for about six months of the year.

DURUM WHEAT
Hard wheat, rich in protein and gluten, which is cultivated in Italy, Spain and parts of North and South America. It makes the best pasta and is widely used in the production of semolina.

à la DUSE
French term for a classic garnish for joints of meat, consisting of tomatoes, French beans and potatoes.

DUST
The smallest commercial grade of black tea leaf. It is often used for making tea-bags and is the fastest-brewing of all grades.

DUST (TO)
To sprinkle food lightly with sugar, ground nuts, cocoa powder and so on.

DUTCH SAUCE
(Mock Hollandaise)
Béchamel sauce, flavoured with lemon juice and enriched with egg yolk and cream. It can be served with poached and steamed fish dishes, roast or boiled chicken and vegetables such as asparagus, broccoli and cauliflower.

DUXELLES
French term for a mixture of chopped mushrooms and sometimes shallots or onions, fried in butter or margarine until most of the liquid has evaporated. It is used as a flavouring in sauces and stuffings.

DWARF GREEN BEAN
A hybrid French bean which snaps easily when broken and has little or no side strings.

E NUMBERS
Means of identifying food additives. Agreed by the European Community (EC), these refer to food additives such as colourings, which are numbered from E100 to E180, preservatives, between E200 and E290, anti-oxidants, between E300 and E321, and artificial sweeteners, bleaching agents, emulsifiers, stabilizers and thickeners, from E322 onwards.

EAR
Cluster of grains at the top of a cereal stalk, together with their protective structures.

EARL GREY
A blended black tea leaf which is flavoured with bergamot oil. The different brands may be blends of Indian and China teas but all have the distinctive bergamot flavour. It is a delicate tea which may be drunk with or without milk.

EARSHELL
See *Ormer*.

EARTHENWARE
Another term for pottery or stoneware. Many cooking utensils are made from earthenware and some are heat-resistant. To avoid breakages, never immerse a hot dish in cold water and to preserve the glaze, soak off left-over food, rather than scraping it with a knife or coarse scourer.

EASTER BISCUITS
Rich British biscuits containing currants and eaten, traditionally, on Easter morning.

EASTER EGGS
It is an old custom to exchange gifts of eggs — regarded as a symbol of fertility — at Easter. Modern eggs

are usually made from chocolate and are available either large, small, hollow or filled with chocolates. Russia is known for its exquisitely decorated Easter eggs, hand-painted and lacquered.

EATS
A British colloquial term for food.

EAU-DE-COLOGNE MINT
A herb (*Mentha piperita citrata*) of the mint family which smells distinctly of eau-de-Cologne with an overlay of mint. The leaves are darkish green, shading to purple towards the edges. It is excellent in fruit cups and drinks such as Pimms.

ECCLES CAKES
These originated in Eccles, Lancashire, and are almost identical to Banbury cakes but larger. They contain currants, mixed chopped peel, butter, brown sugar and spice. They are brushed with milk and caster sugar before being baked, giving them their characteristic glaze and slight crunchiness.

ÉCHAUDER
French term meaning to scald or bring a liquid, such as milk, to a temperature just below boiling point.

ECHOURGNAC
Made by Trappist monks in Aquitaine, this is a delicately flavoured cows' milk cheese from France. It has a pale yellow paste, is dotted with tiny holes and the rind is deep beige in colour. It is a relatively small cheese.

ÉCLAIRS
Finger-shaped pastries, made by piping lengths of choux pastry on to greased baking trays. After baking and cooling, the éclairs are split lengthwise and filled with lightly sweetened whipped cream or confectioner's custard. The tops are usually iced with coffee or chocolate glacé icing.

à l'ÉCOSSAISE
French term meaning in Scottish style, usually denoting the inclusion of barley and also mixed vegetables.

EDAM
One of Holland's most popular and emulated cheeses, Edam dates back to the 14th century and originated in the town of Edam. Now almost entirely factory-produced from cows' milk, the cheese is ball-shaped with a bright red wax coat and has a slightly lower butterfat content than similar cheeses — about 40%. It has a firm and supple texture and is creamy-yellow in colour. It is easy to slice, has a mild and pleasant flavour and is sold when about 3–4 months old.

EDAMER
(Loaf Cheese)
German equivalent of Dutch Edam, but loaf-shaped with rounded corners.

EDDO
A vegetable tuber (*Colocasia* species) of the arum family cultivated in the West Indies. It grows as a cluster of swollen stems with light brown skin and white flesh, rather like an elongated potato. The flavour is bland and the starchy flesh may be cooked as a vegetable on its own or used in local Caribbean dishes. Eddo and similar tuberous species are known variously as dasheen, taro, coco and cologassi, depending on type and region, and all should be boiled or baked to eliminate possible harmful chemicals. In most kinds the green leaves, often large, are also edible when cooked.

EDELPILZKÄSE
See *Pilz*.

EDIBLE CRAB
See *Common Crab*.

EDINBURGH ROCK
A sweetmeat from Edinburgh, in Scotland, developed during the last century. It is soft, pastel-coloured

and flavoured with peppermint, raspberry, lemon or orange; some is spiced. It is usually sold in short lengths.

EEL

(Common Eel)
A fish (*Anguilla* species) with a snake-like body which is unusual in that it is catadromous, meaning that it is born at sea, lives most of its life in fresh or brackish water and returns to the sea to spawn and die. Both the European and American eel start life in the region of the Sargasso Sea. They have black to muddy-brown backs, shading to yellow sides and are yellowish-white on the underside. When the eel is ready to return to the sea to spawn, the underside becomes silvery. The length can reach as much as 130 cm/50 inches and the weight up to 8 kg/18 lb but as eels are eaten from the time when they are very young (elvers), there is no average shop size. Eels are caught throughout the year with heaviest catches in the autumn. The flesh is oily and the fish may be poached, baked, fried, grilled or smoked. Smoked eel is considered a delicacy.

EFFERVESCE (TO)

To bubble, ferment and/or foam.

EGG

An egg is an ellipsoid (meaning egg-shaped or oval), packed neatly into its own calcium shell. Eggs have been eaten since the beginning of civilization and were the symbol of fertility and birth for the ancient Chinese and the peoples of India, Greece and the Middle East. They were also associated with prophecy, foretelling the future and regarded as a token of good fortune. Eggs were surrounded by many superstitions; for example, it was considered unlucky to take eggs into or out of the house after dark; the Romans thought the egg shells were enchanted and so destroyed them; and in the 16th century, it was felt that witches used egg shells as boats and it was supposed that spells were written on them. In an 1881 edition of her cookbook, Mrs Isabella Beeton wrote: 'Many of the most learned philosophers held eggs in a kind of respect approaching to veneration, because they saw in them the emblem of the world and the four elements. The shell, they said, represented the earth; the white, water; the yolk, fire; and air was found under the shell at one end of the egg.' Eggs are a versatile food and useful for many different cooking purposes. When beaten, they capture millions of tiny air bubbles and help to aerate sponges, soufflés, choux pastry and meringues (whites only). They thicken hot mixtures, such as sauces and white stews, by coagulating in the heat and holding the liquid in suspension. They behave as emulsifiers by holding oil or melted butter in suspension, thus enabling, for example, mayonnaise and Hollandaise sauce to be made successfully. They bind together stuffings, rissoles, fish cakes and croquettes. They adhere immediately to foods to be freid and prevent the coating from falling off. They act as a glaze when brushed on to breads, pastry and some biscuts before baking.

EGG (TO)

To coat food with raw beaten egg.

EGG CUP

A small container for boiled eggs. It can be made from wood, metal, plastic, porcelain or pottery.

EGG FLIP

A hot drink, dating back to the 19th century or even earlier, and containing beer, spirit and eggs, heated with a hot iron which was known as a flip iron.

EGG MAYONNAISE

An *hors d'oeuvre* or light main course consisting of halved hard-boiled eggs coated with mayonnaise, garnished according to taste and served with salad.

EGG NOODLES

Narrow ribbons of pasta which contain eggs, available fresh or dried. They are well suited to central, southern and northern European dishes, as well as Jewish and North American recipes.

EGG PASTA

(Pasta All'uovo)

Pasta which has been made with varying amounts of flour and eggs. It is tinted golden-yellow and is available in assorted shapes fresh or dried.

EGG POACHER

A deepish pan containing a little water, topped with a round disc of metal in which four cups have been indented. The cups must be well-greased to prevent the eggs sticking. The poacher is sometimes covered while the eggs are cooking.

EGG PRICKER

(Egg Piercer)

A small implement for making a tiny hole in the wide end of the shell of an egg intended for boiling. This releases air and reduces the chance of the shell cracking during cooking.

EGG ROLL

See *Chinese Egg Roll*.

EGG SALAD

Hard-boiled eggs, usually halved or sliced, served with mixed salad, mayonnaise or salad cream.

EGG SEPARATOR

A utensil designed to separate the whites of eggs from the yolks. It is a round, spoon-like implement with slots or holes to allow the egg white to fall through to a container held underneath. The yolk remains intact in the bowl of the 'spoon'.

EGG SHELL

This constitutes about 10% of an egg's weight and is made up of calcium. The colour is dependent on the feed and breed of hen and may be white or beige (brown). The colour of the shell makes no difference to the flavour or nutritional value and although the British tend to prefer brown-shelled eggs, North Americans like the shells to be as white as possible.

EGG SIZES

In Britain, eggs are officially graded in seven sizes, each of a specified weight. Size 1 denotes the largest eggs, size 7 the smallest. For general cooking or baking purposes, size 3 is ideal.

EGG SLICER

A utensil designed to slice hard-boiled eggs thinly and cleanly. The egg is put into a hollow in the base and when the hinged top, consisting of a frame with thin cutting wires stretched across, is lowered it slices through the egg and the wires rest in slots in the base.

EGG STORAGE

Eggs should be placed in racks or boxes, points downwards, so that the air pockets at the rounded ends can cushion the yolks as they rise in the eggs. This prevents the yolks from sticking to the porous shells and picking up odours from stronger-smelling foods. Eggs should be kept in a cool place to prevent fairly rapid deterioration. If stored in a refrigerator, they should, for general cooking purposes, be removed 30 minutes before use. Surplus yolks should be put into a cup and gently covered with water to avoid dryness; the cup should be covered and the yolks refrigerated for no more than 2 days. Surplus whites can be kept in a small dish, covered and refrigerated for up to a week. Any surplus whole eggs should be beaten with either 2.5 ml/½ teaspoon salt or sugar per egg (depending on whether they will later be used for a savoury or sweet dish) to prevent the edges from congealing, then covered and refrigerated for up to a week. Eggs to be frozen should be prepared in the same way but the yolks must also first be beaten with salt or sugar. All frozen eggs should be thawed in the refrigerator. Because eggs readily pick up bacteria when opened, they should be used straight away or covered and kept in the refrigerator. It is interesting to note that the smaller the air pocket, the fresher the egg.

EGG WASH
A glaze for unbaked pastry, made from egg yolk beaten with a little water. Lightly beaten egg whites may be used for the same purpose.

EGG WEDGER
A utensil working on the same principle as an egg slicer but which cuts the egg into wedges instead of slices.

EGG WHITE
This constitutes about 60% of an egg's total weight. It contains 10.6% protein, 0.03% fat, 0.9% carbohydrate, and 0.6% trace elements together with B group vitamins, the balance being water. Thick, viscous whites are best for frying and poaching; thinner ones for beating to a characteristic snow.

EGG YOLK
This constitutes 30% of an egg's total weight. The yolk can be light or dark, depending on what the hen has been fed. It contains 16.6% protein, 32.6% fat, 1.0% carbohydrate and 1.1% trace elements, the balance being water. It is also a good source of vitamins A, D, E, K and the B group.

EGGNOG
A lightly sweetened egg and milk drink, frequently flavoured with sherry, brandy or rum.

EGGPLANT
North American term for aubergine.

EGGS BENEDICT
A rich North American dish of rashers of mild gammon, fried or grilled, placed on a muffin or slice of toast, topped with poached eggs and coated with Hollandaise sauce. The garnish is a piece of truffle.

EGGS FLORENTINE
A classic dish consisting of a layer of cooked spinach, a layer of poached eggs and a covering of cheese sauce. Grated cheese and sometimes breadcrumbs are sprinkled over the top and the dish is browned under the grill before serving.

EGGS FOO YUNG
Chinese omelettes to which cooked, shredded meat and pieces of cooked vegetables are added. The omelettes may be deep- or shallow-fried and flavoured to taste with soy sauce, garlic, chopped spring onions and sherry.

EGYPTIAN BEAN
See *Hyacinth Bean*.

EIN GEDI
An Israeli version of Camembert, made from cows' milk.

EINKORN
A type of wheat (*Triticum monococcum*) which has only one grain in each row of the ear. It is sometimes considered the most primitive of all wheat and is grown in central Europe, usually in areas of poor soil.

EISBEIN
Pickled pig's knuckles which are boiled in water and served hot. This German speciality is served with *sauerkraut* and potatoes.

ELASTIN
Tough and rubbery connective tissue in meat which will not soften, however much it is cooked.

ELBO
Related to Danish Samsø, this is a mild and pleasant cheese made from cows' milk. The paste is interspersed with a few holes and it is usually covered with red wax.

ELBOW MACARONI
Short lengths of fairly thin, hollow pasta which are usually curved.

ELDERBERRY
The fruit of a tree or shrub (*Sambucus nigra*) which is native to northern Europe and North America and is found both in the wild and as a garden plant. The elderberry is a small, seeded, round fruit which grows in clusters on slender stems and, when ripe, is a shiny black colour. Popular as a fruit from which to make country wine, it may also be cooked with other fruits or used in preserves. In North America there are two main kinds of native elderberry; on the eastern side there is the golden elderberry (*S. canadensis*), and on the western side the western elderberry (*S. caerulea*). All these plants produce larger and juicier fruits than the European varieties and some are red or golden. Commercial production is developing in North America due to the increasing popularity of this fruit. Elderflowers (or blossoms) are sometimes used in speciality fruit dishes and deep-fried for decoration.

ELEVENSES
British term for a mid-morning drink sometimes accompanied by a light snack.

ELMO CHEESE
A North American novelty semi-soft cows' milk cheese, with a creamy texture and hickory nut flavour.

ELVER
A young eel at the time when it leaves the open sea for the river where it will spend most of its life. At this stage it may be as little as 7.5 cm/3 inches long and is almost transparent.

EMEK
An Israeli cows' milk cheese which is relatively hard. Red-rinded, it resembles Dutch Edam and is the country's most widely used and popular cheese.

EMMENTAL
(Emmentaler, Swiss Emmental)
A very large cows' milk cheese, traditionally from Switzerland. It is produced in the Emmental valley and in the adjacent German-speaking part of the country. Cherry-sized holes characterize the cheese and the taste is mild yet full-flavoured and almost nutty. It is a firm cheese, easy to slice and the dry rind is a brownish yellow colour. Emmental is one of Switzerland's finest cheeses and is copied worldwide.

EMPANADAS
Eaten throughout Mexico and Latin America, pastry turnovers containing sweet or savoury fillings. They are either baked or shallow-fried and eaten hot.

EMPANADITAS
Small *empanadas*, eaten as appetizers.

EMPEROR'S OMELETTE
See *Kaiserschmarren*.

EMULSIFIERS
Added to certain foodstuffs to bind them together and prevent separation. The majority of emulsifiers are harmless, and many are of natural origin, derived from plants. Others are chemicals or synthetic copies of natural substances.

EMULSIONS
Mixtures where tiny globules of fat or oil are held in suspension by a liquid. Examples are mayonnaise (oil and eggs), Hollandaise sauce (melted butter and eggs) and creamed ingredients for a cake (fat, sugar and eggs).

EN
French word meaning, in its culinary sense, 'served in'.

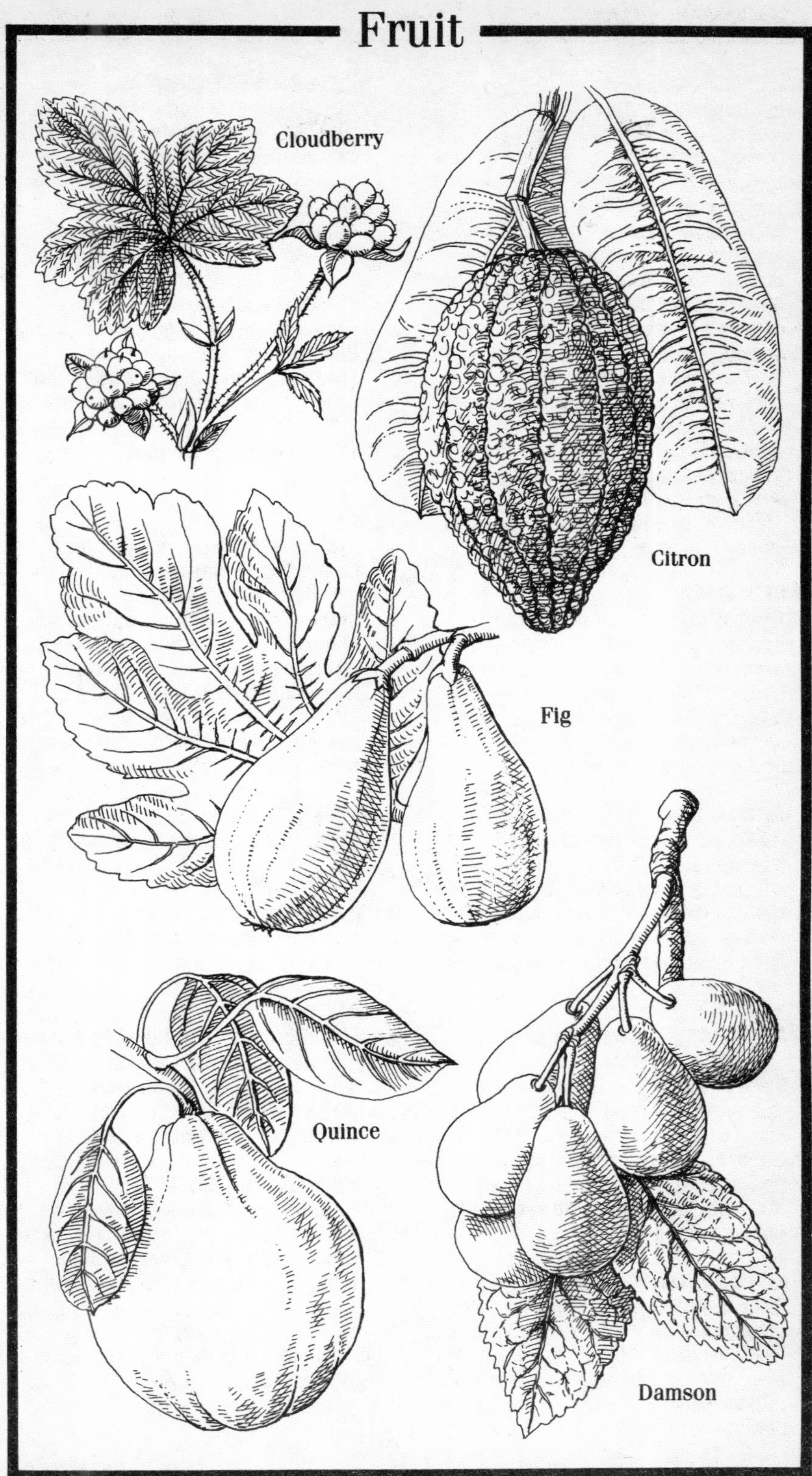
Fruit
Cloudberry
Citron
Fig
Quince
Damson

ENAMEL SAUCEPAN
Available in a good selection of shapes, colours and designs, this type of pan is extremely hygienic and the enamel finish does not retain the smell of the food. They are however heavier, in some cases much heavier, than aluminium pans. Enamel pans require careful handling and they are liable to chip and/or craze if dropped. Neither the inside nor outside should be cleaned with anything liable to scratch the surfaces. Stirring with metal spoons should also be avoided. If light-coloured enamel pans develop inside staining, they should be filled with water and a little household bleach and brought to the boil, then rinsed and dried.

ENCHILADAS
Quickly fried Mexican *tortillas* brushed with chilli or tomato sauce, then rolled up around fillings of cooked meat, poultry or grated cheese. They are coated with more sauce and served with *guacamole* and/or refried beans.

ENCHILADO
A Mexican cows' milk cheese which is white, salty, crumbly and block-shaped. It is sometimes covered with chilli powder, or the outside dyed orange with annatto. It is widely used in cooking, especially in *enchiladas*.

ENDIVE
North American term for chicory.

ENDOSPERM
The white, inner portion of the wheat grain that is turned into white flour after the wheatgerm and bran have been removed. It constitutes 85% of the grain and is the main source of carbohydrate and protein.

ENGLISH BREAKFAST
A cooked meal including a selection of eggs, bacon, sausages, tomatoes, fried bread, kidneys and mushrooms. Fruit juice or fruit and cereals with milk are also included, as are tea and coffee.

ENRICHED BREAD
Usually white breads, enriched with generous amounts of fat, sugar, milk and egg, such as bun loaves and Jewish *cholla*.

ENSALADA DE ARROZ
Spanish rice salad.

ENTRAMMES
French farmhouse type of Port-Salut cheese, made by Trappist monks of the Port-du-Salut Abbey at Entrammes in Brittany.

ENTRECÔTE BEEF STEAK
See *Sirloin Steak*.

ENTRÉE
Although this French word means beginning or entrance, this definition does not apply to an entrée course on a formal French menu. The entrée usually follows the relevé (or 'remove') and is frequently a dish served with a classic white or brown sauce. At its simplest, an entrée can be almost anything other than a roast.

ENTREMETS
French term for desserts, which in France always follow the cheese.

EPICURE
Someone who appreciates fine foods; a gastronomic connoisseur.

EPICURIENNE SAUCE
Mayonnaise flavoured with chopped gherkins and chutney (such as smooth mango). It can be served with cold meats and poultry, hard-boiled eggs and salmon trout.

ERWENTEN SOEP
Holland's national very thick and filling winter soup, made from a base of split green peas, mixed vegetables and meat bones. It is cooked, refrigerated for 1–2 days, then reheated with frankfurter sausages. It is usually accompanied by rye bread.

ESAÜ
French term for any dish containing lentils.

ESCALOPE
A boneless slice of meat, such as veal or pork, cut from the fillet. It is usually beaten until very thin.

ESCALOPE DE VEAU
Classic French veal dish made from a slice or escalope cut from the fillet. The escalope is beaten until very thin, then coated with flour, egg and breadcrumbs prior to frying. Alternatively, it may be coated with flour only, fried briskly and subsequently simmered briefly in stock and/or wine.

ESCARGOT
French term for snail. The best are those from Burgundy which have nibbled on the abundance of vine leaves in the area. Snails are usually served hot as an hors d'œuvre, packed with butter containing garlic and parsley.

ESCAROLE
See *Batavia Endive*.

ESKDALE
A British cows' milk cheese, produced in Yorkshire, resembling Camembert.

à l'ESPAGNOLE
French term for food cooked in Spanish style, denoting the inclusion of peppers, tomatoes, garlic and onions.

ESPAGNOLE SAUCE
(Spanish Sauce)
A classic French brown sauce made from mixed fried vegetables, seasonings, tomato purée and/or fresh tomatoes, flour and either meat or poultry stock or water. It is strained before use and can be served with red meat dishes, game and offal.

ESPRESSO
Coffee which is made from dark-roasted ground beans by using super-heated steam, produced under pressure. A stronger than usual and more bitter drink is the result. The earliest *espresso* coffee machines date from the early 1900s, with the modern versions appearing from about 1946. The Italians were the inventors of these machines and this kind of coffee is most popular in the Mediterranean area. The addition of hot, foaming milk produces the drink called *cappuccino*.

ESROM
A rectangular, brick-shaped Danish cheese with a softish texture and irregularly-shaped holes. It is a light creamy colour, with a mild, piquant and slightly aromatic taste, and is often eaten with its thin, orange rind. It is easy to slice, fits neatly into sandwiches, and is made from cows' milk.

ESSENCE
An extract or essential oil, possessing the natural aroma and flavour of herbs, vegetables, fruit or meat in concentrated form.

ESSENTIAL OIL
Any of several oils that impart characteristic odours to plants. They readily vaporize and are used especially in flavourings.

ESTONSKI
(Estonsky)
A firm, cows' milk cheese from Estonia. It is mild and fairly delicate in flavour.

ESTOUFFADE
(Estouffat, Estoufflet, Étouffat)
French term for a beef or pork pot-roast cooked with vegetables, herbs, seasoning, stock, sometimes wine and beans.

à l'ESTRAGON
French term for any dish containing tarragon.

ESTRAGON SAUCE
A velouté sauce made with fish stock and flavoured with tarragon. It can be served with all fish dishes.

ETHIOPIAN HARRAR
See *Harrar*.

ÉTOUFFAT
See *Estouffade*.

ETOUFFÉ OF BEEF
(Smothered Beef)
A Creole dish from Louisiana in the USA, related to the French *estouffade*. It is a beef pot roast containing a whole piece of meat with onions, celery, green pepper, tomatoes, garlic and seasonings.

à l'ÉTOUFFÉE
French term for food cooked in a pot with a tightly fitting lid; minimal liquid is added and the heat is kept very low.

ÉTUVER
French term meaning to stew.

EUROPEAN FLAT OYSTER
See *Oyster*.

EVAPORATED MILK
(Unsweetened Condensed Milk)
Milk which is evaporated in a vacuum container under reduced pressure at approximately 66°C/150°F, resulting in 60–65% water reduction. The fat in the milk is homogenized and the milk sterilized in cans. When diluted, this milk is sometimes recommended for infant feeding and also has many culinary applications. Undiluted, evaporated milk is an excellent topping for a variety of desserts. The cans of milk keep for a considerable time.

EVERTON TOFFEE
A traditional English toffee, full-flavoured and dark.

EVE'S PUDDING
An old-fashioned British pudding made from layers of sliced apples and sugar, topped with a Victoria sandwich cake mixture and baked.

ÉVORA
A Portuguese mountain cheese made from a combination of ewes' and cows' milk. It has a crumbly texture and is a robust, full-flavoured cheese, generously seasoned with salt. Évora is pale yellow.

EXCELSIOR
A French double cream cheese from Normandy. It is produced from cows' milk, is relatively small and shaped like a cylinder. The texture is close; the flavour mild.

EXPLORATEUR
A French triple cream cheese made from cows' milk in Île-de-France and shaped like a small cylinder. The flavour is delicate and the rind looks white and downy.

EXTENDED-LIFE CREAM
Usually pasteurized double cream, this is packed into vacuum-sealed bottles and keeps for about 3 weeks in refrigeration. It is thick enough to be spooned over desserts and fruit, or may be whipped before use.

EXTENDER
A substance added to a food to increase its bulk or improve its physical properties.

EXTRACT (TO)
To obtain the natural juices and flavour of an ingredient by simmering with a small amount of liquid; to squeeze citrus fruits so that the juice is extracted; to allow an ingredient to absorb flavour from another by slow extraction, for example, by placing cinnamon or vanilla sticks in a jar of sugar.

EXTRACTIVES
In reference to meat, these are muscle or flesh juices which dissolve in cooking liquor and give stews, braised dishes and casseroles their characteristic meaty flavour.

EXTRACTS
Flavourings in concentrated form which have usually been extracted, sometimes by distillation, from a herb, root, plant, flower, fruit, meat, yeast and so on.

EXTRA-THICK DOUBLE CREAM
An already-whipped, very thick and heavy pasteurized cream which is recommended for spooning over desserts and ice cream. It is homogenized and generally sold in glass jars.

EXTRAWURST
(Fleischwurst)
A German scalded sausage which is moist, mild and has a fine, smooth texture. It is made from a well-spiced combination of beef and pork and is pale pinky-beige in colour. It may be sliced and eaten cold, or used in salads or cooked dishes such as stews or casseroles.

à la FAÇON DE
French term meaning in the style or manner of.

FADGE
(Irish Potato Cakes)
These are Irish potato cakes made from potatoes, salt, flour and butter or margarine. The mixture is rolled out, cut into triangles and fried until golden brown on both sides. The cakes are sandwiched together with butter and eaten hot.

FAGGOT
See *Bouquet Garni*.

FAGGOTS
(Fagots, Poor Man's Goose)
Resembling small haggis, these are made from a mixture of minced liver, salt pork, breadcrumbs, spices, seasonings and minced onion bound together with egg. Small amounts of mixture are wrapped in pieces of pig's caul and either simmered in water or baked. Faggots should be served with creamed potatoes and swede.

FAIRY CAKES
Small individual cakes baked in bun tins or paper cake cases. They are made from a creamed cake mixture to which currants have been added.

FAIRY RING MUSHROOM
An edible mushroom (*Marasmius oreades*) which grows during spring, summer and autumn with a small, fawn-coloured, hump-backed cap on a slender stem. It is found in meadowland and other open spaces, including gardens, and it grows in clusters in a circular pattern on a ring of dark green grass. This mushroom is found in both Europe and North America and was one of the earliest kinds regularly picked for eating. It has a pleasant flavour and is useful for making soups, stews or sauces.

FANESCA
A soup from Ecuador, containing spring vegetables, salt cod, peanuts, cheese, milk, cream, stock and seasonings. It is served in Lent.

FANNINGS
One of the smaller grades of black tea leaf, often used in tea-bags.

FÅR I KÅL
A Norwegian stew of lamb and cabbage which is served with boiled potatoes.

FARCE (TO)
To stuff; also, the stuffing or forcemeat used for poultry, meat, game, fish and vegetables.

FARCI
French term for any food filled with a savoury stuffing or forcemeat.

FARFALLE
Bow-tie and butterfly-shaped pasta.

FARFALLINI
Small versions of *farfalle*.

FARFEL
Jewish pasta, shaped like small pellets.

FARINA
A granular meal similar to semolina. Farina is usually produced from ground hard wheat (but not durum) minus the germ and bran. The term also applies to other meals or powders made from potatoes, nuts and cereal grains such as maize and rye.

FARINACEOUS
Containing, or rich in, starch.

FARINOSE
Yielding or resembling farina.

FARL
(Farle)
A Scottish speciality, small, thin triangular-shaped cakes or biscuits made with wheat flour or oatmeal.

FARMED SALMON
Since the 1970s, salmon farming has become an important business in both Scotland and Norway; there are now at least ten times more farmed salmon than wild. They are hatched in fresh water and the small fish are taken in summer to deep pens moored in sheltered sea water where they remain for about a year or until considered big enough to be harvested and sold, either to be eaten fresh or used for smoking. Farmed salmon has most of the qualities of wild Atlantic salmon and only experts can tell the difference.

FARMERS'
A North American cottage cheese, made from cultured cows' milk enriched with cream. It is seasoned with salt and sold in tubs. The characteristic curds may vary in size from small to medium and the cheese has a mild and delicate taste.

FARMHOUSE ENGLISH CHEDDAR
A 16th-century cows' milk cheese which was originally produced in Somerset's beautiful Cheddar Gorge. This traditional cheese is now only made on about 24 farms in the south-west of England. It is allowed to mature for up to 2 years which gives it a characteristic and distinctive flavour, mellow and slightly nutty.

FARMHOUSE LOAF
Made from white bread dough which is placed in oblong loaf tins to rise and, just before baking, dusted lightly with flour and slit lengthwise down the centre with a sharp knife. As the loaf bakes, the slit opens out.

FAST FOOD
Ready-prepared food which can be taken away hot from shops and restaurants and eaten immediately (fish and chips, for example) or made-up dishes sold in supermarkets and food shops which need only to be reheated before serving.

FAST-FREEZE (TO)
To freeze food rapidly in order to avoid the formation of large ice crystals which can cause cell rupture and accompanying loss of natural juices and flavour.

FASULYA PLÂKI
A Turkish bean salad made from cooked haricot beans, chopped onions, oil, chopped tomato, chopped red or green pepper, seasonings and fresh chopped parsley or dill.

FAT MOUSE
Any of several tropical and South African short-tailed mice (genus *Steatomys*) which are considered a delicacy in the locality.

FATÁNYÉROS
A Hungarian mixed grill of three or four meats and offal, usually accompanied by chips and pickles.

FATLESS SPONGE
See *Sponge Cake*.

FATS AND OILS
These, like carbohydrates, are energy-giving food and behave as body insulators. Mainly mixtures of triglycerides, fats are composed of glycerol and fatty acids; a single molecule of fat comprises 1 unit of glycerol (glycerine) and 3 units of fatty acids. Like carbohydrates, fats are also made up of carbon, hydrogen and oxygen but the proportions are different and the ratio of oxygen is lower. Animal fats come from animal foods (meat, poultry, milk, cheese, eggs and certain fish), while vegetable fats and oils come from plants and are frequently converted into margarines.

FATTY
Food which has a high fat content and is greasy.

FATTY ACIDS
A prime constituent of all fats, whether saturated or polyunsaturated.

FAUX-FILET
(Contre-filet)
French term for a cut of beef steak from the top of the sirloin.

FAVA BEAN
See *Broad Bean*.

à la FAVORITE
French term to describe a 'favourite' garnish for steaks and consisting of asparagus tips, *pâté de foie gras* and truffles; also a garnish of artichoke hearts, potatoes and celery for roast meat.

FAZOLIA BEAN
See *Cannellini Bean*.

FEATHER BEEF STEAK
Fairly tender beef steak cut from near the chuck and blade of beef, between the neck and fore rib. The steak is oval, fairly small and has a feathery line of gristle running down the centre. It is recommended for frying, stewing, braising and casseroling.

FECULA
Another name for chlorophyll, the green matter contained in plants. Also a starchy sediment left from washing ground roots in water; examples of fecula include potato flour and arrowroot.

FEIJAO BEAN
Name for the butter (lima) bean in Brazil where it is an important part of the staple diet for much of the population.

FEIJOA
(Brazilian Guava, Pineapple Guava)
The fruit of an evergreen shrub (*Feijoa sellowiana*) native to South America, particularly Brazil, and now cultivated in parts of the USA and Australia. It is oval and about 5 cm/2 inches long. The skin is green and inedible. The flesh is white or greeny-yellow and surrounds an inner core of softer, seed-filled pulp. The flavour is similar to guava with a hint of pineapple, hence its other names. Once peeled, the feijoa may be eaten by itself, sliced in fruit salads or used in preserves.

FEIJOADA COMPLETA
Brazil's national dish; a hearty stew of black beans, dried and salted beef, fresh beef, tongue, bacon, sausages, onions, garlic, tomatoes, parsley, hot pepper, pigs' trotters, pigs' ears, pig's tail and seasonings.

FELAFEL
(Falafel)
Small chickpea balls. Soaked but raw chickpeas are finely minced and mixed with burghul or cracked wheat, garlic, spices, seasonings and egg, then shaped into balls and

fried. In the streets of Israel and in Israeli restaurants, they are served tucked inside pitta bread, layered with salad and topped with *tahina*; they are also speared on to sticks and served as a cocktail savoury.

FELISOWKA
A soured buttermilk from Poland which is mildly alcoholic.

FENNEL SEEDS
Fennel seeds come from the dried fruit of a perennial herb (*Foeniculum vulgare*), native to Europe and belonging to the parsley family. The seeds are small and dark yellow, and the flavour resembles mild aniseed. Much used in Italy in baking, fennel's pleasant aroma and taste makes it a useful addition to mackerel and salmon dishes, beef and pork stews, rich cakes, fruit and cooked apple combinations. It was believed to be one of nine sacred herbs which could counteract nine causes of disease. It is also mentioned in Greek mythology.

FENUGREEK
(Methi)
The seed of an annual plant (*Trigonella foenum graecum*) belonging to the pea family, native to southern Europe, but now grown in India, the Lebanon and the Argentine. The seeds are oval, short and dark yellow with a pleasantly mild flavour resembling burnt sugar or caramel, and are used both whole and ground in chutneys, pickles, curries, various meat stews, spice blends and curry powders. Fenugreek seeds were prized by the Ancients because they were said to stimulate the digestive processes.

FERMENT
A chemical compound which causes fermentation.

FERMENTATION
A chemical reaction in which an organic compound is broken down by the action of an enzyme; for example, when sugar is added to alcohol or lactose to lactic acid. Yeast also causes fermentation, as can be seen from the foaming of the yeast liquid used in making bread.

FERMENTED BLACK BEANS
A strong Chinese flavouring made from salted and fermented soy beans mixed with garlic, used in pork and fish dishes.

FERMIER
The French term for a farmhouse cheese, generally made from unpasteurized milk.

à la FERMIÈRE
French term meaning in the style of a farmer's wife, denoting a meat dish containing a mixture of carrots, onions, celery and turnips.

FESEJAN
(Faisinjan)
An Iranian speciality consisting of fried chicken or duck portions with a pomegranate and crushed walnut sauce.

FETA
(Fetta)
An extremely old Balkan cheese principally from Greece, and made originally from ewes' milk. Now also produced from cows' and goats' milk, Feta is a white and fairly firm cheese with a crumbly texture. Cut into blocks and matured in brine, it has a sharp, salty and slightly acidic flavour. Widely used throughout Greece, it adds character to local salads, puff pastry cases and hors d'oeuvre dishes such as stuffed vegetables or vine leaves. It is generally sold in vacuum packs and is now factory-produced in Denmark and Britain to meet demand. In its countries of origin, Feta is often sold still floating in its brine bath.

FETTUCINE
Flat ribbon noodles from the Italian city of Rome. They are fairly narrow, not too thin and available fresh or dried. They are generally made from an egg-based pasta dough.

FEUILLETAGE
French term for puff pastry.

FIBRE
Ingredient in bran and other vegetable matter which, with liquid, bulks up in the alimentary canal, creating a feeling of fullness. It also enables stools to be passed more quickly and easily through the body, helping to prevent constipation. The daily recommended allowance may come from bran, fruit, dried figs and apricots, crispbreads, brown bread and vegetables.

FIDDLEHEADS
A fern-like vegetable, a speciality of New Brunswick in Canada. The young, coiled fiddleheads are boiled in a minimal amount of water, then drained and tossed gently with butter. They are sometimes mixed with almonds and coated with white or Hollandaise sauce. When cold, they are often added to salads.

FIELD BEAN
(Horse Bean)
A vegetable (*Vicia faba*) native to Asia and probably the first primitive member of the broad bean family of legumes. It has been cultivated in Europe and Asia for thousands of years. It is hardier than most beans and can be grown in both hot and relatively cold climates, and also in poorish soil. The shape is round or oval and the tough skin is brown. It can be removed from the pod and cooked as a fresh vegetable or dried for use as a pulse. Although rather inferior to the more modern broad bean, the field bean is an important crop in some countries. It must be boiled briskly for the first 15 minutes of cooking time to destroy harmful toxins which can prove dangerous to the human body.

FIELD MUSHROOM
An edible and flavoursome mushroom (*Agaricus campestris*) with a white cap which has a pink underside when young, turning to red and brown as it matures; the stem is white. It grows in the late summer in grassland and may be used in recipes instead of the common or cultivated mushroom.

FIG
The fruit of a tree or large shrub (*Ficus carica*) related to the mulberry, which grows in warm and semi-tropical regions from the Mediterranean eastwards across Asia. Probably native to the Middle East, it is now also cultivated in places as far apart as California, Australia and South Africa. The shape of the fruit depends on the type and can vary from almost spherical to an elongated pear shape. Similarly, the skin colour can range from off-white through red to almost black, and the sweet and soft seed-filled flesh is just as variable. The skin may sometimes look as though it were ribbed, and on ripe fruit is often delicate enough to be eaten raw with the flesh. Apart from being an excellent dessert fruit, the fig can be used in preserves and made-up dishes. Although fresh figs are widely available, dried and canned varieties are much in demand.

FIGGY PUDDING
A traditional English steamed suet pudding containing minced apples and figs. It is a Christmas speciality.

FILBERTS
See *Hazelnuts*.

FILBUNKE
Soured milk from Sweden.

FILÉ POWDER
(Gumbo Filé)
Used to thicken gumbos in the southern states of the USA, powder made from dried sassafras leaves.

FILET MIGNON
French term for a small fillet of beef steak, usually grilled or fried. This term is also used in the USA.

'FILLED' MILK
Dried milk powder, skimmed or semi-skimmed, to which vegetable fats have been added.

FILLET (TO)
To cut the flesh of meat, poultry and fish away from the bones.

FILLET BEEF STEAK
(Tournedos)
Thick or fairly thick round steak, cut from a whole piece of fillet of beef. The meat is moist and very tender but has less flavour than rump. It is usually grilled or fried.

FILLET OF BEEF
A superior and expensive cut of boned beef, very tender and highly esteemed. It is the 'core' of the sirloin, located on the inside of the back bone. Sometimes fillet is roasted as a joint but is more usually cut into steaks and grilled or fried.

FILLET OF LAMB
A prime cut of lamb for roasting, cut from the top of the leg. It is known by this name throughout England.

FILLET OF PORK
A prime cut from the top of the leg, oval in shape with a small piece of bone in the centre. It is generally roasted, either left plain or boned and stuffed. Sometimes the boned joint is cut into slices for grilling or frying.

FILLET OF VEAL
A prime and expensive cut of veal, found in the areas of the loin and rump of the calf. The fillet can be roasted as a whole piece, but is more usually cut into slices and beaten thinly to form classic escalopes.

FILLING
Substances in a food case such as cream in éclairs, spreads in sandwiches, jam in layer cakes, etc.; also, food which tends to be heavy and readily sates the appetite.

FILO
(Fillo, Phyllo)
Very thin pastry, closely related to the wafer-thin pastry used to make strudels. It is the basis of many Balkan speciality cakes, desserts and savoury dishes.

FILTER (TO)
To separate a liquid from a solid by straining through muslin or filter paper.

FILTER COFFEE
(Drip Coffee)
Coffee prepared by standing a metal or plastic filter (lined with a paper filter bag) over a cup or jug, adding the required amount of coffee and then pouring through water, just off the boil. The filter itself may have a base of fine mesh, in which case filter bag is required.

FIN DE SIÈCLE
A French double cream cheese made in the Normandy area from cows' milk.

à la FINANCIÈRE
French term meaning financier's style, denoting a lavish garnish for chicken and sweetbreads comprising cockscombs, kidneys, slices of truffles, mushrooms and sometimes olives.

FINE CHINE OF BEEF
Term used in north-east England to describe fore rib of beef.

FINE END AND LOIN OF LAMB
Term used in north-east and north-west England for best end neck of lamb.

FINES HERBES
French term for mixed herbs.

FINGER
A strip of food such as a 'finger' of toast.

FINGER KOMBU
North American term for sea girdle.

FINGERLING
Term used to describe a small fish of up to one year old.

FINNAN HADDOCK
(Finnan Haddie)
Smoked haddock cured in the traditional Scottish manner.

FIORE SARDO
A Sardinian ewes' milk cheese which is eaten young as a dessert cheese and used in cooking when mature (about 6 months old).

FIRST CUTTING OF BEEF
Alternative term used in north-west England for the cut of beef also known as thick flank or top rump.

FISH
Cold-blooded, aquatic, vertebrate animals and their edible flesh. Typically, fish have a streamlined body, either flattened or spindle-shaped, usually covered in scales, with fins instead of limbs. Oxygen is obtained from the water through the gills, which are set at the back of the head. Eels are also classed as fish in spite of their snake-like appearance.

FISH AND CHIP SHOP
(Chippy)
A shop selling freshly fried fish and chips which may be taken off the premises and frequently eaten at home. It is a British innovation and, at one time, the food was always wrapped in newspaper. The traditional seasonings are salt and vinegar.

FISH AND CHIPS
A British take-away meal comprising a piece of fried fish and a portion of potato chips. It is usually sprinkled with salt and vinegar before being wrapped. Fish and chips can also be fried at home.

FISH CUTLETS
Portions cut crosswise from the head half of round-bodied fish down to the 'waist'. This leaves an opening where the fish has been gutted and this space can be filled with stuffing or seasonings.

FISH FILLETS
Boneless pieces of fish, skilfully cut away from the central and side bones. Fillets of large fish are often cut up and sold in pieces.

FISH FINGERS
Fingers of compressed white fish with a breadcrumb coating. They are sold frozen and may be fried, grilled or baked.

FISH KETTLE
A large, oblong saucepan capable of accommodating a whole fish. It is usually made of aluminium and can be up to 60 cm/24 inches long. Shorter, squarer versions are designed for fish like turbot and halibut.

FISH OIL
A healthy and nutritious oil, found primarily in the liver of such fish as halibut and cod. It is usually available in capsule form.

FISH SLICE
A flat, oblong slatted implement with a long handle, very useful for removing foods such as cutlets or fillets of fish, poached eggs, fried meats, fritters and rissoles from the pans in which they were cooked. Slices not only ensure that the food will not break up, but also that any excess water or fat drains away through the slats.

FISH SOUP
A British soup consisting of strained fish stock thickened with a *roux* of fat and flour and enriched with milk. Cooked fish, either in flakes or small pieces, is added to the soup immediately before serving and each portion is topped with a sprinkling of chopped parsley.

FISH STEAKS
Portions cut crosswise from the 'waist' to the tail of round-bodied fish.

FISH STICKS
North American term for fish fingers.

FISH STOCK
See *Court-bouillon*.

FISHCAKES
(Fish Cakes)
Small round cakes made from well-seasoned, cooked mashed potatoes and cooked fish. They are generally coated with breadcrumbs or seasoned flour and are fried until golden and crisp.

FISKEBOLLER
Norwegian fish balls made from minced raw cod and haddock mixed with breadcrumbs, egg, cream and seasonings, which are poached in fish stock and served with a white or cheese sauce.

FIVE SPICE POWDER
(Chinese Five Spice)
A Chinese spice blend made from ground cinnamon, cloves, star anise, ginger and fennel seeds. It smells of liquorice and is widely used in Chinese cooking. It also goes well in baked goods, fruit pies and marinades.

FIZZ
Effervescence in a drink such as the bubbles found in mineral water, champagne and lemonade.

FJORDLAND
A Norwegian cheese, made from semi-skimmed cows' milk. It resembles Swiss Emmental and Norwegian Jarlsberg.

FLAGEOLET BEAN
A vegetable (*Phaseolus vulgaris*) of the kidney bean family produced mainly in France and Italy where it was first developed. It grows as a legume and is removed from the pod when young and either cooked as a fresh vegetable or dried as a pulse. The flageolet has the typical kidney shape of beans of this family with a light green skin. It has a distinctive and delicate flavour and is considered to be a superior variety of bean. It can also be used for sprouting.

FLAKE
A platform or tray for drying fish or other products; also, the flesh of certain small Australian sharks.

FLAKE (TO)
To break up cooked fish along the natural divisions, thus forming flakes; to cut fat into thin pieces.

FLAKED RICE
See *Rice Flakes*.

FLAKY PASTRY
A light, puffy, golden-brown pastry with distinctive and usually even flakes. Its success relies upon the way in which the fat is incorporated into the mixture by special techniques of rolling and folding. It is recommended for sweet and savoury turnovers, pies, pasties, sausage rolls and flans.

à la FLAMANDE
French term meaning in the style of Flanders, denoting a garnish for joints of meat composed of cabbage, root vegetables, boiled potatoes, boiled bacon and slices of sausages; also a clear soup or consommé made from a purée of Brussels sprouts with the addition of peas and chervil; also a coating of chopped hard-boiled eggs and melted butter served over heads of cooked chicory or asparagus.

FLAMBER
French term meaning to sprinkle food with warmed alcohol and ignite it immediately before serving.

FLAN
French term for an open tart filled with custard; also another name for crème caramel, much used in Spain and Portugal.

FLAN PASTRY
(Biscuit-crust Pastry, Sweet-crust Pastry)
A variation on shortcrust pastry, enriched with egg yolk and sweetened with a little sugar. The pastry is fairly fragile and needs care in handling and it is used for sweet flans and other desserts.

FLAN RING
A ring of metal, fluted or plain, which is placed on a flat tray and lined with pastry prior to baking.

FLANK OF LAMB
Term used in Scotland for breast of lamb.

FLANK OF VEAL
A cut from the underside of the animal, suitable for stewing, braising and casseroling.

FLAPJACK
Crunchy biscuits made with oats, fat, syrup and sugar. They are baked in a shallow tin and cut into squares or fingers. Also, North American term for a thick pancake cooked on a griddle.

FLAPJACK SCONES
See *Dropped Scones*.

FLASH
A very rapid means of browning the top of a dish. This can be done under the grill, in the oven or with a salamander. A good example of flash-cooked food is baked Alaska.

FLASH-FRY BEEF STEAK
(Minute Beef Steak)
Lean slices of coarse beef which are passed through rollers covered with knives. This has the effect of breaking down the fibres in order to tenderize the meat and enable it to cook 'in a flash', or quickly. The usual cooking methods are frying or grilling.

FLAT MUSHROOM
See *Common Mushroom*.

FLAT PARSLEY
See *Parsley*.

FLATFISH
A seawater fish with a flattened body which lives on or near the sea bed. In the adult fish both eyes are on one side (back or upper side), which is generally coloured to act as a camouflage against the sea bed. The underside is usually paler than the back. Although born with eyes on both sides of the head, one eye soon 'migrates' to join the other on what has become the back of the fish (upper side). In some species the eye on the right side moves to join that on the left and the fish is called a sinistral flatfish. When the eye on the left side moves to join that on the right, the fish is called a dextral flatfish.

FLAVOUR
The blend of taste and smell sensations evoked by food and drink in the mouth.

FLAVOURED CRISPS
Crisps with added flavourings such as cheese and onion, bacon, vinegar, barbecued beef and prawn cocktail.

FLEISCHWURST
See *Extrawurst*.

FLESH
The soft tissue (sometimes referred to as muscle) underneath the skin of a backboned animal, chicken or fish; also the inside of a plant, fruit or vegetable used for food.

FLESHY
Succulent and pulpy.

FLESHY END OF BEEF
(Flesh End of Beef)
Term used in the east and west of Scotland for a beef cut also known as thick flank and top rump.

FLEUR DE MAQUIS
See *Brin d'Amour*.

à la FLEURISTE
French term meaning in the style of a florist, referring to a garnish of tomatoes and potatoes stuffed with mixed vegetables.

FLEURONS
Small pieces of puff pastry cut into decorative shapes, baked or fried and used as a garnish.

FLIP IRON
A hot iron, used in the last century for stirring drinks such as egg flips.

FLIPPER PIE
A speciality of Newfoundland, made from the flippers of young harp seals during April and May. According to one source of reference, 'Many organizations have flipper pie suppers where pies, several feet in diameter and holding 15 to 20 pounds [7–9 kg] of seal meat and gallons of vegetables, are served.'

FLOATING ISLANDS
A cold dessert consisting of a custard sauce topped with 'islands' made from spoonfuls of poached meringues.

FLOATS
Trinidadian yeasted bread which is rolled into thin rounds and fried. It is served hot with *accra*.

FLORENCE FENNEL
(Bulb Fennel)
A vegetable which is a member (*Foeniculum vulgare* var. *dulce*) of the carrot family and related to the herb fennel. It was developed in Italy but is now widely cultivated both in Europe and North America. It grows as a tight cluster of stalks with a wide base which forms a heart or bulb. Above the bulbous part, the stalks spread out like fingers and are topped with fern-like fronds of foliage. Florence fennel is usually sold with the tops removed and only the bulb and short stalks remaining. The bulb is cream or pale green in colour and the slender stalks are green. The flesh of the bulb is crisp and tastes and smells of aniseed. It may be eaten raw in salads, boiled as a vegetable or used in savoury dishes. If available, the green tops may be used for seasoning. In North America, this vegetable is also called sweet anise.

FLORENTINE
A term taken to mean any dish containing spinach. Eggs Florentine is one example.

FLORENTINES
Luxury biscuits containing dried fruits and nuts. One side of each is usually coated with chocolate.

FLØTEKARAMELLER
Norwegian caramel cream, one of the country's most popular desserts.

FLOUNDER
A flatfish (*Platichthys flesus*) caught all year round in the shallower waters of the North Atlantic from the Kola Peninsula in the USSR to the Mediterranean. It is particularly popular in Scandinavia. It measures up to 50 cm/19 inches in length and is coloured a dullish grey, green or brown (sometimes spotted) on the upper side; the underside is white. The flesh is white and lean and the fish is best steamed or fried. Apart from the European flounder, there are various members of the family found in the seas off Canada and the USA, both west and east, and also near Japan. In all, nearly 200 local names are used and in North America the term flounder can apply to most flatfish, including plaice and sole.

FLOUR
A fine meal ground from cereal such as wheat. All flour should be stored in lidded, airtight containers. As brown flours deteriorate more rapidly than white due to a higher fat content, they should be used as soon as possible after purchase.

FLOUR (TO)
To cover the surface of food with flour by sifting or dredging. This is done before frying, grilling and sometimes roasting to absorb moisture and prevent sticking. The term also applies to the flouring of pastry boards, rolling pins or baking sheets to prevent food from sticking.

FLOUR DREDGER
See *Dredger*.

FLOURY
Coated with flour; good quality boiled potatoes when mashed (as opposed to glutinous potatoes); the taste of some flour-thickened sauces which have been under-cooked; a sweet or savoury sauce which has been over-thickened.

FLUMMERY
A dessert of Welsh origin, flummery used to consist of a fermented and soured oatmeal and water mixture. Over the years it has become slightly more sophisticated; the term is now used for various dishes ranging from a creamy blancmange to a light gelatine dessert.

FLUORINE
A mineral which, like calcium, helps in the formation of strong bones and teeth. It also helps to reduce dental decay. Small quantities only are necessary, and it is found in fish and, in varying amounts, in British drinking water.

FLUTE
Indentation pressed into the edge of a pastry pie for decorative effect.

FLYING FISH
Name given to various species of fish which have enlarged pectoral fins, enabling them to glide through the air for considerable distances when escaping from their enemies. Flying fish are found in tropical and semi-tropical seas and they are highly prized as food in the Caribbean where they are boiled, fried or soused.

FOIL
See *Aluminium Foil*.

FOLD (TO)
To add one mixture to another by gently working it in with a metal spoon or spatula.

FOLIC ACID
A member of the B group of water-soluble vitamins, folic acid is necessary in the synthesis of nucleic acid. It is also considered an aid to fertility and helps prevent anaemia in pregnancy. It is found in brewer's yeast, eggs, soya flour, wheatgerm, bran, nuts, liver and leafy green vegetables such as cabbage. Lack of folic acid results in megaloblastic anaemia, diarrhoea, weariness, depression, insomnia, irritability and shortness of breath. A deficiency may be the result of a diet containing too many over-cooked foods, pregnancy, the contraceptive pill, other forms of medication such as aspirin, and excessive consumption of alcohol.

FONDANT
Made from a simple sugar syrup which is boiled, cooled and stirred until it thickens and whitens. Flavourings such as peppermint and colourings are then added and the mixture formed into assorted shapes as confectionery.

FONDANT ICING
A useful speciality icing for cakes, made from a beaten mixture of heated sugar syrup and powdered glucose. This icing is pliable, very white and easy to handle.

FONDU AU MARC
See *Tomme au Raisin*.

FONDUE
French term for melted; for example, cheese in Swiss Fondue.

FONDUE AU FROMAGE NEUCHÂTEL
(Fondue Neuchâtel)
See *Cheese Fondue*.

FONDUE BOURGUIGNONNE

A meat dish from Switzerland which is cooked at the table. Diners spear cubes of beef on to fondue forks or skewers and cook them in a pot of very hot oil. The cooked meat is accompanied by potato chips, 6–8 mayonnaise-type sauces and a selection of pickles.

FONDUE CHINOISE

A Swiss speciality which is cooked at the table. Wafer-thin slices of beef are rolled, speared on to fondue forks or skewers and cooked in stock or bouillon. The meat rolls are accompanied by 6–8 mayonnaise-type sauces and raw egg yolks. Finally, at the end of the meal, the stock or bouillon is divided between the diners, the remaining egg yolks are added and the soup is flavoured with soy sauce; sometimes cooked rice is also added to the soup.

FONDUTA

An Italian version of Swiss Fondue.

FONTAINEBLEAU

A French cows' milk cream cheese from Île-de-France. It is mixed with whipped cream and served for dessert with sugar and/or fruit.

FONTAL

A factory-produced cheese from the north of Italy. It is made from pasteurized cows' milk and resembles Fontina.

FONTINA

An Italian Alpine cheese, made from unpasteurized cows' milk. It is like a mild and delicate Gruyère, though the holes are smaller throughout its texture. It has a rich, warm flavour and is much used for *fonduta*, the Italian version of fondue.

FOOD

Nutrients taken into the body from products made up of protein, fat, carbohydrates, vitamins, trace elements, fibre and water; also inorganic substances (carbon dioxide or phosphates) absorbed in the form of gases or solutions by plants.

FOOD COLOURINGS

Both natural and synthetic. Among natural colourings used to enhance the appearance of food are pure cochineal, paprika, saffron, tea, coffee, beetroot, onion water (which turns yellow), cocoa, carob, chocolate, tomato purée, caramel and gravy browning. However, the majority of food colourings are synthetic; many belong to the azo dye group and include bright yellows (tartrazine is the best known), reds, browns and blues. These are said to trigger off allergic reactions in sensitive people, especially children.

FOOD DISPENSER

See *Automat*.

FOOD FIBRE

See *Fibre*.

FOOD HYGIENE

All foods should be kept clean and cool, washed before use (unless bought pre-washed) and stored either in a refrigerator or well-ventilated larder. Cooked food should be wrapped to prevent dryness. Uncooked food should not be covered closely as this tends to make it sweat and deteriorate quickly; some air should be allowed to circulate round it. All areas used for food storage should be kept very clean and food used in rotation and according to date stamp. To prevent stomach upsets, such things as pork, bacon and poultry should be cooked thoroughly; slices of roast meat or poultry should never be kept warm in a cool oven as food poisoning bacteria multiply fast in a tepid atmosphere. The most perishable foods are offal, mince, sausages (except hard salami), pies and pasties, milk and milk dishes, gravies and sauces, egg dishes and batters. Unless frozen, these foods should be eaten as fresh as possible. Chipped or cracked dishes harbour germs and should be thrown away.

FOOD LAWS
Government legislation protects the British public from defective foods, inaccurate weights and false descriptions of produce and products. Further details are available from Her Majesty's Stationery Office (HMSO) publications.

FOOD PROCESSOR
An electrically driven machine which, by using different discs, blades and other attachments, is capable of performing most food preparation tasks. Ingredients are placed in a plastic bowl and then beaten, chopped, sliced, grated, minced or puréed by means of a central rotating spindle which turns the relevant attachment.

FOOD SAFE
(Meat Safe)
A ventilated cupboard with a door made of wire mesh set into a wooden frame. It is useful for keeping flies and other insects away from foods and, ideally, should be placed in a cold larder, well-ventilated cellar or airy outhouse.

FOODSTUFF
A substance with food value; also, the raw material of food before and after processing.

FOOL
An old English dessert made from equal quantities of fruit purée and either custard or lightly whipped cream. The most popular fruits for fools are apple, rhubarb and gooseberry.

FOOT SUGAR
(Pieces Sugar)
An old-fashioned term for brown sugar which appears moist.

FORCEMEAT
See *Stuffing*.

FORCING BAG
(Icing Bag, Piping Bag)
A triangular-shaped bag with a hole at the pointed end in which assorted-shaped icing nozzles, tubes or pipes can be fitted to produce a variety of decorative effects. A forcing bag may be used for piping meringue, whipped cream, duchesse potatoes and other mixtures in addition to cake icings.

FORE RIB OF BEEF
A prime cut of meat and the traditional British roasting joint. The whole fore rib consists of four bones but can be bought as single or double ribs on the bone. It is frequently boned and rolled. The cut comes from the top of the animal, between the sirloin and chuck and blade. It is characterized by fairly long bones and is known by the name fore rib in London and the South-East, the West Country and Wales.

FORELEG OF BEEF
See *Shin of Beef*.

FORELLE BLAU
This famous Austrian dish is made from a freshly caught and freshly killed trout which, with slime still on its body, is plunged into gently boiling salted water mixed with vinegar and lemon juice. The skin turns a characteristic blue and the drained trout, the head left on, is served with melted butter and boiled potatoes. Unless the fish is absolutely fresh, the skin will not turn blue.

FOREQUARTER OF MEAT
The front half of a four-legged animal carcase including the leg.

FORESHANK
See *Shin of Beef*.

FORFAR BRIDIES
Scottish pastry turnovers containing beef, suet and onions, originating from the town of Forfar.

FORK LUNCHEON
A buffet-type midday meal eaten with a fork, usually while standing up.

FORK-MIX SHORTCRUST PASTRY
A quick and easy method of making shortcrust pastry which by-passes the traditional rubbing-in technique. Whipped-up, softened fat (white cooking fat or margarine) is put into a bowl, the balance of ingredients are added and the pastry is worked quickly to a dough with a fork.

FORMAGELLE
Small farmhouse cheeses, hand-made in the north Italian mountains from cows', ewes' or goats' milk.

FORMAGGIO
The Italian word for cheese.

FORMOSA OOLONG TEA
See *Oolong Tea*.

FORTIFIED WINE
Wine to which spirit has been added (usually brandy) to increase the alcoholic strength. Sherry and port are two examples.

FORTIFY (TO)
To add stength to an ingredient or mixture by enriching it with fat, cream, eggs, alcohol, etc.

FORTUNE COOKIE
North American term to describe a Chinese biscuit containing a slip of paper on which is printed a prediction of future events, a proverb or a humorous statement.

FORTUNÉS
Miniature cakes, served as *petits fours*, which are made from an almond mixture similar to that for macaroons. They are baked in small paper cases and usually topped with halved glacé cherries. They are dusted with icing sugar and served in their cases.

FOUETTER
French term meaning to whip or whisk; for example, cream or egg whites.

au FOUR
French term meaning baked in the oven or roasted.

FOURME D'AMBERT
A cylindrical French blue cheese which is rather like British Stilton. It is produced in the Auvergne from cows' milk.

FOURME DE CANTAL
See *Cantal*.

FOURME DE LAGUIOLE
See *Laguiole*.

FOWL
Term particularly applied to a hen bird which is suitable for boiling; also, a general term for the domestic chicken which is used for food.

FRAIS
The French term for fresh cheeses, such as fromage blanc and cottage cheese.

à la FRANÇAISE
French term meaning in French style, denoting a garnish of spinach and potatoes, sometimes also cooked lettuce and asparagus.

FRANGIPANE
French term for confectioner's custard containing chopped or ground almonds. It is used as a cake or pastry filling.

FRANGIPANE TART
(Frangipane Flan)
Italian in origin, the tart was supposed to have been introduced to France in the 16th century by Catherine de Medici. A pastry case is spread with jam, then filled with a cooked cream containing crushed ratafias, butter heated until light brown, rum and lemon rind. It is traditionally decorated with whipped cream and chopped pistachio nuts.

FRANK
North American term for frankfurter.

FRANKFURTERS
Genuine frankfurter sausages should, in theory, come only from Frankfurt in Germany or its immediate surroundings; however, the sausages are now imitated worldwide and sold under the name of frankfurter. Made from top-quality pork, ground to a fine paste, frankfurters are scalded sausages which are subsequently cold-smoked, giving them their characteristic golden-bronze colour. Flavoursome and well-seasoned, frankfurters are the vital ingredient in hot dogs and are often eaten as a snack with mustard and bread. In northern Europe and parts of France, the sausages are cut into pieces and added to winter soups and casseroles. To prevent splitting, frankfurters should be placed in water which has just boiled and left to stand away from the heat for about 5 minutes and should be well-drained before serving.

FRAPPER
French term meaning, in its culinary sense, to put chilled food and drinks on or surrounded by crushed ice. For example, *crème de menthe frappé* means the liqueur is poured into a glass over crushed ice.

FREE-RANGE EGGS
Laid by poultry which are non-battery reared and allowed freedom of movement in their environment and a natural diet.

FREEZE (TO)
(Deep Freeze (to))
To preserve food by storing it at a temperature of –18°C/0°F in a specially-designed deep-freeze cabinet (freezer). The action of freezing holds back the growth and multiplication of harmful bacteria.

FREEZE-DRIED
Food which is dried from the frozen state. It usually retains its original colour, flavour and texture better than food dried by traditional methods.

FREEZER KNIFE
(Freezer Saw)
A strong-bladed knife with a scalloped or saw-toothed edge which is used for slicing or cutting up frozen food. It may have two differently serrated edges and sometimes a hooked tip. One type has a blade which will cut through small meat or poultry bones as well as the flesh.

FREEZER-BURN
Coloured or white patches on deep-frozen food which has been inadequately wrapped.

FREEZING: CREAM
Whipping and double cream freeze well for up to 2 months in the domestic deep-freeze. They should be partially whipped with the addition of 15 ml/1 tablespoon milk to every 150 ml/¼ pint and then frozen in plastic containers, securely covered. Before use, the cream should be thawed completely and carefully whipped to the desired consistency; it easily over-whips, hence the need to take care.

FRENCH BEAN
A vegetable (*Phaseolus vulgaris*) which is the fruit of various plants, both dwarf and climbing, probably native to South America and now cultivated worldwide. It grows as a long green or golden-yellow pod enclosing a number of seeds or beans. The term French bean is used for immature, thin and almost stick-like pods which are picked before the beans mature.

FRENCH BREAD
A basic white bread dough which is formed into long sticks before baking. It is characteristically very crusty and golden-brown.

FRENCH COFFEE
Term used to describe coffee which contains added chicory.

FRENCH DRESSING
A classic salad dressing made from oil, salt, pepper and either lemon juice or vinegar or a mixture of both. It is suitable for all salads.

FRENCH FLAN
See *Crème Caramel*.

FRENCH FONDU
Processed cheese from France, with a minimum butterfat content of 40%.

FRENCH FRIES
North American term for chips.

FRENCH FRITTERS OR PUFFS
See *Beignets*.

FRENCH MERINGUE MIXTURE
Method whereby egg whites are put into a basin over a pan of hot water and beaten until thick and stiff with double their weight of sifted icing sugar, a little vanilla essence and a pinch of salt. This process can take as long as 30 minutes. The mixture can be piped in different shapes including baskets to hold soft fruit. It is baked in a very cool oven.

FRENCH SORREL
See *Sorrel*.

FRENCH STICK
See *Baguette*.

FRENCH TOAST
See *Pain perdu*.

FRESH CHEESE
Drained curd cheeses (usually through muslin) which are eaten fresh and immature. Cottage cheese is a typical example. This kind of product must be kept under refrigeration.

FRESH CHICKEN
Chicken which has had all its innards removed, is oven-ready and usually chilled. It comes with or without the giblets.

FRESH FRUIT SALAD
See *Fruit Salad*.

FRESH PASTA
Home-made or shop-bought, this is freshly made, soft pasta, sometimes containing eggs, found in a more limited variety of shapes than dried. It cooks in a comparatively short space of time, from 3 to 5 minutes, depending on type and size.

FRESH SAUSAGES
Lightly salted and often unsmoked sausages which have been prepared from fresh meat and seasonings without added preservatives. They do not have a long shelf-life and should be eaten as soon as possible after purchase.

FRESHNESS OF EGGS
When broken, a fresh egg will have a domed yolk, fairly centrally placed, surrounded by a thick and viscous portion of white which is translucent. Outside this will be found a thinner ring of white which is almost transparent. The white of a stale egg tends to separate from the yolk rather than cling to it and the yolk itself moves to one side and is not as domed. Another test is to lower an unbroken egg into a bowl of cold water. If the egg lies parallel to the base and sinks to the bottom, it should be quite fresh. If the egg appears to be moving upwards in a lop-sided fashion with the pointed end facing down, it is probably stale.

FRESHWATER BREAM
A fish (*Abramis brama*) related to the carp family, mainly of interest to the sporting fisherman as the flesh tends to have a muddy flavour and is full of awkward bones. It bears no comparison to the sea bream as a fish for eating.

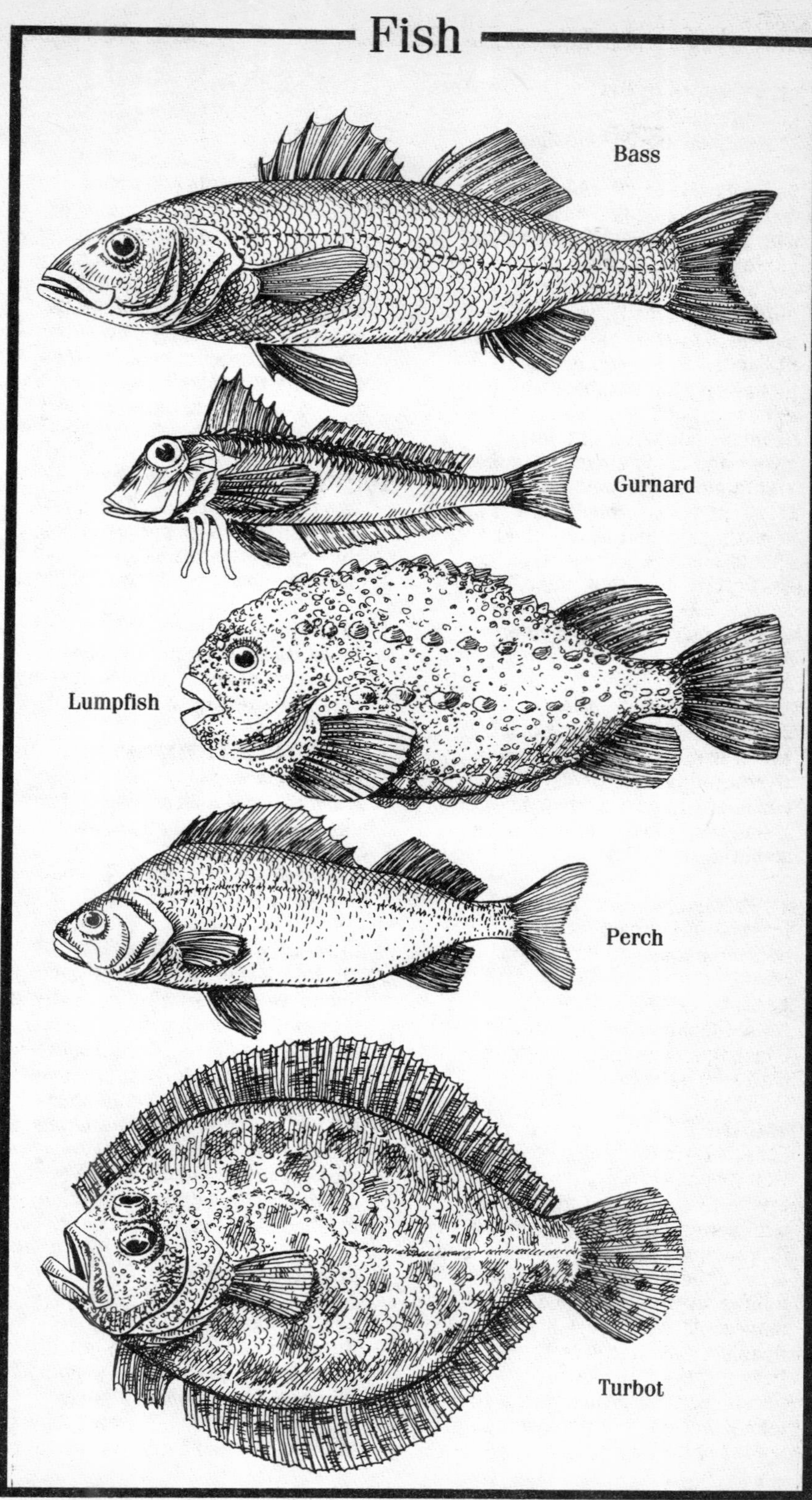
Fish
Bass
Gurnard
Lumpfish
Perch
Turbot

FRESHWATER DRUM

(Sheepshead)

The only member (*Alpodinotus grunniens*) of the drum family of fish which lives all its life in fresh water. The back is pearly coloured with blue or bronze tints, shading to silver on the sides and white on the underside. It has a deep, hump-backed body, and the average length of the whole fish in the shops is 30–40 cm/12–16 inches and the weight about 450 g/1 lb. It is caught, mainly in the summer months, in the larger rivers and lakes of North America and in particular the Great Lakes. In the mid-western states it is sometimes called sheepshead but should not be confused with the seawater fish of that name. The flesh is mild and light-coloured and the fish may be baked or fried.

FRESHWATER FISH

Term used to describe those fish which live in salt-free waters in rivers and lakes and also those which spend part of their lives, usually for spawning, in similar conditions.

FRIANDISES

Petits fours served as an accompaniment to ice cream.

FRIAR'S OMELETTE

An old-fashioned English dish consisting of a baked omelette with stewed apples.

FRICASSÉE

French term for a classic stew of veal or poultry which is pale cream in colour and thickened with a roux. It is flavoured with cloves, onion, mace or nutmeg and is well-seasoned with salt and pepper. It frequently contains mushrooms. It is enriched with double cream and lemon juice before serving. It may be garnished with grilled bacon rolls, lemon wedges and parsley and served with plain boiled rice.

FRIED EGGS

Eggs gently fried in hot butter, margarine, dripping, lard or white vegetable fat. There should be sufficient fat in the pan to baste the eggs while frying in order to cook the tops. To avoid using fat, the eggs can be cooked in a non-stick pan and covered; this way the top and bottom will be cooked simultaneously. The eggs may also be turned over carefully in order to cook the tops. To ensure the yolks do not break, the eggs to be fried should be at room temperature.

FRIED RICE

A combination of cooked rice stir-fried in oil with spring onions and egg. It is served as an accompaniment to Chinese dishes.

FRIES

The testicles of lambs and calves. They can be fried or cooked in stews, casseroles and braised dishes.

FRIESE KANTERKAAS

(Kanter Cheese)

A Dutch cows' milk cheese and an unspiced version of Nagelkaas.

FRIJOLES NEGROS

See *Black Bean*.

FRIJOLES REFRITOS

The literal translation is refried beans. This important Mexican side-dish is served with *tortillas*, as an accompaniment to main courses (*chilli con carne*, for instance) and as a dip. It consists of either red kidney, pinto, pink or black beans boiled until tender with onions, garlic, chillies and occasionally tomatoes. The beans are drained, mashed like potatoes and mixed with fried onions. They are then reheated and served.

FRIKADELLER

A Danish national dish, meatballs made from minced beef and pork, flour, allspice, grated onion, egg, milk and seasoning. They are fried until cooked and golden brown in colour, then served with potatoes and either cooked red cabbage or salad.

FRILL
(Cutlet Frill)
Shaped like a tiny chef's hat, a food frill consists of a small paper roll curled or fluted at one end. The other end is open and is slipped over the protruding tip of a meat bone (often a chop) by way of decoration. Frills are always used on crown roasts of lamb and guards of honour.

FRISCH
(Frischkäse)
This translates from the German as 'fresh cheese' and refers to such products as Quark and cream cheese which are not left to mature.

FRISÉE
(Frisé)
Name under which some kinds of curly endive are sold.

FRITTATA
An Italian-style omelette which is fried on both sides and served flat. Some varieties contain vegetables or offal.

FRITTER BATTER
A thick batter used to coat foods prior to frying. It is made from a flour, oil and warm water mixture into which stiffly beaten egg whites are blended. It is light, crisp and always a warm golden brown after frying.

FRITTERS
Either pieces of sweet or savoury food coated with fritter batter and deep-fried, or diced cooked food stirred into fritter batter and then deep-fried, in small spoonfuls, in hot fat or oil. The latter are usually served hot as appetizers with drinks.

FRITTO MISTO DI MARE
An Italian speciality, consisting of small pieces of assorted fish and sea food and vegetables which have been fried or deep-fried.

FRITURE
French term for fried food.

FRIVOLITÉS
French term for small savouries served at the beginning of a formal meal or banquet.

FRIZZES
North American dried sausages made from minced pork and beef, flavoured with peppercorns and garlic.

FRIZZLE (TO)
To fry until very crisp and brown; almost overcook.

FROG
See *Grenouilles*.

FROGS' LEGS
See *Grenouilles*.

FROMAGE
The French word for cheese.

FROMAGE AFFINÉ
French term for a cheese which has matured and ripened.

FROMAGE BLANC
(à la Pie)
French version of curd cheese, made from cows' milk, with a low or medium butterfat content. It is soft, white, light and spreadable, sometimes containing herbs, pepper, etc, and is very similar to Quark in flavour and consistency. It is often served with soft berry fruits in place of cream.

FROMAGE DE BRUXELLES
(Brusselkaas, Hettekees)
A Belgian cheese made from pasteurized skimmed cows' milk and therefore low in fat. It has a tangy flavour and is rindless.

FROMAGE DE TÊTE
French term for brawn made from the head of an animal such as a calf or pig.

FROMAGE FORT
A French mixture of over-ripe dessert cheese, blended with herbs, spices, alcohol and oil. It is sealed into pots and left to mature according to personal taste. The cheese is strong and piquant. Sometimes the basic mixture also contains Gruyère cheese.

FROMAGE FRAIS
Fresh white curd cheese from France with a very soft consistency and bland taste. It is widely used in cooking and also forms the basis of a variety of desserts. This is very similar to German Quark. It is generally low fat.

FROMAGE-DE-TRAPPISTE
A Belgian semi-soft cheese, similar in texture and flavour to Port-Salut. It is made from cows' milk.

FROMEZ
A mild Israeli goats' milk cheese.

FROST (TO)
North American term meaning to ice a cake.

FROSTING
A thick and fluffy cake icing and filling, usually a North American term.

FROTH
Foam seen on the top of liquids.

FROZEN CHICKEN
An oven-ready chicken, fast-frozen by the producers and sold with or without a pack of giblets in the cavity. Frozen chicken must be thoroughly thawed before cooking.

FROZEN CREAM
Single, whipping and double creams are commercially frozen and usually sold in packets. They can be kept several months in a domestic deep-freeze and should be completely thawed before use.

FROZEN YOGURT
Produced commercially, this is a useful product in that it can be bought and kept in the home freezer until required. It should be defrosted for about 24 hours in the refrigerator.

FRUCTE COAPTE LA FLAMĂ
Romanian fruit fritters which are dusted with icing sugar, sprinkled with alcohol and flamed at the table.

FRUCTOSE
A monosaccharide or simple sugar which, as its name would suggest, is found naturally in fruit. It is also found in honey and cane sugar.

FRÜHSTÜCKSKÄSE
Its German name meaning 'breakfast cheese', this is a relative of Limburger.

FRUIT
The reproductive body of a seed plant. Starting usually as a flower, the ripe fruit comprises skin, flesh and either a seed (or seeds) or a stone containing a seed (or seeds). The edible parts may be any or all of these. The term also applies to any edible product of plant growth.

FRUIT BATTER PUDDING
A baked Yorkshire pudding mixture, containing pieces of fresh fruit (usually apples or rhubarb) and sugar. It is served hot with custard.

FRUIT BRANDIES
Produced like brandy, these are colourless and non-sweet spirits made from fruit wines such as cherry, pear, peach, blackberry, apple and plum. They are produced primarily in France, Germany, Switzerland and the Balkans and are stronger than coloured and sweet liqueurs; 70–78° proof (40–44.5° GL) as opposed to 70° proof (40° GL). They are used as a flavouring and often added to fresh fruit — for example, kirsch with pineapple.

FRUIT BREAD
A loaf made from either a plain or fairly rich white yeasted dough to which dried fruit has been added. Spices and grated orange and/or lemon peel are sometimes also included.

FRUIT BUTTER
See *Fruit Cheese*.

FRUIT CAKE
A general term to cover creamed or rubbed-in cakes containing varying amounts of dried fruit.

FRUIT CHEESE
(Fruit Butter)
A thick, purée-like preserve made from fruit pulp and sugar which are cooked together slowly until most of the liquid has evaporated.

FRUIT CRUMBLE
A dessert made from fruit and sugar placed in a greased ovenproof dish and topped with a crumble mixture made from flour, fat and sugar and sometimes spices. The dessert is then baked and eaten hot with cream, custard or ice cream.

FRUIT CUPS
A name given to non-alcoholic fruit drinks which are served in large bowls, similar to those used for punch. Pieces of fresh and/or canned fruit are added and the drink is lightly chilled before serving in tumblers. The base can be apple juice, grape juice, diluted squashes and cordials, fresh orange juice and so on.

FRUIT ESSENCES
See *Extract (to)* and *Cordials*.

FRUIT FRITTERS
Rings of peeled raw apple, slices of peeled fresh pineapple or chunks of peeled bananas or other prepared fruits coated with fritter batter and fried in deep fat until golden-brown. They are drained, sprinkled with sifted icing sugar and eaten hot.

FRUIT JELLY PRESERVE
Made from the strained and clear juice of cooked fruit, boiled with sugar until setting point is reached.

FRUIT JUICE
Liquid extracted from raw or cooked fruit.

FRUIT PIE
A pie containing fruit, usually sweetened.

FRUIT SALAD
(Fresh Fruit Salad)
A variety of fresh fruits cut, peeled, seeded or stoned as necessary, mixed with cold sugar syrup or fruit juice.

FRUIT SNOW
A combination of lightly sweetened fruit purée, beaten egg whites and sugar.

FRUIT SOUP
Very popular in Austria, Germany, Poland, Yugoslavia and Scandinavia, this is made from sweetened stewed fruit, thickened with either potato flour, arrowroot, fine semolina or cornflour and often flavoured with wine, lemon juice or vanilla.

FRUIT SPONGE PUDDING
A baked pudding in which sliced fruit, such as apples, rhubarb, gooseberries or pears, and sugar are topped with a Victoria sandwich mixture before cooking.

FRUIT SQUASH
A sweetened fruit concentrate in liquid form, which can be turned into a long drink by the addition of soda, mineral or tap water.

FRUIT STREUSEL
North American term for fruit crumble.

FRUIT SUGAR
See *Fructose*.

FRUIT SYRUPS
Sweet and concentrated syrups made from fruits and sugar. Sometimes preservatives are added. The syrups are either used in cooking or mixed with water or mineral water to make long drinks.

FRUIT TURNOVERS
Triangles of pastry filled with fruit which are usually brushed with milk and sprinkled with caster sugar before baking.

FRUIT YOGURT
Fruit yogurt is the most popular variety in Britain. It contains pieces of real fruit which are added after the milk has been inoculated with the yogurt culture and subsequently incubated. The fruit is first cut into suitably-sized pieces, mixed with water and sugar and heat-treated to destroy yeasts. The cartons are then filled with the yogurt and stored at a temperature of 4.5°C/40°F.

FRUITARIAN
Someone who eats only plant foods which do not involve the death of the plants.

FRUIT-FLAVOURED YOGURT
Plain yogurt mixed with natural flavourings and/or fruit juice. It is sweetened (with sucrose or with sugar substitutes) and sometimes coloured with acceptable food dyes. The texture is smooth, and the consistency fairly thick and creamy.

FRUITS DE MER
French term used to describe seafood, or shellfish, but excluding oysters, from Mediterranean, Adriatic and Atlantic waters. The literal translation is 'fruits of the sea'.

FRUMENTY
(Furmety, Fumenty, Thrumety)
A mediaeval British pudding made from wheat cereal with milk. Additions included currants, raisins, beaten egg yolks, sugar and spices. It used to be served hot in cups with brandy as an additional flavouring, and was traditionally eaten during Lent.

FRY (TO)
To cook in hot fat or oil, usually in a frying pan.

FRYER
(Deep-fryer, Frier)
A deep pan used for deep-frying foods. Also, North American term for a young chicken suitable for frying.

FRYING BASKET
(Chip Basket)
Usually part of a deep-frying pan and designed to fit inside it, this is a wire mesh basket that facilitates the removal of small pieces of fried food such as chips or fritters from the pan and allows the hot fat to drain off.

FRYING PAN
A circular pan with shallow, outwardly sloping sides and a long, narrow handle. It should have a heavy base and is best if made from mild steel or enamelled cast iron, rather than aluminium. The heavier the base, the better the transference of heat for effective fast frying. A frying pan should be used for food which is both thin and flat and requires frying in the minimum amount of oil or fat. Many brands have non-stick coatings.

FRY-UP
British term for an informal meal of assorted fried foods.

FUDGE
A semi-soft sweet which appears to be peculiar to Britain, the Commonwealth countries and the USA. It is made from boiled sugar and/or syrup, milk, butter or margarine and flavouring. Sometimes dried fruit and nuts are also included.

FUDGE CAKE

(American Fudge Cake)
A rich North American chocolate cake which has a fudge-like and almost sticky texture. It is moist, finely-flavoured and very popular in its country of origin.

FUDGE ICING

A thick, fudge-like icing, popular in North America. It usually contains chocolate and/or cocoa powder.

FUEL FOODS

Carbohydrates and fats.

FUFU

A West African speciality made from a purée of yams or sweet potatoes, mounded into a dish and served with meat. It is sometimes made with plantains.

FUKIEN COOKING

The food of this region, situated between Shanghai and Canton on the eastern coast of China and opposite Taiwan, includes delicate soups, sucking pig, seafood and egg rolls. Soy sauce is used extensively.

FUL MEDAMES

(Foule Medames)
A vegetable of the broad bean family. It is grown mainly in the Middle East and is particularly popular in Egypt, where it forms the basis of a national dish of the same name. This is made from cooked beans and lentils mashed with crushed garlic, oil and lemon juice. The dish is well seasoned and garnished with chopped hard-boiled eggs.

FULL-CREAM MILK

(Whole Milk, Ordinary Milk, Silver-top Milk)
Pasteurized, unskimmed milk sold in Britain in silver-topped bottles with a clearly visible cream-line. It is an all-purpose milk and may be used for all drinking and cooking purposes. It has a minimum butterfat content of 3%, but the average is 3.8%.

FULL-FAT SOFT CHEESE

A soft white cheese with a butterfat content ranging between 20% and 45%. It is fairly creamy and rich-tasting and excellent both as a spreading or cooking cheese. It is generally made from cows' milk.

FUMER

French term meaning to smoke, applied to foods such as fish, meat or cheese which are smoked.

FUMET

French term for a concentrated fish stock, similar to *court-bouillon* but including fish trimmings.

FUNGUS

A member of a family of plant life which developed many millions of years ago and is distinct from other vegetation in that it has characteristics of both plant and animal life. As fungus does not contain chlorophyll, it cannot feed as other plants do but rather in the manner of animal life from vegetable organisms, living or dead, or on animal manure. In other ways it acts like most plants with fruit-bodies and reproduces by distributing spores as seeds. Most fungi play an important rôle in the process of decay in the earth's natural life cycle. There are many thousands of varieties of fungi and they include moulds and other inedible growths like toadstools, as well as useful kinds such as yeast fungi used in bread and wine-making and fermented milk products. From a culinary point of view, the mushroom and the truffle are the best-known fungi.

FUSILLI

(Rotelle, Tortiglione, Tortiglioni)
Long ringlets or twists of thin macaroni, sometimes described as corkscrews.

FUZZY MELON

(Hairy Melon, Summer Melon)
A Chinese vegetable which looks like a courgette. Its skin is covered with

fine down and the melon must be peeled before use. It is often added to soup and can also be stir-fried or steamed.

FYNBO
A member of the Danish Samsø family, this cows' milk cheese comes from the island of Fyn and is smooth, creamy and fairly firm-textured, with a rich and buttery flavour. It contains a sprinkling of holes and is flattish and round, generally coated with red or yellow wax.

GAD
An Israeli cows' milk cheese with the flavour and texture of Danish Danbo. It has fairly large holes throughout.

GADO-GADO
An Indonesian mixed vegetable salad served with a peanut sauce flavoured with garlic and lemon. The seasonal vegetable mixture is partially cooked and can contain as many as 8–10 different vegetables.

GAENG KAREE
A thick curried Thai shrimp soup which is flavoured with citrus and has a slightly sweet-sour taste. It is yellow in colour, due to the addition of turmeric and other spices. Meat or chicken are sometimes used instead of the fish, and the soup is usually served with rice.

GAENG MUSSAMAN
A renowned Thai curry which is heavily spiced and contains beef, coconut and peanuts. It was supposed to have been introduced to Thailand by Muslim civil servants from India during the early part of the 19th century, hence its English name, 'Muslim Curry'.

GAGE
A group of fruits of the plum family (*Prunus* species) noted for their relatively small size, sweetness and pleasant smell. Two of the popular varieties are the greengage and the golden mirabelle.

GAJI JIJIM
A Korean speciality of fried aubergine slices sandwiched together with thinly carved roast beef. The 'sandwiches' are served with soy sauce sharpened with vinegar.

GAJJAR HALWA
(Gajjar ka Halva)
An Indian sweetmeat resembling fudge made from a mixture of dried milk, carrots and spices.

GALACTOSE
Part of a monosaccharide or simple sugar which occurs during the digestion of milk sugar (lactose).

GALANGAL
A culinary spice (*Alpinia galanga* or *officinarum*) from the Far East which is similar to ginger with a strong and slightly peppery taste.

GALANTINE
Term for a roll made from boned meat or poultry with a minced meat filling in the centre. It is securely tied and simmered in stock until tender. When cold, it is usually pressed. Finally the string is removed and the galantine glazed with aspic and attractively garnished. It is popular on a buffet table.

GALETTE
French term for a type of pancake, often made in Brittany with buckwheat or brown flour, with a sweet or savoury filling. The term is also used for thin, round pastry biscuits which may be sweet or savoury. Some are 20 cm/8 inches in diameter and form layers of a

gâteau with assorted fillings; they are eaten in France in this form on Twelfth Night.

GALIA MELON
A variety of Mediterranean musk or netted melon, distinguished by the 'net-work' pattern on the skin. The skin is yellow and the sweet, juicy and fragrant flesh is a pale greeny-yellow.

GALIC
(Gaelic)
A rich, full-cream soft cheese, produced in Scotland from cows' milk. It is flavoured with the chopped leaves of wild garlic and covered with rolled oats and chopped nuts.

GALIL
A blue-veined Israeli cheese made from ewes' milk. It resembles French Roquefort.

GÁLIT
See *Na'ama*.

GALLIMAUFRY
Said to be a corruption of the French word *galimafrée*, meaning hotch-potch or a 'combination of many things without regard to order or reason'.

GALLINACEOUS
General term for an order of birds (*Galliformes*) which have heavy bodies and live mainly on the ground, including domestic fowl, turkeys, pheasants and grouse.

GAMBREL
A term used for the hock of an animal.

GAME
In general, this refers to certain birds and animals hunted by sportsmen. There are seasons for each and all game is protected by stringent laws, prohibiting hunting during the 'close season' when the birds and animals are breeding and raising their young. Broadly speaking, hunting takes place in Britain from August to March. Rabbits, pigeons and hares are not protected by game laws, although the sale of hare is not permitted between March and July. Game of all types is generally hung in a cool and airy place (cellar, larder or outhouse) in order to tenderize the flesh and improve the flavour. The length of time game should be hung is very much a question of personal taste and those who appreciate game with a high, gamey and strong flavour will allow it to hang for longer than those who prefer their game to be mild. Another factor is age; older, tougher game needs to hang longer than younger birds or animals. Birds have been hung sufficiently when the tail and breast feathers pull out easily and droplets of blood fall from the bills. For maturity of flavour, partridge, pheasant and hare should be hung for up to 8 days; venison up to 14 days; other game 2–5 days.

GAME CHIPS
(Straw Chips)
Thin strips of potato, fried like chips and served with game.

GAME FISH
Fish caught by rod and line for sport as well as food.

GAME PIE
A traditional British raised pie made with hot-water crust pastry and filled with cubed and boned game, rump steak, lean ham, pork sausage-meat and seasonings. It is baked in an oval and hinged ornamental metal mould. Liquid aspic jelly is funnelled into the hot pie through a small hole in the top and sets as the pie cools. Game pie is usually served in portions with salad.

GAME PIE MOULD
See *Game Pie*.

GAMECOCK
Male game fowl.

GAMEY
(Gamy)
Having the flavour or smell of game, especially applicable to birds or meats which have been allowed to hang uncooked until slightly high.

GAMMELOST
A very strong and highly-esteemed Norwegian blue cheese made from skimmed cows' milk.

GAMMON
The hind leg and thigh of cured bacon, smoked or unsmoked, which is served hot.

GAMMON HOCK
(Gammon Knuckle)
The knuckle end of gammon, recommended for boiling, stewing and braising. The meat is also suitable for cutting up and using in pies.

GAMMON SLIPPER
A triangular-shaped cut resembling corner gammon, though it is smaller. It is lean and recommended for boiling.

GAMMON STEAKS
Almost circular and usually cut from the joint known as middle gammon.

GAMONEDO
A strong and potent blue-veined Spanish cheese, which is similar to Cabrales and produced in the same area from a mixture of cows', ewes' and goats' milk. It is smoked for 2–3 weeks, wrapped in fern leaves, matured in caves and eaten after about 2 months.

GAPRON
(Gaperon)
A dome-shaped French cheese from the Auvergne province, this is produced from skimmed cows' milk or buttermilk. It is low-fat and richly endowed with garlic. The texture is fairly soft and supple.

GARAM MASALA
An Indian blend of spices comprising coriander, cloves, cinnamon, cumin, fenugreek, turmeric, pepper and ginger. It is used in curries and other spiced dishes, and available ready-prepared in jars or tins.

GARBANZO
(Garbanzo Pea)
See *Chickpea*.

GARBURE
A thick French vegetable soup containing beans, garlic, herbs, occasionally chestnuts and a piece of preserved meat (duck, goose, turkey or ham). The soup is ladled over slices of bread and the remaining few spoonfuls of each serving are mixed with the last mouthful of red wine left in the diner's glass. *Garbure* is a speciality of Béarn.

GARFISH
(Garpike, Longnose)
An elongated, round-bodied seawater fish (*Belone belone*). The back is greeny-blue in colour, shading to silver on the sides and underside. The fish measures 35–60 cm/14–24 inches when sold. Members of the species are caught in the Mediterranean, in the eastern Atlantic as far north as Iceland and in the Baltic Sea. Similar fish are found in North American, Atlantic and Pacific waters, where they are called needlefish. The green colour of the bones may be offputting, but the flesh is firm and the fish may be poached, steamed, baked or fried.

GARIBALDI BISCUITS
Sweet biscuits containing currants, supposedly named after the 19th-century Italian patriotic leader, Giuseppe Garibaldi.

GARLIC
A herb valued since time immemorial, garlic (*Allium sativum*) is said to have been given to men building the Egyptian pyramids to keep them healthy. It was also very

popular in Britain during the reign of Elizabeth I. Extensively cultivated worldwide and also found wild, the herb is a perennial member of the onion family and grows in bulbs, each containing individually wrapped cloves. The flavour is strong and penetrating and is something of an acquired taste.

GARLIC BUTTER
Softened, whipped butter to which boiled and crushed garlic, together with lemon juice, are added. It is shaped into a 2.5 cm/1 inch diameter roll, wrapped and refrigerated until hard, then cut into rounds of about 5 mm/¼ inch in thickness. These are used to garnish grilled steaks of beef.

GARLIC CLOVE
A segment or individual wedge of garlic taken from the head or bulb. It is always covered with its own layers of fine, papery skin.

GARLIC DRESSING
Either French or vinaigrette dressing flavoured with crushed fresh garlic. It can be served with all types of vegetable salads.

GARLIC POWDER
Garlic powder is made from cloves of garlic which have been dehydrated and finely ground.

GARLIC PRESS
Small implement used to crush garlic cloves. It generally consists of a pair of hinged handles with a perforated cup on one handle and a facing pressing foot on the other. The garlic clove is put into the cup and when the handles are squeezed together, the foot presses the garlic against the cup and forces the juice and pulp through the perforations.

GARLIC SALT
Garlic salt is a mixture of table salt and garlic powder.

GARNIR
French term meaning, in its culinary sense, to garnish with or be accompanied by. For example, when fish is followed by the word *garni* on a menu, it means that vegetables are included.

GARNISH
Decorative trimmings used to ornament sweet and savoury dishes.

GARNITURE
French term for garnish.

GARUM
A fish paste much used as a condiment by the Romans.

GASPEREAU
See *Alewife*.

GASTEROPOD
A mollusc, such as the snail, with the 'foot' situated at the hole in the shell.

GASTRONOME
(Gastronomist)
Someone who is a connoisseur of fine food and wine.

GASTRONOMY
The study and knowledge of good eating and drinking, particularly wines.

GÂTEAU
The French word for cake, now used internationally for rich, elaborate cakes.

GÂTEAU NOIR
See *Créole Christmas Cake*.

GÂTEAU PITHIVIERS
A speciality of Pithiviers, a town to the south-west of Paris. It consists of two layers of puff pastry with a rich cream filling containing almonds and rum.

GÂTEAU SAINT-HONORÉ
A fancy French gâteau, made from a base of shortcrust pastry with a ring border of choux pastry. When

cooked, the ring is split and filled with sweetened whipped cream. It is then brushed with sieved apricot jam and topped with small, cream-filled choux puffs which are decorated with halved glacé cherries. Finally, more whipped cream is mounded into the centre of the *gâteau*.

GAUCHO
A firm and rich-tasting cheese from Argentina made from skimmed cows' milk. It tastes a little like Port-Salut and also resembles it in texture.

GAUFFRES
Belgium's famous waffles, usually served warm with butter and syrup and sometimes accompanied by summer fruits and whipped cream.

GAY-LUSSAC
The French chemist who developed the system of measuring alcohol in liquids by percentage of volume. For example, 40° GL means 40° on the Gay-Lussac alcoholmeter, indicating 40% alcohol content. This is probably the easiest system of classifying drinks as it is based on a simple metric scale of 0° to 100° (as against British and American systems) with the zero reading meaning no alcohol and the 100° reading meaning pure alcohol.

GAZPACHO
A chilled Spanish tomato soup which originated in Andalucia. It is a smooth blend of tomatoes, red pepper, garlic, onion, oil, vinegar, breadcrumbs, water, seasoning and herbs. The *gazpacho* is traditionally accompanied by side dishes of *croûtons*, diced cucumber, diced green pepper and chopped onion.

GEFILTE FISH
(Gefillte Fish)
A Jewish speciality consisting of fish balls made from raw fish, or cutlets of fish stuffed with the same raw fish mixture. The *gefilte* fish is simmered in water with seasonings, onions, sliced carrots and saffron, and served hot or cold.

GEHEIMRATS
A cows' milk cheese produced in southern Germany. It has a yellow rind and is closely related to Dutch Edam.

GEL (TO)
To reach the consistency of jelly by setting.

GELATINE
(Gelatin)
A glutinous substance made by cooking the bony and muscular parts of the animal (head, feet, legs, tails and trotters) with water. The resulting liquid is then evaporated and purified and turned into either powder, granules, leaves or sheets. All gelatine is soluble in water and can be used to set or stiffen sweet or savoury mixtures. Gelatine is a member of the protein family but is not in itself a complete protein. Vegetarian, non-meat gelatine is also available.

GELÉE
French term for anything, sweet or savoury, made or garnished with jelly, hence the phrase '*en gelée*'.

en GELÉE
See *Gelée*.

GELLANT
(Gelant)
Substance used to produce gelling, such as aspic or jelly.

GEMELLI
Named after Gemini, the twins, these are short lengths of *spaghetti* twisted together in pairs.

GEN FURAY
A Gambian snack consisting of small fried fish coated with a mixture of fried onions, tomatoes, garlic and chillies.

GEN STEW
A Gambian fish stew containing onions, green peppers, tomatoes, garlic and chilli.

GENOESE
French term for a light sponge cake mixture which is used in a number of classic desserts.

GENOESE CAKE
(Genoese Sponge)
A whisked sponge cake mixture enriched with melted butter and said to have originated in Italy. It is widely used by top chefs as a basis for gâteaux and some desserts.

à la GÉNOISE
French term meaning in the style of Genoa in north-west Italy, denoting the inclusion of tomato sauce in or over a dish.

GENTIAN
Perennial herb (*Gentiana lutea*) primarily used for medicinal purposes. It grows in the Alpine regions of Europe and has light green leaves and vivid yellow flowers. It is sometimes added to bitters, which are said to relieve stomach upsets.

GENTLEMAN'S RELISH
A British commercial preparation which is a brownish-coloured savoury spread, strongly flavoured with anchovy and heavily salted. It is sometimes used for cocktail snacks or as a savoury at the end of a meal and is generally spread on fingers of hot buttered toast.

GEODUCK
Pronounced 'gooey-duck', this is a large Pacific clam (*Panope generosa*) with an average weight of 1.5 kg/3½ lb. It is gathered all year round. The flesh is lean and is usually fried.

GEORGE'S BANK FLOUNDER
See *Winter Flounder*.

GERANIUMS
Garden flowers (*Pelargonium capitatum*) whose leaves are used to add a subtle scent to preserves. They are also shredded and used in salads, or left whole and treated as a garnish.

GERARDMER
See *Lorraine*.

GERM
See *Wheatgerm*.

GERM BREAD
Baked from white or wheatmeal flour with added wheatgerm, this is usually sold under proprietary brand names and is available as a tin loaf, either wrapped or unwrapped, sliced or unsliced.

GERMAN COFFEE
A mixture of kirsch and hot, sweetened coffee topped with a floating layer of cream. It is drunk unstirred.

GERMAN SALAMI
A hard, slicing sausage, of the preserved variety, generally made from finely minced pork and beef. It is speckled with small pieces of fat, is highly seasoned and often contains garlic. Salami has excellent keeping qualities and the colour ranges from pink to red through to beige and brown. It has an appetizing, smoky flavour and some of the newer kinds are loaf-shaped and sometimes coated with crushed black peppercorns.

GÉRÔMÉ
French cheese, produced from cows' milk in Lorraine. It is similar to Munster.

GÉRÔMÉ ANISE
Gérômé cheese spiced with caraway seeds. It is produced in Lorraine in France.

GEROOKTE PALING
The renowned smoked eel of Holland, which is eaten as a street

snack or restaurant *hors d'oeuvre*. When eaten formally, it is garnished with lemon and thin slices of gherkin.

GESCHNETZELTES
A Swiss speciality consisting of fried pieces of veal and chopped onions which are simmered in a sauce containing stock, wine, seasoning and cream. *Geschnetzeltes* is usually accompanied by *rösti*.

GETMESOST
(Mesost)
A Swedish version of Norwegian Gjetost cheese, made with goats' milk whey.

GHAW-BE-THOT
A strongly flavoured, Burmese fried cabbage dish, flavoured with *blachan*.

GHEE
(Ghi)
The Hindi term for clarified butter, which is widely used in Indian cooking. As all the milky solids have been removed, it keeps well without refrigeration. It also has a higher smoking point than non-clarified butter.

GHERKINS
Pickled cucumbers with a fairly sharp taste which can be midget-sized or a little larger. They are used as a garnish and cocktail savoury.

GHIVECI CĂLUGĂRESC
A Romanian speciality, known internationally as Monk's Hotchpotch, which comprises fried onions stewed gently with potatoes, carrots, celery, aubergines, courgettes, French beans, garlic and salt. It is generally served with roast meat and fresh bread.

GIANT PUFFBALL
An edible fungus (*Lycoperdon giganteum*) which grows during summer and autumn as a white-skinned ball and is found in forests and on grazing land. It is among the largest of all fungi when mature, though it is usually eaten when young; an old giant puffball is full of brown spores and is useless as food. The firm white flesh is generally sliced and fried.

GIBLETS
The offal of poultry including heart, neck, gizzard and liver.

GIEN
Made from a mixture of goats' and cows' milk, this is a soft and creamy cheese from the Orleanais, in France. It is matured for about 3 weeks in leaves or wood ash, has a sprightly flavour, is firm in texture and quite small.

GIGHA
A firm Scottish cheese, named after the island where it is produced. It is made from cows' milk.

GIGOT
French term for a leg of lamb or mutton.

GIGOT LAMB CHOPS
Term used in north-west and north-east England for chump chops of lamb.

GIGOT OF LAMB
Term used in Scotland for a leg of lamb which includes both the fillet end and shank.

GILBOA
A fairly firm Israeli cows' milk cheese, styled on Dutch cheeses.

GILD (TO)
To brush the tops of pastry pies with beaten egg yolk before baking. The object is to produce a rich, golden glaze.

GILDENEH YOICH
Traditional Jewish chicken soup.

GILEAD
A distinctively-flavoured Israeli cheese made from ewes' milk and resembling Balkan Kashkaval.

GIN
A colourless, grain spirit flavoured with juniper berries and sometimes other fruits and herbs as well. It was first produced in Holland in the 16th century. It varies in strength from country to country; British gin is 65° proof (37 GL), Dutch gin is 70° proof (40 GL).

GINGER
A spice native to Southern Asia, ginger (*Zingiber officinale*) is now cultivated in the West Indies, West Africa and India. It is the rhizome (underground stem) of a tuberous perennial plant which is dug up at about a year old, then washed, dried and bleached in the sun until it becomes light beige in colour. Ginger has a distinctive, penetrating flavour with a pungent aroma. Available fresh, dried and in powder form, the spice is used in pickles, chutney, baked and stewed fruit dishes, marinades, Oriental cooking, bakery and as an ingredient of curry powder. It is also used to flavour wines, cordials and other soft drinks. The fresh green roots are crystallized or preserved in syrup for use in confectionery. Ginger tea is said to aid digestion.

GINGER ALE
A sweetened and carbonated non-alcoholic drink, flavoured mainly with ginger extract.

GINGER BEER
A very slightly alcoholic fizzy drink of light and opaque appearance, made by the fermentation of ginger and syrup.

GINGER NUTS
Small biscuits, strongly flavoured with ginger.

GINGER SNAPS
Round sweet biscuits which are crisp, crunchy and strongly flavoured with ginger.

GINGERBREAD
A dark brown, gingery cake made with treacle by the melting method.

GINKGO NUTS
Used in Oriental cooking in soups and stews, these small and creamy-fleshed nuts grow on the maidenhair tree (*Ginkgo biloba*), which is considered a living fossil.

GINSENG
A Chinese plant (*Panax schinseng*) belonging to the Araliaceae or ivy family; its aromatic root is widely valued as a tonic.

GIRDLE
See *Griddlė*.

GIZZARD
The second stomach of a bird, which it uses for grinding food. The gizzard adds flavour to stock and is usually part of the giblet pack found inside a dressed bird.

GIZZARD SHAD
See *Shad*.

GJETOST
(Norwegian Whey Cheese)
The colour of fudge and tasting of lightly sweetened caramel, this is one of Norway's most interesting cheeses. It is usually shaved into very thin slices and served with dark rye bread or crispbread. It is made from a combination of cows' and goats' milk; or sometimes only goats' milk when it is stamped *ekte*, meaning real. The Norwegians use Gjetost in cooking, sometimes adding the cheese to a white sauce, but it remains a popular cold buffet (open table) and breakfast cheese, much favoured by children.

GL
See *Gay-Lussac*.

GLACE
French term for ice cream; also used for cake icing.

GLACÉ CHERRIES
Stoned red cherries preserved with sugar and glucose syrup, widely used in baking and confectionery. Frequently they contain added preservatives and colourings.

GLACE DE VIANDE
French term for a shiny, syrupy sauce, achieved by the reduction (by boiling) of meat, poultry and game stock and/or juices.

GLACÉ FRUITS
See *Candied Fruits*.

GLACÉ ICING
(Water Icing)
A thinnish icing made by mixing sifted icing sugar with water, alcohol or fresh, strained fruit juice such as lemon or orange to a smooth and fairly thin consistency. Glacé icing is flavoured and coloured to taste and used to cover large and small cakes, biscuits and pastries.

GLÄRNERKÄSE
See *Sapsago*.

GLASGOW PALE
A small, lightly smoked haddock from Scotland.

GLASMÄSTARSILL
The Swedish name of this dish means 'Glass Blower's Herring' and it consists of pieces of herring marinated in white vinegar and sugar for 2 days. The fish is then placed in a glass jar (hence the name) with slices of carrot, onion, grated horseradish, crumbled bay leaves and pickling spices and the marinade is heated and poured over the herrings. Once cold, it is kept in the refrigerator until ready to eat.

GLASS BLOWER'S HERRING
See *Glasmästarsill*.

GLASSWORT
(Marsh Samphire)
A plant (*Salicornia* and *Salsola* genera) found in salt marshes in various species on both sides of the Atlantic. It grows as a stem with closely packed thick leaves. The young shoots are eaten raw, cooked or pickled. In Britain, this plant is also called marsh samphire; in North America, it is known as samphire, although it is not related to the European samphire.

GLAZE (TO)
To give food a shiny finish by brushing with egg yolk before baking or with prepared glaze (for example, jam) afterwards.

GLOBE ARTICHOKE
A vegetable which is an edible thistle (*Cynara scolymus*) and belongs to the daisy family. Believed to be native to Asia, it was cultivated in the Mediterranean region for many centuries. It came to Britain during the reign of Henry VIII and, more recently, was introduced to other parts of the world with suitable climates such as northern California. The edible parts are contained in the green-coloured, cone-shaped head which, when it is ready to eat, looks like an unopened flower bud on a thick stem or stalk and can be 5–15 cm/2–6 inches in diameter. The artichoke head consists of three main parts: the outer, multi-layered petals or scales which have a partly edible, fleshy base; the inedible central choke which is a mass of fine bristles; and the tender base or heart which is the main edible portion and is located underneath the choke. Some varieties of globe articoke are eaten raw when very young, particularly in Mediterranean countries, but it is more usual to boil or parboil the whole head and then dismember the plant to be eaten as an *hors d'oeuvre*, in salads or used in cooked dishes. Artichoke hearts are available canned.

GLUCOSE
(Dextrose)
A monosaccharide or simple sugar found naturally in ripe fruits, some vegetables and honey. All starch foods and complex sugars have to be converted into glucose by the digestive processes before they can be absorbed through the blood-stream and used by the body. Glucose provides almost instantaneous energy and is therefore useful in treating fatigue, shock and lethargy. Insulin from the pancreas controls the amount of glucose in the blood; when there is insufficient insulin to maintain the correct balance, diabetes occurs.

GLUTEN
Stretchy, elastic-like substance found naturally in flour. During baking, gluten is stretched by steam and air and, like a skeleton, supports the body of a loaf, cake or pudding. Gluten absorbs water and the more it absorbs, the bigger amount of dough it yields. Therefore strong flour, with more gluten than soft, is recommended for making bread.

GLUTEN-FREE
Any food which contains no gluten, the stretchy substance found naturally in flour and to which a small minority of people are allergic; hence, gluten-free food products and diets.

GLUTINOUS RICE
A speciality of Japan, sticky rice which features in a number of traditional dishes.

GLYCERINE
(Glycerol)
Formed by the direct hydrolysis of fat, it is a clear, colourless liquid occurring during the manufacture of soap. Glycerine has limited culinary use but is sometimes added to royal icing to prevent it from becoming rock hard and difficult to cut.

GLYCEROL
See *Glycerine*.

GLYCOGEN
A polysaccharide or complex sugar derived from starchy foods. The body converts glycogen into glucose, which is stored in the liver as an energy reserve.

GNOCCHI
An Italian dish made from a thick mixture of semolina, milk, eggs and cheese. When set, it is cut into rounds, layered in a dish, sprinkled with grated cheese and browned in a hot oven. It is sometimes eaten as an *hors d'oeuvre* with tomato sauce. Other versions are made with choux paste and potatoes; spinach is also sometimes included.

GOAT
Lean and mild-tasting in a similar way to veal, goat is available in Britain in very limited quantities. It is sometimes found in pâtés and sausages. The milk is used for drinking, cheese-making and yogurt.

GOATS' MILK
General English term to describe cheese made only from goats' milk, used in the same way as French Chèvre.

GOBSTOPPER
An old-fashioned British boiled sweet which is large, round and hard.

GOCHU JEON
A Korean dish made from fried green pepper rings and halved chillies which are stuffed with a meat mixture, dipped in flour and beaten egg and deep-fried in sesame oil.

GOETBORG
A Swedish-style sausage, flavoured with cardamom, widely eaten in North America, which resembles German *cervelat*.

GOETTINGER
A German-style sausage, widely eaten in North America, made from spiced pork and beef, which is hard in texture and similar to *cervelat*.

GOGI JEON-GOL
A Korean stir-fry of beef strips, mushrooms, white radish, onion, strips of fresh pear and eggs.

GO-HAN
The Japanese word for rice.

GOHANMONO
A general Japanese term for all types of rice dishes.

GOLAN
An Israeli ewes' milk cheese, styled on Italian Provolone.

GOLD 'N' RICH
A North American cows' milk cheese which is similar to Port-Salut. It originated in Illinois, and is now produced all over the Mid-West.

GOLDEN BUCK CHEESE
North American term for buck rarebit.

GOLDEN FILLETS
(Smoked Fillets)
Small, thin fillets of smoked haddock.

GOLDEN GAGE
See *Mirabelle*.

GOLDEN GRAM
Indian term for mung bean.

GOLDEN PASSION FRUIT
See *Yellow Passion Fruit*.

GOLDEN SYRUP
A by-product of sugar refining in which the presence of invert sugar prevents crystallization. It is thick and very sweet. It is used in baking, added to some sweet dishes (such as stewed apples) and spread on buttered bread, toast, muffins or crumpets.

GOLUBTSY
A Russian dish of stuffed cabbage leaves filled with minced beef, cooked rice, bacon and seasonings. They are shaped into rolls, fried in lard, then baked in tomato juice.

GOMBO
(Gumbo)
See *Okra*.

GOMOLYA
(Homolky, Hrudka)
A Hungarian and Czechoslovakian ewes' milk cheese which closely resembles Liptó. It is also converted into Brynza.

GOOSE
A large bird (genus *Anser*) belonging to the duck family.

GOOSE EGGS
Relatively large eggs which should be treated in exactly the same way as duck eggs and are best used in cooking.

GOOSE LIVER PÂTÉ
See *Pâté de Foie Gras*.

GOOSEBERRY
The fruit of a deciduous, prickly bush (*Ribes grossularia*) native to Europe and North Africa and of the same family as black- and redcurrants. The cultivation of gooseberries is widespread but is particularly popular in Britain where, in the past, many clubs were formed to improve and develop the various kinds. The gooseberry may be oval or globular-shaped and the skin smooth or covered in fine hairs or down. It has a small calyx (the remnants of the original flower) opposite the stalk. The colour when ripe varies from green to yellow to red and the size varies from 1 cm/ ½ inch to about 4 cm/1½ inches in length. The flesh reflects the skin colour, is juicy and full of soft, edible seeds. Cooking gooseberries are best when small, green, sharp and firm and may be cooked by themselves or used in preserves and

pies. The dessert kinds are the large, colourful types which are softer, generally much sweeter and usually thinner-skinned. The very largest kinds tend to have least flavour.

GOOSEBERRY SAUCE
A sharp sauce made from gooseberries, water and a little sugar. It can be served with mackerel, duck and goose.

GOOSE-NECKED BARNACLE
See *Barnacle*.

GORGONZOLA
A superior Italian blue cheese, related to British Stilton and French Roquefort. It is produced in the Lombardy region from cows' milk and is pale creamy-yellow, richly-flavoured and smoothly soft. It is said to have been produced for over a thousand years.

GORNOALTAYSKY
A cheese from the USSR, named after the mountain area where it is produced. It is made from cows' or ewes' milk and is pungent and hard. There is also a smoked version of the cheese.

GOSLING
A young goose.

GOTHAER
A German sausage, popular in North America, which is air-dried and resembles *cervelat*.

GOUDA
One of Holland's oldest cheeses, Gouda can trace its ancestry back 700 years and is a large, fairly flat cheese produced from full-cream cows' milk. It makes up two-thirds of the country's cheese production and is either exported or copied worldwide. Young Goudas, sold when 1–4 months old, are pleasantly mild and creamy but older Goudas, left for up to one year to ripen, have a much deeper, stronger flavour and increased piquancy. All Goudas tend to have a supple texture which is interspersed with a number of irregularly-shaped holes. When young, the cheese is a deep cream colour, but deepens in tone as it ages. Most Gouda cheese is factory-produced but some is still made on farms in the traditional way, often from unpasteurized cows' milk — the distinguishing mark is *Boeren*, meaning farmer, printed on the yellowy rind.

GOUGÈRES
Savoury choux pastry containing cheese.

GOUJON
French term for strips of sole, coated with egg and crumbs, deep-fried and served hot as a cocktail snack or hors d'œuvre.

GOULASH SOUP
The same as the Hungarian *gulyás*, which is not a stew as is so often assumed but a meat and vegetable soup.

GOURD
The fruit of trailing plants of the Cucurbita family; many gourds are inedible but the family also includes pumpkin, squash and vegetable marrow varieties.

GOURMET
Connoisseur who appreciates fine food and drink.

GOURNAY
A type of Camembert cheese from Normandy in France. This one is mild and lactic in flavour.

GOÛTER
French term meaning to taste or sample wine or food.

GOYA
An Argentinian cheese, a version of Italy's Asiago.

GRAÇAY
A goats' milk cheese from the province of Berry in France, Graçay

is a soft, white cheese which is matured for about 6 weeks and coated with charcoal powder. It has a marked goat-like flavour, a dense texture and is shaped like a stubby cone.

GRADAOST
A factory-produced Icelandic blue cheese made from cows' milk.

GRAHAM CRACKER
North American biscuit, somewhat similar to a British digestive.

GRAHAM FLOUR
North American term for wholemeal flour.

GRAHAM RUSKS
Swedish rolls made from Graham flour which are split in half after baking and then dried out slowly in a cool oven.

GRAIN
The seeds or fruit of food plants. Cereal grasses are one example.

GRAINS OF PARADISE
A West African plant (*Afromomum melegueta*) which yields pungent, pepper-like grains. They were, at one time, added to hot alcoholic drinks, such as spiced wine, to intensify the flavour.

GRANA
An Italian family of rock-hard and granular cheeses from the Po Valley, which can be traced back to the 10th or 11th century. They are used as grating cheeses and include the famous Parmesan and Parmigiano Reggiano. They are full-flavoured and widely used in cooking, for sprinkling over pastas and other Italian specialities and, when young, for eating as dessert cheeses at the end of a meal. Granas are made from semi-skimmed cows' milk and matured for 1–4 years.

GRANADILLA
(Granadillo, Grenadilla)
The fruit of some of the plants of the passion flower family (*Passiflora* species).

GRANARY BREAD
Malted wheat bread made from malted brown flour, such as granary.

au GRAND-DUC
French term meaning in the style of the Grand Duke, referring to a garnish for chicken composed of asparagus, truffles, sometimes crayfish tails and also Mornay sauce.

à la GRAND-MÈRE
French term meaning in the style of a grandmother, denoting the inclusion of croûtons in scrambled eggs; mixed vegetable soup with pasta; also food cooked with onions or shallots, bacon, mushrooms and usually cubes of potatoes.

GRANITA
A type of water ice made from coffee or fruit juice. A speciality of southern Europe, it is served half-frozen.

GRANOLA
A breakfast food, originally from North America, made from oats, nuts, honey, butter or margarine, cinnamon and raisins, baked until golden-brown in colour. When cold, it is stored in an airtight container.

GRANULATE (TO)
To form or crystallize into tiny grains or granules.

GRANULATED SUGAR
General-purpose refined white sugar with small gritty granules.

GRAPE CHEESE
See *Tomme au Raisin*.

GRAPEFRUIT
The fruit of an evergreen tree (*Citrus paradisi*) which is now second only

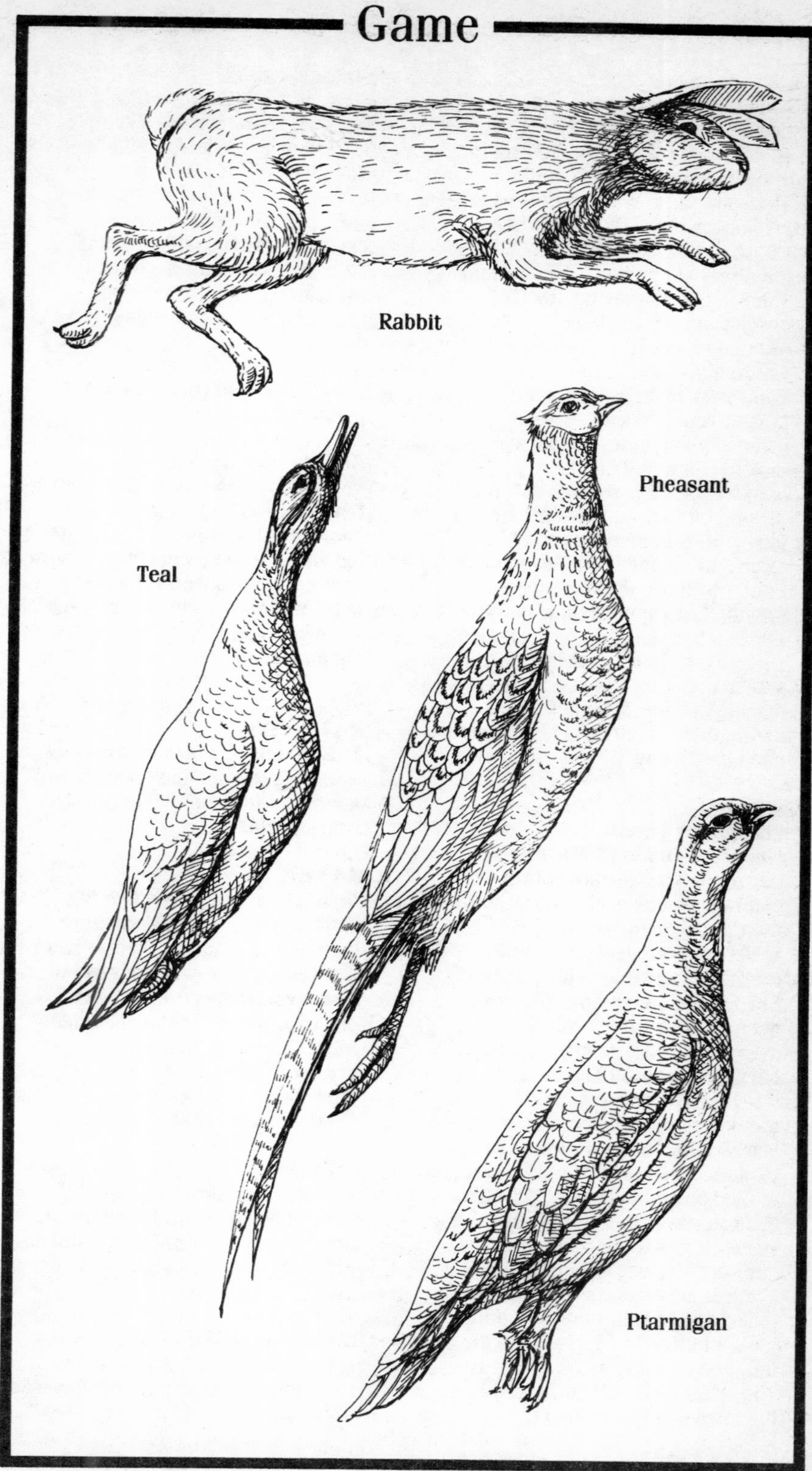
Game
Rabbit
Pheasant
Teal
Ptarmigan

to the sweet orange as the most widely cultivated citrus fruit. It originated either in the Far East as a species on its own or as a variation of the shaddock, which until Victorian times was the only widely known variety of this group of related fruits. It is one of the larger members of the citrus family, almost spherical in shape and 10–13 cm/4–5 inches in diameter. There are two main varieties: those with yellow skins and yellowish flesh and those with pinky-yellow skins and pink or reddish flesh. The skin consists of an outer yellow or pinky-yellow rind and an inner lining of paler pith. The flesh is naturally divided into segments contained in fairly thick membranes and has a tangy, sharp and fresh flavour. It is generally juicy and very rich in vitamin C. Grapefruit is widely eaten at breakfast, halved and sprinkled with sugar, syrup or honey. Its juice is also popular. It is used for making marmalade but, because of its distinctive flavour, it is not widely used in cooking.

GRAPES

The fruit of a deciduous climbing vine (*Vitis vinifera*). The origins of the vine are uncertain but the common vine is probably native to the Caucasus region; other varieties, both deciduous and evergreen, grow wild in Africa, Europe and North America and have been domesticated for assorted uses. Cultivation is known to date back at least 6,000 years; the vine was among the first plants to be grown by man for food and drink and is now to be found wherever the climate is suitable. The fruit is round or oval and comprises a thin skin, sometimes with a 'bloom', and pulpy sweet flesh with or without seeds. The varieties are numerous and the skin colour can vary from pale green to red to purplish-black although, for simplification, grapes are divided into two classes: black and white. The grape grows in elongated bunches on the vine and the size is generally 1–2.5 cm/ ½–1 inch in diameter. The dessert or table grape is eaten as it is or used in fruit salads and desserts. A substantial proportion of grapes grown are used in the production of currants, raisins and sultanas. Many grape varieties grown for wine-making are sweet and juicy and may also be used for desserts.

GRASMERE SHORTBREAD

(Grasmere Gingerbread)

A speciality of the small town of Grasmere, which lies between Kendal and Keswick in the English Lake District. It is a form of shortbread containing chopped mixed peel, sweetened with brown sugar and flavoured with ginger. It is traditionally dusted with some of its own crumbs (made while mixing), then baked and cut into wedges for serving.

GRATE (TO)

To shred or divide solid foods by rubbing them up and down against a grater which has different-sized, sharp perforations.

GRATER

An implement for fragmenting firmish foods without crushing them. In its simplest form it can be a sheet of metal with jagged holes which will reduce food to small pieces when it is rubbed against them. There are specialized versions for nutmeg, cheese or ginger and some graters have slicing blades as well.

GRATIN

French term for a dish which has been sprinkled with breadcrumbs and/or cheese, topped with flakes of butter and browned under the grill.

GRATIN DAUPHINOIS

A classic French potato dish made from thin slices of potatoes layered in an ovenproof dish with garlic, generally cheese (usually Parmesan), seasoning and milk or cream, baked fairly slowly until the top is golden brown and the potatoes tender.

GRAVIERA
A Greek cows' milk cheese, resembling Gruyère.

GRAVLAX
Swedish marinated or sugar-cured salmon made from the raw fish. The whole salmon is filleted and the flesh sides are rubbed with salt, sugar, crushed peppercorns and sometimes saltpetre to intensify the colour. The two sides are sandwiched together with a generous amount of fresh dill, wrapped tightly in foil and refrigerated for a minimum of 3 days. The salmon is then thinly sliced and served with bread, butter and mustard sauce. It will keep for up to 2 weeks in the refrigerator. For a hot dish, the cured salmon is cut into thick slices and fried.

GRAVLAXSÅS
See *Scandinavian Sweet Mustard Sauce*.

GRAVY
A thin British sauce made from pan juices, flour or cornflour, stock or water and seasoning. It is usually served with roast meat or poultry. Gravy for meat should be thicker than that for poultry.

GRAVY BROWNING
A colouring for soups, stews and gravies, usually made from a base of caramel.

GRAYLING
A trout-like freshwater fish (*Thymallus* species) which is found throughout Northern and Central Europe, North America and New Zealand. The colour is silvery with blue and red tints. The average weight is 500 g–1 kg/ 18 oz–2¼ lb and seldom exceeds 1.5 kg/3½ lb. Grayling are often found in the same waters as trout and are caught in the autumn and early winter after the trout season is over. The flesh is firm and white, with a delicate flavour similar to that of trout, and has the unique distinction of smelling faintly of thyme (hence the Latin name). The fish may be poached, steamed, baked, fried or grilled.

GRAZ
(Gratz)
An Austrian cows' milk cheese, farm-produced in the town of Graz near the Yugoslav border. It is firm and full-flavoured.

GRAZALEMA
A Spanish ewes' milk cheese resembling Manchego, which is produced in the Cadiz area of Spain.

GREASE
Fat or oil; also, to brush cake tins (or lining of tins), casseroles, soufflé dishes or paper covers with melted butter, margarine, lard, dripping or oil to minimize sticking.

GREAT NORTHERN BEAN
See *Haricot Bean*.

à la GRECQUE
French term meaning in Greek style, usually referring to vegetables which have been cooked with oil, vinegar or lemon juice, and herbs and spices; also a garnish of rice flavoured with peppers, sausage, peas and onions or shallots.

GREEN BACON
(Pale Bacon, Plain Bacon)
Regional term used to describe cured but unsmoked bacon with fairly deep pink flesh and a pale-coloured rind. It tends to be mild in flavour.

GREEN CHEESE
See *Sapsago*.

GREEN COFFEE BEAN
Term used to describe coffee beans which are ready for roasting. In this

state and coloured greyish-green, the beans may be kept for an indefinite period and many grades improve with age. Some varieties are matured for 5 years or longer.

GREEN DRESSING
English term for *Salsa Verde*.

GREEN FIG
Term commonly used to describe the fresh fig, whether the skin is green or not.

GREEN GODDESS DRESSING
A Californian salad dressing made from a base of mayonnaise and soured cream flavoured with chopped anchovies, onion, mixed fresh herbs and seasonings. It is often used in seafood dishes.

GREEN GOOSE
A spring gosling or young goose.

GREEN GRAM
(Golden Gram)
Indian term for mung bean.

GREEN LAVER
See *Sea Lettuce*.

GREEN MAYONNAISE
English term for *Sauce Verte*.

GREEN OLIVE
See *Olive*.

GREEN ONION
See *Scallion*.

GREEN PEPPERCORNS
See *Madagascan Green Peppercorns*.

GREEN SALAD
Composed primarily of lettuce leaves tossed with French dressing. Sometimes cress, green pepper strips, cucumber and other green vegetables are either added or used for garnishing.

GREEN SAPOTE
See *Sapote*.

GREEN TEA
One of the three main types of tea produced from the original green leaves, found mainly in China, Taiwan and Japan. As the name suggests, the leaves retain some of their green colour as they are not fermented. Instead, they are steamed, rolled and heated. Green tea is lighter in aroma and flavour than black tea and is usually drunk without the addition of milk. It is graded according to the age of the leaf and the preparation which it receives. The most superior grade is young leaves which have been tightly rolled. Green tea is almost exclusively consumed in Arab and Eastern countries, with very little being imported by Europe and North America.

GREEN TOMATOES
Under-ripe tomatoes, frequently used to make chutney.

GREEN TURTLE
A large edible sea turtle (*Chelonia mydas*) which is found in warm seas.

GREEN VEGETABLES
See *Greens*.

GREEN WALNUTS
Young walnuts which are pickled when fresh and before the shell has had time to develop. Once pickled, they turn almost black in colour, have a tangy flavour and make a good accompaniment to cold meats and cheese.

GREENGAGE
A fruit of the gage group of the plum family (*Prunus* species), introduced from France to England by a member of the Gage family in the 18th century. It is spherical in shape, with the typical plum indentation running down one side, and is 2.5–4 cm/1–1½ inches in diameter. The skin colour is green tinged with yellow and the scented, sweet flesh is golden-yellow and surrounds a central stone. It is an

excellent dessert fruit and may also be used in fruit salads and cooked dishes.

GREENLAND HALIBUT
(Greenland Turbot, Black Halibut)
A very close relation (*Reinhardtius hippoglossoides*) of the halibut, caught in Arctic and sub-Arctic waters of the North Atlantic. It is smaller than the true halibut and reaches about 1 metre/39 inches in length. Apart from the size, the main difference is that the Greenland halibut is almost as dark grey or brown on the underside as it is on the upper side. Many countries distinguish this halibut from others by calling it 'black halibut' in their various languages. In North America it is known commercially by the name of turbot, although it bears little resemblance to the European turbot. The flesh is dense and oily; available both fresh and frozen, it is at its best when smoked.

GREENS
(Green Vegetables)
General British term for leafy, green vegetables which are cooked.

GRENADILLA
See *Granadilla*.

GRENADINE
A syrup made from pomegranates. It is deep pink, very sweet and delicately flavoured. It is used in mixed drinks, ice cream, mousses, sweet soufflés and other desserts.

GRENADINS
French term for small thick slices of fillet of veal, which are interlarded with bacon and braised. Turkey breast can also be treated in the same way.

à la GRENOBLOISE
French term meaning in the style of Grenoble in south-eastern France, referring to fish, such as red mullet or hake, floured and fried, then served with a garnish of lemon, capers and chopped parsley. Melted butter is sometimes poured over the top.

GRENOUILLES
French term for frogs. The only edible parts are the legs, which are considered a delicacy. They may be baked or fried and served on their own or with an appropriate sauce.

GREVÉ
A mild Swedish cows' milk cheese.

GREY GURNARD
See *Gurnard*.

GREY MULLET
A round-bodied seawater fish (*Mugil* species) with a good streamlined shape and small head. Its teeth are tiny, or absent altogether, as it feeds on small invertebrates and vegetation on the sea bed. Various species of the grey mullet are found worldwide in warm waters, particularly in the Black Sea, the Mediterranean and on both sides of the Atlantic as far north as the Bay of Biscay on the east, and North Carolina on the west. The length can be 30–70 cm/12–27 inches and the weight 500 g–1 kg/18 oz–2¼ lb. It is covered with broad scales and the back is silvery-grey, becoming lighter on the underside. The species *Mugil cephalus* has longitudinal lines of darker shading on the sides and in the USA is called a striped mullet. The flesh is white, delicate and oily and may be steamed, baked, fried or grilled.

GREY MULLET ROE
The roe traditionally used for Greek taramasalata, though smoked cod's roe makes an excellent substitute.

GREYLAG GOOSE
Most domestic geese are descended from this variety of the bird.

GRIBICHE SAUCE
A French sauce, similar to mayonnaise, made from mashed hard-boiled egg yolks blended with

oil, vinegar and/or lemon juice. It is then well-flavoured and seasoned with chopped capers, chopped gherkins and chopped fresh herbs including tarragon, chervil and parsley. Thin strips of egg white are finally added. It can be served with fried or grilled fish.

GRIDDLE
(Girdle)
A thickish iron sheet which is heated over gas, electricity or solid fuel until hot, and used for cooking griddle cakes and scones of various types. Both a solid electric hot plate and a large, heavy-based frying pan make excellent substitutes.

GRIDDLE CAKES
(Girdle Cakes)
Identical to dropped scones but generally cooked on a hot griddle or girdle, heated by gas, electricity or sometimes over an open fire.

GRIDIRON
Term sometimes used for the rack inside a grill pan.

GRIÈGES
See *Pipo Crème*.

GRIESSNOCKERLSUPPE
An Austrian soup consisting of a clear meat or chicken stock with tiny dumplings made from semolina.

GRILL
The part of a cooker under which food is cooked, browned or toasted by radiant heat from a gas or electric power source set in the roof of the cooker.

GRILL (TO)
To cook food fairly quickly under radiant heat produced from either gas or electricity. The grill radiants should be heated until red-hot before the food is put underneath to cook. Food for grilling should not exceed 2.5 cm/ 1 inch in thickness.

GRILL PAN
A shallow metal pan, fitted with a removable metal rack, designed to go under a grill, sometimes with detachable handles.

GRILLADE
French term to describe grilling; generally, a mixed grill or any food which has been grilled.

GRILLADES
A Creole dish from Louisiana in the USA, consisting of a light stew of thinly sliced veal cooked with green peppers, celery, onions, tomatoes and seasoning and served with rice.

GRILLED GRAPEFRUIT
Halved grapefruit, with loosened and segmented flesh, sprinkled with brown sugar and flakes of butter and browned under the grill. It is usually served hot as a starter.

GRILLING SAUCE
See *Barbecue Sauce*.

GRILSE
The name for young salmon, approximately 3 years old and weighing 900 g–4 kg/2–8 lb, which return to rivers to spawn after one year at sea.

GRIND (TO)
To pound or break down dry foods into a coarse or fine powder by means of a pestle and mortar, electric blender or a hand-operated mechanical grinder.

GRISETTE
An edible mushroom (*Amanita vaginata*) with a greyish cap and a tall white stem. It is a slender and delicate plant and grows in damp parts of woods during the summer and autumn. Because it is fragile, the grisette does not travel well but is much prized in regions where it is found. Great care must be taken when picking the grisette not to confuse it with poisonous members of the Amanita family which it resembles.

GRISKIN
The lean part from a loin of bacon.

GRISSINI
(Italian Bread Sticks)
Thin, crisp, golden-brown sticks, Italian in origin, made from white yeasted dough.

GRISTLE
Connective tissue or cartilage found in meat. The more gristle, the tougher the cut, and long, slow cooking is therefore recommended. Uncooked gristle tends to be white but takes on a gelatinous appearance when cooked.

GRITS
Grains, oats in particular, which are husked and coarsely ground; also, see Hominy Grits.

GROATS
Seeds or kernels of oats, stripped of their husks and left whole or broken.

GROENTESOEP
A Dutch mixed vegetable soup, containing vermicelli.

GROUND ALMONDS
A meal made from pure sweet almonds which has many culinary applications.

GROUND RICE
Fairly fine meal, ground from white rice and used to make milk puddings.

GROUNDNUT OIL
(Arachis Oil)
Made from groundnuts (peanuts) and a popular oil for all culinary purposes. The oil clarifies when kept at low temperatures and in winter can be difficult to pour; however, it liquefies quickly. It also has a high smoking point and may therefore be used for deep-frying. It is relatively high in polyunsaturated fatty acids and is useful for those on a low-cholesterol diet.

GROUNDNUTS
See *Peanuts*.

GROUPER
A number of related species of seawater fish (*Epinephelus* species) of the same family as the sea bass, found in the warm waters of the Mediterranean sea and the Atlantic and Pacific Oceans. The colours vary from grey-green to reddish-brown and even blackish-green depending on species and location. The weight in the shops is usually 2–7.25 kg/ 4½–16 lb. The flesh is firm and lean and the fish may be poached, steamed, baked or grilled.

GROUSE
A popular game bird, in season in Britain from early August to early December. One bird is sufficient for two people.

GROUT
Sediment, such as tea leaves or coffee grounds, at the bottom of a container; also, coarse meal such as groats.

GRUEL
A thin form of porridge made from oats, barley, wheat or any other cereal.

GRUTH DHU
See *Black Crowdie*.

GRUYÈRE
Produced in the Gruyère district of western Switzerland and in the adjacent French-speaking part of the country, Gruyère is a grand and classic cheese, internationally renowned. Made since the 12th century, it is relatively large with a smooth, firm texture interspersed with occasional pea-sized holes. The main ingredient of the classic Swiss fondue, Gruyère is made from cows' milk and has a rich, mild and creamy taste with a distinctive piquancy. It is pale yellow in colour with a brownish rind. It is an excellent slicing cheese.

GRYSTEK
Swedish 'Sunday lunch' consisting of a pot-roasted piece of beef or reindeer with a thickened sauce enriched with cream. It is served with boiled potatoes, mixed vegetables and redcurrant jelly.

GUACAMOLE
A Mexican avocado 'mash' which is served as an accompaniment to many Mexican dishes and also eaten as a dip. It is made from avocados, lemon or lime juice, chopped onion, chopped tomatoes, chopped green chillies, chopped fresh coriander or parsley and seasonings.

GUARD OF HONOUR
A lamb joint comprising two best end necks of chined meat, joind in such a way that the bones cross each other to form a typically British Guard of Honour. The fat side of the bones always faces outwards and stuffing may be packed into the joint, between the bones, before roasting. Cutlet frills should be placed over the top of each bone before serving.

GUAVA
The fruit of a small deciduous tree (*Psidium guajava*), related to the eucalyptus and myrtle, native to tropical America and cultivated in many other regions of the world with suitable climates, both tropical and sub-tropical. The fruit is shaped rather like a pear or large plum and may measure up to 10 cm/4 inches from top to bottom. The skin is green turning to pale yellow when ripe. The highly scented flesh can vary in colour from white to deep pink and contains edible seeds which may be too hard for some people's taste. The flavour is unique with an elusive strawberry aftertaste. Guavas may be eaten raw, cut in half and spooned from the skin, or used with other ingredients. They are also available canned. There are several varieties of this and other related species, some of them evergreen shrubs and with fruits of various sizes and colours.

GUAYMAS SAUCE
Mayonnaise flavoured with tomato purée (made from fresh tomatoes) and chopped stuffed olives. It can be served with cold meats and poultry.

GUDGEON
A small European freshwater fish (*Gobio gobio*) of the carp family. The fish is usually dipped in batter or egg and crumbs and deep-fried.

GUGELHUPF
(Gugelhopf, Kugelhopf)
A yeasted speciality from Germany, Austria and Alsace, this is a spongy mixture containing flour, sugar, eggs, lemon peel, chopped almonds, seedless raisins and milk, traditionally baked in a deep, fluted ring mould and iced when cold. Sometimes baking powder is used instead of yeast. It is said to have been a favourite of Emperor Franz Josef I of Austria and is named after the turbans worn by the Turkish invaders of Austria in the 17th century.

GUINEA FOWL
Originating from West Africa and related to the pheasant, guinea fowl (*Numida meleagris*) is in season in Britain from late spring to early summer. It should be roasted and treated in exactly the same way as chicken.

GUINEA FOWL EGGS
Fairly small eggs which make an attractive garnish. They can also be used in *hors d'oeuvres* and take about 5 minutes to hard boil.

GUISO DE DORADO
A fish stew from Paraguay containing dorado, the famous river fish of the country.

GUISO DE REPOLLO
A robust Bolivian dish in which cooked cabbage is mixed with a rich tomato sauce containing onion, potatoes, chilli, coriander and seasonings. It usually accompanies grilled or fried meat or poultry.

GULAB JAMON
(Gulab Jamun)
An Indian dessert composed of dumplings made from dried milk and flour which are deep-fried and then soaked in syrup containing rose essence and cardamom pods. *Gulab jamon* are a Bengali speciality.

GULAI
The Malaysian term for curry.

GULÉ
(Gulai)
Indonesian term for curry.

GULE AERTER
A Danish soup containing yellow split peas, mixed vegetables and belly of pork and served in winter.

GULLET OF BEEF
Term used in the west of Scotland for clod of beef.

GULLS' EGGS
Usually sold already cooked, gulls' eggs have turquoise blue, speckled shells and are surprisingly non-fishy in flavour. They are fairly small, are available in the summer and make a pleasant addition to an *hors d'oeuvre*.

GULYÁS LE LEVES
Hungarian meat soup made from beef shin, onions, paprika, tomatoes, green peppers and potatoes.

GUM
Chewing gum. Also a hard, gelatinous sweet such as a gum drop.

GUM ACACIA
See *Gum Arabic*.

GUM ARABIC
(Gum Acacia)
A water-soluble gum obtained from several species of acacia and used in confectionery.

GUM DROP
See *Gum*.

GUMBO
A soupy stew from Louisiana in the USA made from either chicken or prawns with tomatoes, rice, peppers, spices, herbs and seasonings; okra, by nature mucilaginous, is added to thicken the dish and to add flavour. The name gumbo is supposed to have come from *guin gômbo*, the African name for okra.

GUMBO FILÉ
See *Filé Powder*.

GUNPOWDER
A grade of China green tea leaf which is among the finest of its kind. Gunpowder tea has one of the lowest percentages of caffeine of any tea, a delicate flavour and does not need milk.

GURNARD
Family of bony fish (*Friglidae*), from the Mediterranean and North Atlantic regions with extremely ugly, oversized heads and enormous spiny fins. They have glittering scales and are highly coloured. They may be poached or steamed and are popular in France.

GUSH HALAV
An Israeli cows' milk cheese with the characteristic flavour and aroma of Dutch cheese.

GÜSSING
An Austrian cheese made from semi-skimmed cows' milk and similar to Brick.

GUT (TO)
To clean a fish by removing its intestines.

GUTSLEBERWURST
A German liver sausage which is coarse-textured but mild and contains pieces of liver, meat (usually pork) and fat.

GÜVEÇ
A Turkish speciality very similar to the Bulgarian *agneshka guvetch*. It is named after the covered casseroles used in the kitchens of the Turkish sultans.

GUVETCH
Balkan-style *ratatouille* made from onions, garlic, sunflower oil, multi-coloured peppers, green beans, tomatoes, chillies and seasoning, usually served with rice or pasta.

GYPSY'S ARM
A Spanish version of Swiss roll, filled with jam or strawberries and cream.

GYULAI
A Hungarian smoked pork sausage flavoured with paprika.

HABITANT PEA SOUP
A classic thick soup from Quebec in Canada, made from special dried peas, yellow and whole, with onions, salt pork, herbs and seasoning.

HACHER
French term meaning to chop up, generally applied to meat.

HADDOCK
A fish (*Melanogrammus aeglefinus*) of the same family as the cod, which it resembles although it is smaller and has more scales. It is about 60 cm/24 inches long and it can weigh 1–4 kg/2¼–9 lb. The back is coloured greyish-brown and the belly white. It is mainly a coastal fish and found on both sides of the Atlantic ocean, covering the New England coast in North America and stretching as far south as the Bay of Biscay on the European side, including the North Sea. It is caught all the year round but is in its prime from autumn to spring. The flesh is lean, rather softer than that of cod, and the fish may be poached, steamed, baked, fried or grilled. Haddock is easily recognizable because of a dark spot on either side of the body near the head, located just behind the gills and supposed to be the finger and thumb print of St Peter; this biblical legend is also applied to the dory.

HAGGIS
A Scottish speciality made from minced heart, liver and lungs of sheep. The mince is mixed with oatmeal, suet, minced onion, spices and seasonings and the mixture is sewn into pieces of well-cleaned sheep's stomach. Traditionally haggis is cooked slowly in water, then carried to the table on a white table napkin to the sound of bagpipes. It is served very hot, accompanied by Scotch whisky. So that the contents may be easily removed, a slit is made in the skin and a serving spoon inserted. Haggis is generally accompanied by swede and potatoes.

HAIRY LYCHEE
See *Rambutan*.

HAJDÚ
A type of Hungarian Kashkaval cheese, made from cows' milk.

HÁKARL
Icelandic ripened shark meat, which is described in a local guidebook as 'a curious food'. The taste for it, most say, is an acquired one. The guidebook continues, 'Because fresh shark meat is not edible, there is need for a highly unusual kind of processing. The shark is cut into strips that are placed on a clean

gravel bed and covered up with stones. After ripening for several weeks, the strips are removed, washed and hung up in sheds to dry. All in all, it's a complex procedure, and only people with a long experience manage to turn out first grade stuff. Like all other ripened foods, Hákarl has a fairly pungent odour; some have remarked that the most ticklish part of eating shark is getting it past the nose. Most Icelanders are convinced that Hákarl tastes best when chased with a liberal schnapps of ice-cold brennivin, a domestic liquor named Black Death.'

HAKE
A fine-quality fish (*Merluccius merluccius*) of the cod family. The long, streamlined body has a slate-grey or bluish back and the underside is silvery-white. The large mouth is grey-black inside and the lower jaw is longer than the upper. It is caught in the western parts of the North Atlantic, mainly off the coasts of Ireland, France and the Iberian Peninsula. It is caught all year round but is at its best from autumn to spring. It is sold whole if small, and in fillets or cutlets if larger. The very white, lean flesh is said to have the same delicacy as chicken breast or baby Scotch salmon and is considered by many connoisseurs to be the best fish of the cod family. The fish may be poached, steamed, baked or fried. There is a Pacific hake, but this fish is mostly used in prepared products such as fish cakes.

HALAL (TO)
(Hallal)
To slaughter an animal for food according to Muslim law; also, the meat from an animal slaughtered in this way.

HALDI
Indian name for types of turmeric.

HALF A LEG
See *Knuckle of Lamb*.

HALF CREAM
A cross between top-of-the-milk and single cream, this has a legal minimum butterfat content of 12%. It is used for coffee and pouring over desserts such as fruit salad, steamed puddings and crumbles. The cream is also recommended for pouring over breakfast cereals and may be added to sauces and dressings. It is pasteurized, will not whip and should not be frozen.

HALF-AND-HALF
North American term to describe a fairly light cream with a butterfat content of 12%. It is known in Britain as half cream.

HALIBUT
This fish (*Hippoglossus hippoglossus*) is the largest of the flatfish and is found in the northern waters of both the Atlantic and Pacific Oceans. It is caught throughout the year but mainly in the summer and autumn. Because of its size, the adult halibut is sold as steaks and fillets. The colour of the upper side is dark green or greenish-brown, and the underside white to grey. The flesh is firm, white, very well-flavoured and medium-oily and the fish may be poached, steamed, baked, fried or grilled. Halibut is considered a luxury fish.

HALOUMI
(Halumi)
Middle Eastern and Greek cheese made from ewes' or goats' milk. It is hard and salty, preserved in whey and used for cooking.

HALVA
A North African and Middle Eastern sweetmeat made from sesame seeds. It is sold in slices, cut from blocks.

HAM
The hind leg and thigh of cured bacon, smoked or unsmoked, which is boiled or baked and served cold.

HAM SAUSAGE
A German scalded sausage made from finely ground beef and pork, interspersed with chunky pieces of ham and bacon. It has a marbled appearance, is well-spiced and often contains garlic. The sausage is ideal for slicing and may be served cold in salads, sandwiches or as part of a mixed meat platter. It may also be grilled or fried, and used in stews, casseroles and hot-pots. Legally, only sausage containing 50% ham may be called ham sausage.

HAMANTASCHEN
The name of this Jewish speciality means 'Haman's purses' and they are named after the Old Testament biblical character, Haman. They are made for the festival of Purim or the Feast of Lots which falls in February or March. The *Hamantaschen* are small, sweet, triangular pastries traditionally filled with black poppy seeds mixed with chopped walnuts, syrup, raisins, butter and milk.

HAMBURGER BUNS
Round and fairly flat yeasted buns which are split open, toasted or not, filled with hamburgers, ketchup, mustard and so on, then sandwiched together.

HAMBURGERS
Said to have originated in Germany, round patties made from minced beef and seasonings which are either grilled or fried. Traditionally served with fried onions, they are now very often left plain and served in flat white buns.

HAMMERHEAD SHARK
See *Shark*.

HAND
(Handkäse, Sauermilchkäse)
German cheeses usually made from naturally curdled, sour cows' milk and moulded by hand into assorted shapes. They can be gently mild or powerfully strong and are sometimes flavoured with spices and herbs. They are light cream or golden-yellow in colour and often look shiny and opaque when cut. The soft rind varies from almost white to light brown. They are generally low in butterfat content and are a rich source of protein.

HAND AND SPRING OF PORK
A large joint from the foreleg, suitable for roasting. It is also cut up and used for stewing, braising, casseroling and mincing. Because of its size, it is often divided into two joints, known as hand and shank. It is called by this name in London and the South-East.

HAND OF PORK
An alternative term used in the West Country of Britain for hand and spring of pork.

HANGIKJÖT
Icelandic smoked lamb, usually eaten with boiled potatoes and a slightly sweetened white sauce.

HANGING MEAT
Freshly killed meat, stiffened by *rigor mortis*, is usually allowed to hang in order to give the flesh and connective tissue a chance to tenderize. This occurs naturally through chemical changes which take place over a period of days. Hanging time depends on the size and type of meat and can vary from 2 days to 1–2 weeks.

HARAK MAS
A Sri Lankan beef curry containing onions, garlic, ginger, vinegar, spices and coconut.

HARD
Term to describe a firm cheese such as Cheddar which is incapable of being spread; also a drink, usually a spirit, having a high percentage of alcohol.

HARD CLAM
See *Quahog*.

HARD FLOUR
Produced from hard wheat, cultivated in countries with hot, dry climates such as Italy, Spain and parts of North and South America. Because of its high gluten content, it is recommended for making bread and pasta. It is also an excellent source of protein.

HARD SAUCE
North American term for rum or brandy butter.

HARD WHEAT
See *Durum Wheat*.

HARD-BOIL (TO)
To cook something until hard. This usually applies to an egg cooked in the shell until white and yolk have solidified.

HARDFISKUR
According to a local guidebook, 'This is dried fish from Iceland and although haddock is the most common, many other fish are used as well. The fish are cleaned, cut and stretched into triangular form, then hung up in airy sheds to dry until hard and brittle; ideally the fish should freeze slightly in the early stages of processing. The end result will keep for years in good, dry storage. Before being served, the dried fish is pounded until it gets soft and crumbly; it is torn from the skin into strips and eaten with butter (no cooking, ever). A special delicacy is Riklingur: halibut cured as outlined above.'

HARDSHELL CLAM
See *Quahog*.

HARDUF
(Hoduf)
An Israeli cheese made from ewes' milk. It is semi-soft, spreadable and resembles Liptó.

HARE
A swift, four-legged, fur-covered animal not unlike a large rabbit with very long hind legs, hare is a member of the rodent family. It is in season in Britain from August to March and may be roasted, braised or stewed.

HARICOT BEAN
(American Navy Bean, Great Northern Bean, Navy Bean)
A vegetable (*Phaseolus vulgaris*) native to Central and South America and now cultivated worldwide, with North America being the major producer. It grows as a legume and the small and oval bean, greyish-white in colour, is best known as the one used in canned baked beans. It is a well-flavoured and nutritious bean, high in vegetable fibre. The haricot bean is an important part of many national dishes in Europe and the Middle East, where it is mainly used as a pulse in its dried form, and it is used in the traditional North American dish, Boston baked beans.

HARICOT LAMB
A British lamb stew containing soaked haricot beans, onions and turnip.

HARISSA
A fiery North African chilli sauce, similar in appearance to tomato purée. It is treated as a condiment.

HARRAR
(Ethiopian Harrar)
Name of a top-quality Ethiopian coffee bean of the *arabica* type with a pronounced flavour. When unblended, Harrar is very suitable for making Turkish coffee, but it is also used for blending with milder beans, often from Central America.

HARZ
(Harzer, Harzerkäse)
Powerfully pungent and fairly small German cheese made by hand from soured cows' milk. It is often eaten with black bread and goose fat and takes its name from the Harz mountains. It is generally round, quite firm, low in butterfat and an excellent source of protein.

HASH
An old English dish made by heating small pieces of leftover cooked meat in well-seasoned gravy or brown sauce. It is served with mashed potatoes and cooked vegetables.

HASH (TO)
To cut or chop food into small pieces; also, a reheated dish containing chopped meat.

HASHED BROWN POTATOES
A North American potato dish which resembles Swiss *rösti*. It consists of grated raw potatoes fried like a pancake in bacon fat, then turned out on to a warm platter. The potatoes are served instead of chips with eggs, bacon or hamburgers.

HASLET
An old English offal-based meat loaf which is cut into slices and served hot or cold. Other versions from Hampshire and Lincolnshire are based on mixtures of pork, onion, rusk and seasonings such as salt, pepper and sage.

HASSELBACK POTATOES
Probably unique to Sweden, these are made by peeling medium-sized, oval-shaped potatoes, then scoring them downwards into thin slices without cutting right through. They are then transferred to a dish, brushed with butter or margarine and baked in the oven until tender. Halfway through the cooking time, they are sprinkled with grated cheese.

HAUNCH
A cut of meat generally comprising the leg with part of the loin attached.

HAUTE CUISINE
French term for top-grade cooking and food.

HAVARTI
A rindless Danish cheese which resembles Tilsit, Havarti is named after the farm where it was first produced. It is a creamy-coloured, cows' milk cheese of medium firmness which can be round like a Dutch Gouda or oblong and loaf-shaped. It is peppered with numerous holes and is full-flavoured with a pungent after-taste. There are two versions of the cheese; one contains 60% butterfat and the other 45%. It is vacuum-packed in pieces and sometimes contains caraway seeds.

HAYBOX
An airtight box, well-insulated, traditionally with hay, used to maintain the temperature of a heated cooking container and its contents, thus enabling slow cooking to continue.

HAYMAKING CHEESE
See *Single Gloucester*.

HAZEL HEN
A woodland grouse (*Tetrastes bonasia*) native to Europe.

HAZELNUTS
(Cobnuts, Filberts)
A thick-shelled nut from either of two hazels (*Corylus avellana pontica* and *C. maxima*) found in Europe and North America. Hazelnuts are internationally popular. The nuts are small with firmly attached skins immediately beneath the shells. To remove the skins, the nuts should be roasted in a moderate oven for about 20 minutes, then rubbed between the hands protected by oven gloves. Hazelnuts are used in both sweet and savoury dishes and are an important ingredient in many Central and Northern European cakes. In North America, hazelnuts are known as cobnuts or filberts.

HDL
(High-density Lipoproteins)
See *Cholesterol*.

HEAD
The foam or froth that rises on a fermenting or effervescing liquid such as a glass of beer, or a yeast

mixture (yeast with milk or water and sugar).

HEAD CHEESE
Brawn made from a pig's head, onion, seasonings and herbs.

HEALTH FOODS
Natural foods, often fibrous, which are available from health food shops and supermarket chains. Many such foods are organically grown without the use of artificial substances to fertilize the soil or kill pests. Some are also free from additives and are unrefined; molasses sugar and brown rice are just two examples of the many natural foods that are available.

HEART
An economical, high-protein food and also a good source of iron, vitamin A and vitamins of the B group. The types of hearts most readily available come from lambs, pigs and oxen. Calf's heart, probably the most delicate, is rarely available. Ox hearts are the largest and about 175 g/6 oz should be allowed per person. One lamb's heart will serve one person; one calf's or pig's heart is sufficient for two. Because hearts are a tough, well-worked muscle, they respond best to gentle roasting in the oven. To prepare heart, blood vessels and fat should be removed and the centre walls, dividing the chambers of the heart, cut through. It should then be well-washed and left to soak for 1 hour in cold, salted water. If the heart is to be roasted, it should be parboiled first, then filled with a suitable stuffing. The traditional accompaniments to roast heart are creamed potatoes, rich brown gravy and redcurrant jelly. Ox heart may also be cubed, then stewed or braised until tender. As with all offal, hearts become stale quickly and should be cooked as soon as possible after purchase.

HEART OF PALM
See *Cabbage Palm*.

HEAT (TO)
To warm through, without boiling, a liquid or cooked dish. This can be done on top of a cooker, under the grill or in an oven.

HEAVY
Digested with difficulty, usually because of excessive richness; also, a cake, loaf or pudding which has risen insufficiently or sunk in the centre.

HEAVY CAKE
See *Cornish Heavy Cake*.

HEAVY CREAM
(Whipping Cream)
North American term for a pasteurized cream which equates to British whipping cream although it has a higher butterfat content of up to 40%. It can be made by combining equal quantities of double and whipping cream.

HEDGEHOG
A small and greasy animal, sometimes eaten in a stew by the Romany community.

HEMI-CELLULOSE
Basically pectin, necessary for the setting of jam, found naturally in some fruits and vegetables and also artificially produced. It is a carbohydrate and falls into the polysaccharide category.

HEN
A female bird.

HERBAL
Anything made of or containing herbs.

HERBAL TEA
An infusion using any part of plants other than tea leaves or coffee beans. Most herbal teas are made from the flowers or leaves of plants, either fresh or dried. Originally prepared for their medicinal properties rather than for their refreshing qualities, herbal teas offer a pleasant and usually milder

alternative to tea and coffee, especially for people with a low tolerance of caffeine.

HERBES DE PROVENCE
A Provençale mixture made from herbs grown in the South of France, including thyme, marjoram, oregano, basil and sometimes savory. The herbs may be fresh or dried.

HERBS
Aromatic plants and/or their leaves which are grown in temperate climates. Many are available both fresh or dried.

HERKIMER
A North American cows' milk cheese from New York, which resembles Cheddar. It is factory-produced.

HERMIT CRAB
(Bernard l'Hermite, Bernard) Edible crabs eaten primarily in France.

HERRGÅRDSOST
Sweden's most popular cheese, Herrgårdsost is factory-produced from cows' milk and closely resembles Emmental. At one time it was made on small farms and called 'manor' cheese. The skimmed-milk version contains 30% butterfat; the whole-milk cheese contains 45% butterfat and is stamped *elite*.

HERRING
A round-bodied, streamlined fish (*Clupea harengus*) that is caught in huge shoals in the North Atlantic, from North Carolina in the USA to the Bay of Biscay, and also in the North Pacific. It is the most important fish in the herring family (which includes pilchard and sprat) and can vary in size from under 20 cm/8 inches for most of the Pacific varieties to an average 25 cm/10 inches for the European kinds, and 40 cm/16 inches for those caught off the North American Atlantic coast. The back is a steely-blue colour and the belly silvery-white. Although it can be caught all the year round, the main Atlantic fishing is in the summer, and the Pacific in the winter. The flesh is oily, firm and highly nutritious and the fish can be baked, fried, grilled, salted, smoked or pickled. The vast number of herring which can be found in a shoal is indicated by the name, which derives from an old Teutonic word *heer* meaning army.

HERVE
A group of Belgian cheeses, notorious for their overwhelming smell. They are produced from cows' milk in northern Liège and date back to the 16th century.

HEUK BONE OF BEEF
Term used in the east of Scotland for rump.

HICKORY
North American hardwood related to the walnut family. Used in the USA for smoking food, especially hams.

HICKORY NUTS
Widely grown in North America, these are the sweet, edible nuts of the hickory tree (genus *Carya*) and are related to pecan nuts. They resemble walnuts and are used mainly in confectionery and baking.

HIGH TEA
A cooked or uncooked meal popular in the North of England and Scotland served during the early part of the evening. It is often followed by supper about three hours later, consisting of a light snack plus a hot drink. These two meals replace dinner, which is more favoured in the South.

HIGHLAND CHOICE
A novelty Dunlop-type cheese from Scotland. It contains flaked almonds and Drambuie.

HIGHLAND HERBS
A Scottish Dunlop-type cheese, containing local mustard and chives.

HIGH-MOISTURE JACK
See *Monterey Jack*.

HIJIKI
(Hiziki)
A sea vegetable (*Hisikia fusiforme*) of the brown algae group of plants, found in shallow coastal waters in the Far East, particularly around Japan. It is blanched and dried before being sold either in pieces or shredded. *Hijiki* has a high mineral content and a strong flavour.

HIMMEL UND ERDE
The name of this dish means 'heaven and earth'. It is a German speciality comprising creamed potato mixed or served with an equal quantity of fresh apple purée and flavoured with chopped, fried onions. The mixture is transferred to a dish, then topped with fried liver.

HINDLEG OF BEEF
See *Leg of Beef*.

HIP BONE OF BEEF
Alternative term used in the Midlands of Britain for rump.

HOB
See *Cooker*.

HOCK OF MEAT
The joint or part of the hind limb of an animal, corresponding to the ankle of man but raised and bending backwards.

HOCK OF PORK
A bony and small cut of pork, the meat from which may be diced and used in stews, braised dishes and casseroles. It may also be minced and used in pâtés and terrines.

HODGE-PODGE
See *Hotch-Potch*.

HOG
Term for a male pig.

HOG PLUM
(Jamaica Plum)
The fruit of a tree (*Spondias* species) of the same family as the mango and native to the West Indies, tropical America and the Pacific islands depending on the species. It is now cultivated widely in its several forms in South-East Asia and South America. It is either plum- or egg-shaped and 4–7.5 cm/1½–3 inches in length. The skin colour may be yellow or red and the flesh, surrounding a large seed like that of the mango, is yellow and generally flavoursome. Some varieties may be eaten raw and others are more suited to preserves and meat dishes. The variety that is very popular in the Pacific region is called the Otaheite-apple (*S. dulcis*).

HOI SIN SAUCE
Chinese barbecue sauce made from a base of soy sauce flavoured with spices and garlic. It looks like brown ketchup.

HOKKAIDO
A Japanese version of Cheddar, made from cows' milk.

HOKKIEN MEE NOODLES
Chinese egg noodles.

HOLISHKES
(Galuptzes, Holipce, Praakes)
Said to be of Romanian origin, *holishkes* are a traditional Jewish speciality and consist of cabbage leaves or sometimes vine leaves, packed with meat and rice, rolled up into parcels and simmered in a sweet-sour tomato sauce containing vinegar and sugar.

à la HOLLANDAISE
French term meaning in Dutch style, referring to any dish served with Hollandaise sauce; also, poached fish coated with melted butter and served with potatoes and sometimes wedges of hard-boiled eggs.

HOLLANDAISE SAUCE
A classic French sauce, a golden-yellow heated emulsion made from butter, egg yolks and either lemon juice or vinegar or a combination of the two. It is custard-like in consistency, should be thick enough to coat the back of a spoon and eaten warm. It can be served with poached or grilled fish dishes, vegetables such as asparagus or broccoli, and roast or boiled chicken.

HOMARD
French term for lobster.

HOMARD À L'AMÉRICAINE
(Homard à l'Armoricaine)
A classic French *haute cuisine* dish, made by combining pre-cooked and diced lightly fried lobster with a *mirepoix*, then flaming the ingredients with brandy. Tomato purée, white wine, stock, chopped tomatoes and lobster coral (roe) are then added and the dish flavoured with tarragon. It is finally thickened with *beurre manié*.

HOMARD À LA BORDELAISE
Almost identical to *homard à l'Américaine* but the liquid is thickened with egg yolks instead of *beurre manié*.

HOMARD CARDINAL
A classic French speciality. Lobster boiled in *court-bouillon*, shelled and diced, combined with a sauce containing the red lobster coral, sprinkled with cheese and browned quickly under the grill.

HOMARD THERMIDOR
A much-loved classic French dish, made by adding cubes of cooked lobster to a Béchamel sauce which is well-flavoured with French mustard. The dish is sprinkled thickly with grated cheese and browned under the grill.

HOMINY
Hulled maize (corn) from which the germ has been removed, widely eaten in North America although it has minimal nutritional value.

HOMINY GRITS
(Grits)
Made from hominy, ground into uniform granules. In North America, grits are eaten as a breakfast cereal or treated as an accompaniment to main dishes. They have minimal nutritional value.

HOMOGENIZED MILK
Pasteurized milk sold in Britain in red-topped bottles. Because homogenization distributes cream throughout the milk, there is no visible cream-line and the milk requires no shaking. It is whiter in appearance than ordinary milk.

HOMOLKY
See *Gomolya*.

HONAN COOKING
North-east of Szechuan and inland, this region of China specializes in fried Yellow River carp and full-flavoured, hearty dishes containing wine and a great number of spices.

HONEY
A thick, sweet and syrupy substance made naturally by bees from nectar found in an assortment of flowers and herbs, hence the flavour variations. Honey is a compound of fructose and glucose, is energizing and is also reputed to be valuable medicinally. The lighter the colour, the milder the taste. Honey can be thick and curd-like or clear and syrupy and the latter kind may be substituted for golden syrup in cooking.

HONEY FUNGUS
An edible fungus (*Armillaria mellea*) which grows in clusters at the foot of both live and dying trees and is generally found in the autumn. The slender stem curls out from a swollen base attached to the tree and the cap is golden-brown and scaly when young, becoming light

brown with maturity. Honey fungus needs to be well cooked to remove its bitter taste and unpleasant smell and, in mature mushrooms, only the caps are suitable for eating.

HONEYCOMB
A light, open-textured and crunchy sweet made from honey or syrup, sugar, butter or margarine, and vinegar. It rapidly becomes sticky on exposure to air.

HONEYCOMB MOULD
A typically British moulded pudding made from a mixture of jelly and cold custard sauce into which stiffly whipped egg whites are folded. If two layers are required, hot jelly is added to warm custard, the whites are whisked in and then the mixture is set in a mould. Once set, two layers are clearly visible.

HONEYCOMB TRIPE
This comes from the second stomach of an ox and has a honeycomb appearance, hence the name.

HONEYDEW MELON
A variety of melon noted for its thick skin and good keeping qualities. The skin is yellow or green and characterized by uneven, longitudinal ridges, usually close together. The flesh is pale green, relatively firm and often not as sweet as that of melons which ripen more quickly.

HONEY-ROAST HAM
A term used to describe commercially produced ham, which owes its individual character and flavour to the special curing and smoking techniques employed by the manufacturer. It is usually prepared with a coating of honey or a combination of brown sugar, breadcrumbs and honey.

à la HONGROISE
French term meaning in the style of Hungary, usually referring to a dish cooked with onions, tomatoes, paprika and soured cream.

HOP
A plant (*Humulus lupulus*) used in the brewing of beer. The surplus young shoots are sometimes cut and used in the same way as asparagus spears.

HOPPER
A Sri Lankan speciality, a pancake made with rice flour and coconut milk, which is deep-fried until crisp. Treated as a bread, the *hopper* is served either as an accompaniment to meals or, with a fried egg, as an appetizer.

HORIATIKI
Traditional Greek salad, containing Feta cheese, tomatoes, olives, cucumber, onion, olive oil and vinegar.

HORN OF PLENTY
An edible fungus (*Craterellus cornucopioides*) which looks like a ragged-edged and upward-facing trumpet, browny-black on the inside and grey on the outside. It grows mainly in beech woods in the summer and autumn and, despite its unappetizing appearance, it is used for flavouring and may also be dried for later use.

HORS D'OEUVRE
Although the term now refers to any first course of a formal meal, the authentic *hors d'oeuvre* was once synonymous with the rotating trolley in a restaurant, with its twenty or more savoury items ranging from egg mayonnaise to salami. All were contained in small dishes and a selection was chosen by the diner.

HORSE BEAN
See *Field Bean*.

HORSE CLAM
A large Pacific clam (*Thesus nuttalli*) with an average weight of 1–1.5 kg/2¼–3½ lb. It is gathered all year round and the meat is light-coloured, lean and is eaten raw, particularly in Japan, or fried.

HORSE MUSHROOM
An edible mushroom (*Agaricus arvensis*) with a white stem and a cap which is cream-coloured to yellow on top and greyish underneath. It grows during summer and autumn in woodland as well as open grassland and can be found alongside its close relative, the field mushroom, from which it can be distinguished by the fact that it turns yellow when cut or damaged and gives off a smell similar to aniseed. It can be used in any recipe suited to the common or cultivated mushroom but it has a slightly stronger flavour.

HORSEMEAT
Highly prized meat in France, Italy and Spain, where it costs about the same as beef. Shops selling horsemeat in France usually carry the emblem of a horse on the shop front for easy identification. Horsemeat is not eaten in Britain.

HORSERADISH
Native to the Far East and eastern Europe, horseradish (*Armoracia rusticana*) is now grown all over the world and it belongs to the cabbage family. It is a brown, cylindrical root which resembles a thin parsnip and the flesh is hard, creamy-white and usually grated before use. Hot, pungent and with a characteristic flavour, horseradish has many culinary applications and is the basis of horseradish sauce, traditionally served with roast beef. It is very popular in Scandinavia, Northern Europe and the USSR.

HORSERADISH SAUCE
A strongly-flavoured creamy sauce made from cream, lemon juice, vinegar, grated horseradish and seasonings. It is suitable for serving with roast beef and smoked mackerel or trout.

HOT AND SOUR SOUP
A Peking speciality, a shredded pork soup containing vegetables, Chinese dried mushrooms, eggs, soy sauce, vinegar, seasonings and cornflour.

HOT BISCUIT
See *Biscuit*.

HOT CROSS BUNS
Traditionally, eaten hot in Britain for Good Friday breakfast or during the morning. They are yeasted, fruited, spiced and usually have a cross of pastry on the top, hence their name.

HOT DOG
North American term for a frankfurter sausage.

HOT DOG SANDWICH
(Hot Dog)
Usually a long roll which is split, spread lightly with mustard and sandwiched together with a frankfurter or wiener sausage.

HOTCH-POTCH
(Hodge-Podge)
A British stew of lamb or mutton, very similar to Irish stew. It is thought that the name is derived from the Dutch word *hosten*, meaning to shake, and also the word pot.

HOTEL ROLLS
Crusty rolls, usually white, with a cross cut in the centre of each.

à l'HÔTELIÈRE
French term meaning in the style of a hotelier, referring to a garnish for fish comprised of *maître d'hôtel* butter or sauce and chopped, fried mushrooms.

HOT-SMOKING
A technique whereby foods are smoked fairly quickly at relatively high temperatures ranging from 38°C/100°F to 110°C/225°F. The process cooks and smokes the food simultaneously and it may be safely eaten without further cooking. Hot-smoked foods include some sausages, mackerel, trout, poultry, game, beef and cheese.

HOT-WATER CRUST PASTRY
A robust pastry, made from flour, egg yolks and boiling milk, water

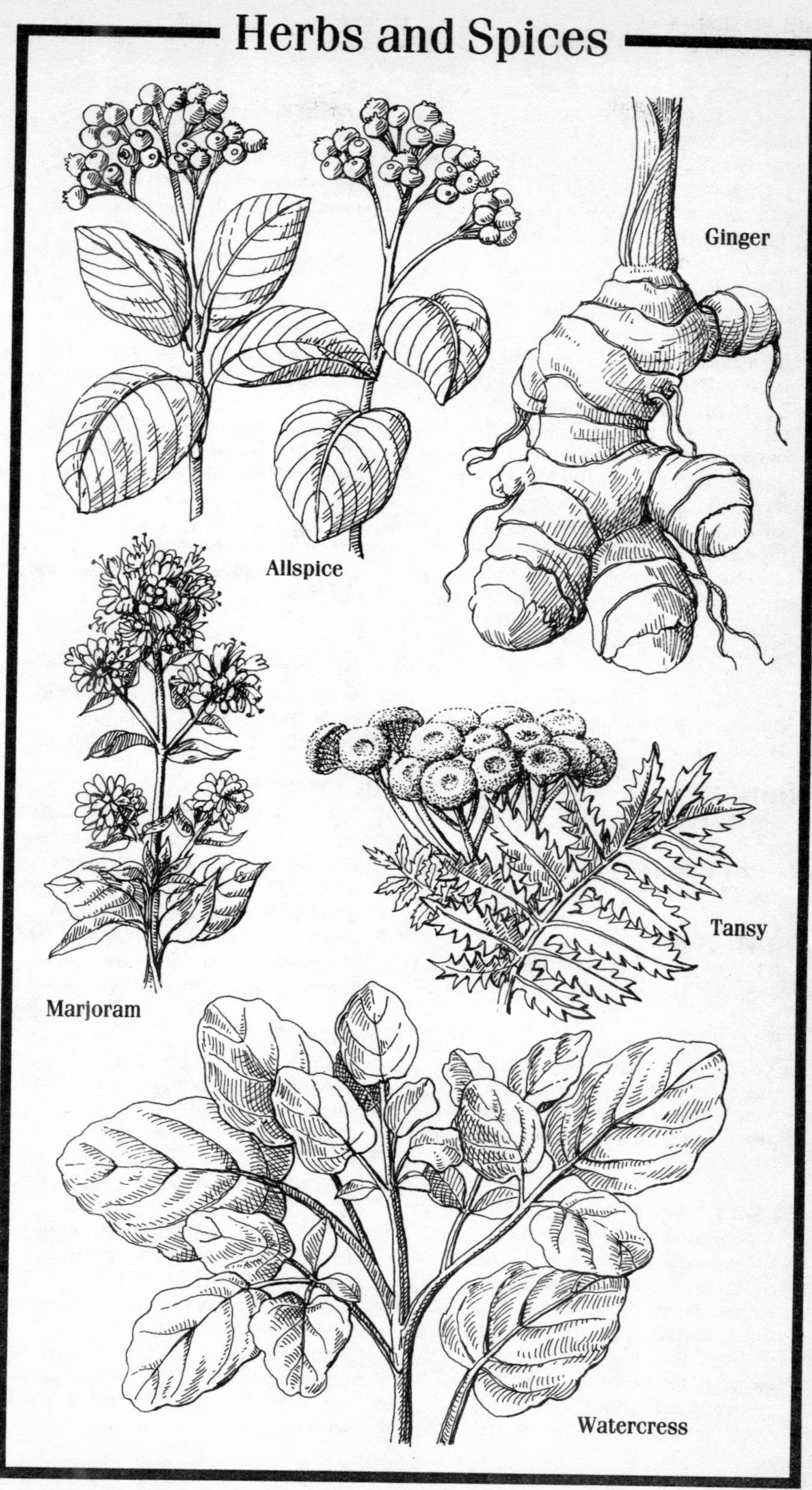
Herbs and Spices
Ginger
Allspice
Marjoram
Tansy
Watercress

and fat, which is strong enough not only to support itself, but also the filling it contains. It is the pastry used traditionally for British raised pies such as game, veal and ham, and pork, known as raised pies because they can be raised or shaped by hand. However, to make this operation speedier and easier, the warm pastry is moulded round a cake tin (if allowed to become cold, the pastry is difficult to handle) or used to line a decorative, hinged raised pie mould. Because raised pies have to be cooked longer than most other pies, hot-water crust pastry is used fairly thickly. As the meat filling inside a raised pie shrinks when cold and leaves gaps, liquid aspic jelly should be poured into the pie through a small hole in the top and left to set before serving.

HOUGH OF BEEF
(Skink of Beef)
Term used in Scotland for shin of beef (foreleg) and leg of beef (hindleg).

HOUMOUS
See *Hummus*.

HOUSEHOLD FLOUR
See *Plain Flour*.

HOWGATE
A top-quality Scottish cream cheese, coated with oatmeal.

HRAMSA
A Scottish cream cheese, very rich and smooth, which is flavoured with local wild garlic. It is classed as a dessert cheese and made from cows' milk.

HUBBARD SQUASH
A vegetable (*Cucurbita maxima*) of the squash family native to North America. It is one of the winter squash group which matures slowly and is usually eaten in the winter months. The shape varies from round to oval with an uneven and ribbed green skin. The hubbard squash contains inedible seeds when ripe, and is often too large to use whole so is generally sold in pieces. The deseeded piece may be cooked with or without the skin and the orangey-yellow flesh is used by itself as a vegetable or in savoury dishes.

HUCKLEBERRY
The fruit of a small bush (*Gaylussacia frondosa*) related to the blueberry and native to eastern America where it grows wild in cool and shady conditions. The berry is black or blue-black, spherical and grows in clusters. It is about 1 cm/½ inch in diameter and the flesh is sweet and juicy. The berry may be eaten raw or used in cooked dishes suited to the blueberry.

HULL
The outer covering of a fruit or seed; also the green or leafy parts of the base of berry fruits that protected the flower when in bud.

HUMBLES
The internal organs of a deer and, according to a Victorian encyclopaedia of cooking, 'these are excellent when made into a pie, and have no doubt suggested the expression "eating humble pie", the viscera usually falling to the lot of the huntsmen's servants'.

HUMBUG
A hard, peppermint-flavoured sweet with stripes. It is made from boiled sugar.

HUMMUS
(Homos, Houmous, Houmus, Humus)
A Middle Eastern appetizer, made from *hummus* (chickpea purée) mixed with *tahina* (a sesame seed paste). Portions are spooned on to plates, topped with a trickle of olive oil then garnished with black olives and chopped parsley. The *hummus* is traditionally mopped up with pitta bread.

HUNDREDS AND THOUSANDS
Multi-coloured fine sugar strands used for sprinkling over iced cakes and desserts as a decoration.

HUNGARIAN BUTTER
(Paprika Butter)
Softened, whipped butter to which paprika, onion and wine vinegar are added. It is shaped into a 2.5 cm/1 inch diameter roll, wrapped and refrigerated until hard, then cut into rounds of about 5 mm/¼ inch in thickness. These are used to garnish grilled veal or pork chops, shellfish dishes and grilled gammon.

HUNGARIAN GOULASH
See *Borgrácsgulyás*.

HUNGARIAN SAUCE
A velouté sauce made with fish, poultry or meat stock and flavoured with lightly fried onions and paprika. It can be served with freshwater fish, roast and grilled poultry, and roast veal.

HUNTER'S SAUCE
English term for Chasseur sauce.

HUNTER'S SAUSAGE
See *Jagdwurst*.

HUNTSMAN
A British cheese from the Vale of Belvoir, composed of layers of Blue Stilton and Double Gloucester.

HUNZA APRICOTS
Grown in the vast area of the Himalayas, these are wild fruits, quite small, which are well suited to drying. They have an especially delicious flavour.

HUSH PUPPIES
A traditional dish from the southern states of the USA, these used to be scraps of fried cornmeal batter which were thrown to nagging puppies to keep them quiet, hence 'hush puppy'. Today, hush puppies are onion-flavoured, round dumplings made from cornmeal which are deep-fried and served with fried fish.

HUSHÅLLSOST
A Swedish cows' milk cheese which is shaped like a cylinder. It is pale in colour with a slightly open texture, laced with elongated, round holes. It is mild and creamy and sometimes spiced with cloves and cumin.

HUSK
See *Bran*.

HUSS
See *Dogfish*.

à la HUSSARDE
French term meaning in the style of a hussar, referring to a garnish (usually for joints of meat) of aubergines, stuffed potatoes, grated horseradish and sometimes mushrooms.

HUTSPOT
A casserole of meat and vegetables and one of Holland's national dishes.

HYACINTH BEAN
(Egyptian Bean)
A vegetable (*Dolichos lablab*) native to India and cultivated in many parts of the world with suitable warm climates. It is a legume which is cooked as a fresh vegetable, using the pod as well as the beans. The beans may also be dried and used as a pulse.

HYDROCHLORIC ACID
Sometimes referred to as a digestive juice, which is secreted by cells in the stomach walls and changes pepsinogen into pepsin, an enzyme partially responsible for the digestion of protein.

HYDROMETER
Weighted glass tube for measuring the density of sugar syrup.

HYSSOP
An ancient herb (*Hyssopus officinalis*) valued for its medicinal

properties. It is a Eurasian plant of the mint family with spikes of small blue, white or pink flowers and dark green, slender leaves. It is rarely used as a culinary herb.

I'A LAWALU
A Hawaiian speciality consisting of local fish baked in taro leaves.

IÇ PILAV
(Turkish Pilav, Pilaff, Pilaf, Pilau)
A Turkish *pilav* made from round-grain rice, fried onions and pine nuts, chopped lamb's liver, currants, tomato, cinnamon, stock or water and seasonings.

ICE (TO)
To use icing to cover or decorate cakes, buns and biscuits.

ICE CREAM
A flavoured and coloured frozen food usually made from custard or cream (or cream substitute), sugar and often eggs.

ICE CREAM SODA
See *Soda*.

ICE CREAM SUNDAE
(Sundae)
Individual portions of ice cream topped with fresh or canned fruit, sauce, whipped cream and a sprinkling of chopped nuts.

ICE LOLLY
(Lolly)
An individual block of sweetened, frozen fruit juice on a stick.

ICEBERG LETTUCE
A type of lettuce which is ball-shaped, pale green in colour with crisp, closely packed leaves. It is very mildly flavoured.

ICEBLOCK
New Zealand and Australian term for an ice lolly.

ICED FANCIES
Small sponge cakes, completely covered with fondant icing in assorted colours and flavours. Sometimes they are decorated with piped glacé fruits, crystallized flower petals and silver balls.

ICELAND MOSS
An edible lichen (*Cetraria islandica*) of mountainous and Arctic regions that yields an extract used especially in the preparation of size.

ICES
First made in Roman times when flavourings were added to snow, ices are said to have originated in Naples in Italy and were based on fruit juice, fruit pulp, dairy products and sugar.

ICING
Usually a sweetened covering or filling for a cake or cakes; also, a stiff mixture, such as royal icing, used for decorative purposes.

ICING BAG
See *Forcing Bag*.

ICING SUGAR
Refined white sugar which is pulverized into a fine powder. It is not only used in making cake icings and confectionery but is also sifted over desserts, sweet yeasted goods and cakes for a decorative finish. To eliminate lumps, icing sugar should be sifted before use.

IDIAZÁBAL
(Aralar, Urbasa, Urbia)
A Spanish smoked cheese from the Basque country produced from ewes' milk. It is one of the most popular of the country's mountain cheeses and is matured for 3–4 weeks in caves. It tastes faintly of herbs and also has a mild, smoky flavour. It is a relatively firm cheese, interspersed with a few holes.

IDLI
Small Indian steamed rice cakes served with spiced coconut and other sambals.

IKAN BERINTI
A Malaysian dish of stuffed fish.

IKAN BILLIS
The Malaysian version of Bombay duck, made from tiny fish which are cooked, dried in the sun and then deep-fried before being sprinkled over traditional vegetable and other dishes.

ILHA
Produced in the Portuguese Azores, a cows' milk cheese which resembles Cheddar.

à l'IMPÉRIALE
French term meaning in Imperial style, denoting a garnish of *foie gras*, mushrooms and sometimes cockscombs, used for chicken.

INCANESTRATO
See *Canestrato*.

INCISE (TO)
To make slits in raw food before cooking. This is often done to enable sprigs of herb, or slivers of garlic, for example, to be inserted into the flesh to impregnate it with flavour during cooking.

INCONNU
(Connie, Coney)
A Canadian freshwater fish (*Leucichthys mackenzii*) found in the larger lakes. It has a silvery-grey back, lightening to whitish on the underside, and a pronounced, protruding lower jaw. The average shop weight is about 4 kg/9 lb and it is caught all year round. The flesh is white, oily and tender and the fish may be poached, steamed, baked, fried or grilled. Although inconnu is a white fish, it can be used as an alternative to salmon in most recipes.

INDIAN CORN
North American term for maize.

INDIAN CRESS
See *Nasturtium*.

INDIAN DATE
See *Tamarind*.

INDIAN FIG
See *Prickly Pear*.

INDIAN NUTS
See *Pine Nuts*.

INDIAN PUDDING
A milk pudding from North America made with cornmeal, milk, butter, treacle, spices and eggs. It dates back to the time of the Pilgrim Fathers who named sweetcorn Indian corn.

INDIAN RICE
North American term for wild rice.

à l'INDIENNE
French term meaning in Indian style, denoting food served in a mild curry sauce and accompanied by rice.

INFUSE (TO)
To extract flavour from such items as tea leaves, ground coffee and herbs, by steeping them in a liquid which is usually hot.

INFUSER
Small, perforated, closed container which is fitted with a handle or a chain and in which enough tea is placed to produce a single serving. The filled infuser is placed in a cup and covered with boiling water. When the required strength of tea is achieved, the infuser is removed from the cup by the handle or chain.

INK CAP
See *Shaggy Cap*.

INKFISH
See *Squid*.

INLAGD GURKA
A sweet-and-sour Swedish cucumber salad made from thinly sliced cucumber marinated in a mixture of vinegar, sugar and water. It is refrigerated, covered, for a minimum of 3 hours, then garnished with chopped parsley or dill before being removed from the liquid and served.

INLAGD SILL
Swedish pickled herring, made from well-soaked, salted herrings marinated in a spicy vinegar mixture containing chopped onions. The herrings are garnished with dill and extra onion, then served with boiled potatoes or bread and butter.

INNARDS
Colloquial term for the internal organs or viscera of an animal.

INSTANT
Immediately soluble in hot or boiling water, such as instant coffee; also, pre-mixed or pre-cooked food for easy final preparation, instant potato, for example.

INSTANT COFFEE
Coffee powder or granules which dissolve totally in hot water without any residue or grounds and are made commercially by removing the water from a strained coffee solution. This is done by evaporation using hot air or freeze-drying methods and leaves the coffee in the required dry powder form, not unlike the original ground coffee bean, or in small granules. Instant coffee is usually manufactured from cheaper beans, often *robusta* types, but with better modern methods the use of the finer *arabica* bean has increased. By this means the manufacturers are now producing an instant coffee tasting more like that made from freshly ground beans. The same brand of instant coffee will differ slightly in flavour around the world as the original beans are blended to suit national tastes and water.

INTERLARDING
A method of keeping meat moist as it cooks by threading it with thin strips of fat, called lardons, by means of a special needle.

INTESTINES
Animal intestines, used in stewing and braising and also as a casing for sausages.

INVERT SUGAR
A simple sugar or monosaccharide, consisting of a compound of glucose and fructose. Its presence prevents crystallization in syrups and some types of confectionery.

IODINE
Important to the body because it controls the action of the thyroid gland situated in the neck, iodine, a mineral, constitutes part of the hormone thyroxin which controls metabolism. Those deficient in iodine can develop goitre, which used to be more familiarly known as 'Derbyshire neck' because water in the area lacked iodine. Iodine is found in sea fish, shellfish and drinking water; also in foods which have been grown near the sea, because they automatically absorb sea spray carried by the wind. The earth also contains iodine. Many brands of table salt have iodine added.

IRIO
An East African speciality made from a basis of mashed potatoes mixed with sweetcorn, green peas, cooked green bananas, seasoning and butter or margarine.

IRISH COFFEE
A mixture of Irish whiskey and hot, sweetened coffee topped with a floating layer of cream. It is drunk unstirred.

IRISH MOSS
See *Carrageen*.

IRISH POTATO CAKES
See *Fadge*.

IRISH SODA BREAD
See *Soda Bread*.

IRISH STEW
A typical Irish dish made by stewing lamb with potatoes, onions, water and seasoning. Individual portions are sprinkled with chopped parsley before serving.

IRISH SWISS CHEESE
See *Blarney*.

IRON RATIONS
Emergency food rations, usually supplied to the armed forces.

ISCHLER BISCUITS
Austrian biscuits, made from a ground almond and flour mixture, which are rich, buttery and sweet. They are cut into rounds before baking, allowed to cool, then sandwiched together with red jam. They are traditionally covered with chocolate icing.

ISINGLASS
A solid, jelly-like substance made from fish bladders. It is used as an egg preservative.

IŞKEMBE ÇORBASI
A Turkish tripe soup flavoured with garlic and vinegar and thickened with egg yolks, lemon juice and cream.

ISLAY
A fairly firm, Scottish cheese which resembles some kinds of Cheddar. It is made from cows' milk.

ITALIAN BREAD STICKS
See *Grissini*.

ITALIAN COFFEE
A mixture of Strega liqueur and hot, strong unsweetened coffee topped with a floating layer of cream. It is drunk unstirred. The term may also be used to describe strong black coffee made from very well-roasted beans.

ITALIAN MERINGUE MIXTURE
Used primarily by professional chefs. It is prepared from a sugar syrup boiled to the soft ball stage and then beaten into egg whites until the mixture is cold and peaky.

à l'ITALIENNE
French term meaning in Italian style, denoting any dish served with or containing pasta and sometimes artichokes.

JABUKE U RUMU
A speciality of Slovenia in Yugoslavia, syrup-poached apples served chilled with a topping of whipped cream, glacé cherries and a sprinkling of rum.

JACKET
Term used to describe the skin of a potato when baked.

JACKFISH
See *Pike*.

JACKFRUIT
(Jakfruit)
The fruit of a large tree (*Artocarpus integrifolia*) native to parts of India and Malaya and now cultivated in many wet, tropical areas around the world. The fruit is large, oval or cylindrical in shape and generally sold when about the size of a football. The skin is yellowy-brown, rough and prickly and the fruit may take over six months to ripen fully after it has been picked. The inside consists of pockets of sweet, juicy flesh, eaten raw, set in a kind of edible 'pith' which, in some countries, is treated as a vegetable and boiled or baked. The seeds, from inside the pockets, are roasted like nuts or finely ground and used in cooking.

JAFFA
A general term to describe citrus fruit from Israel.

JAGDWURST
(German Garlic Sausage, Hunter's Sausage)
A German scalded sausage which is made from finely minced pork, dotted with pieces of pork and bacon fat and flavoured with garlic. The sausage is light pinky-beige, relatively large and easy to slice, with an appetizing flavour.

JAGGERY
See *Palm Sugar*.

JALAPENO PEPPERS
Large and fiery green chillies, widely used in Mexican cooking.

JALEBI
(Jelabi)
An Indian dessert consisting of deep-fried spirals of batter soaked in a rose-flavoured syrup.

JALOUSIE
A French double-crust jam tart which is oblong-shaped and characterized by narrow slits on its lid. It is glazed with egg white and caster sugar and baked until golden-brown.

JAM
A preserve made by boiling fruit (often precooked with water) and sugar until setting point is reached.

JAM PUFFS
See *Puffs*.

JAM ROLY-POLY
See *Roly-Poly Pudding*.

JAM SAUCE
An almost transparent sauce made from jam, heated with a little water and thickened to a pouring consistency with arrowroot, sometimes sweetened with sugar and sharpened with lemon juice. It is typically British and served with steamed and baked sponge-type puddings.

JAM SUGAR
A white sugar containing citric acid and added pectin. Its purpose is to help to set jams and marmalades reliably and more quickly than if conventional sugar were used.

JAM TART
A pastry case filled with jam.

JAM TURNOVERS
Triangles of pastry filled with jam which are usually brushed with milk and sprinkled with caster sugar before baking.

JAMAICA BLUE MOUNTAIN COFFEE
See *Blue Mountain Coffee*.

JAMAICA PEPPER
See *Allspice*.

JAMAICA PLUM
See *Hog Plum*.

JAMBALAYA
A Creole dish from Louisiana in the USA, this is related to Spanish *paella* and is a mixture of fried onions, celery, green pepper and garlic cooked with long-grain rice, tomatoes and either prawns or chicken. It is mounded on to plates and served with Tabasco sauce.

JAMBERRY
See *Tomatillo*.

JAMBON BLANC
See *Jambon de Paris*.

JAMBON CUIT DE PRAGUE
(Prague Ham)
A French version of cooked ham, Prague style. It is a relatively small ham, left on the bone and is used to make speciality dishes.

JAMBON D'ARDENNES
See *Ardennes Ham*.

JAMBON DE PARIS
(Jambon Blanc)
French cooked ham with a mild, delicate flavour. It is generally boned.

JAMBON PERSILLÉ
(Parsley Ham)
A French speciality ham from Burgundy, this consists of shoulder and leg meat mixed with wine-flavoured jelly and a generous amount of chopped parsley. It is cooked in moulds.

JAMBOS
See *Surinam Cherry*.

JAN COUDE MAI MARGE
A speciality stew from St Lucia which is a Caribbean 'labourer's lunch'. It is made from salt beef and pork, red kidney beans, yellow yams, other tropical vegetables, onions, coconut oil and thyme.

JANHAGEL
Dutch finger biscuits flavoured with cinnamon and topped with flaked almonds and granulated sugar.

JANSSON'S TEMPTATION
A crusty, golden Swedish casserole made from grated raw potatoes, chopped onions, butter, anchovy fillets, cream and breadcrumbs. It is named after Erik Jansson, a 19th-century religious fanatic who, when confronted with the casserole and its tempting aroma, succumbed to its charms, despite his sworn promise to give up all earthly pleasures.

JAPANESE MEDLAR
See *Loquat*.

JAPANESE MILLET
A coarse grass (*Echinochloa frumentacea*) cultivated in Asia for its edible seeds.

JAPANESE OYSTER
(Pacific Oyster)
See *Oyster*.

JAPANESE PEAR
See *Asian Pear*.

JAPANESE WINEBERRY
See *Wineberry*.

JAPONICA RICE
See *Short-grain Rice*.

à la JARDINIÈRE
French term meaning in the style of a gardener's wife, referring to a garnish or accompaniment of young spring vegetables, sometimes cut into fancy shapes.

JARLSBERG
Based on an old recipe, Jarlsberg was reintroduced in the late 1950s and has become one of Norway's most popular and well-known cheeses. It is a cross between Gouda and Emmental, is interspersed with a sprinkling of round holes and has a firm texture, making it easy to slice. It is deep cream in colour and produced from pasteurized cows' milk.

JASMINE
Any of numerous climbing shrubs (genus *Jasminum*) of the olive family with very fragrant flowers. Jasmine is used to flavour some Oriental dishes and is also added to tea.

JASMINE TEA
A classic China green tea which is flavoured with jasmine blossoms. It has a delicate taste, does not need milk, and is traditionally served with *dim sum* dishes.

JÁTERNICE
Czechoslovakian offal sausage which is designed for boiling or frying.

JAVA COFFEE
One of the finest *arabica* coffee beans in large-scale cultivation outside Africa and America, and particularly popular during the 19th century. Plant disease and other factors have reduced the importance of this coffee, but a good, matured

Java has a distinctive flavour; strong and slightly smoky. Similar quality beans from nearby islands may be found labelled as Java. The increased introduction of the hardier but relatively inferior *robusta* bean and its hybrids means that the name Java no longer guarantees a coffee from the *arabica* bean unless labelled as such.

JBANE
A Moroccan cheese made from goats' milk. It is either eaten fresh or left to harden on straw racks.

JELITA
Czechoslovakian blood sausage which is boiled or fried.

JELLIED EELS
A traditional British dish made by simmering pieces of fresh eel in a little water. As they cool, the liquid becomes jellied. Vinegar and spices are sometimes added to the water for extra flavour and individual portions are seasoned to taste with salt and pepper.

JELLIES
See *Pastilles*.

JELLY
North American term for jam.

JELLY BABY
A small, soft gelatinous sweet in the shape of a person.

JELLY BAG
A cloth bag used to strain the juice from cooked fruit. The juice is boiled with sugar to make a jelly preserve.

JELLY BEAN
A bean-shaped sweet, in assorted colours, which is sugar-coated and popular in the USA.

JELLY CUBES
(Packet Jelly)
A concentrated block of coloured, fruit-flavoured gelatine divided into cubes which are dissolved in hot water according to the instructions on the packet. It is then left to cool and set. A liquid jelly can be poured into a mould, first rinsed with cold water or lightly oiled, to set. Additions can be made to a half-set jelly to include fruits, nuts, beaten egg whites, milk and cream but never fresh pineapple as it prevents the jelly from setting; canned pineapple is quite safe to use with jelly cubes. This kind of jelly dessert is typically British.

JELLY MOULD
See *Mould*.

JELLY ROLL
North American term for Swiss roll.

JELLYFISH
A Chinese speciality, appreciated for its crispness in cold dishes. Sold in dried form, it must be soaked, drained and shredded before use.

JERKED BEEF
(Chipped Beef)
North American term for strips of air-dried beef.

JERKED MEAT
Sun-dried and smoked strips of beef or venison, sometimes known in North America as charqui or chipped beef.

JERSEY WONDERS
Still to be found in Jersey, Channel Islands. These are fried twists or rings of a light dough mixture which, like French *beignets*, are dusted with sugar and eaten warm. They date back to the beginning of the 20th century.

JERUSALEM ARTICHOKE
A tuber (*Helianthus tuberosus*) of a vegetable which is a member of the sunflower family and native to America. It was introduced to Europe in the 16th century and has been widely cultivated ever since both as a domestic vegetable and as animal feed. It looks like a knobbly

potato in shape and in colour which may be either light brown or purplish, and it should be scraped or thinly peeled and boiled. Though like the potato in character, it contains less starch, is easy to digest and is excellent in soup and as a vegetable in sauce. It is not related to the globe artichoke; the name came into use because of a similarity in taste.

JESUIT'S CRESS
See *Nasturtium*.

JÉSUS
A large, coarse-textured, dried sausage from France, made from pork meat packed into pig gut (intestine).

JEWISH CHICKEN SOUP
See *Gildeneh Yoich*.

JEWISH SALAMI
A kosher salami, made from beef only, which is well seasoned and sometimes flavoured with garlic.

JEW'S EAR
A fungus (*Auricularia auricula*) which grows on elder trees in North America. It resembles a small, misshapen saucer and the colour varies from beige to brown.

JOCHBURG
An Austrian cheese from the Tyrol. It is made from a mixture of cows' and goats' milk and has a rustic and distinctive flavour. It is shaped into large, shallow discs.

JODDA
The name used in Sicily for yogurt.

JOHNNYCAKE
A North American bread or cake made from maize meal.

JOINT
A large piece of meat, usually for roasting; also to cut a chicken into pieces.

JOINTS
Portions into which a carcass is cut. These cuts vary from country to country and even from district to district within a country.

JOJOBA
A shrub or small tree (*Simmondsia californica*) of the box family from the south-western states of North America. The edible seeds yield a valuable liquid wax.

JOLLOF
A West African speciality made from beef, chicken or mutton simmered with fried onions, tomatoes, rice and seasonings.

JORDAN ALMOND
(Sugared Almond)
A large Spanish almond that is coated with sugar of various colours and flavours.

JOULE
A metric unit of energy, sometimes used in place of kilocalories or Calories. One kilocalorie equates to 4.2 kilojoules.

JOWL
The cheek meat of a pig.

JUBES
(Jujubes)
Originally cough sweets, made from an extract of the fruit of the jujube tree, which has a soothing effect on the throat and chest. Jubes tended to be jellied; some also contained liquorice.

JUDIC
French term for a garnish for entrées comprising stuffed tomatoes, braised lettuce, potatoes and sometimes truffles and kidney.

JUG (TO)
To cook in a heavy jug (old-fashioned) or heavy earthenware casserole. This term usually refers to a hare, but may also be applied to any rich stew cooked in these containers.

JUG COFFEE
An old-fashioned but simple method of preparing coffee. About 10 ml/ 2 tsp of medium-ground coffee per person are put into a warmed jug, water (just below boiling point) is added and the coffee left to brew for about 4 minutes. It is then poured into a cup through a strainer.

JUGGED HARE
A rich British stew of sectioned hare in which the blood of the animal is incorporated into the gravy. The term 'jugged' is an old one and dates back at least a century to when hare was cooked in a 'jug', a large vessel with a large body and a narrow mouth.

JUG-JUG
A stew from the Caribbean containing fresh or salted beef and pork and pigeon pea purée.

JUHLA
A sharpish-flavoured Finnish cheese which resembles Cheddar. It is made from cows' milk.

JUICE EXTRACTOR
This can be as uncomplicated as a simple conical-shaped lemon squeezer on to which halved lemons, oranges or grapefruits are pressed and turned to extract their juice, or it can be an electrically operated piece of equipment which presses out juice from fruit and vegetables.

JUICES
Natural liquid found in meat, poultry, game, fish, fruit and vegetables.

JUJUBE
The fruit of a family of trees (*Ziziphus jujuba* and species), both deciduous and evergreen, native to either the Middle East or China and India and widely grown in its many forms in Europe, Asia, Australia and North America. The fruit is usually the size and shape of an olive with slight variations for the associated species. The green skin turns to brownish-red or dark brown as it ripens, sometimes almost black. The jujube has a single, hard central stone and the surrounding flesh is white, sweet and sticky when newly ripe. The fruit is left to dry out slightly before use. The flesh may be eaten raw or used in preserves or with other ingredients in both sweet and savoury dishes. The juice is a good source of vitamin C, soothing to sore throats, and is used in some medicines.

JULEFROKEST
The Danish Christmas cold table, characterized by a whole cooked Danish gammon (*skinke*).

JULIENNE
French term for food, especially vegetables, cut into strips the length and thickness of wooden matchsticks.

JULSKINKA
A Swedish presentation of ham served hot or cold at Christmas time. When cold, the words *God Jul* (Happy Christmas) are piped on to the ham with *chaud-froid* sauce.

JUMBLES
Lemon-flavoured biscuits containing almonds. They are quite rich and popular in North America.

JUMBO OATS
Large oat flakes.

JUNEBERRY
(Serviceberry)
The fruit of a shrub or tree (*Amelanchier* species) of the rose family, found mostly in North America and also in parts of Europe and Asia. It is often used as a decorative tree in gardens and parks and the fruit is a similar size and shape to a blackcurrant, with a skin colour ranging from red to black. It is juicy and pleasant to eat on its own but may also be used in pies and tarts. The juneberry is one of the native North American fruits much used by early settlers.

JUNIPER BERRIES
The blackish berries of small evergreen trees or shrubs (genus *Juniperus*) which are related to the conifer family and native to Europe. Juniper berries are available fresh or dried and used in the distillation of some kinds of gin and other European spirits. They are popular in Scandinavia and northern Europe and go well in some beef stews, game dishes and pickles. Juniper berries are mentioned in the Bible and, historically, were regarded as a symbol of protection against evil spirits and wild animals.

JUNK FOOD
Calorie-laden food and drink which is considered unhealthy as it usually contains excessive amounts of sugar, fat and salt.

JUNKET
A traditional British dessert made from warmed, sweetened milk and thickened by the addition of rennet. The dish was, and sometimes still is, flavoured with brandy, sherry or liquor and sprinkled with powdered spice before serving.

JUS
French term to describe fruit or tomato juice, pan juices left behind after roasting a joint and natural juice occurring in such foods as oysters.

au JUS
French term for roast meat served with gravy.

JUS LIÉ
French term for gravy which has been thickened with flour, cornflour or similar substance.

à la JUSSIÈRE
French term for a garnish for entrées comprising onions, braised lettuce, potatoes and sometimes carrots.

JUUSTOLEIPÄ
(Leipäjuusto)
An eastern Finnish and Lapland speciality, this is a low-fat cows' milk cheese produced by hand on local farms. It is loaf-shaped, sliced and toasted and is often eaten for breakfast, broken into small pieces and dunked in hot coffee.

K RATION
A lightweight packaged ration of emergency foods developed for the US armed forces in World War II.

KABABS
The Indian term for pieces of meat or seafood threaded on skewers, usually wooden, and charcoal-grilled or cooked in a special oven called a *tandoor*.

KABAK DOLMASI
A Turkish speciality of young marrows or courgettes stuffed with a mixture of onions, raisins, pine nuts, seasonings and chopped parsley or dill. They are baked in the oven, then served lightly chilled.

KABAK TATHSI
A Turkish dessert made from cooked pumpkin flesh soaked in syrup and sprinkled with chopped walnuts.

KABANOS
Long and slender Polish-style dried pork sausages which are fairly hard, well-seasoned and smoked. They are generally eaten as a snack.

KADIN GÖBEĞI
The Turkish name means 'lady's navel' and these are small fried Turkish biscuits, resembling navels, which are soaked in syrup and eaten for dessert.

KAGGOST
A Swedish cows' milk cheese which is medium-mild and medium-soft. It is yellow in colour and sometimes spiced with cumin.

KAHA BATH
Spiced rice, coloured yellow with turmeric, prepared for festive occasions in Sri Lanka.

KAHVE
The Turkish word for the strong black coffee of the country, made in a long-handled and lidded pot called a *džezva*.

KAIL
See *Kale*.

KAISERSCHMARREN
An Austrian speciality made from a thick, sweetened batter containing raisins or sultanas, which is poured into a large pan and fried fairly briskly, simultaneously being pulled into strips with two forks. When all the strips are golden and crisp, they are piled on to a plate and sprinkled with sugar. The *Kaiserschmarren*, meaning Emperor's Omelette in English, is eaten as a dessert with stewed plums.

KAKAVIA
A Greek fish soup related to the French *bouillabaisse*.

KAKI
(Kakee)
See *Persimmon*.

KALAKEITTO
A milky Finnish soup containing assorted lake fish, onions, water, rye bread, potatoes and milk, thickened with cornflour. Each portion is sprinkled with chopped fresh dill.

KALAKUKKO
Described as Finland's national Karelian dish (Karelia lies to the east of Finland), this is made from a hollowed-out rye loaf filled with *muikko*, tiny white fish which are smaller than sardines and similar to whitebait, fat pork and seasonings. The loaf is then baked slowly to cook the filling. It is sliced and eaten hot, everyone being given crust and filling. The word in English means fishcock.

KALBSHAXEN
Loosely translated into English, this means a calf's knee joint. It is an Austrian and Bavarian speciality, consisting of large veal or pork joints, roasted until they are golden brown, tender and crisp. They are served with boiled potatoes and salad. The *kalbshaxen* are sometimes spit-roasted or fried.

KALBSLEBERWURST
A superior German liver sausage made from pork, veal and a high proportion of top quality calves' liver. The texture is smooth and creamy and the flavour mild and delicate.

KÅLDOLMAR
Swedish cabbage rolls stuffed with minced beef, rice, milk, water and seasonings. They are lightly fried, placed in a casserole and coated thinly with syrup. Stock is added and the rolls are baked, covered, until tender. The gravy is thickened with soured cream and cornflour and the *kåldolmar* are served with boiled potatoes and cranberry sauce.

KALE
(Borecole, Curly Kale, Kail)
A vegetable (*Brassica oleracea*, var. *acephala*) which is a member of the cabbage family and a descendant of the wild or sea cabbage native to Europe. It is a hardy plant, less developed than other modern members of the family. The name kale is given to any form of cabbage with sprouting leaves which are curled and finely dented and do not form a solid head or heart. The dark green leaves sprout on stems growing from a central stalk which may be up to 60 cm/2 feet tall and they are harvested when young as

mature kale has a very strong flavour. It is generally eaten boiled as a vegetable. Kale, in its various forms, has been part of the staple winter diet for many of the poorer people in north-west Europe for hundreds of years; it is known in Holland and Germany as 'peasant's cabbage'.

KALLALOO
See *Callaloo Soup*.

KALUA PUAA
A Hawaiian dish consisting of shredded roast pork which is well-seasoned and roasted in taro leaves.

KAMANO LOMI
A Hawaiian appetizer made from chopped smoked salmon (or salted and soaked salmon), chopped tomatoes, chopped onions and salt. The dish takes its name from the word *lomi*, meaning to crush, squeeze or chop.

KANGAROO TAIL
An Australian speciality, kangaroo tail is treated in the same way as oxtail.

KANGAROO TAIL SOUP
An Australian soup made in the same way as oxtail.

KANTER
See *Friese Kanterkaas*.

KAPI
See *Blachan*.

KARELA
See *Bitter Gourd*.

KARELIAN HOT-POT
See *Karjalanpaisti*.

KARELIAN OPEN PASTIES
Finnish pasties which look like flat, elongated ovals. They are made from rye dough, filled with a cooked rice mixture. They are served warm, each topped with a mixture of chopped hard-boiled eggs and butter.

KARJALANPAISTI
A classic Finnish dish, a casserole made from diced beef, pork, lamb, black peppercorns, bay leaves, onions, carrots, water and salt, cooked in the oven very slowly and served with boiled potatoes and mashed swedes.

KARTANO
A Finnish version of Dutch Gouda cheese made from cows' milk.

KARTOFFELPUFFER
Large potato pancakes associated with the Rhineland but eaten all over Germany. They are served sizzling hot and are usually accompanied by cold apple purée.

KÄSE
The German word for cheese.

KASERI
(Kasseri).
A semi-hard ewes' milk cheese from Greece. It is mild and white and resembles Italian Provolone. It is used for a Greek version of pizza, served as a dessert cheese or cut into pieces, coated with flour and fried in hot oil for an hors d'oeuvre.

KASHA
See *Buckwheat*.

KASHKAVAL
(Kaskaval)
A Balkan cheese which dates back to Roman times. It resembles Italy's Caciocavallo and is made from ewes' milk or a mixture of ewes' and cows' milk. It is a useful, all-purpose cheese for eating and cooking.

KASHRUTH
(Kashrut)
The state of foods being Kosher and permissible for orthodox Jews to eat; also, Jewish laws concerning foods and the slaughter of animals.

KASSLER
(Kaseler Rippenspeer, Kaseler)
A speciality pork product from Germany, kassler is made from

lightly salted loin of pork which is mildly smoked with juniper berries. It originates from Berlin and is named after its inventor, a butcher called Kasel. It can be roasted, cut in slices and fried (as gammon) or thinly carved and used in *hors d'oeuvre*, cold buffets and sandwiches. Hot kassler is served with creamed potatoes or noodles and pease pudding.

KATENRAUCHWURST
(Farmer's Cottage Sausage)
A German preserved sausage, made from coarse pieces of pork. It is slowly smoked over juniper branches, heather, pine or beechwood and develops a dark skin and powerful flavour and is often served accompanied by black bread and beer.

KATENSPECK
A German speciality pork product which closely resembles streaky bacon in appearance but has a dark, brownish rind and is sold pre-cooked in the piece. It has a distinctive, delicate, smoky flavour and may be sliced and eaten cold or used in a variety of stews, casseroles and soups.

KATSUOBUSHI
The Japanese term for dried bonito flakes, which are used extensively in stock.

KEBABCHÉS
Bulgarian meat balls, usually served on top of thick slices of grilled veal, beef or pork.

KEBABS
(Kebobs, Shashlik, Shish Kebabs)
An eastern Mediterranean speciality consisting of small pieces of meat, traditionally lamb, threaded on to skewers and grilled, often over an open fire. The meat is frequently marinated before cooking and the kebabs are well-seasoned and served with rice and salad. Westernized versions of kebabs also include pieces of vegetables such as mushrooms, red or green peppers, onions and small skinned tomatoes.

KECAP MANIS
Indonesian soy sauce.

KEDGEREE
An old British breakfast dish dating back to the days of the Indian Raj. It is made from smoked and fresh haddock, cooked rice, chopped hard-boiled eggs, cream and/or butter and seasoning to taste, sometimes with the addition of curry powder. Kedegeree is served piping hot with a sprinkling of chopped parsley.

KEEMUN
The traditional tea of old Imperial China, this is one of the finest of the Congou black teas of northern China. It is used in some Breakfast Blend teas and is also available unblended. With or without milk, it is a good accompaniment to Chinese food.

KEFALOTIR
A Yugoslav version of Greek Kefalotiri cheese.

KEFALOTIRI
(Kefalotyri)
A hat- or skull-shaped ewes' milk cheese from Greece which is firm-textured and distinctively-flavoured. It is a cooking cheese and similar to Parmesan.

KEFIR
Originally from the Caucasus in Southern Russia, between the Black and Caspian Seas, it is a slightly alcoholic, soured milk drink treated with culture which contains both bacteria and lactose-fermenting yeasts. It is a low-fat product produced in Scandinavia.

KEFTEDES
Greek meat balls, made from well-seasoned minced beef or veal which are fried and served as a main course.

KEFTEJI
The North African version of meat balls.

KEFTETHAKIA
(Keftedakia)
Small *keftedes* which are eaten in Greece as an appetizer.

KEFTETHES
Greek meat rissoles or patties, made from well-seasoned minced beef or veal. The mixture is shaped into egg-sized balls, coated with flour, fried until well-browned and served with salad and bread.

KELEPA SAYUR
A Malaysian dish of chopped mixed vegetables cooked in coconut milk.

KELP
See *Kombu*.

KEMIRI NUTS
See *Candlenuts*.

KENYA COFFEE
One of the finest African coffees when obtained from the *arabica* bean, combining the qualities of flavour and aroma to be found in the best coffees from other countries. Although a later starter in the commercial coffee market, Kenya has become one of the most popular types in the UK.

KENYA TEA
A relatively recent producer of tea, Kenya grows some black teas at high altitudes which are similar in quality to those from Sri Lanka. Although mostly used in blends with teas from other countries, some solely Kenyan mixtures are available.

KERN MILK
Scottish term for buttermilk.

KERNEL
The edible part of a nut. Although the stones from peaches and apricots are referred to as kernels, this is actually incorrect as it is only the inner, nut-like portions which should bear that name.

KERNHEM
A recently introduced Dutch cows' milk cheese which is creamy, rich, very soft and pale yellow in colour. It coats the knife when cut and has a tacky orange-brown rind. It is full-flavoured, with a butterfat content of around 60%, and is based on a traditional monastery cheese.

KEŞKÜL
A Turkish milk pudding flavoured with almond essence and chopped almonds and topped with chopped pistachio nuts and desiccated coconut.

KESTI
A Finnish version of Tilsit cheese, flavoured with caraway seeds.

KETAN
Indonesian glutinous rice which is served as a dessert with grated desiccated coconut and a syrup made from brown sugar.

KETCHUP
(Catsup, Catchup)
Commercially prepared bottled sauce which is a fairly strongly flavoured condiment and served with cold foods and salads, or grills and roasts. Tomato ketchup is an international favourite and, in Britain, brown sauce (such as HP) is also very popular. In Victorian times ketchup was much sought-after and used as an essence to flavour and enliven bland foods. It was made from the then inexpensive oysters, lobsters, eels, anchovies and mushrooms, and had a shelf life of 20 years.

KETJAP SAUCE
The Indonesian term for soy sauce.

KEY LIME PIE
A Florida speciality, made from a baked pastry case with a filling of sweetened condensed milk, egg yolks and lime juice. The filling sets

when cold and is sometimes topped with meringue, which is then browned quickly in a hot oven. The limes used were originally from the Florida Keys.

KIBBEH
The Middle Eastern term for dishes made with burghul (cracked wheat).

KIBBEH NAYÉ
(Kibbeh Nayyeh)
A Middle Eastern speciality made from a mixture of raw minced lamb, minced onions and burghul. The ingredients are minced or pounded together until very smooth, seasoned to taste and eaten as an appetizer accompanied by lettuce leaves.

KIBBLED WHEAT
(Cracked Wheat)
Coarsely roller-crushed grains of wheat which are cooked for 20–25 minutes and eaten hot as a breakfast cereal or served as an accompaniment to main dishes. Sometimes the raw wheat is sprinkled on top of bread or rolls prior to baking to improve both their flavour and appearance.

KICKSHAW
An old-fashioned British term to describe a delicacy or fancy dish.

KID
Term for a young goat.

KIDNEY BEAN
See *Red Kidney Bean*.

KIDNEY FAT
(Suet)
The fat or suet surrounding kidneys is of a very high quality and is frequently chopped and used in steamed puddings, mincemeat and for frying.

KIDNEYS
These should be bought as fresh as possible and their 'overcoat' of fat left on as this improves their keeping qualities. They should be mid-brown in colour (the colouring will vary slightly with type) and be free from dark patches, which indicate staleness. Kidneys are best used within 12 hours of purchase and are a good source of protein, iron and vitamins of the B group.

KIELBASA
A Polish sausage, popular with the large Polish community in the Midwest of the USA. It is a boiling ring made from beef, pork, garlic and spices.

KILIMANJARO
A Tanzanian coffee which, when made from the *arabica* bean, is similar in quality to Kenya coffee but slightly less sharp in flavour.

KILKIS
The Norwegian name for anchovies.

KILLARNEY
An Irish version of Cheddar cheese.

KILOCALORIE
See *Large Calorie*.

KILOCALORIFIC VALUE
(Calorific Value)
The amount of energy derived from a specific amount of food or food nutrient.

KILOJOULE
See *Joule*.

KING CRAB
A large, long-legged crab (*Paralithodes camtschatica*) caught on the Alaskan coast. It is light brown in colour and average weight is 2.5–3.5 kg/5½–8 lb.

KING PRAWN
Any of several species (*Penaeus* species) of large prawns found in Australian waters.

KINOKO
The Japanese word for mushroom.

KIPPER
A fish, usually herring, which has been split, gutted, salted and smoked.

KIPPER (TO)
To preserve fish by smoking after splitting and salting. The fish most commonly treated in this way in Britain is the herring and the resultant kipper has made the name its own, although it can also apply to other fish.

KIPPER FILLETS
Fresh or frozen fillets of kipper which are boneless.

KIPPERED HERRING
See *Kipper*.

KIR
See *Crème de Cassis*.

KIRI BATH
A thick rice and creamed coconut mixture which is spread out, cut into diamonds and served with jaggery or dark brown sugar at Sri Lankan festivals.

KIRSCH
Dry and colourless fruit brandy based on cherries.

KISHKA
(Stuffed Derma)
A Jewish version of haggis in which beef intestine is stuffed with a mixture of flour, onion, chopped suet and seasonings and is then simmered over a low heat with onions and water. The *kishka* is served hot with horseradish sauce, usually as an appetizer.

KISSEL
A Russian blancmange made from fruit juice (often currant juice), water and sugar. The *kissel* is thickened with cornflour or potato flour, set in dishes and topped with cold milk or cream. It is a summer dessert and is served well chilled.

KISZKA KASZANKA
A Polish blood sausage, containing buckwheat groats.

KIWANO
Native to New Zealand, oval fruit about the same size as a large pear. The skin is deep yellow and spiky. The seedy pulp is green and tastes like a mixture of orange, lemon and passion fruit.

KIWI FRUIT
(Chinese Gooseberry)
The fruit of a deciduous, vine-like climbing plant (*Acinidia chinensis*) native to the fringes of the forests in the Yangtse Valley in China and once known only as Chinese gooseberry. It is now cultivated in many parts of the world, even under glass on Guernsey in the Channel Islands, but most successfully in New Zealand, where the climate and soil are ideal. The shape is generally oval with flattened ends and the skin is brown, thin and hairy. The length is about 7.5–10 cm/3–4 inches and the soft flesh, with its tiny black and edible seeds, is a distinctive peridot green. The flavour is sweet, bearing no resemblance to a gooseberry, but more reminiscent of a melon or strawberry. Kiwi fruit is very rich in vitamin C. It may be sliced across the middle and eaten with a spoon like a boiled egg. If desired, the hairs may be removed from the skin by rubbing. The unusual colour of the peeled flesh is useful in decorating salads and the flavour is suitable for adding to both sweet and savoury foods. Preserves and drinks can also be made from this versatile fruit. The skin contains enzymes which make it useful as a meat tenderizer but the fruit itself stops gelatinous mixtures from setting.

KLÖSSE
(Knödel)
Heavy German dumplings which can be made from potatoes, flour, breadcrumbs or semolina (or a combination), mixed with milk, fat

and sometimes bacon. They are generally boiled and served as an accompaniment to sweet or savoury dishes.

KNACKWURST
A German scalded sausage, related to frankfurters and bockwurst but spicier than both. The name refers to the cracking sound it sometimes makes when the skin splits open during heating.

KNAIDLECH
Jewish Passover soup dumplings made from unleavened *matzo* meal, eggs, water, salt, and either melted margarine, chicken fat or oil.

KNAOST
See *Pultost*.

KNEAD (TO)
To work with the hands, or the dough hook attachment of a mixer, any dough or pastry mixture to the consistency described in the recipe.

KNEADED BUTTER
English term for *Beurre Manié*.

KNEDLÍKY
Traditionally heavy, Czechoslovakian dumplings which are served with soup, meat and as desserts. They are made from flour and/or semolina; sometimes breadcrumbs are included.

KNICKERBOCKER GLORY
A large and elaborate dessert presented in a conical glass and consisting of chopped jelly, canned fruit and custard. It is topped with whipped cream and a glacé cherry and appears to be unique to Britain.

KNIFE SHARPENER
There are three types of knife sharpener. The simplest is a silicone carbide stone on which the edge of the knife is honed. The second type is a steel, which is a carbon steel rod with a handle of bone, wood or metal. The knife blade is drawn across the finely-ribbed rod until sufficiently sharpened. The third type is a patent sharpener, basically a V-shaped slot with a milling or grinding device across which the blade is drawn, which may be hand-held, table-mounted or wall-mounted. Electrically driven types of patent sharpener may also be used to sharpen scissors.

KNISHES
(Pirogen)
Half-moon-shaped Jewish pastry turnovers. Fillings can be based on cheese, liver, buckwheat groats, *kasha* or even *sauerkraut*. Different types are made for specific Jewish festivals.

KNOCK DOWN (TO)
To knead any yeasted mixture lightly after it has risen and before it is shaped into specific loaves, rolls, buns or cakes.

KNÖDEL
See *Klösse*.

KNOL-KOHL
See *Kohlrabi*.

KNOTTED MARJORAM
See *Marjoram*.

KNUCKLE
A cut of meat consisting of the lowest leg joint of a pig or sheep, together with the adjoining flesh.

KNUCKLE OF LAMB
(Half a Leg)
The end of the leg from which the thick fillet joint has been removed. It is suitable for roasting.

KNUCKLE OF PORK
The lower part of a leg of pork, recommended for roasting.

KNUCKLE OF VEAL
Part of the leg, it is a bony cut which is usually stewed, braised or casseroled. It is also cut into rounds and used in the famous Italian dish, *osso bucco*.

Meat

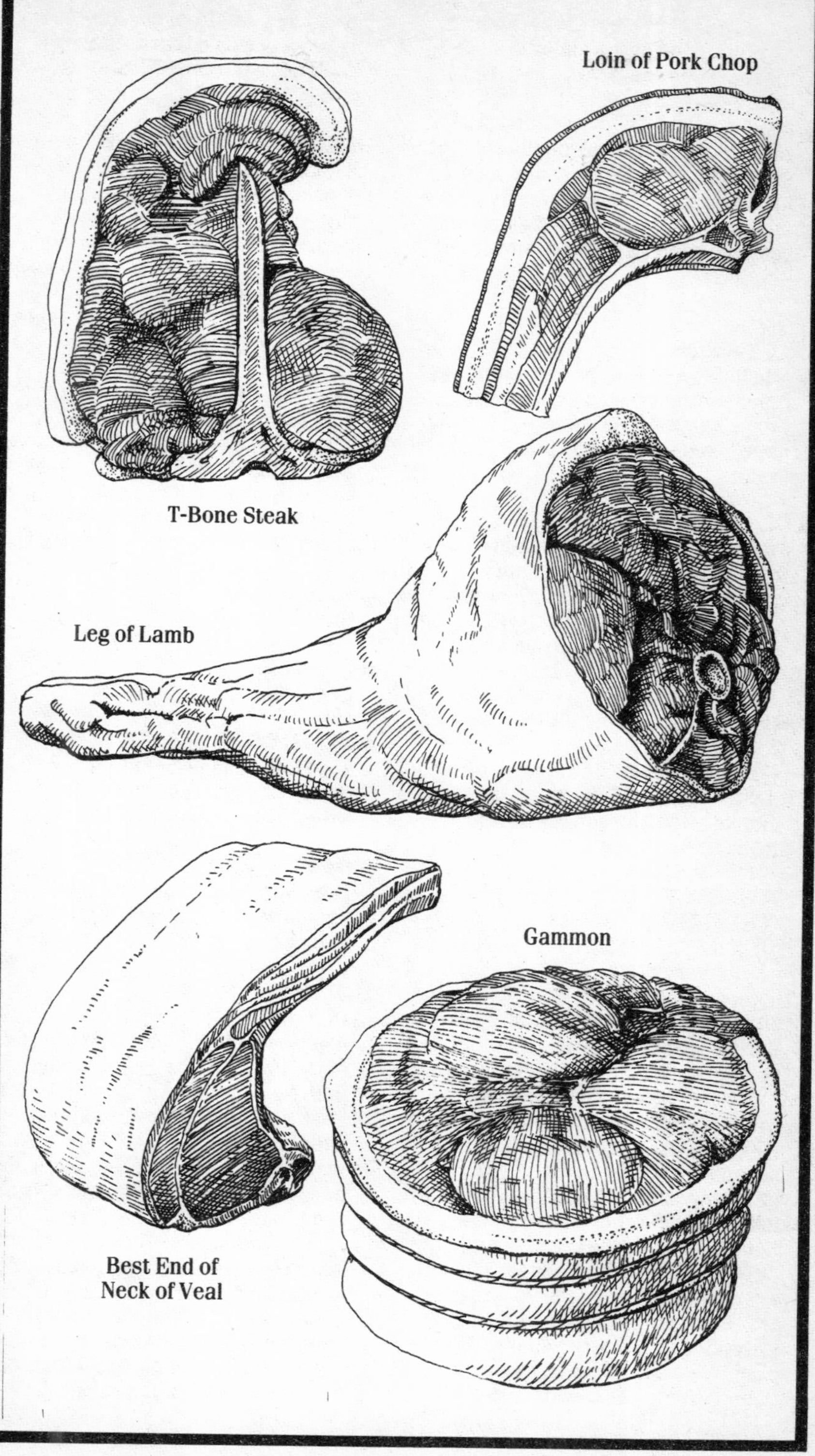

Loin of Pork Chop

T-Bone Steak

Leg of Lamb

Gammon

Best End of
Neck of Veal

KOCHWURST
German sausages made from tongue, liver and blood, produced from well-seasoned mixtures of cooked meats which are filled into skins. They are subsequently steamed or boiled and sometimes lightly smoked. Cooked sausages are perishable and should be eaten as soon as possible after purchase.

KOFTA
(Kofte, Kufta)
Middle Eastern minced meat and onion patties cooked on skewers over a barbecue or under a grill and served with rice or pitta bread.

KÖFTE
Turkish fried meat balls made from minced beef, white bread, onions, water and seasonings. Large *köfte* are served as a main meal with chips; small *köfte* are eaten as an appetizer.

KOFTES
(Koftas)
A central and northern Indian dish of minced meat, fish or vegetables shaped into balls and deep-fried or grilled.

KOHLRABI
(Knol-kohl)
A vegetable (*Brassica oleracea* var. *caulorapa*) which is a member of the cabbage family and, although well-known in Continental Europe and parts of Asia, is less popular in Britain and North America. It grows as a swollen round bulb from which sprout thin stalks topped with leaves. It is usually sold with the stalks partly or totally removed, although the leaves may be eaten when young. Kohlrabi has a pale green, white or purple skin colour and is at its best when immature, 5–7.5 cm/ 2–3 inches in diameter. The mild flavour of the cream-coloured flesh resembles a combination of cabbage and turnip with nutty overtones. Kohlrabi may be eaten raw, cooked as a vegetable or used in recipes suitable for celery or turnip.

KOKOSKA U UNAKU OD SLAČICE
A speciality from Croatia in Yugoslavia, this is a roast chicken dish coated with a thickened sauce made from giblet stock, egg yolks, vinegar, soured cream, sometimes a little alcohol and seasonings. It is served with dumplings.

KOKT TORSK
A classic Swedish dish of thick slices of cod which are poached and served with melted butter or a hot white sauce to which chopped hard-boiled eggs have been added. The usual accompaniment is boiled potatoes.

KOLA NUTS
See *Cola Beans*.

KOL-BEE
See *Colbi*.

KOLDEBORD
The Danish equivalent to the Swedish open table, the *smörgåsbord*.

KOLDTBORD
Norway's open table, which is very similar to Sweden's *smörgåsbord* and just as lavish.

KOMBU
(Kelp)
A sea vegetable (*Laminaria* species) of the brown algae group of plants, found in the colder waters of the Far East, particularly around Japan. Other members of this family grow in waters off the Atlantic shores and have a number of local names. This is a broad-leafed group of sea vegetables, varying in size and shape from region to region. *Kombu* is a natural source of monosodium glutamate (MSG) and is used to make the stock called *dashi* used in many Japanese dishes; it is also rich in minerals and is a particularly

good source of iodine. *Kombu* is sold in the West as packeted dried strips but in Japan is available in many forms, including powdered. The Western name for the *kombu* family of sea vegetables is kelp.

KÖNIGSBERGER KLOPSE
Speciality meat balls from Königsberg in Germany, which are simmered in well-flavoured stock. The stock is subsequently thickened, flavoured with capers and served with the meat balls. Freshly boiled rice is the traditional accompaniment.

KOPANISTI
A strong blue cheese, produced from cows' milk on the Aegean islands in Greece. It has a smooth and creamy texture.

KOPENHAGENER
The German term for Danish pastries.

KORMA
A term for a fairly dry, mild Indian curry cooked with cream or yogurt. *Kormas* containing meat are a speciality of northern India; vegetarian *kormas* are a speciality of southern India.

KOSHER
Food prepared according to Jewish dietary laws; a shop or restaurant serving Kosher food.

KOSTROMSKOÏ
(Kostromskoy)
A Gouda-type cheese produced in the USSR from cows' milk.

KOTLETI
Russian meat cutlets made from equal amounts of minced beef and pork, bread soaked in milk or water, salt and egg. The mixture is shaped into rounds or ovals, coated with breadcrumbs and fried. The cutlets are traditionally served with mashed or chipped potatoes, macaroni, mixed vegetables and either a white or tomato sauce.

KOTLETI IZ RYBI
Russian fish cakes made with raw minced cod or pike, milk, white bread and seasonings. The mixture is enriched with butter, shaped into round cakes, coated with breadcrumbs and fried. Before serving, the cakes are coated with extra melted butter and served with vegetables in a white sauce.

KÖTTBULLAR
Swedish meat balls, made from minced beef. They are fried and served with creamed potatoes and cranberry sauce.

KOULIBIAK
See *Coulibiac*.

KOUMISS
(Kumiss)
A thick, soured drink from Central Russia based on asses' and camels' milk which is very slightly alcoholic (about 3%). Originally, it was made from asses' milk by the nomadic peoples of Central Asia and was used both medicinally and as a beverage.

KRAKAUER
A Polish-style ham sausage, highly esteemed in Germany.

KRAPIVNIE SHCHI
A Russian soup made from young nettles, sorrel, meat or vegetable stock, sausages, onions and seasonings. It is served with soured cream.

KRÄUTEKÄSE
See *Sapsago*.

KRÄUTERLEBERWURST
A German sausage which contains chunky pieces of liver and is well seasoned with herbs.

KREIVI
A Finnish cheese resembling Tilsit but without caraway seeds. It is generally loaf-shaped.

KREPLACH
The Jewish version of *ravioli*. The filling is generally based on chicken or meat and the *kreplach* are usually served in clear chicken soup. Cheese *kreplach*, filled with cottage or curd cheese, soured cream and eggs, are boiled gently and tossed in melted butter; salt is added for a savoury dish, sugar turns them into a dessert.

KRUMPLI
(Burgonya)
The Hungarian colloquial term for a vegetable stew containing onions, bacon, potatoes, paprika, green peppers, water, tomatoes, continental sausages and seasonings.

KRUPUK
Indonesian prawn crackers which are eaten either as a snack or as part of the traditional *rijst-tafel* (rice table) with its many dishes.

KRYDDOST
A popular Swedish cheese, produced from cows' milk and spiced with caraway seeds and cloves.

KUCHAI
(Kuichai)
See *Chinese Chive*.

KUGEL
A Jewish baked rice pudding with dried and fresh fruits, chopped nuts, eggs, sugar, spices and margarine or melted chicken fat. Noodles may sometimes be substituted for the rice. There is also a savoury *kugel* based on potatoes.

KUGELHOPF
See *Gugelhupf*.

KULFI
Indian ice cream which generally contains nuts and rose water.

KUMARA
New Zealand name for a locally grown sweet potato.

KÜMMEL
A caraway-flavoured liqueur, first produced in Holland in the late 16th century. Its production has now spread to Russia, Germany and Denmark.

KUMQUAT
(Cumquat)
The fruit of an evergreen tree (*Fortunella* species) related to the citrus family and native to the Far East. The several species are named after a Mr Fortune who introduced them to Europe in the mid-19th century. The kumquat looks like a miniature orange but has fewer segments of flesh. The shape is round or oval, about the size of a small fig, and the skin is a golden-orange colour. The flavour is bitter-sweet and the whole fruit may be eaten as the skin is thin and edible when ripe. It makes excellent marmalade and in the southern USA, the fruit is grown on a commercial scale for preserving. Kumquats are also used in many cooked dishes, both sweet and savoury.

KWARK
The Dutch equivalent of German low-fat Quark, made from skimmed cows' milk.

LABLAB BEAN
West Indian name for hyacinth bean.

LABNA
(Labneh)
A goats' milk cream cheese from the Middle East, coated in olive oil and paprika.

LABSKAUS
The name of this dish from northern Germany means 'seaman's hash'. It is made from mashed potatoes,

onion, chopped corned beef and seasoning. It is served when very hot and each portion is topped with a fried egg. The usual accompaniments are slices of pickled beetroot and gherkin.

LACE (TO)
To enliven a soup, sauce, stew, casserole, braised dish or hot and cold drinks by the addition of alcohol and/or assorted condiments and spices.

LACHSSCHINKEN
(Laxschinken)
The name of this Germany speciality meat means 'salmon-ham', although it tastes of neither. It is deep pink in colour, rather like darkish smoked salmon, and is made from mildly smoked pork loin, rolled in thin sheets of bacon fat to preserve flavour and moisture. It is an exclusive product, finely flavoured, always eaten raw and very thinly sliced. It is often served as an *hors d'oeuvre* with horseradish sauce, or used as a sandwich filling and *canapé* topping.

LACTALBUMIN
One of the three main proteins found in milk.

LACTIC ACID
Mild acid found in milk, cream and some butters which have turned sour naturally or been commercially soured.

LACTIC BUTTER
Butter, such as Danish, to which a culture has been added. The resultant butter has a mild and delicate tang, sometimes with a hint of salt. Lactic butters are excellent for cake-making.

LACTOGLOBULIN
One of the three main proteins found in milk.

LACTOSE
(Milk Sugar)
A disaccharide, or double sugar, composed of one part each of glucose and galactose. It is known as milk sugar and is found in the milk of all mammals. It is less sweet than sucrose.

LACTO-VEGETARIANISM
Vegetarianism that permits the consumption of certain animal products such as milk, cheese and sometimes eggs.

LADIES' CHEESE
(Butterkäse, Damenkäse)
A rich, German cows' milk cheese which is also known as 'butter cheese'. It is the colour of butter with a delicate taste and aroma, and has a light brown rind. It is usually shaped into loaves and sometimes spiced with caraway seeds.

LADIES' FINGERS
(Ladyfingers)
See *Okra*.

LADLE
A long-handled scoop which is made in various sizes, ranging from the large soup ladle to the small gravy ladle. Ladles originated around 1200 BC and it is interesting to note that the basic shape has undergone minimal change over the centuries.

LADY BALTIMORE CAKE
A 19th-century North American white layer cake which is filled with a meringue-like icing laced with dried fruits and nuts. It is then completely covered with more white icing. It is a very sweet confection and popular in its country of origin.

LADYFINGERS
See *Langues de Chat*.

LADY'S FINGERS
A short, fat, sweet variety of banana (*Musa* species). This spelling is sometimes used as an alternative name for okra, instead of the more usual ladies' fingers.

LAGER
Light-coloured beer with a distinctive piquancy, originally from Munich and subsequently from Pilsen in Czechoslovakia.

LAGUIOLE
(Fourme de Laguiole, Laguiole-Aubrac)
A cows' milk mountain cheese from Aquitaine in France. It resembles Cantal.

LAHANI DOLMASI
A Turkish speciality of cabbage leaves stuffed with a mixture of rice, onions, raisins, pine nuts, seasoning and chopped parsley or dill. They are baked in the oven and served lightly chilled.

LAITIER
French term for a commercial food product made from milk.

LAKE BASS
Several species of freshwater fish (*Micropterus* species) caught throughout most of North America (with the exception of Alaska). It is an important game fish and is best for the table at 1–1.5 kg/2¼–3½ lb as larger fish have less flavour. The flesh is firm, lean and white and the fish may be baked or fried. Lake bass are also bred on fish farms and this practice has spread to parts of Asia.

LAKE HERRING
(Cisco)
A freshwater fish (*Leucichthys* species) caught in the lakes of North America. The various species have the streamlined shape of the herring and similar silver-grey colouring but are in fact members of the whitefish family. The weight can vary from less than 500 g/18 oz to about 1 kg/2¼ lb and the fishing is all year round. The flesh is medium-oily and the fish may be poached or fried.

LAKE TROUT
(Great Lake Trout)
The largest of the trout species (*Salvelinus namaycush*), caught all year round in North American lakes and rivers. The back can range from near black to light green in colour and the average weight in the shops is 2 kg/4½ lb. The flesh is oily and the colour varies from ivory to pink. The fish may be poached, steamed, baked, fried or grilled.

LAKE WHITEFISH
A freshwater fish (*Coregonus clupeaformis*) of the same family as trout and salmon. The colour of the back is light brown, sometimes tinged with blue, becoming paler on the underside. The average length is 25–35 cm/10–14 inches and weight 1–2 kg/2¼–4½ lb. It is caught in the North American Great Lakes and the larger Canadian lakes all year round, but the main season is from April to November. The flesh is white, medium-oily, delicate and with large flakes and the fish may be poached, steamed, baked, fried or grilled.

LAKSA ASAM
A Malaysian sour fish soup containing noodles.

LAMB
The meat of sheep, usually under one year old. The flesh is light pink in colour and fairly fatty.

LAMB RIBLETS
Breast of lamb separated into riblets by cutting in between the ribs. The strips of bone and meat are used for stewing, braising or casseroling.

LAMBS' BRAINS
Lambs' brains tend to be small and one set, comprising two brains, is sufficient for only one serving.

LAMBS' FRY
Consisting of lambs' liver, kidney, heart and brains which are briefly simmered, drained and cooled. They are then cut into pieces, coated with

egg, tossed in breadcrumbs and fried until crisp and golden. Sometimes fresh chopped parsley is added to the crumbs for extra flavour and colour.

LAMBS' KIDNEYS

Fairly small kidneys with a thin membrane or skin covering each. This should be carefully removed and the kidneys either left whole or split in half by cutting through with a sharp knife. If halved, the white 'cores' and tubes radiating from them should be removed with kitchen scissors. Lambs' kidneys may be grilled, fried or used to make kebabs; they are also the kidneys used in a traditional mixed grill and two should be allowed per person. Overcooking should be avoided as it toughens the flesh.

LAMB'S LETTUCE

(Corn Salad)

A vegetable (*Valerianella olitoria*) which is not a member of the lettuce family but is descended from a weed native to Europe. It was developed as a salad ingredient mainly in France and Italy and grows as a cluster of small and elongated oval green leaves which are picked when young. It has a rather bitter taste and is generally used in mixed salads or as a garnish. Lamb's lettuce is also known as corn salad or as *mâche*, its French name.

LAMBS' LIVER

Light brown with a smooth texture, lambs' liver is popular and reasonably priced. It may be grilled, fried or stewed, but overcooking must be avoided or it will become tough and leathery. It is a first-class protein food with a fairly mild but distinct flavour.

LAMB'S QUARTERS

A wild vegetable, profuse in the New Brunswick region of Canada, which is a cross between Swiss chard and spinach. It has a faint flavour and aroma of lamb, is cooked in the same way as spinach and served with butter or a little vinegar.

LAMBS' TONGUES

These are small compared with ox tongues, weighing about 225 g/8 oz. They are pale pink and springy when fresh and are generally sold unsalted. They have a good flavour and are recommended for stews and casseroles. They can also be boiled like ox tongue, packed into a saucepan or round cake tin and coated with the stock in which they were cooked. Once jellied and set, the tongues can be turned out and served cold with mustard and/or salad.

LAMINGTONS

An Australian speciality consisting of small squares of sponge cake coated with chocolate icing and desiccated coconut.

LAMPARI

A Sri Lankan speciality, curried rice baked in banana leaves.

LANCASHIRE

A classic, English cows' milk cheese which is lightly pressed and scalded. It has a soft, crumbly texture and a fresh, mild flavour with a hint of acid. It has excellent cooking properties and may be crumbled over food without grating. Lancashire also makes an appetizing dessert cheese when served with fresh fruit.

LANCASHIRE HOT-POT

A British North Country stew made in a casserole with alternate layers of lamb, potatoes and onions, interspersed with sliced lamb's kidneys and, traditionally, fresh oysters. Seasoning is sprinkled between the layers, the casserole is half-filled with stock or water and it is topped with a layer of potatoes dotted with small flakes of butter or margarine. The hot-pot is covered and baked in the oven; the lid is removed for the last 30 minutes of cooking time to allow the potatoes to brown.

LANCASHIRE PARKIN
Similar to gingerbread but containing fine or medium oatmeal, mixed chopped peel, demerara sugar and caraway seeds.

LANDJÄGER SAUSAGE
A fairly small, smoked, scalded sausage from Germany, with square sides due to the shape of the wooden frame into which it is pressed for smoking. It is made from a well-spiced mixture of pork and beef and often includes garlic and caraway. Sometimes red wine is used for mixing.

LANDRAIL
See *Corncrake*.

LANGOUSTE
French term for crawfish.

LANGOUSTINES
French term for large prawns such as the Dublin Bay.

LANGSAT
The fruit of a tree (*Lansium domesticum*) native to Malaysia and cultivated in the East Indies and the Philippines. It is round or oval, averaging 4 cm/1½ inches in diameter, and grows in grape-like clusters. The skin is tough and yellow-coloured with brown blotches. The flesh is white, juicy and fragrant, containing one or two large, bitter, inedible seeds. It is usually peeled and eaten raw.

LANGSKAILL
A Scottish cows' milk cheese which resembles Dutch Gouda.

à la LANGUEDOCIENNE
French term meaning in the style of Languedoc in south-west France, referring to a garnish for entrées composed of aubergines, mushrooms, tomatoes and parsley.

LANGUES DE CHAT
(Cats' Tongues, Ladyfingers)
The French name for biscuits which are long, slim and slightly waisted in the middle. They are dry, crisp and sweet and said to resemble cats' tongues. They are sometimes served with tea or coffee but more generally now are used in desserts, such as a Charlotte Russe, when they are arranged round the dish or mould for both lining and decorative purposes.

LAOS POWDER
Similar to ground ginger in both flavour and colour, a powder (*Alpinia galanga*) which is much used in Oriental cooking, especially Malaysian.

LAP OF LAMB
Term used in north-west and north-east England for breast of lamb.

LAPSANG SOUCHONG
A large-leaf black China tea from the province of Fujian (Fukien), this has a highly individual smoky flavour and is served black with an optional slice of lemon. Lapsang Souchong is strong enough for only a minimal quantity to be needed per cup and even a small amount in a blend is very noticeable. This tea needs to be kept in an airtight container to prevent its strong aroma affecting other food or teas.

LARD
A soft white pigs' fat, much used in cooking. It is very high in saturated fatty acids and therefore unsuitable for those on a low-cholesterol diet.

LARD (TO)
To dress meat for cooking by inserting or covering with pork fat or bacon to prevent dryness.

LARDING NEEDLE
A needle specially designed for threading thin strips of fat through meat.

LARDON
(Lardoon)
Strip of pork or bacon fat, inserted into the flesh of lean meat, to add flavour and moisture.

LARDY CAKE
A slightly sweet, flaky pastry cake from Oxfordshire based on lard. It is baked in a Yorkshire pudding tin with rounded corners and the top is always scored into diamonds. It is traditionally eaten warm with butter.

LARGE CALORIE
Heat unit, used to measure energy value derived from food. A Calorie written with a capital C is the amount of heat required to raise the temperature of 1 kg of water by 1°C; alternatively, this heat unit may be referred to as a kilocalorie.

LASAGNE
Wide, flat strips of pasta. The shape depends very much on the manufacturer or cook and some pieces are oblong while others are almost square; few are under 5 cm/ 2 inches in width. The edges may be left plain or crimped and sometimes each piece of *lasagna* is finely ribbed. Some manufactured *lasagne* are made with a flour and egg dough.

LASAGNE PASTICCIATE
(Lasagne)
The Italian name for a dish made from *lasagne*. The leaves of pasta are layered with cheese and *Bolognese* sauces, topped with a final layer of cheese sauce and covered with grated cheese. The dish is reheated and browned in a hot oven. The finished *lasagne* is cut and served in wedges. It is often made with green *lasagne*.

LASAGNE VERDI
Lasagne which have been tinted green with spinach purée. They are a speciality of Emilia-Romagna in Italy.

LASAGNETTE
Wide ribbons of flat pasta that are somewhere between *lasagne* and *tagliatelle* in size. They are usually made from a pasta dough mixed with eggs, and the edges are crimped.

LASSI
A cool Indian drink made by whisking soured milk or plain yogurt with salt or sugar, water and sometimes spices. It is widely drunk throughout the country and very refreshing.

LATVIISKI
(Latviysky)
A strong-smelling cheese with a pungent taste produced from cows' milk in the USSR.

LAUGHING COW
(La Vache Qui Rit)
Brand name of a French cows' milk processed cheese which is foil-wrapped in individual squares and sold in boxes.

LAULAU
A Hawaiian speciality, parcels of taro leaves containing a filling of salt pork and either butterfish, mackerel or salmon. They are steamed and served hot.

LAVER
A sea vegetable (*Porphyra* species) of the red algae group of plants, found in the shallower waters off the coasts of north-west Europe, and particularly those of Scotland and South Wales. It is rather like spinach in appearance and it is most popular in Wales where it is cooked to a purée to produce laver bread. Some alternative names used for laver in other parts of the British Isles are sloke, stake and stoke. Laver is related to the Japanese sea vegetable, *nori*.

LAXSCHINKEN
See *Lachsschinken*.

LDL
(Low-density Lipoproteins)
See *Cholesterol*.

LE COLOMBO
A Caribbean curry containing a selection of tropical vegetables in addition to the main ingredient which can be meat, poultry, fish or shellfish. It is flavoured with rum, coconut and lime.

LE MOINE
A Canadian monastery cheese produced by monks at the Abbey of Saint-Benoît-du-Lac, which is in the south of Quebec. It resembles Port-Salut.

LEA AND PERRINS
See *Worcestershire Sauce*.

LEAF BEET
See *Swiss Chard*.

LEAF FAT
Animal fat lining the cavity of the abdomen and also covering the kidneys. It usually comes from a pig and is used in the production of leaf lard.

LEAF LARD
Fine quality lard (pork fat) produced from leaf fat.

LEAN CUBES OF LAMB
A new and leaner British cut of meat, suitable for kebabs. The cubes can also be used in stews, braised dishes and casseroles.

LEAN FISH
The flesh of fish is considered lean if the fat content is about 2% or less.

LEAVEN
Agent, such as yeast, used to raise dough.

LEBANON BOLOGNA
A North American smoked beef bologna sausage from Lebanon in Pennsylvania.

LEBEN
(Leban)
Term used to describe yogurt in Iraq, the Lebanon and Israel.

LEBEN RAID
The name used in Saudi Arabia for yogurt.

LEBERKÄSE
Although its German name means 'liver cheese', this is a precooked meat loaf from Bavaria which resembles luncheon meat in appearance. It is made from a mixture of minced liver and sausage meat and served cut into thick slices which are grilled or fried.

LEBERKNÖDELSUPPE
A classic Austrian and Bavarian clear soup, such as a chicken consommé, containing small dumplings made from breadcrumbs, liver, herbs and seasonings. The garnish is either finely chopped parsley or chives.

LEBERWURST
German term for liver sausage.

LEBKUCHEN
German ginger biscuits, a speciality of Nuremberg, and eaten throughout the country from Advent to Twelfth Night. They are very spicy, brown in colour and often covered with hard white icing or chocolate.

LECHON DE LECHE
A speciality of the Philippines, a barbecued suckling pig, usually presented whole.

LEEK
A vegetable (*Allium porrum*) which is a member of the onion family and native to Europe. It was well-known in Roman times and has been widely cultivated in Britain for many centuries. The leek grows as a

multi-layered cylinder of tightly packed, curved leaves which open out towards the top. Although the natural colour is green, the leek is earthed-up to blanch the stem to a very pale green or off-white. Large specimens are produced for exhibition purposes but the size in the shops is 20–25 cm/8–10 inches long, with some of the fibrous green top removed, and about 2.5 cm/ 1 inch in diameter. If eaten raw, the leek has a strong taste but, when cooked, it is the mildest and sweetest of the onion family and may be eaten on its own or used in savoury dishes.

LEFTOVERS

Food which is left over from a meal and can be re-used, for example, cold roast or boiled meat in sandwiches; fish in fishcakes; potatoes, sliced or diced and fried; bread for toast.

LEG CHOPS OF LAMB

Term used in the Midlands of Britain for chump chops of lamb.

LEG OF BEEF

(Hindleg of Beef)

This cut comes from the hindleg of beef and has a high proportion of gristle. It therefore responds best to long, slow and moist methods of cooking such as stewing, braising and casseroling. The cut is known by this name in London and the South-East, the Midlands, north-east and north-west England and the West Country.

LEG OF LAMB

A prime cut of lamb for roasting which comes from the back leg and is often divided into two joints: fillet of lamb and knuckle of lamb. Both contain bone and the joint is known by all three names (leg, fillet and knuckle) in London, the South-East and the West Country. The whole leg may be boned, stuffed and rolled.

LEG OF MUTTON CUT

A term sometimes used to describe top rib of beef, a fairly coarse but lean cut suitable for stewing, braising and casseroling. When boned and rolled, it can also be pot-roasted.

LEG OF PORK

A large cut of prime and tender pork, from the hindquarter of the pig, designed for roasting. It is often divided into two joints known as fillet of pork and knuckle of pork.

LEG OF VEAL

A prime cut for roasting, leg may be boned and stuffed prior to cooking.

LEG STEAKS OF LAMB

A new and leaner British cut of meat which is divided into steaks for grilling or frying.

LEGUME

The edible pod or seed of a leguminous plant, such as a pea or bean, which is used as a vegetable. The pod typically contains several seeds and, if unpicked, splits lengthwise into two halves to disperse the seeds on to the ground. When dried, legume seeds are called pulses. The term legume also refers to any of a large family (Leguminosae) of climbing plants, shrubs or trees which bear fruits that are legumes. Legumes are an important source of protein to both humans and animals worldwide. There are over 10,000 known species in the family and nearly all produce edible seeds. A few, such as those of the laburnum, are poisonous.

LEGUME SOUPS

A general term for soups made from the dried seeds of leguminous plants, such as whole or split peas, butter beans, haricot beans and lentils. Often the soups are puréed and enriched with milk, cream or butter.

LEGUMINOUS

Consisting of, resembling, or being plants that are legumes.

LEIDEN

(Leyden)

A classic Dutch cheese made from semi-skimmed cows' milk mixed with buttermilk. It is generally spiced with cloves and exported when it is a minimum of 4 weeks old. It is coated with red or yellow wax and is a crumbly, firm cheese which is fresh-tasting and slightly salty. Farmhouse varieties are stamped with two crossed keys, the arms of the city of Leiden, and contain about 30% butterfat. Factory-produced cheeses have a butterfat content of 20–40% and are sometimes flavoured with cumin or anise in addition to cloves.

LEIPAJUUSTO

See *Juustoleipä*.

LEKACH

(Honiglekach)

Jewish New Year honey cake, containing spices, raisins and chopped mixed peel.

LEMON

The fruit of a tree (*Citrus limon*) native to the Far East, cultivated in the Middle East, America, Australia and, most successfully, in the Mediterranean region. The fruit is oval or round with a nodule at one or both ends and is an average of 7.5 cm/3 inches in length. The light and oily yellow skin or rind is fairly smooth. The flesh is divided into segments contained in membranes with bitter seeds and is juicy, paler than the skin and, in most varieties, has a sharp and acidic taste. The lemon is probably the most versatile of the citrus fruits because the culinary uses of its rind, flesh and juice in both sweet and savoury dishes, drinks, baking and confectionery are endless. In suitable climates the lemon tree may fruit several times a year, ensuring a steady supply.

LEMON BALM

(Melissa)

Originating in the Middle East, this herb spread to areas bordering the Mediterranean and now grows widely almost everywhere. The long leaves of this perennial plant (*Melissa officinalis*) have a distinct lemon scent when bruised and add a fragrant and refreshing tang to alcoholic fruit cups, China tea, Indian tea and cold summer drinks. The leaves can also be chopped and added to stuffings for light meats and fish and make pleasant additions to salads, apple jelly, quince jelly and stewed fruits.

LEMON BARLEY WATER

Home-made drink comprising strained barley water (left over after cooking the cereal) mixed with sugar and lemon juice. It is a refreshing summer drink.

LEMON BUTTER SAUCE

English term for meunière butter sauce.

LEMON CURD

A sweet preserve made from lemons, eggs, sugar and butter. Commercial varieties have a longer shelf-life than home-made, but both keep better if stored in the refrigerator, especially after opening.

LEMON ESSENCE

Culinary lemon essence, in concentrated form, is available in small bottles and is used in cakes, desserts and confectionery.

LEMON GRASS

Resembling slim spring onions, lemon grass (*Cymbopogon citratus*) is Oriental, related to the citronella and has a strong taste of lemon. The white, fleshy bulbs have a more concentrated flavour than the fibrous green stems and it is a highly-esteemed herb in the Orient, where it is added to a wide variety of dishes. It is also available in the West and is sold by some major supermarket chains.

LEMON JUICE
Natural acid which is not only rich in vitamin C, but also more delicate than any vinegar or commercially produced acid. It is useful in preventing oxidation and cut apples, pears, bananas and avocados will not turn as brown if sprinkled with lemon juice. A dash of lemon juice added to the water when cooking root vegetables helps them to stay a good colour.

LEMON MERINGUE PIE
A British pie, not North American as is sometimes supposed, consisting of a baked pastry case filled with thick, lemon-flavoured sauce. It is topped with meringue, baked until light brown and is generally served cold.

LEMON SOLE
(Long Flounder, Witch Sole)
A flatfish (*Microstomus kitt*) which, in spite of its name, is a member of the same family as plaice and halibut. The colour of the upper side is brownish-yellow, marbled with lighter and darker oval and round spots. It has a regular shape, similar to the sole family, but with a very small head. It grows to a maximum length of about 60 cm/24 inches and is caught, mainly during the winter months, in the shallow waters of the North Atlantic from Iceland to France. The flesh is white, lean and although not as fine as the Dover sole, the fish may be poached, steamed, baked, fried or grilled. It is called 'lemon' sole because of the slight lemony smell it has when it has just been caught.

LEMON SOUFFLÉ
See *Milanese Soufflé*.

LEMON SQUASH
A non-carbonated, non-alcoholic drink base, made from a sweetened lemon concentrate, usually diluted with water.

LEMON SQUEEZER
See *Juice Extractor*.

LEMON THYME
A cultivated variety of the common European lemon thyme (*Thymus citriodorus*), highly regarded for its lemon-scented leaves which are used in fresh fruit salads, dips and stuffings.

LEMON VERBENA
A native of Chile and introduced in Britain towards the latter part of the 18th century, this perennial shrub (*Lippia citriodora*) has long, pointed, crinkly leaves which taste strongly of lemon. It may be used fresh or dried in white meat dishes and with fish. Lemon verbena also improves the flavour of summer drinks, jams and jellies.

LEMON ZESTER
See *Zester*.

LEMONADE
A soft drink consisting of sweetened lemon juice mixed with water; also a carbonated soft drink, flavoured with lemon.

LENTIL
A vegetable (*Lens culinaris*) which is one of the oldest known to man. Its ancestry is uncertain, though it possibly originated either in the Middle East or Asia, and it is now cultivated from Europe to the Far East. It is a legume which grows as a pod on a branching plant from which the bean is extracted; the bean is then dried and used as a pulse. There are several main types of lentil. The tiny, bright orange variety, often sold as a split lentil, is a brown-skinned bean with the casing removed; it may also be bought in the unskinned state as a brown lentil. The green or continental lentil has a greeny-brown skin, is creamy-orange inside and is much larger than the red lentil. There are many other cultivated types of varying sizes and assorted colours.

Lentils can be eaten whole when young as a vegetable, but they are most commonly used as a pulse. Lentils are high in protein, have a pleasant flavour, are easy to purée when cooked and are a popular ingredient in many Mediterranean and Asian dishes. Lentils which retain the outer skin must be boiled briskly for the first 15 minutes of cooking time to destroy harmful toxins found in the outer skin which can prove very dangerous to the human body.

LESCH V PERGAMENTE
A Russian speciality consisting of fillets of bream, first soaked in hot water for 5 minutes, then drained. They are then transferred to a large piece of greaseproof paper, foil or parchment paper, topped with a mixture of grated carrot, onions and butter and sprinkled with lemon juice and herbs. The paper is folded round the fish to make a tight parcel and the fish is simmered until cooked. *Lesch v pergamente* is served with boiled potatoes, white sauce and sometimes pickled cucumber.

LESCÓ
(Letscho)
A condiment used in Hungary to flavour paprika dishes in winter when the fresh ingredients are unavailable. It is made by simmering green peppers slowly in lard with chopped bacon and onions, paprika, tomatoes and salt, and cooking to a purée-like consistency. When cold, it is stored in the refrigerator or freezer.

LETTUCE
A vegetable (*Lactuca sativa*) probably native in its various forms to both Europe and Asia. It was known to the Greeks and Romans and was introduced to Britain about 2,000 years ago when it was used for medicinal purposes and as a vegetable. Lettuce grows as a cluster of green leaves, sometimes tinged with red, direct from the root with little or no stalk or base. All types share a distinctive flavour and are widely grown both commercially and in gardens. Principal categories to be found in the shops are the cabbage or round lettuce, the long cos or Romaine lettuce and the type called Webb's Wonderful. Normally eaten raw as a salad ingredient, lettuce may also be used in savoury dishes such as soups and stews or cooked as a vegetable.

LEVERET
A young hare.

LEVULOSE
See *Fructose*.

LIAISE (TO)
To bind together soups, sauces, stews and other dishes by means of a thickener such as flour, cornflour, potato flour, arrowroot, cream or eggs.

LIAISON
French term for a liquid thickened with either flour or cornflour mixed with water, a roux of fat and flour, Beurre Manié, eggs, cream or butter.

LIBERICA
Variety of coffee plant grown in Liberia. The production of beans is relatively small and the quality lies somewhere between that of *arabica* and *robusta*.

LICHEE
(Litchee, Litchi)
See *Lychee*.

LIČKI KUPUS
A Yugoslavian peasant dish from Croatia made with three or more different cuts of pork which are simmered with *sauerkraut*. Boiled potatoes are the traditional accompaniment.

LIEDERKRANZ
A top-ranking, North American cheese made from cows' milk and developed in 1892 by Emil Frey of

Monroe in New York. It is a soft, Limburger-related cheese, but is milder in taste and the colour is a warm, golden-yellow. The rind is deeper-toned and the name means 'ring of song'. The cheese is now mainly produced in Ohio.

à la LIÈGEOISE
French term meaning in the style of Liège in Belgium, denoting the inclusion of gin or juniper berries in a cooked dish.

LIFRARPYLSA
See *Blódmör*.

LIGHT
A cake that is well-risen and not heavy in texture; also, food which is easily digested and mildly flavoured; drinks with a low alcohol content.

LIGHT CORN SYRUP
(Light Syrup)
See *Corn Syrup*.

LIGHT CREAM
(Coffee Cream)
North American term for a pasteurized cream with a butterfat content of 18–22%.

LIGHT MUSCOVADO SUGAR
An unrefined soft brown sugar which is naturally a warm golden colour. It has a fine but gritty texture and is used in cakes and biscuits as an alternative to caster sugar.

LIGHTS
See *Lungs*.

LIGONBERRY
See *Lingonberry*.

à la LIGURIENNE
French term meaning in the style of Liguria in northern Italy, denoting a garnish of stuffed tomatoes, risotto flavoured with saffron and duchesse potatoes.

LILY BUDS
A component of Chinese cooking, 5 cm/2 inch-long dried lily buds which are light brown in colour. They are generally soaked in hot water for 30 minutes before being used and have a woody, elusive scent for which there is no substitute. They are available in packets from Oriental food shops.

LIMA BEAN
A variety of butter bean.

LIMBURGER
A strong-tasting German cheese which originated in Belgium but began to be made in Bavaria during the 19th century. Produced from cows' milk, Limburger has a very strong, unmistakable and potent smell and is full-flavoured and piquant. It has a yellow-brown rind and is loaf-shaped. The cheese is a warm gold colour and the butterfat content ranges from 20% to 50%.

LIME
The fruit of a small tree (*Citrus aurantifolia*) native to South-East Asia and now cultivated in tropical and semi-tropical regions in the Middle East, Africa and North and South America. It varies from oval to an almost spherical shape, with a blunt nodule at one end, and measures about 5 cm/2 inches in diameter. The skin is thin and has little pith. The colour is a rich green and the flesh is a lighter shade of greeny-yellow. The flavour is very distinctive, rather like that of a lemon but more aromatic, and often slightly less sharp. The lime is a rich source of vitamin C and may be used as a flavouring or garnish for many sweet and savoury dishes, in cocktails and also for making preserves. The juice may be used in dressings, refreshing drinks and as a marinade for fish. The zest of the skin adds a subtle flavour to cooked dishes.

LIMEADE
A sweetened, non-alcoholic drink, made from a mixture of lime concentrate with plain or carbonated water.

à la LIMOUSINE
French term meaning in the style of Limousin in central France, denoting the addition or an accompaniment of red cabbage, *cèpes* and chestnuts.

LIMPA BREAD
A Swedish speciality, this is a dark, yeasted rye bread containing anise or crushed fennel. It is sweetened with an equivalent to black treacle and has a distinctive flavour.

LIMPET
A single-shelled mollusc (*Patella* species) found on rocky shores on both sides of the North Atlantic and the Mediterranean. It has a conical shell about 5 cm/2 inches in diameter which is coloured various shades of brown. The flesh may be eaten raw, boiled or fried.

LINE (TO)
To cover the insides of tins with non-stick parchment paper, greaseproof paper or foil to prevent sticking; to cover the insides of flan rings, pie plates and sandwich tins with pastry; to coat the insides of moulds with a thin layer of jelly mixture; to cover the insides of baking dishes with strips of bacon before filling with pâté-type mixtures.

LING
(Common Ling)
A long, round-bodied fish (*Molva molva*) of the cod family which is caught in the North Atlantic from August to May. The average length of the whole fish as seen in the shops is 75 cm–1 metre/30–39 inches. The fish has a brownish back and a paler underside. The flesh is well-textured and flavoured and ling may be poached, fried, baked or barbecued. A related fish called the Spanish ling is to be found in the western Mediterranean and the Bay of Biscay.

LINGCOD
A slender, round-bodied fish (*Ophiodon elongatus*) which, in spite of its name, is not a true member of the cod family. It is sold in the shops at about 1 metre/39 inches long and 5 kg/11 lb in weight. It is coloured a mottled brown and dark grey, becoming paler on the underbelly, and has a large mouth with prominent teeth. It is caught off the Pacific coast of North America from Alaska to California all the year round but is less abundant in the winter months. The lean, mild, moist and flavoursome flesh changes colour when cooked, losing its greenish tinge and turning white. The fish can be cooked whole or as fillets or steaks and may be poached, steamed, baked, fried or grilled.

LINGONBERRY
(Ligonberry)
A kind of wild Arctic cranberry (*Vaccinium* species). In parts of Scandinavia, the berry is used in desserts, sauces and also to produce a deep pink-coloured liqueur which is both rare and delicately flavoured.

LINGUADO COM BANANAS
A Portuguese and Madeiran dish consisting of baked sole fillets topped with bananas. The traditional accompaniment is boiled potatoes and salad.

LINGUE DI PASSERO
(Sparrows' Tongues)
Thin strips of flat pasta, resembling noodles.

LINGUINE
Small, tongue-shaped pieces of flat pasta, said to resemble birds' tongues.

LINK SAUSAGES
North American term for frying or grilling sausages (such as pork) which are joined or linked.

LINQUISA
(Linguica)
A heavily spiced and brined Portuguese pork sausage which

contains garlic, cumin and cinnamon. It should be cooked thoroughly and is often fried or baked.

LINSEED BREAD

A German speciality bread (*leinsamenbrot*) made from coarse wholemeal flour and whole seeds of the linseed plant, said to be an aid to digestion. It complements strong-tasting sausages and cheeses.

LINZ CAKE

(Linz Tart)

See *Linzertorte*.

LINZERTORTE

(Linz Cake, Linz Tart)

A speciality from Linz in Austria, this is a very superior jam tart and is made from a rich pastry containing ground almonds or hazelnuts. The top is decorated with a trellis of pastry strips.

LIPTAUER CHEESE SPREAD

A Hungarian cheese spread speciality, traditionally based on soft and creamy ewes' milk Brynza cheese, originally produced in Liptov in the Tatra mountains. It can be reproduced with ordinary curd or cream cheese and should contain paprika, capers, caraway seeds, onions, anchovies and butter.

LIPTÓ

A soft and creamy ewes' milk cheese, made in Liptó in the north of Hungary.

LIQUEURS

Coloured spirits which are fruity and/or aromatic and usually sweet and syrupy. They are widely used in cooking worldwide both for flavouring and flaming and are popular as an after-dinner drink or as an ingredient in cocktails.

LIQUID PARAFFIN

A by-product of coal-tar which is not digested or absorbed by the body. It is illegal to include paraffin in edible foodstuffs, but liquid paraffin is well known as a laxative and is contained in many proprietary emulsions for constipation. Taken in excess, it can cause a deficiency of vitamins A and D.

LIQUIDIZE (TO)

To pulverize fruits and vegetables into a purée and/or liquid.

LIQUIDIZER

See *Blender*.

LIQUOR

A liquid in which food has been cooked; a liquid used to preserve food; an alcoholic drink such as spirit or liqueur.

LIQUORICE

(Licorice)

A European plant (*Glycyrrhiza glabra*) of the pea family; the word liquorice appears to come from a combination of two Greek words, *glukus* and *rhiza*, meaning sweet root. The plant itself grows mainly in Spain and Sicily, hence the old word 'Spanish' to describe long sticks of liquorice, the popular sweetmeat. Liquorice has laxative properties.

LITTLE TUNNY

A saltwater fish (*Euthynnus alletteratus*) of the world's tropical waters which resembles an immature albacore. The colour of the back is steely-blue or green with irregular stripes, shading to a silvery underside. It is caught at about 45 cm/18 inches in length and can weigh 2–7.25 kg/4½–16 lb. The main season is during the summer months. The flesh is dark, firm and oily and the fish may be baked or grilled.

LITTLE-NECK CLAM

A small Pacific clam (*Venerupis japonica*) which is only about 6 cm/2½ inches across and is slightly oblong in shape. It is gathered mainly in the winter months. The meat is lean and it may be eaten raw, baked, fried or used in made-up dishes.

LIVAROT

A French cows' milk cheese from Normandy, which is disc-shaped, rather like Camembert. It has a pronounced taste and smell, the texture is fairly firm and resilient and the rind shiny, verging on brown. In Normandy, the cheese is sometimes accompanied by a glass of Calvados.

LIVE

Containing living organisms, for example, live yoghourt.

LIVE YOGURT

All yogurt manufactured and sold in Britain is made from milk to which a live culture is added. After incubation and cooling, the yogurt is kept at a low temperature which arrests the growth of the culture but does not kill it. This should help to dispel the myth that only those yogurts labelled 'live' or 'true' contain the live culture yogurt.

LIVER

Liver makes a valuable contribution to the diet and a minimum of 10 g/ 4 oz is recommended per person per week. All liver, apart from calf's and chickens', benefits from being soaked in milk for about an hour before cooking and this applies particularly to imported, frozen liver which sometimes has a strong flavour. Liver should be cooked carefully, avoiding overcooking, which will result in the 'shoe leather' texture associated with badly prepared liver.

LIVER PUDDING

See *Maksalaatikko*.

LIVER SAUSAGE

A cooked sausage of either firm or spreadable consistency, made from liver and pork meat. The texture can be fine or coarse. It is generally well seasoned and occasionally smoked and sometimes herbs, garlic and onion are added for flavouring. Liver sausage is always beige in colour.

à la LIVORNAISE

French term meaning in the style of Livorno in Italy, referring particularly to poached fish accompanied with shallots or sometimes onions, tomatoes and truffles.

LOACH

European river fish (*Cobitidea* family), of which there are three main types. The flesh has a good flavour but is packed with bones. It is usually fried and is particularly popular in France.

LOAF

A term, generally used in connection with bread, which is said to be derived from two Anglo-Saxon words: *hlif-ian* meaning to raise or lift up, and *hlaf* meaning a raised loaf.

LOAF CHEESE

See *Edamer*.

LOAF SUGAR

Old-fashioned British term for cube sugar.

LOBIA

(Lobya)
See *Blackeye Bean*.

LOBSCOUSE

See *Scouse*.

LOBSTER

The largest European crustacean (*Homarus vulgaris*) with a large claw and four legs situated behind the head on each side and reaching halfway down the elongated, jointed body. The colour is usually dark blue or green, with reddish tinges, and varies according to the region. As the lobster is slow-growing, it is caught at various weights between 250g/9oz and 2 kg/4½ lb. It is caught on both sides of the Atlantic, with large catches on the Canadian coast, and the main seasons are late spring and early winter. It is usually sold boiled (the shell turns a vivid red) and sometimes frozen. The flesh is lean and rich and can be eaten boiled (as bought) or poached, baked, fried or grilled and used in made-up dishes. The North American lobster (*Homarus americanus*) is larger than the European kind and is widely exported.

LOBSTER MAYONNAISE
An internationally popular dish of half a cold boiled lobster, usually served in the shell, accompanied by mayonnaise and salad.

LOBSTER NEWBURG
A North American speciality first made in New York's Delmonico restaurant, this dish is prepared by cutting cooked lobster meat into cubes which are fried in butter, adding sherry and thickening the mixture with double cream and egg yolks. It is served on a bed of rice, sprinkled with paprika.

LOCRO
A speciality of Ecuador, a potato soup containing cheese, garnished just before serving with pieces of avocado.

LOCUST BEAN
See *Carob*.

LOGANBERRY
The fruit of a plant related to the rose family (*Rubus* species), a hybrid first developed by a Judge Logan in California in the 1880s. It is also grown in Britain, both commercially and in gardens, but is limited to the south and west because it is not as hardy as other related plants. It is a cross between a raspberry and either a blackberry or the closely related dewberry. It is mainly oval and may measure up to 5 cm/2 inches in length. The colour is dark red and the individual, tiny, single-seeded globules which make up the fruit are larger than those of the raspberry. The flesh is juicy and has a fragrant, sweet-sour flavour. It may be eaten raw or used in any recipe suited to the raspberry or blackberry. The loganberry is very suitable for canning and freezing.

LOHIKEITTO
Traditional Finnish salmon soup containing potatoes and leeks.

LOHIPIIRAS
A Finnish salmon pie which is related to the Russian *koulibiac*.

LOIN OF LAMB
A prime cut between the best end neck and chump, the loin can be often divided into chops, roasted as a whole joint on the bone, or boned and stuffed before roasting.

LOIN OF PORK
A prime cut of pork from the top of the pig, situated roughly between the neck and chump area. It can be cut into chops (with or without kidney), roasted on the bone, or boned and rolled before roasting. The joint may also be stuffed and produces excellent crackling.

LOIN OF PORK CHOP
Cut from the loin of pork, which runs along the top of the pig, roughly between the neck and the chump area. It frequently contains a piece of kidney. The chop can be fried or grilled and is known by this name in London and the South-East, the Midlands, north-east and north-west England.

LOIN OF VEAL
A rib cut of veal which is either divided into chops, roasted on the bone, or boned out and rolled prior to cooking. It is a prime cut, well-flavoured and tender.

LOIN OR SINGLE LOIN OF LAMB
Term used in Scotland for best end neck of lamb.

LOIN STEAKS OF LAMB
A new and leaner British cut of meat which is divided into steaks for grilling or frying.

LOKSHEN
A Jewish term for *vermicelli*, usually served in clear chicken soup.

LOKUM
The Turkish name for Turkish delight.

LOLLY
See *Ice Lolly*.

LOLLYPOP
(Lollipop)
A large and flat round or oval sweet on the end of a stick.

LONG BACK BACON
Long rashers from the hindquarter of the pig. They are suitable for grilling or frying.

LONG FLOUNDER
See *Lemon Sole*.

LONG LIFE CREAM
See *Ultra-Heat Treated Cream*.

LONGAN
(Dragon's Eye, Lungan)
The fruit of a tree (*Nephelium longana*) native to India and related to the lychee and rambutan. It is cultivated in China and other tropical and sub-tropical countries. The appearance is similar to that of the lychee with a rough, brown shell and sweet white flesh surrounding a brown stone. Although not so well known in Europe as the lychee, the longan, with its slightly stronger, grape-like flavour, is preferred by some people, particularly when canned. The longan is also available in dried form and is used in Chinese dishes.

LONGAZINA
A Portuguese sausage, similar to Spain's *chorizo*.

LONG-GRAIN BROWN RICE
A non-sticky rice, much used in the Orient and Middle East, which tends to fluff up in the same way as white rice with the grains staying separate and firm.

LONGNOSE
See *Garfish*.

LONZA
Italian pork loin (fillet), treated in a similar way to *prosciutto crudo*. It is eaten raw, cut into thin slices.

LOQUAT
(Japanese Medlar)
The fruit of an evergreen tree (*Eriobotrya japonica*) which is one of the few sub-tropical members of the apple and pear family. It is native to China and Japan and cultivated in North America, Australia and the Mediterranean region. It is plum-shaped with a yellow-orange, slightly downy skin like an apricot, and is about 4 cm/1½ inches long. The fragrant flesh may be coloured from white to orange and surrounds from one to four brown seeds, depending on the variety. Loquat may be eaten raw, including the skin, or used in salads and preserves.

LORRAINE
(Gerardmer, Gros Lorraine)
A French cows' milk cheese from Lorraine which looks like a thick, flat cylinder. It is a whitish cheese with a distinct, lactic flavour and is related to Munster and Gérômé cheeses.

LOTHIAN
Scottish version of Camembert.

LOTUS
(Chinese Water Lily, Indian Lotus)
A vegetable (*Nelumbo nucifera*) of the water-lily family native to Asia and important in the cooking of that region, particularly in China and Japan. It is found below water as a string of elongated, connected, swollen roots with leaves and

Nuts

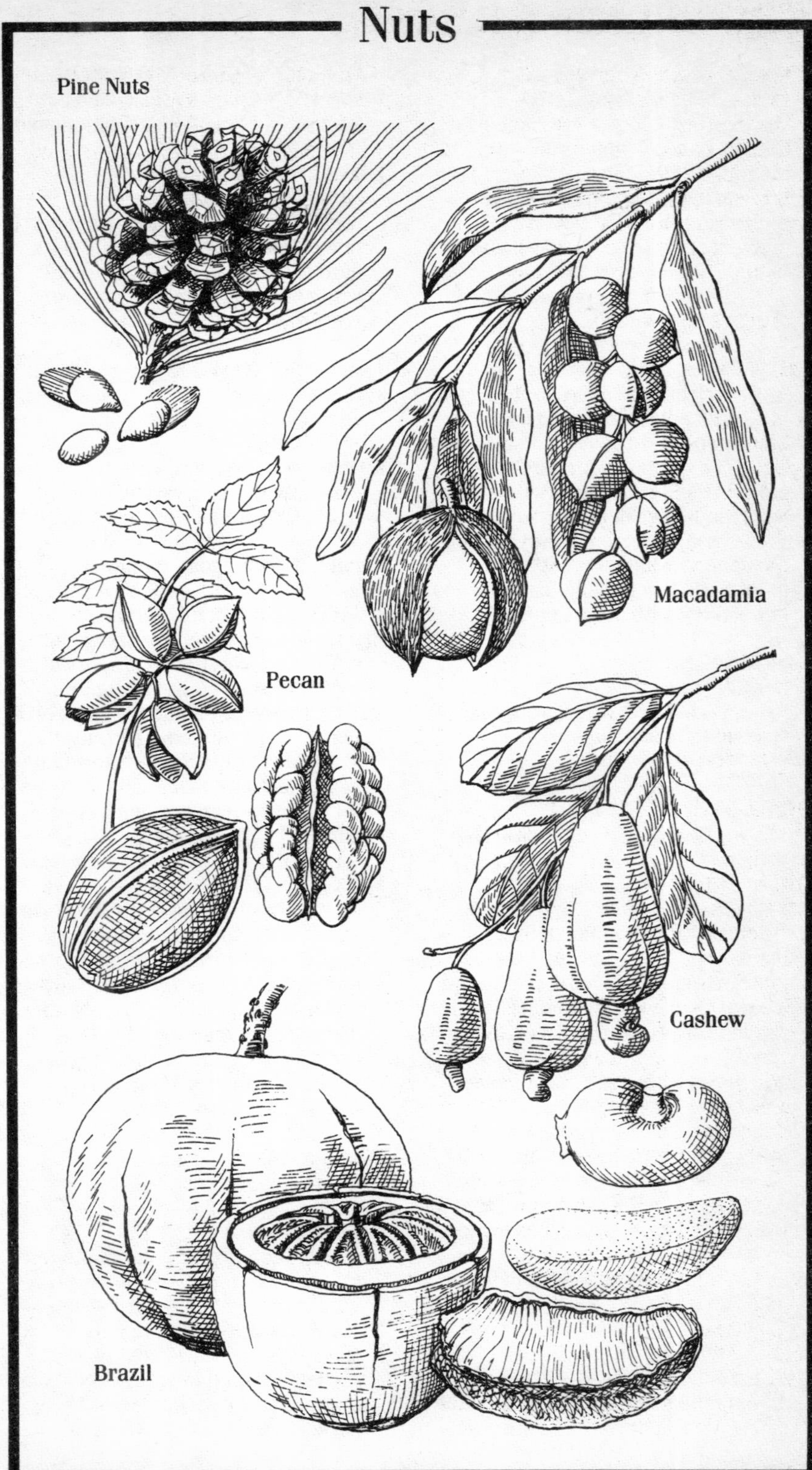

flowers growing upright above the surface. The root segment is characterized by a symmetric pattern of holes which run lengthwise through it, producing a lacy design when the root is cut crosswise. The root, flower, seed and leaf are all used in Far Eastern recipes. Dried roots and leaves are sold in specialist shops and canned root is also available.

LOUIS SAUCE
An American sauce, created early in the 20th century by a chef called Louis in a San Francisco restaurant. Designed originally for serving with crab, the sauce is basically mayonnaise flavoured with chilli sauce, whipped cream, very finely chopped green pepper, spring onions and lemon juice. The sauce is now served with other seafoods.

LOUKANIKA
A fairly small, dried sausage from Greece made from pork, red wine, coriander, seasonings and a selection of herbs.

LOUKOUM
The North African term for Turkish delight.

LOVAGE
Originally grown in the gardens of the Benedictine monks in France, this herb spread to northern Europe where it is now cultivated (there are no wild varieties). It is a tall and spreading perennial (*Levisticum officinale*) with large green leaves which taste slightly of yeast. It is popular in Germany, Austria and Switzerland for soups, stews, casseroles and hot-pots and is also appreciated in France and Italy. The Greeks and Romans chewed lovage seeds as an aid to digestion; additionally, it is supposed to have aphrodisiac and deodorizing qualities.

LOVE IN DISGUISE
An old English dish which originated in the West Country, consisting of stuffed and baked calves' hearts, served with brown gravy and bacon.

LOVING CUP
Old-fashioned British term to describe a type of party punch made from sherry, Madeira, port, claret, lemon juice, sugar and water. It should be served very cold.

LOW-FAT QUARK
(Speisequark)
See *Quark*.

LOW-FAT SOFT CHEESE
A soft, white cheese with a butterfat content ranging from 2% to 10%. It can be made from the milk of cows, goats or ewes.

LOW-STARCH FLOUR
Specially prepared for those suffering from diabetes, most of the starch is removed from the wheat leaving behind a flour which is rich in protein and gluten. It is available from some health food shops and pharmacists; directions for its use are given on the packets.

LOX
North American term for the local smoked salmon which is a deep orange colour and both mild and flavourful. A New York speciality is lox and cream cheese bagels. The name is a corruption of the German word *lachs*, meaning smoked salmon and the Scandinavian word *lax*.

LOZENGE
A medicated sweet.

LUAU SOUP
A Hawaiian cream soup made from a base of puréed taro leaves.

LUGANEGHE
(Luganega)
A northern Italian version of Cumberland sausage made from pork.

LUMACHE
Snail-shaped pasta.

LUMP SUGAR
Old-fashioned British term for cube sugar.

LUMPFISH
A seawater fish (*Cyclopterus lumpus*) which is hump-backed, deep-bellied and knobbly. The colour is generally grey or green and the length 45–60 cm/18–24 inches. It is caught in the North Atlantic and the Baltic in spring and early summer. Lumpfish is peculiar in that it is mainly used to supply roe from the female, which is used as an alternative to caviar. The flesh of the male is oily and may be poached, but the female fish is not really edible for most of the year.

LUNCH
A mid-day meal, usually less formal than luncheon.

LUNCHEON
A formal meal, usually eaten at mid-day.

LUNCHEON MEAT
A precooked mixture of meat, such as pork, which usually contains cereal, fat and certain permitted preservatives. It is shaped into a loaf and is usually eaten thinly sliced with salad.

LUNGFISH
See *Barramunda*.

LUNGS
(Lights)
Also known as lights, these are found in all animals and are either used for pet food or occasionally added to stuffings.

LUOSTARI
A Finnish cows' milk cheese which resembles Port-Salut.

LYCHEE
(Chinese Cherry, Lichee, Litchee, Litchi)
The fruit of an evergreen tree (*Litchi chinensis*) native to southern China but now cultivated in many parts of the world with suitable climates. It is round, about 4 cm/1½ inches in diameter and its brownish-red skin, which is rough and brittle, can be easily peeled away to reveal translucent and firm white flesh enclosing a small, hard, dark kernel. The flesh has a delicate flavour like a muscat grape and is very sweet. It may be eaten by itself, poached in syrup and then served cold, or used in fruit salads or other desserts. Lychees canned in syrup retain most of the particular aroma and flavour of the fresh fruit and are a speciality of many oriental restaurants.

LYMESWOLD
A British blue cheese which is soft, creamy-gold and mild when fresh.

à la LYONNAISE
French term meaning in the style of Lyons in eastern France, denoting the inclusion of fried onions in a dish or as a garnish.

LYONNAISE SAUCE
An Espagnole sauce, well-flavoured with fried onions. It can be served with grilled and roast red meat, pork, game and offal.

LYRE OF BEEF
Term used in the east of Scotland for clod of beef.

MAASDAM
A factory-made cows' milk cheese from Holland which resembles Swiss and German Emmental. It has

a nutty, mild flavour and is coated with yellow wax.

MAATJES HARING
Small herrings, similar to the German *matjes*, which are lightly cured. They are eaten in Holland from May until the autumn, as a street snack or in restaurants as an appetizer with toast or bread, or as a main course with boiled potatoes and a green salad. *Maatje* is derived from the word *maagde* meaning virgin and these speciality Dutch fish are young herrings which have not yet developed roes.

MACADAMIA NUTS
These rich, almost buttery-textured and hard-shelled nuts are native to south and north-eastern Australia; the trees belong to two families, *Macadamia ternifolia* and *M. integrifolia*. They were discovered about a hundred years ago and are now cultivated in Hawaii, the southern states of the USA, South Africa and the Caribbean. They are round, skinless and creamy-coloured, highly priced and are regarded as a delicacy. Macadamia nuts may be roasted and salted and eaten as a snack or used in cooking.

MACARONI
(Maccheroni)
Hollow pasta, thicker than *spaghetti*.

MACARONI CHEESE
An English dish, popular since the beginning of the 20th century, made from cooked macaroni mixed with cheese sauce. The top is covered with grated cheese and browned under a hot grill.

MACAROONS
Slightly chewy, round biscuits made from egg white, almonds, sugar and flavourings. They are often decorated with almonds and are thicker than rolled biscuits; the mixture is placed on baking trays with a spoon or piped on in rounds. They are in the luxury class.

MACCHERONCINI
A more slender version of macaroni.

MACCHERONI
A generic Italian word to describe all types of dried pasta, irrespective of size or shape. It also refers to hollow spaghetti, perhaps better known in Britain as macaroni.

MACE
A spice obtained from the lacy mesh skin covering the nutmeg (*Myristica fragrans*). Native to Molucca or the Spice Islands, mace is now exported from Indonesia and the West Indies. It is bright red, lightening to pale orange after drying and is sold either ground or in pieces known as blades. Resembling nutmeg in flavour but less pungent, the blades make an interesting addition to fish stocks, pickles, stewed fruits and marinades. Ground mace is generally used in baked goods, chocolate puddings and cakes, meat loaves and chicken dishes.

MACÉDOINE
French term for an assortment of diced mixed fruits or vegetables.

MACÉDOINE DE FRUITS
French term for a fruit salad.

MACERATE (TO)
To soften food by soaking in a liquid.

MÂCHE
See *Lamb's Lettuce*.

MACKEREL
(Atlantic Mackerel)
A round-bodied and streamlined seawater fish (*Scomber scombrus*) with a silvery underside and dark bluey-green back bearing a cross-wise pattern of darker, irregular zig-zag lines. It can reach a length of 55 cm/21 inches and a weight of 2 kg/4½ lb, but is usually sold in the shops as whole fish of half this size or less. It is caught all year round on both sides of the Atlantic, in the Mediterranean and Black Sea. The flesh is oily, firm and

well-flavoured and the fish may be poached, baked, fried, soused or grilled; commercially smoked mackerel is also very popular. The Pacific mackerel (*Scomber japonicus*) is caught in great quantities off California and is an important fish in Japanese cookery.

à la MÂCONNAISE
French term meaning in the style of Mâcon in eastern France, referring especially to freshwater fish poached in Mâcon wine and garnished with croûtons, small braised onions or shallots and button mushrooms.

MACQUE CHOUX
Adapted from an Indian recipe by the Acadians (Cajuns) in the Louisiana Bayou country of the USA, this is a Christmas dish made by stewing tomatoes with sweetcorn, hominy, green peppers, celery, lemon juice and seasonings. It generally accompanies duck.

MACQUÉE
A Belgian skimmed milk cheese which is generally soft, mild and brick-shaped. It is made from cows' milk.

MACROBIOTIC
Term to describe a specific diet, consisting chiefly of whole grains and vegetables. It is followed with the intention of promoting health and prolonging life.

MADAGASCAN GREEN PEPPERCORNS
(Green Peppercorns)
Soft, dark green and under-ripe peppercorns, usually from Madagascar. They are pickled, preferably in brine, or in vinegar, and are sold in jars or cans. They are also sometimes available in Britain fresh, on stalks. They are mild yet fine-flavoured and subtle, suitable for beef and game dishes and in marinades. Dried green peppercorns lack the piquancy of the under-ripe ones but are a pleasing condiment ground over fish and steak dishes.

MADAGASCAR BEAN
A variety of butter bean.

MADEIRA
A group of fortified wines which have been produced in Madeira since the middle of the 18th century and can be dry, medium-dry, medium-sweet and sweet. The drier Madeiras can be added to soups such as oxtail and consommé; also to stews, braised dishes and sauces. Sweet Madeiras are used in many desserts and are excellent in trifles.

MADEIRA CAKE
A large, round cake made from a creamed cake mixture flavoured with finely grated lemon peel and/or vanilla. Traditionally, it is topped with slices of citron peel halfway through baking.

MADEIRA SAUCE
An Espagnole sauce, flavoured with Madeira wine and meat extract such as Bovril. It can be served with grilled and roast beef, offal and game.

MADELEINES
(Madelines)
In Britain, these are light cakes shaped like chimney pots which are coated in jam and covered with desiccated coconut. In France, they are vanilla-flavoured sponge cakes baked in special scalloped madeleine moulds.

MADÈRE
French term for Madeira wine, indicating that a dish includes some or is served with Madeira sauce.

à la MADRILÈNE
French term meaning in the style of Madrid in Spain, denoting a garnish or addition of tomatoes.

MAFALDA
Long, flat ribbons of pasta with crinkly edges.

MAGGI
Proprietary name of a brown liquid food colour and flavouring made, like Marmite, from hydrolysed vegetable protein.

MAGNESIUM
A mineral important for normal metabolism. It is also necessary for the sound formation and maintenance of bones and teeth.

MAH MEE
A Singaporean noodle soup containing shellfish, pork, vegetables, herbs and seasonings.

MAHÓN
A centuries-old Spanish cheese from the Balearic islands made from cows' milk. It is white when young, also creamy and soft. It hardens as it matures, becoming darker and developing a more pronounced taste. The rind is a brownish colour. Mahón cheese is brined, matured for 3 weeks, then coated with olive oil, which improves its keeping qualities.

MAIDS OF HONOUR
Originally from Richmond in Surrey, these small cakes consist of puff pastry cases filled with a sweetened mixture of curd cheese, almonds, lemon, egg yolks, butter and spice. Sometimes the cakes are sprinkled with currants before baking.

au MAIGRE
French term meaning lean or cooked without meat, offal or poultry. It is a popular form of cooking during Lent.

MAIGRELET
A Canadian cheese made from skimmed cows' milk. It is medium-soft and produced in Quebec.

à la MAILLOT
French term for a garnish for entrées comprising turnips, carrots, French beans, braised lettuce and peas.

MAIN COURSE
See *Course*.

à la MAINTENON
French term for a garnish of onion sauce containing puréed onions and chopped mushrooms.

MAINZ
A German Hand cheese, similar to Harz, but often flavoured with cumin. It, too, is powerful and an acquired taste.

de la MAISON
French term meaning house style, often abbreviated on a restaurant menu to 'maison'; for example, *pâté maison*. Also applied to any other speciality of the restaurant, made on the premises.

MAÎTRE D'HÔTEL
French term for a head waiter.

MAÎTRE D'HÔTEL BUTTER
Softened, whipped butter to which chopped parsley and lemon juice are added. It is shaped into a 2.5 cm/1 inch diameter roll, wrapped and refrigerated until hard, then cut into rounds of about 5 mm/¼ inch in thickness. These are used to garnish poached, steamed, grilled or baked fish.

MAIZE
(Corn)
Yellow or white corn (*Zea mays*) from which cornflakes, cornflour, cornmeal and cornstarch are produced. Maize is grown all over the world and is one of the most important and widely distributed cereals.

MAIZE MEAL
North American term for coarsely ground maize (corn).

MAKO SHARK
See *Shark*.

MAKSALAATIKKO
A Finnish liver pudding, also common to Sweden, made from rice,

milk, water, onion, liver, golden syrup, raisins, eggs, marjoram and seasonings. Each portion of pudding is topped with butter and served with boiled potatoes and cranberry sauce.

MÁLAGA
A Spanish cheese produced from the milk of the goats which inhabit the mountains around Malaga. It is rich in character with a distinctive but delicate goaty flavour. The texture is close and cream-coloured and the cheese is covered with a yellow rind.

MALAKOFFTORTE
A French cake from the Parisian suburb of Malakoff. It is made by layering sponge fingers soaked in rum with a rich cream mixture made from butter, sugar, eggs, ground almonds, cream and either coffee or almond flavouring.

MALIC ACID
Acid found in most under-ripe fruits but especially in apples, rhubarb and some berries. If such fruits are used for jam-making without the addition of either lemon juice, citric acid or tartaric acid, the set will be unsatisfactory.

MALLARD
See *Wild Duck*.

MALNUTRITION
The literal meaning of this word is 'bad feeding' and, if someone is suffering from malnutrition, it is an indication that their meals are improperly balanced and lacking in certain nutrients: proteins, fat, carbohydrates, vitamins, trace elements, fibre and liquid, usually water.

MALT
Made from fermented barley. Certain enzymes in the grain turn the starch present into maltose and dextrine. The grains are then dried and crushed and used in the preparation of alcoholic drinks such as beer.

MALT BREAD
Made from a fairly plain, white yeasted dough to which malt extract, black treacle and mixed dried fruit have been added. It has a characteristically rich and malty flavour, is light brown in colour and is usually served sliced and buttered.

MALT EXTRACT
A sweet, light brown syrup prepared from an infusion of malt and water.

MALT VINEGAR
A brandy-coloured, strong vinegar which has an acetic acid content of 50–60%. It is widely used for pickling, in the making of chutneys and sometimes for sousing.

à la MALTAISE
French term meaning in Maltese style, denoting the addition of orange peel and juice to a dish; also Hollandaise sauce flavoured with strained blood orange juice.

MALTED BROWN FLOUR
Used to make malted wheat breads such as granary, the flour contains kibbled and whole grain wheat.

MALTED MILK DRINK
A drink made by combining malted milk powder with milk.

MALTED MILK POWDER
A soluble powder prepared from dried milk and malted cereals.

MALTESE SAUCE
(Maltaise Sauce)
A Hollandaise sauce, flavoured with grated orange rind and tinted with strained orange juice. It can be served with asparagus or broccoli.

MALTOSE
A disaccharide or double sugar which is basically malt sugar resulting naturally from starch in the production of beer.

MĂMĂLIGĂ
Romania's national dish, *mămăligă* is made from boiled polenta, sometimes enriched with butter, served as a base for poached eggs, grated cheese and soured cream.

MAMMEE
(Mamey)
The fruit of a tree (*Mammea americana*) native to South America and grown in the Caribbean area and some neighbouring countries. It is spherical and can be over 15 cm/6 inches in diameter. It has a double skin; the rough outer skin is brown or grey and the thin inner skin bitter-tasting and yellowy-white. The flesh, which surrounds up to four seeds, is yellowish in colour and reminiscent in flavour of a mixture of raspberry and apricot. It may be eaten raw after carefully removing both skins, or used in dessert dishes.

MAMSELL BABETTE
A rich German cows' milk cheese produced in Bavaria. It is loaf-shaped, contains small pieces of smoked ham and has a fairly firm texture. The flavour is mild.

MANCHEGO
A Spanish ewes' milk cheese produced in La Mancha, the finest coming from Ciudad Real. It is Spain's most popular cheese with a rich, fairly mild and creamy taste. The colour is ivory-gold and the texture firmish with a sprinkling of small holes.

MANDARIN
See *Tangerine*.

MANDARIN COOKING
A Chinese cuisine of a high order, once reserved for aristocratic Mandarins. It is a combination of Peking and Shanghai specialities.

MANDOLINE
An implement for slicing and paring which consists of stainless steel blades set in slots in an oblong framework of wood or metal. By pressing firm vegetables and fruits across the various blades, plain or fancy designs can be produced. The thickness of the slices is controlled by adjustable blade settings.

MANGE-TOUT
(Chinese Pea, Snow Pea, Sugar Pea)
Type of peapod in which the seeds hardly develop and the whole pod is eaten as a vegetable. The French name means literally 'eat it all'.

MANGO
The fruit of an evergreen tree (*Mangifera indica*) native to South-East Asia, important in India for several thousand years and now cultivated throughout the world wherever the climate permits. It is estimated that more mangoes are eaten than any other fruit and production is steadily increasing. Although the mango varies in size, the commonest is egg- or kidney-shaped and weighs 225 g–1 kg/ 8 oz–2¼ lb. The skin, usually smooth, changes from green to a range of colours as it ripens and often an individual fruit has an attractive combination of shades comprising yellow, red and purple. The flesh is light orange in colour and the finest kinds have little of the natural stringiness sometimes associated with the mango. Often described as the world's most delicious fruit, the main disadvantage is the difficulty experienced in removing the flesh from the large and flat central stone. Once this is overcome, the flesh is excellent on its own, in fruit salads and other desserts. It can be used in jams and preserves and green mangoes are widely used in making chutney.

MANGOSTEEN
(Mangostan)
The fruit of an evergreen tree (*Garcinia mangostana*) native to South-East Asia, mainly Malaysia, and suited only to certain wet, tropical regions. It is about the same

size as a small orange and when ripe has a thick, purply-brown skin. The flesh consists of about six white segments, each usually containing a seed. This juicy flesh has a delicious, delicate taste and is best eaten straight from the opened skin or used in a fruit salad. Mangosteen is not suitable for cooking purposes other than preserves. The juice from the skin contains an indelible dye, so the fruit must be handled and opened with care.

MANHATTAN CLAM CHOWDER
See *Chowder*.

MANICHE
Wide tubes of pasta, resembling shortened *cannelloni*.

MANIOC
Another name for the cassava plant; also the dried meal made from its tuber and used in the making of tapioca.

MANIZALES
One of the finest of Colombian coffee beans.

MANJAR BLANCO
See *Dulce de Leche*.

MANJU
A Japanese cake, eaten at teatime accompanied by green tea.

MANOORI
(Manouri)
Ewes' milk cheese from Crete, which is usually eaten with honey for a dessert.

MANTI
A Turkish dish of fresh *ravioli*, which are cooked and drained, then coated with a sauce made from yogurt, garlic, melted butter and paprika.

MANUR
(Mandur)
A Yugoslav farm cheese made from whole cows' and ewes' milk whey. It is mixed with whole milk or buttermilk and turns into a hard cheese, suitable for grating.

MAPLE SUGAR
Light golden-brown sugar produced from the sap of Canadian rock maple trees.

MAPLE SYRUP
A thin, light brown sweet syrup derived from the sap of Canadian rock maple trees.

MAPLE SYRUP PIE
A Canadian speciality, consisting of a double-crust pie with a filling of maple syrup, cornflour, butter and chopped nuts.

à la MARAÎCHÈRE
French term meaning in the style of a market gardener, referring to a garnish for joints of meat comprising salsify, Brussels sprouts, potatoes, onions and carrots.

MARANTA
See *Arrowroot*.

MARASCHINO
A colourless liqueur, produced in Yugoslavia and northern Italy for over 200 years. It is made from maraschino cherries and their crushed kernels and sold in straw-covered bottles. It has a distinctive taste and is used as a flavouring in some southern European dessert dishes.

MARASCHINO CHERRY
A cherry preserved in maraschino liqueur and used to decorate food or drinks.

MARBLED
A term which generally refers to the flesh of beef which is slightly intergrained with fat, giving it a marbled appearance.

MARCHAND DE VIN SAUCE
Similar to Chasseur sauce but flavoured with dry red wine. It can

be served with grilled or roast meat dishes, roast duck and offal.

au MARÉCHAL
French term meaning in the style of a marshal, referring to a garnish for entrées comprising asparagus tips, truffles and sometimes cockscombs and peas.

MAREDSOUS
A Belgian cows' milk cheese, similar to Saint-Paulin. It is usually rectangular.

MARGARINE
A butter substitute, this is made from a combination of animal and/or vegetable fats and/or oils. These include hydrogenated coconut oil, palm oil, cottonseed oil and sometimes groundnut oil. Some margarines also contain whale oil, sunflower oil and soya derivatives. Vitamins A and D are added.

MARIBO
A firm, Danish cheese which is flattish, large, rounded and creamy-coloured. It is peppered with numerous irregular holes, giving the cheese an open texture and it is generally coated with yellow wax. It is made from cows' milk and the flavour is mild and very slightly acidic.

à la MARIE-LOUISE
French term meaning in the style of Marie-Louise, referring to a garnish for entrées comprising onion purée, artichoke hearts, mushrooms and potatoes.

MARIENHOFER
An Austrian version of Limburger, made in the Tyrol.

MARIGOLD
A bright yellow or orange self-seeding, annual flower (*Calendula officinalis*), native to Asia and southern Europe but also grown in temperate zones of the world. It is the festival flower of India and the tangy petals are often used in cooking as a substitute for the more expensive saffron; young marigold leaves can be added to salads.

MARINADE
From the French word *mariner*, meaning to soak in a piquant liquid prior to cooking. The liquid can consist of wine, cider or an acid such as vinegar which is then flavoured with herbs, spices and onions and enriched with oil. Some Oriental and Balkan marinades also contain yoghurt. The mixture is frequently strained and used as a base for sauce to accompany the food which was marinated.

MARINATE (TO)
To treat with a marinade.

à la MARINIÈRE
French term meaning in the style of a boatman, referring to mussels cooked in white wine with onions, garlic and herbs; also fish garnished with mussels.

MARJORAM
(Knotted Marjoram, Sweet Marjoram)
A herb native to western Asia and the Mediterranean, marjoram (*Origanum majorana*) comes mainly from France, Chile and Peru and is also grown in California. The grey-green leaves are dried and are slightly aromatic with minty overtones. Marjoram is excellent in lamb and Italian dishes and also goes well with chicken and strong fish like mackerel and herring.

MARKET CRAB
See *Dungeness Crab*.

MARMALADE
A preserve made by boiling pre-cooked citrus fruits (usually chopped up) with sugar until setting point is reached. Seville or bitter oranges are popular for marmalade due to colour and flavour.

MARMALADE SAUCE
Made from marmalade which is heated with a little water and thickened to a pouring consistency with arrowroot, sometimes sweetened with sugar and sharpened with lemon juice. It is usually served with steamed or baked sponge-type puddings.

MARMELADE
French term for a thick purée of stewed fruit.

MARMITE
A brand name to describe a thick, dark brown paste which is yeast extract. It can be used as a spread, a flavouring in soups, stews, gravies and sauces, or diluted with water to make drinks. It is suitable for vegetarians.

MARMITE DISH
An earthenware pot with handles and a lid, widely used in France. Large *marmites* are flameproof and used on top of the cooker. *Petite marmite* describes not only a clear *consommé*-style soup, but also the individual-sized, earthenware pot in which it is served.

à la MAROCAINE
French term meaning in the style of Morocco, referring to a garnish of courgettes, peppers, rice flavoured with saffron and sometimes tomatoes or tomato sauce.

MAROILLES
A Flemish/French cows' milk cheese, it is named after the Maroilles monastery where it was first produced by an anonymous monk in the 10th century. This popular cheese is small, square-shaped and about 5 cm/ 2 inches in thickness. It has a forthright taste and aroma, with a fleshy, elastic and pale yellow texture. The ruddy-brown rind is smooth and slightly glossy.

MARQUISE
A frozen French dessert made from a sorbet containing alcohol (a sherbet) with the addition of whipped cream.

MARRONS
French term for chestnuts.

MARRONS GLACÉS
French term for candied chestnuts, a luxurious speciality.

MARROW
See *Vegetable Marrow*.

MARROW BONES
Thigh and shin bones of beef which contain rich, delicate marrow, much appreciated by gourmets. The bones are usually cut up into shortish lengths and boiled gently to soften the marrow, which is then carefully removed and often served on toast. Traditionally, one or two pieces of bone were presented to the diner on a napkin-lined plate so that the marrow could be scooped out with a spoon and spread over hot toast. Silver marrow scoops have become highly collectable antiques.

MARROWFAT PEA
A large green pea of the same family as the garden pea and grown mostly in northern European countries. It is usually sold canned or dried and is used in the British North Country dish called mushy peas. All peas were of the marrowfat type until three or four hundred years ago, when the 'modern' pea was developed.

MARSALA
Produced in Sicily, this is the finest and best-known Italian fortified grape wine. It is much used in Italian cooking and is the basis of *zabaglione*. Marsala is a dessert wine, frequently served with nuts and fruit at the end of a formal meal.

à la MARSEILLAISE
French term meaning in the style of Marseilles in southern France, denoting a garnish for steaks

composed of tomatoes, anchovies and olives.

MARSHMALLOW

A pink-flowered, hairy Eurasian plant (*Althaea officinalis*) of the hollyhock family that grows in marshes, usually near the sea, and has a root containing a sweet gum-like substance sometimes used in confectionery and medicine; a soft confection made from the soft, gum-like substance contained in the root of the plant; a commercially made soft sweet prepared from sugar, gelatine, water and egg white.

MARYLAND COOKIES

See *Chocolate Chip Cookies*.

MARZIPAN

A sweetmeat. Also used to cover a cake prior to the addition of icing. It is fairly rich, the basic proportion being equal quantities of ground almonds and sugar plus egg yolks or whites for mixing. It is pliable and can be moulded into various shapes. It can be coloured with food colourings.

MASA HARINA

A particular type of cornflour treated with lime water. It is used in Mexico and South America for making classic *tortillas*.

MASALA DOSA

Southern Indian vegetarian pancakes filled with a fairly hot and spicy potato mixture. They are accompanied by a creamy coconut 'pickle'.

MASCARPONE

(Mascherpone)

A rich northern Italian cream cheese made from cows' milk. It is usually eaten fresh as a dessert with sugar, fruits and spices.

à la MASCOTTE

French term for a garnish for chicken and roast joints composed of artichoke hearts, truffles and potatoes.

MASH

Crushed malt or grain meal steeped and stirred in hot water to ferment prior to the production of beer or whisky; also, a British colloquial term for mashed potato.

MASH (TO)

To break down cooked food into small particles or a purée, usually with the aid of a fork or patent masher.

MASHED POTATOES

Freshly boiled potatoes which are strained and finely broken down by mashing with a large fork or potato masher. Butter, milk or cream are sometimes added, as well as salt and pepper.

MASK (TO)

To coat food completely with sauce, glaze, jelly or mayonnaise.

à la MASSÉNA

French term for a garnish for steaks composed of artichoke hearts, Béarnaise sauce and bone marrow.

MAST

The name used in Iran for yogurt.

MATAMBRE

An Argentinian meat roll which is stuffed with spinach, onion rings, sliced carrots and quarters of hard-boiled eggs and simmered in stock until tender. When cold, it is sliced and served as an appetizer.

MATÉ

Although strictly speaking a herbal tea, *maté* is produced rather like tea leaves and was widely drunk in Latin America for the stimulating effect of its high caffeine content before the introduction of coffee. It is prepared as an infusion and drunk with sugar and milk or lemon. The rather elaborate native ritual of preparation and drinking of *maté* has been largely superseded by the modern teapot, cup and saucer.

MATELOTE
French term for a freshwater fish stew containing a selection of local fish including eel. It derives its name from the French for sailor.

MATJES
These lightly cured small herrings are caught in May and at their best during the summer months. They are usually served with raw onion and boiled potatoes.

MATOKE
An East African speciality made from a thick mash of boiled plantains, butter and seasoning.

MATSUTAKE
An edible mushroom (*Tricholoma matsutake*) which grows in Japanese pine woods in autumn. It is the most desirable fungus in Japan and although it is exported fresh to some countries, for example North America, it is generally only available dried or canned outside the Far East. The matsutake dried mushroom has a very distinctive flavour and is best suited to Japanese-style dishes.

MATURE
Ripe and/or ready for eating or drinking.

MATURE GOUDA
Dutch Gouda cheese which is a minimum of 3 months old.

MATZO
See *Passover Bread*.

MATZOON
The name used in Armenia for yogurt.

MAXIMILIAN SAUCE
A mayonnaise flavoured with tomato purée, chopped gherkins, chopped capers and chopped parsley. It can be served with fried, baked and grilled fish dishes.

MAYONNAISE
A classic French sauce, the consistency of softly whipped cream, based on an uncooked emulsion of egg yolks, oil and either lemon juice or vinegar or a combination of both. It can be served with all cold, savoury foods and salads.

MCHUZI
An East African beef and mixed vegetable stew, very lightly seasoned with curry powder.

MEAL
Any grain which has been coarsely ground.

MEAL (A)
Food taken or provided at one time to satisfy appetite.

MEASURING CUP
A standard measure in North America, Australia and New Zealand, used for measuring both liquid and solid ingredients.

MEASURING JUG
Handled jug, made from heat-resistant glass, metal or rigid plastic, with markings on the sides for measuring different quantities of liquids. The most useful kind has Imperial, metric and cup measures (used in North America and some other countries). The lidded version is suitable for storage in a refrigerator or deep-freeze.

MEAT
The flesh of animals, the most common in Britain being that of cow, lamb, pig and calf. Meat is a first-class, body-building food and is made up of muscle tissue consisting of bundles of fibres which contain meat juices (or extractives) and valuable protein. The fibres are joined together by protein-rich connective tissue which, although insoluble in water, can be tenderized by moist heat, when it is converted into gristle which is a type of gelatine. There are two types of connective tissue; one is called

collagen and the other elastin. The latter is exceptionally tough and rubbery and not softened by cooking. When the fat cells in meat are interspersed between the fibres, as, for instance, in pork, they are termed invisible. Visible fat lies directly under the skin of the animal or round its vital organs and is sometimes marbled through the flesh, as in beef.

MEAT CLEAVER
A heavy meat chopper, capable of cutting through bone.

MEAT LOAF
Minced meat usually mixed with onion, seasonings, breadcrumbs and eggs. It is frequently baked in a loaf tin and served in slices, hot or cold.

MEAT PIE
Pie with a meat and gravy filling.

MEAT SAFE
See *Food Safe*.

MEAT TENDERIZER
See *Meat Tenderizing Powder*.

MEAT TENDERIZING POWDER
(Meat Tenderizer)
A white powder, used to make tough cuts of meat softer and therefore more edible. The powder is most likely to contain the enzyme papain. The directions on the bottle or jar should be followed carefully.

MEAT TEXTURE
Fine-grained meat flesh usually indicates that the cut is tender and may be grilled, fried, roasted or barbecued. Coarse-grained meat comes from either older animals or the neck and leg cuts, and is suitable for mincing, stewing, braising, casseroling and pies. Some recipes specify whether meat is cut with the grain or across it.

MECHOUI
The North African version of roast lamb.

MECHOUIA
A Tunisian speciality, a salad made from assorted vegetables.

MECKLENBURG
An East German cheese which is produced from skimmed cows' milk and classified as hard.

MEDAILLONS
French term for food which is cut or shaped by hand to resemble a medal, either round or oval. Beef tournedos are one example.

MEDELLIN
One of the finest kinds of Colombian coffee beans.

à la MÉDICI
French term for a garnish for steaks named after Catherine de Médici and comprising artichoke hearts, peas, carrots, turnips and sometimes tomatoes; also Choron Sauce consisting of Béarnaise sauce flavoured with tomatoes or tomato purée.

MEDITERRANEAN MEDLAR
See *Azarole*.

MEDIUM
British term to describe steak which is partially cooked with some red meat in the centre.

MEDIUM-FAT QUARK
A German soft cheese product, the richest of its kind, containing 10–12% butterfat. Ideal for eating and cooking purposes (it makes excellent cheesecake), this creamy Quark yields 160–180 kilocalories per 100 g/4 oz.

MEDIUM-FAT SOFT CHEESE
A soft white cheese with a butterfat content ranging from 10% to 20%. It can be made from the milk of cows, goats or ewes.

MEDIUM-OILY FISH
The flesh of a fish is considered medium-oily if it has a fat content of between 2% and 6%.

MEDLAR
The fruit of a deciduous tree (*Mespilus germanica*) of the same family as apple and pear, native to Iran and found growing wild in most European countries. Medlar trees are not commercially grown but are popular in gardens both for their decorative appearance and for their fruit. The fruit is the size of a small apple with a very prominent calyx (the remnants of the original flower), which gives it the appearance of a large rose-hip. The skin colour is brown and the flesh, which turns from white or pale green to brown, is only edible when over-ripe and on the verge of decay. When ready for eating, the flesh can be scooped out of the skin with a spoon and the seeds discarded, but the medlar is most commonly used in preserves.

MEE KROB
(Mi Krob)
Crisply fried, puffed-up *vermicelli* (rice noodles) which are mixed with stir-fried fish, pork and vegetables, then flavoured with lemon juice, vinegar and sugar. This Thai dish is garnished with omelette strips, spring onions and fresh coriander.

MEE NOODLES
Chinese egg noodles.

MEGRIM
A deep-water flatfish (*Lepidorhombus whiffiagonis*) caught mainly from September to February in European waters from Iceland to the Mediterranean. Fully grown, it is 50–60 cm/19–24 inches in length and the upper side is brownish or grey. Although the flesh is not as fine as other fish in the same family, such as turbot, the fish may be poached, steamed, baked or grilled.

MEIN NOODLES
Chinese egg noodles.

MEKABU
The Japanese sea vegetable *wakame* (*Undaria pinnatifida*) has a root or base with a high mineral content known as *mekabu* which is sold as a separate vegetable and is particularly suitable for adding richness to stews. It is available whole or shredded.

MELBA SAUCE
Created by the famous chef, Escoffier, during the latter part of the 19th century for the operatic star, Dame Nellie Melba. A purée of lightly sweetened raspberries, sometimes thickened slightly with arrowroot and water. It is served cold, traditionally with fresh peaches and vanilla ice cream.

MELBA TOAST
Wafer-thin slices of crustless white bread, cut into triangles and baked in a very cool oven until the edges curl and the bread turns a pale golden-brown and becomes very crisp. Melba toast is frequently served as an accompaniment to *hors d'oeuvre* and is said to have been named after Dame Nellie Melba for whom the toast was originally made. Uncurled slices of commercially prepared melba toast are available in packets.

MELBURY
A British cows' milk cheese, sold in small blocks. It is rich and creamy with an edible crust which is white, soft and almost downy in appearance. The texture is relatively firm, rather like under-ripe Brie.

MELILOT
A fragrant herb (*Melilotus officinalis*) which is a member of the clover family. Once grown for cattle feed, melilot is now dried and used to flavour stuffings and white-meat stews in the Alpine regions of Europe. Its taste is reminiscent of dried grass.

MELISSA
See *Lemon Balm*.

MELITZANOS SALATA
A Greek salad made from chopped, cooked aubergine flesh, onions, garlic, tomatoes, oil, vinegar, lemon juice and seasonings. It is usually garnished with black olives, parsley and rings of green pepper, and served as an appetizer or as an accompaniment to grilled or fried meat or fish.

MELKTERT
A South African custard tart, lightly flavoured with cinnamon.

MELON
From the same family of trailing plants as the cucumber and gourds, the melon (*Cucumis melo*) is the only one considered to produce a fruit rather than a vegetable. Its origin is obscure and it may be native to either Asia or Africa. It was certainly cultivated in ancient Egypt and is now grown in many varieties all around the world. The shape may be spherical or oval and the general characteristics are a thick skin, either hard or soft when ripe, sweet, soft and juicy flesh and a central cavity filled with seeds. The size varies with type and will generally be 10–15 cm/4–6 inches in diameter. The skin colour is usually green, yellow or a mixture of both and the flesh green, yellow or orange. The seeds are edible and may be toasted or roasted. The melon may be cut in half or segmented and the flesh scooped out with a spoon, or used in fruit salads or other dishes, both sweet and savoury. Important varities of melon include the musk or netted melon, of which the galia is an example; the cantaloupe melon represented by the charentais and ogen; and the winter melon best known as the honeydew.

MELON BALLER
(Baller)
An implement with a hollow scoop at either end, one of which is larger than the other. It is generally used to cut decorative, spherical shapes from the flesh of the melon. However, it can also be used on any fruit or vegetable with suitable flesh, such as apple, pear, potato or avocado.

MELT (TO)
To turn a solid ingredient into a liquid through the application of direct or indirect heat. This applies especially to fat and chocolate.

MELTED CAKES
(Melting Method)
Cakes, like gingerbread and parkin, made by what is known as the melting method; namely, the fat, sugar, golden syrup and treacle are all melted together before being added to the dry ingredients.

MELTING MOMENTS
Oat-covered, round biscuits which are pale in colour and crisp.

MELTON MOWBRAY PIE
A famous British raised pork pie from Melton Mowbray in Leicestershire, made with hot-water crust pastry filled with minced pork, seasonings, ground mace and ground ginger and brushed with egg during the last 15 minutes of baking for a golden glaze. After cooking, liquid aspic jelly is poured through a small hole in the top and it sets as the pie cools.

MENAQUIONE
(Phytomenadione)
See *Vitamin K*.

MENRUI
A general Japanese term for all the various types of noodle.

à la MENTONNAISE
French term meaning in the style of Menton in southern France, referring to a garnish for joints composed of marrow or courgette, potatoes and artichokes.

MENU
A list of dishes, usually with prices against each, indicating what is

available to eat and drink at a restaurant; also, a card or folder provided at formal functions, setting out the dishes that are to be served.

MERGUEZ
A scalded sausage from North Africa which is popular in France. It is slim, heavily spiced and usually served grilled. Merguez are sometimes available from specialist shops in Britain.

MERIENDAS
The Filipino term for snack, from the Spanish.

MERINGUE
(Swiss Meringue Mixture)
A thick and aerated mixture made by beating egg whites until very stiff before adding caster sugar gradually. It can be shaped into fingers, ovals, individual or large baskets and baked very slowly until completely dry in a very cool oven. When baked and cold, these meringues keep well in an airtight container.

MERMEZ
A Tunisian speciality, a mutton stew.

MESOST
A low-fat Swedish cheese, made from the whey of cows' milk. It is fudge-coloured and sweet and is popular with children.

METABOLISM
The digestion and absorption, or the breaking down and then building up again, of essential nutrients derived from food, which in turn play their various rôles in the body functions.

METCHNIKOFF
(Mechnikov)
A Russian soured milk product, named after the bacteriologist Metchnikoff who isolated *lactobacillus bulgaris* at the Pasteur Institute in Paris during the early part of this century.

METHI
See *Fenugreek*.

METTWURST
A small to medium-sized German preserved sausage, made from mildly smoked pork and beef. It may be smooth or coarse, depending on type: some sausages are hard and resemble salami, while others are soft and easy to spread. All have a delicate piquancy.

MEUNIÈRE
French term meaning literally a miller's wife, used to describe a buttery sauce served especially with sole.

MEUNIÈRE BUTTER SAUCE
Clarified butter, heated slowly until it turns light brown, then flavoured with chopped parsley, lemon juice and white pepper and poured over poached, baked and steamed fish.

à la MEXICAINE
French term meaning in the style of Mexico, referring to a garnish of tomatoes, mushrooms, peppers and sometimes aubergines; also rice.

MEXICAN BLACK BEAN
See *Black Bean*.

MEZE
A selection of Greek *hors d'oeuvres* which may include stuffed vine leaves (*dolmathes*), smoked cod's roe paste (*taramasalata*), hummus, aubergine salad, an assortment of shellfish including prawns, baby squid and clams, fried liver, small meat balls, a selection of cheeses, raw vegetables and warm bread.

MEZETER
Turkish *hors d'oeuvre* consisting of an assortment of dishes, including caviar, smoked sturgeon, smoked meats, shrimps or prawns, lobster, aubergine and other vegetable salads, sardines in oil, the cheese or meat pastries called *börek* and stuffed vegetables.

MICHAELMAS GOOSE
An old-fashioned name for roast goose served on 29 September, Michaelmas Day.

MI-CHÈVRE
French cheese, made from a minimum of 25% goats' milk and 75% cows' milk. The label is sometimes banded with a yellow stripe for quick identification.

MICROWAVE
See *Microwave Oven*.

MICROWAVE OVEN
(Microwave)
A compact cabinet in which food is rapidly cooked by microwave energy or microwaves — electromagnetic, short-length, high-frequency radio waves at the top end of the radio band. They are emitted from a smallish device called a magnetron (usually placed at the top of the oven, to one side), then pass down a channel known as a waveguide. Thus the microwaves enter the oven, bounce off the sides and beam on to the food from all directions. At the same time, the microwaves are absorbed by the food and force the water molecules within the food itself to vibrate vigorously, about 2400 million cycles or vibrations per second. This creates rapid friction and sufficient heat to cook the food. It should be noted that microwaves are only capable of penetrating food by 2.5 cm/1 inch in all directions which is why stirring and standing times are recommended in microwave cook books.

MIDDLE BACON
Combination of streaky and back bacon which comes from the centre of the pig. It can be boiled or baked as a joint, or cut into long rashers for frying and grilling. Because of its shape, it can also be stuffed.

MIDDLE GAMMON
A prime cut which is neat, round and usually tied in place with string. It is found between the hock and corner gammon in the middle of the pig. It is lean and fleshy, suitable for boiling, braising, stewing or casseroling. The joint may also be cut into rashers for grilling or frying.

MIDDLE NECK OF LAMB
A bony cut of lamb, often divided into chops. It comes from the shoulder area of the animal and is recommended for stewing, braising, casseroling and hot-pots.

MIGNONETTE PEPPER
White peppercorns which have been coarsely crushed and are said to resemble the seeds of the mignonette plant.

à la MILANAISE
French term to describe a dish cooked in Milanese style, such as escalope of veal which has been egg-and-crumbed, then fried.

MILANESE SOUFFLÉ
(Lemon Soufflé)
A classic French term for a cold soufflé flavoured with finely grated lemon rind.

MILD CURE BACON
A term used to describe quick-cured bacon, which owes its particular flavour, colour, mildness and texture to the ingredients contained in the curing solution.

MILDEW
Green furry mould which settles on food such as jam, bread and cheese if they are stale or have been stored in the damp. The mildew is caused by tiny organisms which flourish in a warm, humid atmosphere and although mildew is not necessarily harmful, the food should be thrown away for reasons of hygiene.

MILK
Milk is one of the most valuable liquid foods available to man. It is rich in first-class, body-building protein (containing all the essential amino acids) and calcium for the healthy formation of bones and

teeth. It is also a good source of vitamin A and vitamins of the B group, and contains some vitamins C and D. The natural sugar in milk, known as lactose, aids the absorption of calcium and also provides energy; the fat content, in very small globule form, is easily digested, contributes to the flavour of the milk and has a high energy value: 600 ml/1 pint of milk yields approximately 380 kilocalories and contains a legal minimum of 3% butterfat and 8.5% non-fat solids. It is one of the few foods that provides satisfying, easily-digested and instant nourishment at a low cost. Fresh milk should not be left in sunlight as this is liable to destroy some of its vitamins. It is best stored, in its own bottle, in the refrigerator but may be transferred to a rinsed-out jug which should not be dried. To prevent contamination, old milk should not be added to fresh milk. All milk should be kept covered and away from strong-smelling foods as it readily picks up odours.

MILK BREAD
A white loaf containing 6% full-cream milk solids.

MILK CHOCOLATE
Chocolate to which milk has been added by highly technical processes.

MILK JELLY
A typically British dessert made from warm milk, flavoured to taste with coffee, chocolate or vanilla for example, into which melted, cooled but still liquid gelatine is added. The mixture is poured into a mould and turned out when cold and firmly set.

MILK LOAF
Bread made from a basic white dough in which milk, or milk and water, has been used for mixing.

MILK PUDDING
A typically British pudding made from rice, sago, tapioca, semolina, barley or macaroni, baked or cooked in milk with sugar.

MILK SHAKE
Made by shaking milk with either non-acid fruit juice or fairly thin fruit purée and sugar, or fruit syrup. Sometimes ice cream is shaken with the milk or added to the drink afterwards. It is best to make a milk shake in a blender goblet; alternatively, the ingredients may be shaken together in a vacuum flask. Milk shakes are also made with chocolate, coffee or vanilla flavourings, instead of fruit.

MILK SUGAR
See *Lactose*.

MILK TART
See *Melktert*.

MILL
An implement used for grinding pepper, salt, herbs or spices. It is usually a small cylinder with a mechanism which dispenses the ground product through the top or bottom of the mill.

MILLE FEUILLES
The French name means 'a thousand leaves' and these are a classic pastry speciality, made from oblong pieces of baked puff pastry which are split twice between the 'leaves' and filled with jam and either sweetened whipped cream or confectioner's custard. The tops are covered with pink or white glacé icing, sometimes with a feathered pattern drawn in chocolate icing.

MILLET
Ancient grain or cereal grass which is an annual plant (*Panicum miliaceum*) and an important staple food in Africa and parts of the Orient. A relative of sorghum, it is a small, yellow, seed-like cereal which is easy to cultivate and grows happily both in hot climates and the more temperate climates of the West. It tastes like a cross between semolina and cornmeal when cooked, and makes a nutritious hot breakfast cereal. It is rich in fat and trace elements but has a limited

shelf-life. It is worth noting that it absorbs a vast amount of water as it cooks.

MILLET KASHA
A Russian 'porridge' made from millet, milk, a little sugar and salt.

MILT
The soft roe of fish; also, spleen of a mammal.

MIMOLETTE
The French name for a Dutch Edam-type cheese made from cows' milk and dyed dark orange with annatto.

MIMOSA
A French garnish of sieved or grated egg yolk which is said to resemble the flower.

MINAS
A Brazilian cows' milk curd cheese which is either eaten fresh or allowed to mature and turn golden-yellow. It is both a dessert and cooking cheese.

MÎNCARE CU BANE
A Romanian stew made from fried onions, diced pork, tomato juice, okra, seasonings and herbs, generally served with bread.

MINCE
A colloquial British term for finely chopped raw meat, usually beef.

MINCE (TO)
To cut or chop into very fine pieces, best carried out in a mincing machine or food processor; also, a term for minced beef, commonly used by butchers.

MINCE OF LAMB
A new and leaner British lamb product, suitable for a variety of dishes.

MINCE PIES
(Mynce Pies (Old English), Shred Pies)
Small British pies filled with dried fruit (mincemeat) and topped with a lid of pastry, eaten at Christmas. In Elizabethan times, the filling contained minced beef or lamb and was heavily spiced. They were once known as shred pies and thought to be imitations of the paste images given away on Christmas Eve.

MINCEMEAT
A typically British Christmas confection used for mince pies. In the Victorian period, and even earlier, the mincemeat used was a combination of minced beef, beef suet, apples, currants, sugar, spices, grated rind and juice of oranges and lemons, port and brandy. The meat has long been omitted from mincemeat and what is made today is a much less glorious combination of fruit (dried and fresh), sugar, suet, spices and sometimes alcohol.

MINCER
A piece of equipment fitted with cutting blades, designed to break down food finely or coarsely. Some are hand-operated, others are an optional attachment to an electric mixer.

MINEOLA
A hybrid of a grapefruit and a tangerine, with bright orange skin and a protrusion which gives it a bell-like shape. The juicy flesh has a spicy flavour. It is one of the more recent developments in the cultivation of soft-skinned, easily peeled citrus fruits.

MINERAL WATERS
Still or bubbly waters from natural sources such as spa springs, containing trace elements. Typical examples are Perrier, Vichy and Apollinaris.

MINERALS
See *Trace Elements*.

MINESTRONE
The classic soup of Italy, originally from the north of the country, made

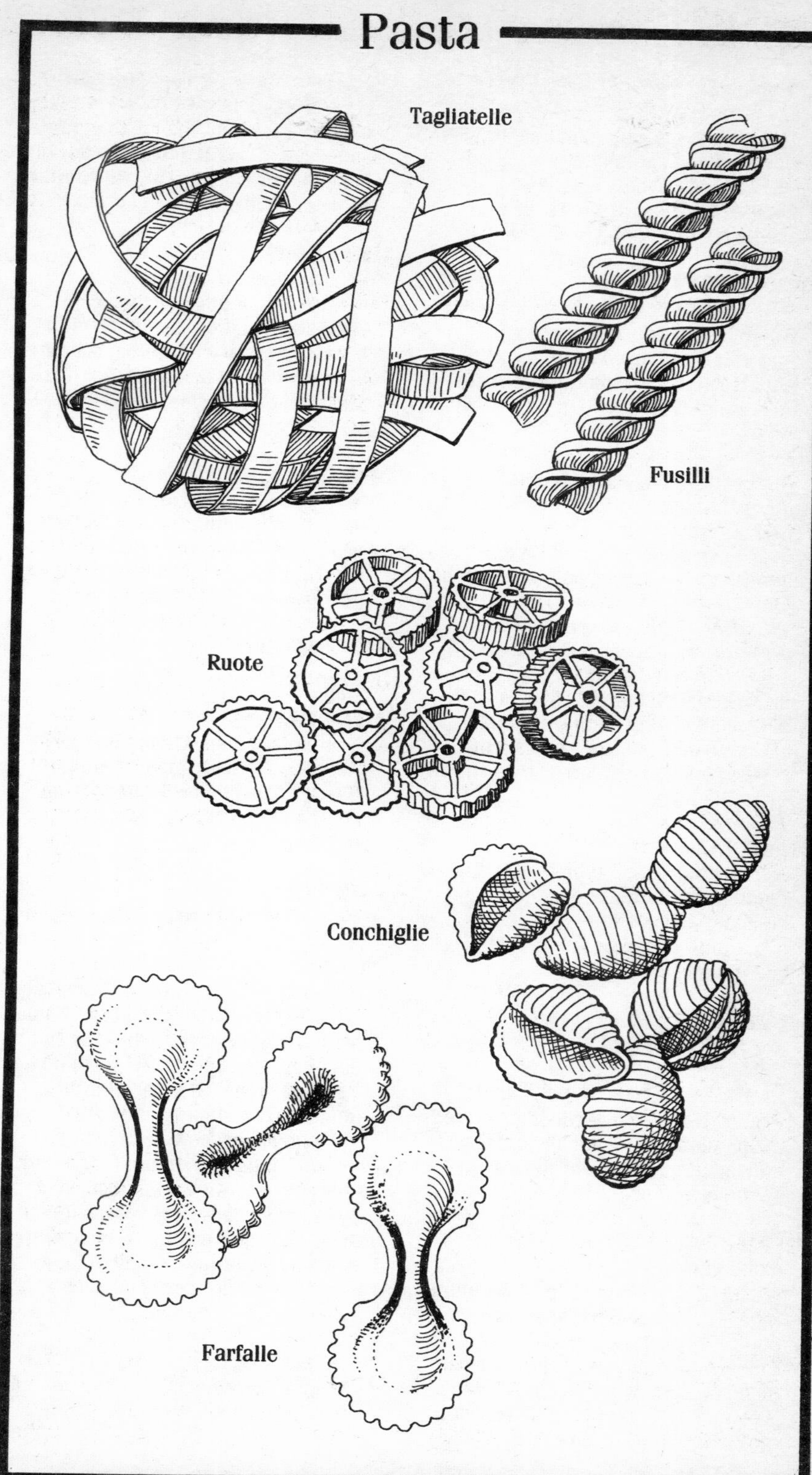
Pasta
Tagliatelle
Fusilli
Ruote
Conchiglie
Farfalle

from meat, vegetables and dried beans laced with tomatoes and herbs. Pasta is added or sometimes rice, and each portion is sprinkled with grated Parmesan cheese. Recipes for *minestrone* vary according to region.

MINNESOTA SLIM
A North American cows' milk cheese which is fairly open-textured and moist. It is coloured orange with annatto and is excellent in cooking as it melts easily.

MINT
Any of the genus *Mentha* of the family Labiateae, these herbs grow in temperate zones of the world and bear deep green leaves with an unmistakable strong and tangy scent and flavour. Spearmint (*Mentha spicata*) and peppermint (*Mentha piperita*) are the varieties most commonly used for cooking. Popular in Britain with lamb dishes, mint is also used in long summer drinks, added to new potatoes and spring vegetables and treated as a garnish for cold dishes.

MINT SAUCE
A thin, cold sauce, typically British, made from finely chopped mint, vinegar, water, sugar and seasoning. It can be served with roast lamb.

MINUTE BEEF STEAK
See *Flash-fry Steak*.

à la MIRABEAU
French term for a garnish for grilled meats comprising anchovies, olives and butter pats flavoured with anchovy essence.

MIRABELLE
(Golden Gage)
A fruit of the gage group of the plum family (*Prunus* species) and very popular as a dessert fruit in European countries. It is spherical in shape and averages a little over 2.5 cm/1 inch in diameter. The skin colour is golden-yellow. The yellowish flesh surrounding the central stone is sweet, juicy and has a pleasant scent. The name golden gage is also applied to a number of closely related hybrids with similar skin colouring.

MIREPOIX
French term for a lightly fried mixture of chopped or thinly sliced vegetables and chopped bacon or ham, seasoned with herbs. It is used in braised meat and some shellfish dishes such as *homard à l'Américaine*.

MIRIN
A very sweet rice wine from Japan, used extensively in cooking as it gives food a translucent glaze. It is used almost exclusively for culinary purposes.

MIRLITON
See *Chayote*.

MISCHLING
A mountain cheese from Western Austria with a strong and piquant flavour. The cheese is made from cows' milk and contains a few irregular-sized holes.

MISHIKAKI
East African charcoal-grilled meat.

MISO
A Japanese staple, *miso* is basically *tofu* (bean curd) which is combined with a grain (barley, wheat or rice) and impregnated with a certain type of yeast mould. It is then left to mature from months to years, depending on the type of *miso* required: light, medium (or red) or dark brown. Most Japanese have some *miso* daily; it is served for breakfast in the famous *miso* soup, used as a coating on grilled foods and thinned down and used as a dressing for vegetables.

MISO-SHIRU
A Japanese soup containing *miso*.

MIX
A commercial product, designed for making up in the home with suggested additions; examples are sauce mixes, soup mixes and cake mixes.

MIX (TO)
To combine two or more ingredients.

MIXED GRILL
A typically British dish, consisting of meat, offal and vegetables. Usually each portion includes a loin of lamb chop, a lamb's kidney, a chipolata sausage, 3–4 button mushrooms, half a tomato and a bacon rasher. Sometimes a piece of steak is also added. All the ingredients are grilled and are served garnished with potato crisps and watercress.

MIXED HERBS
Term to describe a mixture of herbs, including parsley, chives, chervil, sage, savory and basil.

MIXED SALAD
Comprising an assortment of prepared vegetables, sometimes also fruit, tossed with a suitable dressing.

MIXED SPICE
A combination of finely ground cinnamon, nutmeg, cloves, coriander, ginger, cassia and pimento.

MIXER
See *Beater*.

MIXER DRINK
A non-alcoholic soft drink (tonic water or ginger ale, for example), usually combined with a spirit to make a long drink such as gin and tonic, whisky and ginger and so on.

MIZITHRA
Greek cheese made from the whey of ewes' milk, resembling German Quark or Italian Ricotta. The same cheese is made in Cyprus under the name of Anari.

MOA LUAU
A Hawaiian speciality, boiled chicken dice mixed with cooked taro leaves, butter and seasonings.

MOA NIU
A Hawaiian speciality, boiled chicken heated in a white sauce, then packed into halved coconuts, covered with foil and baked in a tin containing a small amount of water.

MOCHA
(Moka, Mocca)
Mocha is the name of an old seaport in the Yemen through which coffee was shipped. True mocha coffee is that grown in what is now the Yemen and is very scarce, but the name is often used for certain coffee beans grown in Ethiopia from where the original Yemeni trees came. These types are ideal for making Turkish coffee. The term mocha is also used to describe a coffee-chocolate mixture for both drinks and some types of cake, but this does not mean that mocha coffee is used. In some recipes mocha is used to indicate the inclusion of coffee.

MOCK CREAM
Made during the Second World War, this consisted of a combination of thick cornflour sauce and a creamed mixture of fat and sugar. It is still made today and provides a relatively low-fat and pleasant cake filling which is also economical.

MOCK HOLLANDAISE
See *Dutch Sauce*.

MOCK TURTLE SOUP
An imitation of green turtle soup made with a calf's head.

à la MODE DE
French term meaning 'in the style of'. For example, *Tripe à la mode de Caen* means tripe cooked in the characteristic style of the town of Caen, in northern France.

à la MODERNE
French term meaning in modern style, referring to a garnish of cauliflower coated with cheese sauce, tomatoes and duchesse potatoes.

MOHINGHA
A Burmese national dish. A heavily spiced fish soup served with noodles, hard-boiled eggs, raw onions, fresh chillies and lemon.

MOHNKUCHEN
A central European speciality cake made from a base of white yeasted dough filled and topped with a sweet, rich mixture containing poppy seeds. It is served in pieces, dusted with icing sugar.

MOISTEN (TO)
To dampen ingredients slightly by the addition of liquid (sweet, savoury, milky or watery) without allowing them to become saturated.

MOLASSES
North American term for a variant of black treacle.

MOLASSES SUGAR
Deep brown in colour and closely resembling black treacle in both taste and smell, this is a sticky, unrefined sugar with fine crystals. It is rich and soft and recommended for rich fruit cakes and Christmas puddings.

MOLBO
Danish version of Edam, usually covered in red wax and made from cows' milk.

MOLE
(Molli)
A special Mexican sauce, used for meat and poultry, made from chillies, onions, garlic, tomatoes, an assortment of spices, *tortillas* which thicken, raisins which sweeten and chocolate which darkens. Sometimes almonds or sesame seeds are added.

MOLE POBLANA DE GUAJALOTE
Mexico's national dish which consists of roast turkey with *mole* sauce.

MOLLUSC
Animal belonging to the soft-bodied, hard-shelled species such as snail, oyster and mussel, with the shell outside the body, or to the family of cephalopods, such as cuttlefish and squid, with the shell inside the body.

MONASTERY
A general term to describe cheese made in monasteries by monks.

MONDSEER
An Austrian cows' milk cheese from Salzburg which is similar to Münster.

MONGOLIAN FIRE POT
(Mongolian Hot-Pot)
Related to the Swiss *fondue chinoise*, this is based on a classic Chinese dish cooked at the table in a pot with a central funnel. A burner beneath the pot keeps the contents warm.

MONKEY NUTS
See *Peanuts*.

MONKFISH
(Angler-fish)
An odd-looking, round-bodied seawater fish (*Lophius* species) with an enormous, broad mouth in a head that is almost half the size of the whole body. It has dorsal fins which resemble fishing rods above its head which lure smaller fish within reach. The colour of the back tends to match the local sea bed as part of its camouflage. It is caught all year round in the Mediterranean and the North Atlantic. Various members of the family can be up to 2 metres/6½ feet long and weigh up to 30 kg/67 lb. The tail of the monkfish is the only part marketed and the flesh is lean and white with a good texture

and a flavour reminiscent of lobster. It may be poached, baked, grilled or fried. In North America, this fish is also called goosefish.

MONOSACCHARIDES
See *Carbohydrates*.

MONOSATURATED FATTY ACIDS
These are an intermediate variety of fatty acid, liquid at room temperature and found in an extensive range of foods. Olive oil is an especially rich source.

MONOSODIUM GLUTAMATE
See *Aji-no-moto*.

MONSIEUR
(Monsieur Fromage)
A small, French double cream cheese, produced in Normandy from cows' milk. It is shaped like a tall cylinder and is fairly strong in flavour. The cheese was originally created by a farmer called Fromage at the end of the 19th century.

MONSTERA
See *Ceriman*.

MONT BLANC
A classic French dessert, made from sweetened chestnut purée topped with whipped cream.

MONTASIO
A north Italian cheese made from semi-skimmed cows' milk. It resembles Asiago.

MONTEREY JACK
(High-moisture Jack, Dry Jack)
A Californian cheese somewhat similar to Cheddar which began to be mass-produced at the beginning of this century. High-moisture Jack is a young cheese made from whole cows' milk, matured for up to 6 weeks, with a mild flavour and creamy texture. Dry Jack is a 6-month-old cheese, made from skimmed or semi-skimmed cows' milk, which is rather hard and suitable for grating. It has a more distinctive flavour than High-moisture Jack.

à la MONTMORENCY
French term for a garnish for steaks composed of artichokes, carrots and potatoes; sometimes Madeira sauce. It may also denote the inclusion of cherries, especially with duck.

MONTPENSIER
French term for a steak garnish composed of artichokes, asparagus, truffles and potatoes.

MONTRACHET
A small, cylindrical, goats' milk cheese from Burgundy in France. It is wrapped in grape or chestnut leaves and is delicate and creamy.

MOOLI
(Mouli, Muli)
See *Daikon*.

MOORFOWL
This can refer to a red grouse or any of various game birds.

MOOSE
Eaten in certain parts of the world such as Newfoundland in Canada, it should be treated exactly as beef. The membrane around the muscles, which causes the gamey odour and taste, should be peeled off before the moose meat is cooked as steaks. If roasted, the meat should be marinated for 24 hours prior to cooking.

MORAVSKÝ BOCHNIK
Czechoslovakian version of Emmental, produced from cows' milk.

MORAY EEL
A warm seawater fish (*Muraena helena*) particularly favoured in the Mediterranean. The colour varies but is always mottled. The length can be up to 1.5 metres/5 feet. The

flesh can be poached or boiled, and is often used in prepared dishes such as soup.

MORCILLA
A Spanish blood sausage and a speciality of Asturia.

MOREL
An edible mushroom (*Morchella* species) which has a short, creamy-white stem and a hollow, brownish-yellow, domed cap and grows in open land, meadows, parks or clearings in forests in the spring. It resembles a piece of sponge or light-coloured lava in appearance and collects sand or grit in the crevices; it needs careful cleaning and should be split and washed thoroughly under cold, running water. The morel is a much-prized fungus and usually served in a white sauce. It is available dried, canned and sometimes fresh.

MORELLO CHERRY
The fruit of a deciduous tree (*Prunus* species). Best-known of the sour cherries, the morello is smaller than the sweet dessert varieties and tastes too sharp to be enjoyed raw. The skin is bright red, the flesh dark red and the central stone quite small. It is much prized in northern, central and eastern Europe where it is widely used in cooking.

MORNAY SAUCE
A Béchamel sauce, flavoured with Gruyère, Parmesan or Cheddar cheese, with a little cayenne pepper and mustard. It can be served with fish dishes, egg dishes, vegetables such as cauliflower and broccoli, grilled and roast veal, and poultry.

MORÓN
A Spanish cheese, produced in Morón de la Frontera, near Seville. It is made from either goats' milk or a mixture of cows' and ewes' milk. Often left to mature for only 24 hours, it is a mild and delicate white cheese with a fresh flavour. If left to mature for longer, it is steeped in olive oil, then removed and rubbed with paprika.

MORTADELLA
(Bologna)
A very large, pale Italian sausage with a smooth texture and mild flavour, made from lightly spiced minced pork, dotted with pieces of pork fat and peppercorns. It originated in Bologna and was once based on donkey meat. The sausage should be thinly sliced and served cold as an *hors d'oeuvre*.

MORTAR
See *Pestle and Mortar*.

MORVEN
A soft cows' milk cheese from Scotland, it is similar to German Butterkäse (or Ladies' Cheese) and spiced with caraway seeds. It is produced in square blocks which have a pale yellow rind.

MOSKOVSKI
A cows' milk cheese from the USSR which is hard and full-flavoured. It is left for 3–4 months to mature.

MOTAL
A farm cheese from the USSR, produced in the Caucasus Mountains. It is made from the milk of ewes or cows and matured for 3–4 months. It is a salty cheese, due to brining.

MOULD
A container used for setting sweet or savoury jellies, blancmanges, ice creams, sorbets and so on. A mould may be completely plain, for example a pudding basin, or ornamental, and can be made from metal, porcelain, glass, earthenware or plastic.

MOULD (TO)
To shape with the hands into the form required; also, a jellied or cornflour mixture, sweet or savoury, left to set in a plain or fancy mould.

MOULES MARINIÈRES
A stew of fresh mussels cooked in white wine, garlic, onions and parsley. It is very popular in both Belgium and France and always served in deep soup plates.

MOUNTAIN CHEESE
See *Berg*.

MOUNTAIN CHICKENS
A Caribbean term for frogs' legs, usually served fried.

MOUNTAIN CRANBERRY
See *Cowberry*.

MOUNTAIN HOLLYHOCK
See *Wasebi*.

MOUNTAIN OYSTERS
(Prairie Oysters)
The testicles of the male ox which may be boiled, braised or stewed.

MOUNTED BUTTER
See *Beurre Monté*.

MOUSETRAP
British colloquial term to describe Cheddar cheese.

à la MOUSQUETAIRE
French classic term for food which is heavily spiced, so called because of the boisterous activities and behaviour of the Three Musketeers.

MOUSQUETAIRE SAUCE
(Musketeer Sauce)
A mayonnaise flavoured with chopped onion or shallot simmered in dry white wine. It can be served with cold meats.

MOUSSAKA
A Greek casserole made from layers of fried aubergine slices and seasoned minced meat, topped with white sauce enriched with eggs, sprinkled with cheese and baked until heated through and browned. *Moussaka* is served in wedges.

MOUSSE
French term for a light, foamy dessert usually containing eggs, sugar, gelatine, cream, flavouring and/or fruit, which is served cold; also a savoury poultry or fish mixture lightened with egg whites and sometimes cream, set with gelatine.

MOUSSELINE
French term for a small mousse, either sweet or savoury.

MOUSSELINE SAUCE
Hollandaise sauce to which softly whipped cream is added. It can be served with fish soufflés, poached salmon and salmon trout, poached or boiled chicken, asparagus and broccoli.

MOZZARELLA
A 400-year-old Italian cheese, traditionally made from buffaloes' milk but now more commonly produced from cows' milk. It is the classic topping for pizza but may also be served cold and sliced as part of an Italian hors d'oeuvre. It is a pale, pliable and small cheese with a delicate flavour and, when exported from Italy, is generally packed in bags of whey. The cheese is much used in traditional cookery and is characterized by its elasticity and stringiness. Imitations are made throughout Europe and North America.

MOZZARELLA AFFUMICATA
A smoked version of Italian Mozzarella cheese.

MUESLI
Originally a breakfast food developed by a Swiss health clinic and consisting of soaked oats, condensed milk, lemon juice, grated unpeeled apple and nuts. Other mixtures are now available, ready-prepared in packets, containing many different combinations of cereals, dried fruit and nuts.

MUFFINS

A traditional British North Country speciality made from rounds of white yeasted dough, cooked either on a griddle or baked in the oven. Before serving, the muffins are gently eased apart with the fingers and toasted on both sides. They are then spread with butter, pressed together again and eaten immediately. Also, North American cupcakes served warm or hot.

MUGWORT

A wild perennial herb (*Artemisia vulgaris*) which was used to add bitterness to beer before the introduction of hops. It was known to the ancients and John the Baptist is said to have worn a garland of mugwort in the wilderness as protection against pain. Mugwort has deep green leaves with downy undersides and its flowers are small, flat, round and coloured deep mauve or yellow. To counteract greasiness and prevent stomach upsets, it is recommended that dried and crushed mugwort be sprinkled very sparingly over fatty meats and poultry prior to roasting.

MUKTUK

The tough outer flesh of a whale, used by the Eskimos as food.

MULBERRY

The fruit of a deciduous tree (*Morus nigra*) of the same family as the fig and native to South-West Asia, probably from the region of ancient Persia. Because of the delicacy of the ripe fruit, the mulberry is not ideally suited to commercial usage but is widely grown in Europe and Asia for its decorative appearance and luscious berries. It is oval, up to 2.5 cm/1 inch long and looks rather like an elongated blackberry (although the actual construction of the fruit is different). The colour turns from green to purple as it ripens. The very juicy flesh has a sweet-sour taste and readily stains anything with which it comes into contact. Because the mulberry is fragile, it is best eaten on its own or gently mixed into fruit salads. There is a white version of the mulberry, but the fruit is not as good as the red; the leaves of this variety are used to feed silkworms.

MULL (TO)

To heat wine or beer with or without spices and sugar. The word 'mull' comes from the old English 'mold', meaning 'mold-ale' or ale that was served at a funeral gathering.

MULLIGATAWNY SOUP

(Mullagatawny)

Brought back to Britain from India during the latter part of the 19th century. The name is said to have come from the Tamil word *milakutanni*, meaning hot or peppery water. Less fiery than it used to be, mulligatawny soup is made from a base of chopped and fried onions, carrots and celery. It is flavoured with curry powder and simmered with stock and pieces of apple. It is finally strained and thickened with cornflour or rice flour. A small quantity of lemon juice is added to bring out all the flavours. Sometimes pieces of chicken or lamb are also included.

MUNG BEAN

A vegetable (*Phaseolus aureus*) native to Asia, probably India, and widely cultivated in most Far Eastern countries and in Australia. It is a legume which may be eaten whole as a vegetable when young, but usually the bean is extracted and dried to be used as a pulse, either whole or as a split bean. The very small and hard dried bean is usually olive-green in colour but yellow and black-skinned varieties are also grown. The flesh is yellowish and in India the mung bean is also known as green gram and golden gram. The shape is almost spherical and there is a tiny white stripe showing where the bean was joined to the pod. The mung bean is more easily digested than many other pulses and, apart from being used in soups and cooked dishes, it is also one of the most popular beans for sprouting. The mung bean must be boiled briskly for the first 15 minutes of cooking time to destroy harmful toxins found in the outer skin which can prove very dangerous to the human body.

MUNNAJUUSTO
A Finnish egg cheese made from cows' milk mixed with eggs. It is a rich golden-yellow with a mild and delicate flavour.

MUNSTER
A French cheese from Alsace, this is closely related to German Münster.

MÜNSTER
A German cows' milk cheese, originally from Alsace and still produced in France as Munster without the umlaut. It has a strong smell although the taste is mild and delicate. The colour is pale cream and the thin skin encasing the Münster is yellowy-red.

MURGH MUSALLAM
Spicy roast chicken, a speciality of Pakistan.

MURLINS
See *Alaria*.

MURTABAK
Singaporean fried pasties with a savoury meat and vegetable filling. They are a national speciality, eaten as a snack.

MUSACA
Romania's version of the Greek *moussaka*, which is topped with soured cream instead of cheese and egg sauce.

MUSAKKA
A close relation of the Greek *moussaka*, the Turkish version omits the sauce and eggs and consists of layers of fried sliced aubergines, fried onions, minced lamb or beef, sliced tomatoes and halved green peppers. It is either simmered slowly on the hob or baked in the oven and is always covered while cooking to prevent excess evaporation.

MUSCAT GRAPE
A very distinctive seedless white grape with a musky flavour. When dried, it is known as a muscatel raisin.

MUSCATEL RAISINS
Dried muscat grapes which retain the unique flavour of the fruit. They may be purchased de-seeded as individual raisins or (rarely) with seeds as a bunch on the stalk.

MUSCOVADO SUGAR
An unrefined, dark brown, soft sugar tasting and smelling slightly of treacle. The crystals are fine and the sugar is recommended for rich fruit cakes and Christmas puddings.

MUSH
North American term for a type of porridge made with cornmeal (maize meal).

MUSHIMONO
The Japanese word for steaming, a cooking technique which is widely used throughout the country.

MUSHROOM
An edible plant of the fungus family, descended from some of the earliest forms of plant life. Although many kinds are widely cultivated, it is generally the wild varieties which are most highly esteemed. In Europe alone, over 60 species are to be found in the natural state, though relatively few are available on the market. Mushrooms grow in a wide variety of shapes, sizes and colours and some knowledge is required to avoid picking unpalatable and/or poisonous fungi.

MUSHROOM KETCHUP
A dark brown sauce made from mushrooms and salt. The salt extracts the juices from the

mushrooms. The sauce is bottled and sold commercially. Some brands also contain soy sauce to increase the flavour.

MUSHROOM SAUCE
A white sauce to which sliced mushrooms are added. It can be served with dishes made from eggs, cheese, meat, poultry and fish.

MUSHY PEAS
Processed marrowfat peas, usually canned, which are bright green and coarsely mashed. They are a traditional dish in the north of England and are served with fish and chips and sometimes pies.

MUSK MELON
(Netted Melon)
A group of melons distinguished by the 'net-work' pattern found on the skin. In the USA, this type of melon is classed as a cantaloupe.

MUSLIM CURRY
See *Gaeng Mussaman*.

MUSSEL
A bivalve saltwater mollusc (*Mytilus* species) with an elongated shell which can range in colour from brown through blue to black, depending on location. The usual length of mussels in the shops is 5–7.5 cm/2–3 inches. It can be gathered in spring, autumn and winter from rocks, seaweed and pebbles to which it attaches itself. More and more mussels are being produced by methods of aquaculture where they can be reared in ideal conditions. The flesh is lean and may be eaten raw, poached, baked, steamed or fried.

MUSTARD
Originally from Europe and Asia and used since prehistoric times, mustard (*Brassica nigra* and *B. alba*) is a member of the cabbage family and grown in North America, East Africa, northern Europe and Britain. The name is said to be a corruption of mustseeds, as the seeds were processed in Britain during the Roman occupation by being steeped in must, or grape juice. It is an annual plant yielding hot-tasting seeds; the two varieties most commonly used are the black (or brown) and the white (or yellow). Mustard has a distinctive flavour, is fairly sharp and pungent but only slightly aromatic. It goes well as a condiment with pork, beef, cheese and eggs and also makes a flavoursome additive to stews, casseroles, pies, flans and in baked dishes such as savoury loaves and scones.

MUSTARD AND CRESS
See *Cress*.

MUSTARD BUTTER
Softened, whipped butter to which English or French mustard and lemon juice are added. It is shaped into a 2.5 cm/1 inch diameter roll, wrapped and refrigerated until hard, then cut into rounds of about 5 mm/ ¼ inch in thickness. These are used to garnish grilled gammon steaks, grilled beef steaks, grilled pork chops, grilled mackerel and grilled herring.

MUSTARD OIL
A deep yellow oil extracted from mustard seeds. It is much used in Indian cooking for frying and as a preservative in pickles and chutneys.

MUSTARD PICKLE
See *Piccalilli*.

MUSTARD PICKLE SAUCE
The yellow, mustard-flavoured sauce used for piccalilli.

MUSTARD SAUCE
A white sauce flavoured to taste with strong mustard and vinegar. It can be served with pork, ham and cheese dishes, fried or grilled herring or mackerel, and hot boiled tongue.

MUSTARD SEEDS
The whole seeds of the mustard plant; the dark variety (*Brassica nigra*) being much more pungent than the light (*B. alba*). These small seeds are used in pickles, sauerkraut, marinades and stocks, also in Indian cooking.

MUTTON
The fairly strongly flavoured flesh of a mature sheep.

MUTTONFISH
Type of abalone (*Haliotis naevosa*) found in Australian waters.

MYCELLA BLUE
Danish Blue cheese which is deep cream-coloured, soft, mild and smooth. It is streaked with blue-green veining and the crust is a soft, whitish-brown. It is a superior dessert cheese and made from cows' milk.

MYRTLE
A wild plant (*Myrtus communis*) common to the Mediterranean area. Its leaves and berries have a pleasing scent and both are used in marinades and stews; the leaves resemble bay leaves and the berries are like a mild version of juniper.

MYSOST
A Norwegian cheese made from the whey of cows' milk. The end-product is similar to Gjetost.

MYSUOST
An Icelandic cheese made from the whey of cows' milk. It is firm and easy to slice and resembles Norwegian Gjetost. It is light brown with a fudge-like texture and is usually shaved into thin slices.

NA'AMA
(Tomer, Horesh, Gálit, Levavit)
Brand names of Israeli processed cheeses, sold in boxes of varying weights.

NAAN
(Nan)
Indian leavened bread from the Punjab made with white flour, yeast and yogurt. It is a puffy bread, generally served with *tandoori* dishes and *kababs*.

NAARTJE
The South African version of the tangerine and one of the finest citrus fruits from that region.

NABEMONO
(Nabe-mono)
Japanese one-pot meals, cooked at the table.

NACHOS
A Mexican snack made from pieces of fried *tortilla*, topped with cheese and browned under the grill. The traditional garnish is green chilli.

NAGELKAAS
(Friese Nagelkaas)
Dutch cows' milk cheese which is firm, comparatively strong and spiced with cumin and cloves. The rind is very hard, the cheese pale and Nagelkaas is generally matured for a minimum of 6 months. The unspiced version of this is called Kanter.

NAM PLA
The national sauce of Thailand, produced from the liquid of salted and fermented fish. It is mild but very salty, brown in colour and has a thin consistency. It is used in Thai cooking in the same way that soy sauce is used in Japanese and Chinese cooking.

NAM PRIK
A very fiery chilli sauce from Thailand, used as a dip.

à la NANTAISE
French term meaning in the style of Nantes in north-west France, referring to a garnish for roasts composed of peas, potatoes and turnips.

à la NANTUA
French term meaning in the style of Nantua in eastern France, referring to a garnish for fish composed of crayfish tails and sometimes truffles.

NAPLES MEDLAR
See *Azarole*.

NAPOLEON BISCUITS
Sandwich biscuits with hollow centres filled with red jam. They are usually dusted with sifted icing sugar.

à la NAPOLITAINE
French term meaning in Neapolitan style, denoting a garnish of spaghetti in tomato sauce, grated cheese and sometimes chopped tomatoes.

à la NARBONNAISE
French term meaning in the style of Narbonne in southern France, referring to a garnish of haricot beans, aubergine and sometimes tomatoes.

NASEBERRY
See *Sapodilla*.

NASHI
See *Asian Pear*.

NASI GORENG
Indonesian fried rice which contains strips of pork, ham, finely chopped onions and sometimes garlic, seafood and seasonal vegetables. It is served with *acar* (mixed pickles), *krupuk* (prawn crackers) and fried eggs.

NASTURTIUM
(Jesuit's Cress, Indian Cress)
An annual plant (*Tropaeolum majus* or *minus*), brought to Europe by the Jesuits. The leaves, which resemble watercress in flavour, are bright green and round and, when shredded, can be added to salads. The vivid orangey-yellow flowers may also be torn up and mixed into salads or used for a garnish or decoration. The seeds can be pickled and treated as capers.

NATILLAS PIURANAS
See *Dulce de Leche*.

NATIVES
A name used to describe oysters from Kent and Essex beds, particularly those from near Colchester.

au NATUREL
French term meaning plain and without adornment; simply cooked; food and drink in their natural state.

NAVARIN
A French lamb stew with root vegetables, peas, onions, green beans, tomatoes, garlic, herbs and seasonings.

NAVEL
A sweet orange distinguished by the 'navel' on its underside which contains a small secondary fruit.

NAVY BEAN
(American Navy Bean)
See *Haricot Bean*.

NDIZI NA NYAMA
An East African beef or mutton stew containing plantains, onions, tomatoes, coconut and seasonings.

NEAPOLITAN ICE CREAM
See *Cassata*.

NEAPOLITAN SAUCE
An Italian tomato sauce from Naples flavoured with onion, basil and parsley. It can be served with meat, poultry and pasta.

NECK BONE
The curved and sectioned neck bone of chicken, duck, turkey or other fowl. It adds flavour to stock and is usually part of the giblet pack found inside a dressed bird.

NECK END OF PORK
A large, economical roasting joint near the head of the animal which may be boned and rolled prior to cooking. The joint is often cut in two to make blade of pork and spare rib of pork.

NECK OF BEEF
A tough cut of beef near the head of the animal and above the clod. The meat is tough, coarse and requires long, slow cooking such as stewing, braising and casseroling. It is often minced and used in recipes requiring fresh minced beef.

NECTAR
Supposedly a delicious drink of the Greek and Roman gods; also, a sweet liquid secreted by the nectaries of a plant that is the chief raw material of honey.

NECTARINE
The fruit of a deciduous tree (*Prunus persica nectarina*), generally accepted as being a variant of the peach with a similar history and worldwide distribution, although it is not quite as hardy and needs a slightly better climate to flourish. Usually smaller than the peach, the nectarine has a smoother, shinier skin which is an orange colour, tinted with tones of red. The firm, sweet, often perfumed flesh may be coloured from white to red and there is a large, rough, central stone. Nectarines can be divided into two main categories: the free-stone variety, where the flesh does not stick to the stone, and the cling variety, where it does. The nectarine may be eaten raw or used in fruit salads, cooked dishes (both sweet and savoury), and in preserves. An occasional nectarine may appear on a peach tree or a peach on a nectarine tree as the variation may occur in either direction.

NEEDLEFISH
See *Garfish*.

NEEDLES
Special needles are used in cooking for larding, barding and trussing. Others, resembling darning needles, are useful for stitching pieces of meat and poultry after stuffing.

NEEP
Scottish dialect term for turnip.

NEESEBERRY
See *Sapodilla*.

NETTED MELON
See *Musk Melon*.

NETTLE
(Stinging Nettle)
A plant (*Urtica dioica*) which grows in clusters as a weed in many parts of the world and is one of the members of the nettle family which is covered with stinging hairs. However, this does not prevent the young tips being carefully gathered in the spring and used as a vegetable in the same manner as spinach; boiling literally takes the sting out of the nettle. It can also be used for brewing a home-made, beer-like drink.

NEUFCHÂTEL
(Coeur, Bondon, Briquette, Carré)
A cows' milk cheese from Normandy in France. It is white in colour, creamy in texture and the skin is covered with bloom. It is relatively salty and tastes of sour cream. It is produced in small, assorted shapes (hence its many names) and is considered a very superior cream cheese.

NEW CHEESE
See *Caerphilly*.

NEW ENGLAND CLAM CHOWDER
See *Chowder*.

NEWBURG SAUCE
A rich coating sauce, based on a roux of fat and flour, made with cream and sherry, flavoured with onion and enriched with egg yolks. It can be served with hot lobster.

NIACIN
(Nicotinic Acid, Nicotinamide)
See *Vitamin B_3*.

NIB
Small pieces of any hard food but particularly almonds, hence almond nibs.

NIBBLES
Small pieces of any food, eaten between meals.

à la NIÇOISE
French term meaning in the style of Nice in southern France, denoting food cooked with tomatoes, garlic, capers, olives, lemon and sometimes French beans.

NICOTINAMIDE
See *Niacin*.

NICOTINIC ACID
Acid which is part of the vitamin B family and found especially in brewer's yeast, yeasted goods, brown flour, liver, beef, pork, white fish, cheese, eggs and potatoes. As the acid is water-soluble, some of it will be lost in the water when foods are boiled. The function of nicotinic acid in the body is to help to release the energy from carbohydrate foods.

NIGHTCAP
A hot, milky drink or an alcoholic drink taken at bedtime.

NIMONO
The Japanese word for simmering, the most widely used cooking method throughout the country.

NIOLO
A French goats' milk cheese, produced in Corsica. It is rich and strong.

NITRATE
See *Saltpetre*.

NITRE
See *Saltpetre*.

NIVA
A blue cheese from Czechoslovakia based on cows' milk. It is familiarly known as 'Roquefort'.

NOGGIN
A British measurement of approximately 150 ml/¼ pint; also used colloquially for a small alcoholic drink.

NOISETTE
French term for hazelnut and also used to describe anything nut-shaped, particularly lamb and veal, or nut-coloured.

NOISETTES OF LAMB OR PORK
A prime and boneless cut taken from the loin of lamb and pork, this is usually rolled, tied and cut into slices for grilling or frying.

NOKKEL
An unusual and heavily-spiced Norwegian cheese.

NON-CALORIFIC
Food that is either extremely low in calories or yields none at all.

NON-DAIRY
Containing no milk or milk products.

NON-FAT
Lacking fat solids or having had fat solids removed.

NONPAREILS
French term for hundreds and thousands, the multi-coloured tiny sugar strands used to decorate cakes and desserts.

NOODLE PASTRY
Similar to a strudel pastry and containing eggs. It is cut into strips or squares and cooked briefly in boiling salted water until just tender. It is then drained and used as required, either in soup or as an accompaniment to main courses.

NOODLES
Generic term to cover an assortment of flat pasta strips of varying widths, lengths and thicknesses. Some contain egg.

NOPALES
The fleshy leaves of the prickly pear cactus plant (*Opuntia* species) which are included in many Mexican dishes. After careful removal of the prickly spines, the leaves are cut up and used as a vegetable.

NORBO
A recently introduced Norwegian cows' milk cheese. It is mild, creamy, warm gold in colour and interspersed with holes.

NORFOLK APPLE CAKE
(Apple Cake)
A shortcrust pastry pie with lid, baked in a sandwich tin. The filling consists of well-stewed apples, orange marmalade and currants.

NORI
A sea vegetable (*Porphyra tenera*) which is the Japanese variety of laver. It is an excellent source of minerals and protein.

NORI-MAKE
A Japanese dish of rice and seaweed.

NORMANDY SAUCE
A velouté sauce made with fish stock and enriched with egg yolk and extra butter. It can be served with all grilled, poached or baked fish dishes.

NORTH AMERICAN SHORTCAKES
Large scones which are split, buttered and filled with fruit and sometimes whipped cream.

NORTHERN FLUKE
See *Summer Flounder*.

NORWAY HADDOCK
See *Redfish*.

NORWAY LOBSTER
See *Dublin Bay Prawn*.

NORWEGIAN OMELETTE
See *Baked Alaska*.

NORWEGIAN WHEY
The name by which the Norwegian fudge-coloured cheese, Gjetost, is known in Britain.

NOSH (A)
A colloquial term for a meal taken informally.

NOSH (TO)
A colloquial term meaning to tuck into an informal meal or spread; also, to pick at food between meals.

NOSH-UP
A colloquial term for an informal meal of generous proportions.

NOUGAT
Any sweetmeat made with nuts combined with syrup, honey, sometimes egg whites and glacé fruits such as cherries. Nougat varies throughout the world and can be white (French type) or light brown-coloured and smooth (German type). It can also be hard or soft.

NOUILLES
French term for ribbon-like strips of noodles made from pasta dough.

NOURISHMENT
This is provided by food which is nutritious and contains the essentials for growth, maintenance

and repair: protein, fat, carbohydrate, vitamins, trace elements, fibre and water.

NOUVELLE CUISINE
French term meaning literally new cooking; a recently developed French technique, now adopted almost worldwide, whereby fresh, top-quality food is lightly and delicately cooked (often undercooked), served in small portions, then garnished decoratively in the artistic style of China and Japan. Rich sauces have no rôle to play in *nouvelle cuisine*, nor do butter, cream and alcohol though these ingredients are sometimes used very sparingly; much depends on the chef.

NOZZLE
An open-ended, cone-shaped tube used with a piping bag. There are many types of small nozzles in assorted shapes for piping cake icings and larger ones for vegetable purées and other mixtures of similar texture.

NÜDELN
German, Austrian and German-Swiss word for egg noodles.

NUOC MAM
The basic Vietnamese sauce made from the liquid of salted and fermented anchovies.

NUSSTORTE
A Central European speciality cake containing ground almonds or walnuts and breadcrumbs. It is usually filled and coated with whipped cream or butter cream.

NUT BRITTLE
See *Brittle*.

NUT MEAL
Finely ground nuts, such as almonds and hazelnuts, used in some northern and central European *torten*.

NUT YOGURT
A sweetened yogurt which contains chopped nuts.

NUTCRACKER
British Cheddar cheese with walnuts.

NUTMEG
The seed of a peach-like fruit which grows on a tall, tropical evergreen tree (*Myristica fragrans*) with leaves like those of the rhododendron. Available whole for grating or already ground, the flavour is exotic, sweet and unmistakable. It is frequently used in Italian dishes and also in milk puddings, baked goods, egg custards, some sauces, marinades and occasionally meat stews and casseroles.

NUTRIA
(Nutria Rat)
A vegetarian animal, which is considered a luxury meat in the Louisiana Bayou region of North America. It is generally cooked in a highly flavoured tomato sauce.

NUTRITION
The science of correct feeding and how the various food nutrients work in the human body.

NUTRITIONAL NEEDS
(RDI, Recommended Daily Intake)
Often expressed as recommended daily intake (RDI), this refers to essential nutrients required by the body to function satisfactorily and includes protein, fat, carbohydrates, vitamins, minerals, fibre and water. The amounts needed vary from person to person.

NUTRITIONIST
Someone who specializes in the study of food and nutrition.

NUTRITIVE RATIO
The ratio of digestible protein to other nutrients in a foodstuff.

NUTS
Nuts are of two main basic types: either seeds, such as walnuts, or tubers, such as peanuts. All nuts have an outer shell enclosing a kernel and are rich in protein and fat (the exception is the chestnut which is starchy and not as valuable nutritionally as other nuts). The nuts most widely used worldwide are sweet almonds, Brazils, cashews, coconuts, chestnuts, hazelnuts, peanuts, pecans and walnuts. The term nut is also used for a small amount of food, for example, a nut of butter.

NUTTY
Having the flavour and/or consistency of nuts.

NYANYA CREOLE
A Gambian dish, made from oysters stewed with onions, green peppers, tomatoes, oil, garlic and chilli and served with boiled rice or crusty French bread.

OAK LEAF LETTUCE
With bronze-green, oak leaf-shaped leaves, this is a decorative variety of lettuce which tastes similar to cos, though it is slightly more bitter.

OAT FLAKES
(Rolled Oat Flakes)
See *Porridge Oats*.

OAT FLOUR
Flour produced from oats which is often combined with wheat flour and used for making bread and other kinds of baking.

OATCAKES
Traditional Scottish biscuits based on oatmeal. They are unsweetened and may be eaten with sweet or savoury foods.

OATEN
Anything made from or containing oats or oatmeal.

OATMEAL
(Scottish Oatmeal)
Made from husked grain and available in three types: coarse, medium and fine. Individual recipes stipulate which one to use.

OATS
An annual cereal grass (*Avena sativa*), apparently first cultivated in Bronze-Age Europe and now grown extensively in Europe, Asia and throughout America. Oats are one of the richest sources of soluble fibre, which is said to help the body break down excess cholesterol in the bloodstream. They are also a protein and energy food and available in six main forms: whole grain or groats, jumbo oats, rolled oats, crushed oats, oatmeal and oat flour.

OBERS
(Schlag Obers)
A colloquial Austrian term for whipped cream.

OBESITY
A term to describe excessive overweight, due either to an unsuitable diet or medical problems.

OCEAN PERCH
North American term for redfish.

OCTOPUS
A seawater mollusc (*Octopus vulgaris*) of the cephalopod family with eight 'arms'. The colour varies with location and circumstance from almost transparent, when trying to evade an enemy, to the normal bluey shades of some Pacific and Indian Ocean species. The Mediterranean and Atlantic varieties of octopus are usually caught at 30 cm–1 metre/

12–39 inches. There are many related species throughout the world in tropical and sub-tropical waters and the main season is during the summer months when the octopus moves inshore. The tentacles are generally the preferred part of the flesh and may be poached, steamed, baked or fried.

ODALSOST
An Icelandic cows' milk cheese which resembles Emmental.

OELENBERG
(Trappiste d'Oelenberg)
A mild and supple French cows' milk cheese, made by Alsatian monks in the Oelenberg monastery. It is used for both cooking and eating.

OEUFS À L'AGENAISE
A French dish of eggs fried in goose fat with aubergines and onions.

OEUFS À LA COQUE
French term for soft-boiled eggs, eaten from the shell.

OEUFS À LA NEIGE
French term for floating islands.

OEUFS BROUILLÉS
French term for scrambled eggs.

OEUFS EN COCOTTE
Eggs baked in a greased cocotte or ramekin dish.

OEUFS FLORENTINE
A French interpretation of an Italian-style dish, consisting of freshly poached eggs on a bed of spinach and coated with cheese sauce. The dish is sprinkled with cheese, and sometimes breadcrumbs, then browned under a hot grill and eaten with hot toast.

OEUFS FRITES
French term for fried eggs.

OEUFS MOLLETS
French term for boiled eggs, which are usually served shelled and eaten like poached eggs. The consistency is between a soft- and hard-boiled egg, the white being fairly firm and the yolk soft.

OEUFS POCHÉS
French term for poached eggs.

OEUFS SUR LE PLAT
(Shirred Eggs)
Eggs baked in a well-greased, shallow, heatproof dish.

OFF
Term to describe any food or drink that has gone bad.

OFFAL
Derived from the term 'off-fall', offal describes those parts of the animal which are cut away from the carcase when it is prepared for sale. The parts from inside the carcase include liver, kidneys, heart, sweetbreads, brains and tongue. Parts from outside the carcase include pig's head, ox cheek, calf's feet, pig's trotters, cowheel and oxtail. Also classified as offal are animal blood, bone marrow, intestines and tripe.

OGEN MELON
A variety of melon of the cantaloupe type developed in Israel. The skin is mottled greeny-yellow and grooved to give a wide panelled effect. The flesh is pale green, fragrant, sweet and juicy. It is excellent eaten on its own.

OGGY
Cornish term for a pasty.

OGOPOGO APPLE DUMPLINGS
Canadian apple dumplings, based on an old English recipe. Squares of pastry are folded over the apple filling to resemble envelopes, which are coated with syrup and baked. They are named after the strange monster many people claim to have seen in Okanagan Lake, which runs down the famous apple-growing valley in British Columbia.

OI GIMCHI
A Korean dish of radish-stuffed cucumbers which are pickled with ginger, garlic, chillies and salt.

OIL
A grease or fat, of animal or vegetable origin, which is liquid at room temperature. See also entry for Fats and Oils.

OIL PASTRY
A type of shortcrust pastry made with oil instead of fat, and recommended for use in savoury dishes. It is fairly delicate and should be rolled out between two sheets of non-stick parchment paper.

OILY FISH
The flesh of a fish is considered to be oily if it has a fat content of over 6%.

OISEAUX SANS TÊTES
'Birds without heads', a Belgian and Dutch version of beef olives.

OKA
A cows' milk cheese limited to the Montreal area of Canada and made near the town of Oka. It was first produced just over a hundred years ago by French monks in their monastery in Quebec. High demand has made this cheese comparatively rare. It resembles Port-Salut.

OKANAGAN SAVOURY TOMATOES
A speciality of British Columbia in Canada, tomatoes stuffed with fried onions, flour, milk, herbs, spices, grated Cheddar cheese and breadcrumbs.

OKASHI
The Japanese term for sweets and desserts.

OKRA
(Ochro)
A vegetable which is the fruit of a tall plant (*Hibiscus esculentus*) of the same family as cotton and hollyhock. It is native to Africa and widely grown in tropical and sub-tropical regions round the world. It grows as a pod, tapering to a point at one end. The pod is light or dark green in colour and, in most varieties, has five to seven ridges running lengthwise. Okra is best eaten when young and fresh and the size can vary with kind and country of production from about 7.5 cm/ 3 inches to the 30-cm/ 12-inch giant known in North America as Chinese okra. The okra pod is very mucilaginous inside and each country has different ways of either removing the stickiness or using it to advantage as, for example, in Creole gumbo dishes in which the vegetable is treated as a thickener. Okra may be cooked as a vegetable or used in many ethnic dishes. This vegetable is known as *bindi* in Hindi and *bamiya* in Arabic.

OLALLIEBERRY
A fruit which is a cross between a loganberry and a youngberry. It is black in colour and mostly grown in the south-west of the USA.

OLD HEIDELBERG
A fairly small North American cows' milk cheese, produced in Illinois. It resembles Liederkranz cheese.

OLD-SMOKEY HAM
A term used to describe commercially produced ham, which owes its individual character and smoky flavour to the special curing and smoking techniques employed by the manufacturer.

OLEIC ACID
Fatty acid, capable of making fats soft or liquid. Lard, for example, contains oleic acid and is considered a soft fat when compared with beef fat. Oleic acid is also found in olive and other oils.

OLENDA
The Italian version of Dutch Edam.

OLIVE

The small, firm-textured and bitter-tasting fruit of the evergreen tree (*Olea europaea*) which is widely cultivated in the warmer parts of Europe and in Africa and Asia. The majority of olives are used in the production of olive oil, but olives are also eaten as a cocktail snack, an appetizer and used in various savoury dishes and salads. The green fruit turns black when fully ripe and both black and green olives are available, whole or pitted, and may be purchased loose, in jars or vacuum-packed. Green olives are available as stuffed olives, pitted and stuffed with pieces of pimiento or anchovy.

OLIVE OIL

A golden-green oil with a rich and fruity flavour. The best is known as virgin oil and comes from the first pressings of small, ripe black olives from Mediterranean and Balkan countries. In Latin countries, it is used for general cooking and frying purposes; in other areas, it is generally reserved for salad dressings and mayonnaise. The oil is a good source of monosaturated fatty acids.

OLLA PODRIDA

A rich, highly seasoned Spanish stew containing assorted meats, poultry, game birds, sausages and vegetables.

OLMÜTZER

An Austrian cows' milk cheese, similar to German Hand cheese. It is quite strong and sometimes spiced with caraway. The aroma is potent.

OLOMOUC

(Olomoucký)

The Czechoslovakian version of Olmützer cheese.

OMELETTE

See *Plain Omelette*.

OMELETTE PAN

(Omelet Pan)

A frying pan made in heavy metal with a thick base and curved sides which is ideally suited to the making and serving of omelettes. Before using for the first time, it is advisable to prove the pan to prevent the egg mixture from sticking. If possible, keep the pan only for omelettes and wipe, rather than wash, after every use. Omelette pans with non-stick coatings should never be proved.

OMELETTE SOUFFLÉ EN SURPRISE

See *Baked Alaska*.

OMNIVORE

One who feeds on both animal and vegetable substances.

ONIGIRI

Japanese filled rice balls, often wrapped in toasted seaweed. They are a typical picnic food and take the place of western sandwiches.

ONION

A vegetable which is a member (*Allium cepa*) of the same family as garlic, chives and leeks, believed to be native to Asia and now growing in wild and cultivated varieties all over the world. It is one of the oldest and most widely used flavouring plants; the Ancient Egyptians placed it as an offering to their gods. Most types of onion begin as tender green shoots which develop into bulbous swellings at or near ground level. When lifted at an early stage, often to thin out the crop and before the bulb is properly formed, it is sold as a spring or salad onion. The onion differs from most vegetables in that it is edible at all stages up to maturity. The fully grown onion consists of tightly-packed and multi-layered head or bulb with an outside, papery covering which is either pale bronze, yellow or light violet-red in colour. The ripe onion, usually pale cream inside, may be cooked whole and eaten as a

Pastry and Pies

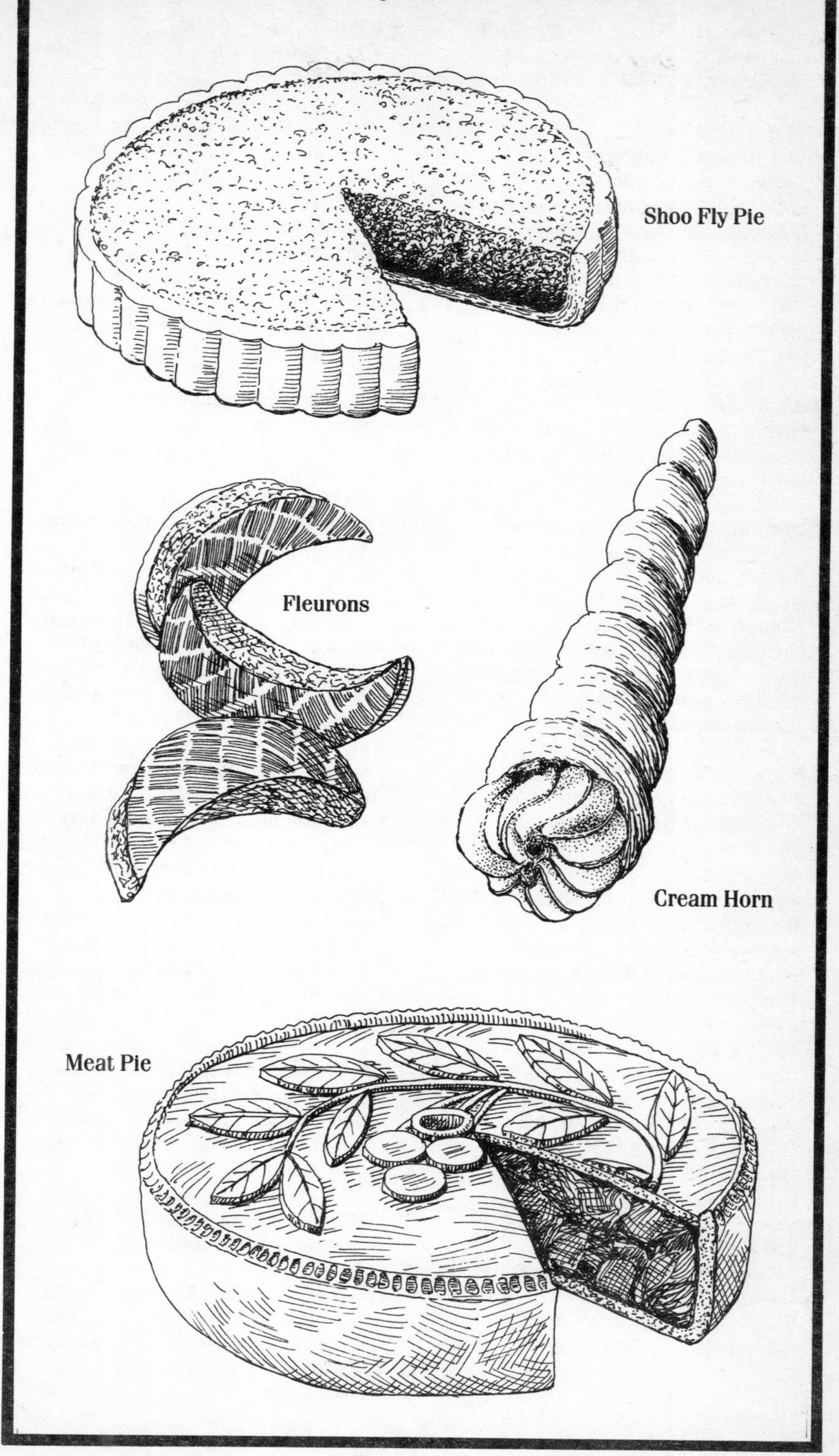

Shoo Fly Pie

Fleurons

Cream Horn

Meat Pie

vegetable on its own, or used in innumerable savoury dishes either as a flavouring or main ingredient.

ONION SAUCE
A white sauce flavoured with chopped, boiled onions and a little nutmeg. It can be served with tripe (as in the British dish of tripe and onions), grilled and roast lamb, boiled bacon and grilled liver. For extra flavour, half the milk may be replaced with the water in which the onions were cooked.

OOLONG
One of the three main kinds of tea produced from the original green leaves, oolong is halfway between green and black teas as it is only partially fermented. It is greeny-brown in colour and has a full flavour, more subtle than that of black tea but fuller than green tea. Oolong tea is produced in China in the province of Fujian (Fukien) and on the island of Taiwan (Formosa). The finest Formosa oolongs are among the best teas in the world.

OPEN SANDWICH
Scandinavian in character and a speciality of Denmark, these sandwiches are made without a top slice of bread. The single slice is spread with butter or margarine and the food and garnishes arranged on top in a decorative manner. To facilitate eating, knives and forks should be provided.

OPEN TABLE
(Cold Table)
This is the same as Sweden's *smörgåsbord*, Russia's *zakuski*, Denmark's *koldebord*, Norway's *koldtbord* and Finland's *voleipäpöytä*.

à l'OPÉRA
French term meaning in opera style, referring to a garnish of chicken livers, duchesse potatoes and asparagus tips.

OPOSSUM
(Possum)
A small marsupial, eaten in certain areas of North America, but especially in the Louisiana Bayou region.

ORANGE
(Sweet Orange)
The fruit of an evergreen tree (*Citrus sinensis*) native to South-East Asia but now cultivated in many of the warmer parts of the world, particularly in the countries bordering on the Mediterranean. The orange is globe-shaped or slightly oval and can be 5–10 cm/ 2–4 inches in diameter. The skin is a bright orange colour, consisting of the outer, orange-coloured rind and an inner lining of whitish pith. The flesh is naturally divided into segments contained in thin membranes and is sweet, juicy and rich in vitamin C. In each segment a variable number of seeds (pips) are normally found. Most commonly eaten as a dessert fruit, the orange is very versatile and may be used raw in salads and in many cooked dishes, both sweet and savoury. Orange juice is a very refreshing and nutritious drink and a substantial proportion of oranges are grown especially for the production of orange juice. Sweet oranges may be used in making marmalade, either by themselves or with the Seville or bitter orange.

ORANGE ESSENCE
Culinary orange essence, in concentrated form, is available in small bottles and is used in cakes, desserts and confectionery.

ORANGE PASSION FRUIT
See *Sweet Granadilla*.

ORANGE PEKOE
One of the larger grades of black tea leaf. The term is also used for a particular large-leaf, scented China tea.

ORANGE SAUCE
English term for Bigarade sauce.

ORANGEADE
A sweetened, non-alcoholic drink made from a mixture of orange juice with plain or carbonated water.

OREGANO
(Wild Marjoram)
With origins in ancient Rome, oregano (*Origanum vulgare*) is both a wild and cultivated perennial herb which is found throughout Europe and Mexico. The flavour of the green leaves is strong and pungent and particularly suited to Italian and Spanish dishes.

ORGANIC
This term describes any food or drink product which has been produced without chemically formulated fertilizers or pesticides.

ORGEAT
A non-alcoholic syrup made with almonds or barley and scented with rose or orange flower water. It is used in cocktails.

à l'ORIENTALE
French term meaning in Eastern style, referring to a garnish of rice, tomatoes and sometimes peppers.

ORKNEY
A Scottish cows' milk cheese, produced in island creameries. It is a firm cheese resembling Dunlop and is sometimes smoked. It is either left white or coloured orange with annatto.

à l'ORLÉANAISE
French term meaning in the style of Orléans, south of Paris, referring to a garnish of braised chicory and potatoes.

ORMER
(Earshell, Sea Ear)
The European version (*Haliotis tuberculata*) of the Pacific abalone, this is a single-shelled mollusc found mainly in the Mediterranean. The shell may be up to 10 cm/4 inches long and is shaped rather like an ear. The edible part is the white 'foot' which is lean and may be eaten raw or fried. Ormers are also found in Britain's Channel Islands.

ORRECCHIETTE
The Italian name of these small shell-like pasta shapes means 'little ears'.

ORT
A small scrap of food left after a meal.

ORTANIQUE
A cross between an orange and a tangerine (mandarin), developed in Jamaica and now a speciality of that country. Ortaniques vary in size and the skin colour is pale orange. There may be slight blemishes on the thin skin which is tough, scaly, shiny and sometimes difficult to peel. The flesh is sweet and very juicy, divided into segments like an orange and containing up to 10 pips. It may be eaten as a dessert fruit or used in fruit salads and sweet and savoury dishes.

ORTOLAN
A small brown and greyish-green European wild bunting (*Emberiza hortulana*), a bird measuring about 15 cm/6 inches in length. It is much appreciated by epicures, particularly in France, and is treated in exactly the same way as quail.

ORZO
Rice-shaped pasta, used in soups.

OSSO BUCCO
An Italian speciality from Lombardy which consists of shin of veal, cut into slices, cooked in a tomato and wine sauce with vegetables and stock. Each serving is sprinkled with a mixture of parsley, crushed garlic and finely grated lemon peel. The traditional accompaniment is *risotto alla Milanese*.

OTAHEITE-APPLE
See *Hog Plum*.

OTAK-OTAK
A chopped raw fish mixture, containing herbs, spices, onions, coconut and eggs, from Malaysia, which is steamed in banana leaves or foil.

ÓVÁR
(Ovari)
A Hungarian cows' milk cheese with a supple, yellow texture and reddish-brown rind. It resembles Tilsit.

OVEN
A box-like cavity designed for cooking food which may be heated by solid fuel, oil, gas or electricity.

OVEN-READY CHICKEN
A cleaned and trussed chicken, ready to go into the oven.

OVERDO (TO)
To cook too much.

OVOLI
Small, ball-shaped Mozzarella cheese which the Italians sometimes eat with Parma ham.

OX
A domestic species of bovine mammal.

OX BRAINS
A little less delicate than calf's brains, a set of two will serve two people.

OX CHEEK
A rich, gelatinous and immensely tasty cut of beef offal which can be made into soups, stews and casseroles. It needs careful cleaning and long, slow cooking.

OX KIDNEY
A large, strongly flavoured, dark red kidney which has a core of fat running through the middle. It is a tough offal and is best used in stews, casseroles, hot-pots and braised dishes, when long, slow cooking is required. Ox kidney usually forms part of the steak and kidney mixture used for traditional British pies and puddings. To remove some of the strong flavour, ox kidney should be soaked for about 45 minutes in warm salted water to which a little vinegar has been added. About 100 g/4 oz per person should be allowed.

OX LIVER
Smooth and glossy, deep brown in colour with a reddish sheen, ox liver is a high-protein food with very little fat. It is a very important source of iron in the diet and also contains vitamin A. Although ox liver is considered less of a delicacy than liver from other animals, it is excellent in stews, braised dishes, casseroles and coarse *pâtés*. A reasonable amount to allow is 100 g/4 oz per person and, when choosing it, pieces with large veins and tubes should be avoided. Ox liver is usually sold sliced to the thickness requested by the customer. To counteract its strong flavour, ox liver should be soaked in milk for about 1 hour prior to cooking.

OX TONGUE
The largest of all domestic animal tongues, weighing about 3 kg/6½ lb, ox tongue may be bought fresh or already brined. When cooked, it has a soft and velvety texture, a rich flavour and is traditionally served hot with mustard or Madeira sauce. It may also be served cold with salad or thinly sliced and used as a sandwich filling. Tongue is a first-class protein food but contains more fat than other offal such as heart and liver.

OXALIC ACID
An acid found in spinach, rhubarb and some leafy green vegetables. The acid appears to serve no useful

purpose and is even thought to aggravate rheumatic conditions. When oxalic acid links with calcium in the body, it forms insoluble salts which cannot be absorbed.

OXFORD

A British cheese which is a cross in texture and flavour between Cheddar and Cheshire. A smoked variety is available.

OXFORD JOHN

Lamb steaks cut from the leg, usually fried with onion, thyme and parsley, then served with brown gravy flavoured with port and lemon juice. Oxford John is a speciality of the Oxfordshire area of England.

OXFORD SAUCE

A cold sauce made by heating port, redcurrant jelly, orange juice, lemon juice, spices and seasonings. The mixture is then strained, allowed to cool and served with game. It is similar to cold Cumberland sauce.

OXFORD SAUSAGES

Skinless sausages made from minced pork and veal mixed with suet, white breadcrumbs, mixed herbs, lemon peel and seasonings. The meat mixture is shaped into sausages, fried until golden and served hot.

OXTAIL

Oxtail is sold already skinned and cut into joints of various sizes. Each tail weighs about 1.5 kg/3 lb and there should be a good proportion of red meat to fat. The tail should be cooked within 24 hours of purchase and it can be braised, stewed or made into soup. Oxtail is high in protein but, because of the high ratio of bone to meat, one tail will serve no more than 3–4 people.

OXTAIL SOUP

A rich brown soup made from a *mirepoix* of vegetables, herbs, water, oxtail and beef. The soup is strained and thickened, then flavoured with dry sherry. Often pieces of cooked oxtail are added.

OYSTER

A bivalve mollusc (*Ostreidae* family) with a shell which is basically fan-shaped but which grows to fit its environment; the colour also varies according to the environment. The average length when harvested is about 10 cm/4 inches but the Pacific or Japanese oyster (*Crassostrea gigas*) can be as long as 30 cm/ 12 inches. Harvesting takes place all year with the heaviest catch in the winter months and, apart from widespread natural oyster beds, commercial hatcheries are increasing to meet growing demand. The meat is lean and rich and is customarily eaten raw but may also be poached, baked or fried. Three of the main species of oyster are the Pacific, the European flat (*Ostrea edulis*) and the Portuguese (*Crassostrea angulata*).

OYSTER BACON

A cut from the end of the long back. It is a round and chubby joint, well-endowed with fat and may be boiled or cut into rashers.

OYSTER MUSHROOM

An edible mushroom (*Pleurotus ostreatus*) which grows from autumn to spring, temperatures permitting, on deciduous trees. The shape is somewhat oyster-like and the cap, when young, is a delicate blue-grey colour. The short stalk is on one side of the cap, joining it to the tree. When cooked, the oyster mushroom has a distinctive, slightly fishy flavour and it is now cultivated commercially to meet demand.

OYSTER OF VEAL

A prime cut of veal, from the forequarter of the calf, which is suitable for roasting. It is generally boned and rolled prior to cooking.

OYSTER PLANT

(Vegetable Oyster)
See *Salsify*.

OYSTER SAUCE
Soy sauce flavoured with oysters, a popular additive to Chinese dishes and also a table condiment.

OYSTERS ROCKEFELLER
A speciality from New Orleans in the USA, oysters in the half shell are topped with a savoury breadcrumb mixture flavoured with Pernod. The oysters are baked quickly in a hot oven and served as an appetizer.

PAAN
Indian breath fresheners which are taken after a meal.

PABELLÓN CARAQUEÑO
Venezuela's national dish, a mixture of steak, rice, black beans and plantains or bananas. Each portion is topped with a fried egg.

PABULUM
Formal term for food, more frequently referring to intellectual sustenance.

PACA
A common edible rodent of northern South America which has a brown coat spotted with white. The hide is used locally to make leather.

PACIFIC COD
A round-bodied seawater fish (*Gadus macrocephalus*) closely related to the Atlantic cod. The back is brown to grey, lighter and mottled on the sides and shading to light grey to white on the underside. The average length is 40–60 cm/16–24 inches and the weight 2–4 kg/4½–9 lb. It is caught all year round in the seas off north-west America from Alaska to northern California, with main catches in the winter months. The flesh is lean and white and the fish may be poached, steamed, baked, fried or grilled.

PACIFIC DOGFISH
See *Spur Dog*.

PACIFIC HALIBUT
See *Halibut*.

PACIFIC MACKEREL
See *Mackerel*.

PACIFIC OYSTER
(Japanese Oyster)
See *Oyster*.

PACIFIC THREAD HERRING
See *Atlantic Thread Herring*.

PACKET JELLY
See *Jelly Cubes*.

PADDY RICE
Freshly harvested rice with very hard and arid cellulose husks.

PADDY STRAW MUSHROOM
(Straw Mushroom)
An edible mushroom (*Volvariella volvacea*) grown in China on beds of straw. It is mainly available dried or canned and is recommended for use in Chinese and Japanese dishes.

PAELLA
A famous Spanish dish which is a savoury mixture of rice, vegetables, chicken and shellfish. Saffron is often included as a seasoning and colouring agent.

PAGLIA E FIENO
Fairly slim green and yellow noodles, sold mixed in a packet.

PAIMI
See *Conkies*.

PAIN AU SUCRE
A French-Canadian speciality, made from bread toasted on one side only, the untoasted side then sprinkled

thickly with maple sugar and grilled until the sugar half-melts. The toast is served coated with cream.

PAIN D'ÉPICE
French term for well-spiced gingerbread.

PAIN FIG BANANE
Caribbean banana bread containing local spices including cinnamon, nutmeg, ginger and cloves. It is cut like a cake and is a speciality of St Lucia.

PAIN PERDU
The literal translation from the French name is 'lost bread' and refers to slices of bread which are dipped in a mixture of beaten eggs, milk (often evaporated) and vanilla, fried until brown on both sides, then served with icing or caster sugar and either syrup or honey. In North America, it is known as French toast and is served for breakfast or supper.

PAK-CHOI
(Chinese Leaves)
A vegetable (*Brassica chinensis*) which is a member of the cabbage family native to China, now widely cultivated round the world. It looks rather like a bunch of white celery, intermingled with dark green and fluted cabbage leaves. It may be used in salads, cooked as a vegetable or used in savoury dishes. This vegetable should not be confused with its very close relative, Chinese cabbage, which is also sometimes called Chinese leaves; although with some varieties the differences are small. In North America *pak-choi* is known as *bok choy*.

PAKORAS
(Pakorhas)
Indian vegetable fritters made from batter containing besan or chickpea flour. They are deep-fried and served hot with chutney.

PALAČINKY
A Czechoslovakian national dish, pancakes made from a light batter and filled with grated chocolate, apricot jam or a sweetened cream cheese mixture containing sultanas.

PALATSCHINKEN
Austrian pancakes served in the same way as French crêpes.

PALE BACON
See *Green Bacon*.

PALETTE KNIFE
A wide, flexible, blunt-bladed knife with a round end which is used for removing foods from trays and containers and for smoothing icings and toppings.

PALM HEART
See *Cabbage Palm*.

PALM KERNEL OIL
(Palm Butter)
The kernels of tropical palms yield a white oil which, like coconut oil, is sometimes used in the manufacture of margarine. It is free from fatty acids and is known in some parts of Africa as palm butter.

PALM OIL
A fatty substance from the fruit of several palms, most of which are grown in West Africa. It is used mainly for soap and candle-making.

PALM SUGAR
(Jaggery)
A dark brown sugar made from the sap of Oriental palm trees; generally coconut and palmyrah. It is sold in flat round cakes or lumps and is available from Oriental food shops.

PALMIERS
French sweet biscuits, shaped like palm leaves, made from puff pastry.

PALMITIC ACID
(Stearic Acid)
Acid responsible for the firmness of beef and lamb fats.

PAN
A term generally used for a metal cooking vessel which may be round, oval or rectangular and may have either two small handles, one long one or, in some cases, none.

PANACHÉ (PANACHÉE)
French term for multi-coloured, applied to a salad, a garnish of flageolets mixed with French beans (for entrées) or assorted ice creams.

PANADA
A Spanish word from the Latin *panis* (bread). Originally, panada was a pulp made from bread and water but it was later refined by the French into a roux of fat and flour to make a white sauce which is double the thickness of a coating sauce. In this form it is used as a binding ingredient and is the basis of soufflés and croquettes.

PANAMA ORANGE
See *Calamondin Orange*.

PANCAKE PAN
A heavy-based frying pan with shallow, sloping sides which is ideally suited to the baking and serving of pancakes or *crêpes*. Before using for the first time, it is advisable to prove the pan to prevent the mixture from sticking. If possible, keep the pan only for pancakes and wipe, rather than wash, after every use. Pancake pans with non-stick coatings should never be proved.

PANCAKE ROLL
See *Chinese Egg Roll*.

PANCAKES
Thin, flat cakes cooked in a frying pan and usually made from a pouring batter. They may contain sweet or savoury fillings. In Britain pancakes are traditionally served simply with lemon juice and sugar on Shrove Tuesday.

PANCETTA
Italian term for belly of pork, cured with salt and spices, then rolled up like a large sausage and eaten either raw in very thin slices or cut more thickly and used in cooking.

PANDORO
(Pandolce)
A sweet, yeasted bread and a speciality of Verona in Italy.

PANDOWDY
An old-fashioned American dessert made by covering stewed sliced apples with pastry, then baking the dish until golden.

PANEER
(Panir)
Indian milk curds made from boiling milk which has been curdled with the addition of lemon juice. The curds are used to make a variety of Indian desserts and also feature in some vegetable dishes.

PANER
French term meaning to coat food with breadcrumbs.

PANETIÈRE
French term for a baked pastry case filled with pre-cooked food or a small bird and served hot.

PANFORTE
A rich Italian cake which is a speciality of Sienna. It contains glacé fruits and nuts.

PANNARONE
(Pannerone)
An Italian cows' milk cheese, produced in Lombardy. It is closely related to Gorgonzola but contains no blue mould. The cheese is rich, soft and creamy.

PANNETONE
An Italian yeasted cake from Milan containing nuts, sultanas and spices.

PANOCHA
(Panoche)
A coarse Mexican sugar.

PANSOTTI
(Pansoti, Panzerotti)
Triangular-shaped pockets of pasta, stuffed with meat, offal or cheese.

PANSY
Plant (*Viola tricolor*) with multicoloured, edible flowers which are highly decorative and subtle-tasting.

PANTHE KAUKSWE
A mild Burmese chicken curry containing onions, garlic, chillies, coconut milk and turmeric. It is served with noodles, hard-boiled eggs, sliced fresh onions, wedges of lemon and prawn crackers.

PANTOTHENIC ACID
See *Vitamin* B_5.

PANZEROTTI
See *Pansotti*.

PAP
Soft food, for example, bread soaked in milk or mashed potatoes mixed with gravy. This type of food is often given to invalids.

PAPADUM
(Pappadam, Pappadum, Poppadom, Puppadom)
A very thin, round pancake made from lentil flour which is fried briefly until it is crisp. Papadums are served as an appetizer or, more traditionally, are crumbled over curries.

PAPAIN
An enzyme found in the juice of unripe pawpaw. It quickens the breakdown of proteins to simpler compounds and is used as a tenderizer for meat.

PAPAYA
See *Pawpaw*.

PAPER FRILL
See *Frill*.

en PAPILLOTE
(Papillote)
French term for any food baked in greaseproof paper or aluminium foil.

PAPPARDELLE
Wide egg noodles, usually with crimped edges.

PAPRIKA
A mild spice powder made from the pods of the red capsicum (*Capsicum annuum*), better known as the red (sweet) pepper, an annual plant grown in Hungary, southern Europe and North America, where they are known as bell peppers. Bright orange in colour, paprika is always added to goulash and other Hungarian dishes and is also very popular in dishes from central and eastern Europe and the Balkans. It is widely used as a garnish, sprinkled over savoury dishes which benefit from such a splash of colour.

PAPRIKA BUTTER
See *Hungarian Butter*.

PAPRIKÁS CSIRKE
A rich Hungarian chicken stew containing onions, peppers, tomatoes, paprika, seasonings and soured cream. It is usually served with pasta or the Hungarian *tarhonya*.

PARADISE CAKE
See *Carrot Cake*.

PARADISE NUT
(Sapucaya Nut)
South American nut (*Lecythis sabucajo*) which resembles the Brazil but has a more delicate taste and a thinner shell.

PARASOL MUSHROOM
(Umbrella Mushroom)
An edible mushroom (*Lepiota procera*) which grows during late summer and autumn on a tall,

slender, striped stem topped by a cap which, when mature, resembles a light brown parasol with a bump in the centre. It is found in grassy areas near or in woods. The cap, which may measure 15 cm/6 inches or more in diameter, has a scaly surface which should be removed before use. This mushroom is at its best before the cap is fully open.

PARATHA
Flaky Indian bread made from a combination of brown and white flour, butter, water and salt. The dough is formed into rounds and fried until golden.

PARBOIL (TO)
To boil foods, usually vegetables, until they are half-cooked.

PARBOILED RICE
(Pre-fluffed Rice, Easy Cook Rice)
From North America, this is white rice which has been subjected to a steam-pressure process which helps the rice to retain much of its natural mineral and vitamin content. This technique hardens the grain, lessening the possibility of overcooking. The raw rice has a yellow tinge but separates into creamy-white grains when cooked. It is the same length as regular-milled white rice.

PARCHED CORN
See *Pinole*.

PARE (TO)
To peel thinly.

PARENYICA
(Ribbon Cheese)
A Hungarian and Czechoslovakian ewes' milk cheese which is cut into long strips, rolled up and smoked.

PAREVE
A Jewish term to describe foods made without milk or meat, or their derivatives.

PARFAIT
A rich, mousse-like, frozen dessert, often flavoured with coffee or chocolate and enriched with cream. Other flavourings include praline and vanilla.

PARIS-BREST
A French speciality cake composed of three rings of choux pastry, sprinkled with flaked almonds before baking. When cold, it is split and filled with confectioner's custard flavoured with crushed nut brittle. Before serving, the top is dusted with sifted icing sugar.

à la PARISIENNE
French term meaning in the style of Paris, referring to a garnish of braised lettuce, potatoes and sometimes mushrooms.

PARKIN
Traditionally baked in the North of England for the celebration of Guy Fawkes Night. This is a dense ginger cake containing flour, oatmeal, ginger, other spices, brown sugar, treacle, golden syrup, fat, bicarbonate of soda, eggs and milk. It is given at least a week to mature before being cut.

PARMENTIER
French term for any dish with potatoes.

PARMESAN
A member of the Grana family, this is a hard, Italian cows' milk cheese produced in the north of the country. It is either grated and widely used in cooking, or treated as a dessert cheese and eaten with shelled walnuts at the end of a meal. The colour is pale creamy-grey, the flavour pungent and the texture rock-like and grainy, hence the name Grana by which Parmesan is known in Italy.

à la PARMESANE
French term for a dish containing or garnished with Parmesan cheese.

PARMIGIANO REGGIANO
(Parmesan, Parmigiano)
The best of Italy's Parmesan cheeses, this one is protected by law and may only be called Parmigiano Reggiano when made in and around the area of Parma, Reggio, Bologna, Mantua and Modena under clearly laid down conditions. It is one of the country's finest cheeses, eaten when young for dessert and grated for cooking as it matures. It is a large cheese and can weigh as much as 40 kg/90 lb.

PARR
(Samlet)
The name for a young salmon, in its second or third year, before it leaves the river for the open sea. It is still tiny at that age and must not be caught.

PARRILLADA
The Argentinian word for barbecue, a popular method of cooking in this Latin American country.

PARSLEY
A nutritious herb, packed with trace elements and vitamins. There are two main types in common use: curly (*Petroselinum crispum*) and flat-leafed (*P. sativum*), which has a superior flavour. There is also a third type which has a fern-like appearance. Parsley grows worldwide and is used both in cooking and as a garnish. It is bright green when fresh but turns a greenish-brown when dried.

PARSLEY SAUCE
A white sauce flavoured with finely chopped fresh parsley and a trace of nutmeg. It can be served with grilled, baked, poached and steamed fish dishes, boiled bacon and cooked vegetables such as cauliflower or broccoli.

PARSNIP
A root vegetable (*Pastinaca sativa*) native to Europe and cultivated for over 2,000 years. It was introduced to North America during the 16th and 17th centuries and is now found there both in wild and cultivated forms. Parsnip grows as a tapering, conical root with green foliage above the ground. The size varies widely and may be 15–25 cm/6–10 inches in length and 4–7.5 cm/1½–3 inches at the widest part. The more mature the parsnip, the sweeter the taste but it is best eaten before it reaches full growth as its central core becomes hard and woody with age. The crisp flesh is white in colour and the thin skin is creamy-yellow. The parsnip may be boiled, roasted, baked or fried, used for flavouring soups and stews or in savoury recipes.

PARSON'S NOSE
(Pope's Nose)
The fatty extension of the rump or tail of a cooked fowl.

PARTAN BREE
Scottish puréed soup containing crab and rice.

PARTRIDGE
Well-known game bird which is in season in Britain from early September to the beginning of February. It is at its best during October and November and one partridge should be sufficient for two servings.

PARWAL
(Palwal)
The Hindi name for tindori.

PASIEGO PRENSADO
A Spanish cheese from Santander, produced from semi-skimmed cows' milk mixed with ewes' milk. Left to mature for up to 2 weeks, the cheese is white, creamy, smooth and relatively mild, and has a golden-yellow rind.

PASIEGO SIN PRENSAR
A fresh Spanish cheese, similar to Pasiego Prensado, but hand-moulded into assorted shapes. It is produced in Santander.

PASKHA
A traditional Russian Easter cake, shaped like a four-sided pyramid. It is made in a mould from curd cheese, soured cream, eggs, almonds and glacé fruits. It is then turned out and decorated with more glacé fruits.

PASSION FRUIT
The fruit of the passion flower family of plants (*Passiflora* species). These include the purple passion fruit (*P. edulis*), the yellow passion fruit (*P. edulis flavicarpa*) and the sweet granadilla (*P. ligularis*). The names passion fruit and granadilla are often interchanged to describe the fruits of the passion flower plants.

PASSOVER BREAD
Called *matzo* in Hebrew, the Jewish unleavened bread eaten at the time of the festival of Passover. It is available in packets and resembles oblong sheets of water biscuits.

PASTA
Pasta is the Italian word for a staple food made, in its simplest form, from a paste of flour and/or semolina with water. The best quality is produced from high-protein, hard durum wheat which grows mainly in Canada, North America, North Africa and the USSR. To make egg noodles and egg pasta, eggs are used for mixing in conjunction with, or instead of, water. The word *verdi* means green and refers to pasta into which spinach purée has been incorporated. Wholewheat pasta is made from wholewheat flour. Although Marco Polo is attributed with 'discovering' pasta and taking it back to Venice after his visit to China in the latter part of the 13th century, modern food historians maintain this is a myth and that pasta was eaten and enjoyed in Italy long before this time and was also part of the Chinese diet some 3,000 years ago. The amount of pasta per serving depends on appetite but, as a general guide, allow 450 g/1 lb of uncooked pasta for 4 people for a main course; the same amount will serve 6–8 people as a starter.

PASTA ALL'UOVO
See *Egg Pasta*.

PASTA FILATA
An important term in cheese-making to describe curds that have been dipped into hot water, then kneaded until they become elastic and easy to shape, rather like bread dough.

PASTA SECCA
See *Dried Pasta*.

PASTA TWISTS
Twisted lengths of pasta; *fusilli* are an example.

PASTA-MAKING MACHINES
Hand-operated or electric machines which are able to produce a limited variety of pasta shapes from home-made pasta dough.

PASTE
A fat-enriched dough such as pastry; also, almond paste, the traditional mixture used for covering cakes and making sweets; a smooth preparation of meat or fish used for spreading on bread or toast; a smooth preparation made by evaporation or grinding, such as tomato purée.

PASTELILLOS
Caribbean pasties, containing meat or cheese, which are deep-fried. They are generally served as an *hors d'oeuvre* or appetizer.

PAŠTETICE OD SIRA-SKUTE
Yugoslavian pastry turnovers from Serbia, filled with ham. The pastry is made from flour, butter and cottage cheese.

PASTEURIZATION
When applied to milk, this is a form of heat treatment which ensures that any disease-causing organisms

are killed off. Milk is therefore made safe and hygienic with satisfactory keeping qualities, with no adverse effect on the flavour of the milk. During the process, milk is brought up to a temperature of 72°C/161°F, held there for 15 seconds and then rapidly cooled to not more than 10°C/50°F. The cream from pasteurized milk rises to the top (unless homogenized) and is clearly visible. The milk itself is virtually all-purpose and can be used for both drinking and cooking purposes.

PASTEURIZED MILK
(Pasteurised Milk)
See *Pasteurization*.

PASTILLE
French term for a small sweet.

PASTILLES
(Jellies)
Soft or hard jellied sweets, frequently fruit-flavoured and coated with sugar. Peppermint and a variety of aromatics are also used in the making of pastilles. The name comes from the Latin *pastillus*, which is the diminutive of *pastus*, meaning food.

PASTINE
(Pastina)
General name for small pasta shapes.

PASTRAMI
North American salted and spiced beef which is smoked before boiling.

PASTRIES
See *Pâtisserie*.

PASTRY
A stiffish, paste-like mixture made from flour, fat and water with the occasional addition of eggs, sugar, raising agent and milk. It is the way in which these ingredients are combined and worked together that makes one pastry different from another. With the exception of choux, all pastry is rolled out on a floured surface with a rolling pin.

PASTRY BOARD
A square or oblong of wood or marble, with a smooth surface, used for rolling out pastry. A marble board is preferable since it remains cold, thus keeping the pastry cool.

PASTRY CASE
An uncooked or baked pastry container for a sweet or savoury filling.

PASTRY CREAM
See *Confectioner's Custard*.

PASTRY CUTTERS
See *Cutters*.

PASTY
A pastry case enclosing a savoury filling, usually meat-based, baked on a metal sheet and not moulded to fit a container.

PAT
A small mass of something such as butter, shaped as if by patting.

PATA DE MULO
See *Villalón*.

PATAGRAS
A South American cheese, made from cows' milk, which resembles Dutch Gouda.

PATAKUKKO
A Finnish speciality from Karelia, a double-crust pie made from rye dough and filled with tiny white fish called *muikko*, fat pork and seasonings. It is baked very slowly to soften the fish and pork almost to a purée. The word in English means potcock.

PÂTE
French term for all types of pastry, including yeasted dough.

PÂTÉ
An authentic *pâté*, as eaten in France, is very similar to a British raised pie with a meat filling completely enclosed in pastry. It is

generally served hot, as opposed to a *terrine* or *pâté maison*, which are served cold.

PÂTE BRISÉE
French version of British shortcrust pastry, made with butter and flour and mixed to a paste with egg yolk and a little water. It is used for both sweet and savoury dishes.

PÂTÉ DE FOIE
See *Pâté de Foie Gras*.

PÂTÉ DE FOIE GRAS
This exclusive speciality of Strasbourg in France is made from enlarged goose livers, delicately flavoured with slivers of truffles. It has a fine, smooth texture and is much favoured in gastronomic circles. However, many people are offended by the way in which the geese are treated and refuse to eat it.

PÂTÉ MAISON
French term for a pâté, such as liver, made to a specific restaurant recipe. It is served cut in slices and accompanied by fingers of hot toast.

PÂTE SUCRÉE
A sweet speciality pastry similar to British shortcrust pastry, made with butter, flour and sugar mixed to a paste with egg yolk and a little water. It is fragile and requires careful handling. The pastry is widely used in France for sweet flans, tarts and other *pâtisserie*.

PATERNOSTRI
Fairly small squares of flat pasta.

PATIENCE
A herb (*Rumex patientia*), related to sorrel, with a slightly acidic taste. It can be used in all recipes requiring sorrel or spinach.

PÂTISSERIE
French term for sweet items, generally made of pastry, which are filled, for example, with cream, chocolate or jam, and decorated with icing or nuts.

PÂTISSIÈRE
French term for a pastry cook.

PATLICAN DOLMASI
A Turkish speciality consisting of aubergine halves stuffed with minced beef, onions, tomatoes, rice, water and seasonings. They are baked in the oven and served hot.

PATLICAN SALATASI
A Turkish aubergine purée salad, flavoured with lemon juice and salt and enriched with olive oil. It is garnished with tomato wedges, strips of green pepper and black olives.

PATNA RICE
Long-grain white rice from Patna, in India, similar in size to Basmati rice but slightly less aromatic and tasty.

PATRA
Leaves of the dasheen, used as a vegetable and reminiscent of spring greens.

PATTY
A small pie or pasty.

PATTY TINS
(Bun Tins)
Individual tins, either set into trays or free-standing, used for baking small cakes, tartlets, tartlet cases and miniature Yorkshire puddings (North American popovers).

PATTYPAN SQUASH
(Cymling, Scalloped Squash)
A vegetable (*Cucurbita pepo*) of the squash family native to North America. It is one of the summer squash group which is eaten when young and tender with skin, flesh and seeds all being edible. The pattypan is roughly disc-shaped with a scalloped edge and swollen middle. The skin and flesh are creamy-white and the squash is usually cooked and used as a vegetable on its own.

PAUA
An edible shellfish (*Haliotis iris*) found in New Zealand. It has a rainbow-coloured shell that is often used as an ornament.

PAUPIETTES
French term for meat cuts, such as beef olives.

PAVLOVA
An Australian dessert, consisting of meringue piped rather like a shallow basket, usually filled with cream and decorated with strawberries, fresh pineapple or passionfruit.

PAWPAW
(Papaya)
The fruit of an herbaceous plant (*Carica papaya*) native to the American tropics but now cultivated in most tropical and sub-tropical areas. Although the different species vary in shape, the most common kinds are rather similar to a melon with the stem end elongated. The size varies with the species but most of those on sale average 10–13 cm/4–5 inches in diameter and about 18–20 cm/ 7–8 inches in length. The skin is green and inedible and usually turns to yellow as the fruit ripens. The ripe flesh is soft and juicy, and tastes and smells like a mixture of roses, peaches and strawberries. Its colour ranges from orange to salmon-pink. The central cavity in the flesh is filled with inedible blackish seeds. As the flesh is not recommended for cooking, the fruit is eaten raw or as part of a fruit salad. The pawpaw plant and fruit skin contain an enzyme which acts as a meat tenderizer and the flesh itself, when under-ripe, may be used as a vegetable.

PAYSANNE
French term for any food, particularly vegetables, cut into tiny triangles.

à la PAYSANNE
French term meaning in peasant style, referring to a fairly simple dish containing onions, bacon and sometimes carrots.

PAZLACHE
See *Agnolotti*.

PEA
(Garden Pea)
A vegetable (*Pisum sativum*) which grows as the fruit of a climbing plant, possibly native to northern India. It was also known to the Greeks and Romans, and was introduced to Britain in the 16th century. It is now cultivated worldwide except in tropical and sub-tropical regions. Peas grow in an elongated flat pod or shell which becomes tubular in shape as the peas inside swell and mature. Both pod and pea are green in colour and the pod has a thin, fibrous, inedible lining. There are many varieties and all are sweetest and best when the pea itself is relatively small. Most pea pods are sold at 7.5–10 cm/3–4 inches long and about 1 cm/½ inch wide. Fresh young peas may be eaten raw by themselves or in a salad, lightly boiled or used in cooked dishes; older peas should be cooked. The pods of some varieties such as mange-tout do not have an inedible lining and these are picked before the pea seed has developed, to be eaten whole and unshelled. Peas are particularly well-suited to freezing and are also processed and sold in cans. Dried peas are available as pulses in the form of whole green peas and as yellow or green split peas.

PEA AUBERGINES
Tiny aubergines (*Solanum torvum*) from Thailand which look like straggly bunches of grapes. The green ones are sometimes available in Britain though there are other colours including white, yellow and mahogany-purple. Pea

aubergines are picked while still unripe and used raw in hot sauces and chutneys.

PEABERRY
A mutation of the *arabica* coffee bean which develops as a single round bean and not a matching pair, each with a flattened, creased side. These spherical beans are sorted from the main crop and treated and sold as Peaberry coffee, coupled with the name of the producing country — Kenya, Jamaica, etc. Although considered a superior type, Peaberry coffee depends for quality more on the reputation of the country of origin than the shape of the bean itself.

PEACH
The fruit of a deciduous tree (*Prunus persica*) which is one of the rose family and native to China. The peach was introduced to Persia (Iran) a very long time ago and is now cultivated in temperate climates round the world with the greatest production in the USA and Italy. Most of the varieties of peach are globular in shape, with an indentation running down the side from the deep stalk cavity. The size varies with the type and the country of origin and may be 5–7.5 cm/2–3 inches in diameter. The soft, downy skin may range in colour from cream to orange flushed with pink; some are even pale green. The sweet, juicy flesh may be white, yellow or orange and surrounds a large, rough, central stone. Peaches can be divided into two main categories: the free-stone variety, where the flesh does not stick to the stone, and the cling variety, where it does. A ripe peach (especially the white-fleshed kind) in perfect condition should be eaten raw, for it is among the most succulent and delicious of all fruits. Peaches may also be used in fruit salads, cooked dishes (both sweet and savoury) and preserves. Peaches are also used in liqueurs.

PEACH MELBA
Named after the opera singer, Dame Nellie Melba, this dessert is usually served in individual glass dishes and contains vanilla ice cream, cold peach halves previously poached in syrup and a topping of raspberry sauce, made from fresh raspberry purée sweetened with sugar.

PEANUT BUTTER
Spread made from a purée of peanuts, oil and salt. Sometimes coarsely chopped peanuts are included to give the butter more texture.

PEANUT OIL
See *Groundnut Oil*.

PEANUTS
(Groundnuts, Monkey Nuts)
Resembling small beans in appearance, peanuts are native to South America and were introduced to other parts of the world by Spanish and Portuguese explorers. Peanuts grow in pairs inside light-coloured, brittle shells beneath the ground on very slim twigs. Although nutritionally valuable and a good source of protein, they are the least costly of all nuts and may be eaten plain or roasted and salted. Peanuts are sometimes called groundnuts, due to the manner in which they grow underground.

PEAR
The fruit of a deciduous tree (*Pyrus communis*) of the same family as the rose, native to Europe and western Asia and growing wild and in cultivated species throughout temperate parts of the world. Over many centuries, the varieties of pear have multiplied to over 3,000, but only a relative few have been carefully nurtured to produce the best of today's fruit. The thin, usually smooth skin may range in colour from pale yellow through green to brown, often mottled. The flesh is firm, delicately flavoured, juicy, sweet and pale cream in colour and the centre contains a

core of small seeds enclosed in scaly pockets. The pear is bred in many shapes and sizes consistent with the soil and climate of its country of origin, and is either a dessert or cooking variety, seldom suitable for both purposes. The sweet-tasting dessert pear may be eaten on its own, peeled or unpeeled, or added to fruit salads. The good keeping qualities of the cooking pear makes it more suitable for storing and using in cooked dishes. Some pears are cultivated exclusively for the making of perry and pear brandy.

PEARL BARLEY
Barley with its outer husk removed. It is then steamed, rounded and polished.

PEARL MOSS
See *Carrageen*.

PEARL ONIONS
Tiny white onions, usually pickled in colourless vinegar, used as a cocktail savoury and garnish.

PEARL SAGO
See *Sago*.

PEASE PUDDING
A British dish, traditionally made from split peas which have been soaked overnight. They are then boiled, drained and mashed with butter or margarine, egg yolks and seasoning. The mixture is reheated in the oven for about 30 minutes before serving.

PEAT-SMOKED
A Scottish cows' milk cheese which is peat-smoked on a straw mat. Each one is made individually and the texture is smooth and creamy. The flavour is smoky and mild.

PECAN NUTS
The stones of fruit growing on a variety of the hickory tree (*Carya pecan*) and native to the southern states of the USA. They resemble elongated walnuts but with smooth, reddish-brown shells. The flesh is markedly wrinkled and the flavour of the nuts is mild, delicate and more subtle than the walnut. Pecans tend to be fairly costly and may be eaten as they are or used in cooking.

PECAN PIE
A popular North American pie which is very sweet and traditionally eaten at Thanksgiving.

PECKISH
A British term meaning slightly hungry, ready for a snack or meal.

PECORINO
(Pecorino Romano)
An Italian ewes' milk cheese with a fairly pungent flavour and usually hard texture. It is produced throughout the country from unpasteurized milk and used in cooking and for dessert. It is most popular in southern Italy.

PECTIN
See *Hemi-cellulose*.

PEEL
The skin or rind of fruit and some vegetables; also, a long-handled shovel used by bakers to move bread, buns and pies into or out of the oven.

PEEL (TO)
To remove skin (and pith) of fruits and vegetables; to remove lining paper from cakes, hence 'to peel away paper'.

PEELER
(Potato Peeler)
An implement for removing the skin or surface of vegetables and fruit. The handle may be of wood, plastic or metal, but the peeling head is always made of steel with a sharp-edged slot which accurately controls the depth of cut. Some models have a point or loop at the tip to remove blemishes.

PEELINGS
Skin or rind that has been removed from fruit or vegetables, for example, potato peelings.

PEKING COOKING
The food from this cool, north-eastern region of China is relatively robust. Specialities include meat hot-pots, unleavened wheat bread and an abundance of noodles. Crabs, giant prawns and carp are the most common fish. Flavourings include garlic, spring onions, chives, leeks and ginger. The internationally known gourmet dish, Peking duck, originated in this area.

PEKING DUCK
One of China's most renowned dishes, consisting of a specially prepared and cooked duck with crisp skin. Pieces of the duck meat and skin, with spring onions and cucumber strips, are rolled in small pancakes, first brushed with Chinese barbecue sauce. They are then eaten with the fingers.

PEKOE
A grade of black tea leaf.

PELAGIC
Term used to describe fish which live in shoals or large groups in the middle and surface layers of the open seas.

PELARDON
A small and mild goats' milk cheese from Languedoc in France. It has a smooth, close texture and is usually white.

PELAU
A Caribbean version of *pilaf* made from boiling fowl and salt beef, almonds, sugar, water, butter, olives, rice, onions, tomatoes, herbs, spices and seasonings.

PEMMICAN
(Pemican)
A concentrated food, traditionally made by North American Indians. It consists of lean dried meat, finely pounded and mixed with melted fat. Another version made from beef and dried fruits is used for emergency rations.

PENETELEU
(Dobrogea)
A Romanian cheese which closely resembles Kashkaval. It is always made from ewes' milk.

PENNE
Hollow lengths of slim macaroni, about 4 cm/1½ inches in length, cut crosswise at both ends. They resemble pens or quills in shape, hence their name.

PENNE RIGATE
Finely ribbed *penne*.

PENNETTE
(Pennine)
Thin version of *penne*.

PENNY BUN
See *Cep*.

PENNYROYAL
A member (*Mentha pulegium*) of the mint family, this herb yields a strong, mint-flavoured oil which is used as a flavouring.

PEPATO
An Italian Pecorino-type cheese, spiked with crushed peppercorns.

PEPERONATA
An Italian vegetable stew, related to the French *ratatouille*, made from sweet red peppers, tomatoes, onions, garlic, herbs and seasonings cooked in olive oil. It is frequently served cold as an *antipasta* (appetizer).

PEPO
(Pepos)
A hard-rinded, fleshy member of the marrow family that contains many seeds.

PEPPARKAKOR
Traditional Swedish Christmas biscuits spiced with cinnamon, powdered cloves and ground cardamom.

PEPPER
A spice native to the East Indies, pepper (*Piper nigrum*) is now exported from India, Indonesia, Sri Lanka and Brazil. Pepper berries, considered the world's most important and useful spice, grow on perennial vines which are trained to climb in the same way as grape vines. When ready for gathering, the clusters of berries are red. Pepper dates back to the year 3000 BC and was introduced to the West by Columbus.

PEPPER (TO)
To sprinkle, season or cover with pepper.

PEPPER JELLY
A fiery jelly for hot and cold meats, also served with cream cheese, made by the Cajuns in the Louisiana Bayou country of the USA. It consists of chillies, green peppers, sugar, vinegar, pectin and both red and green colourings.

PEPPER POT SOUP
A Caribbean soup made from beef, oxtail, pig's trotters, chicken and mixed vegetables including okra, pumpkin, yams and chillies. It often contains cassava juice.

PEPPER SALAMI
A variety of salami which is coated with crushed black peppercorns.

PEPPER SAUCE
See *Poivrade Sauce*.

PEPPER STEAK
(Steak au Poivre)
Beef steak coated with crushed black peppercorns before frying, usually in butter. A sauce is made with the pan juices, cream and ignited brandy.

PEPPERMINT
Plant (*Mentha piperita*) of the mint family that has dark green tapering leaves and small flowers in pink or purple. It is cultivated for its aromatic oil.

PEPPERMINT CREAM
See *Fondant*.

PEPPERMINT OIL
A strong-smelling oil extracted from the flowering tops of the peppermint plant. It is used to flavour confectionery and some liqueurs.

PEPPERONE
A salami-type sausage from Italy made from beef and pork, mixed with red peppers and seasoned with fennel.

PEPSI-COLA
A popular brand of cola.

PERCH
An oval-bodied freshwater fish (*Perca* species) caught in rivers and lakes in most of the temperate parts of the northern hemisphere, mainly from June to December. The back is generally greeny-yellow, becoming paler on the underside. An average length is 30 cm/12 inches and weight about 500 g/18 oz. The flesh is lean and delicate and considered to be among the finest of freshwater fishes in spite of the number of bones. The fish may be poached, steamed, baked, fried or grilled.

PERCIATELLI
See *Bucatini*.

PERCOLATED COFFEE
Made in a jug fitted with a narrow, central tube and perforated, covered basket situated just under the lid. As the water boils, it repeatedly circulates through the tube and basket, which contains medium-ground coffee. The strength of the coffee is determined by the length of time it is left to percolate. Most percolators are electric but some models can be used on the hob.

PÉRIGORD BLACK TRUFFLE
See *Truffles*.

à la PÉRIGOURDINE
French term meaning in the style of Périgord in south-west France,

referring to the inclusion of local truffles and sometimes *foie gras*.

PÉRIGUEUX SAUCE
An Espagnole sauce to which port and chopped truffles are added. It can be served with meat dishes such as croquettes, poultry, roast chicken and omelettes.

PERIWINKLE
See *Winkle*.

PERRIER WATER
See *Mineral Waters*.

PERRY
A cider-like drink produced from fermented pear juice. It can be used in exactly the same ways as apple cider and is particularly delicious in stewed fruit.

PERSILLADE
French term for chopped shallots or garlic mixed with chopped parsley. It is added to an assortment of stews and braised dishes to increase flavour.

PERSIMMON
(Kakee, Kaki)
The fruit of a large group of trees and shrubs (*Diospyros* species), evergreen and deciduous, native to Asia and North America and increasingly cultivated in the Mediterranean area, South America and Australia. The main Asian varieties (*Diospyros kaki*) are shaped rather like a large tomato, averaging 7.5 cm/3 inches in diameter, with a prominent calyx (the remnants of the original flower). The green skin turns to a glossy, yellow-orange as the fruit matures and most kinds are not edible until very ripe indeed; even then, they are somewhat astringent. The flesh reflects the colour of the skin and is generally pulpy when ripe for eating. The central seeds, rather like those of an apple have, in some varieties, been eliminated by careful breeding, although the skin is usually inedible. The ripe persimmon is eaten as a dessert fruit or added to fruit salads. It may also be used in preserves, some dishes and for decoration.
The native American persimmon (*D. virginiana*) is only half the size of the Asian varieties and may have a much redder skin and flesh. The fruit can be ripened more quickly if placed in a closed bag with an apple.

PESTLE
See *Pestle and Mortar*.

PESTLE AND MORTAR
A short, stumpy stick-like implement (pestle) and a bowl (mortar) which are used together to crush or grind foods to a powder or paste. A pestle and mortar can be made from earthenware, stone, glass or metal.

PESTO
A paste-like Italian condiment from Genoa which melts over hot pasta and oils it. It is made from fresh basil, garlic, pine nuts, Pecorino or Parmesan cheese and olive oil. It should be prepared in a pestle and mortar, hence its name.

PETCHA
(Fisnoga, Pilsa)
A traditional Jewish Sabbath appetizer, made from calves' foot jelly flavoured with garlic, vinegar and seasoning, then studded with wedges of hard-boiled eggs.

PETIT DÉJEUNER
French term for breakfast although it translates literally into small lunch.

au PETIT-DUC
French term meaning in the style of the little duke and referring to a garnish of creamed chicken in tartlet cases, asparagus tips, truffles and sometimes mushrooms.

PETITE MARMITE
A French meat and vegetable soup, sometimes clear, served in a lidded earthenware pot, also called a *petite marmite*.

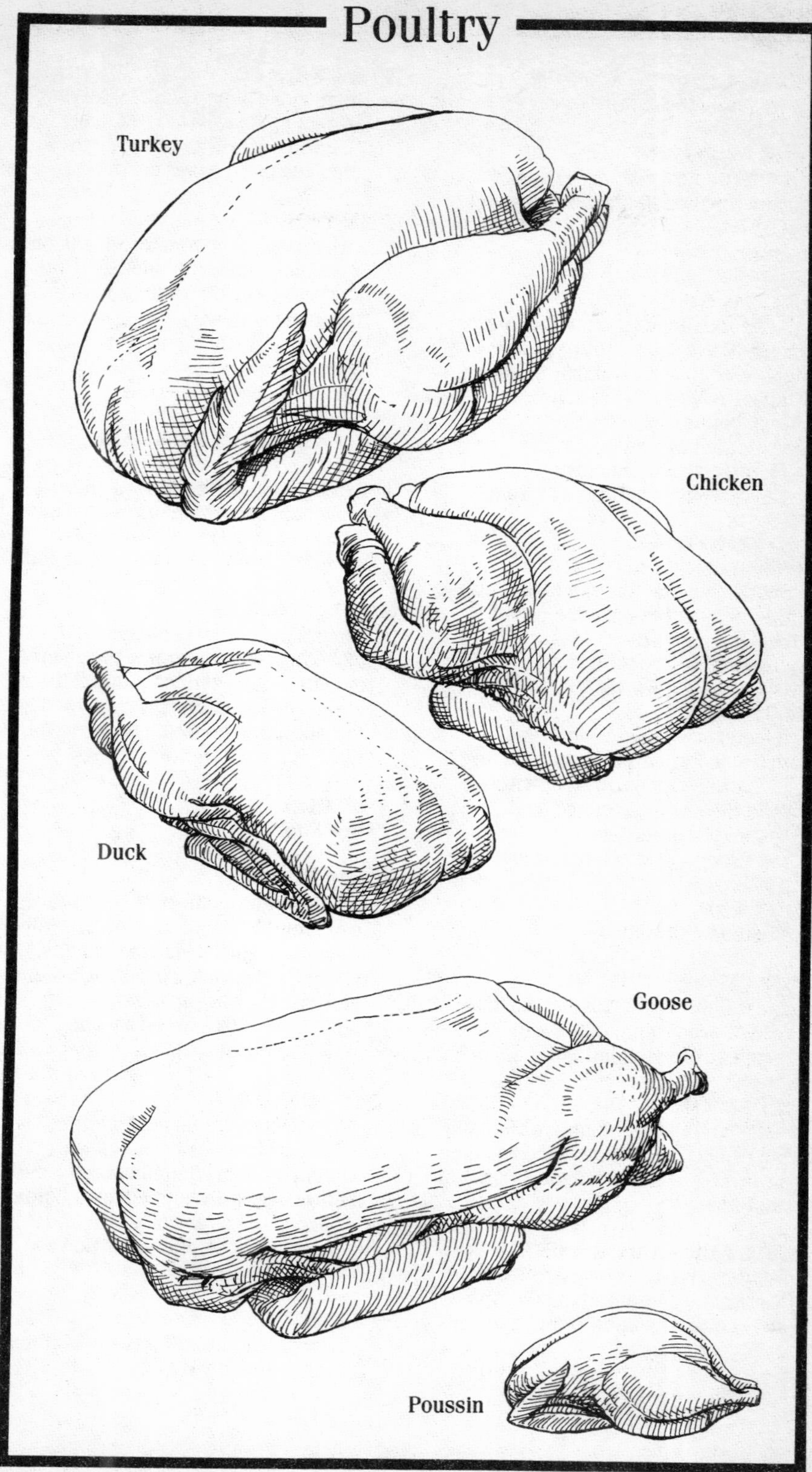
Poultry
Turkey
Chicken
Duck
Goose
Poussin

PETIT-LAIT
French term for milk whey.

PETITS FOURS
A term to describe the range of sweetmeats and chocolates which are served with coffee at the end of a formal meal.

PETITS POIS
A European vegetable which dates back to the 16th century, these tiny green peas are available fresh in the early summer and frozen throughout the year. They originated in Italy and were adopted with enthusiasm in both Italian and French Court circles.

PETIT-SUISSE
A French cheese created in Switzerland during the last century, this is a double or triple cream cheese made from pasteurized cows' milk.

PETRUS
A Belgian monastery cheese, produced in Loo from cows' milk. It has a fairly strong smell, with a mild flavour and orange rind. The texture is supple, pale yellow and interspersed with a few tiny holes.

PE-TSAI
See *Chinese Cabbage*.

PETTICOAT TAILS
Skirt-shaped shortbread biscuits which are crisp, golden and originally from Scotland.

PETTITOES
The feet of sucking pigs which may be braised, grilled or used to make jellies for pies such as pork or veal and ham.

PFÄLZER LEBERWURST
A speciality liver sausage from Germany, containing medium to coarse pieces of offal and specially selected spices.

PFANNKUCHEN
The German word for pancakes. German *pfannkuchen* tend to be thicker than British and French pancakes and *crêpes*.

PHEASANT
With its very long plumes, this is one of the most colourful and beautiful of all the game birds. In season in Britain from the beginning of October to the beginning of February, one pheasant should be sufficient for four servings.

PHILADELPHIA CREAM CHEESE
Brand name of a rich cows' milk cream cheese which originated in the USA in the last century. It is white in colour and packaged in foil.

PHOSPHORUS
An important inorganic element, classified as a mineral, which works in conjunction with calcium. It helps in the release of energy from food in the body, and maintains the body fluid vital for life.

PHYLLO
See *Filo*.

PICADILLO
A savoury filling from Mexico made from minced pork, beef, onions, oil, tomatoes, garlic, vinegar, raisins, chopped almonds, spices, herbs and seasonings. The *picadillo* is sometimes also served as a main course with rice.

PICADINHO
A Brazilian minced beef mixture which is simmered in stock with chopped onions and tomatoes. Just before serving, chopped hard-boiled eggs and olives are mixed in and it is generally accompanied by rice or mashed potatoes.

PICATA
Term for a small round or medallion of meat, usually veal.

PICCALILLI
(Mustard Pickle)
Pieces of cauliflower, cubes of marrow, green beans, pickling onions and pieces of cucumber which are all brined for 24 hours, then pickled in a sauce made from white vinegar, sugar, mustard, ginger, flour and turmeric. The pickle is characteristically bright yellow in colour and piquant in flavour.

PICCATA
Thin slices of fried veal escalope, accompanied by lemon.

PICKEREL
A young pike; also the name of a small relative of the pike family caught in fresh water over most of North America.

PICKLE (TO)
To preserve foods by keeping them in brine or an acid such as vinegar with the addition of appropriate spices, sugar and salt.

PICKLED CUCUMBER
(Sour Cucumber)
Cucumbers which are pickled in spiced brine and vinegar. Available in delicatessens.

PICKLED EGGS
Hard-boiled eggs which are cooled and shelled, then pickled in spiced and seasoned vinegar. Pickled eggs are usually ready to eat after a month but may stay in their pickling solution for a further two.

PICKLED TESTICLES
Testicles pickled in whey, an Icelandic dish.

PICKLING SPICE
A mixture of herbs and spices, often available ready packeted, which can include one or two red chillies, a bay leaf, black and white peppercorns, ginger and white mustard seed.

PICNIC
An outing on which food is taken to be eaten in the open.

PIE
A sweet or savoury filling encased or covered with pastry and baked in a pie dish or other container.

À LA PIE
See *Fromage Blanc*.

PIE DISH
A round or oval dish with rim which may be made from glass, earthenware or sometimes metal. The rim is important as it gives support to the pastry lid.

PIE VEAL
Diced veal for stewing, braising, casseroling and mincing. It comes from the clod, shin and neck of the calf.

PIÈCE DE RÉSISTANCE
French term used in its culinary sense to describe the highlight of a meal. This is usually the main course.

PIECES SUGAR
See *Foot Sugar*.

PIECRUST
Pastry used for lining a dish in which a pie is to be made; also the pastry lid of a pie.

à la PIÉMONTAISE
French term meaning in the style of Piedmont in northern Italy, referring to a garnish of polenta or risotto, white truffles and sometimes tomato sauce.

PIEROGI
The Polish version of Italian *ravioli*, generally served in soup.

PIG
The term used in Britain to describe any of various short-legged and rotund mammals (family *Suidae*) with thick, bristly skins and long mobile snouts. The name applies especially to a domesticated pig belonging to the same species (*Sus scrofa*) as the European wild boar. In North

America, the word pig refers to a sexually immature young pig, also known as sucking pig.

PIGEON
(Wood Pigeon)
Although this is a wild bird, it has no close season and may be shot and eaten throughout the year. One pigeon per person is the usual allowance and it can be roasted, casseroled, stewed or braised.

PIGEON PEA
(Red Gram, Tuware)
A vegetable (*Cajanus cajan*) native to North Africa and cultivated in many parts of the world with suitably warm climates. It is a legume and is used either as a fresh vegetable or dried as a pulse. The colour of the dried pea varies from white to red to black.

PIGNOLIAS
See *Pine Nuts*.

PIGS' EARS
In the Victorian era, pigs' ears were partially boiled and stuffed with a mixture of breadcrumbs, suet, egg yolks, herbs and seasoning. They were then fried until 'bright brown' and stewed for 45 minutes in very rich brown gravy. Today, the ears are usually cooked with the head.

PIG'S FRY
The heart, liver and sweetbreads of a pig which are cut into pieces, boiled until tender, drained, coated in flour mixed with sage and seasonings and fried. Pig's fry is traditionally served with fried potatoes, green vegetables and gravy.

PIG'S HEAD
The head of a pig which may be boiled and used for brawn, or boned after cooking and added to pies.

PIGS' KIDNEYS
Comparatively small kidneys which are a little more elongated and slightly larger than lambs' kidneys. Darkish brown and well-flavoured, they may be fried, grilled or diced and added to stews, casseroles, pies and puddings. The usual allowance is one kidney per person.

PIGS' LIVER
Almost as strongly flavoured as ox liver, pigs' liver should be soaked in milk for a minimum of 1 hour before cooking. As it is fairly coarse, pigs' liver should be stewed, casseroled or made into a terrine or country-style *pâté*. It can also be minced and used in stuffings. Like other livers, it is an excellent source of protein.

PIGS' TROTTERS
The most readily available of all animal feet and sold fresh or salted. They may be boned, stuffed and then roasted or, because of their gelatinous nature, used to make brawn. Cold boiled trotters are generally served with a sharpish French dressing; hot boiled trotters with well-flavoured white sauce laced with plenty of English mustard.

PIIMA
A Finnish version of buttermilk.

PIKE
(Jackfish)
A large, round-bodied, pointed-nosed freshwater fish (*Esox* species) caught in rivers and lakes in most of the temperate parts of the northern hemisphere, mainly from August to February. The back is greeny-yellow in colour, lightening on the underside. Pike seen in the shops would weigh 1.5–3.5 kg/3½–8 lb and not exceed 90 cm/3 feet in length. The flesh is lean, white and flaky, but is rather dry and very bony. The fish may be poached, steamed, baked, fried or grilled.

PIKELETS
British North Country term for a thinner version of crumpets.

PIKE-PERCH
A round-bodied freshwater fish (*Stizostedion* species) which looks very much like a cross between a pike and a perch; its body shape is like a perch but it has the pike's pointed nose. It is caught in rivers and lakes in most of the temperate parts of the northern hemisphere, mainly in the latter half of the year. The colour of the back is brownish with darker transverse bars, lightening on the underside. An average length would be 50 cm/19 inches. The flesh is white, firm and delicate and the fish may be poached, steamed, baked, fried or grilled.

PILAF IZ RYBI
A Russian *risotto* made from rice, fish, tomatoes, onions and butter or margarine.

PILAFI
Similar to *pilav*, this is a Greek dish made by frying rice in butter until creamy-coloured, then simmering it in stock until tender.

PILAKI
A Turkish dish of fish cutlets, braised with vegetables and garlic. They are served cold with a garnish of chopped parsley and lemon juice.

PILAU
(Pilao, Pillau, Pulao)
A savoury boiled rice dish from India which resembles *pilaf* and *risotto*, usually made with Basmati rice.

PILAV
(Pilaff, Pilaf, Pilau)
Turkish round-grain rice, cooked until tender, then forked with butter.

PILCHARD
A round-bodied seawater fish (*Sardina pilchardus*) of the herring family. The back is green, the sides yellowish and the underside silver. The length is about 25 cm/10 inches. The European pilchard is caught in the western Mediterranean, and the Atlantic as far north as the south of England. The main season is April to November. Related species are caught in waters off South Africa and Australia. The flesh is oily and soft and the fish may be baked, fried, grilled or canned.

PILE O'BONES TURKEY
A speciality of Saskatchewan in Canada, Pile O'Bones is the English meaning of the Cree word Wascana, which was the original name of the city of Regina, the provincial capital. Pile O'Bones is also what is left when you serve meaty, broad-breasted Saskatchewan turkey.

PILZ
(Edelpilzkäse)
A German blue-veined cheese which is strong, pungent and distinctive. The texture is crumbly and the colour deep cream. It makes an excellent dessert cheese, especially when eaten with black grapes. It is produced from cows' milk.

PIMIENTO
(Pimento)
See *Sweet Pepper*.

PIMMS
(Pimms No 1)
Proprietary mixture based on gin to which lemonade, ice and mint are added to make a long drink.

PIN BONE OF BEEF
Term used in Wales and the West Country for rump.

PINDOS
Greek cheese, similar to Kefalotiri.

PINE NUTS
(Indian Nuts, Pine Kernels, Pignolias)
Found inside cones growing on pine nut trees (*Pinus pinea*) in the southern Mediterranean and North America, pine nuts have a rich and wax-like consistency, are long, needle-shaped and creamy white. They are widely used in the Middle

and Far East and tend to be expensive. Italy's famous *pesto*, a soup and spaghetti condiment, is based on pine nuts.

PINEAPPLE
The fruit of an herbaceous plant (*Ananas comosus*) native to Brazil. Because of its adaptability to any reasonably suitable climate, it is now cultivated in many tropical and semi-tropical areas. Hawaii is by far the largest exporter. It is shaped rather like a tapered cylinder and the skin has a rough, honeycomb appearance, topped with a crown of spiky leaves. It is one of the larger types of fruit and different varieties can weigh 1–4 kg/2–9 lb and measure up to 30 cm/12 inches in length. The skin colour varies as the fruit matures, turning from green to mixtures of yellows, greens and reds, depending on the variety. The flesh is firm, juicy and fibrous, and the colour of the sweetest varieties is golden-yellow. Fresh pineapple is a good dessert fruit and may also be used in preserves and with other ingredients in both sweet and savoury dishes. Large quantities are canned, a process that tends to eliminate any natural tartness in the fruit. Raw pineapple prevents gelatinous mixtures from setting.

PINEAPPLE CHEESE
A pinky-coloured and soft-textured cows' milk Cheddar-type cheese from the USA. It originated in Connecticut over a hundred years ago and at one time was shaped like a pineapple.

PINEAPPLE FRITTERS
See *Fruit Fritters*.

PINEAPPLE GUAVA
See *Feijoa*.

PINEAPPLE MELON
Originally from Japan, this is a new variety of Israeli melon with a hard rind which is striped in light and dark green. The flesh is golden and, like the watermelon which it closely resembles, interspersed with brown seeds. It is refreshingly crisp, fairly sweet and tastes very faintly of pineapple.

PINION
The wing of poultry or game.

PINK SALMON
The smallest member (*Oncorhynchus gorbuscha*) of the Pacific salmon family, caught from Alaska to Oregon. The colour of the back is dark blue, shading to silver on the sides and undersides, with oval spots on the tail fins and the back. The average weight is 1.5–2.25 kg/3½–5 lb. The main fishing season is July to September. The flesh is pink and oily with a fine texture and small flakes, and the fish may be poached, steamed, baked, fried, grilled or canned.

PINK SHRIMP
See *Shrimp*.

PINK TROUT
See *Salmon Trout*.

PINKEL
Sausages from Bremen in north Germany, popular in North America and made from beef and/or pork, oats or other groats, onions and seasonings, and frequently lightly smoked. Pinkel are generally used in recipe dishes but may also be boiled and eaten plain with vegetables.

PINOLE
A finely ground flour made from parched maize (corn) and used, especially sweetened, in Mexico and the south-western states of the USA.

PIÑON
An edible, nut-like seed found on a number of low-growing pine trees.

PINT
British measurement of 20 fl oz; North American measurement of 16 fl oz; 'a pint' also refers informally to beer served in a public house in Britain.

PINTA
A colloquial British term for a pint of milk.

PINTO BEAN
A vegetable (*Phaseolus vulgaris*) of the kidney bean family which is widely grown in North America and in Latin American countries. It is a legume which is generally dried and used as a pulse. The bean is kidney-shaped with a browny-pink, mottled skin which turns pink when cooked. It may be used instead of the red kidney bean in cooking but has its own distinctive flavour. It must be boiled briskly for the first 15 minutes of cooking time to destroy harmful toxins found in the outer skin which can prove very dangerous to the human body.

PINZGAUER BIER
An Austrian cows' milk cheese produced in the mountains around Salzburg. It is full-flavoured and distinctive.

PIP
A small seed, usually found in fruits such as oranges, apples, grapes and melons.

PIP (TO)
To remove the seeds or pips from fruit and vegetables.

PIPE (TO)
To decorate large and small cakes, biscuits, buns and so on, with cream or icing applied with an icing nozzle fitted to a fabric or paper bag or metal syringe.

PIPÉRADE
A dish from the Basque region of France consisting of eggs scrambled with chopped tomatoes, peppers and ham.

PIPI
Either of two marine shellfish which are smooth-shelled bivalves and found in New Zealand (*Mesodesma novae-zelandiae*) and eastern Australia (*Plebidonax deltoides*).

PIPING
Decorative, sometimes ornate swirls or lines of icing piped on to a cake with an icing bag (made from paper or cloth) fitted with a fancy tube or nozzle. Sometimes roses and other decorative items are piped individually on to greaseproof paper and added to the cake afterwards.

PIPING BAG
See *Forcing Bag*.

PIPO CRÈME
(Grièges)
A French blue cheese made from cows' milk. It is produced in Grièges and called by that name in France. It is creamy-textured with a distinctive flavour.

PIQUANT (PIQUANTE)
French term for anything appetizing, tangy and spicy.

PIQUANT SAUCE
An Espagnole sauce, flavoured with extra fried onion or shallot, wine vinegar, chopped capers, chopped gherkins and chopped parsley. It can be served with pork and bacon dishes, grilled or fried offal and fried sausages.

PIRI-PIRI
A hot condiment, akin to tabasco, originating in the old Portuguese colonies in Africa.

PIROGEN
See *Knishes*.

PIROSHKI
Small Russian patties, served with *borsch*, or by themselves as part of the *zakuski* (*hors d'oeuvre*). They can be made with a variety of pastes — puff, sour, or paste made with milk, eggs and butter. The fillings can also be varied with meat, fish, cereals, vegetables or fruit. If intended for eating with soup, the *piroshki* should be made small, a knob of paste for each *piroshki*. A milk, egg and yeast paste can be used for fried *piroshki*, puff paste for

baked *piroshki*. The fillings can vary widely; sweet cream cheese and chopped cabbage or sago and carrot are typical examples.

PISSALADIÈRE

A Provençal version of pizza. A large flat tart or flan, made from bread dough, is covered with softly fried onions and garnished with anchovies, black olives and tomatoes. It is well-seasoned and flavoured with local herbs. It is served hot or cold as a snack or light meal, cut into squares.

PISTACHIO NUTS

Native to Syria, these are also grown in other areas of the Middle East, the Balkans, Italy and the USA. Peridot green in colour and uniquely bright, the nuts have a subtle taste and aroma and are related to the cashew family. They are the seeds of fruit grown on a small tree (*Pistacia vera*) and have pale, creamy-coloured shells which split naturally at one end. They are expensive and generally available roasted and salted, still in their shells. They have many culinary applications and need blanching to remove their skins.

PISTOU

A Provençal version of the Italian *pesto*.

PIT

North American term for a fruit stone.

PIT (TO)

To remove stones from fruits, olives and dates.

PITCAITHLY BANNOCK

A Scottish shortbread, containing chopped mixed peel, often topped with flaked almonds before baking.

PITH

A spongy layer, usually white, beneath the rind of citrus fruits, forming an inner layer of the skin and surrounding the flesh and seeds.

PITHIVIERS CREAM

A classic French cake filling made from butter, sugar, eggs, ground almonds and flavouring.

PITTA BREAD

(Pita)

Lightly leavened Middle Eastern bread which is generally shaped into small flattish ovals.

PIZZA

A flattish, open tart originating in Italy made from a base of yeast dough topped with a savoury mixture. One of the most popular pizzas is the Neapolitan, topped with tomatoes, garlic, Mozzarella cheese, black olives and anchovies.

PIZZA BASE

Generally made from a white or brown yeasted bread dough, fairly thinly rolled.

PIZZAIOLA SAUCE

An Italian tomato sauce made from crushed tomatoes, oil, crushed garlic, chopped parsley, oregano and seasonings. It is frequently served with steaks, hence Steak Pizzaiola.

PIZZOCCHERI

Noodles made from buckwheat flour which are short and stubby and beige in colour.

PLA TOO

Fried, salted mackerel, trout or herring from Thailand. The fish is served with *nam prik*.

PLĂCINTĂ CU BRÎNZĂ DE VACĂ

Romanian curd cheese dumplings which are poached in water, then coated with melted butter, breadcrumbs and caster sugar.

PLAICE

The most important flatfish (*Pleuronectes platessa*) found in the shallower European waters, from the North Atlantic near Iceland to the western Mediterranean. It is caught all year round and its average length is about 30–40 cm/12–16 inches and it weighs about 1.5 kg/3½ lb. It has a ridge of between 4 and 7 knobs running from between the eyes back over the head. The colour is basically grey or brown with red or orange spots on the upper side and white on the underside. The flesh is lean and white and the fish can be poached, steamed, baked, fried or grilled either whole or in fillets.

PLAIN
Undecorated; simply prepared and cooked; made with small quantities of fat and sugar in proportion to flour, yielding a plain cake; flour without raising agent.

PLAIN BACON
See *Green Bacon*.

PLAIN CAKES
So called because of the fairly low ratio of fat and sugar to flour, usually half or just under half. In other words, 75–100 g/3–4 oz of both fat and sugar to 225 g/8 oz plain flour with the addition of 15 ml/3 teaspoons baking powder. Alternatively, self-raising flour may be used. Other ingredients may be added such as coconut or spice. Plain cakes are made by the rubbing-in method.

PLAIN FLOUR
(Household Flour)
This flour has a gluten content of 7–10% and is recommended for baked goods, steamed sponge-type puddings and all pastries except puff. Baking powder or other raising agents are often used in conjunction with plain flour.

PLAIN OMELETTE
(Omelet, French Omelette)
A simple omelette made from eggs beaten with 5 ml/1 teaspoon water per egg and seasoning to taste. It is fried quickly in an omelette pan, folded into thirds and slipped out on to a warm plate.

PLANKED
North American term for food cooked and served on wood.

PLANTAIN
A species of banana (*Musa*) which is grown in most tropical areas and is a staple food of those regions. It is larger than the dessert banana and has green skin, often with blemishes. The skin is difficult to remove and the edible fruit is not soft and sweet but rather firm and starchy. It is eaten mainly as a vegetable, either boiled, baked or fried.

PLASTIC ICING
(Australian Fondant Icing)
A thick, paste-like cake icing which resembles fondant in appearance and can be rolled out like pastry. It is an Australian speciality made from granulated and icing sugars, water, gelatine, lemon juice and cooking fat or butter. It is left to rest overnight in a plastic bag, then rolled out on icing sugar and used as required. This icing can be coloured and moulded into flowers, figures, and so on.

PLAT DU JOUR
French term for the day's speciality (sometimes specialities), featured on a restaurant menu.

PLATE
A flat, usually round piece of crockery on which food is served; also, food and service supplied to one person.

PLATE OF BEEF
Term used in Scotland for a piece of beef cut from the shoulder of the animal. It is lean but tough and requires long, slow cooking such as stewing, braising or casseroling.

PLATEAU
A medium-strong Belgian cheese with a smooth texture. It has been likened both to Saint-Paulin and Herve cheeses and is made from cows' milk.

PLÄTTAR
Swedish pancakes which are rolled up and served with jam. They are a traditional dessert served after split pea and pork soup on winter Thursdays.

PLATTEKAAS
A Belgian version of curd cheese, generally made from cows' milk.

PLATTER
A large serving plate; also a main course on a plate.

PLAVA
A Jewish Passover cake which is often flavoured with almond. It is like a fatless sponge and made from *matzo* meal.

PLJESKAVICE
Yugoslavian grilled hamburgers, a Serbian speciality.

PLOAT (TO)
To pluck or remove feathers from birds.

PLOCKWURST
A German preserved sausage with a somewhat flaky texture, made from a high ratio of beef which, after smoking, develops a deep red colour.

PLOUGHMAN'S LUNCH
A traditional British 'Pub lunch' which usually consists of a piece of cheese, crusty bread and butter, pickles and beer.

PLOVER
Pigeon-sized game birds in season in Britain from August until March. Only the grey and golden varieties are eaten. They are generally roasted undrawn and served on toast with melted butter, slices of lemon and a garnish of watercress. One plover per person is the usual allowance.

PLOVERS' EGGS
A gastronomic delicacy.

PLUCK
The entrails and other internal organs, such as heart and liver, which are removed or plucked from an animal after slaughtering.

PLUCK (TO)
To remove feathers from poultry.

PLUM
The fruit of a tree (*Prunus* species) of the rose family. Many species have grown wild in the northern hemisphere for thousands of years and have been cultivated and cross-bred for nearly as long and the numerous varieties of the fruit may be oval or spherical and differ considerably in size. Most plums have an indentation running from top to bottom down one side. The skin may be any colour from yellow to black and the flesh is basically yellowish but, to some extent, may reflect the skin colour. All plums have a central stone, either oval or round. The flesh of the dessert varieties is juicy and sweet and these are best eaten raw; cooking plums are much less palatable in their raw state. All plums may be used in cooked dishes such as pies and tarts, but tend to be rather bland when cooked compared to close relatives such as damson and gage. However, plum jam is universally popular.

PLUM DUFF
A traditional British suet pudding which contains currants, raisins, spice and brown sugar. It is usually boiled in a floured cloth and the ball-shaped pudding is served hot with custard or cream.

PLUM PUDDING
Traditionally British, plum pudding dates back many centuries and was originally a porridge-like mixture made at Christmas with 'plumbs' or raisins, other dried fruits, spices, oranges and lemons, sugar, minced veal and beef, sherry and bread, which acted as a thickener. During the reign of Queen Victoria, because

it was popular with Prince Albert, plum pudding developed into the traditional Christmas pudding known today.

PLUM SAUCE
A Chinese condiment made from water, sugar and dark red plums.

PLUMBS
An old English word for raisins.

POACH (TO)
To cook delicate foods, such as eggs and fish, in very gently simmering liquid.

POACHED EGGS
Shelled eggs, simmered gently for about 3 minutes in a pan of slowly bubbling water, then lifted out with a draining spoon. If preferred, the liquid used for poaching may be milk, stock or wine, which can then be incorporated into a classic sauce to coat the eggs. For ease and convenience, an egg poacher may be used; this ensures that the eggs are cooked in a neat shape.

PO-BOY
A sandwich made by the Cajuns in the Louisiana Bayou country of the USA. It consists of a whole French loaf, split lengthwise, then packed with a savoury filling.

POCHE
See *Caecum*.

POD
Seed shell, generally elongated, of a fruit or vegetable which splits lengthwise into two parts when fully ripe to release the seeds for propagation. For use as food, the pod is usually picked before maturity for maximum flavour and tenderness. The term pod is used for the shell whether with or without the seeds; it is most often applied to the legume family of vegetables.

POD (TO)
To remove peas, for example, from their outer casing, which is more commonly called a pod.

POI
A paste made from the boiled, pounded tubers of the taro plant which is a staple food in the Pacific area.

à POINT
French term for a grilled rump, sirloin or fillet steak which is partially cooked through, known in Britain as medium.

POIRES BELLE HÉLÈNE
A classic French dessert composed of poached pear halves, vanilla ice cream and chocolate sauce.

à la POIVRADE
French term for any dish containing freshly milled black and white pepper; also dried green peppercorns.

POIVRADE SAUCE
(Pepper Sauce)
An Espagnole sauce, sharpened with dry red wine and wine vinegar, then flavoured with ground black pepper. It can be served with grilled and roast beef, also game dishes.

au POIVRE
French term for any dish with pepper. Steak is one example.

POKEWEED
A shrub (*Phytolacca americana*) with poisonous and inedible roots native to North America. Provided the leaves are young and up to about 15 cm/6 inches in length, they may be boiled and treated like asparagus. The red berry of the mature plant is used as a food colouring.

POLE DAB
A flatfish (*Glyptocephalus cynyglossus*) caught on both sides of the North Atlantic. It resembles

the winter flounder but the body is thinner. The fish may be poached, steamed, baked, fried or grilled.

POLENTA
Bright yellow maize (corn) meal which is like a coarse version of semolina. It is an Italian speciality, cooked until very thick with water and salt. Cooked *polenta* is served with meat stews, *Bolognese* sauce, or simply topped with butter and grated Parmesan cheese.

POLISHED RICE
White rice from which the outer husks have been removed during the milling process. It is lower in vitamin B than some other types of rice.

POLLACK
A member (*Pollachius pollachius*) of the cod family, similar in shape but with a protruding lower jaw. The back is dark green, shading to light green on the sides and white on the underside. It can measure up to 1 metre/39 inches, but is usually sold in the shops at half that length. It is very much a coastal fish and is found in rocky waters from Iceland to Spain where it is caught all year round. The flesh is lean, white and is of good quality although it is less delicate than cod. The fish may be poached, steamed, baked or fried.

POLLO ALLA CACCIATORA
An Italian chicken stew containing tomatoes, stock, seasonings, mushrooms and Marsala. It is usually served with fresh pasta.

POLLO ALLA MARENGO
An Italian chicken stew containing tomatoes, stock, white wine, seasonings, mushrooms, parsley and black olives.

POLLO REBOZADO
A Bolivian speciality. Chicken joints, coated in an egg and milk batter containing polenta, are first fried, then simmered until tender in a sauce made from tomatoes, wine, seasonings and spices.

POLLOCK
A North American name for coley.

à la POLONAISE
French term meaning in Polish style, referring to cooked vegetables sprinkled with melted butter, breadcrumbs, chopped hard-boiled eggs and sometimes parsley.

POLONY
(Poloney)
The British term for hot-smoked bologna sausage.

POLYSACCHARIDES
See *Carbohydrates*.

POLYUNSATURATED FATTY ACIDS
Found in many vegetable oils such as corn, rapeseed, soy and sunflower, these differ in nature chemically from fats and oils with saturated fatty acids, such as hard butter, lard, suet and cocoa butter, and are suitable for those on a low-cholesterol diet. They have a different number of carbon atoms from saturated fatty acids and contain two or more double bonds, forces that hold atoms together.

POMEGRANATE
The fruit of a tree (*Punica granatum*) probably native to Iran and grown in the Mediterranean area and as far east as India. It is now cultivated in other tropical and sub-tropical regions including South America. The fruit measures up to 7.5 cm/ 3 inches in diameter and is spherical, with a calyx (the remnants of the original flower) that is part of the skin and looks like a miniature crown. The skin is hard and leathery and becomes more so as the fruit ripens. It is yellow, tinged with red-brown on the side which faced the sun, and usually with small brown markings. The skin or rind is most important to this fruit as it protects a multitude of creamy-white seeds, the size of apple pips, embedded in glistening pellets of pink flesh which are juicy

and sweet. These fleshy seeds are contained in segments of yellow, bitter-tasting pith which extend inwards from the skin. The pomegranate is eaten by cutting it in half and easing out the pink pellets of flesh and seed. The flesh may also be used for food decoration, in salads and in cooked dishes. The juice has been appreciated since biblical times and is made by squeezing the pink flesh without crushing the pips, as they may add a bitter taste to the liquid.

POMELO

(Pummelo)
The fruit of an evergreen tree (*Citrus grandis* or *C. maxima*) native to the Far East and now cultivated in the Caribbean region (where it is also known as 'shaddock' after the man who introduced it to the West Indies) and in the eastern Mediterranean. The largest member of the citrus family, the pomelo looks rather like an elongated, pear-shaped grapefruit with goose-pimpled skin. This skin consists of an outer yellow rind and an inner lining of lighter pith. The sweetish flesh is naturally divided into segments contained in a thick membrane which should be removed before use. Pomelo can be eaten in its natural state or used in salads and other sweet or savoury dishes, and the skin can be used in preserves or made into candied peel.

POMMES ANNA

A classic French potato dish composed of layers of hair-thin slices of potatoes, melted butter and seasonings. It is baked until the top is golden brown, then inverted on to a warm dish. It is cut into wedges to serve.

POMMES DUCHESSE

A classic French potato dish used in *haute cuisine* as a garnish in the form of a border piped round large serving dishes. It is made from very finely mashed potato beaten until completely smooth with butter, egg yolks and a little milk. The mixture is carefully brushed with beaten egg yolk, then browned in a hot oven.

POMMES SAVOYARD

Similar to *gratin Dauphinois* but made with stock instead of milk.

POMPANO

A seawater fish (*Trachinotus* species) with a high back, deep belly and a deeply forked tail. The colour of the back may vary from yellow to greeny-blue, graduating to a silvery underside. Small fish of 500 g–1 kg/18 oz–2¼ lb are best for eating but the weight may reach up to 3.25 kg/7 lb. Pompano is caught in warm and tropical waters off the western coasts of North America. The flesh is white, tender and rich and the fish may be baked, fried or grilled.

PONTEFRACT CAKE

(Pomfret Cake)
A round and flat liquorice sweet.

PONT-L'EVÊQUE

Available in 200-g/7-oz boxed squares, French Pont-l'Evêque is a plump cheese which shares a similarity in flavour to Camembert, though there is more strength and nuttiness to its taste. Produced from cows' milk and said to be one of Normandy's oldest cheeses (it dates back 300 years), it bears the *Appellation Controlée* label of origin, an indication of its superior quality. Its speckled golden-orange rind is serrated and cross-hatched from the mats on which it has lain, and the soft, pale, yellow interior reveals countless holes. It is a full-flavoured and hearty cheese, best eaten with a knife and fork.

POOR KNIGHTS OF WINDSOR

A British version of *pain perdu*, popular in both Britain and France from the Middle Ages onwards. The egg and milk mixture, into which fingers of bread are dipped before frying, is sometimes flavoured with alcohol. The hot fingers are frequently sprinkled with caster sugar and cinnamon.

POOR MAN'S BEEF STEAK
See *Beefsteak Fungus*.

POOR MAN'S GOOSE
See *Faggots*.

POP
A British colloquial term to describe fizzy, sweet drinks.

POPCORN
Special kind of maize (corn) which pops and bursts when heated, due to soft starch and steam in the kernel. Popcorn has been a popular food for thousands of years and even before Columbus set sail for the New World, North and South American Indians, together with Mexican Indians, were popping corn in hot sand, on hot stones in shallow clay pots or, on the cob, directly over an open fire.

POPE'S EYE OF BEEF
Term used in the west of Scotland for rump.

POPE'S NOSE
See *Parson's Nose*.

POPOVERS
North American term for small Yorkshire puddings baked in bun or patty tins.

POPPADOM
(Puppadom)
See *Papadum*.

POPPER
North American term for a utensil used to prepare popcorn.

POPPY SEEDS
Obtained from the bright red field poppy (*Papaver rhoeas*), poppy seeds are native to Asia but are also cultivated in Europe, particularly in Holland, Poland and Turkey. It takes about 900,000 of the gun-metal grey seeds to produce 500 g/18 oz. Although they are a product of the poppy plant, the seeds have no narcotic properties and are crunchy with a pleasing flavour of nuts. They were known to the Egyptians around 1500 BC and are widely used in baking and in some Jewish and Oriental specialities.

PORBEAGLE SHARK
See *Shark*.

PORCINI
Italian term for cep.

PORK
The flesh of pig, beige in colour and considered rich due to its high fat content.

PORK CHOP
Term used in Wales and the West Country for loin of pork chops.

PORK CRACKLING
(Crackling)
The crisp and golden bands of the scored skin of roast pork.

PORK PIE
A British raised pie which may be large or small and similar in character to Melton Mowbray pie. The main difference is that the meat in a traditional pork pie is cubed, not minced, and hard-boiled eggs are sometimes included.

PORK SAUSAGES
British sausages containing pork, cereal and seasonings, which are fried or grilled.

PORKER
A hog specially fattened for eating.

PÖRKÖLT
Described in Hungary as a combined sauté, stew and braised dish, a thick beef mixture containing tomatoes, green peppers, onions, and paprika. Water is added in small amounts. The dish is traditionally served with boiled potatoes or rice and either a

green salad or pickled cucumber. In Hungary, other meats, game and poultry are also used.

PORRIDGE OATS
(Oat Flakes, Rolled Oat Flakes, Rolled Oats)
Produced from whole grain oats which are husked and then rolled. They are used as a hot breakfast cereal, notably in Scotland, a basis for muesli, a thickener in savoury dishes and for baking.

PORT
A blended and fortified grape wine from Portugal which is popular as an after-dinner drink. It can be red or white in colour and ranges from dry to sweet in taste. It is often added to soups, sauces and hot wine cups and, at formal lunches and dinners, is served with the cheese at the end of the meal.

PORT WINE JELLY
A typical British dessert made from port, sugar, spices and gelatine. The mixture is poured into a mould, turned out when cold and set and served with whipped cream.

PORTERHOUSE STEAK
Beef steak cut from the fillet end of the sirloin. It is always boned, is relatively large and either grilled or fried.

PORT-SALUT
(Port-du-Salut)
Originally a French monastery cheese, made by Trappist monks of the Port-du-Salut Abbey at Entrammes. It dates back 200 years and closely resembles Saint-Paulin. After the Second World War, the monks sold the name of Port-du-Salut to commercial enterprises and much of this famous and popular cows' milk cheese is now factory-produced under the name Port-Salut.

à la PORTUGAISE
French term meaning in Portuguese style, referring to a garnish of tomatoes, potatoes, shallots or onions and mushrooms.

PORTUGAISE SAUCE
(Tomato Sauce)
Similar to Espagnole sauce but containing more fresh tomatoes to produce what is basically a classic tomato sauce. It can be served with pasta and dishes made from meat, poultry, fish and eggs.

PORTUGAL CABBAGE
(Braganza Cabbage, Couve Tronchuda)
A hardy member (*Brassica oleracea*, var. *Tronchuda*) of the cabbage family, developed in Portugal and used in the national soup called *caldo verde*.

PORTUGUESE BOILED DINNER
See *Cozido à Portuguesa*.

PORTUGUESE OYSTER
See *Oyster*.

POSSET
An old-fashioned British dessert, made from a rich egg custard mixture with the addition of sherry, lemon and sometimes almonds; also, a hot drink made from spiced, sweetened milk containing alc or wine.

POSSUM
See *Opossum*.

POSTNY FARSHIROVONI KABACHOK
A Russian speciality, consisting of aubergines stuffed with their own pulp mixed with fried onions, tomatoes, chopped hard-boiled eggs, parsley and seasonings. The stuffed aubergines are sandwiched together in pairs, then baked in a little water and lard.

POT
A cylindrical-shaped container, usually deep and fitted with a lid and two small handles. It is made from earthenware or metal and is

especially useful for the gentle simmering of stews.

POT (TO)
To put paste-like mixtures of meat, fish, poultry and game into smallish pots and seal them by covering the tops with a layer of melted fat which solidifies on cooling (such as butter); to put freshly made jams, marmalades and pickles into jars.

POT CHEESE
A North American term for cottage cheese.

POT LUCK
Sharing the food of one's host or hostess, be it humble or *haute cuisine*, hence taking pot luck or a gamble when making unplanned social calls.

POT MARJORAM
A perennial herb (*Origanum onites*), native to Sicily, which came to Britain in the middle of the 18th century. It is a close relation of marjoram and has a similar flavour.

POTAGE
French term for a thickened soup.

POTAGE À L'ALBIGEOISE
A sturdy soup from Albi in south-west France, usually with a base of beef stock and containing preserved goose, sometimes calves' feet, ham, sausage and mixed vegetables.

POTASSIUM
Chemically, this behaves in a very similar way to sodium, but potassium is contained in muscle cells and red corpuscles. Potassium is lost from the body through urine, but not from sweat. Most foods contain potassium and a deficiency of this mineral is rare.

POTASSIUM BROMATE
See *Bleaching Agents*.

POTASSIUM NITRATE
See *Saltpetre*.

POTATO
A vegetable (*Solanum tuberosum*) which is the tuber of a plant native to South America. In the 16th century it was introduced to Europe where it was regarded with a mixture of interest and suspicion before becoming established as a major food crop. It is now cultivated worldwide except in regions of extreme heat or cold. There are many varieties of potato and the skin colour varies from fawn to red. The potato is an irregular, elongated ball-shape and the starchy flesh is generally a creamy-white colour and is either waxy or floury in texture. Main crop potatoes in the shops usually measure 4–7.5 cm/1½–3 inches across the middle and no more than about 15 cm/6 inches in length; early or 'new' potatoes are generally much smaller. From a culinary point of view the potato is very versatile and may be boiled, baked, steamed or fried and used in many savoury recipes. Much of the goodness lies in the layers just beneath the skin so peeling or scraping should be avoided where possible.

POTATO CHIPS
See *Chips*.

POTATO CRISPS
See *Crisps*.

POTATO CROQUETTES
Fried balls of mashed potato.

POTATO LATKES
Closely related to Germany's *kartoffelpuffer*, Jewish potato pancakes made from grated raw potatoes, chopped onions, eggs, flour and seasoning. They are fried until crisp and usually served with Jewish salt beef and pickled cucumbers.

POTATO MASHER
A flat piece of perforated metal or plastic with an upright handle. The potatoes are mashed by plunging the masher up and down.

POTATO PEELER
See *Peeler*.

POTATO SALAD
Consisting of cooked, diced potato tossed with mayonnaise. Sometimes a little grated onion is also included and the salad is generally garnished with chopped parsley.

POT-AU-FEU
The literal translation is 'a pot over heat'. A two-in-one French meal consisting of a beef and vegetable soup (first course) in which a large piece of beef has been boiled (second course).

POTÉE
A substantial French soup containing mixed vegetables including cabbage and potatoes, beans, lentils, salt pork and sausages.

POTHERB
Any of various plants whose leaves or stems are cooked as green vegetables; also a herb, such as parsley, which is used to flavour food.

POT-ROAST (TO)
To cook a less tender cut of meat slowly, with a small amount of liquid and seasonings, in a covered container in the oven.

POTTAGE
A thick vegetable soup.

POTTED HOUGH
A type of brawn made in Scotland from shin of beef, a piece of knuckle, peppercorns and seasonings, all simmered slowly together in water.

POTTED MEAT
Meat, such as shin of beef, cooked slowly in water with bones and trotters. It is then coarsely chopped and mixed with some of the cooking liquor which sets on cooling. Traditionally, the meat and gelatinous liquor are packed into pots, hence the name.

POTTED SHRIMPS
A typically British *hors d'oeuvre*, made by mixing peeled shrimps with melted butter and transferring the mixture to small pots for serving.

POUDING DIPLOMATE
French term for diplomat or cabinet pudding.

POUDING NESSELRODE
Created for the Russian Count Nesselrode, it is uncertain whether this pudding was the masterpiece of the French chef Mony or of Carême. A sweetened chestnut purée is combined with an egg custard, flavoured with maraschino. Raisins and currants are added. The mixture is half frozen, cream is folded into it and it is then transferred to a mould. It is turned out when firm and served with maraschino-flavoured custard.

POUILE DUDON
A chicken stew from St Lucia in the Caribbean containing coconut oil, garlic, onions, pepper, caramelized sugar and spices. It is served with pigeon peas and rice.

POULARDE ALBUFÉRA
An ornate French chicken dish which owes its name to one of Napoleon's generals.

POULET NOIR
A type of French chicken, now available in Britain, with black feathers and a very slightly gamey flavour.

POULTRY
Domestic birds, including chickens of all types, turkey, duck and goose. Chicken and turkey are first-class protein foods and their flesh is lighter in texture and more digestible than dark meats such as beef or lamb. Chicken and turkey are comparatively lean, but duck and goose contain more fat and are therefore richer. Poultry may be roasted, braised, boiled, steamed, poached or fried according to the recipe.

POULTRY SHEARS
Heavy scissors with serrated blades designed for cutting through joints of raw or cooked poultry and game.

POUND (TO)
To break down food with a pestle and mortar; also to beat meat with a special meat mallet or rolling pin, either because the recipe requires thin slices of meat, or because the meat itself is tough and needs pounding to break down the fibres and tenderize the flesh.

POUND CAKE
A rich cake made with equal weights of eggs, sugar, fat and flour. It is made by the creaming method and usually no raising agent is required.

POURING BATTER
A thin batter which is made from flour, seasonings, sometimes sugar, egg and milk. It is used for pancakes or Yorkshire pudding.

POURING SAUCE
Either a brown or white thin sauce used for moistening dry foods. The usual proportion is 15 g/½ oz thickening agent to every 300 ml/½ pint milk or other liquid.

POURLY
A French goats' milk cheese from Burgundy. It is a fairly recent addition to the family of goat cheeses and is white, creamy, mild and covered with a pale blue-grey rind.

POUR-ON CHEESE
Bottled processed cheese toppings from North America which are described as being either mild or sharp.

POUSSIN
A 4–6-week-old chicken weighing about 450 g/1 lb. One bird will serve one person.

PRAGUE HAM
(Pragerschinken)
Speciality ham from Prague, in Czechoslovakia, which is cured for some months in a mild brine solution, then wood-smoked. It is now difficult to find, even in its country of origin.

PRAIRIE OYSTER
A hangover remedy made from brandy, Worcestershire sauce, vinegar, ketchup, Tabasco, bitters and a whole egg yolk. The mixture is swallowed in one gulp.

PRAIRIE OYSTERS
See *Mountain Oysters*.

PRALINE
Almonds set in caramel, sometimes crushed to a powder and used in ice cream, desserts and confectionery.

PRÄSTOST
A Swedish cheese made from cows' milk. It is factory-produced and is a firm and creamy cheese with a somewhat open texture. It dates back about 200 years and the name translates into English as 'Priest's cheese'.

PRATIE
Irish term for potato.

PRATO
The name of this Brazilian cows' milk cheese means 'plate'. It is fairly flat and resembles the Dutch family of cheeses.

PRAWN
A small, clawless, saltwater crustacean with an elongated, curved tail and large head with antennae. The names prawn and shrimp are sometimes interchangeable in Britain, but in the USA and elsewhere, the term shrimp is widely used for all the assorted species. The prawn is found worldwide and is caught primarily in the summer months. The main British kind is the common prawn (*Palaemon serratus*); on Canada's west coast, the spot prawn (*Pandalus platyceros*) is the most important. The colour varies widely from whitish to red or brown and the

average length is 7.5–20 cm/ 3–8 inches. In most cases the prawn is washed and boiled when caught. The tail meat can be used in a variety of dishes or eaten in its plain, boiled state.

PRAWN COCKTAIL
Served as an *hors d'oeuvre*, shelled prawns are combined with a cocktail sauce, usually made from mayonnaise flavoured with tomato ketchup, Worcestershire sauce, Tabasco, lemon juice and a little grated horseradish or horseradish sauce. This mixture is put into individual dishes or glasses, already partly filled with shredded lettuce and garnished with lemon wedges. Crabmeat, shrimps and other types of shellfish or cooked white fish may be used in a similar way to make fish cocktails.

PRAWN COCKTAIL SAUCE
See *Cocktail Sauce*.

PRAWN CRACKERS
The Chinese version of crisps, which can either be served as a cocktail savoury or as an accompaniment to Chinese dishes. Available in packets in assorted pastel colours, the crackers look like opaque plastic discs but puff up as they are deep-fried. When cooked, they are almost white and bear no resemblance to potato crisps.

PRE-COOK (TO)
To cook in advance; to cook one or more ingredients and then use them in another dish which is further reheated. Pre-cooking is also used for foods which are subsequently to be incorporated into salads such as rice, pasta, eggs, meat, poultry, fish and vegetables.

PREHEAT (TO)
To heat in advance, especially an oven.

PREPARED MUSTARD
(Continental Mustard)
Almost every country has its own variety of prepared mustard and those from France and Germany are best known, often referred to as continental mustards. Generally, prepared mustards are made from a base of ground mustard seed (dark and/or light) mixed with selections of vinegars, herbs, spices and seasonings. They are used as condiments and also added to a wide variety of dishes.

PRE-PRANDIAL
Usually referring to a pre-dinner drink.

PRESERVATIVE
A substance (or substances) that helps to prevent food spoilage, decay and discoloration. It can be an anti-oxidant such as sulphur dioxide.

PRESERVE (TO)
To can, bottle, deep-freeze or otherwise treat perishable foods for future use; a jam or jelly consisting of fruit preserved by cooking with sugar.

PRESERVED SAUSAGES
Called *rohwurst* in German, preserved sausages are made from lean fresh pork and beef which are smoked and air-dried to prolong their keeping qualities. Seasonings vary according to type and region of production. All preserved sausages keep for many months in a cool place; refrigerator storage is required if the sausages have been sliced and vacuum-packed.

PRESERVING SUGAR
Refined white sugar especially recommended for jam- and marmalade-making as it forms minimal scum.

PRESS (TO)
To weigh down cooked tongue, boned joints of meat and boned poultry so that they retain a neat

and attractive shape when cold; also, to squeeze juice out of fruit.

PRESSED CHEESE
A cheese-making process whereby milk curds are moulded and pressed during production. The longer and harder the pressing, the firmer the cheese becomes.

PRESSED OX TONGUE
Made by cooking a whole tongue, stripping it of skin, removing bones and gristle near the root end, then curving the tongue snugly into a round saucepan or cake tin. It should be covered with a plate, then weighed down with a brick or heavy stone. When cold and set, the tongue is unmoulded, thinly sliced and served with salad.

PRESSURE COOKER
A lidded saucepan made of thick aluminium in which food is cooked under pressure. Both the base and the lid of the cooker have sturdy handles and the lid has a pressure gauge and a safety valve. Food is cooked quickly, thus saving time and fuel. Manufacturer's instructions should always be read carefully before using a pressure cooker.

PRESSURE COOKING
Cooking by means of pressure produced by steam from water within a pressure cooker. The major advantages of this method are speed, fuel economy and flavour retention as no steam escapes from the hermetically-sealed cooker.

PRETZELS
(Bretzels, Salt Sticks)
A German type of savoury biscuit, available in a variety of shapes including figures of eight and knots. They are dry, slightly salty, and popular with apéritifs.

PRICKLY CUSTARD APPLE
See *Sour Sop*.

PRICKLY PEAR
The fruit of cactus plants (*Opuntia* species) native to Central and South America, now both cultivated and growing wild in countries bordering the Mediterranean, India, Australia and south-western North America. The fruit is oblong rather than pear-shaped and has a tough, thin skin covered in barbed prickles. As the fruit ripens, the skin colour turns from green to greeny-orange and even to a purply-red, depending on the type. The length can be 4–7.5 cm/1½–3 inches. The flesh is a seed-filled pulp which may be white, yellow or orange and is sweet and juicy when ripe. The seeds may be eaten if soft. Although usually eaten raw, the flesh may be used in cooked dishes. Because the seeds become hard during cooking, they should be removed from the flesh before use. The prickles are difficult to dislodge if they become stuck into the hands and, therefore, care should be taken when handling the fruit. An alternative name for one of the varieties of prickly pear is Indian fig.

PRIME
Term for a choice and top-quality cut, especially applied to meat or fish.

PRINCE ALBERT PUDDING
An old-fashioned British pudding, in which a Victoria sandwich mixture is steamed in a basin lined with cooked prunes. Sometimes half the flour is replaced by breadcrumbs.

à la PRINCESSE
French term meaning in the style of the princess, referring to a garnish for steaks and sweetbreads composed of artichokes, asparagus tips, potatoes and sometimes Béchamel sauce.

à la PRINTANIÈRE
French term meaning in the style of spring, denoting an addition or garnish of mixed spring vegetables.

Puddings and Desserts

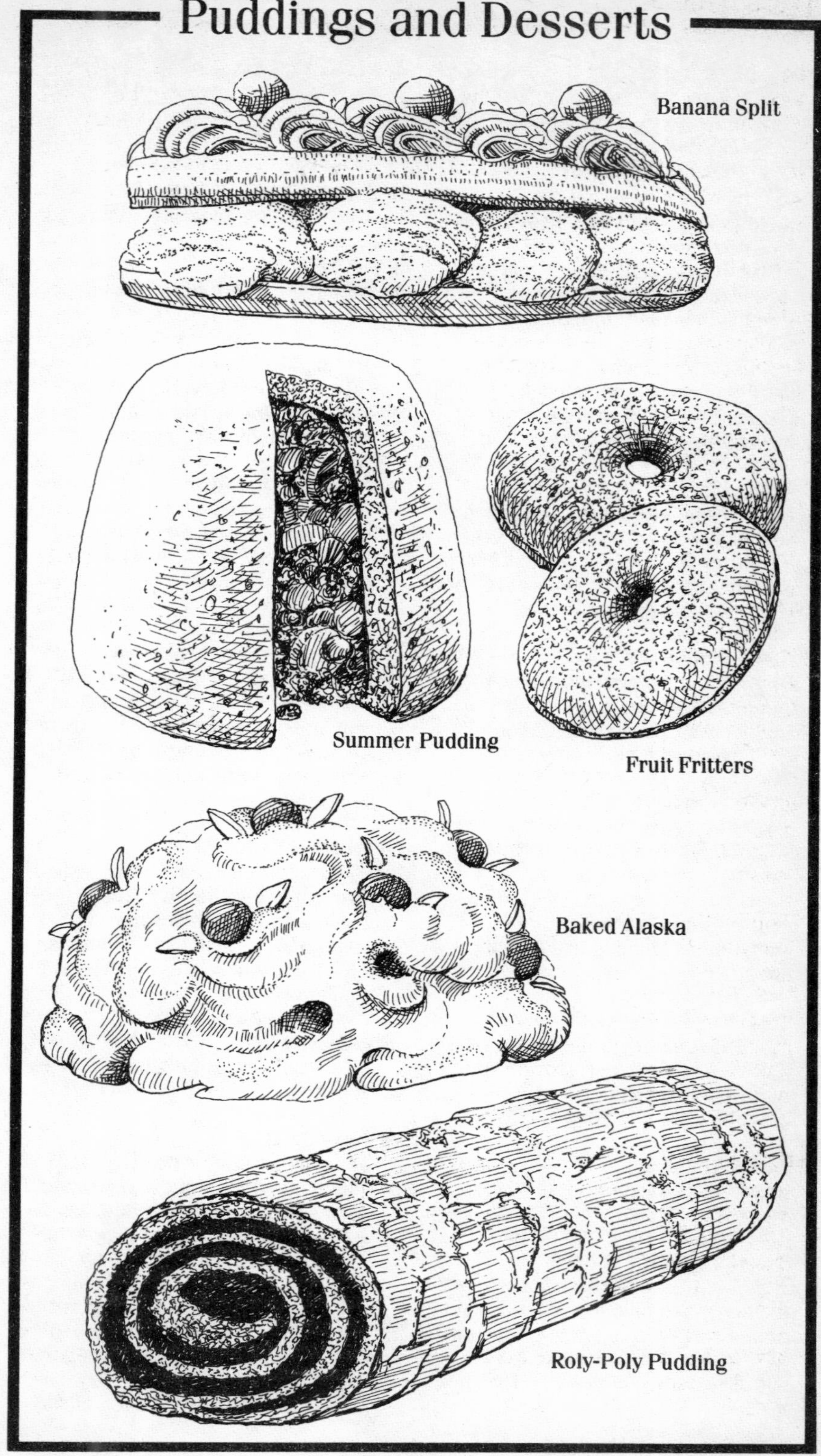

PRIX FIXE
French term for fixed price, usually seen on restaurant menus.

PROCESSED CHEESE
Relatively bland-tasting cheese, made by melting down one or more cheeses, then re-shaping the mixture while still warm. Processed cheese may be fairly firm or spreadable and is sometimes sold already sliced in vacuum-packs or in tubes. The technique of making this cheese was developed in Switzerland during the early part of this century and the most widely used varieties are Cheddar, Emmental, Gouda or Edam. Additives include emulsifying agents and legally laid-down limits of other flavouring ingredients such as herbs and tomato. These cheeses have good keeping qualities.

PROCESSED PEAS
Bright green marrowfat peas, canned with added water, salt and sugar, which are drained, heated and served with main meals.

PROFITEROLES
A popular dessert of small choux pastry buns, filled with lightly sweetened whipped cream. Chocolate sauce is the traditional coating. The *profiteroles* are sometimes mounded in a pyramid shape.

PROPRIETARY FLOURS
Flour mixtures containing assorted amounts of wheatgerm, bran, soy flour, malt and sometimes other cereals, including rye and barley.

PROSCIUTTO
Italian term for ham, generally smoked and spiced.

PROSCIUTTO CRUDO
Highly esteemed salted and air-dried Italian ham such as Parma ham. *Prosciutto crudo* is eaten raw in very thin slices as an *hors d'oeuvre*. Often served with figs or melon.

PROSCIUTTO DI MONTAGNA
A relation of Parma ham but more powerfully flavoured and darker in colour.

PROTECTIVE FOODS
An old-fashioned term for vitamins.

PROTEINS
These are vital in providing material for the growth, repair and maintenance of body tissue. Spare protein also provides energy and can sometimes be converted into fat. Most proteins are not soluble in water, although a fair number of common food proteins do dissolve in brine solutions of various densities. Proteins are compounds of carbon, hydrogen, oxygen, nitrogen and sometimes also contain sulphur and/or phosphorus.

PROVE (TO)
To leave a yeast mixture to rise; to treat a frying pan (without a non-stick coating) by heating with salt and oil so that certain mixtures, such as pancake batter or omelettes, will not adhere to the base and sides.

à la PROVENÇALE
French term meaning in the style of Provence in southern France, referring to dishes cooked with tomatoes, garlic, olive oil, onions, olives and sometimes mushrooms and anchovies.

PROVISIONS
Foodstuffs bought to eat; groceries for the store cupboard.

PROVOLONE
Originally from the south of Italy, cows' milk Provolone is now made throughout the country and may be mild or piquant, depending on the rennet used in production. It is hand-moulded into assorted shapes and matured for either 2–3 months for a mild variety, or 6 months to 2 years for a zestier and stronger cheese. Young Provolone is treated as a dessert cheese and the more

mature types are used in cooking. It is generally accepted as being a hard cheese.

PROVOLONE AFFUMICATA
A smoked version of Provolone.

PRUNES
Dried plums, brownish-black in colour with wrinkled skin. Some varieties are sold already stoned.

PTARMIGAN
Game bird found in parts of Scandinavia and the Scottish Highlands. In Britain it is in season from late August until early December. It is generally roasted and one ptarmigan per person is the usual allowance.

PUDDING
Originally, a mixture of minced meat and cereal, packed into a skin and boiled, for example, black pudding and haggis; also, a light, spongy sweet cake mixture which is steamed, boiled or baked in a basin, tin or dish; a steak and kidney pudding in which the meat and offal are steamed in a basin lined with suet crust pastry; the sweet or dessert course served at the end of a meal.

PUFF PASTRY
A rich, melting, multi-layered connoisseur's pastry which bakes to a flaky, golden-brown crispness in a hot oven. Its success relies upon the way in which the fat (usually butter) is incorporated and the number of times the pastry is rolled and folded. It is recommended for *vol-au-vent* cases and pastries such as *mille feuilles*.

PUFFBALL
A fungus (*Lycoperdon* species) which is edible in its various forms when young. The giant puffball is the most impressive of the family, and grows during summer and autumn in forests or on grazing land. All types of puffball are eaten young, when the flesh is still white and before the brown spores form inside the body. The puffball is usually sliced and fried.

PUFFED
Food which is mechanically aerated, such as puffed cereal grains.

PUFFS
(Jam Puffs)
Hollow rounds of puff pastry filled with jam and/or whipped cream.

PUI LA CEAUN CU MUJDEI
Romanian roast chicken served with a sauce made from chicken stock and crushed garlic cloves.

PULAO
See *Pilau*.

PULLAN
(Pollan)
An Irish freshwater herring caught in lakes during spring and summer. It is similar to vendace.

PULLET
A young hen.

PULP
A thick and sometimes coarse purée of fruit or vegetables; also, the residue of cooked fruit or vegetables after sieving.

PULSE
Term for dried seeds of legumes such as the bean, pea and lentil. Pulses are a rich source of protein and a staple food in vegetarian diets.

PULTOST
(Knaost, Ramost)
A Norwegian cows' milk cheese which is made all over the country. It is tangy and often contains caraway seeds.

PUMMELO
See *Pomelo*.

PUMPERNICKEL
A speciality German bread made from rye flour and cooked in steam chambers for as long as 20 hours. It

is very dark in colour, strongly flavoured with a slightly sticky texture and is always thinly sliced.

PUMPKIN
A vegetable (*Cucurbita pepo*) of the squash family. It is native to North America and grown on both sides of the Atlantic, but is more highly regarded in North America than in Europe. The shape is usually round and the skin colour is generally orange, but elongated varieties exist and the colour can vary from white to yellow. The flesh contains edible seeds. The pumpkin is a large vegetable and is mostly sold in sections. It is used in both sweet and savoury dishes and as a vegetable.

PUMPKIN PIE
A North American dessert, traditionally served at the Thanksgiving celebrations, comprising a pastry shell filled with cooked pumpkin purée, eggs, sugar, spices, cream or evaporated milk and treacle or molasses. It is baked until firm and set, then cut into wedges and served with whipped cream.

PUMPKIN SEEDS
The nutritious, edible kernels of the pumpkin which are covered in cream-coloured husks. When the husks are removed, oval flat seeds are revealed which are green-skinned with ivory flesh. The seeds are sold fresh or roasted, with or without the husk, and may be eaten as they are or used both in cooking and as a garnish.

PUNCH
The name is derived from the old Indian word meaning 'five' and alludes to the ingredients which frequently are used in a punch: spirit (rum, for example), water, sugar, lemon and spice.

PUNNET
A small square or oval basket, woven from strips of thin wood, plastic or reinforced card, often with a handle, used to hold soft fruits such as strawberries and raspberries.

PUR CHÈVRE
The French term for cheese made only from goats' milk.

PURÉE
A thick pulp made from raw or cooked fruit and vegetables, rubbed through a sieve or worked until smooth in a blender goblet or food processor; also, a thick smooth soup made usually from puréed vegetables, stock or water, seasonings, milk and cream.

PURIS
Indian bread, basically deep-fried *chapatis* which puff and swell as they cook. *Puris* should be served hot with assorted curries.

PURPLE PASSION FRUIT
The fruit of a plant (*Passiflora edulis*) native to Brazil, cultivated in Australia and Africa. Round or egg-shaped, this particular fruit of a passion flower is 5–7.5 cm/2–3 inches in diameter. It has a green, tough and leathery skin which turns browny-purple and very wrinkled as the fruit ripens. The juicy flesh consists of a light orange-coloured pulp dotted with small and edible black seeds. It has a distinctive flavour with a sweet-sharp taste which is noticeable even in small quantities in fruit salads or ice cream. It is often eaten as a dessert fruit cut in half and spooned out of the skin.

PURSLANE
(Common Purslane, Green Purslane)
A herb-type plant (*Portulaca oleracea*) which probably originated in Asia and is found both wild and cultivated in many parts of the world. It has green, fleshy leaves which, when young, are suitable for use in salads. The flavour is mild but sharply distinctive and the texture is

slightly sticky. Purslane is also used as a flavouring and can be dried and made into a tisane.

PUTREFACTION
See *Decomposition*.

PYRÉNÉES
A French cheese produced from cows' or ewes' milk in the mountainous south-west. The cows' milk version is wrapped in a black rind; the ewes' milk cheese has an orange coat. Both types are peppered with small holes and are supple with gentle yet somewhat tangy flavours.

PYRIDOXINE
(Pyridoxal, Pyridoxol)
See *Vitamin* B_6.

PYTT I PANNA
A Swedish hash made from fried potato cubes, fried onions, fried ham and fried beef cubes. Each portion is sprinkled with parsley and topped with a raw egg yolk which is stirred into the hash.

QUADRUCCI
Small squares of egg pasta used in soup.

QUAHOG
An Atlantic clam (*Mercenaria mercenaria*) which can reach a length of 13 cm/5 inches but is sold at various sizes by volume rather than weight. In North America it is gathered all year round along the whole of the east coast. It may be eaten raw, particularly if very small, steamed or used in made-up dishes. In the USA it is also known as hard clam and hardshell clam.

QUAIL
A small, migratory game bird which visits Britain between May and October. Quail is a protected species in Britain, so only birds specially reared for the table are available. They are usually wrapped in strips of bacon or in vine leaves and roasted and are sometimes served on buttered toast, garnished with watercress.

QUAILS' EGGS
Small eggs, exactly the same shape as hen's eggs but with smoother and creamier yolks. Hard-boiled and shelled, they may be served with a dip of mayonnaise as an appetizer. They may also be used for garnishing cold dishes on a buffet.

QUARK
A German, low-fat, soft cows' milk cheese which can be compared to smooth cottage cheese or a cross between thick yogurt and cottage cheese. It is a fresh and mild-tasting product which is completely natural and free from preservatives and colouring. Because it is bland, it can be used for sweet or savoury purposes. It is an excellent source of proteins, vitamins and minerals, with some varieties containing fresh herbs, vegetables and fruit. It resembles Italian Ricotta and French Fromage Frais.

QUARTER OF MEAT
Limb of a four-legged animal with the adjacent parts.

QUARTIROLO
An Italian cows' milk cheese which resembles Bel Paese.

QUATRE-ÉPICES
A French version of mixed spice made from four spices: cloves, white pepper, nutmeg and ginger. It is generally used for savoury dishes.

QUATRE-QUARTS CAKE
The French version of British and North American pound cakes. See *Pound Cake*.

QUEEN CAKES
A Victorian speciality, these are small, rich cakes containing currants and flavoured with nutmeg and lemon. They are baked in individual bun tins.

QUEEN OF PUDDINGS
A British pudding consisting of a baked breadcrumb mixture containing sugar, milk, eggs and essences. The mixture is spread with jam while hot, topped with meringue and baked slowly until golden-brown.

QUEEN SCALLOP
(Queenie)
A small, bivalve shellfish (*Chlamys opecularis*) of the scallop family with a maximum shell size of 10 cm/4 inches in diameter. The shell colour varies from pink to brown. As with the larger scallops, the muscle controlling the shell is the main edible part. It is lean and rich and may be poached, baked, shallow-fried or grilled.

QUENELLES
Very finely minced raw fish, meat, game, chicken's or calf's liver combined with egg whites, seasonings and sometimes brandy and/or whipped cream. Tablespoonfuls of the mixture are poached very gently in stock or water, drained thoroughly and served with a classic French sauce. *Quenelles de brochet*, served with *sauce Nantua*, are a renowned example of this treatment.

QUESADILLAS
Fried *tortilla* 'sandwiches', filled with cheese, onions and chillies. A Mexican speciality, they must be served hot.

QUESILLOS
A South American cream cheese which is rather like Asadero. It is made from cows' milk and wrapped in leaves of corn or banana.

QUESUCOS
A Spanish cheese from Santander, made from a mixture of cows', ewes' and goats' milk. It is pleasantly mild and often smoked.

QUICHE
A French sweet or savoury open tart or flan, the most famous being *quiche Lorraine* with its traditional filling of eggs, cream and bacon.

QUICHE LORRAINE
See *Quiche*.

QUICK CURE (OF BACON)
(Canadian Style, Mild Cure, Sweet Cure, Tender Cure)
A fast method of curing bacon which takes 2–3 days. The curing solution, of syrup, sugar and spices, is injected mechanically into the muscles of the carcass and the end product, whether smoked or not, is vacuum-packed.

QUICK-MIX CAKES
Quick-mix cakes have the same consistency, texture, flavour and appearance as creamed cakes but are termed 'quick-mix' because all the ingredients are put into a bowl and beaten together for 2–3 minutes. This is undoubtedly a short-cut method and, for success, it is essential to use easy-cream or soft margarines, or whipped-up white cooking fat.

QUINCE
The fruit of a deciduous tree (*Cydonia vulgaris*) of the same family as the apple and the pear, native to South-West Asia and grown in many temperate regions around the world, both commercially and as a garden plant. The different varieties can be round like an apple, elongated like a pear or a rather knobbly shape somewhere between the two. The size can vary from that of a plum to cultivated giants of over 1.5 kg/3 lb in weight. The skin colour is yellow and sometimes has a light down, and the flesh is slightly paler with a central core of many

brown pips. The fruit has a pleasant fragrance when ripe, but the flesh is too hard and bitter to be eaten raw. When cooked, the flesh turns pink and may be used in both sweet and savoury dishes. Quince makes excellent preserves.

QUININE
Alkaloid found in the bark of cinchona, a tropical evergreen tree. It is used both as a medicine and also to flavour tonic water.

QUINOA
A small, seed-like grain which is golden in colour and not unlike millet in appearance. It has been cultivated in the South American Andes since 3000 BC and was the basic food of the Incas. Pronounced 'keenowa', the plant is a tall annual (*Chenopodium quinoa*) with pink stems, grown primarily in altitudes unsuitable for corn. Quinoa is a high-protein food which has nourished and sustained the native populations of Chile and Peru for centuries; it is rich in phosphorus, calcium and vitamins B and E. The grain may be used in the same way as rice and makes an excellent breakfast cereal. It has a nutty and delicate flavour and a grainy texture.

RABAÇAL
A Portuguese curd cheese made in the mountains from a mixture of ewes' and goats' milk. It has a mild yet full flavour and is white and soft. Sometimes it is allowed to mature for up to 4 weeks, causing its taste to intensify.

RABBIT
A four-legged, fur-covered animal which is sold either whole or divided into portions. The strong flavour of the flesh may be toned down by soaking the skinned animal in salted water for 1 hour and then blanching it for 1–2 minutes. Rabbit may be fried, roasted, stewed, casseroled or braised. The traditional accompaniment to roast rabbit is onion sauce.

RACCOON
A small, carnivorous mammal of North America, sometimes eaten by Cajuns in the Louisiana Bayou region.

à la RACHEL
French term meaning in the style of Rachel, referring to a garnish for steaks of artichokes, bone marrow and parsley.

RACK OF LAMB
Consists of one best end neck of lamb, chined and fat-trimmed, which is generally lightly coated on the outside with a breadcrumb mixture containing mustard, herbs, seasonings and butter or margarine. It is then roasted and cut into chops for serving. A single rack serves 2 people.

RACLETTE
A Swiss cheese made from unpasteurized cows' milk and similar to Gruyère in both texture and taste. It has given its name to *raclette*, a classic Swiss dish made by halving a Raclette cheese, toasting it in front of a fire, scraping it on to plates and eating the melted cheese with boiled potatoes and pickles.

RADICCHIO
A vegetable which is a member (*Cichorium endivia*) of the endive family, developed in Italy, and looks like a small red cabbage. Its crisp leaves have white spines and veins and the taste is distinctive and slightly bitter. Comparatively expensive, radicchio is used in salads and as a garnish.

RADISH

A root vegetable (*Raphanus sativus*) of the mustard family probably native to southern Asia and cultivated for thousands of years in many European and Asian countries. The radish is grown in many forms with skin colours from white to red to black and shapes from bulbous to conical. The size ranges from small young round radishes which are about 1 cm/½ inch in diameter to the elongated varieties which may be up to 30 cm/12 inches in length. In many cases the green foliage is also edible when young. The radish has a crisp texture and distinctive peppery flavour which may be strong or mild, depending on type and size. It is usually eaten raw as an appetizer or part of a salad, although some radishes such as the daikon, particularly popular in Japanese dishes, may also be cooked.

RAGI

(Ragee, Raggee, Raggy)
The seeds of an East Indian cereal grass (*Eleusine coracana*), yielding a main food crop in the Orient.

RAGOÛT

French term for an appetizing stew made from meat or poultry and therefore either dark or light. Other foods may be included such as offal or sausages. It is quite thick without too much sauce or gravy.

RAINBOW SMELT

See *Smelt*.

RAINBOW TROUT

A trout (*Salmo gairdneri*) which lives mostly in fresh water, only occasionally venturing out to sea. It is the most highly coloured of the family with a silvery-green, lightly spotted back, banded with pink along the body. The average weight is about 500 g/18 oz.

RAISE (TO)

To lighten baked goods by the addition of baking powder or yeast.

RAISED PIE

See *Hot-Water Crust Pastry*.

RAISING AGENTS

Substances which force baked goods to rise as they cook. The two main raising agents are baking powder and yeast; eggs and carbon dioxide are also important.

RAISINS

Drying grapes to produce raisins may well date back to biblical times in the areas in and around Iran, and the practice of drying spread with the vine in places where the sun was hot enough to dehydrate the fruit naturally. Today, about one-third of the world's supply comes from California and the three main kinds of raisin are natural seedless and golden seedless produced from the Thompson seedless grape and muscat from the muscatel grape. In North America the currant is sometimes called a currant raisin.

RAITA

An Indian side-dish or *sambal* based on thick yogurt mixed with chopped cucumber, onions or bananas. The *raita* is usually flavoured with cumin, coriander and pepper and seasoned with salt. Sometimes *raita* contains a combination of vegetables or fruits.

RAMBUTAN

(Hairy Lychee)
The fruit of a tree (*Nephelium lappaceum*) native to Malaysia and cultivated in other parts of the Far East, the Philippines and tropical regions of Central America. It is oval and about 5 cm/2 inches long and derives its common name of hairy lychee from its covering of soft spines. The green skin changes to red as it ripens and the glossy flesh is white or off-white and has a central inedible brown and oblong seed or stone. The flesh has a delicate taste, similar to a muscat grape, and is very sweet. It may be eaten by itself or used in fruit salads or other desserts.

RAMEKIN
(Ramekin Dish)
Small, individual ovenproof dish, usually round and sometimes with handles, which is used for baked eggs, egg custards, mousses and *pâtés*.

RAMOST
See *Pultost*.

RAMPION
A flowering plant (*Campanula rapunculus*) of the harebell family native to Europe which is cultivated both for its leaves and its fleshy, edible root.

RANCID
A term commonly used to describe stale fat, especially butter. Foods become rancid when the glycerol breaks away from the fatty acids.

RAPE
A vegetable (*Brassica napus*) which is a member of the cabbage family native to Europe and increasingly grown in Britain both as animal feed and for its seeds, which yield rapeseed oil. The leaves are also edible as a vegetable or as a sprout with cress, producing rape and cress as an alternative to mustard and cress. The dense yellow flowers of rape make this species very distinctive and different in appearance from the swede and the rutabaga, which are close relatives.

RAPESEED OIL
Oil containing monosaturated fatty acids made from sun-ripened seeds of the vivid yellow flowering rapeseed plant, native to Europe and a member of the cabbage family (*Brassica napus*). It is a bright golden colour with a light and delicate flavour and is ideally suited to cooking or for making salad dressings.

RARE
Meat cooked so that the inside is still red.

RARE BEEF STEAK
(Rare Beef)
British term to describe underdone beef steak.

RARHAR
See *Arhar*.

RAS GULAS
An Indian dessert comprising curd cheese balls poached in spiced, rose-flavoured syrup.

RASHER
See *Bacon Rasher*.

RASP (TO)
To make crumbs from dry bread.

RASPBERRY
Fruit of a deciduous plant (*Rubus* species) related to the rose and native to both the old and new worlds. Cultivated and wild varieties flourish in the relatively cooler and wetter regions of the world such as Scotland and are not so successful in warmer, drier climates such as North America. Improved hybrids have been developed in recent years but in some European countries, particularly Greece and Italy, the wild varieties are much preferred. Wild raspberries are mostly about 5 mm/¼ inch long but cultivated varieties can be up to 2.5 cm/1 inch long. The deep red fruit is more extensively grown than the newer white and black varieties. Generally conical in shape, the fruit consists of a cluster of tiny one-seeded globules loosely attached to a cone-shaped central core from which it is separated before use. The flavour and texture depend on the variety but all are best if picked and eaten when fully ripe. Raspberries may be eaten on their own or used in desserts, preserves and to flavour vinegar.

RAT
The North American nickname for cheese which the British call 'Mousetrap'; plain Cheddar or processed cheese.

RATAFIA
A sweet and strong liqueur made with fruit kernels and bitter almonds. It has a distinct almond taste and is used mainly for flavouring.

RATAFIAS
Very small, round biscuits which are almond-flavoured and almost the same as miniature macaroons. They take their name from the liqueur, ratafia. They are widely used in Italy.

RATATOUILLE
(Ratatouia)
A Provençal vegetable stew containing aubergines, tomatoes, onions, peppers, courgettes, garlic, oil and seasoning.

RAVIGOTE DRESSING
A vinaigrette dressing to which chopped onion, chopped hard-boiled egg, chopped capers, chopped parsley, chopped tarragon, chopped fresh chervil and French mustard are added. It can be served with all vegetable salads, cold roast meat and canned fish such as tuna or salmon.

RAVIGOTE SAUCE
A velouté sauce made with either meat, poultry or fish stock, then flavoured with shallot, wine vinegar and chopped fresh herbs including parsley, chervil, chives and tarragon. It can be served with assorted cold meats, roast or grilled poultry, and fish.

RAVIOLI
Cushions of pasta filled with meat or cheese mixtures.

RAVIOLINI
Small versions of *ravioli* used in soup.

RAW
Uncooked; not processed or purified and in the natural state; neither diluted nor blended.

RAZNJICI
Yugoslavian grilled meat kebabs, a Serbian speciality.

RØDGRØD MED FLØDE
A Danish speciality made from soft summer fruits, stewed and sweetened, then thickened with arrowroot. The mixture is placed in individual dishes to set and served topped with sweetened whipped cream.

RØDKAAL
Danish red cabbage, either cooked by itself or with chopped apples, flavoured with caraway seeds. It is served with duck, goose, pork and meatballs.

READY-MEALS
Usually available frozen or chilled, pre-cooked meals which only require reheating. Many are suitable for the microwave.

REBLOCHON
A mountain cheese from the Haute Savoie region and one of the oldest cows' milk cheeses in France. Packed between hair-thin wooden discs, Reblochon is shaped something like Camembert but is wider and thinner. Its crust varies from deep orangey-yellow to reddish-chestnut in colour and the cheese itself is light cream, supple, soft and finely-flavoured yet exquisitely mild. Unlike a Camembert it is never runny but does turn unpleasantly bitter when stale.

RECHAUFFÉ (RECHAUFFÉE)
French term for any reheated dish.

RECIPE
Instructions (or formula) with a list of ingredients and detailed method, describing how a dish can be made.

RECOMMENDED DAILY INTAKE (RDI)
See *Nutritional Needs*.

RECONSTITUTE (TO)
To restore dried foods to their fresh state; for example, by mixing milk powder or potato powder with water.

RED BEAN SAUCE
A pungent Chinese condiment made from soy beans, available from Oriental food shops.

RED CHESHIRE
The deep orange-coloured version of Cheshire cheese, dyed with annatto.

RED COOKING
Sophisticated Chinese form of braising, turning food mahogany-red in colour as it cooks in dark soy sauce, sherry, tangerine peel, sugar and Chinese spices.

RED FLANNEL HASH
A North American speciality, this is made from a mixture of onions, bacon, corned beef, chopped cooked beetroot and coarsely mashed potatoes, fried in a large pan. The hash is turned out on to a plate and served in wedges with fried or poached eggs.

RED GRAM
See *Pigeon Pea*.

RED GROUSE
A dark, reddish-brown grouse that is found in abundance on Scottish and North Country moors.

RED GURNARD
See *Gurnard*.

RED HERRING
The product of an old technique of commercially curing whole herring. The herrings are left in a strong brine solution for some weeks and then slowly smoked for a further 2 weeks, or until they become mahogany-coloured. They are fairly strong, very salty and should be soaked before eating. They are usually served as part of a mixed hors d'oeuvre, or as a decoration on egg-based canapés.

RED KIDNEY BEAN
(Mexican Bean, Chilli Bean)
A vegetable (*Phaseolus vulgaris*) native to Central America and cultivated mainly in the Americas and Africa. It is a legume from which the bean is extracted then dried and used as a pulse. It is a medium-sized, mahogany-coloured bean with the characteristic kidney shape which typifies most American beans. Although kidney beans can be grown in colours ranging from white to black, the red version is the best known and used in such dishes as the Mexican *chilli con carne*. The red kidney bean is well-flavoured and a good source of protein and minerals. It must be boiled briskly for the first 15 minutes of cooking time to destroy harmful toxins found in the outer skin which can prove very dangerous to the human body. Ready-cooked beans are sold in cans.

RED LEICESTER
(Leicester Cheese)
A large English cheese which is dyed a deep orange colour with annatto. It is left to mature for 2–3 months to produce a flaky, medium-hard cheese with a softer texture than Cheddar. It has a clean, fresh flavour and can be used as both a dessert and a cooking cheese. Its splendid colour is especially recommended for dishes such as Welsh Rarebit or Quiche. It is made from cows' milk.

RED MEAT
A term which usually refers to the flesh of cattle and sometimes lamb.

RED MULLET
A round-bodied seawater fish (family *Mullidae*). Members of this family are found worldwide and have a reddish back, becoming paler on the underside. The length is 20–40 cm/8–16 inches and the weight can be up to 1.5 kg/3½ lb. The red mullet has always been highly regarded and the flesh is white, oily and delicate and the fish is best fried, baked or grilled.

RED PEPPER
A fine pepper made from dried and ground red peppers (genus *Capsicum*), including paprika, cayenne and chilli peppers.

RED PEPPERS
General term to describe all manner of peppers, hot or mild, which are coloured bright red. Chillies are one example, sweet pimientos another.

RED PORGY
North American term for sea bream.

RED SALMON
The reddish flesh of the sockeye salmon, most of which is canned.

RED SEA BREAM
(Tai, Dai)
A type of sea bream which is regarded as a great delicacy in Japan, where it is used raw in sushi dishes and is called tai or dai.

RED SNAPPER
The best (*Lutjanus campechanus*) of the family (*Lutianidae*) of warm seawater fish called snappers, of which there are about 200 species world-wide. It has a distinctive red skin and the average weight in the shops is 500 g–2 kg/18 oz–4½ lb. The flesh is white and rich and the fish may be baked or grilled. Oriental recipes for snapper include stir-frying, or marinating and then deep-frying.

REDCURRANT
The fruit of a bush (*Ribes* species) native to parts of Europe and Asia. It is hardier than its relative, the blackcurrant, and is widely cultivated. It is a small, red, round and juicy seeded berry which grows in clusters on the bush. It has a small calyx (the remnant of the original flower) at the opposite side to the small, thin stalk on which it grows. Even when ripe the redcurrant is seldom pleasant to eat raw but it has many culinary applications and may be used in preserves, drinks and cooked dishes.

REDFISH
A stubby-bodied, bony-cheeked, deep-sea fish (*Sebastes* species) which is sold in the shops at 20–25 cm/10–19 inches in length and is coloured bright orangey-red. The species are found in the cold waters of the North Atlantic in an arc from the north-east of the USA to the North Sea, including Greenland and Iceland. The flesh is white, flaky and with a delicate flavour and the fish may be poached, steamed, baked, fried or grilled. The North American species is called ocean perch and the smaller of the European varieties is also known as Norway haddock.

REDUCE (TO)
To boil down liquid until it is reduced in quantity. The amount of reduction required will depend on the recipe.

RÉDUIRE
French term meaning, in its culinary sense, to reduce liquid by boiling.

REFINED OILS
Oils which have been treated with chemicals to extend their life, to make the texture lighter and to enable them to reach a high temperature for frying. They are less beneficial than virgin oils for health reasons.

REFORM SAUCE
Named after London's Reform Club where it was introduced in the late 19th century by the then famous chef, Alexis Soyer. It is an Espagnole sauce, sharpened with dry red wine and wine vinegar, well-peppered and flavoured with strips of egg white, chopped gherkin, chopped cooked tongue, chopped mushrooms and truffles.

à la RÉFORME
French term for a garnish of strips of carrot and ham, slices of truffle, mushrooms, gherkins and egg white, for lamb cutlets. An Espagnole or Réforme sauce accompanies.

REFRESH (TO)
To encourage wilted herbs and vegetables to freshen by leaving them in cold or iced water until they show signs of rejuvenation; to immerse blanched vegetables into cold water.

REFRESHMENTS
Light informal food and drink taken between meals or instead of a formal meal.

REFRIED BEANS
See *Frijoles Refritos*.

REFRIGERATOR
The old name for a refrigerator was ice-box, an apt term to describe the modern equivalent which is a mechanically-operated cold cabinet. It is designed to store foods at 2–7°C/35–45°F, the temperature range at which harmful bacteria cannot grow and multiply.

REFRIGERATOR BISCUITS
Made from a thick, sausage-shaped biscuit dough mixture which is wrapped and kept in the refrigerator. Biscuits can then be thinly sliced from the roll, as and when required, and baked. The idea is North American.

REGENSBURGER
A German speciality sausage from Bavaria, made from pork and beef with small pieces of bacon. Short in length, *regensburgers* are heated in water like frankfurters and eaten with German rye bread.

REGULAR-MILLED WHITE RICE
(American Long-Grain Rice)
From North America, a rice from which the husk, bran and germ have been removed. The grain is slim, translucent in appearance and about four or five times as long as it is wide. When cooked, the grains stay separate.

REINDEER MEAT
Smoked and salted meat, a speciality of northern Scandinavia. Reindeer tongues are considered a delicacy.

à la REINE
French term for any dish made from chicken; also cooked chicken coated with Allemande or Velouté sauce and garnished with button mushrooms and truffles.

REINO
A Brazilian cows' or goats' milk cheese which resembles Serra cheese from Portugal.

RELEVÉ
French term for the course which, in a formal menu, comes after the fish (or after the soup if there is no fish course) and precedes the entrée.

RÉLIGIEUSE
An individual choux pastry puff filled with cream and topped with a second, smaller, choux puff. When coated with coffee or chocolate icing, the *réligieuse* is said to resemble the head and shoulders of a French nun, hence the name. A larger cone-shaped version is made from rounds of small choux buns, topped with an additional bun. It, too, is coated with coffee or chocolate icing.

RELISH
North American term for pickles and highly seasoned sauces and condiments.

REMOUDOU
A very strong-smelling Belgian cows' milk cheese related to German Romadur, a member of the potent Limburger family. It has an orangey-brown rind and a rich and mature flavour.

RÉMOULADE SAUCE
Mayonnaise flavoured with anchovy (essence or chopped canned fillets), French mustard, chopped gherkins, chopped capers and chopped fresh herbs including parsley, tarragon and chervil. It can be served with cold meat and poultry, shellfish and hard-boiled eggs.

REMOVE
See *Relevé*.

RENDER (TO)
To melt pieces of fat until the fat itself changes from a solid into a liquid. This is usually done in a heavy pan over a low heat.

RENNET
Gastric juices responsible for curdling milk, used for junket and cheese-making, obtained from the fourth stomach of an unweaned calf. Vegetarian varieties are now available from health food shops.

RENNIN
See *Rennet*.

REPAS
French term for a meal.

REPAST
An old-fashioned term to describe a formal meal.

REPOLLO RELLENO
A Bolivian speciality consisting of a whole cabbage stuffed with a savoury meat mixture, simmered in stock and served with rice.

REQUEIJÃO
A Portuguese and Brazilian cheese, made from ewes' milk whey. It is white, smooth, fresh-tasting and similar to Italian Ricotta. Often butter and cream are added to enrich the cheese.

RESTAURANT
A place where meals are eaten on the premises.

RÉTES
The Hungarian term for apple strudel.

RETINOL
See *Vitamin A*.

RETTICH
See *Daikon*.

RHUBARB
A vegetable (*Rheum* species) which is a member of the dock weed family and native to northern Asia, used medicinally in China over 4,000 years ago and known to the Greeks and Romans. Its cultivation spread through Europe reaching Britain in the 16th century and was used primarily for medicinal and decorative purposes. Its culinary uses were not appreciated in Britain until the 18th century when better hybrids were developed. By the mid-19th century, its cultivation had spread to North America. Rhubarb grows as a straight grooved stem, 20–30 cm/8–12 inches or more long, and up to 2.5 cm/1 inch in diameter. The stem is bright pink in colour when young and divides at the top into finger-like stalks which are linked by an oval and crinkly yellow-green leaf, shaped rather like a webbed foot. In older rhubarb, the stem colour deepens to red or greeny-red, as do the veins in the leafy top. The leaf is poisonous and the stem has a very sour taste. Although classed as a vegetable, rhubarb owes its popularity to the fact that it ripens early in the year and is used as a fruit in northern countries when other native fruits are scarce. It may be eaten raw when young, but is not to everyone's taste; it is best when cooked by itself with a sweetener or combined with other fruits. It can also be incorporated into desserts and used in preserves where its distinctive, sharpish flavour is a bonus.

RIB ROAST OF BEEF
Term used in Scotland for fore rib of beef.

RIBBON CHEESE
See *Parenyica*.

RIBOFLAVIN
See *Vitamin* B_2.

RICE
This cereal (*Oryza sativa*) is the staple diet of those living in the Far East. It thrives in a warm, moist climate and is cultivated in parts of North America, Asia, Africa, Australia and southern Europe. It has a high starch content and is easy to digest. Varieties include long-, medium- and short-grain, polished, Carolina, Basmati, Patna, risotto, brown, white, regular-milled, parboiled, ground, flakes, flour and wild.

RICE (TO)
To mash a cooked vegetable, such as potato, with a patent masher.

RICE FLAKES
(Flaked Rice)
White or brown rice, converted into flakes during milling. The flakes may be eaten cooked as a cereal or uncooked in a home-made muesli.

RICE FLOUR
A low-gluten flour, produced from white rice. It may be used in the same way as potato flour and cornflour.

RICE NOODLES
Thick rice flour noodles available dried in Oriental food shops.

RICE PAPER
Smooth, wafer-thin, edible white paper made from the pith of a small tree (*Tetrapanax papyriferum*) of the ivy family, growing in Formosa. It is used for lining baking trays on which macaroons and florentines are cooked. Food cooked on rice paper does not usually stick to the tray.

RICE PUDDING
A popular British pudding made by baking a mixture of short-grain rice, sugar and milk slowly. The top is usually sprinkled with grated nutmeg.

RICE VERMICELLI
Very fine pasta threads made from rice flour available, dried, from Oriental food shops.

RICE VINEGAR
Mild, sweetish vinegar made from rice. It is used in the Orient to sour dishes and also for pickling and preserving. It can be light or dark.

RICE WINE
Chinese wine made from fermented rice. It resembles sherry in taste and is used both as a drink and in cooking. It is available in two varieties: light amber and clear.

RICH
Food that is highly seasoned, fatty, oily or very sweet and lavishly decorated.

RICH CAKES
See *Creamed Cakes*.

à la RICHELIEU
French term meaning in the style of Cardinal Richelieu, referring to a garnish for roasts composed of stuffed tomatoes, mushrooms, potatoes and braised lettuce.

RICOTTA
A mild and bland Italian cheese which is white in colour, smooth in consistency and very fresh-tasting. It has no British equivalent but slightly resembles German Quark which, like Ricotta, is high in protein and easy to digest. Ricotta is not made from milk but is a by-product of cheeses such as Provolone, Mozzarella and Pecorino; the surplus whey (from either cows' or ewes' milk) is used up in its manufacture. For increased richness and nutritional value, whole or skimmed milk is sometimes added during production. In Italy there are two more versions of Ricotta; a salted and dried soft

cheese, and a mature one which is hard enough to grate. The cheese is most commonly pressed into a flat-based dish with sloping sides, then unmoulded for retail sale.

RIDDER
A rich Norwegian cows' milk cheese which is similar to Saint-Paulin.

RIGATONI
Ridged macaroni, about 1 cm/½ inch in diameter and 5 cm/2 inches in length.

RIJST-TAFEL
(Rijsttafel)
A meal comprising many savoury dishes, all accompanied by rice and noodles. This Indonesian custom is widely followed in Holland, one of the only European countries presenting an authentic *rijst-tafel*. The object is to provide contrast: crisp and soft, mild and hot, fish and meat and so on.

RIKLINGUR
See *Hardfiskur*.

RILLETTES
A French meat spread made by simmering pork in its own fat with herbs until very tender. The mixture is then pounded until fairly smooth and packed into containers. It is a speciality of the Loire valley and quite rich.

RIND (TO)
To remove the thick skin from bacon rashers, bacon joints and cheese; to cut away crusts from bread.

RING DOUGHNUTS
See *Doughnuts*.

RING MOULD
(Border Mould)
A shallow, ring-shaped tin with curved sides and a funnel in the centre. It is usually made of aluminium or tinned steel and can be used for baking cakes or setting jellied mixtures.

RIPE
Fully grown and developed, therefore ready for eating; also, cheese which has reached maturity.

RIPEN (TO)
To allow food, especially fruit and vegetables, to reach maturity.

RIS DE VEAU
French term for sweetbreads.

RISENGRØD
A Danish rice soup or porridge which is served at Christmas before the main course, sprinkled with sugar and cinnamon, then topped with flakes of butter. One almond is added to the mixture; whoever gets it is rewarded with a present of marzipan.

RISI E BISI
(Risi Bisi)
An Italian *hors d'oeuvre*, a mixture of cooked rice and peas, rather like thick soup, served sprinkled with grated Parmesan cheese.

RISOTTO
A savoury Italian rice-based dish; the recipe varies according to region.

RISOTTO ALLA MILANESE
The most famous of all Italian *risottos*, this version consists of lightly fried chopped onions and short-grain rice simmered in stock and white wine until tender. It is flavoured with saffron and grated Parmesan cheese. *Risotto alla milanese* is usually served as a course by itself or as an accompaniment to *osso bucco*.

RISOTTO KALAMARA
A speciality from Dalmatia in Yugoslavia, consisting of a rice and squid mixture, similar to an Italian *risotto*, darkened with the ink from the fish. Each portion is sprinkled with grated Parmesan cheese.

RISOTTO RICE
A special kind of white Italian rice, recommended for making successful

risotto. It is a short-grain variety, with a capacity for absorbing more liquid than many other kinds of rice.

RISSOLE
See *Boulettes*.

RIVER TROUT
See *Brown Trout*.

au RIZ
French term for any dish served with rice.

RIZ À L'IMPÉRATRICE
A cold French rice dessert dish which was created for the Empress Eugénie, wife of Napoleon III.

ROACH
A small, bony freshwater fish (*Rutilus rutilus*) which is a member of the carp family. It is a silvery colour with red fins. It is usually fried but is difficult to eat because of the numerous forked bones.

ROAST (TO)
To cook in an oven by means of a combination of convection and radiation. The heat causes coagulation of the protein contained in meat, poultry and game, resulting in the characteristic brown surfaces associated with roasted foods.

ROAST BEEF
A classic British dish, consisting of a suitable cut of beef (sirloin, for instance) roasted in the oven. Roast beef is traditionally served with Yorkshire pudding and horseradish sauce or mustard.

ROASTED CHEESE CANAPÉS
Similar to Welsh rarebit, a speciality of Ontario in Canada, consisting of a well-flavoured cheese and breadcrumb mixture spread over toast slices, which are then grilled and cut into fancy shapes. The canapés are served hot as appetizers.

ROBALO
General name used for a number of pike-like fish caught in tropical seas off North America in Atlantic, Pacific and Caribbean waters. Another general name for these kinds of fish is snook and the common snook (*Centropomus undecimalis*) is caught as a game fish off the south-east coast of North America.

ROBERT SAUCE
An Espagnole sauce, lightly flavoured with dry white wine and French mustard. It can be served with cold roast meat and poultry, also game.

ROBIOLA
(Robbiola)
A north Italian cheese which closely resembles Taleggio.

ROBUSTA
Type of coffee bean grown mainly in Africa and of a less delicate quality than *arabica*, the other main variety. Suitably blended, *robusta* is widely used, particularly in the making of some instant coffee. About 75% of coffee grown in Africa is of this type and the plants are hardier, more prolific and with a higher caffeine content than the *arabica* beans.

ROCAMBOLE
A vegetable (*Allium scorodoprasum*) of the onion family which grows wild in Europe and is cultivated in some countries. It resembles a thin leek in appearance and tastes of garlic. Rocambole is used as a flavouring in savoury dishes.

ROCK
A sweetmeat in the shape of a stick, usually highly-coloured, particularly popular in seaside resorts.

ROCK CAKES
Individual-sized, plain cakes containing dried fruits. They are baked in rough, irregularly shaped mounds on greased baking trays.

ROCK EEL
See *Dogfish*.

ROCK SALMON
See *Dogfand Spur Dog*.

ROCK SOLE
(Roughback)
A flatfish (*Lepidopsetta bilineata*) of the flounder family. The back varies from brown to grey in colour and the fish is usually about 20 cm/8 inches long. It is caught all year round off the Pacific coast of Canada, where it is the most important of the smaller flat fish; it is also in demand in Japan. The flesh is lean and white and the fish may be poached, steamed, baked, fried or grilled. Because of the rough scales on its back, this fish is also called roughback in Canada.

ROCKET
A salad vegetable (*Eruca sativa*) native to Europe and now found in both wild and cultivated forms. It is most popular in the Mediterranean area, particularly Italy. It grows as a cluster of small oval or heart-shaped green leaves and, when mature, produces yellowish-white flowers. Rocket has a distinctively strong flavour which is less aggressive in the cultivated kinds.

ROCKFISH
The common name of a large group of related fish (*Sebastodes* species) numbering about 200 species. They are found on rocky coastlines in most parts of the world and the length may be 30–90 cm/1–3 feet. The weight averages 1–2.5 kg/2¼–5½ lb. Some of the best specimens are caught off the North American Pacific coast. The flesh is white or pink when caught, turning white when cooked, and is firm, flaky and mildly oily. The fish may be poached, baked or grilled.

ROE
Hard roe are the eggs of the female fish; soft roe are the milt or sperm of the male fish. Both are edible and highly nutritious. Hard roe may be fried, and soft roe poached, steamed or fried.

ROE BUCK
A small Scottish deer.

ROGAN JOSH
The name of a curry blend and also the Indian dish to which it is added: a mild lamb curry containing yogurt, additional herbs and spices and tomatoes. It is served with rice and sprinkled with chopped mint or fresh coriander.

ROGNONS BLANCS
French term for veal testicles. They are usually coated with flour and fried briefly in butter.

ROLL
Any type of food which has been rolled up for cooking and/or serving, such as a Swiss roll, pastry rolled up with jam (roly-poly), Chinese egg roll and so on; also, a small piece of yeasted dough, rather like a tiny loaf of bread.

ROLL (TO)
To flatten pastry or dough by pushing backwards and forwards lightly with a rolling pin, usually made from wood.

ROLLED OATS
See *Porridge Oats*.

ROLLED PORK AND SHOULDER
Term used in Scotland for spare rib of pork.

ROLLER-MILLED FLOUR
Wholemeal or wholewheat flour produced by a commercial technique.

ROLLING PIN
A wooden or porcelain pole about 5 cm/2 inches in diameter and 25–50 cm/10–19 inches in length. It is used for rolling out pastry, biscuit and scone mixtures, and

also for crushing food such as praline. More elaborate versions are available for special purposes.

ROLLMOP
Filleted herring which has been marinated in a salt and vinegar solution for 7–10 days. They are then rolled, packed into containers with additions such as onions and spices, and are sold in jars, cellophane packs, or individually from delicatessens or delicatessen counters in supermarkets.

ROLLS
Miniature loaves.

ROLY-POLY PUDDING
A typically British pudding, made from suet-crust pastry which is spread with jam, syrup or marmalade, rolled up and either steamed or baked.

ROMADUR
A German cows' milk cheese which is highly spiced, fairly strong and quite pungent. It resembles Limburger but is milder and sweeter. The consistency is soft and smooth, with a few holes throughout the texture. The colour is a warm gold and the rind a reddish-brown.

à la ROMAINE
French term meaning in Roman style, referring to a garnish for roasts composed of tomatoes or tomato sauce, spinach and sometimes potatoes.

ROMAINE LETTUCE
North American term for cos lettuce.

ROMAN POT
See *Chicken Brick*.

ROMAN SNAIL
An edible European snail (*Helix pomatia*).

ROMANESCO
A beautiful variety of cauliflower, pale green and reminiscent of a domed cluster of molluscs, each with its own peak. This decorative vegetable is grown in the Netherlands and other European countries.

ROMANO
A member of the Pecorino family, this is a hard Italian cheese made from cows' milk. It has a pungent flavour.

RÖMERTOPF
See *Chicken Brick*.

RONCAL
A Spanish cheese made from ewes' or cows' milk. It is produced at Roncal and is hard and full-flavoured with a dark, reddish-brown rind. It is frequently smoked; also grated like Parmesan and used in cooking.

ROOT BEER
A sweet, fizzy North American drink which is flavoured with herbs and sassafras oil.

ROOT GINGER
See *Ginger*.

ROOT VEGETABLE
The enlarged edible underground root of a leafy vegetable.

ROQUEFORT
A French ewes' milk blue cheese of momentous quality and flavour. It defies duplication because the milk from which it is made comes from areas strictly designated by law and it is ripened in caves unique in formation, mineral composition and air currents. Roquefort cheese is rich and creamy, golden-yellow in colour and remarkably smooth. It is also surprisingly mild for a blue cheese.

ROSE APPLE
A fruit (*Syzygium malaccense*) from the Far East, which grows in clusters. The small, pink and white fruit are pear-shaped. They taste rather similar to European apples but are full of seeds and have a pappy texture.

ROSE HIP
The fruit of various members of the rose family (*Rosa* species), native to many parts of the northern hemisphere and cultivated around the world in suitable climates. The hip may be round, oval or more elongated and measures 1–2.5 cm/ ½–1 inch in length. The colour can be orange-red to dark red and there is usually a calyx (the remnant of the original flower) at the end opposite the stalk. It is the fleshy skin of the hip which is edible, not the hard and often bristly seeds it contains. Because of the very high vitamin C content, the hip is useful for making syrups and preserves and combines well with other fruits in dessert dishes.

ROSE HIP CATSUP
A ketchup from Alberta in Canada, made from rose hips, onions, garlic, water, sugar, spices and vinegar.

ROSE HIP SYRUP
An extract of rose hips, available in syrup form. It is one of the richest sources of vitamin C and lends a mild, delicate flavour and pink colour to drinks and some desserts.

ROSE OIL
A fragrant oil obtained from roses and used mainly as a flavouring.

ROSE WATER
Diluted essence made from the petals of roses which grow in abundance in Iran and the Balkans. Bulgaria is famous for its own 'Valley of the Roses' and is an important exporter of the essence to both the food and perfume industry. Rose water is used as a flavouring in confectionery and desserts.

ROSECOCO BEAN
(Rose Cocoa Bean)
See *Borlotti Bean*.

ROSEMARY
A herb native to the Mediterranean, rosemary grows successfully in Britain though some is also imported from southern Europe and the Balkans. The leaves, from an evergreen shrub (*Rosmarinus officinalis*) of the mint family, resemble curved pine needles and are fragrant, pungent and aromatic. Available fresh or dried, as needles or ground, the herb is excellent in lamb dishes, meat loaves, casseroles and meat or strong fish soups. Said to have been introduced to Britain by Queen Philippa of Hainault in the 14th century, this herb has more legends attached to it than any other: Ophelia talks of 'rosemary for remembrance' in *Hamlet* and it was favoured in Tudor times as a herb of remembrance and fragrance; it is said to grow only in the gardens of the righteous; it is a symbol of fidelity; rosemary flowers were said to have been originally white, but changed to blue when the Virgin Mary hung her linen out to dry on a rosemary bush.

ROSETTE
Coarse-textured, dried sausage from France, made from pork and encased in animal gut (intestine). It is a relatively large sausage and is eaten raw.

ROSII UMPLUTE CU CASTRAVETI
Romanian dish of tomatoes stuffed with tomato pulp, chopped cucumber, chopped onion, chopped parsley and seasoning. It is served in summer with cold meats.

ROSTBRATWURST
See *Bratwurst*.

RÖSTI
A famous Swiss potato pancake made from grated cooked potatoes, chopped onion and seasonings, fried in oil or dripping.

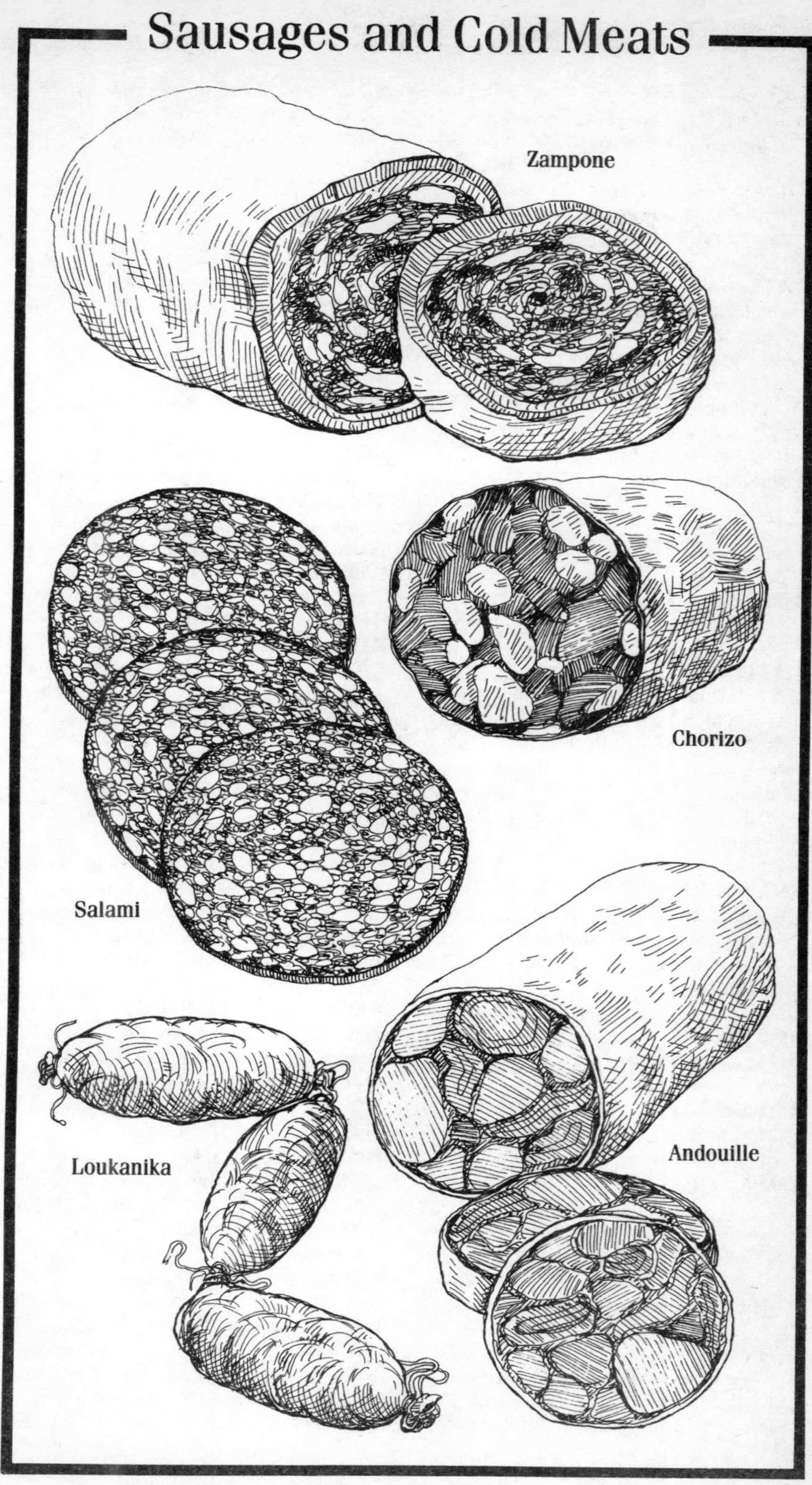

Sausages and Cold Meats
Zampone
Chorizo
Salami
Andouille
Loukanika

ROTARY BEATER
(Rotary Whisk)
A hand-held implement for beating, mixing and aerating, consisting of metal loops which are rotated by means of a notched wheel driven by a small handle.

ROTE GRÜTZE
A German soft-fruit blancmange made from strained fruit juice sweetened with sugar and thickened with potato flour or cornflour. It is set in individual dishes and cold milk or cream is poured over the top before serving.

ROTELLE
See *Fusilli*.

ROTINE
See *Ruote*.

ROTISSERIE
A rotating fitting in an oven or grill which turns joints of meat as they are cooking. Rotisserie roasting results in well-flavoured, succulent and tender meat which is always evenly browned on the outside.

ROUGH PUFF PASTRY
A quick and easy-to-make type of flaky pastry, recommended for savoury dishes such as meat pies and pasties.

ROUGHAGE
See *Cellulose*.

ROUGHBACK
See *Rock Sole*.

ROULADE
A rich, rolled cake, usually chocolate, filled with sweetened whipped cream and dusted with icing sugar; savoury mixtures may also be presented in this way.

ROULÉ
A Swiss-roll type of soft white cream cheese with added parsley or other herbs, chopped nuts, etc. It can be made from cows' or goats' milk and is a fairly new cheese attraction from France.

ROUND GOURD
See *Tinda*.

ROUND OF DRINKS
A set of drinks, usually alcoholic, served at one time to each person in a group.

ROUND OF TOAST
Usually a slice of buttered toast.

ROUX
A French culinary term for a mixture of equal amounts of melted fat and flour used for thickening liquids for sauces. The proportions vary depending on the required consistency.

ROWANBERRY
The fruit of the mountain ash (*Sorbus aucuparia*) or rowan tree, which is native to Europe and parts of western Asia. Although widely grown as an ornamental tree, its clusters of tiny, bright orange, pectin-rich berries are too bitter to be eaten raw but are useful in making preserves, both on their own or combined with other fruits. Gathering rowanberries can be a problem as birds will strip a tree as soon as the berries ripen.

ROWANBERRY JELLY
A Scottish jelly, generally served with venison. It is made from ripe rowanberries, apples, water and sugar.

ROYAL CUSTARD
Made by steaming eggs beaten with milk until firm and set. The mixture is subsequently cut up into small cubes and usually added to a clear consommé as a garnish.

ROYAL ICING
A hard white icing made from icing sugar and egg white. It is often used to cover and decorate wedding, birthday, christening and Christmas

cakes. Sometimes glycerine is added to make the icing less hard and easier to cut.

à la ROYALE
French term meaning in royal style, referring to food, such as chicken or fish, coated with a rich white sauce and garnished with truffles and sometimes button mushrooms; also a garnish for chicken consommé made from a very firm poached egg custard, cut into assorted shapes.

ROYALP
A Swiss cows' milk cheese, dating back to the 19th century, and produced in the cantons of Thurgau, Saint-Gall and Zurich. It has a smooth, fresh taste with a well-rounded, creamy flavour and the pale yellow texture is dotted with small holes. Royalp, known as Tilsit in Switzerland, is a fairly firm cheese and cuts easily into slices or cubes. The rind is reddish-brown.

RUB IN (TO)
To break down pieces of fat by rubbing into a mixture of dry ingredients with the finger-tips until the mixture resembles fine breadcrumbs.

RUE
A herb (*Ruta graveolens*) with small, bluish-green leaves which are used as a garnish and in summer salads. It has a pungent aroma and the flavour is strong and somewhat bitter. Rue oil is used for medicinal purposes.

RULADĂ DE NUCI
A Swiss roll from Romania with a filling of ground walnuts mixed with sugar, milk, grated lemon peel and rum.

RUM
A strong spirit (70° proof or 40° GL), distilled from a base of sugar cane (molasses) after fermentation. It is produced in most sugar-growing countries and ranges in colour from colourless to deep amber. It is non-sweet, has a distinctive taste and is used to flavour chocolate dishes, Christmas puddings, rum butter, rum babas and other sweet items.

RUM BABAS
Shaped like chimney pots, these are made from a light and sweet white yeast dough. They are baked either in special *baba* ring moulds or in castle pudding tins, also known as dariole moulds. The *babas* are then soaked in rum-flavoured syrup, left until cold, and traditionally decorated with whipped cream, glacé cherries and pieces of angelica.

RUM BUTTER
A solid sauce made from butter, sugar, rum and sometimes cinnamon. It is traditionally served in Britain with hot mince pies or Christmas puddings and melts over the food, providing flavour and moisture.

RUM SAUCE
A sweetened white sauce flavoured with rum. It can be served with Christmas pudding or mince pices.

RUMP
This comes from the rear end of the animal and generally applies to beef which is sliced into steaks for grilling or frying. It is a prime cut and has the advantages of being lean, tender, juicy and flavourful. The cut is known by this name in London and the South-East, the Midlands, north-east and north-west England and the West Country.

RUMP STEAK
A slice of meat, for grilling or frying, cut from the rump or hindquarter of beef.

RUMP TOP
Alternative term used in north-east England for a beef cut also known as thick flank or top rump.

RUNNER BEAN
(Scarlet Runner Bean)
A vegetable (*Phaseolus multiflorus*) which is the fruit of a climbing plant native to South America. It was introduced to Britain in the 18th century as a decorative, outdoor wall-climber and it was not until about 100 years later that the runner bean was appreciated as a food. Since then it has become widely cultivated both commercially and in kitchen gardens. It grows as a long and narrow green pod enclosing a number of seeds or beans, and is best eaten young as the pods become tough with maturity. The runner bean may be boiled whole or sliced and eaten as a vegetable with main meals.

RUOTE
(Rotine)
Rounds of cartwheel-shaped pasta, a little larger than *ruotini*.

RUOTINI
Small rounds of pasta, patterned like cartwheels and used in soups.

RUSKS
Dried, golden-brown and very crisp slices of bread. The slices tend to be small, brittle and crumbly.

à la RUSSE
French term meaning in Russian style, denoting the inclusion in a dish or garnish of beetroot, soured cream, hard-boiled egg, gherkins and sometimes salt herring.

RUSSIAN COFFEE
A mixture of vodka and hot, sweetened coffee topped with a floating layer of cream. It is drunk unstirred.

RUSSIAN FISH PIE
A British version of the classic Russian dish *coulibiac*, this is a combination of cooked fish, rice and hard-boiled eggs inside an envelope of puff pastry which is brushed with egg and baked.

RUSSIAN SALAD
A classic salad made from equal quantities of cooked, diced potatoes and carrots mixed with half the amount of cooked peas and sliced green beans. The vegetables are tossed with mayonnaise or salad cream and mounded on lettuce-lined plates. The traditional garnishes are sliced hard-boiled egg, sliced gherkins and diced beetroot.

RUSSIAN TEA
(Lemon Tea)
Term used to describe tea drunk in the Russian fashion, fairly weak and served with lemon instead of milk. Sugar may be added, or even jam in the style of Imperial Russia.

RUTABAGA
A root vegetable (*Brassica campestris* var. *rutabaga*) which is a variety of swede with yellow flesh. In North America, the common swede is also called rutabaga or sometimes turnip.

RUTLAND
British Cheddar cheese flavoured with chopped parsley and garlic. It is also laced with beer.

RYE
A cereal (*Secale cereale*), popular in Scandinavia and eastern and northern Europe. It originated in the region between the Austrian Alps and the Caspian Sea, and is a kind of grass allied to wheat. It now grows primarily in northern Germany and areas round the Baltic. It has a distinctive taste and is widely used in the production of crispbreads and dark breads, which are often eaten with salami, cheeses and smoked fish. Rye is also used in the distillation of some spirits.

RYE FLAKES
Flakes made from rye. They may be cooked and eaten as a breakfast cereal, used to thicken soups and stews or mixed into muesli.

RYE FLOUR
This flour, which can be light or dark, is made from either the partially husked rye grain or the whole grain. It is used for making bread but, as its gluten is more sticky than stretchy, it is often combined with wheat flour for lightness. Bread made only with rye flour tends to be dense and moist with a distinctive taste. Unleavened crispbread, based almost exclusively on rye flour, is tasty, crisp, dark and low in calories.

RYE LOAF
Originally from Scandinavia, this is a cigar-shaped baton made from a mixture of white and rye flours. Caraway seeds are sometimes added for extra flavour.

SAANEN
A Swiss cows' milk cheese similar to Sbrinz.

SAANICH FRUIT PLATE
A dessert from British Columbia in Canada, made from local fresh fruits including apples, peaches, pears, apricots, strawberries, raspberries, blackberries, cherries and loganberries. The fruits are served thickly covered with 'Devonshire' cream from Victoria on Vancouver Island.

SABAYON SAUCE
A French version of the Italian *zabaglione* sauce based on egg yolks, sugar, sherry and water. Sometimes whipped cream is folded into the sauce which is served cold with fruit desserts.

SABLÉ BISCUITS
(Sand Biscuits)
French biscuits made from a rich and buttery dough which is rolled into a thick 'sausage' and chilled. Thin slices are cut from the dough and then baked until golden.

SAC
See *Caecum*.

SACCHARINE
A very sweet sugar substitute derived from coal-tar. It is available in powder, tablet and liquid form and is used by slimmers and diabetics.

SACCHAROMETER
A device for measuring the percentage of sugar in a mixture.

SACCHAROSE
See *Sucrose*.

SACHERTORTE
A famous Austrian chocolate cake, coated with thick chocolate icing. It was created by Frau Sacher, who owned a restaurant of the same name, still in existence in the heart of Vienna.

SAD
A term used to describe a heavy, sunken loaf or cake.

SADDLE
A large cut of meat from a sheep, hare, rabbit or deer, consisting of both sides of the unsplit back of the carcase to include both loins.

SADDLE OF LAMB
A large joint of lamb, comprising the whole loin from each side of the animal. It is left unseparated as a complete piece and sometimes the kidneys are also included, usually appearing at one end of the saddle. The joint is generally tied before roasting for security reasons. It is traditionally a British dish and served with redcurrant jelly.

SAFFLOWER OIL
An oil containing polyunsaturated fatty acids, made from the seeds of a widely cultivated plant (*Carthamus tinctorius*) belonging to the daisy

family. It is used in the manufacture of some margarines and cooking fats. It is a greasy oil and should therefore be combined with lighter varieties (such as corn or rapeseed) if used as a salad dressing. It is useful for those on a low-cholesterol diet.

SAFFRANSBRÖD
A Swedish yeasted fruit bread, flavoured and coloured with saffron. It is traditionally served on 13 December, the festival of Santa Lucia.

SAFFRON
Said to be the most expensive spice in the world, saffron comes from the dried stamens of the cultivated crocus (*Crocus sativus*), a bulb which originated in the East and was introduced to Spain by the Arabs. The stamens are dark orange in colour, as is the powdered saffron made from them. The flavour, slightly exotic and pleasantly mild, is unique and the herb 'dyes' food a deep yellow; a little goes a long way and saffron is prized as much for its colour as for its flavour. Each crocus plant yields three stamens and it takes approximately 225,000 to produce 500 g/18 oz, hence its high cost. Saffron is an important part of Spanish, Middle Eastern and Asian cookery and is also used in some Jewish dishes. It dates back to the Old Testament and is supposed to have grown in King Solomon's garden. In Greece, saffron yellow was the royal colour, and the Romans used it to perfume their baths.

SAFFRON CAKE
(Cornish Saffron Cake)
Yeasted fruit cakes, usually round, containing saffron. They originated in Cornwall.

SAFFRON MILK CAP
An edible mushroom (*Lactarius deliciosus*) which has a circular cap with a slightly irregular edge and a central depression. The colour of the cap is basically orange with faint, narrow and concentric green circles. It is found in late summer and autumn on grassland near to trees. When cut, this mushroom releases a yellow liquid which turns green on drying, a particular characteristic of the species. It has an agreeable aroma and flavour and is sometimes pickled in vinegar or used in cooking.

SAGANAKI
A Greek appetizer consisting of thick slices of lightly floured Kasseri or Kefalotiri cheese which are fried in hot oil and served with wedges of lemon.

SAGE
A member (*Salvia officinalis*) of the mint family, sage is grown and used worldwide. The leaves are a silvery-green when fresh but take on a greyish tinge when dried. The flavour and aroma are pungent and distinctive and the herb can be used successfully in all kinds of pork dishes, strong fish dishes and fish soups, salad dressings and marinades.

SAGE DERBY
Version of Derby cheese which is marbled with green from the juice of sage which has been steeped in chlorophyll.

SAGE LANCASHIRE
Lancashire cheese, flavoured with chopped sage.

SAGO
(Pearl Sago)
A cereal prepared from the starchy pith of several types of palms of the *Metroxylon* family which grow in Malaya and the East Indies. The soft and fibrous pith from the hollow trunk is beaten in water to remove the starch. The starch is subsequently dried and granulated to form tiny balls, known as pearl sago. Sago is used chiefly for milk

puddings and, when cooked, becomes transparent. It is also used as a thickening agent in some soups.

SAIGNANT
French term for bloody, used to describe grilled rump, sirloin or fillet steak which is quickly and lightly cooked, very underdone and known in Britain as rare.

SAILOR'S BEEF
See *Sjömansbiff*.

ST GEORGE'S MUSHROOM
An edible mushroom (*Tricholoma gambosum*) with a creamy-coloured, uneven cap on a thick stem. It is found in the spring and early summer in grassy places anywhere outside woods, one of the few fungi available so early in the year. The mushroom is often used as a flavouring for soups and stews and has a characteristic floury after-taste and aroma.

SAINT LAURENCE
The patron saint of cooks.

SAINT-ALBRAY
Shaped like a six-petal flower with a central hole, this is a large French cows' milk cheese. It is delicately mild with slight piquancy, covered with a downy rind flecked with yellow and orange.

SAINT-CHEVRIER
A fairly recent, fresh goats' milk cheese from France, covered with ash. It is relatively mild and very creamy.

à la SAINT-GERMAIN
French term meaning in the style of Saint-Germain near Paris, denoting the use of peas in a dish.

SAINT-PAULIN
Closely resembling Port-Salut, this is a French cows' milk cheese factory-produced all over the country. It has a deep orange rind, mild flavour and supple texture. It is used both as a dessert and cooking cheese.

SAITHE
See *Coley*.

SAKE
(Saki)
A Japanese rice wine, usually served hot. It is also widely used in cooking.

SALAD BURNET
A herb introduced to Britain during the 16th century, salad burnet has been known since the beginning of time. Growing on evergreen plants (*Sanguisorba minor*), the green leaves taste of cucumber and make an excellent addition to fruit drinks, fruit cups and cocktails.

SALAD CREAM
A bottled mayonnaise substitute, sharper in flavour and less rich. It is a popular accompaniment to all types of salads.

SALAD DRESSINGS
Even as early as the 15th century, salads were mixed with a dressing of oil and sharp vinegar seasoned with salt and pepper. The basic concept remains the same today and the classic French and vinaigrette dressings are still made with oil, acid (vinegar and/or lemon juice), seasonings, herbs and spices such as mustard. The main object of any dressing is to moisten the salad and enhance the flavours of the ingredients. A salad should be tossed with the chosen dressing immediately before serving; if done in advance, any green leaves will become limp and soggy. There should only be just sufficient dressing to lubricate and moisten the ingredients, not enough to leave a pool in the base of the salad bowl. Salad dressings can be made quickly by putting all the ingredients into a screw-top jar and shaking vigorously. Dressings with acid should not be kept in containers

with metal tops but transferred to plastic containers with airtight, plastic lids. To prevent the flavour being spoiled, additions to the dressings in the form of garlic and herbs should be removed after 24 hours.

SALAD ONION
See *Spring Onion*.

SALAD SHAKER
A round plastic or metal basket with a handle in which freshly washed salad can be shaken free of excess water. An enclosed version is made with a plastic body and a hand-driven rotating basket inside.

SALADE NIÇOISE
A classic salad from Nice, in France, made from a base of lettuce leaves topped with mounds of cooked, diced potatoes, chunks of canned tuna, anchovy fillets, cooked green beans, capers, wedges of hard-boiled egg, black olives and slices of tomato, moistened with vinaigrette dressing.

SALADE TIÈDE
A salad with a warm dressing, found mostly in restaurants serving *nouvelle cuisine*.

SALADS
Raw and/or cooked vegetables either shredded, sliced or diced and tossed in suitable dressing. Alternatively, the ingredients can be arranged decoratively on a plate and coated with dressing. Also, dishes made up from assorted cold foods combined with a dressing.

SALAMANDER
A device for browning or crisping the surface of dishes without spoiling the rest by overheating. It consists of a small circular cast-iron block at the end of a metal rod, fitted to a wooden handle. The block is heated till red hot and then applied to the food surface until, for instance, a sugar coating turns to caramel. The block is small enough to be used on individual servings.

SALAMI
Sausage with excellent keeping qualities, made worldwide, which is brined and usually smoked. The texture can be fine or coarse, the flavour mild or spicy, the colour pale pink to light brown and the meat used can be pork and/or beef and sometimes veal. The salami is interspersed with pieces of fat and is always served sliced, as part of an *hors d'oeuvre*, main meal, open sandwich topping or cocktail savoury; it may also be added to certain cooked dishes to increase piquancy. Because salami is characteristically hard, it is possible to slice it very thinly.

SALERATUS
Raising agent used in baking which consists of the chemical compound potassium bicarbonate or sodium bicarbonate.

SALERS
See *Cantal*.

SALICYLIC ACID
White, crystalline acid which comes naturally from willow-bark or is produced synthetically from phenol. It is used as an antiseptic and also in the production of aspirin.

SALLY LUNN
Dating back to the 18th century, this was first eaten in the spa town of Bath and is said to be named after the girl who sold it. It is made from a white yeast dough enriched with eggs and butter. After baking and glazing, it is split in half horizontally, sandwiched together with thick cream or butter, and eaten while still warm.

SALMAGUNDI
(Salamagundi)
A very old English recipe, the original ingredients and presentation have been obscured by

time. According to *Cassell's Dictionary of Cooking* published in 1896, 'Salmagundi is a sort of vegetable mosaic made with pickled herrings, cold dressed chicken, salt beef, radishes, endive, olives etc. all arranged with regard to contrast in colour as well as flavour, and served with oil, vinegar, pepper and salt.'

SALMIS
A rich, brown stew of game in which the bird or animal has first been partially roasted in the oven. It is a British speciality.

SALMON DACE
See *Bass*.

SALMON TROUT
(Pink Trout)
A fish-trade name for sea trout. Although in common use, this name contravenes the British Trade Descriptions Act as it is not a salmon.

SALMONELLA
Rod-shaped bacteria of the *salmonella* genus that cause food poisoning. The bacteria can affect both humans and warm-blooded mammals.

SALOIO
A Portuguese cheese made from cows' milk which is pleasantly fresh and creamy. It is produced by dairy farmers near Lisbon.

SALPICON
French term for a savoury mixture, not unlike that for croquettes, usually combined with a thick white or brown sauce. It is used as a stuffing or filling.

SALSA ALLA PIZZAIOLA
A Neapolitan tomato sauce, heavily flavoured with garlic and herbs including basil or oregano and chopped parsley. It can be served with meat, poultry and pasta.

SALSA VERDE
An Italian salad dressing, based on *vinaigrette*, flavoured with crushed garlic, chopped canned anchovies or anchovy essence, chopped parsley and drained capers. It can be served with all types of salads but especially those with cold meat, poultry and hard-boiled eggs.

SALSICCIA
An Italian term for sausage.

SALSIFY
A root vegetable (*Tragopogon porrifolius*) related to the lettuce and native to central and southern Europe but relatively rare in Britain and North America except in cans. Salsify grows as a slender and tapering root, rather like a narrow-shouldered parsnip, and its leaves may be used in salads when young. The skin and tender flesh are white or creamy-white in colour. The delicate flavour is very distinctive and has, in the past, been compared to that of the oyster, hence the old alternative names of oyster plant or vegetable oyster. Salsify may be eaten raw or used in savoury dishes but is probably at its best when boiled as a vegetable on its own. The name salsify or black salsify is sometimes used for a related vegetable called scorzonera.

SALT
See *Sodium Chloride*.

SALT BEEF
Jewish salt beef is prepared in the same way as corned beef but the cut of meat is always brisket.

SALT OF HARTSHORN
(Ammonium Carbonate)
A Swedish raising agent, formerly obtained from the antlers of deer. Ammonium carbonate is now used as a substitute.

SALT PORK
Fat pork cured in salt or brine.

SALT STICKS
See *Pretzels*.

SALTIMBOCCA
Literally translated from the Italian, this means 'jump-in-the-mouth' and consists of rolls of very thin pieces of veal with ham and fresh sage leaves fried in butter or oil. The rolls are then simmered in wine for about 15 minutes before being served.

SALTINE BISCUITS
Similar to thin cream crackers, sprinkled with salt.

SALTPETRE
(Nitre, Sodium Nitrate)
The common name for nitre, or sodium nitrate, a white saline substance found naturally in the soil of India and other parts of the world where the soil is porous. Its main culinary purpose is for preserving meat.

SALTSPRING LAMB
Baby lamb from British Columbia in Canada, raised on the salty marshes of Saltspring Island, which are then roasted and served with mint sauce, peas and potatoes.

SALTWATER FISH
Fish which live in the open sea and include haddock, sole and cod.

SALZBURGER NOCKERLN
See *Austrian 'Pancakes'*.

SAMBAL GORENG SOTONG
A Malaysian side-dish made from fried squid flavoured with chilli.

SAMBAL MANIS
A fairly mild Indonesian condiment containing mixed herbs, onions and sugar. It is dark brown in colour.

SAMBAL OELEK
Fiery Indonesian condiment made from red peppers.

SAMBALS
(Sumbols)
Small dishes of pickles, coconut, yogurt, chutney and so on which are served as an accompaniment to Indian foods.

SAMLET
See *Parr*.

SAMOSAS
Triangular Indian pasties containing savoury fillings which are deep-fried and eaten hot as a snack.

SAMPHIRE
(Rock Samphire)
A plant (*Crithmum maritimum*) which is a member of the carrot family and native to Europe. It grows in rocky coastal districts and has fleshy green leaves and yellow flowers. It is strongly flavoured and is used as a cooked vegetable or for pickling. In North America, the name samphire is used for the unrelated plant known in Britain as glasswort or marsh samphire.

SAMSØ
A Danish cheese, made from cows' milk, which is a cross between Emmental and Cheddar. It is matured for 8–10 weeks before it reaches the shops and is considered a mild cheese. The paste is interspersed with a few holes.

SAN SIMÓN
A pear-shaped cheese from Galicia in Spain, similar to Tetilla. It is made from cows' milk and produced in the area of Lugo.

SANCOCHE
A thick Caribbean broth made from salted meats (pork and beef), fresh meat, tropical vegetables, green figs, yellow split peas and coconut. It is served with dumplings.

SANCOCHO
A Colombian meat and vegetable stew, related to the Spanish *cocido*.

SAND BISCUITS
See *Sablé Biscuits*.

SAND CAKE
A rich cake, similar to Madeira, but containing a mixture of flour and either cornflour or potato flour. It is widely eaten in Scandinavia and Germany, where its somewhat crumbly texture and dryish consistency is popular.

SAND DAB
See *American Plaice*.

SAND SMELT
(Silverside)
A slender, torpedo-shaped seawater fish (*Atherina presbyter*) caught mainly in the Mediterranean. It grows to a length of 13–15 cm/5–6 inches. The back is a semi-transparent green, a silver horizontal line runs along the side and the underside is whitish. The flesh is oily and the fish may be fried or grilled.

SAND SOLE
(French Sole)
A flatfish (*Pegusa lascaris*) of the sole family, somewhat smaller than the Dover sole, with a speckled, brownish upper side. It is caught in shallow waters from the Mediterranean to the English Channel. The flesh is lean, not as fine as the Dover sole, and the fish may be poached, steamed, baked, fried or grilled.

SANDKAGE
See *Sand Cake*.

SANDWICH
Said to have been the 18th-century creation of the Earl of Sandwich who, while in the middle of a game of chance, wanted to be disturbed as little as possible and therefore ate his meat dinner between two slices of bread.

SANDWICH ROUND
Refers to one sandwich made from two slices of bread with a filling in the centre.

SANTOS
(Brazilian Santos)
Probably the most popular of Brazilian coffee types, mild in flavour and generally low in acidity. It blends well with stronger coffees from other countries.

SAPODILLA
(Chico, Chiku, Chikku, Naseberry, Neeseberry)
The fruit of an evergreen tree (*Achras sapota*) native to Mexico and Central America and cultivated in South-East Asia and Ceylon. It is round or oval and 5–7.5 cm/2–3 inches in diameter. The green skin turns brown and rough as it ripens. The skin is thin and sticky and the flesh is light or dark brown with a number of rough, inedible black seeds in the central core. The flesh in a good, well-ripened fruit should be almost paste-like in consistency and with a sweet, burnt-sugar taste. It may be eaten as a dessert fruit, the flesh scooped out of the skin and deseeded, or carefully peeled to avoid the stickiness of the skin, or deseeded and used in fruit salads and other dishes. The tree itself is the source of chicle, the basis of chewing gum.

SAPOTE
The fruit of a deciduous tree (*Calocarpum mammosum*) native to Central America. It is roughly oval and is 7.5–15 cm/3–6 inches in length. The skin is brown and rough and the generally sweet and spicy flesh surrounds a large seed. The flesh may be eaten on its own, used to make a drink or added to salads and preserves. The green sapote (*C. viride*), a related fruit, grows in less hot climates, is round and green-skinned; the flesh is more reliably sweet and juicy than that of the true sapote.

SAPSAGO
(Glärnerkäse, Kräutekäse, Schabzieger, Green Cheese)
A novelty Swiss cheese with a slightly green tinge. It is made from cows' milk, flavoured with a herb (*Melilotis coerulea*) unique to its area of production and is exceptionally hard. Dating back 500 years, Sapsago is grated and used as a condiment. It is characteristically shaped like a truncated cone.

SAPUCAYA NUT
See *Paradise Nut*.

SARACEN CORN
See *Buckwheat*.

à la SARDE
French term meaning in the style of Sardinia, referring to a garnish for roasts composed of rice, tomatoes, stuffed cucumber and sometimes mushrooms.

SARDINE
The sardine (*Sardina pilchardus*) is a young pilchard and is a round-bodied fish of the herring family. The back is green, the sides yellowish and the underside silver. The length is about 10–13 cm/ 4–5 inches. Beyond this size it becomes a small pilchard. The European sardine is caught mainly around the Iberian peninsula and in the western Mediterranean and the main season is from April to November. The flesh is oily and soft and the fish may be baked, fried or grilled. In Europe, the sardine is a specific fish, but in North America the term is applied to any small fish which are used in the same way as European sardines, by the canning industry, for example.

SARRASIN
See *Blé Noir*.

SARSPARILLA
(Sarsaparilla)
An old-fashioned flavouring for non-alcoholic fizzy drinks. It is produced from the dried roots of a climbing plant (*Smilax officinalis*), native to Central and South America, and has an unusual, distinctive flavour.

SASHIMI
A Japanese dish consisting of a selection of raw fish. The fish is very fresh, thinly sliced and served early in the meal so that diners may appreciate its delicacy. It is artistically arranged on individual plates with appropriate garnishes. It is always accompanied by sake or rice wine.

SASSAFRAS
A tall North American tree (*Sassafras albidum*) of the laurel family with aromatic leaves, small clusters of yellow flowers and dark blue berries. Its dried root and bark are ground into powder and used as a flavouring and thickener for Creole dishes.

SATÉ
(Satay)
Indonesian or Malaysian *kebabs*. Small cubes of meat, poultry or fish are threaded on to special *saté* sticks made from thin bamboo and grilled. *Satés* are often accompanied by peanut sauce.

SATÉ STICKS
(Satay Sticks)
Thin wooden sticks used for *satés*.

SATSUMA
A cultivated version of the tangerine and one of the many citrus varieties developed to produce finer fruit. The satsuma is one of the smaller members of the group and has no pips.

SATURATED FATTY ACIDS
Found in suet, lard, cocoa butter and cows' milk butter, these differ in nature chemically from monosaturated and polyunsaturated fatty acids. They are termed 'hard' fats, and are unsuitable for those on a low-cholesterol diet.

SATURATES
Fats in foods, or fats on their own, which contain saturated fatty acids, mainly of animal origin. They solidify at room temperature.

SAUCE SPOON
Resembling a large teaspoon with a flattened bowl, this sometimes forms part of a cutlery place setting in elegant restaurants and is used to eat the sauce accompanying fish, meat or poultry dishes.

SAUCE VERTE
A mayonnaise flavoured with chopped fresh herbs including tarragon or chervil, chives and watercress. It can be served with cold fish dishes.

SAUCEBOAT
A boat-shaped dish with a handle at one end and lip at the other which may be made from porcelain, earthenware, glass or metal. The sauceboat should stand on an oval plate to prevent spillage and may also be used with a ladle.

SAUCEPAN
Generally a cylindrical container with one long handle and a lid. A saucepan can be made from a light metal like aluminium or from a heavier one such as copper, cast-iron or stainless steel. Occasionally, saucepans are made from specially treated porcelain or glass. Capacity can range from 600 ml/1 pint to as large as 5–6 litres/ 9–10½ pints.

SAUCES
Liquid embellishments, of various thicknesses, used to accompany sweet and savoury dishes.

SAUCISSE
French term for an uncooked sausage which needs to be grilled or fried before eating.

SAUCISSE SÈCHE
From upland regions of France, a coarse-textured sausage which is either completely or partly dried and is sometimes lightly smoked.

SAUCISSON
French term for cooked sausages, usually large, which are sold sliced or in a piece ready for eating. In France they are eaten as an hors d'œuvre. Some sausages under this heading, such as frankfurters or saveloys, need reheating before serving hot.

SAUCISSON SEC AU POIVRE
(Pepper Sausage)
Coarse-textured, dried sausage from France, usually made from pork and coated with crushed black peppercorns. It is eaten raw.

SAUCISSON SEC AUX HERBES
(Herb Sausage)
Coarse-textured, dried sausage from France, usually made from pork and coated with herbs from Provence. It is eaten raw.

SAUCISSON SEC D'ARLES
Coarse-textured, dried sausage from France, originally made from horse and donkey meat but now made from fat pork and lean beef. It is eaten raw.

SAUCISSON SEC DE MÉNAGE
Coarse-textured, dried sausage from France, made either from pork or a mixture of pork and beef. It is eaten raw.

SAUCISSON SEC DE MONTAGNE
Coarse-textured, dried sausage from France, containing a high proportion of pork, together with pork fat. It is irregularly shaped and eaten raw.

SAUERBRATEN
A famous German dish made from beef which has been marinated in spiced vinegar for up to three days, then cooked with vegetables and ginger biscuits or cake, giving a unique flavour to the meat. The sauce is sweet-sour and deep brown.

SAUERKRAUT
Finely shredded pickled white cabbage, a speciality of northern and eastern Europe, which may be eaten hot or cold.

SAUERMILCHKÄASE
See *Hand*.

SAUMURE
French term for brine, as used for salting or pickling food.

SAUR (SAURE)
French term to describe food that has been both salted and smoked; herrings, for example.

SAUSAGE MACHINE
A machine that shapes and encases sausage-meat and produces sausages in a linked string.

SAUSAGE MEAT
British pork or beef sausage meat mixture sold without casing. It is especially popular at Christmas when it is often used for stuffing poultry.

SAUSAGE ROLLS
Universally popular in Britain, sausages are wrapped in shortcrust or flaky pastry, then glazed with egg and baked. They may be large or small and eaten hot or cold.

SAUSAGES
A vast variety of sausages are made throughout the world, ranging in size from the small chipolata to the giant *mortadella*. Their shape is the principal common characteristic. Pork is the main ingredient of the better quality sausages. The best British sausages are made by individual pork butchers and are superior in flavour to those that are mass-produced. Skinless sausage meat is also available and can be used for stuffing and for making Scotch eggs, for example.
Salami-type sausages are precooked and eaten cold, thinly sliced. Known in France as a *saucisson*, those from Lyons, Arles, and Strasbourg are highly regarded. Undoubtedly, Germany and Austria are the countries that produce the largest variety of sausages.

SAUTÉ PAN
Either a shallow saucepan or a deepish frying pan used for cooking potatoes, onions and any other foods which need to be sautéed or shallow-fat fried.

SAUTER
French term for frying food lightly in a small quantity of fat or oil, usually in a shallow frying pan.

SAVARIN
A ring cake made from a light, sweet white yeast dough, usually steeped in rum-flavoured syrup and sometimes glazed with melted and sieved apricot jam. Sometimes the centre is filled with whipped cream and fruits.

SAVELOY
Known in France as *cervelas* (after the brains from which the original saveloy was made), this is a scalded sausage produced from pork. It has a smooth texture and, like frankfurters, is smoked and piquant in flavour. It is relatively large and dumpy, and often encased in a bright red skin. The saveloy is best heated through in water or eaten cold.

SAVORY
(Summer Savory, Winter Savory)
A member of the mint family, savory (*Satureja*) is native to southern Europe but now grows worldwide. The leaves become brownish-green when dried and have a delicate yet aromatic flavour which is slightly resinous and reminiscent of thyme. The herb is recommended for use in egg, poultry and some meat dishes. Both the summer variety (*S. hortensis*) and the winter (*S. montana*) have similar culinary uses.

SAVOURY
Something non-sweet; a meal starter or *hors d'oeuvre*; also, cheese and biscuits, Welsh rarebit

or other savoury dish served at the end of a meal in Britain to stimulate the digestive juices.

SAVOURY BUTTERS
Fresh butters to which herbs, pepper or cheese have been added. They are sold in packets in some supermarkets and other grocery outlets.

SAVOY
A dark green cabbage with heavily veined leaves.

SAVOY BISCUITS
(Sponge Finger Biscuits)
Crisp, long and sweet. They are closely related to Langues de Chat.

à la SAVOYARDE
French term meaning in the style of Savoie in eastern France, referring to dishes which contain local cheese and potatoes.

SAW
A useful kitchen tool for cutting through bones of meat, poultry and game. Some new knives, designed for cutting deep-frozen and unthawed food, serve the same purpose as a saw in that their blades are strong, sharp and serrated.

SAWKNIFE
See *Bread Saw*.

SAYYADIYA
A fish, onion and rice stew, especially popular in Kuwait.

SBRINZ
A Swiss cows' milk cheese which is a member of the Grana family, with a grainy texture similar to Parmesan. It is produced in central Switzerland, originally in the region of Brienz, and dates back centuries, becoming famous in and around Switzerland some 300 years ago. It is a hard cheese, made from unpasteurized milk, with a full, piquant flavour and it is used mainly for grating. Sbrinz is said to aid digestion and one is recommended to eat a small piece daily.

SCALD (TO)
To bring a liquid up to a temperature just below boiling point. This term normally applies to milk.

'SCALDED' CHEESE
A semi-soft cheese made by scalding the curds in the whey before draining, but at a lower temperature than that used to make 'cooked' cheese.

SCALDED SAUSAGES
Called *brühwurst* in German, these sausages are made from finely minced fresh meat, usually pork or beef, with added spices and either bacon or bacon fat. The mixture is filled into skins, smoked while hot, then scalded at a temperature of about 80°C/176°F to seal in the flavour. They are classed as fresh sausages and should be eaten within two days of purchase.

SCALES
Equipment for weighing food, of which there are two main types. The first is the balance scale which consists of two pans or plates at opposite ends of a pivoted unit. A metal weight of the required quantity is put into one pan or plate and the ingredient is added to the other until the two balance exactly; or the item to be weighed may be placed in one pan and weights added to the other until the two balance. The second kind of scale has only one pan or container and the weight is indicated on a scale by a pointer operated by a spring.

SCALLION
North American term for spring onion.

SCALLOP
A bivalve shellfish (family *pectinidae*) with a ribbed, fan-shaped shell. There are about 400 related species found worldwide

but only a few are of commercial interest. When harvested, the shell size can be 7.5–20 cm/3–8 inches in diameter and the colour ranges from off-white to black. The muscle controlling the shell is the main edible part and is lean and rich. It may be poached, baked, shallow fried or grilled.

SCALLOPED POTATOES
A North American speciality of raw sliced potatoes baked in a dish with butter, seasonings and milk.

SCALLOPED SQUASH
See *Pattypan Squash*.

SCALOPPINE
The Italian term for thin slices of veal or pork fillet which are either coated in an egg and breadcrumb mixture and fried like *Wiener schnitzel*, or lightly floured and gently fried in oil and/or butter. In Italy, floured *scaloppine* are frequently cooked with Marsala, or Marsala and cream, and are served with tomato sauce.

SCALOPPINE MILANESE
Prepared in the same way as *Wiener schnitzel* but left ungarnished and served with lemon wedges.

SCALY CUSTARD APPLE
See *Sweet Sop*.

SCAMPI
See *Dublin Bay Prawn*.

SCANDINAVIAN SWEET MUSTARD SAUCE
(Gravlaxsås, Gravlax Sauce)
Usually served with Scandinavian marinated salmon, made by mixing mild prepared (usually French) mustard with oil, vinegar, sugar, salt, pepper and chopped fresh dill. Owing to the large amount of mustard used, the sauce is yellow and its characteristic sweetness makes it very much an acquired taste.

SCHABZIEGER
See *Sapsago*.

SCHAFMILCH
A German slicing cheese made from ewes' milk.

SCHAV
A chilled Jewish soup made from sorrel (or spinach), lemon juice, eggs, sugar and soured cream. It originated in Russia.

SCHINKENWURST
The German term for ham sausage.

SCHLACKWURST
Related to German *cervelat*, *schlackwurst* is made from beef and pork, is deep pink in colour, and is noted for its good keeping qualities.

SCHLAG OBERS
See *Obers*.

SCHLOSSKÄSE
(Castle Cheese)
An Austrian cows' milk cheese which is similar to Limburger and Romadur, though often milder.

SCHMALTZ
A Jewish term borrowed from the German, usually applied to chicken fat which has been rendered down with onion.

SCHMELZ
German processed cheese.

SCHNAPPS
(Snapps)
A strong spirit of 70–80° proof (40–45.5 GL) which is colourless, dry and flavoured with caraway or juniper. The base is generally a neutral spirit distilled from grain starch.

SCHNITT
The German term for cheeses (such as Tilsit or Edamer) which are medium-soft but can still be cut cleanly in slices. The consistency is firmer than spreadable cream

cheeses but softer and easier to cut than hard cheese such as Allgäu Emmental.

SCHWARZWURST
A French blood sausage from Alsace which is well spiced and sometimes flavoured with onions.

SCHWYZERKÄSE
This means 'Swiss cheese' and refers to a hard, all-purpose cheese produced in central Switzerland from cows' milk.

SCISSORS
Special scissors are made for specific culinary tasks such as cutting fish, poultry or grapes, and there are also all-purpose kitchen scissors. Handles can be metal or plastic.

SCOFF (TO)
To pounce on food and devour it greedily; also, to eat food quickly in an ill-mannered fashion.

SCONE
A soft, individual 'cake' which is made from a dough of flour, raising agent, a little fat and sugar or salt, and milk. It is typically British and is traditionally eaten for tea with whipped or clotted cream and jam.

SCONE ROUND
Scone mixture which is shaped into a large round, transferred to a greased metal tray and scored into wedges prior to baking. It is then eased apart, each wedge is gently split open and eaten with jam and cream. Sometimes a savoury mixture is used, containing herbs, bacon, cheese and so on.

SCORE (TO)
To mark lightly into divisions with a knife. For example, a scone round is scored into wedges; the fat of boiled bacon is scored after the skin has been stripped off; freshly made fudge is scored into squares.

SCORPION FISH
This ugly, bony-cheeked family of fish (*Scorpaena* species) is found in various parts of the world but is mainly used in the Mediterranean area for fish soups and stews such as bouillabaisse.

SCORZONERA
A root vegetable (*Scorzonera hispanica*) related to the lettuce, native to central and southern Europe but relatively rare elsewhere. Before its culinary potential was realized, it was used for medicinal purposes. It grows as a tapering root, resembling a narrow parsnip, and its young leaves may be used in salads; it is black-skinned with white, tender flesh. The flavour is delicate and distinctive and the vegetable may be boiled on its own or used in savoury dishes. Scorzonera is closely related to salsify and is sometimes sold under that name or, alternatively, as black salsify.

SCOTCH BROTH
A Scottish speciality, this is a thick soup made from lamb, root vegetables, onions, leeks and barley. Each serving is sprinkled with chopped parsley.

SCOTCH EGGS
Hard-boiled eggs encased in pork sausage-meat, coated with egg and breadcrumbs and fried in hot, deep fat. They are served cut in half. They are a traditional British pub and picnic food.

SCOTCH PANCAKES
See *Dropped Scones*.

SCOTCH WOODCOCK
A highly esteemed British savoury served at the end of a formal dinner. It consists of buttered toast spread with anchovy paste or Gentlemen's Relish, topped with scrambled eggs, sprinkled with chopped parsley and served hot.

SCOTS BLACK BUN
A Scottish Hogmanay or New Year's Eve cake. It comprises a pastry case filled with a dense mixture made from dried fruits, almonds, flour, spices, a small amount of brown sugar, eggs, milk and sometimes whisky or brandy. It is slow-baked in a moderate oven to give the filling a chance to cook through and the pastry time to dry out and harden.

SCOTTISH OATMEAL
See *Oatmeal*.

SCOTTISH SHORTBREAD
See *Shortbread*.

SCOUSE
(Lobscouse)
Term generally meaning a sailor's stew containing meat and vegetables.

SCRAG
(Scrag End)
Another term for the neck of any animal.

SCRAG OF LAMB
A cut from the neck of the animal which is bony and somewhat fatty. It is suitable for stewing, braising, casseroling and hot-pots.

SCRAMBLE (TO)
To cook and stir beaten eggs constantly over a gentle heat until they have thickened to a creamy consistency.

SCRAMBLED EGGS
A lightly-cooked mixture of eggs, butter or margarine, milk and seasoning. It must be stirred constantly while cooking and the pan removed from the heat when the eggs still look moist. Over-cooking will result in tough eggs floating in liquid, rather like curds and whey. Perfectly made scrambled eggs should be in thick, creamy flakes which look almost fluffy.

SCRAPPLE
An old North American dish in which a seasoned mixture of meat, such as pork, is cooked with cereal. When set, it is cut into slices and fried.

SCRAPS
Fragments of discarded or leftover food.

SCREWPINE LEAVES
Long pointed leaves, resembling short swords, which add their own rose-like fragrance to a number of Indian and Oriental dishes. The leaves are available in the West, but should be well-wrapped and stored apart from delicate foods as they have a very penetrating fragrance.

SCROD
North American term for a young cod. Scrod is a comparatively new word and its origins are vague. One generally accepted version is that it came from a famous old Boston restaurant which prided itself on offering the freshest fish available. As the menu was prepared a day in advance, when it was uncertain what fish might be available, the manager invented the term 'scrod' to cover what we would now call 'fish of the day'. A more prosaic version claims that it is derived from an old Dutch word describing a small fish prepared for cooking.

SCUM
A thickish grey layer which rises to the top of stock, meat, poultry and some vegetables as they boil; also, the foamy topping which sits on the surface of freshly made jam or marmalade.

SCUP
North American name for sea bream.

SEA BREAM
One of a family of saltwater fish (*Pagrus pagrus*) which are found mainly in tropical and sub-tropical seas round the world. The fish are deep-bodied and blunt-nosed and

the colours range from grey to rosy-pink. The maximum length varies with the species and can be 20 cm–1 metre/8–39 inches. The flesh is pink or white and medium-oily and the fish may be steamed, baked, fried or grilled. In North America the sea bream is called red porgy or scup.

SEA CAT
See *Catfish*.

SEA CUCUMBER
See *Bêche de Mer*.

SEA DRUM
(Black Drum)
A deep-bodied seawater fish (*Pogonias cromis*) which is one of the group called drum in North America because of its ability to make drumming noises with its air bladder. The length averages about 1 metre/39 inches and the usual shop weight is about 4 kg/9 lb. It is caught off the eastern coast of the USA all year round. The flesh is lean and may be poached, steamed, baked, fried or grilled.

SEA EAR
See *Ormer*.

SEA FOOD
A general term covering edible marine animals, including fish, shellfish, molluscs and crustaceans.

SEA GIRDLE
A sea vegetable (*Laminaria digitata*) of the brown algae group of plants, found in the shallow waters of the North Atlantic, which is related to the Japanese *kombu* family of plants. It has a variety of regional names and is called tangle or sea tangle in Scotland and finger kombu in North America.

SEA KALE BEET
See *Swiss Chard*.

SEA LETTUCE
A sea vegetable (*Ulva* species) of the green algae group of plants, found in the shallow coastal waters of Northern Europe, which resembles a rather tired and ragged lettuce. It is also known as green laver and may be used in the same ways as true laver.

SEA OAK
North American name for *arame*.

SEA PIE
An old English dish which is made by lifting the lid off a casserole containing beef stew 30 minutes before the end of cooking time, and topping it with a round of suet-crust pastry. The casserole lid is replaced and the stew and pastry are allowed to cook together for 30 minutes. The pastry is cut into pieces and served with the stew.

SEA ROBIN
North American term for members of the gurnard family.

SEA SALT
(Bay Salt)
Common salt obtained by evaporating sea water.

SEA TROUT
A brown (river) trout which has found its way to the sea, returning to fresh water to spawn.

SEA VEGETABLE
Term used to describe edible vegetation of the algae group of plants which grow in seawater.

SEAKALE
(Sea Kail)
A plant (*Crambe maritima*) which is a member of the cabbage family and native to coastal regions of Europe, where it is found in its wild state as well as being cultivated elsewhere as a garden vegetable. It grows as a cluster of stalks topped with small green leaves. Unless blanched, seakale is generally too bitter to eat and it is best boiled or steamed and treated like asparagus spears or used as a seasoning in savoury dishes.

SEAR (TO)
To seal the surface of a food, usually meat, by the application of fierce or intense heat.

SEASON (TO)
To improve the flavour of an ingredient or dish by the addition of salt, pepper, herbs, spices, pickles, vinegar, lemon juice, liqueurs, wines, sherry, cider, beer or spirits.

SEASONING
Salt, spices, herbs, condiments and so on which are added to foods in order to improve their natural taste; also, a British North Country term for Stuffing.

SEA-URCHIN
An almost spherical, spine-covered sea creature (*Paracentrotus lividus*) which lives on rocky shorelines. It can measure up to 7.5 cm/3 inches in diameter and the colour of the female, which contains the edible ovaries, can vary from green to purple. Members of the sea urchin family are found in the Mediterranean, Atlantic and Pacific and the main demand comes from France and Japan. The sea urchin is sold alive as it must be fresh when eaten. When opened up across the middle, the star-shaped bands of orange-coloured eggs are removed and usually eaten raw or used as a garnish. The spines can cause problems as they readily detach, penetrate the skin of hands or feet and are very difficult to remove.

SEAWEED
Term to describe vegetation which grows in seawater and belongs to the mainly aquatic group of plants known as algae. As most kinds of seaweed are edible and are increasingly being cultivated and harvested, particularly in Japanese coastal waters, the name sea vegetable is becoming more widely used for this form of food. Seaweed is divided into three classes, depending on the depth of water in which it grows. Generally speaking, the deepest waters produce red algae, intermediate waters yield brown algae, and the shallowest waters encourage the growth of green algae. Although in most countries outside the Far East the eating of seaweed is not general, these plants are a rich source of minerals, vitamins and protein and, in Japan, their consumption is regarded as a basic requirement for good health. Seaweed may be eaten fresh from the sea but most is dried before being distributed and sold.

SEA-WOLF
See *Catfish*.

SEC (SÈCHE)
French term for dry or dried, applied particularly to meat, fruit and wine.

SEDGEMOOR EASTER 'CAKES'
A speciality from the south-west of England. They are thin, crisp biscuits containing currants and brandy.

SEDIMENT
Something which settles at the bottom of a liquid.

SEED
The grains or ripened ovules (part containing the egg cell and its food store) of plants; also the fertilized ripened ovule of a flowering plant containing an embryo and normally capable of germination to produce a new plant. In general terms, the part of a plant (for example, a spore or small dry fruit) that can propagate.

SEED CAKE
An old-fashioned rich cake, akin to Madeira, containing caraway seeds and flavoured with lemon and/or vanilla.

SEEDLESS
Term to describe fruits and vegetables without seeds.

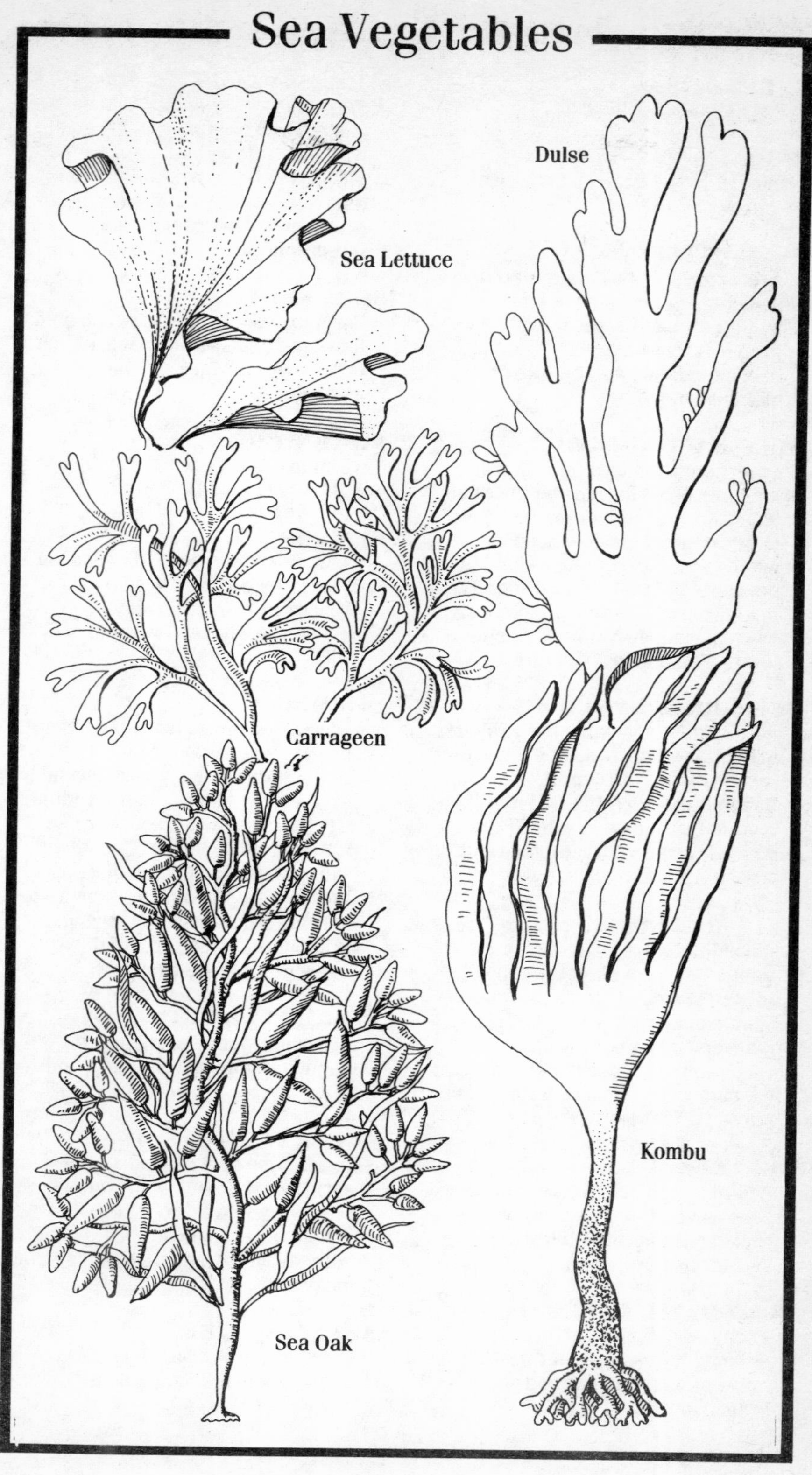
Sea Vegetables
Dulse
Sea Lettuce
Carrageen
Kombu
Sea Oak

SEETHE (TO)
See *Simmer*.

SELAMATAN
Indonesian festival food served at religious and other feasts.

SELF-CATERING
A term to describe holiday or other accommodation with cooking facilities, enabling the tenants to prepare their own meals. The accommodation may be with or without service.

SELF-RAISING FLOUR
Plain flour to which controlled amounts of baking powder have been added during production. It is useful in that it eliminates the need for adding specific amounts of baking powder, but is not suitable for all baking purposes; for example, a rich fruit cake, made from self-raising flour, might fall in the centre.

SELKIRK BANNOCK
A Hogmanay speciality from Selkirk, in Scotland, which dates back to the middle of the 19th century. The bannock is a fairly flat, yeasted cake containing sugar and dried fruits which is usually served sliced and buttered.

SELL-BY DATE
A deadline stamped on packeted food products to show the consumer the latest date by which the foods should be sold. Anything bought inadvertently after this date, especially if it is perishable, must be consumed as soon as possible after purchase for health reasons.

SELTZER
A natural 'medicinal' mineral water such as Vichy; also, an artificially prepared mineral water containing carbon dioxide.

SEMI-DRIED DATES
Partly dried for longer life, available either in boxes, or sometimes in bunches on a small strand or branch.

SEMI-SKIMMED MILK
Partially-skimmed milk, either pasteurized or ultra-heat treated, with a butterfat content of 1.5–1.8%. It is unsuitable as baby food but excellent for those who prefer milk with less fat than full-cream.

SEMI-SOFT
Term to describe a food which holds its shape but is still capable of being cut; a piece of ripe Camembert, for example.

SEMI-SWEET
Term to describe any food which is lightly sweetened.

SEMLOR
Light, spicy, yeasted buns made in Sweden for Shrove Tuesday. They are served as an after-dinner dessert, floating in bowls of hot milk.

SEMOLINA
A cereal produced from hard wheat, the best being that which is milled from the variety known as durum. It is a creamy-yellow colour, granular in texture and a rich source of protein. It is the basis of pasta and is used to make milk pudding, as a thickening agent and, when a crisp and short texture is required, may be substituted for some of the flour in biscuits and shortbread.

SEMOLINA KASHA
A Russian 'porridge' made from semolina, milk, a little sugar and salt.

SEPARATE (TO)
To take one part of a substance away from another. For example, to separate the yolk from the white of egg; to take cream off the top of the milk; to cut fat and gristle away from meat.

SERAI POWDER
Dried and ground lemon grass, widely used in Oriental dishes.

SEROENDENG
Indonesian-style condiment for rice dishes made from fried and shredded coconut mixed with peanuts and Javanese brown sugar.

SERRA
A Portuguese ewes' milk cheese made by farmers in mountain regions, somewhat reminiscent of Emmental in texture and colour. The flavour is marginally fresher but still rich and creamy. It is matured for 4–6 weeks.

SERRATED KNIFE
See *Bread Saw*.

SERVICE
A set of crockery such as a dinner, tea or coffee service; also, attendance from staff to customers in a restaurant.

SERVICEBERRY
See *Juneberry*.

SERVING
A single portion of food or drink.

SESAME OIL
Available light or dark, it is extracted from sesame seeds and is much used in Oriental cookery to flavour traditional dishes at the end of the cooking process. It is rarely used for frying as it has a low smoking point and is relatively costly. It is high in polyunsaturated fatty acids and therefore recommended for those on a low-cholesterol diet.

SESAME SEEDS
Small, creamy-white, shiny, oval-shaped, flattish and resembling seed pearls, the seeds of a fairly small annual bush (*Sesamum indicum*). Once native to the East Indies, sesame is now cultivated in the Far and Middle East, North and Central America and the Balkans. The seeds are contained in 2.5 cm/ 1 inch-long, dark grey hulls which break open when ripe. Sesame oil, produced from the seeds and containing polyunsaturated fat, is widely used in Oriental and Middle Eastern cooking and the seeds are highly prized as a topping for baked goods and confectionery.

SET (TO)
To lay a table; to leave jelly mixtures in a cool place until firm; to freeze ice cream until it is solid.

SET YOGURT
This is firm yogurt which is inoculated, packaged and incubated in its retail container.

SEVEN-MINUTE FROSTING
A North American speciality icing and cake filling which is meringue-like in consistency. It is made by putting egg white, granulated sugar, boiling water, cream of tartar and flavouring essence into a bowl over a pan of hot water and beating steadily for 7 minutes.

SEVILLE ORANGE
(Bitter Orange)
The fruit of an evergreen tree (*Citrus aurantium*) native to South-East Asia, introduced to the Mediterranean earlier than the sweet orange and to Spain by the Arabs. Because of its sharpness, it is not eaten as a dessert fruit but used in conserves such as marmalade and also to add piquancy to meat dishes. It is about 7.5 cm/ 3 inches in diameter and looks like a sweet orange with a slightly darker, coarser skin.

SEW (TO)
To join together two pieces of skin, usually of poultry, to prevent the filling from escaping. This technique is also applied to some thick slices of meat in which a pocket has been cut to hold a filling.

SHAD
(Gizzard Shad)
A group of seawater fish (*Alosa* species) belonging to the herring family which enter fresh water to

spawn and, in some cases, live there. The fish is shaped like a herring but has a thicker body. The colour of the back is blue or green, shading to silver on the underside. The average length varies with the species and can be 20–50 cm/8–19 inches and includes the largest fish in the herring family. It is caught in the Mediterranean and the Black Sea, on both sides of the Atlantic and also in the Pacific. The flesh is oily and delicate and the fish may be baked, fried or grilled. The bone structure of this fish can be troublesome and in Japan the gizzard shad is often marinated in vinegar to loosen the bones before the fish is used in sushi. The roe of most of the species is in great demand.

SHADDOCK
The fruit of an evergreen tree (*Citrus grandis* or *Citrus maxima*) native to the Far East, which was introduced to the West Indies by a Captain Shaddock and named after him. It is now also known as pomelo (pummelo) in its widely cultivated form.

SHAGGY CAP
(Ink Cap)
An edible fungus (*Coprinus comatus*) with a soft, elongated, scaly head, rather like a miniature lawyer's wig, perched on a short stem. It grows in clusters on manure heaps in gardens, grassy strips by the roadside and sometimes in fields. It should be picked and eaten when young and white as it soon discolours, finally turning into a black messy fluid, hence the alternative name.

SHAGGY PARASOL
An edible mushroom (*Lepiota rhacodes*) which grows on a short, off-white stem topped by a cap which, when mature, resembles a light brown and rough-surfaced parasol with a dark bump in the centre. It is mainly found in woods in summer and autumn. The cap has a scaly surface which should be removed before use and the mushroom is at its best before fully open.

SHAKE
North American term for milk shake.

SHALLOT
Native to Syria, the shallot (*Allium ascalonicum*) is similar to garlic and a member of the onion family. Highly prized in cookery, its name is said to be derived from the town of Ascalon (Ashkelon) in Israel. The small bulbs are encased in a papery, tan-coloured skin and each one contains 2–3 individual cloves. They are relatively mild and have a subtle flavour, reminiscent of a mixture of onions and garlic.

SHALLOW-FRY (TO)
To cook in a shallow frying pan containing enough hot fat or oil to half-cover the foods being cooked. The food item should not be more than 2.5 cm/1 inch thick and preferably coated with batter, egg and crumbs, or flour. All food fried in this way should be turned at least twice.

SHAMOUTI
A sweet orange from Israel with a typically oval shape and a skin which is easier to peel than other varieties.

SHANGHAI COOKING
Embracing the specialities of all the regions of China, it is cosmopolitan and sophisticated with a style of its own. In general terms, its nearest equivalent is Peking cooking.

SHANGHAI NUTS
Snack consisting of roasted peanuts covered in crisp, savoury 'shells'.

SHANK
Part of the leg of any animal, but usually the knuckle. The term is also used in Wales for the whole leg, including the fillet end.

SHANK OF LAMB

The end of the leg from which the thick fillet joint has been removed, and often called half a leg. The shank is known by this name in north-east and north-west England, and is suitable for roasting.

SHARK

A family of over 200 kinds of fierce and voracious sea creatures which are really in a class of their own. The edible ones are treated as fish although they lack the main characteristic of true fish, a bony skeleton, and have, instead, one constructed of cartilage. Partly because of size and partly because of their unattractive appearance, sharks usually appear in the shops as steaks or fillets. The various species are caught worldwide and the main edible kinds can measure up to 4 metres/13 feet long and weigh up to 45 kg/100 lb. The flesh is lean and, depending on species, may be poached, baked or grilled. Among the best edible sharks are the porbeagle (*Lamna nasus*), the hammerhead (*Sphyrna zygaena*) and the mako (*Isurus oxyrinchus*). The various dogfish species are also part of the edible shark group.

SHARK'S FIN SOUP

One of China's best-known soups, consisting of pieces of shark's fin cooked in chicken stock with strips of chicken, Chinese mushrooms and seasonings. The soup is thickened with cornflour and garnished with thin strips of ham.

SHARON FRUIT

A modern relative of the persimmon (*Diospyros* species), developed in Israel and grown in the Sharon Valley. The fruit is firm, round (like a large tomato) and orange in colour, and both skin and flesh are edible. It does not have the same kind of astringency as the persimmon and should be eaten while still feeling hard; once over-ripe, the fruit develops dark patches and soon deteriorates. It can be eaten in the same way as an apple, cut up and added to fruit salads, hollowed out and stuffed, or sliced and used to decorate an assortment of sweet and savoury dishes.

SHARP

Anything with a pungent, tart or acid flavour; fine cutting edge on a knife.

SHASHLIK

See *Kebabs*.

SHASHLIK

Russian kebabs made from cubes of lamb marinated in lemon juice, garlic, parsley, dill and seasonings. The cubes are threaded on to skewers and grilled.

SHCHI

A Russian cabbage soup made with beef, chopped cabbage, tomatoes, onions, butter and herbs. It is accompanied by soured cream.

SHEA BUTTER

A pale solid fat obtained from the seeds of the shea tree (*Butyrospermum parkii*). It is used as a food and in the making of soap and candles.

SHEA NUTS

The seeds of a tropical African tree (*Butyrospermum parkii*), related to the sapodilla family, which are used in the production of shea butter.

SHEEPSHEAD

(Fathead)

A deep-bodied seawater fish (*Archosargus probatocephalus*) of the same family as the sea bream. The back is silvery-blue, becoming paler on the underside and marked with seven darker vertical bars on the back and sides. The average weight in the shops is 2.5–4.5 kg/ 5½–10 lb. It is caught mainly in the winter months off the south-east coastline of the USA from Florida to Texas. The flesh is white and firm and the fish may be poached, baked or grilled. (This fish should not be confused with the freshwater drum, which is sometimes also called sheepshead.)

SHELF-LIFE
A term used to describe the length of time a food product will stay fresh in a refrigerator, cupboard, larder or pantry.

SHELL
A pastry case which is generally filled with a sweet or savoury mixture; also, the hard casing round a nut; the outer covering of an egg, known as eggshell; the 'home' of some seafoods such as oysters, mussels and crabs.

SHELL (TO)
To remove the outer covering of nuts, eggs and some vegetables, for example, peas.

SHELLED
Having had the shell removed.

SHELLFISH
A general fish trade term to describe marine animals such as molluscs (snail, oyster and mussels) and crustaceans (lobster, prawn and crab).

SHEPHERD'S PIE
A typically British pie made from cooked minced lamb and gravy, topped with a thick layer of creamed potatoes, then reheated and browned in the oven.

SHERBETS
Eastern in origin, these are similar to sorbets but frequently include alcohol in the form of wine, cider or liqueurs. The word sherbet is derived from the Arabic *sharbat*, meaning a drink.

SHERRY
The family name for a range of Spanish grape wines, all fortified with brandy and carefully blended to produce dry, medium and sweet sherry. Sherry is used for both drinking and cooking.

SHERWOOD
British Double Gloucester cheese, mixed with sweet pickle.

SHIITAKE
An edible mushroom (*Lentinus edodes*) found in Japan and China, both wild and cultivated. The fresh mushroom is popular and abundant in its countries of origin, but is generally only available dried or canned outside the Far East. It is recommended for use in Chinese and Japanese dishes.

SHIN OF BEEF
(Foreleg of Beef, Foreshank)
This cut is taken from beef foreleg and has a high percentage of gristle. It therefore responds best to long, slow and moist methods of cooking such as stewing, braising and casseroling. It is known as shin of beef in the Midlands, north-east and north-west England, the West Country and Wales.

SHIRIN POLO
(Shirini Polo)
An exotic Middle Eastern dish made from rice and chicken flavoured with candied orange peel, almonds and sometimes saffron.

SHIROMONO
The Japanese word for soup.

SHIRR (TO)
To bake eggs in individual dishes, basting them with a little melted butter or margarine before putting them into the oven.

SHIRRED EGGS
See *Oeufs sur le plat*.

SHISH KEBAB
See *Siş Kebap*.

SHOESTRING POTATOES
Very thin and crisp chips, usually served with steaks and game.

SHOO FLY PIE
A sweet North American molasses pie with a crumble topping which is baked and served either warm or cold with cream or ice cream. It is very sweet and attracts flies which one shoos away, hence the name.

SHOPPE KEBAB
A Bulgarian stew made from beef, tomatoes, onions, paprika, butter, marjoram and chillies which is thickened with eggs, yogurt, flour and vinegar. The traditional garnish is chopped parsley.

SHOPSKA
The national salad of Bulgaria, *shopska* is made from dried tomatoes, cucumber and sheep's milk cheese, moistened with French dressing and sprinkled with chopped parsley.

SHORT
Whisky or other spirits (a 'short' drink) as opposed to a 'long' drink of beer; also, a by-product of wheat milling that includes the germ, bran and some flour; also, term describing light-textured and crumbly pastry and biscuits.

SHORTBREAD
A speciality of Scotland. It is rich and buttery, baked in a shallow tin, and becomes crisp as it cools. Depending on the shape of the tin, shortbread is cut into either fingers or wedges. It is often sprinkled with caster sugar and is characterized by holes made with the prongs of a fork over the surface.

SHORTBREAD BISCUITS
Rich, Scottish biscuits made from butter, flour, sugar and beaten egg. They should be fairly thin and crisp.

SHORTCAKE
North American term for scone.

SHORTCRUST PASTRY
Probably the most widely used pastry in the West, this is made in the proportion of half fat to plain flour and is usually mixed to a paste with cold water. The pastry may be sweet or savoury, flavoured or plain and mixed with either water, milk, fruit juice or wine. If it is made with self-raising flour it becomes very light, a little brittle and almost flaky. Shortcrust pastry is used for a wide variety of both sweet and savoury dishes.

SHORTEN (TO)
To add fat to a pastry mixture to make it light and melting.

SHORTENING
A North American term, also used in Australia and New Zealand, to describe fat, usually white vegetable fat, used in cooking and baking.

SHORT-GRAIN BROWN RICE
A type of sticky rice, much used in Japan.

SHORT-GRAIN RICE
(Japonica Rice)
Stubbier than Carolina rice, but with similar characteristics and uses.

SHOULDER OF BEEF
A fairly tough cut of beef, suitable for stewing, braising or casseroling.

SHOULDER OF LAMB
A moist and tender cut which can either be roasted on the bone or boned, stuffed, rolled and then roasted. Depending on size, a shoulder can be divided into two joints, one slightly larger than the other.

SHOULDER OF PORK
Name by which hand and spring of pork is known in the Midlands, north-east and north-west England and Wales.

SHOULDER OF VEAL
A prime cut of veal for roasting which is usually boned, stuffed and rolled prior to cooking. It may also be left unstuffed.

SHOULDER STEAKS OF PORK
A new and leaner British cut of meat which is divided into steaks for grilling or frying.

SHPINATNIE SHCHI
A Russian spinach and sorrel soup containing meat stock, onions and root vegetables. It is served with hard-boiled eggs and soured cream.

SHRED (TO)
To cut into very thin strips.

SHREDDED WHEAT
The tradename of a popular breakfast cereal made from cooked and partially dried wheat, shredded, then moulded into oblong 'cakes' which are baked until golden and crisp. They are eaten with milk.

SHREWSBURY BISCUITS
A speciality of Shrewsbury in Shropshire. They are large biscuits (13 cm/5 inches in diameter), flavoured with lemon peel.

SHREWSBURY EASTERTIDE BISCUITS
(Shrewsbury Eastertide Cakes)
Mentioned in the *Ingoldsby Legends*, rich, crisp biscuits containing caraway seeds, brown sugar, vanilla and sherry.

SHRIMP
A small, clawless, saltwater crustacean with an elongated, curved tail and large head with antennae. The names shrimp and prawn are sometimes interchangeable in Britain, but in North America and elsewhere the term shrimp is widely used for all the assorted species. It occurs worldwide and is caught primarily in the summer months. The colour ranges from a translucent white to grey or brown and the average length is 2.5–10 cm/1–4 inches. In most cases the shrimp is washed and boiled when caught. The lean tail meat can be used in a variety of dishes or eaten in its plain, boiled state. The main British varieties are the brown shrimp (*Crangon crangon*), the pink shrimp (*Pandalus montagui*) and the deepwater shrimp (*Pandalus borealis*).

SHRINKAGE
Term to describe what happens when baked items such as cakes contract in the tin after cooking or when meat and poultry become smaller during the cooking process.

SHROPSHIRE BLUE
A British blue cheese, made from cows' milk and coloured orange with annatto.

SHROVE TUESDAY BUNS
See *Semlor*.

SHUCK
North American term for opening and preparing bivalves, such as oysters, or removing husks from sweetcorn.

SICILIANO
See *Canestrato*.

SIDE DISH
An accompaniment to a main dish; for example, vegetables, salad, rice or some sort of pasta.

SIDE OF MEAT
The right or left half of a meat carcase.

SIEVA BEAN
A variety of butter bean.

SIEVE
A fine-meshed implement, with a handle, used for rinsing, draining, sifting or puréeing food. It can be made of metal or plastic and can be bowl-shaped or conical. A handleless drum-shaped sieve, with interchangeable meshes, is also available.

SIEVE (TO)
To shake dry ingredients through a mesh sieve to remove lumps and ensure smoothness; to rub soft

foods (canned fruits, for instance) through a sieve to form a purée.

SIFT (TO)
To shake dry ingredients through a mesh sieve to remove lumps.

SIFTER
See *Dredger*.

SILBA
A Yugoslav cows' milk cheese which resembles Port-Salut.

SILD
A Scandinavian name for herring and used to describe those canned in oil, like sardines, especially in Norway.

SILLSALLAD
A Swedish herring salad made from finely chopped salted herring mixed with chopped cooked potatoes, pickled beetroot, pickled cucumber, dessert apple and onion. It is mixed with a vinegar and sugar dressing and garnished with wedges of hard-boiled egg and either fresh parsley or dill.

SILOTAKIA TIGANITA
A Greek appetizer consisting of small pieces of fried chicken's or calf's liver, speared on to cocktail sticks and sprinkled with lemon juice.

SILVER BALLS
Small, edible, silver-coloured balls used for cake decoration.

SILVER HAKE
(Whiting)
A fish (*Merluccius bilinearis*) of the cod family. It is slender and round-bodied with a dark grey-to-brown back and silvery underside. When freshly caught, the back has a silvery shine which accounts for its name. The average length is about 30 cm/12 inches and weight about 400 g/14 oz. It is caught off the North American coast from Newfoundland to South Carolina all year round, but the main season is from May to November. The flesh is white, lean and moist and the fish may be poached, steamed, baked, fried or grilled. It is usually chilled or frozen when caught to prevent the naturally firm flesh from becoming flabby and is widely used in the USA in the fish and chip trade. It is also known as whiting in North America and it resembles the European fish of the same name.

SILVER SMELT
(Argentine)
See *Smelt*.

SILVERSIDE FISH
(Atlantic Silverside)
A slender, torpedo-shaped seawater fish (*Menidia menidia*) which grows to a length of 13–15 cm/ 5–6 inches. The back is a semi-transparent green colour, a silver horizontal band runs along the side and the underside is whitish. It is caught mainly in the autumn on the Atlantic coastline and in the estuaries of North America. The flesh is oily and the fish may be fried or grilled. The term silverside is also used for the European sand smelt, which is similar in size and appearance.

SILVERSIDE OF BEEF
Traditional British salt beef, served with carrots and sometimes dumplings. It is a boneless and fairly tough cut of meat, ideal for salting and boiling. Cooked silverside can be served hot or cold with salad. The meat comes from the rear end of the animal, between the leg and rump.

SIMMER (TO)
(Seethe (to))
To keep a liquid bubbling gently at just below boiling point.

SIMNEL CAKE
A traditionally British Easter Cake made from a rich fruited mixture with a layer of marzipan baked in the middle. When cold, the top is decorated with more marzipan and

then edged with twelve marzipan balls to represent Christ's Apostles. Sometimes the centre is covered with a small amount of white glacé icing and little confectionery eggs.

SINGE (TO)
To apply a naked flame to the outside of poultry and game to burn off remnants of feathers and fine hair which remain after plucking.

SINGIN' HINNIES
Because of their high fat-content, the hinnies sing or hiss while cooking, hence their name. They are smallish, round cakes containing currants and cinnamon and are made from a sweet dough which is rolled out and cut into 7.5-cm/3-inch diameter rounds. They are usually cooked on a greased griddle, then spread with butter and sprinkled with caster sugar to serve.

SINGLE CREAM
Pasteurized cream with a legal minimum butterfat content of 18%. It is always homogenized and is used for pouring over desserts and ice creams, and for adding to soups, coffee and hot chocolate. It does not whip, nor should it be frozen.

SINGLE GLOUCESTER
(Haymaking Cheese)
A light-coloured, mild cheese which was once produced from early season cows' milk and was popular at haymaking time. It is now very rare.

SINGLE LOIN OF PORK
Term used in the east and west of Scotland for a loin of pork chop.

SINIGANG
A savoury stew of fish with vegetables which is a speciality of the Philippines.

SINISTRAL
See *Flatfish*.

SINK TIDY
A triangular dish with perforations which is placed in the sink to catch potato peelings and other waste, facilitating their removal and preventing sink blockage.

SIPPET
An old-fashioned term for a small triangle of toast or fried bread used as a garnish.

SIRENE
The most popular cheese in Bulgaria, Sirene is closely related to Brynza cheese and is made from ewes' or cows' milk. It is firm, white, salty and crumbly and, like Feta, is used in salads, pastry cases and breads.

SIRLOIN OF BEEF
A prime cut of beef from the loin, it is tender, moist, well-flavoured and comparatively lean. It is usually sold on the bone but some joints are boned and rolled. Either way it is suitable for roasting and is also the basis of a number of steak cuts including T-bone and fillet.

SIRLOIN STEAK
(Entrecôte Beef Steak)
Prime or tender grilling or frying steak, cut from the upper part of beef sirloin.

SIŞ KEBAP
(Shish Kebab)
The national dish of Turkey, this consists of cubes of meat, usually lamb, threaded on to skewers and grilled. Peppers and tomatoes are cooked on separate skewers and served as a side-dish and the traditional accompaniment is Turkish *pilav*. It is etiquette in Turkey to remove the cubes of food from the skewers before serving.

ŞIŞ KÖFTE
Turkish lamb meatballs which are threaded on to skewers and grilled. The traditional accompaniment is *pilav*.

SISSAY YASSA
A Gambian speciality consisting of chicken joints marinated in lemon juice and oil with onions, garlic, ginger and chilli. The chicken is then fried and served with rice.

SJÖMANSBIFF
A Swedish stew consisting of layers of sliced fried beef, sliced onions, peeled and sliced potatoes and water or beer, seasoned with salt and simmered until tender.

SKATE
A non-bony fish (*Raja batis*) of the ray family with a flattened body and large triangular pectoral (side) fins, like wings, joined to the head. It has a long, slender tail with small fins near the tip. The eyes are on the upper side of the head but the mouth, nostrils and gills are all on the underside. The upper side is greenish-brown with occasional spots and the underside is dark bluish-white. Skate can measure up to 2 metres/6½ feet across the wings. They are caught, during most of the year, in the eastern Atlantic from Iceland to the Mediterranean and close relatives are caught off the shores of Canada and North America. The edible parts of skate are the wings, which are usually sold in skinned pieces ready for cooking. The flesh is white and medium-oily and may be poached, steamed, baked or fried.

SKEWER
A wooden, bamboo or metal rod, often with a ridged surface, which resembles a knitting needle and sometimes has a small, looped handle at one end. It is used to hold the edges of meat together and also for grilling small pieces of meat and fish, for example, kebabs.

SKEWER (TO)
To hold edges of poultry, game and joints of meat firmly together by threading with a metal or wooden skewer; also, to thread pieces of meat and vegetables on to skewers to make kebabs.

SKILLET
North American term for a lidded frying pan.

SKIM (TO)
To remove fat and scum as it rises to the top of a pan while boiling one or more ingredients; to spoon off residual fat floating on top of hot gravy, soup, stews or sauce; to separate cream from milk to make skimmed milk.

SKIMMED MILK
Recommended for slimmers and those on medically-approved diets, this milk has had most of the fat removed and contains just 0.3% butterfat. It is available in three forms: ultra-heat treated (UHT), pasteurized or sterilized. It is a 'thin' tasting milk and burns readily on heating, but is an excellent source of protein and relatively nourishing, despite its low-fat content.

SKIMMED MILK QUARK
(Magerquark)
A German soft cheese product containing less than 1% butterfat. Described as *Magerquark* (German for fat-free) on the label, this cheese yields approximately 75 kilocalories per 100 g/4 oz and is highly recommended for slimmers.

SKIMMED MILK SOFT CHEESE
A soft and pale cheese with a minimum butterfat content of 2% produced from the milk of cows, goats or ewes.

SKIN
The outer covering of an animal; also the film which forms on top of sauces, soups and jams on cooling.

SKIN (TO)
To strip off the skin of poultry; to remove fur from rabbits and hares; to cut away the flesh from the skin of

uncooked fish; to remove the skin of nuts, tomatoes, peaches and so on, after blanching.

SKINK OF BEEF
See *Hough of Beef*.

SKIRT OF BEEF
A thin and lean cut of beef, usually from the diaphragm of the animal. It is fairly tough and should be stewed, braised or casseroled.

SKORTHALIA
(Scorthalia, Skordalia)
Very similar to *aïoli* sauce, this Greek version consists of mayonnaise strongly flavoured with garlic, ground almonds and either lemon juice or vinegar and thickened with breadcrumbs. Sometimes finely chopped walnuts or pine nuts are also added. The sauce can be served with cooked or raw vegetables, freshwater fish and beef, and some salads.

SKYR
An Icelandic speciality dating back several centuries, this resembles French Fromage Frais and can be emulated by beating together one part natural or plain yogurt with two parts German low-fat Quark. It is eaten as a sweet with cream, sugar and berry fruits. In Iceland, Skyr is also a breakfast or snack food and coated with milk. It is made from skimmed milk to which rennet has been added and is ultra-smooth and glossy.

SKYROS
A Greek cheese, similar to Kefalotiri, produced on the Aegean island of Skyros.

SLAKE
See *Blend*.

SLATKA
Serbian preserved fruits, a speciality of Yugoslavia. They are served mid-afternoon in small dishes and are accompanied by glasses of cold water and Turkish coffee.

SLAUGHTERHOUSE
(Abattoir)
A place where animals are killed, usually prior to human consumption.

SLAW
See *Coleslaw Salad*.

SLIP
Australian term for a baking tray.

SLIVER
Thin, narrow strip of food, such as whole almonds.

SLOAT OF BEEF
Term used in north-east England for clod of beef.

SLOE
The fruit of the sloe or blackthorn bush (*Prunus spinosa*) and a member of the plum family. It is spherical in shape and smaller than other types of plum, averaging only about 1 cm/½ inch in diameter. The skin is black and the sharp-tasting flesh is greenish-yellow and surrounds a central round stone. The sloe may be used in preserves or the making of sloe gin.

SLOKE
(Stoke, Stake)
See *Laver*.

SLOW
Term to describe cooking at a low temperature, either on the hob or in the oven.

SLY CAKES
See *Cornish Sly Cakes*.

SMALL CALORIE
A unit of heat for measuring energy value. A calorie written without the capital C is the amount of heat required to raise the temperature of 1 gm of water by 1°C. The term is used in physics.

SMALL GOUDA
A small version of Dutch Gouda cheese which is round with a yellow waxy coat.

SMALLHOLDER
A Scottish Lowland cheese, produced from cows' milk and resembling Cheddar.

SMELT
A number of herring-like fish (*Osmerus* species) found on both sides of the North Atlantic and on the North American Pacific coast. They are caught in shoals in coastal waters, estuaries and sometimes in fresh water. The length can be 13–20 cm/5–8 inches for the rainbow smelt, which is caught from the Bay of Biscay to the Baltic, and up to 55 cm/21 inches for the silver smelt, which is found across the whole of the North Atlantic. The colour of the back varies with the species from bottle-green to dirty yellow and most kinds have a silvery stripe running along the sides; the undersides vary from creamy-white to silver, sometimes spotted. The flesh is firm and ranges from lean to very oily and the fish may be poached, steamed, fried or grilled.

SMETANA
(Smytana)
A type of medium-thick soured cream, widely used in Scandinavia, northern Europe and the USSR. It has a smooth consistency, mildly acidic taste and is a cross between natural yogurt and soured cream. Smetana is relatively low in fat, containing 12% butterfat compared with about 18% in soured cream.

SMITANE SAUCE
(Sour Cream Sauce)
A velouté sauce, made with poultry or game stock, flavoured with vinegar, shallots and white wine. It is enriched with soured cream and can be served with roast poultry and game birds, roast venison and grilled offal.

SMITHFIELD HAM
A North American ham, originally from Smithfield in Virginia, produced from pigs which live on a diet of hickory nuts, acorns and beech nuts, then just before slaughter are fed on peanuts and corn. Smithfield ham is cured with dry salt, then spiced and wood-smoked.

SMOKE (TO)
See *Smoking*.

SMOKED BACON
Cured bacon which is subsequently smoked. The flesh becomes a dull red, the rind amber-coloured and the flavour appetizingly smoky. It has a stronger flavour than green bacon and is also saltier. To remove some of the saltiness, bring the bacon to the boil twice in two changes of cold water. This is more effective than soaking.

SMOKED CHEESE
(Raucherkäse)
High-quality German, often processed, cheese which has been naturally smoked. Sometimes it contains additions such as ham, herbs, vegetables and nuts.

SMOKED COD
Cod treated in much the same way as smoked haddock but, because the cod is so much larger, it is cured in large pieces and frequently dyed during the brining or salting process. It is usually sold ready-skinned so there is virtually no waste.

SMOKED COD'S ROE
The pale orange roe of the cod which is salted and smoked, then used in the preparation of a number of cocktail savouries. The saltiness of smoked cod's roe varies, and while some is very mild and resembles smoked salmon, some is very salty and rather overpowering. It is available in jars from delicatessens and speciality shops and is sometimes sold loose by weight. It is important to remember that any cod's roe bought in the piece will be encased in a type of embryonic skin which is very tough and

should not be eaten. Cod's roe is the basis for taramasalata not made in Greece.

SMOKED EEL
Regarded as a delicacy in many parts of the world. Eels are very lightly salted and smoked and then cut into thin slices ready for serving. As eels are an oily fish, they are usually accompanied by lemon juice and salt and pepper to taste. In the Netherlands they are a popular snack.

SMOKED FILLETS
See *Golden Fillets*.

SMOKED HADDOCK
Produced from either smallish haddock (500–675 g/1–1½ lb) or pieces of larger, unskinned haddock. The fish is first salted or brined, sometimes dyed, and subsequently smoked for some hours. The colour varies from pale straw to yellow. It is eaten poached or baked.

SMOKED MACKEREL
Usually made from very fresh, fleshy fish, hot-smoked in smokeries, sometimes with additions such as crushed peppercorns. Whole smoked mackerel from Britain's West Country are moister and more agreeably flavoured than fillets, which can be artificially coloured and overcooked, making them dry. Any mackerel with a slithery skin should be avoided. The hot-smoking process cooks the fish, which can then be eaten cold without further preparation.

SMOKED OYSTER
Generally available in cans or jars. The oysters are first steam-cooked, then salted, smoked and packed in oil. They are very good speared on to cocktail sticks and served with drinks. They are also delicious if wrapped in half-rashers of streaky bacon, speared on to sticks, grilled and then served hot as an appetizer; this is the modern version of angels on horseback, originally made with raw oysters.

SMOKED SALMON
The most famous smoked salmon of all is that which comes from Scotland and the word Scottish, when prefixed to smoked salmon, puts it into a class of its own. Because of supply and demand, this fish has become an expensive luxury and salmon from Scandinavia and Canada is widely used in addition to fish from Scotland. The basic principles of curing are simply salting and smoking filleted sides of salmon but this is carried out with immense skill, experience and pride. Salmon is usually served thinly-sliced with one or two wedges of lemon. The traditional accompaniments are cayenne pepper and thinly sliced brown bread and butter.

SMOKED SPRATS
These are sprats which have been brined and lightly smoked. They are ready for eating and are usually served as a cocktail savoury or as part of a mixed hors d'oeuvre. Some Scandinavian varieties are canned in oil.

SMOKEHOUSE
A building where meat or fish is cured by smoking, usually by burning wood such as oak chips.

SMOKIES
A Scottish speciality made from haddock and sometimes whiting, which have been beheaded and gutted but not slit from head to tail; consequently they retain their original fish shape. They are tied together in pairs by the tails and mechanically hot-smoked.

SMOKING
An ancient method of preservation in which meat, fish, poultry, cheese and sausages are placed in smokehouses and exposed to smoke from wood, turf or peat.

SMOLT
The name for a young salmon in its second or third year, when it changes shape and colour and swims downstream towards the sea. It is about 13 cm/5 inches long at this stage and should not be caught. In fish farms, the smolts are transferred from freshwater hatcheries to deep pens moored in sheltered seawater in order to emulate natural development.

SMÖRGÅSBORD
Sweden's open table, which ranges from a modest spread in the home to an elaborate feast served in a restaurant or hotel. A large *smörgåsbord* might include a variety of herring dishes, a dozen or so dishes made from other fish or shellfish, 3–4 egg dishes, 15–20 hot and cold meat and poultry dishes, 9–10 condiments or salads, an assortment of crispbreads and breads with cheese, fruit, desserts and coffee. It is impolite to pile up one's plate and guests are encouraged to tackle the *smörgåsbord* piecemeal, collecting a clean plate and cutlery with each portion or helping.

SMØRREBRØD
The world-famous open sandwiches of Denmark, including some six hundred varieties.

SMOTHERED BEEF
See *Etouffé of Beef*.

SNACK
A small amount of food, usually taken between meals.

SNAIL
Edible gasteropod molluscs (*Helix* species) which are either wild or cultivated on farms. Various species are found in many parts of the world and are popular internationally. They may be poached, boiled or fried, depending on the size, type and the country of origin. Snails are often eaten as an appetizer, stuffed with garlic butter mixed with finely chopped parsley.

SNAP
Term to describe any food which breaks easily such as a biscuit; also used in the North of England for lunchtime food taken to work.

SNAP BEAN
(String Bean)
North American term for French bean.

SNAPPER
See *Red Snapper*.

SNIPE
A small game bird which is in season in Britain from the second week in August until the end of January. It should be treated in the same way as plover.

SNIR
A factory-produced cows' milk cheese from Israel, resembling Bel Paese. It is semi-soft with a piquant taste.

SNOEK
The South African name for barracouta.

SNOOK
(Common Snook)
See *Robalo*.

SNOW PEA
See *Mange-tout*.

SO'O-YOSOPY
See *Sopa de Carne*.

SOAK (TO)
To leave in water or other recommended liquids, for varying lengths of time, as specified in recipes.

SOBA NOODLES
Japanese noodles made from buckwheat flour, available, dried, in flat sticks of about 20 cm/8 inches in length.

SOCKEYE SALMON

A member (*Oncorhynchus nerka*) of the Pacific salmon family which is caught in Alaska, Canada and the state of Washington in North America. The back is greenish-blue in colour with fine black specks, shading to silvery on the sides and underside. The average weight is 2.5 kg/5½ lb. The flesh is oily with small flakes and is deep red or orange in colour. The fish may be poached, steamed, baked, fried or grilled but is perhaps best known as the red salmon of the European canned fish trade.

SODA

Soda water; also a North American sweet drink consisting of soda water, flavouring and ice cream.

SODA BREAD

(Irish Soda Bread)

Traditionally made in Ireland, a white or brown bread containing no yeast. Bicarbonate of soda and soured milk or buttermilk are the raising agents.

SODA CAKE

(Somerset Soda Cake)

A light fruit cake from Somerset, well-spiced and raised with bicarbonate of soda and soured milk. If soured milk is unavailable, vinegar is used instead.

SODA SIPHON

A bottle which has a press-down lever on one side and a spout on the other. It contains carbonated water under pressure which, when squirted into glasses, bubbles and retains its effervescence for some time.

SODA WATER

Aerated water which has been artificially carbonated with carbon dioxide under pressure in a soda siphon. Soda water is obtainable ready prepared in siphons and bottles. Also, a fizzy drink taken to ease indigestion, made from a weak solution of bicarbonate of soda dissolved in a little warm water, which is claimed to be an antacid.

SODDEN

(Soggy)

Wet and heavy due to excess moisture. This usually refers to baked goods but fruit on trees, especially cherries and plums, can become sodden with water after heavy rain and show signs of spoilage as a consequence.

SODIUM CHLORIDE

(Salt)

Sodium chloride is essential to life and, together with water, is responsible for the proper composition of body fluids. Salt is lost through urine and sweat and a salt deficiency results in muscle cramp. Consequently, in hot climates or in very hot weather, more salt than usual may be necessary in the diet. Most foods contain natural sodium or salt and it is one of man's oldest preservatives. It occurs in nature as rock salt (a mineral deposit), as well as in brine springs and sea water. Large deposits of rock salt are to be found in central and eastern Europe, and in Cheshire and the neighbouring counties in England. Commercial salt is obtained either from rock salt, from the evaporation of natural brine or from artificial brine obtained by running water into mines to dissolve the salt.

SODIUM NITRATE

See *Saltpetre*.

SOFRITO

A Caribbean and Latin American condiment made by slowly cooking together chopped onions, garlic, green peppers, ham, salt pork, tomatoes, herbs and seasonings. The mixture is stored in jars and used to flavour soups and stews.

SOFT
Having a pliable consistency; also, having a mild, gentle and delicate flavour as opposed to a sharp one.

SOFT-BOIL (TO)
To boil an egg in its shell to the point where the white sets but the yolk remains liquid.

SOFT CHEESES
(British Soft Cheeses, Soft British Cheeses)
General term to describe soft small cheeses, which are easy to spread and pleasantly mellow. They are made by coagulating cows' milk with rennet and adding a starter. In this way, a fresh acid flavour is produced which may be described as 'clean'. The curd is drained slowly by gravity without the application of pressure. The resultant cheeses have a high moisture content (50–70%) and ripen (mature) quickly.

SOFT DRINK
Any of several sweetened and flavoured non-alcoholic drinks that are frequently based on soda water and often served chilled.

SOFT FLOUR
Produced from soft wheat, which is a starchy grain, cultivated worldwide in temperate climates. It is more suited to making cakes and biscuits than to bread.

SOFT FRUIT
General term to describe soft summer fruits including all the berries and currants. They are fairly delicate, easily damaged, perishable and should be used as soon as possible after purchase or picking.

SOFT PASTE CHEESE
Cheese, such as Brie and Camembert, which is gradually softened by its white *penicillium* coat, over a period of 3–5 weeks, depending on the size of the cheese and the type of milk. In France there are at least 100 soft paste cheeses.

SOFT WHEAT
See *Soft Flour*.

SOFTEN (TO)
To leave fats at room temperature to become soft after refrigeration; to tenderize by cooking.

SOFT-SHELLED CRAB
A crab which is eaten just after it sheds its old, hard shell and before the new shell has had time to harden. The American blue crab is the most commonly used in this way but, in theory, any soft crab can be treated similarly.

SOGGY
See *Sodden*.

à la SOISSONAISE
French term denoting the inclusion of white haricot beans in a dish; also a garnish of the beans for a roast.

SOLE
See *Dover Sole*.

SOLE BERCY
A classic French dish of sole cooked in white wine with shallots and parsley, then coated with reduced stock, enriched with butter.

SOLE COLBERT
A classic French dish of egg-and-crumbed sole in which the thick side is slit down the centre and the flesh on either side filleted away from the bone almost to the edges, but not completely detached. After frying, the exposed bone is carefully removed and the cavity filled with *maître d'hôtel* butter.

SOLE DUGLÉRÉ
A classic French dish of sole poached in white wine with skinned, deseeded, chopped tomatoes and mixed herbs. The cooking liquor is reduced by boiling and then lemon juice and butter are added.

SOLE WALESKA
A classic French dish created for the Comtesse Waleska, mistress of Napoleon. It consists of fillets of sole coated with Mornay sauce and garnished with truffles and pieces of lobster.

SOLIANKA
A slightly sour Russian salmon soup containing chopped pickled cucumber, olives, capers, onions and butter.

SOLIDIFIED COOKING OIL
This is oil compressed into a white block. The oils used are generally vegetable.

SOLOMON GUNDY
Salted and pickled herrings from Nova Scotia in Canada. The fish is soaked, filleted and cut into pieces, then packed into jars with chopped onions. The jars are filled with vinegar, sugar and spices and the herrings left for several days to pickle. They are served as appetizers.

SOLUBLE FIBRE
Found in oat bran, peas, beans, citrus fruit and barley, the exact function of this type of fibre is not yet fully understood. Research to date has concluded that as part of a cholesterol-controlling diet it can assist in removing LDL from the bloodstream, thus lowering cholesterol levels.

SOMEN NOODLES
Very thin, almost pure white, Japanese wheat flour noodles which resemble *vermicelli*.

SOMERSET CIDER CHEDDAR
A mild Cheddar, flavoured with cider.

SOMMELIER
French term for a wine waiter.

SOP
A piece of food, especially bread, used for dipping into a hot liquid such as soup.

SOPA DE AGUACATE
Mexican and Latin American avocado soup made from mashed avocados, chicken stock, chopped fresh coriander or parsley, seasonings and sometimes cream. It is served lukewarm or chilled.

SOPA DE ALMEJAS
A Colombian soup, containing clams, white fish and vegetables.

SOPA DE CARNE
(So' O-Yosopy)
A beef and vegetable soup from Paraguay to which rice or *vermicelli* is added. Each portion is sprinkled with grated Parmesan cheese.

SOPA DE MONÍ
A speciality of Ecuador, a peanut and potato soup enriched with cream.

SOPPRESSATE
An Italian sausage from the Basilicata region in the south-west of the country. It is fairly large, with a flattened oval shape well seasoned and flavoured with ginger. It is sometimes preserved in olive oil.

SOPRESSA
See *Coppa*.

SORBET
(Water Ice)
A frozen dessert made from fruit juice, water, sugar and whipped egg white. It is often served at the end of a meal as a sweet, or between courses during a formal banquet to refresh the palate.

SORGHUM
(Sorgo)
A grain related to millet and an important food in parts of Africa and India. The Chinese and Japanese favour it boiled as an alternative to rice, but in the West the sweet sap is extracted from the stalks and used as a food sweetener by manufacturing industries. Sometimes the sap is converted into sugar and syrup before use. The

grain is also used for animal fodder and silage. Like millet, sorghum swells during cooking and, because it has a high fat content, the raw grain should be stored in a cool place to prevent it from going rancid.

SORREL
(French Sorrel)
A perennial herb (*Rumex acetosa*), dating back to around 3000 BC and originally native to Europe and the Middle East. Introduced to Britain during the latter part of the 16th century by the French, the herb is a member of the dock family with large, green and fleshy leaves which taste slightly bitter. It can be used as a substitute for spinach and is much loved in the USSR where, as in France, it is used in soup and salads.

SOSATIES
South African mutton kebabs, originally from Malaysia.

à la SOUBISE
French term denoting the inclusion of onion purée or Soubise sauce in or over a dish.

SOUBISE SAUCE
A Béchamel sauce, flavoured with a purée of boiled onions and nutmeg and enriched with cream. It can be served with roast or grilled lamb, and roast pork.

SOUCHONG
Term applied to a number of black teas of the large-leaf variety produced in the Far East. One of the best known is Lapsang Souchong from China.

SOUFFLÉ
A hot soufflé is a light and puffy dish, sweet or savoury, in which egg yolks and stiffly beaten whites are incorporated into a thick sauce. The mixture is subsequently transferred to a straight-sided, round greased dish and baked until it rises and browns. A soufflé must be eaten straight away as it sinks rapidly once removed from the oven. A cold soufflé is a fruit purée, gelatine and cream mixture into which stiffly beaten egg whites are folded. It is refrigerated until set and is characteristically light.

SOUFFLÉ DISH
A deep, straight-sided ovenproof dish made from earthenware, glass or specially treated porcelain used for both sweet and savoury, hot and cold soufflés.

SOUFFLÉ OMELETTE
Made from beaten egg yolks and seasoning (or sugar), into which stiffly beaten egg whites are folded. The mixture is spread into an omelette pan and cooked gently. The top is then lightly browned under the grill. Two eggs should be allowed per person.

SOUP
A liquid food of varied consistency made from vegetables, meat, fish, poultry, game or offal, combined with water, stock and/or milk.

SOUPE GERMOU
Pumpkin soup from St Lucia in the Caribbean. It is cooked with onions, garlic and celery, thickened with flour and served hot or cold.

SOUR
Having a sharp and/or acidic taste. A lemon is sour; so, to a lesser extent, is soured cream.

SOUR CREAM SAUCE
See *Smitane Sauce*.

SOUR CUCUMBER
See *Pickled Cucumber*.

SOUR DOUGH
A type of leavening which imparts a characteristic sourness to the dark breads of Scandinavia, North America and northern and eastern Europe. Basically, it is bread dough in which the yeast is still alive and active which is reserved from one

baking to use as a leaven in the next. In between baking sessions, the sour dough should be stored in the refrigerator, but should be allowed to reach kitchen temperature before use.

SOUR MILK CHEESE
(Sauermilchkäse)
A general term to describe German cheeses made from cows' milk curds which have been soured by the action of a lactic acid starter as opposed to rennet. All the Hand cheeses are made from sour milk curds.

SOUR SOP
(Prickly Custard Apple)
The fruit of a tree (*Anona muricata*), native to tropical America, which is a member of the custard apple family. It is the largest fruit in this group, 15–23 cm/6–9 inches long, is heart-shaped and has a green spiny skin. It is the most acid-tasting of the custard apples and the texture of the flesh is less appealing than that of the other species. It is, however, very juicy and, when fully ripe, makes an excellent basis for refreshing drinks and desserts.

SOURED CREAM
Pasteurized single cream, with a legal minimum butterfat content of 18%, which is incubated with harmless bacteria and culture to turn it slightly sour. It is recommended for adding to casseroles, stews (such as Goulash), Stroganoff, salad dressings and mayonnaise to reduce thickness. It makes an excellent dip with crudités of raw vegetables and is often used as a topping for cheesecake.

SOURED MILK
Untreated milk which turns sour due to the growth of lactic acid bateria. This converts the lactose in the milk to lactic acid which in turn curdles the milk and gives it a slightly piquant and acid taste.

SOUS CHEF
An assistant to a senior chef.

SOUSE (TO)
To cook in a spicy and acid mixture, usually applied to herring and mackerel.

SOUSED HERRINGS
Rolled-up herrings, baked in a covered dish with onions, herbs, spices, vinegar, water, a little sugar and seasonings. They are eaten cold and are a British speciality.

SOUSED MACKEREL
A British speciality prepared in the same way as soused herrings with mackerel being substituted for the herring.

SOUTHERN FRIED CHICKEN
A speciality of the southern states of the USA, consisting of chicken portions coated with seasoned flour, then fried until brown and tender. They are served with a white sauce and mashed potatoes.

SOUTRIBBETJIE
A South African speciality, ribs of lamb or mutton soaked in a salt solution then drained, hung up and left to dry. *Soutribbetjie* are usually cooked on a barbecue.

à la SOUVAROFF
French term for a casserole of game birds or poultry containing brandy, truffles and foie gras.

SOUVLAKIA
Greek kebabs of lamb, veal or pork which are either grilled or barbecued. They are served with lemon, onions and slices of tomato.

SOWBELLY
Salted fat pork or bacon.

SOY BEAN CURD
See *Tofu*.

SOY BEAN OIL
A mild oil derived from soy beans with a faint taste of soy. It can be

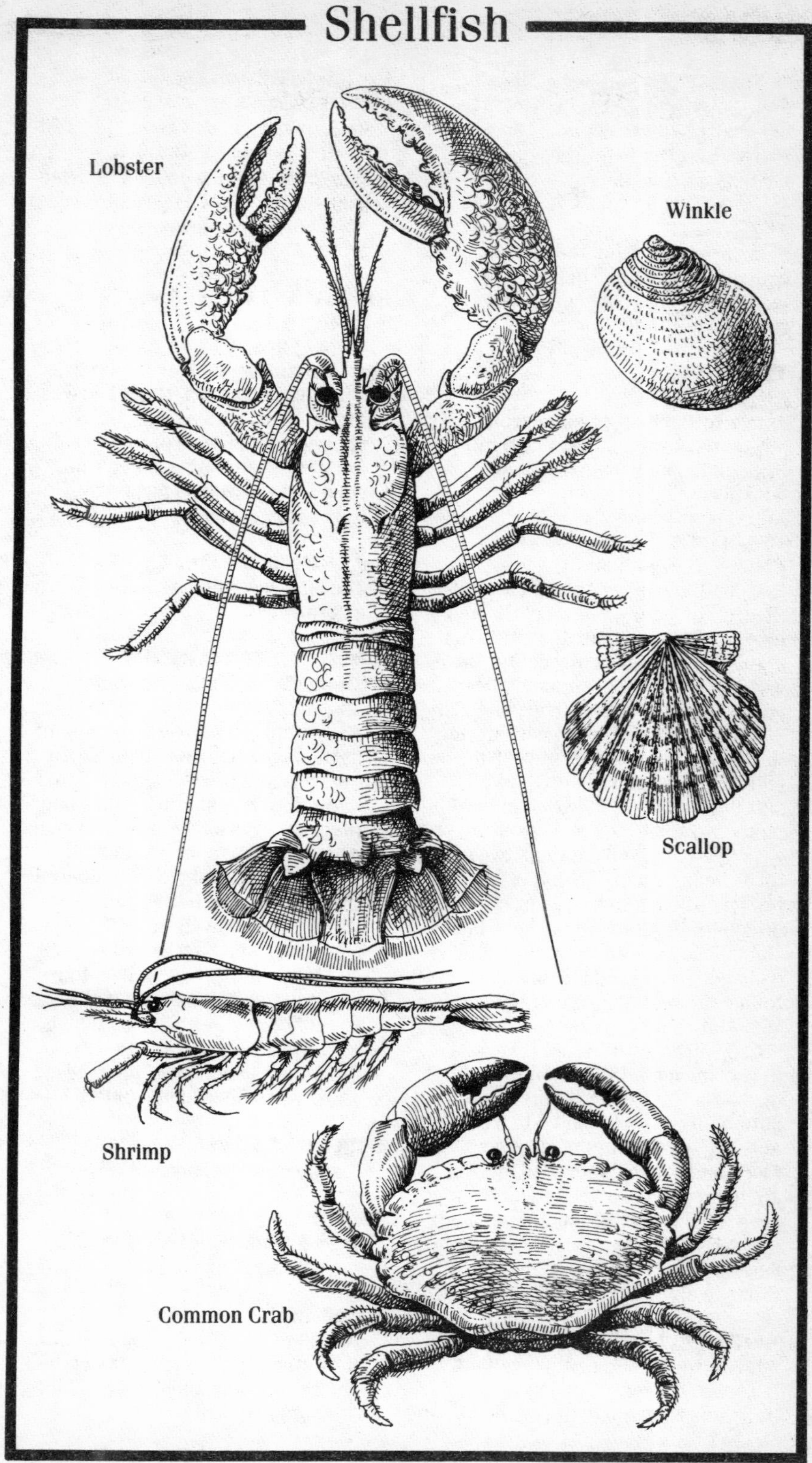
Shellfish
Lobster
Winkle
Scallop
Shrimp
Common Crab

used in cooking and salad dressings. It is a healthy oil, high in polyunsaturated fatty acids and therefore suitable for those on a low-cholesterol diet.

SOY FLOUR
Flour produced from the soy bean, a member of the pea family. It has a high fat and protein content but requires specialist recipes.

SOY SAUCE
(Soya Sauce)
A dark or light sauce made from fermented soya beans pickled in brine. It is much used in oriental cooking.

SOYA BEAN
(Soy Bean, Soja Bean)
A vegetable (*Glycine max*) which is the fruit of an erect plant of the pea family native to China and cultivated in the Far East for many centuries. It was not known in Europe until the end of the 17th century, became established in North America during the 19th century and is now also cultivated in other countries with suitable climates. It grows, in its many varieties, as a pod covered with fine hairs and contains two or three beans which may be yellow, brown, green, black or even bi-coloured. Although the soya bean can be cooked as a vegetable, it is used mainly to produce oil and meal. Unlike the rest of the pea family, it is very high in protein and low in carbohydrates, therefore it is used to replace meat in some national diets. The soya bean is very nutritious, has a bland taste, readily absorbs the flavours of stronger foods and is used, either as meal or oil, in many manufactured food products in place of animal fats and oils. Soya bean is processed as bean curd or *tofu*, a Japanese term for a Chinese discovery.

SPAGHETTI
Slim cords of solid pasta, available in assorted lengths. In southern Italy, it is referred to as *vermicelli*.

SPAGHETTI ALLA CARBONARA
An Italian speciality consisting of freshly cooked and drained *spaghetti* tossed with chopped and fried bacon, beaten eggs and cream. Each portion is sprinkled with grated Parmesan cheese.

SPAGHETTI ALL'AMATRICIANA
(Spaghetti alla Matriciana)
An Italian speciality from Amatrice consisting of *spaghetti* served with a tomato sauce flavoured with chopped onions and pieces of salt pork or bacon. Local sheep's milk cheese, Pecorino, is grated over the top of each serving.

SPAGHETTI FRUIT
The Israeli version of the spaghetti marrow.

SPAGHETTI MARROW
(Spaghetti Squash, Vegetable Spaghetti)
A vegetable (*Cucurbita* species) of the squash family native to North America and widely exported from California. It is shaped rather like a rugby or American football, oval and with flattish panels. The skin is smooth, thick and yellow-coloured. The flesh is pale yellow and characterized by its stringiness; it resembles spaghetti when cooked. The large, flattish creamy-coloured seeds in the flesh are not edible and should be removed. The squash is usually eaten with tomato or Bolognese sauce, or simply tossed with grated cheese and butter.

SPAGHETTINI
A slim version of *spaghetti*.

SPAM
Brand name of a canned luncheon meat made from pork.

SPANISH
An old-fashioned English term for long sticks of liquorice. The plant from which it is made grows chiefly in Spain and Sicily.

SPANISH CHESTNUT
The edible and rather sweet nut of a large and widely cultivated chestnut tree (*Castanea sativa*).

SPANISH LING
See *Ling*.

SPANISH OMELETTE
A flat, hearty omelette containing fried potato cubes, chopped onion, chopped tomato and chopped sweet pepper or canned red pimiento. The Spanish name for the omelette is *tortilla*.

SPANISH ONION
Term for a large, mature onion, generally with a mild flavour.

SPANISH PEPPER
See *Sweet Pepper*.

SPANISH RICE
A North American dish made from rice, onions, green pepper, tomatoes, herbs and seasonings. It is served as an accompaniment to roasts and stews.

SPANISH SAUCE
See *Espagnole Sauce*.

SPARE RIB OF PORK
A cut of pork from the neck end which is either divided into chops or cut up for stews, braises and casseroles. It is known by this name throughout England and Wales.

SPARERIBS OF PORK
A sheet of pork rib bones which may be fleshy or lean and either cooked Chinese-style or barbecued. The bones can be left as a sheet or cut into individual ribs.

SPARLING
North American name for smelt.

SPARROWGRASS
See *Asparagus*.

SPATCHCOCK
A chicken or game bird that is dressed, split open and cooked flat by frying or grilling immediately after slaughter. Sometimes the game bird is allowed to hang for an appropriate length of time before being split and cooked.

SPATULA
Handled bowl-scrapers made from wood, plastic and rubber. They are most effective when the oblong-shaped scraper is flexible.

SPÄTZEL
An Alsatian and southern German egg noodle.

SPAUL OF BEEF
Term used in Scotland for a cut of meat between the neck and the fore rib, more commonly known as chuck and blade steak. It is generally used for stewing, braising and casseroling.

SPEAR
Term used to describe a young blade, shoot or sprout of vegetation such as grass or asparagus.

SPEARMINT
See *Mint*.

SPECK
German pork fat, mildly cured and smoked, much used in traditional German cooking.

SPECULAAS
Dutch spiced biscuits made for the feast of St Nicholas and the ensuing Christmas season.

SPEISEKARTE
German term for a restaurant menu.

SPEISEQUARK
See *Low-fat Quark*.

SPENCER
See *Ulster Roll*.

SPICE BREAD
See *Yorkshire Spice Bread*.

SPICES
Once as precious as gold, spices are obtained from aromatic plants generally grown in tropical countries and available dried, either ground to a powder or in pieces like blades of mace.

SPICKEN SILL MED SUR GRÄDDE
A Swedish speciality consisting of pieces of pickled herring combined with a soured cream and mayonnaise sauce, flavoured with chopped fresh dill or chives.

SPIDER CRAB
(Spiny Crab)
A member (*Maja squinado*) of the family of crustaceans, distinguished by the positioning of the legs which are arranged rather like those of a spider. It is a popular crab in the Mediterranean and the Bay of Biscay. The oval shell, which is coloured reddish to brown, can reach 20 cm/8 inches in length and is covered in little pointed lumps. The meat is lean and the crab, after being killed, is boiled whole. When cold, the edible meat is removed from the shell and used as required.

SPIKE
An ear of grain.

SPINACH
A vegetable (*Spinacea oleracea*) native to Asia and cultivated in Persia over 2,000 years ago. It was introduced to Europe, both for medicinal and culinary purposes, in the 16th century and is now grown in many countries worldwide. Spinach grows as a loose cluster of thick-stalked and crinkly green leaves, oval or triangular in shape, and is ready for picking when about 18 cm/7 inches tall. The main types are a round-leaf summer variety and a prickly-leaf winter kind. Spinach leaves must be thoroughly washed to remove grit and may be eaten raw in salads when young, or boiled and used as a vegetable; it is also used in many savoury dishes.

SPINACH BEET
A vegetable (*Beta vulgaris cicla*) which is a member of the beetroot family cultivated for its greenery rather than its root. It grows as a cluster of stalks topped with oval leaves and is best harvested when young and tender; the leaf is green and the stalk white. Spinach beet has a mild, spinach-like flavour and may be steamed and eaten on its own with seasoning, or used in savoury dishes.

SPINY DOGFISH
See *Spur Dog*.

SPINY LOBSTER
See *Crawfish*.

SPIRIT
The product distilled from a fermented liquid. The liquid can be grape wine, grain wine or sugar wine. This definition covers spirits such as brandy, calvados, gin, rum and whisky. Even though almost any natural product containing sugar can be fermented and then distilled, some of the resultant products may not be drinkable but may have medical or commercial uses.

SPIT
A slender, pointed rod for holding food, generally meat or poultry, over a source of heat such as an open fire or barbecue. The spit should be rotated to ensure even cooking.

SPITCHCOCK
An eel that is split and grilled or fried.

SPIT-ROAST (TO)
To cook on a rotating spit either in front of an open fire or in an enclosed spit which may be part of a cooker or free-standing.

SPLEEN
(Milt)
An oval, vascular and ductless gland situated below the diaphragm in the abdominal quarter to the left of the cardiac end of the stomach. It is a

reddish colour and resembles liver in appearance. It is not widely used, but may be fed to household pets or added to stuffings.

SPLIT ALMONDS
Blanched almonds which have been split lengthwise along their natural dividing line.

SPLIT PEA
See *Pea*.

SPLIT TIN LOAF
A long white loaf with the crust divided lengthwise down the middle. Just before the dough is baked, a lengthwise cut is made in the top with a sharp knife. As the bread bakes, the split opens out slightly and browns.

SPONGE CAKE
A light, rather dry cake which is completely fatless. It becomes stale quickly and should be eaten or used soon after baking.

SPONGE FINGER BISCUITS
See *Savoy Biscuits*.

SPONGE FLAN
A sponge cake with an indented centre which can be filled with fruit, whipped cream or mousse mixtures. The flan is made from a sponge cake mixture or a Victoria sandwich mixture.

SPONGE PUDDING
A steamed or baked pudding, often made from a Victoria sandwich mixture. Jam or golden syrup is sometimes used to line the basin or dish before the mixture is added.

SPONGE SANDWICH
Two layers of sponge cake, usually filled with jam and dusted with caster sugar. Sometimes whipped cream is used instead of jam or added with it.

SPOON BREAD
From the southern states of the USA, spoon bread is a baked savoury pudding made from cornmeal. Due to the inclusion of eggs, it puffs up while baking.

SPOONABLE CREAM
Homogenized cream which is thick rather than whipped and sold ready to spoon over desserts and ice creams.

SPOT PRAWN
See *Prawn*.

SPOTTED DICK
(Spotted Dog)
A typically British pudding made from flour, raising agent, breadcrumbs, dried fruit, sugar, suet, eggs and milk. It is steamed for several hours in a basin, turned out and served with cream or custard.

SPRAT
A round-bodied member (*Sprattus sprattus*) of the herring family but a separate species in its own right. It grows up to 14 cm/5½ inches and has a bluish-green back and silvery sides and belly. It is caught, from September to March, close to the shore from Norway down to the Mediterranean. Close relatives are found in the Black Sea. The flesh is oily and the fish may be baked, fried or grilled.

SPREAD
A large amount of food on a table, a buffet for example; also, a food product which is capable of being smoothed over another, such as cheese spread on bread or pâté on toast.

SPRING CHICKEN
Similar to *poussin* but a little larger; an individual bird can weigh up to 1.5 kg/3½ lb. Spring chicken is usually roasted but may also be grilled, or halved and fried, braised, stewed or casseroled.

SPRING GREENS
Young leaves of vegetables of the cabbage family which are picked before the heads or hearts have formed.

SPRING ONION
(Salad Onion)
An immature onion with little or no bulb formation, white at the base and becoming green towards the top. There are varieties of onion (*Allium fistulum*) which never form a bulb and are used in the same way as a spring onion in salads and some cooked dishes.

SPRING ROLL
See *Chinese Egg Roll*.

SPRINKLE (TO)
See *Dredge*.

SPRITZ BISCUITS
Frequently eaten in Holland and Belgium with cups of tea or coffee. The word 'spritz' means to squirt and the biscuit mixture is piped or squirted on to metal trays in finger-length lines, zig-zags or in 'S' shapes. They are baked until lightly golden brown and crisp.

SPRUE
(Sprue Grass)
Young cultivated asparagus spears, or thin wild ones, generally of rather poor quality.

SPUD
Colloquial English term for a potato.

SPUN SUGAR
Made from sugar syrup which, when cool enough to handle, is spun or pulled rapidly to form fine threads. These are shaped according to requirements, such as a cascade on top of a dessert or clusters of threads in the form of posies. This form of decorative sugar work requires considerable expertise.

SPUR DOG
(Rock Salmon)
A cartilaginous (non-bony) round-bodied, torpedo-shaped fish (*Squalus acanthias*) of one of the shark families. The average length is 60 cm/24 inches and weight 2–3 kg/ 4½–6½ lb. The colour of the back varies with the region fished but is basically slate grey to grey-brown, shading to pale grey or white on the underside. This fish is one of the most widely distributed of the small sharks and is caught in European waters from Norway to the Mediterranean. In North American waters it is found from southern Labrador to Florida and in the Pacific from Alaska to California. The Atlantic spur dog is caught mainly in the summer months but fishing in the Pacific is all year round. The flesh is medium-oily, delicate and white and the fish may be poached, steamed or baked, but is best known as a standard fried fish in fried fish and chip shops, where it is interchangeable with other sharks such as the larger dogfish. In North America, the spur dog is called the spiny dogfish and on the Pacific coast it is known also as the Pacific dogfish.

SPURTLE
A carved wooden stick, traditionally used in Scotland to stir porridge while it is cooking. The cereal should always be stirred clockwise.

SQUAB
North American term for a small, one-portion chicken. Also, a four-week-old pigeon.

SQUAB PIE
See *Devonshire Squab Pie*.

SQUARE MEAL
A full meal as opposed to a snack.

SQUASH
Term mainly used in North America for vegetables which grow as fruits of the plant family Cucurbiteae. They are broadly divided into two

categories: the summer varieties which are eaten at an immature stage, often including the skin and seeds, and the winter varieties which are allowed to grow to maturity and have skins and seeds which are inedible. Squashes all have mild-flavoured, watery flesh and include courgette, vegetable marrow and pumpkin.

SQUASH MELON
See *Tinda*.

SQUID
(Inkfish)
A member (*Loligo* species) of the cephalopod group of seawater molluscs, the squid has a torpedo-shaped body with a transparent inner shell. It has two long tentacles and eight 'arms' which sprout directly from the head. It can measure 30–60 cm/1–2 feet in length, depending on habitat, and is basically semi-transparent, sometimes with reddish spots. It is widely distributed and is in demand in places as far apart as the Mediterranean area and Japan. In European waters the main season is from May to October. The flesh is lean and the edible parts can be poached, steamed, baked or fried.

SQUIRREL
A bushy-tailed member of the rodent family, eaten in some areas of the world and highly esteemed by the Cajuns in the Louisiana Bayou region of North America.

SRPSKA PROJA
Yugoslavian cornbread, served warm and cut in squares with all meals of the day. It is a Serbian speciality.

ST JOHN'S BREAD
See *Carob Powder*.

STABILIZERS
Act in much the same way as emulsifiers and prevent foods from separating. Cornflour is a useful domestic stabilizer and thickener; gelatine is another.

STAFF OF LIFE
A sustaining part of a diet, a term often associated with bread.

STAINLESS STEEL SAUCEPAN
This type of saucepan is tough, hard-wearing and virtually stainproof so manages to retain a good appearance throughout its long life. To ensure even heat distribution, it is advisable to choose a pan with a copper base.

STAMP AND GO
Jamaican salt cod fritters flavoured with chillies, spring onions and thyme. They are eaten hot as a snack.

STANDING RIBS OF BEEF
Term used in north-west England and North America for fore rib of beef.

STAR ANISE
The star-shaped dried fruit of a small evergreen tree (*Illicium verum*) native to China, a member of the magnolia family. Star anise is similar in flavour to aniseed and is used both in Chinese cooking and to flavour certain liqueurs.

STAR APPLE
The fruit of a tree (*Chrysophyllum cainito*) related to the sapodilla, native to the Caribbean and neighbouring countries and cultivated in Sri Lanka and Hawaii, often as a decorative garden plant. It is shaped like a slightly flattened globe and averages 7.5 cm/3 inches in diameter. The skin colour may be white, greenish or purple depending on the type. The flesh is white, sweet and pulpy and contains a number of dark, inedible seeds. If the fruit is cut in half horizontally, the seed pockets form a star shape, hence the name. The star fruit is usually eaten on its own or in a fruit salad. Care must be taken to remove the sticky skin, which has an unpleasant taste.

STAR FRUIT
See *Carambola*.

STARCH
Carbohydrate found mainly in rice, other grains and the potato family. It has neither smell nor flavour.

STARCHY FOODS
Foods which contain starch, such as flour-thickened sauces and soups, potatoes, rice, pasta and baked goods.

STAR-GAZEY PIE
A pilchard pie from Cornwall in the English West Country in which the whole fish are cooked beneath a crust of pastry but with their heads peeping out round the edges, their eyes gazing upwards to heaven. The pie is flavoured with parsley, onion, bacon and vinegar or cider and thickened with breadcrumbs and eggs.

ŠTARJERSKA KISELA ČORBA
A Yugoslavian soup from Slovenia, based on pigs' trotters and tails, vegetables, garlic, water, seasonings and vinegar, thickened with flour.

STARTER
Term used to describe a bacterial culture added to milk which changes its lactose into lactic acid, giving flavour to milk, butter and cheese; also, the first course of a fairly formal meal.

STEAK
A general term for certain cuts of beef; also, the cross-sectional slices from between the centre and tail of a large fish such as salmon.

STEAK AND KIDNEY PIE
There are two different versions of this traditional British pie. The first is a plate pie for which a previously made stew of steak and kidney is baked fairly quickly on a plate between a top and bottom crust of either shortcrust, rough-puff or flaky pastry. The second type is made from raw cubes of steak and kidney which, after being tossed in seasoned flour, are put into an oval pie dish with sliced onions, water and seasoning. The filling is domed in the centre and the pie is covered with a lid of either shortcrust, rough-puff or flaky pastry and baked until the meat is tender — about 3 hours.

STEAK AND KIDNEY PUDDING
A great British favourite, this is made by lining a basin with suet-crust pastry, then filling it with diced stewing beef, diced ox kidney, sliced onions, seasonings and either water, stock or beer, and covering with a lid of pastry. The basin is securely covered and the pudding steamed or boiled for 3–3½ hours. It is traditionally served from the basin with a white napkin tied round the outside.

STEAK AU POIVRE
See *Pepper Steak*.

STEAK BONE OF BEEF
Alternative term used in north-east England for rump.

STEAK DIANE
A classic international meat dish in which thin steaks are fried in butter and flavoured with Worcestershire sauce and chopped parsley. Sometimes cream and/or ignited brandy is also included.

STEAK PIECE OF BEEF
Alternative term used in the West Country for rump.

STEAK TARTARE
A classic international dish made from raw minced fillet of beef mixed with egg yolk, chopped onions and parsley, capers and seasonings.

STEAM (TO)
To cook in steam rising from boiling water.

STEAM TABLE
A catering table with openings to hold containers of cooked food over steam or hot water.

STEAMED PUDDING
General term to describe a range of typically British puddings which can be based on a suet, Victoria sandwich cake or sponge mixture. Steamed puddings are usually sweet, but the classic steak and kidney pudding also belongs in this category.

STEAMER
A traditional steamer is very similar to a double saucepan except that the base of the upper compartment is perforated to enable steam, rising from the boiling water in the saucepan beneath, to circulate around and cook the food which is in the upper compartment. The steamer should always be covered with a lid to prevent excess evaporation of cooking water.

STEARIC ACID
See *Palmitic Acid*.

STEEL
See *Knife Sharpener*.

STEEP (TO)
See *Macerate*.

STEINBUSCHER
An East German cows' milk cheese, produced originally in Steinbusch, near Brandenburg, about 100 years ago. It is similar to Romadur.

STEINPILZ
Term used in parts of eastern Europe for the cep.

STELLETTE
(Stelline)
Minuscule pasta stars, usually added to soup.

STEPNOÏ
(Stepnoy)
See *Steppe*.

STEPPE
(Steppen)
A cows' milk cheese resembling Tilsit, made in East and West Germany, Austria, Scandinavia, western Canada, and in the USSR where it is known as Stepnoï. It has a fairly strong flavour and sometimes contains caraway seeds.

STERILIZED CREAM
Canned cream which lasts a minimum of 2 years in the store cupboard. It is homogenized and thick, and the sterilization process gives it a slight caramel-like after-taste. The cream should be stirred before use but will not whip.

STERILIZED MILK
A golden-coloured milk with a faint but characteristic caramel flavour, enjoyed by many in coffee, milk puddings and other cooked dishes. It is sold in Britain either in long, slender-necked bottles with blue caps or in sealed cartons. It has excellent keeping qualities if unopened and is useful for those without refrigeration. It is made from pasteurized milk which is homogenized, bottled and sealed, then brought to a temperature of just above boiling point and held at that temperature for 20–30 minutes. It is subsequently left to cool. Because of the heat treatment, it is unsuitable for making junket but may be used for home-made yogurt.

STEW (TO)
To simmer meat and poultry, with liquid and vegetables, in a heavy saucepan with a tight-fitting lid to minimize evaporation. Thickening may take place at the beginning or end of cooking time. Also to cook fruit, such as apples, with a little water and sugar until soft.

STEWED FRUIT
Fruit simmered with water and sweetened with sugar, honey or syrup.

STICKJAW

An informal British term to describe a sweet, such as toffee, that is difficult to chew.

STIFADO

(Stifatho)

A Greek stew based on meat, poultry or octopus and containing oil, onions, garlic, tomatoes, vinegar, red wine, seasonings and shallots or small onions.

STILL

Not carbonated and having no effervescence; a distillery; an apparatus used in distillation, especially of spirits, comprising either the chamber in which the vaporization is carried out or the entire equipment.

STILTON

(Blue Stilton)

Rated as the 'King of Cheeses', British Stilton appears to have originated in Leicestershire well over 200 years ago, although its exact birthplace remains uncertain. However, tradition maintains that Stilton was 'invented' by Mrs Elizabeth Scarbrow, a talented cheese-maker and housekeeper to Lady Beaumont at Quenby Hall in Leicestershire. She passed the recipe on to her daughters, one of whom, farmer's wife Mrs Paulet, produced the same cheese for the landlord (her own brother-in-law) of the Bell Inn in the village of Stilton. The Bell Inn was a coaching stop on the Great North Road and Stilton's fame was quickly spread by hungry and appreciative travellers. Stilton was subsequently made for generations in the valley of Belvoir in Leicestershire and also in the Dove valley of Derbyshire. During the First World War, small creameries were established to improve production conditions. As a result, the Stilton Cheese Making Association was formed and it now holds the copyright. Thus strict regulations are enforced by the Association to safeguard Stilton's pedigree and Stilton cheese must come only from the Shire counties of Leicester, Nottingham and Derby. Additionally its shape must be cylindrical and the cheese made from pasteurized whole cows' milk. It must not be pressed during production and has to have a naturally grown rind. Stilton is a smooth and pale-coloured cheese, deepening in tone towards the edges. It is marbled with blue-green veins and has a close-textured consistency which is characteristically creamy. The taste is always mellow but more sharp and zesty when the cheese is young (around 3 months). As it matures, the taste increases in depth and Stilton reaches its prime when 4–6 months old. Its rind is hard and dusty-looking and usually a kind of mushroom-soup colour. Stilton is traditionally accompanied by port at the end of a meal.

STIR (TO)

To agitate or 'move' a mixture to prevent sticking or burning, to discourage the formation of lumps and to ensure a smooth and well-blended consistency. The implement used for stirring is usually a spoon or spatula.

STIRABOUT

A porridge of Irish origin consisting of oatmeal or maize boiled in water or milk.

STIR-FRY

A Chinese method of preparing food, usually in a wok, in which small strips or squares of food are stirred together while being fried rapidly in hot oil or fat.

STOCK

A fairly concentrated liquid made by simmering meat, game, poultry or fish with vegetables, herbs, spices, water and often wine. It is strained and used as a base for sauces and soups.

STOCK CUBE
(Bouillon Cube)
A savoury cube used to flavour soups, gravies, stews and casseroles. It is made from seasoned and evaporated meat, poultry or vegetable extracts.

STOCK POT
An old-fashioned term for a large brew of meat, vegetables, spices, herbs and water which was kept on the kitchen range and boiled and skimmed daily to prevent spoilage.

STOCKFISH
Fish (cod, haddock and hake, for example) which is dried in the open air without salt.

STODGE
A British colloquial term to describe heavy, starchy food such as a steamed or boiled suet pudding.

STOLLEN
A German yeasted Christmas cake filled with fruit, nuts and sometimes marzipan which has excellent keeping qualities. It is folded like an omelette, baked, then coated thickly with melted butter and sifted icing sugar.

STOMNA KEBAB
A Bulgarian stew, made in a clay pot, consisting of lamb, butter, tomatoes, spring onions, herbs and seasonings, thickened with flour.

STONE
Term for the hard, central container which houses the kernel of fruits such as plum, cherry and mango.

STONE (TO)
See *Pit*.

STONEGROUND FLOUR
Wholemeal or wholewheat flour which has been ground between two slowly-rotating stones at a low temperature. It is a traditional technique and helps to conserve some of the heat-sensitive nutrients in the flour. Flours milled between steel rollers are subjected to higher temperatures and possibly lose some nutritional value as a consequence.

STORE (TO)
To keep dry and long-lasting foods in cupboards and perishable foods in a refrigerator or larder. Deep-freezing is another method of storing.

STOUT
Said to have tonic properties, this is a full-bodied and fairly dry, creamy black beer. The best known brand is Guinness, originally produced in Ireland.

STRACCHINO
A north Italian cows' milk cheese, noted for its ability to ripen quickly; it takes only 8–10 days. It is usually brick-shaped or square, mild in flavour and luxuriously creamy. It can be large or small, depending on type.

STRACCIATELLA
(Stracciatelle)
A classic Italian soup from Rome, which contains little ragged-looking threads produced from a mixture of beaten eggs, semolina and grated Parmesan cheese which is whisked into the boiling beef or chicken broth. The mixture then separates into the strands which characterize the soup.

STRAIN (TO)
To drain foods of water after cooking. Careful straining through muslin or filter paper is sometimes necessary to remove sediment from a mixture. Using a jelly bag is another means of straining.

STRAINER
See *Colander* and *Sieve*.

à la STRASBOURGEOISE
French term meaning in the style of Strasbourg in eastern France, referring to food cooked with sauerkraut, bacon and *foie gras*.

STRAW CHIPS
See *Game Chips*.

STRAW MUSHROOM
See *Paddy Straw Mushroom*.

STRAWBERRY
The fruit of an herbaceous plant (*Fragaria* species) related to the rose and native to temperate regions of both the Old and New Worlds and of mountain regions in hotter areas. Although cultivated through the ages, there was little improvement on the wild varieties in Europe until the middle of the 18th century when the larger, succulent hybrids, based on American species, began to emerge. The strawberry now ranges in size from the tiny and delicious wood or wild kind to the largest modern specimen which can measure 5 cm/2 inches or more. The colour of most strawberries is bright red but can vary from almost white to dark red. The shape is also variable but is generally conical. The fruit consists of a cluster of tiny globules on a fleshy stem; each globule is a one-seeded fruit, and the strawberry differs from other soft fruits in that the seeds are on the surface rather than embedded in the flesh. The flavour and texture depend on the variety, but all are at their best if picked and eaten when fully ripe. Strawberries may be eaten on their own or with cream, or used in cooked dishes and preserves.

STRAWBERRY SHORTCAKE
A North American speciality made from large scones which are split while warm and spread with butter. They are then filled and topped with sweetened whipped cream and sliced strawberries. Other berry fruits, such as raspberries, are sometimes substituted.

STREAKY BACON
A cut from the underside of the pig, centre-front, which can be boiled as a whole joint or cut into rashers for grilling and frying. The rashers have stripes of lean meat and fat. They are frequently used to line tins and dishes in which pâtés and terrines are cooked.

STREUSEL CAKE
Central and northern European in origin, this slightly sweet yeasted cake has a crumble topping flavoured with cinnamon or mixed spice.

STRING
(Braid Cheese)
A North American cows' milk cheese which is similar to Mozzarella in both colour and consistency, but sometimes contains caraway seeds. Native to Armenia, it is shaped like a tube and, in its country of origin, is eaten by being divided into thickish threads and mounded on to plates.
It is also a good cooking cheese. In Georgia in the USSR the cheese is packed in brine.

STRIPED BASS
An inshore seawater fish (*Morone saxatilus* and *Roccus saxatilus*) which enters fresh water to spawn. The deep body has an olive-green back and sides with longitudinal stripes which give it its name. The average weight in the shops is 2.25 kg/5 lb. It is caught off the east and west coasts of North America and is also found in some landlocked lakes. The flesh is white, flaky and medium-oily and the fish may be poached, steamed, boiled, fried or grilled.

STRIPED MULLET
North American name for one of the common species of grey mullet.

STRONG PLAIN FLOUR
This flour has a high gluten content of 10–15% and is the best flour to use for yeasted goods, puff pastry, Yorkshire pudding and steamed suet puddings.

STRUDEL PASTRY
Wafer-thin pastry which is a speciality of both Austria and Hungary. It is made from flour, oil, eggs and water and traditionally used for making fruit or cheese strudels.

STUD (TO)
To add decorative touches to certain foodstuffs with pieces of olive, anchovies, gherkin and so on. Cloves, for example, are used to stud the scored and glazed fat layer of a joint of cooked gammon.

STUFATO
(Stufatino)
An Italian dish of beef braised with red wine, onions, celery, tomatoes, garlic and ham.

STUFF (TO)
To fill cavities of meat, poultry and fish with a stuffing or forcemeat. To do exactly the same with vegetables such as tomatoes, marrow, peppers, aubergines, cabbage leaves and mushrooms. Also to fill the cavities in cored apples before baking.

STUFFED DERMA
See *Kishka*.

STUFFED OLIVE
See *Olive*.

STUFFING
(Forcemeat)
A seasoned, savoury mixture, often based on breadcrumbs, used to fill poultry, joints of meat, fish and vegetables.

STURGEON
A family of fish (*Acipenser* species) with armour-plated bodies and skeletons of both cartilage and bone, which has changed little in appearance for many millions of years. Most species have an elongated snout which is used for prodding the sea bed for food. A large female may carry as much as 22 kg/50 lb of eggs (caviar). The colour of the back varies with species but is generally dark grey-green, sometimes becoming paler on the underside. The 16 species which exist are found from the Caspian and Black Seas to the western Atlantic from New England to North Carolina and also in many rivers and lakes where the fish return to spawn. The main catches are from January to March and in the early autumn. The flesh is firm, white to pink in colour and in some species has been compared with veal for flavour and texture. The fish may be baked, fried, grilled or smoked.

SUAN LA TANG
The Cantonese name for hot and sour soup.

SUBMARINE
A North American term for an elongated sandwich made either from long rolls or a French stick which is subsequently cut into pieces.

SUBO BENACHIN
A beef, lamb or fish stew from the Gambia containing onions, chilli, tomatoes, rice and seasonings.

SUBO DOMODA
A Gambian speciality, this is a meat or fish stew containing fried onions, tomato purée, peanut butter, chillies and seasoning.

SUCCORY
See *Chicory*.

SUCCOTASH
A North American dish of Indian origin, this is a combination of small, cooked lima beans and sweetcorn kernels, heated together with cream and seasonings. It is sometimes served with the Thanksgiving turkey.

SUCKING PIGS
Unweaned piglets, said to be at their best when about three weeks old. They are roasted either stuffed or unstuffed.

SUCKLING
A young unweaned animal.

SUCROSE
A disaccharide or double sugar made up of two monosaccharides, consisting of one part glucose and one part fructose. It is found in cane or beet sugar, fruits and root vegetables such as carrots.

SUET
A concentrated, hard animal fat which is added finely chopped to a mixture of dry ingredients. The best suet is said to be that which surrounds the kidneys of an animal. It is high in saturated fatty acids and therefore not suitable for those on a low-cholesterol diet.

SUET PUDDING
A traditional British pudding made from a mixture of flour, breadcrumbs, sugar, suet, flavouring, eggs and milk. It is usually steamed in a covered basin, with or without syrup or jam in the base.

SUET-CRUST PASTRY
A typically British pastry made from strong plain flour with added salt, raising agent and chopped-up beef or vegetable suet, mixed to a stiff but pliable dough with cold water. It is used for traditional steamed steak and kidney pudding and also for roly-poly puddings and dumplings.

SUFFOLK HAM
Traditional English ham, sweet-cured in beer and sugar. The skin is bronzed and the meat a deep reddish-brown, characterized by a 'blue' bloom. Suffolk hams are a rare luxury.

SUGAR
A carbohydrate found naturally in plants which, for commercial purposes, comes either from grass-like canes growing in hot climates such as the West Indies, or from beets growing in more temperate climates such as Britain. All sugar is sweet-tasting and water-soluble and provides energy. There is no difference in taste or appearance between cane and beet sugar.

SUGAR APPLE
See *Sweet Sop*.

SUGAR BEET
A root vegetable (*Beta vulgaris*) which is the palest and sweetest of the beet family. Although some kinds of sugar beet can be cooked as a vegetable, the primary use is in the production of sugar.

SUGAR CANE
(Cane)
One of the larger members of the grass family of plants (*Saccharum officinarum*), native to tropical Asia and cultivated widely in many areas with suitable climates and particularly in the Caribbean region. It grows to 2 metres/6 feet 6 inches or more and looks like thick, purply-brown bamboo cane. It is mostly used for the commercial production of sugar but some kinds may be cut into pieces and the sweet juice extracted by chewing or pressing.

SUGAR PEA
See *Mange-tout*.

SUGAR SUBSTITUTES
See *Artificial Sweeteners*.

SUGAR SYRUP
See *Syrup*.

SUGAR THERMOMETER
A mercury-filled thermometer, capable of reaching a very high temperature and therefore able to record accurately the temperature of preserves and confectionery while boiling. A sugar thermometer is the best indicator as to whether the mixture has cooked for the correct length of time to ensure a satisfactory set.

SUGARED ALMOND
See *Jordan Almond*.

SUGARLOAF
A moulded cone of refined sugar.

SUGARPLUM
A small, round, boiled sweet, usually flavoured and coloured.

SUKIYAKI
A famous Japanese dish which is cooked at the table. It consists of sliced mixed vegetables, squares of *tofu* (bean curd) and paper-thin slices of beef. The beef is fried with soy sauce, rice wine, sugar and water, then the other ingredients are added and lightly cooked. Diners help themselves and add rice to each portion.

SULTANAS
Seedless white grapes which are not only dried but also chemically treated to keep the colour light, enhancing the appearance. Sultanas are produced in countries round the eastern Mediterranean and in the USA, South Africa and Australia.

SÜLZWURST
German version of brawn, made from fairly large pieces of pork set firmly in wine-flavoured aspic. It is usually sliced and served with French dressing.

SUMMER FLOUNDER
(Northern Fluke)
A flatfish (*Paralichthys dentatus*) related to the plaice family. It is the largest of the American flounder family and can be 1 metre/39 inches long and the average weight is 5–6 kg/11–13 lb. The colour of the upper side varies from dark grey to brown and the dark spots may be more defined than on the winter flounder. It is caught from February to October, with main catches in the summer months, in the waters off North America from Nova Scotia to South Carolina. It has firm, lean flesh and the fish may be poached, steamed, baked, fried or grilled. It is called the summer flounder because it tends to seek shallower water during the warm season.

SUMMER PUDDING
A traditional British pudding made in a pudding basin lined with strips or slices of white bread and filled with lightly stewed and sweetened soft summer fruits such as berries and currants. It is refrigerated overnight, turned out and served with cream.

SUMMER SAUSAGE
North American term for a pork and beef sausage of the *cervelat* type.

SUMMER SAVORY
See *Savory*.

SUNDAE
An ice cream and whipped cream dessert, usually topped with sauce, chopped nuts, and so on.

SUNFLOWER OIL
Extracted from sunflower seeds. It is a mild and very healthy oil, more suited to use in salad dressings and mayonnaise than for frying. It is very high in polyunsaturated fatty acids and therefore suitable for those on a low-cholesterol diet.

SUNFLOWER SEEDS
The seeds of the annual sunflower (*Helianthus annuus*), widely grown in the Balkans and eastern Europe. They are a good source of protein and make a delicious snack or topping for salad.

SUNNY SIDE UP
North American term for a fried egg with the yolk facing uppermost.

SUNOMONO
A Japanese salad dressed with vinegar and served in tiny portions as an appetizer. Alternatively, it features at the end of a formal meal, making its appearance before the rice.

SUPA KANGYA
Gambian fried fish and onions simmered with tomato purée, stock, garlic, palm oil, spinach and okra.

SUPPER
A light evening meal served when the main meal of the day is taken around noon; also, an informal term for dinner.

SUPRÊME
French term meaning, in its culinary sense, the breast or fillet of poultry and game birds. Usually the wing is also included.

SUPRÊME SAUCE
A velouté sauce made with vegetable, fish or poultry stock and enriched with cream, egg yolk and butter. It can be served with fish or poultry dishes and roast veal.

SURATI PANIR
An Indian cheese produced in Gujarat from buffaloes' milk. It is a white cheese, matured in whey and fairly pungent and sharp.

SURF CLAM
Found in abundance off the eastern coasts of North America, the flesh of this clam (family *Mactridae*) is generally used in made-up dishes.

SURINAM CHERRY
(Jambos)
The fruit of a small tree or shrub (*Eugenia uniflora*) of the myrtle family grown in tropical or semi-tropical parts of the world. It is round or slightly oval with eight clefts running from the stem end of the cherry. The skin turns from green to red as the fruit matures and darkens almost to black when fully ripe. The red flesh surrounding the single large stone is juicy and soft and may be eaten raw or cooked with other ingredients. The name jambos is often used both for this fruit and others in the same family.

SUSHI
In its simplest form, *sushi* is made from fingers of vinegared rice with decorative toppings of very fresh, raw fish. It is accompanied by hot green tea.

SUSSEX POND PUDDING
A typically British steamed suet pudding in which suet crust pastry lines a basin and acts as a lid; the 'filling' consists of a whole lemon, brown sugar and butter or margarine. Each portion should contain a piece of lemon and the surrounding juices.

SUSUMBER
See *Drumstick*.

SUTTAÇ
A Turkish rice pudding, simmered on the hob, then served with ice cream.

SVECIAOST
A Swedish, all-purpose cows' milk cheese which can be strong or mild, firm or soft and young or 'old', depending on how long it has been allowed to mature.

SWALEDALE
A British cows' milk cheese from North Yorkshire which is mild, creamy and fairly soft.

SWEAT (TO)
To cook chopped or sliced vegetables very slowly in fat over a low heat. The lid should be kept on the pan so that steam builds up inside and the vegetables are able to release their own juices (sweat) without browning.

SWEDE
(Swedish Turnip)
A root vegetable (*Brassica napobrassica*) native to Europe, introduced to Britain during the 18th century and cultivated both for human consumption and animal feed. It grows as a swollen root, is shaped rather like a spinning top with ridges near the base of the foliage and is normally allowed to

mature in the ground to reach a weight of 450 g–1.5 kg/1–3 lb. The skin is coloured purple in most cases and the flesh is dense and yellow in colour. The swede has a delicate, distinctive and slightly sweet flavour and may be grated and eaten raw in salads but is more usually cooked as a vegetable or added to soups, stews, casseroles and other savoury dishes. In North America and northern parts of Britain, the swede is often referred to as a turnip.

SWEDISH ANCHOVIES
(Brisling)
Sprat, canned in oil

SWEDISH HASH
See *Pytt i Panna*.

SWEDISH SAUCE
Mayonnaise mixed with thick apple purée and grated horseradish. It can be served with smoked meats, cold roast pork and continental sausages.

SWEET
Anything containing sugar, syrup, honey or sugar substitute; wine that retains some of its natural sugar; a small piece of confectionery; a dessert at the end of a meal.

SWEET (A)
British colloquial term to describe a dessert or item of confectionery.

SWEET ALMONDS
Dating back to biblical times, sweet almonds (*Prunus amygdalus*) are one of the most extensively used nuts in the world. They can be eaten either fresh from the cracked shells or roasted and salted. The best dessert almonds come from Jordan and Spain.

SWEET AND SOUR PRAWNS
A Chinese speciality consisting of fried prawns in a sauce containing soy sauce, vinegar, sugar, sherry, and cornflour.

SWEET ANISE
North American term for Florence fennel.

SWEET BASIL
See *Basil*.

SWEET CHESTNUT
An edible chestnut from Spain.

SWEET CICELY
(Cicely)
A strong, perennial herb (*Myrrhis odorata*) of the carrot family with fern-like leaves and a distinct taste of aniseed. It can be added to meat dishes, soups and stock.

SWEET CURE BACON
See *Quick Cure*.

SWEET GRANADILLA
(Orange Passion Fruit)
The fruit of a plant (*Passiflora ligularis*) of the passion flower family native to tropical America. The shape is almost globular, slightly tapering at the stem side. The parchment-like skin is orange-coloured with brown mottling and has a soft pith lining. The flesh consists of a loose pocket of grey and flattish edible seeds in a gelatinous 'sauce', rather like frog's spawn in appearance. If the fruit is shaken when ripe, the flesh and seeds appear to rattle in the brittle skin. The flavour is like a ripe dessert gooseberry with a touch of elderberry.

SWEET MARJORAM
See *Marjoram*.

SWEET ORANGE
See *Orange*.

SWEET PEPPER
(Bell Pepper, Capsicum, Spanish Pepper, Pimento, Pimiento)
A vegetable which is the fruit of a plant (*Capsicum annuum*) native to tropical America, now widely grown in various forms in countries with suitable climates. The shape may be squat like a large tomato, elongated

or even tapering to resemble its relative, the hot-tasting chilli pepper. The skin of the young sweet pepper is green and turns to yellow or red as it ripens. There are also varieties which are black, cream and even variegated. The crisp and fairly juicy flesh is the inner layer of the skin. The centre is hollow with a number of small, inedible seeds adhering to ribs of white pith. Sweet pepper has a distinctive flavour, mainly mild but sometimes with quite a kick, and may be eaten raw in salads, fried, stuffed and baked or added to dishes such as stews. Capsicums in the various stages of ripeness are referred to as green peppers, red peppers and yellow peppers.

SWEET PICKLE

See *Chutney*.

SWEET POTATO

A vegetable tuber (*Ipomoea batatas*) of a trailing vine of the morning glory family native to South America and now grown in most tropical regions. There are many varieties but most of those available in Britain are an elongated potato shape, tapering at one end. An average length in the shops is about 15 cm/6 inches. The skin colour is generally red but may vary from off-white to crimson. The flesh is yellow or white, depending on the type, and the sweet potato is sweet enough to be used in dessert dishes as well as being cooked as a vegetable on its own. The sweet potato is sometimes sold under the name of yam but is of a different botanical genus.

SWEET SOP

(Scaly Custard Apple, Sugar Apple) The fruit of a tree (*Anona squamosa*), originally from the American tropics, but now cultivated in many parts of the world in lowland tropical regions. It is one of the main species of the custard apple family and is about 5–7.5 cm/2–3 inches in diameter. The general appearance is rather scaly, resembling a green, unopened fir cone. When ripe the flesh is white, studded with many inedible black seeds. It has a texture like thick custard and may be eaten raw or used with other ingredients in sweet dishes and drinks.

SWEET-AND-SOUR PORK

A typically Chinese dish consisting of pieces of pork coated with egg and cornflour, then deep-fried. The accompanying sweet-and-sour sauce includes fruit juice (pineapple, for example), water, vinegar, sugar, soy and Worcestershire sauces, and salt. It is thickened with cornflour and used to coat the fried pork.

SWEETBREADS

Smooth, pinky-beige glands sold in pairs, made up of the pancreas gland which is associated with the stomach and the thymus gland which is associated with the throat. Sweetbreads come from oxen, calves and lambs. The most delicate and tender are said to be those from lambs, while next in line are calf's sweetbreads. Ox sweetbreads are fairly tough and need long, slow cooking to make them tender and edible. Sweetbreads are an easily digested protein food and are considered an expensive luxury. They are high in cholesterol.

SWEETCORN

A vegetable (*Zea mays sacharata*) which is one of many types of maize native to North and South America and eaten by the peoples of these two continents for thousands of years. Maize seed was brought to Europe during the 16th century but was used to produce animal fodder. Improved varieties over the years encouraged the use of maize in the kitchen and sweetcorn is now cultivated in cooler climates. It grows as a cluster of yellow or white seeds or kernels round a central core or cob, covered with silky threads and enclosed in a husk of green leaves. The plant itself may be 2 metres/6 feet tall and has a number of cobs spaced along its stem. Before being cooked whole, corn-on-the-cob should have the leaves and threads removed. The kernels may be cut off the central cob and either cooked by themselves or used in savoury dishes. Commercially, sweetcorn is sold frozen or canned, on or off the cob.

SWEETCREAM BUTTER
Hard butter which is traditionally prepared in Britain and available either salted or unsalted. The pasteurized cream is churned in stainless steel vats at a carefully controlled temperature to produce large pieces of butterfat. These are washed clean of buttermilk, salted (or not), kneaded until the consistency is correct, then wrapped and packaged ready for distribution. Typical examples of sweetcream butter are any of the British brands or those from New Zealand. They are piquant and fresh-tasting, recommended for pastry-and biscuit-making.

SWEET-CRUST PASTRY
See *Flan Pastry*.

SWEETEN (TO)
To make sweet by the addition of sugar or artificial sweetener.

SWEETGRASS BUFFALO AND BEER PIE
A speciality of Alberta in Canada, consisting of buffalo meat (now very scarce) stewed with sago, vegetables, herbs, spices and beer. The mixture is put into dishes, covered with pastry and baked.

SWEETMEAT
Crystallized fruit, sugar-coated nut or any other item covered in sugar.

SWEETS
A British term to describe any sweet dish served at the end of a meal; also most confectionery except chocolate.

SWEET-SOUR
(Sweet and Sour)
Food mixed with a sauce containing sugar or fruit juice and vinegar or lemon juice.

SWEET-SOUR SAUCE
(Sweet-and-Sour Sauce)
Chinese-style sauce made from stock, soy sauce, often chopped vegetables, sugar, vinegar and sometimes fruit. It is thickened with cornflour, which gives the sauce its characteristic gloss.

SWIRL (TO)
To add one mixture to another so as to achieve a rippled effect; to whisk a sauce gently in a figure-of-eight motion; to move a saucepan of sauce or stew in a slow to-and-fro motion, after *beurre manié* (kneaded butter) has been added to it for thickening purposes.

SWISS
A term widely used, especially in the USA, to describe Switzerland's Emmental cheese.

SWISS BUNS
Buns made from a fairly plain white yeast dough which is shaped into batons measuring about 13 cm/5 inches in length. After baking, the buns are left to cool and later covered with pink or white glacé icing.

SWISS CHARD
(Leaf Beet, Sea Kale Beet)
A vegetable (*Beta vulgaris*) which is a member of the beetroot family cultivated for its greenery rather than its root. It grows as a cluster of stalks topped with crinkly, oval leaves which are wide and thick-veined and best harvested before maturity to eliminate stringiness. The leaf is green and its wide stalk is normally white but red varieties do exist. Swiss chard may be cooked and eaten whole but more often the green leaf is stripped off and used separately

from the white stalk. The leaf is best steamed, as overcooking destroys the mild, spinach-like flavour.

SWISS FONDUE
See *Cheese Fondue*, *Fondue Bourguignonne* and *Fondue Chinoise*.

SWISS MERINGUE MIXTURE
See *Meringue*.

SWISS ROLL
An oblong sponge cake, plain or flavoured (often with chocolate), which is spread with jam or cream and rolled.

SWISS STEAK
A North American term for stewed steak, simply cooked with onions and sometimes garlic.

SWORDFISH
A seawater fish (*Xiphias gladius*) caught all round the world. The sword (snout) can be up to 35% of the total length and makes this fish unmistakable. Even a small swordfish when caught can be 2–3 metres/6½–10 feet long and, because of its length and large size, it is sold mostly as steak portions. The flesh is white, firm and medium-oily to oily. The steaks may be baked or grilled. In Japan, swordfish meat is used raw in sushi dishes.

SYLLABUB
(Sillabub)
An old English dessert which is made by beating double cream with wine, lemon juice, finely grated lemon peel and sugar. When ready, a syllabub should be the consistency of softly whipped cream.

SYRUP
Sweet liquids, of varying densities, used for poaching fruit, soaking *babas* and *savarins*, sweetening fruit purées and so on. Syrups are generally made from a mixture of white sugar and water, gently heated until the sugar melts. The mixture is then boiled until the correct consistency has been reached. Also, the concentrated juice of a fruit or plant, such as maple syrup. The term syrup is also applied to raw sugar juice obtained from crushed sugar cane after evaporation and before crystallization in sugar manufacture.

SYRUP ROLY-POLY
See *Roly-Poly Pudding*.

SZECHUAN COOKING
The food from this hot, humid region of western China is fiercely fiery. Deep-frying, steaming and smoking are the most popular methods of preparing the food. Garlic, salted bean curd, noodles, mushrooms and strongly flavoured pickles are much used.

SZECHUAN PEPPERCORNS
(Szechwan Peppercorns)
Chinese red peppercorns which are milder than black peppercorns and used in pickles, preserves, marinades and meat dishes.

SZEKELYGULYÁS
A Hungarian pork stew containing sauerkraut, onions fried in lard, caraway seeds, garlic, chopped dill, paprika, water, seasonings and soured cream.

TABASCO SAUCE
A fiery sauce/condiment made in Louisiana, USA, from a special kind of red capsicum. It is used to add heat and flavour to Mexican-style dishes and sometimes curries. Traditionally served with oysters, it may also be added to salad dressings, marinades and barbecue sauces.

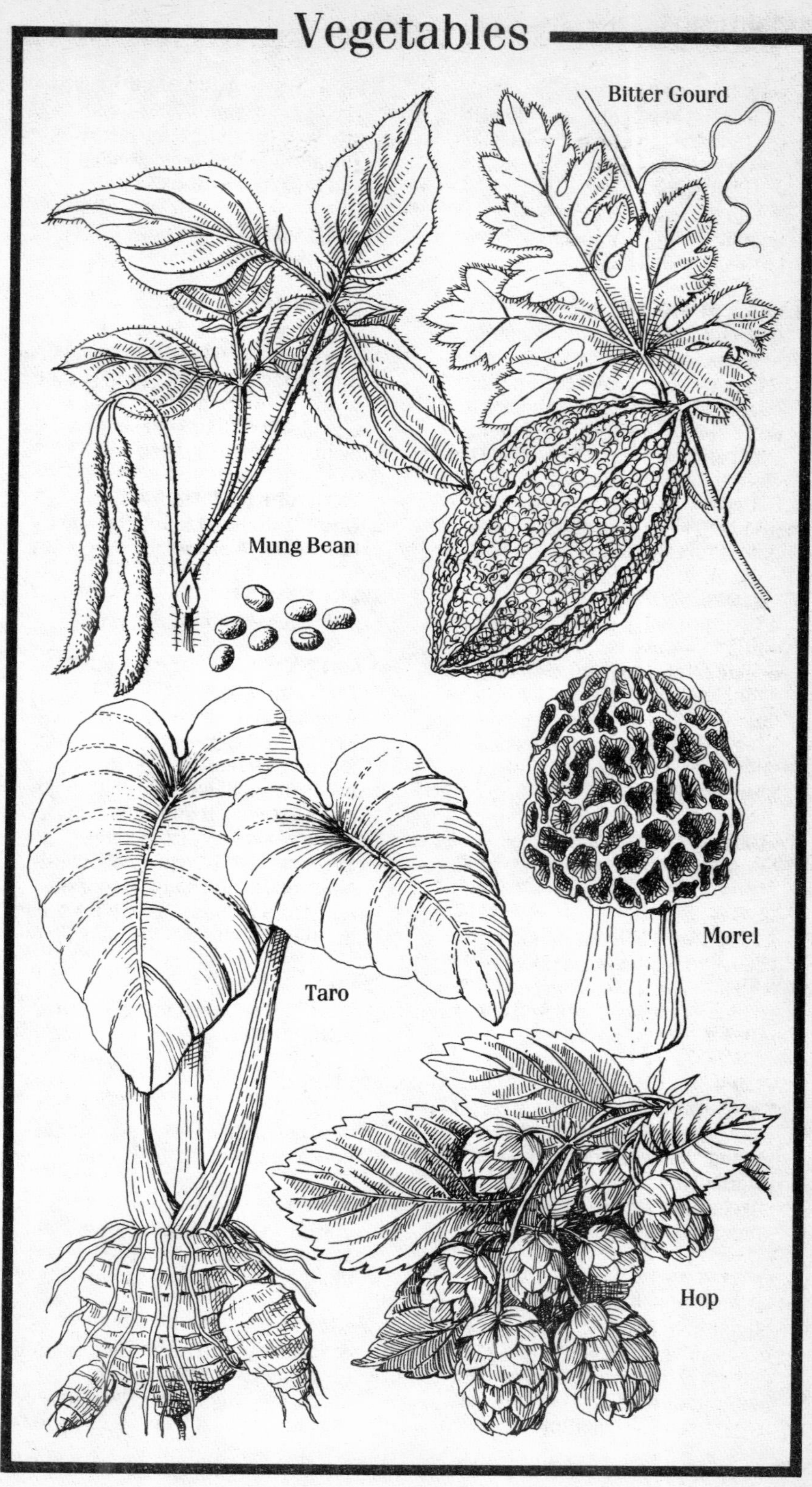
Vegetables
Bitter Gourd
Mung Bean
Morel
Taro
Hop

TABBOULEH SALAD

One of the most enticing salads from the Middle East, made from soaked and drained burghul, grated onion, chopped mint, parsley, olive oil, lemon juice and seasonings. It is usually served in individual, lettuce-lined dishes.

TABLE D'HÔTE

French term for a set menu offered at an inclusive price by a restaurant. It usually covers the starter, main course with vegetables and dessert. Coffee is frequently an optional extra and there may be an additional charge for bread or rolls and butter. In Britain, taxes are part of the fixed price but service is not automatically included.

TABLE SALT

A fine-grained, free-flowing salt suitable for use at the table and in cooking. It is basically refined sodium chloride treated with small quantities of chemical compounds, such as, for example, magnesium silicate or calcium phosphate, to prevent caking.

TABLE WATERS

See *Mineral Waters*.

TACO SHELLS

A 'Tex-Mex'-style dish made from fried *tortilla* shells, usually filled with salad, *chilli con carne, guacamole, frijoles refritos* and other 'Tex-Mex' mixtures.

TACOS

The Mexican term for small *tortillas*. Sometimes the cooked *tacos* are stuffed, rolled up and eaten hot; alternatively, they are fried in oil or lard until crisp and served immediately.

TAFELSPITZ

An Austrian dish of exceptionally tender and delicious boiled beef, prepared from a special cut. Thick slices are coated with the cooking liquor and the meat is served with fried potatoes. Traditional accompaniments include tartare sauce, apple sauce or purée on its own or mixed with whipped cream and horseradish, red cabbage salad and creamed spinach.

TAGLIARINI

See *Tagliatelle*.

TAGLIATELLE

(Tagliarini, Tagliatteli)

Flat ribbon noodles from Bologna in Italy, approximately 5 mm/¼ inch in width. They are made from an egg-based pasta dough and are available fresh or dried.

TAGLIATELLE VERDI

Green-coloured tagliatelle, due to the inclusion of spinach purée.

TAGLIOLINI

A thinner version of *linguine*.

TAHINA

(Taheena, Tahini)

A Middle Eastern sesame seed paste similar in consistency to mayonnaise and used in the preparation of hummus. Tahina by itself is spooned on to small plates in the same way as *hummus*, garnished with a trickle of olive oil, black olives and chopped parsley and eaten with pieces of pitta bread as an appetizer.

TAHU

The Chinese equivalent of tofu or bean curd.

TAI

(Dai)

Japanese name for red sea bream, considered a great delicacy.

TAIL CUT

The tail end of a large fish, such as salmon or cod, shaped like an elongated triangle.

TAJINE

A North African casserole containing local meat, vegetables and chickpeas. *Tajine* is both the name of the casserole and the actual dish.

TAKE-AWAY
In Britain, this term means ready-cooked food taken away from a restaurant or other place of preparation. Fish and chips is a typical take-away meal while others may come from Chinese or Indian restaurants.

TAKO
The Hungarian term for yogurt.

TAL HA'EMEK
An Israeli cheese, styled on Emmental, made from cows' milk.

TALATTOURI
See *Zatziki*.

TALEGGIO
A north Italian cows' milk cheese produced in Lombardy. It closely resembles mild Camembert in texture and taste and is ripened in caves for approximately 6 weeks before being exported. The rind is slightly rough and pinky-orange.

à la TALLEYRAND
French term for a garnish for poultry composed of macaroni with cheese, truffles, *foie gras* and sometimes button mushrooms. Talleyrand was a 19th-century French prince and connoisseur of fine food.

TAMALES
A Mexican speciality dating back to the time of the Aztecs, consisting of parcels of *masa harina* 'porridge' spread on to corn husks, banana leaves, foil or parchment paper. The 'porridge' is topped with chilli-spiced meat or pieces of cheese and rolled up securely. The *tamales* are then steamed and served hot with chilli sauce.

TAMARILLO
(Tomarillo, Tree Tomato)
The fruit of an evergreen shrub or small tree (*Cyphomandra betacea*) related to the tomato family. It is native to South America and cultivated in many tropical and sub-tropical countries including New Zealand and Kenya. It is egg-shaped and averages 5 cm/ 2 inches long. It has a glossy and tough red or yellow skin. The flesh is a lighter version of the skin colour, is divided internally in the same way as a tomato and contains dark, edible seeds. The taste is a cross between that of a tomato and a cape gooseberry and when blanched and skinned, the whole fruit may be eaten raw, cooked with other ingredients or used in preserves.

TAMARIND
(Indian Date)
The fruit of a tropical tree (*Tamarindus indica*) of the pea family native to Africa and possibly India, and cultivated from the West to the East Indies in regions which are not too wet. It is a pod, usually curved and averaging 10–15 cm/ 4–6 inches in length. The pod is dark brown when ripe and contains from one to ten seeds embedded in pulp. This fruit has many uses. When young it is acid-tasting and is used in seasoning, together with the leaves from the tree, particularly in Indian cooking. When ripe it may be eaten as a dessert fruit.

TAMARIND PULP
Much used in Oriental cooking, this bitter, tacky pulp comes from inside the dark brown seed pods which are the fruit of the tamarind tree (*Tamarindus indica*). It gives a sharpish flavour and brown colour to food and is usually dried and sold in packets in Britain. It is used in preserves, but requires dilution, generally in the proportion of one part tamarind pulp to three parts water.

TAMMY
An old-fashioned word for the fine woollen material through which soups and sauces were strained.

TANDOORI
The term for a northern Indian method of cooking in which meat, poultry or fish is first marinated in a

spicy yogurt mixture before being cooked in a special clay oven called a *tandoor*. *Tandoori* dishes are generally served with Indian bread and are garnished with raw onions and lemon slices.

TANDOORI SPICE MIX
A blend of spices, with added orange colouring, which is used to flavour north Indian and Pakistani roasts and grills of poultry, meat or fish, traditionally cooked in a clay oven or *tandoor*. The blend of spices depends on the individual cook or manufacturer but usually includes cinnamon, nutmeg, ginger, ground black peppercorns, turmeric, chilli powder, paprika, cardamom, garlic, cumin and coriander.

TANGELO
Term used in North America for various hybrids of the grapefruit and the tangerine or the grapefruit and the sweet orange. The fruit sold under the name of ugli is one of these hybrids.

TANGERINE
(Mandarin)
The fruit of an evergreen tree (*Citrus reticulata*) native to China, hence its alternative name. This is one of the members of the orange family which has a skin that peels very easily and is slightly darker than that of the sweet orange. The flesh is sweet and juicy and may contain many seeds (pips). It may be eaten as a dessert fruit or used as an alternative in any dishes requiring oranges. This fruit, when canned as segments, is sold as mandarin oranges.

TANGERINE PEEL
Always sold dried in pieces, a popular Chinese flavouring which adds a distinctive fragrance to chicken, duck and meat dishes.

TANGLE
(Sea Tangle)
See *Sea Girdle*.

TANNIA
(Yautia)
A vegetable tuber (*Xanthosoma sagittifolium*) related to taro and coco, native to the Americas and cultivated in tropical and sub-tropical regions. It grows as a tapering root with a hairy skin and white to pink inner flesh. Tannia is used in recipes in the West Indies, South America and West Africa.

TANNIN
The chemical which affects the smell and astringency in tea leaves. In general, green teas have the highest tannin content, oolong teas less and black teas the least. The actual amount of tannin also depends on factors such as the type of plant, where it is grown and when the leaves are picked; freshly picked leaves have the highest tannin content, which gradually reduces as they are processed. Adding milk to tea reduces the astringency because of a protein in the milk which partially neutralizes the tannin content. Tannin slows down the absorption of caffeine into the body, making tea a gentler and longer-lasting stimulant than coffee, less likely to cause insomnia.

TANSY
Known to the Greeks and Romans, a hardy perennial herb (*Tanacetum vulgare*) which bears charming, lacy green leaves and vivid yellow flowers. Due to its somewhat odd taste, it is used more as a garnish or decoration than a culinary herb though it was popular in Victorian times to flavour baked goods and some desserts.

TAPAS
Spanish appetizers or *hors d'oeuvre*.

TAPÉNADE
Thick Provençal paste made with anchovy fillets, capers, olives, garlic and olive oil. It is usually served with hard-boiled eggs as a *hors d'oeuvre*. It is named after *tapeno*, the word for capers in the local dialect.

TAPIOCA
A farinaceous cereal derived from the Brazilian and Far Eastern cassava root. After the crude juice is extracted, the cereal is washed, dried, roasted and sifted into different grades and sizes of tapioca 'pearls' and, less frequently, tapioca flakes. Its culinary uses are the same as sago.

TAQUITOS
Their name meaning 'little *tacos*', these Mexican appetizers are generally filled with *picadillo*, folded in half, secured with cocktail sticks and briefly deep-fried.

TARAMA
The dried and salted roe of grey mullet, used in Greece to make *taramasalata*. In Britain, smoked cod's roe is generally used instead.

TARAMASALATA
(Taramosalata)
A Greek dip traditionally made from dried and salted grey mullet roe (*tarama*), white bread or potatoes, oil, onion, lemon juice, vinegar and seasoning to taste, although smoked cod's roe is often substituted for the mullet roe. It is pale pink and should be very smooth. *Taramasalata* is garnished with black olives and parsley and eaten with warm pitta bread.

TARATOR
A Bulgarian speciality but enjoyed throughout Balkan countries, *tarator* is a chilled soup made from grated cucumber, yogurt, milk, lemon juice, garlic and parsley.

TARATOR OD KRASTAVACA
A Yugoslavian salad from Macedonia made from grated cucumber, green chilli, yogurt and garlic.

TARHONYA
Hungarian pasta pieces which look like small pellets and resemble the Jewish *farfel*.

TARO
A vegetable tuber (*Colocasia* species) native to the Pacific area and grown in many tropical regions. It grows as a cluster of swollen stems with brown skin and starchy white flesh. The flavour is bland and the flesh may be cooked as a vegetable or used in savoury dishes. It is from taro that the Pacific speciality called *poi* is made. Taro and similar tuberous species are known variously as dasheen, eddo, coco and cologassi, depending on type and region, and all should be boiled or baked. In most kinds the green leaves, often large, are also edible when cooked.

TARRAGON
A herb native to Siberia and Asia, tarragon (*Artemisia dracunculus*) was introduced to southern Europe and France about the time of the Middle Ages. The small, perennial plant bears slim green leaves and its distinctive taste is said to be a cross between aniseed and mint. It is the principal flavouring ingredient in tarragon vinegar and Béarnaise sauce and is also used in poultry and shellfish dishes, omelettes and some soups.

TARRAGON VINEGAR
Mild vinegar flavoured with tarragon.

TART
Baked pastry case with a filling, such as jam, but no lid.

TARTARE
A fresh cream cheese from France, made from cows' milk and flavoured with herbs.

TARTARE SAUCE
Mayonnaise flavoured with chopped gherkins, chopped capers and chopped parsley. It can be served with fried, grilled and baked fish.

TARTARIC ACID
Crystalline acid derived from cream of tartar, usually sold in powder

form. It is frequently combined with an alkali such as bicarbonate of soda to make baking powder and dissolves easily in water. It is often substituted for citric acid or lemon juice in jam-making to improve setting qualities. Tartaric acid is also found in some of the sharper fruits.

TARTE AU RIZ

A famous Belgian tart from Liège, filled with a creamy rice mixture containing raisins or sultanas, chopped almonds and nutmeg.

TARTE TATIN

A popular French version of apple tart, in which the fruit is arranged in the base of a flan tin, sprinkled thickly with sugar and covered with sweet-crust pastry (*pâte sucrée*). When baked, the tart is inverted and the apples caramelized under a grill.

TARTLET

A small tart (see entry).

TARTRAZINE

Synthetic food colouring which is classified as an azo dye and adds a yellow colour to food. Tartrazine is numbered E102 in the European Community (EC) coding for food additives. It is believed to aggravate certain allergies, especially in children, and in consequence is now used much less by the food and drink manufacturing industries than it once was.

TASSO

The Acadian version of jerked beef, eaten in the Louisiana Bayou country of the USA.

TASTE (TO)

To put a small amount of food or wine in the mouth to check the flavour.

TATTIE

(Tatty)

Scottish dialect term for potato.

TAYBERRY

The fruit of a climbing plant which is a cross between a North American blackberry and a specially bred raspberry. It was developed in Scotland in the 1960s and '70s and named after the River Tay, near to the nursery. The tayberry resembles the loganberry in many of its essential features but is larger and less acid-tasting. It is long and conical in shape and the colour is a bright, purplish-red when ripe. It matures a little earlier in the year than other related fruits and may be eaten raw or used in jams; it is often canned or frozen. Because of the way the fruit grows on the plant and the smallness of the thorns, picking is relatively easy.

T-BONE STEAK

A very large piece of beef, which looks like an outsize chop, cut from the fillet end of the sirloin and containing a piece of bone. The central portion, near the bone, is generally tender although the end piece can sometimes be tough. It may be grilled or fried.

TEA

(Tea Leaf)

The leaf of an evergreen tropical bush of the camellia family (*Camellia sinensis*). Native to China and parts of India, the tea bush is hardy and will grow almost anywhere, but it is best suited to hot, wet climates. Tea is now cultivated over much of Asia, the wetter parts of Africa and even a little in South America but between 50% and 70% of world exports come from India and Sri Lanka (Ceylon) alone. Although all tea comes from one species of plant, the different kinds depend partly on local differences of soil and weather, and partly on hybrids and varieties developed over the years. Altitude also plays a major part as tea plants grown at high altitudes mature more slowly and produce a finer leaf. The leaf is green and usually glossy with serrated edges; it can be as much as

30 cm/12 inches long but smaller leaves have a more delicate flavour. After picking, the leaf is so treated that it becomes one of the three main kinds of tea: green or unfermented; oolong or semi-fermented; black or fermented. It is not certain when tea drinking began and several legends exist. One describes a Chinese leader who, about five thousand years ago, was boiling water to purify it for drinking purposes when some burning leaves blew into the container, resulting in an interesting beverage. It is, however, fairly certain that the province of Yunnan, either by accident or by experimenting with various plant leaves, produced the first tea, to be drunk as much for medicinal reasons as for pleasure. Today tea may be drunk by itself or with a variety of additives depending on the local customs; for example, lemon or jam in Russia, yak butter in Tibet. Any other plant that is infused is known as herbal tea.

TEA BREAK
A British term for a pause in a working day to have a cup of tea or coffee.

TEA PERSON
A British term for a junior employee whose job it is to make mid-morning and afternoon tea for the staff.

TEA-BAG
A perforated cloth or paper bag holding enough tea leaves to make an individual serving when infused with boiling water.

TEABREAD
A cake-like bread often served in Britain at teatime. If very plain, it is usually served sliced and buttered.

TEAL
This is a small wild duck (genus *Anas*) in season in Britain from the beginning of September to the end of February. It is usually roasted and served with gravy. One teal should be allowed per person.

TEEWURST
A German preserved sausage, made from a smooth mixture of pork and beef. It is salmon-pink in colour with a rust-coloured skin, distinctively spiced and of spreadable consistency.

TEFF
(Teff Grass)
An economically important African cereal grass (*Eragrostis abyssinica*), grown for its grain which yields white flour in addition to a forage and hay crop.

TEISEN LAP
A Welsh fruit and spice cake baked in an oblong tin. When cold, it is sliced and buttered.

TELEME
A Balkan cheese made from the milk of cows, ewes or goats. It is similar to Feta but, in the USA, factory-produced Teleme is a little more like Mozzarella.

TELEME JACK
A Californian cows' milk cheese which is widely used in cooking. It is pliable in the same way as Mozzarella and was introduced to the USA in the 1920s by Greek immigrants.

TEMPURA
Introduced to Japan in the late 16th century by the resident Spanish and Portuguese communities, *tempura* consists of batter-coated, deep-fried pieces of fish and vegetables, dipped in a piquant condiment composed of *dashi, mirin* and light soy sauce with the addition of grated white radish (*daikon*) and fresh ginger. The batter must be thin and light so that it forms a lacy coating over the food.

TENDER CURE BACON
See *Quick Cure*.

TENDER MEAT
Prime and tender cuts of meat from beef, pig, lamb and veal which contain minimum gristle. The cuts

are generally used for roasting, frying and grilling; also for kebabs.

TENDERIZE (TO)
See *Soften*.

TENDERLOIN OF PORK
An elongated, boneless, tender and lean cut of pork which is the equivalent of fillet of beef. It may be roasted, cubed and threaded on to skewers for kebabs, or cut into slices for frying and grilling.

TEPID
Term applied to lukewarm liquid. This temperature is easily achieved by combining one part boiling water with one part cold.

TERASI
See *Blachan*.

TERIYAKI
A Japanese marinade for meat, fish or poultry made from garlic, soy sauce, fresh ginger, sugar, sweet rice wine and sometimes oil.

TERRAPIN
Small American turtle which lives in fresh or nearly fresh waters. Canned terrapin is available in Europe.

TERRINE
French term for a meat pâté, baked like a cake, in an earthenware dish with a lid. The dish is often lined with bacon rashers and filled with one or more coarsely minced meats; a terrine can also be made from poultry, game, liver, fish or shellfish. Additions include herbs, spices, sometimes garlic and occasionally alcohol. A terrine forms part of an hors d'œuvre and is eaten with toast like *pâté maison*.

TERRINE DISH
(Terrine)
A heatproof earthenware dish with lid, plain or fancy, used for baking a terrine.

TESTICLES
The sex organs of male animals, testicles are used in an assortment of meat products.

TÊTE DE MOINE
(Bellelay)
A Swiss mountain cheese made from cows' milk. It was originally produced in the 15th century by monks at the Bellelay Abbey in the Bernese Jura.

TETILLA
Bosom-shaped Spanish cheese, made from cows' milk in the area of Galicia. It is creamy, fresh-tasting, very slightly acidic and relatively salty.

TEXAS RED
A North American grapefruit with red flesh from which cultivated red varieties in other countries have been developed.

TEXTURED VEGETABLE PROTEIN
(TVP)
Plant proteins which have been isolated, flavoured and manufactured into assorted products which are treated as meat substitutes. TVP is produced from beans, especially soy, with trace elements added and is a healthy, nutritious and inexpensive food, highly regarded by vegetarians. It is available from health food shops.

THAMBILI
A Sri Lankan speciality, milk from the king coconut, drunk directly from the shell.

THAUMATIN
A modern sugar substitute used in Britain.

THERMOS
(Vacuum Flask)
A trade name for a cylindrical container, with a vacuum between an inner and outer wall, used to keep soups and beverages hot or cold for prolonged periods of time.

THERMOSTAT
An automatic temperature control attached to cookers, refrigerators, freezers, dishwashers, electric irons and other domestic appliances.

THIAMINE
See *Vitamin* B_1.

THICK FLANK OF BEEF
A cut of beef from the belly of the animal. It is relatively lean but needs tenderizing by long, slow cooking such as stewing, braising and casseroling. It may also be carefully slow-roasted and cut into slices for stewing (medium thick) and frying (fairly thin). It is known by this name in north-east and north-west England, Wales and the West Country.

THICK RIBS OF BEEF
A cut of beef from the rib cage of the animal (side), usually boned and rolled. It is suitable for stewing (in the piece), braising and pot-roasting.

THICK SEAM TRIPE
This comes from the third stomach of an ox and has the same flavour as blanket or honeycomb tripe.

THICK SOUP
An unstrained soup thickened with small pieces of vegetables, meat or poultry, pasta or cereals.

THICKEN (TO)
See *Liaise*.

THICKENERS
Mostly natural products, derived from plants such as algae and seaweed. They are used to thicken and add viscosity to manufactured foods.

THIEBOU DIENE
A Senegalese national dish, consisting of braised fish and vegetables served with rice.

THIN FLANK OF BEEF
A lean and thin cut from the underside (belly) of the animal. It is tough and recommended for stewing, braising, casseroling and mincing. Sometimes it is salted and boiled.

THIN RIBS OF BEEF
A cut of beef from the rib cage of the animal (side), usually boned and rolled. It is suitable for stewing (in the piece), braising and pot-roasting.

THOUSAND ISLAND DRESSING
A North American sauce consisting of mayonnaise flavoured with chilli sauce, chopped gherkins, chopped onion or chives, chopped parsley, tomato purée and sometimes chopped hard-boiled eggs. When home-made, whipped cream may be added if wished.

THROUGHCUT BACON
Combination of streaky and back bacon which comes from the centre of the pig.

THRUSH
Small or medium-sized songbirds (family *Turdidae*) which are usually brown in colour with spotted underparts. They are regarded as a delicacy, especially in France and Italy.

THÜRINGER ROTWURST
A German cooked blood sausage and a variation of *blutwurst*. Its name means 'Thüringer red sausage'.

THYME
A herb native to southern Europe, thyme (*Thymus vulgaris*) is a relative of the mint family and grows abundantly in Mediterranean countries. A hardy perennial, the herb bears small, greenish-brown leaves with a pungent and aromatic flavour and is particularly suited for use in tomato dishes, meat and poultry stuffings, fish soups and croquettes.

TIGER NUT
(Earthnut, Pignut, Rush-nut)
A small tuber which forms on the root of a plant (*Cyperus esculentus*) native to the Mediterranean area. It has a brown skin and white flesh and the flavour sweetens as the tuber dries and shrivels. Although generally eaten as a nut, it is valued in Spain, where it is referred to as *chufa*, for other culinary uses.

TIKKA
An Indian term for small pieces of meat or poultry marinated in yogurt and *tandoori* spices, then roasted or grilled. Indian bread and salad should accompany the dish.

TILLAMOOK
A North American cows' milk cheese, similar to Cheddar, produced in the county of Tillamook in Oregon.

TILSIT
(Tilsiter)
A 19th-century German cows' milk cheese, first made in the town of Tilsit by Dutch immigrants. It is a pale yellow cheese which has a smooth texture, interspersed with very small, irregular holes. It is creamy, mildly pungent and usually loaf-shaped for ease of slicing.

TIMBALE
French term for a cup-shaped mould which, traditionally, is lined with pasta or rice and filled with a creamy meat, fish or vegetable mixture. It also describes a light and creamy puréed mixture which is baked in the mould; it is then turned out and served with an appropriate sauce.

TIMPANA
Malta's national dish, consisting of a pastry pie filled with macaroni mixed with *bolognese* sauce, eggs and pieces of fried chicken's liver. The pie is covered with a lid of pastry and baked.

TIN
A lightweight container used for baking which is made from stainless steel, tinned steel or aluminium. Tins are made in many shapes and sizes to suit the kind of bread, cake or pastry to be baked.

TINAMOU
Eaten in France, any of a family (*Tinamidae*) of South American game birds resembling the partridge.

TINDA
(Round Gourd, Squash Melon)
A vegetable (*Citrullus vulgaris* var. *fistulosus*) of the squash family native to India and an important summer vegetable in that area of the world. It resembles a very small watermelon, about the size of a little apple. The skin is green, either light or dark, and the flesh creamy-coloured with light-coloured seeds.

TINDORI
A vegetable (*Trichosanthes dioica*) of the squash family native to India, which is an important ingredient in Indian cooking. It looks rather like an elongated green olive, sometimes with pointed ends. The skin is thin and the light green flesh is filled with soft, edible seeds. The flavour, when raw, is similar to cucumber and some varieties have a slightly bitter taste. The tindori may be eaten raw or cooked.

TINNED
Sealed in a can (tin) for preservation.

TIPSY CAKE
An old-fashioned British pudding, consisting of a dome-shaped cake moistened with sherry, studded with almonds and coated with egg custard sauce. It is served cold.

TIRGGEL
A Christmas biscuit from Zurich, in Switzerland. It is heavily spiced, of the gingerbread type and baked in a highly ornate, old-fashioned wooden

mould. The result is a 'picture' biscuit of either ancient or contemporary design.

TISANE
A herbal infusion or tea.

TIT-BITS
Small portions of usually savoury foods to whet the appetite.

à la TIVOLI
French term for a garnish for entrées composed of asparagus and mushrooms.

TOAD-IN-THE-HOLE
A well-known British dish consisting of sausages baked in batter.

TOAST
Bread slices grilled on each side until brown, either under a grill or in a toaster.

TOAST (TO)
To brown under a grill.

TOASTED BUCKWHEAT
Buckwheat which has been cooked in an ungreased pan over a moderate heat until it can be heard making popping sounds.

TOCOPHEROL
See *Vitamin E*.

TOFFEE
(Taffy, Toffy)
A traditional English sweet, fairly hard, made from syrup, water, sugar, butter or margarine and vinegar.

TOFFEE APPLE
Popular worldwide, the apples are generally impaled on sticks and covered with a layer of fairly hard and brittle toffee.

TOFU
The Japanese word for the high-protein, low-calorie bean curd which is an ancient and staple ingredient in both Japanese and Chinese cuisines, made from dried soya beans which are first soaked in water until soft, finely crushed and finally boiled. This mixture is separated into pulp and milk, and the milk is coagulated and transformed into a thick creamy paste resembling curd cheese in appearance. Bland-tasting and filling, its uses in Oriental cuisine are infinite. Tofu is economical, an excellent protein extender and is sold in Britain in blocks by health food shops, Oriental food stores and some supermarkets.

TOGGENBURGER
A white cheese from Switzerland, made from naturally-soured skimmed cows' milk. It is shaped into cubes and matured for 6 months.

TOKÁNY
A Hungarian speciality, very similar to *pörkölt* with the additions of garlic, sliced mushrooms, peas and soured cream. It is usually served with rice or pasta.

TOM YAM KUNG
A spicy brown soup from Thailand.

TOMARILLO
See *Tamarillo*.

TOMATES FARCIES
One of the classic *hors d'oeuvres* of Belgium, tomatoes packed with shrimps and topped with mayonnaise.

TOMATILLO
(Jamberry)
The fruit of a plant (*Physalis ixocarpa*) of the tomato family, closely related to the cape gooseberry and grown in Central and South America and parts of the USA. The edible berry is red or yellow when fully ripe and is enclosed in a colourful, multi-part husk with a parchment-like appearance. The berry may be eaten raw but is often used in jam-making.

TOMATO
The fruit of a branching plant (*Lycopersicum esculentum*) native to South America, introduced to Europe in the 16th century. It was regarded with suspicion at that time, considered poisonous and grown mainly for decoration. The first tomatoes cultivated in Europe were yellow-skinned and it was not until the 18th century that the red variety arrived from America; from then on it became widely cultivated both commercially and in gardens. The tomato grows as a hanging fruit, initially green in colour, but turning red or yellow with maturity. The size when ripe varies enormously with type and the fruit may be spherical, round with flattened tops and bottoms or pear-shaped. The thin skin encloses a pulpy flesh with a central core of small, soft and edible seeds. Tomato may be eaten raw by itself or in salads and it is used in numerous cooked dishes where it adds a distinctive flavour. Commercially, the tomato is suitable for canning whole or turning into juice.

TOMATO PASTE
A concentrated paste made from Italian plum tomatoes which is widely used in Italian dishes, as well as adding flavour to many soups, sauces, stews and casseroles. It is usually available in tubes or cans.

TOMATO PURÉE
See *Tomato Paste*.

TOMATO SAUCE
See *Portugaise Sauce*.

TOMER
See *Na'ama*.

TOMME AU RAISIN
(Fondu au Marc, Fromage Fondu, Fondu au Raisin, Grape Cheese) French processed Emmental cheese which is completely covered with dried grape seeds.

TOMME DE SAVOIE
The general term to describe mild, supple cheeses made in the French region of Savoie from whole or semi-skimmed cows' milk.

TONGS
Flexible, U- or scissor-shaped implements used when turning or handling hot or delicate foods. Tongs are made of wood or metal and there are various kinds to suit different cooking or serving needs. Being blunt, tongs do not pierce or damage foods and valuable juices are therefore retained.

TONGUE
Ox and lambs' tongues are readily available and may be bought fresh or already brined. The skin has a roughish appearance, like coarse sandpaper, and is relatively thick; it is peeled away from the tongue after cooking.

TONIC WATER
Carbonated water with a small amount of bitter quinine added. It is a good mixer for gin.

TONKA BEAN
The seed of any of several trees (genus *Dipteryx*) of the pea family, which contains coumarin. This has the scent of new-mown hay and is used as a flavouring.

TOP AND TAIL (TO)
To remove stalks from the top and bottom of certain fruit and vegetables.

TOP RIB OF BEEF
A fairly coarse but lean cut of beef, suitable for stewing, braising, casseroling and pot-roasting when boned. It is sometimes known as leg of mutton cut.

TOP RUMP
Term used in London and South-East England for a beef cut also known as thick flank.

TOPAZ
The fruit of a tree of the citrus family which is a hybrid of an orange and a tangerine. It is one of the recent developments in the cultivation of soft-skinned, easily peeled citrus fruits.

TOPE
A shark (*Galeorhinus galeus*) which is found mainly in Atlantic waters off the coasts of Europe and is caught as a game fish around Britain in spring and summer. The flesh tends to have a strong smell of ammonia when fresh but this odour lessens or disappears with cooking.

TOPPING
A covering of crumbs, cheese, sauce, cream and so on over the surface of a prepared dish; also, a garnish for savoury foods or a decoration for sweet dishes.

TOPSIDE LEG STEAKS OF PORK
A new and leaner British cut of meat which is divided into steaks for grilling or frying.

TOPSIDE OF BEEF
A boneless cut of beef from the rear end of the animal, between the rump and leg. It is relatively lean and usually wrapped in a sheet of fat, secured with string. It is suitable for pot-roasting, braising and slow-roasting.

TORBAY SOLE
See *Lemon Sole*.

TORRONE
A kind of nougat from Cremona in Italy.

TORTE
A fancy cake, usually from the German-speaking countries of Europe.

TORTELLI
Small dumplings of stuffed pasta which are available fresh or dried. The filling is made from either meat or cheese.

TORTELLINI
Smaller versions of *tortelli* and a speciality of Bologna in Italy.

TORTIGLIONE
See *Fusilli*.

TORTILLA
See *Spanish Omelette*.

TORTILLA CHIPS
(Corn Chips)
Also known in Mexico as *totopos* and *tostaditas*, these are made by cutting *tortillas* into small triangles, then frying them in hot lard or oil until crisp. They are served with dips such as *frijoles refritos* or *guacamole*.

TORTILLAS
The national pancakes of Mexico made with *masa harina* or maize flour. They are shaped between the hands into paper-thin rounds or are flattened in a special *tortilla* press, widely available in Mexico. They are then dry-fried on a griddle or in a large frying pan. Tortillas can also be made with white flour instead of *masa harina*.

TORTONI
An Italian-style ice cream speciality made from thick cream, sugar, maraschino cherries, chopped almonds and rum.

à la TOSCANE
French term meaning in the style of Tuscany in central Italy, referring to a garnish of pasta, *foie gras* and truffles. The basic food is usually fried chicken or sweetbreads coated with egg, crumbs and Parmesan cheese.

TOSS (TO)
To turn hot vegetables over in a dish with two spoons so that they become coated with butter or margarine; to turn salads over in the bowl so that they become coated in salad

dressings; to run rubbed-in dry ingredients through the fingers and turn them over; to shake pieces of meat, fish or poultry in a bag containing flour so that they are well-coated prior to frying; to turn pancakes.

TOSTADOS
Medium-sized Mexican *tortillas*, fried until crisp and topped with salad, meat, poultry, cheese or fish and seasoned with chilli sauce. Small *tostados* are served as cocktail snacks.

TOSTONES
Fried plantain chips from the Caribbean which are flavoured with garlic. They are served as an appetizer.

TOTOPOS
See *Tortilla Chips*.

à la TOULOUSAINE
French term meaning in the style of Toulouse in south-west France, referring to a garnish for chicken composed of truffles, mushrooms, cockscombs, kidneys and Suprême sauce.

TOULOUSE SAUSAGE
Fresh sausage from France, usually made from pork or chicken.

à la TOURANGELLE
French term meaning in the style of the Touraine in the Loire Valley, denoting a garnish of French beans mixed with flageolet beans and Velouté sauce.

TOURNEDOS
Individual round steaks, cut from the thickest part of the beef fillet. They are usually grilled or fried.

TOURNEDOS ROSSINI
A French speciality created for, and named after, the Italian composer, Rossini, a gourmet as well as a musician and who was said to have had a great fondness for *fois gras*. The *tournedos* are usually butter-fried and stood on rounds of fried white bread. The meat is topped with a lightly floured and quickly fried slice of *foie gras* and garnished with a piece of truffle. Madeira sauce is served with the *tournedos*.

TOURRÉE-DE-L'AUBIER
Brand name of a large French cows' milk cheese with a thin crust. It has a velvety texture with a delicately earthy taste, both sweetish and nutty. It serves excellently as a cooking and dessert cheese and is a comparatively new addition to French cheeses.

TOURTIÈRE
A famous pork pie from Quebec in Canada, consisting of two layers of pastry containing minced pork, chopped onion, water, herbs and seasonings.

TRACE ELEMENTS
Natural and basic chemicals, tiny quantities of which are vital for the maintenance of sound health in all living things. They are present in the soil and are transferred to plant and animal life via the absorption of liquid and food.

TRANSPARENT ICING
This is made slightly thinner than glacé icing by the addition of extra liquid and forms a semi-transparent covering over fancy breads, buns and cakes.

TRANSPARENT NOODLES
See *Cellophane Noodles*.

TRAPPIST
Cheese made by Trappist monks in parts of Europe (Germany, France and Austria) and also in North America. In general it is a mild cheese, with a medium-soft texture and a golden colour. It is easy to slice.

TRAPPISTE DE CHAMBARAND
See *Chambarand*.

TREACLE
See *Black Treacle*.

TREACLE TART
A typically British open tart, made from shortcrust pastry filled with a mixture of golden syrup, breadcrumbs, grated lemon peel and a little spice, topped with a trellis of pastry strips prior to baking.

TREACLE TOFFEE
A traditional English sweet, similar to toffee but also including black treacle.

TREE TOMATO
See *Tamarillo*.

TRENCHER
Originally, a thick slice of bread on which food was served but now a term for a wooden serving dish.

TRENCHERMAN
Someone who is a healthy eater and drinker.

TRENETTE
Similar to *tagliatelle*, *trenette* are a speciality of Genoa in Italy and they are frequently served with *pesto* sauce.

TREPANG
See *Bêche de Mer*.

TRIFLE
A popular British dessert, traditionally made with sponge cake soaked in sweet sherry, topped with an egg custard sauce, softly whipped cream and decorated with hundreds and thousands. There are now innumerable variations and modern trifles often contain jelly, fruit, chocolate cake, liqueurs and so on.

TRIGLYCERIDE
See *Fats and Oils*.

TRIM (TO)
To neaten; to remove unwanted extras from any piece of food or dish; to cut to shape; to remove surplus fat from meat.

TRIMMING
An additional garnish or accompaniment to a main dish.

TRIPE
The stomach lining of an animal, generally the ox, which is one of the most easily digested protein foods. It is sold bleached or dressed by the butcher and any fat adhering to it is easy to remove. A minimum of 100 g/4 oz should be allowed per person and, as tripe deteriorates rapidly even in refrigeration, it should be bought, cooked and eaten within 8–12 hours of purchase. Although the butcher will have cleaned, blanched and partially cooked the tripe, it should be very well washed before cooking. Whatever dish is being prepared with the tripe, it should be pre-cooked in salted water until tender: about 30 minutes. The tripe should then be cut into pieces and cooked as specified in the recipe. All tripe should be firm, thick and creamy white; any that is dull beige in colour, limp and smelly is stale.

TRIPE AND ONIONS
A famous, classic British dish consisting of boiled tripe and boiled onions in a white sauce. It is well-seasoned, flavoured with a little nutmeg and accompanied by boiled potatoes or toast.

TRIPES À LA MODE DE CAEN
A world-famous casserole from Caen in north-west France, consisting of tripe, calf's foot, onions, herbs, spices, brandy, Calvados and cider.

TRITICALE
A cereal grass that is a hybrid between wheat and rye. It gives a high yield and is rich in protein. The name is derived from the Latin *Triticum* meaning wheat and *Secale* meaning rye.

TROTTERS
See *Pig's Trotters*.

TROUT
A round-bodied, streamlined fish (*Salmo trutta*) of the salmon family. It exists in a confusing variety within the species, with saltwater trout growing up to 1 metre/39 inches in length and the freshwater ones usually rather smaller. The weight is generally 175 g–2 kg/6 oz–4½ lb, but with exceptions, such as the North American lake trout, which can reach 35 kg/78 lb. The colour of the back can vary from almost black to light green. The flesh is oily and can vary in colour from ivory to deep pink depending on diet. The fish may be poached, steamed, baked, fried or grilled.

TRUFFLE
An edible fungus (*Tuber* species) which grows just below the surface of the earth on tree roots and is the rarest of all the fungus family, and also the most expensive. The French black truffle (*Tuber melanosporum*) from the Périgord region is wrinkled, warty and much-prized by gourmets for its strong, distinctive fragrance, rather than its mild flavour. The Italian 'white' truffle (*T. magnatum*), from the Piedmont region, is smooth and beige-pink in colour with a more pronounced aroma than its French relation. There is also an English truffle (*T. aestivum*), which is relatively small and lacks the strong aroma of the French and Italian varieties. The truffle is treated mainly as an exclusive flavouring, in *pâté de foie gras* for instance, and the white Italian kind is best left uncooked and either sliced or grated over such dishes as spaghetti tossed with butter. In most countries, truffles are principally available only in cans but much of the unique quality of the fungus is lost in the process. As truffles are invisible above ground, trained dogs or pigs have been used for centuries to locate them by their scent.

TRUFFLES
Marble-shaped sweets, which are rich, sweet, soft and made from a base of chocolate. They are sometimes flavoured with coffee or alcohol and coated with cocoa powder or chocolate vermicelli.

TRUMPETER
See *Agami*.

TRUSS (TO)
To tie or skewer poultry and game birds into neat, compact shapes before roasting.

à la TSARINE
(à la Tzarine)
French term meaning in the style of the Tsarina, denoting a garnish for chicken breasts composed of cucumber cooked in butter and mixed with cream.

TSATSIKI
See *Zatziki*.

TSUKEMONO
The Japanese word for pickles, which play an important part in daily meals.

TUB
See *Vat*.

TUB GURNARD
See *Gurnard*.

TUBER
The underground part of a plant from which both the roots and stems grow.

TUBETTI
(Tubellini, Tubettini)
Very small pasta tubes, used in soups.

TUCK
A colloquial British term sometimes used to describe snacks taken to school by children.

TUCK IN (TO)
To eat with pleasure and gusto.

TUCKER
An Australian and New Zealand term for informal food.

TUILES
French-style wafer biscuits, sometimes covered in almond flakes, which are traditionally pressed lightly over a rolling pin when just baked to give them a characteristic curve.

TUMBLERS
Flat-bottomed, cylindrical drinking glasses for water and mineral water. Some are in plain glass, others in cut crystal.

TUNA
(Tunny, Bluefin Tuna)
Also known as bluefin tuna, this fish (*Thunnus thynnus*) is the largest of the tuna family and the average length as seen in the shops is 1–2 metres/39 inches–6½ feet. The back is blue, shading to silver-grey on the sides and belly. It is caught worldwide in warm seas and the principal landing season is late autumn. Part of the flesh is light and lean; part is dark and oily. In Japan, tuna is often eaten raw in such dishes as sushi and sashimi; in the West, it is baked or grilled. It is readily available canned.

TUNNY
See *Tuna*.

TURBAN
French term for a ring mould, shaped like an Eastern turban. It is used either to set or to bake food such as fish, veal or chicken.

TURBAN SQUASH
(Turk's Cap Squash)
A vegetable (*Cucurbita maxima*) of the squash family native to North America. It is one of the winter squash group which matures slowly and is mainly eaten during the winter months. The turban squash is one of the most decorative of all edible squashes with a large, slightly flattened circular base from which grows a smaller, grooved and globular top which resembles a four-humped hat of turban-like appearance, sporting a depression on the crown. The colour is eye-catching; the base is orange with yellow mottling and the top basically orange with streaks of green and yellow. It is thick-skinned, and the firm, slightly sweet flesh is orange-yellow with a scattering of seeds towards the centre. The turban squash may be boiled or baked as a vegetable or used in North American winter squash dishes.

TURBOT
(Bannock Flute)
A diamond-shaped flatfish (*Psetta maxima*) which can be 1 metre/39 inches in length and weigh 15 kg/33 lb or more. The colour of the back is generally sandy, to match the sea bed, and tends to be spotty. It has no scales but has little bumps on the surface of the skin. It is caught in the shallower waters of the North Atlantic, the Mediterranean and the Black Sea all year round but is best during the summer months. The flesh is firm, white and medium-oily and the fish may be poached, steamed, baked, fried or grilled. Supplies of this highly regarded fish are limited and it is relatively expensive.

TUREEN
A large, lidded dish from which soup is served at the table.

TURKEY
A large North American bird (*Meleagris gallopavo*) with a heavy, rounded body, lustrous plumage and a distinctive, featherless head. Popular in most parts of the world, turkey is farmed for its high-protein and comparatively low-fat meat.

TURKEY COCK
A male turkey.

TURKEY EGGS
Not often available, these are fairly large eggs with speckled shells.

TURKEY LIVERS
Generally available during the Christmas season, either frozen in tubs or fresh. They are larger and darker than chickens' livers and are marginally less delicate in flavour. They are useful for *pâtés*, terrines, meat loaves, stews, casseroles and braised dishes.

TURKISH COFFEE
Coffee prepared as a dark, frothy, thick, almost mud-like liquid. It is drunk in small cups without milk or cream but sometimes with sugar and more often cardamom pods or seeds. Alternatively, cinnamon, nutmeg or clove may be added. For Turkish coffee, the beans are very finely ground and these grounds may be consumed with the liquid if desired. Although coffee does not grow in Turkey, it is recognized as the country that introduced a ritualistic approach to the preparing, serving and drinking of coffee which has become traditional, not only in Turkey, but wherever Middle Eastern people meet.

TURKISH DELIGHT
A Middle Eastern sweet, usually pink and white squares coated with icing sugar. The flavours are rose-water and vanilla. Sometimes chopped nuts are included and a green version contains peppermint flavouring.

TURK'S CAP SQUASH
See *Turban Squash*.

TÜRLÜ
A Turkish mixed vegetable stew, similar to Bulgarian *guvetch* but incorporating more vegetables to include courgettes, marrow, aubergines and okra.

TURMERIC
A bright, yellowy-orange spice native to Indonesia and China but now cultivated in India, the West Indies and South America. Turmeric is produced from the aromatic roots of a plant (*Curcuma longa*) belonging to the ginger family and is fresh-tasting and mild with a distinctive hint of pepper. Ground turmeric is an ingredient of curry powder, adds colour to some prepared mustards and is used in the manufacture of certain varieties of pickles, especially piccalilli. As a colouring agent, it makes an acceptable substitute for saffron. In Biblical times turmeric was used both as a spice and a perfume.

TURN (TO)
To make acid or sour; to curdle; to ferment.

TURN OUT (TO)
To unmould jellies, blancmanges, caramel creams and steamed or baked puddings from the containers in which they were chilled or cooked; to remove cakes, buns and loaves from the tins in which they were cooked.

TURNIP
A root vegetable (*Brassica rapa*) native to Europe or western Asia and known before the times of Ancient Greece. It was probably introduced to Britain by the Romans, but became more popular when Flemish immigrants introduced better varieties in the reign of Elizabeth I. The turnip grows as a swollen root topped by a cluster of hairy leaves. The shape is either globular or cylindrical and the colour of the smooth skin may range from white to green to purple and may sometimes be bi-coloured. The young leaves are edible and the turnip itself is at its best if harvested when immature, often small enough to be sold by the bunch. The white flesh has a pleasant flavour and tender, young

specimens may be grated and eaten raw, but the turnip is usually cooked and eaten as a vegetable. It is also used in savoury dishes, such as soups and stews, where it adds its own distinctive flavour.

TURNOVER
A small, semi-circular or triangular piece of pastry with a sweet or savoury filling, made from a round or square of pastry folded in half to enclose the filling.

TURRON
A Spanish sweet, resembling halva. The basic ingredient is usually ground almonds.

TURTLE
Aquatic versions of the tortoise found in most of the warmer waters of the world. Most kinds have edible flesh and the large species, called the green turtle (*Chelonia mydas*), is used to make the best turtle soup.

TUSK
(Cusk, Torsk)
A member (*Bromse bromse*) of the cod family although it resembles the hake in shape. It is caught in the colder waters of the North Atlantic all year round, with main catches in June and July. The average length of the whole fish in the shops is about 50 cm/19 inches. Depending on the region, the colour of the back will vary from dark red to pale yellow, shading to a creamy-yellow on the underside. The flesh is lean and white and the fish may be steamed, poached, grilled, fried, baked or barbecued. It is becoming increasingly popular in North America.

TUTTI-FRUTTI
Ice cream containing a mixture of dried or glacé fruits, always chopped.

TUWARE
See *Pigeon Pea*.

TV DINNER
Any pre-cooked, pre-packaged meal that can be eaten informally in front of the television. Some are designed for reheating, others for eating cold.

TVP
See *Textured Vegetable Protein*.

TWELFTH NIGHT CAKE
A rich fruit cake, traditionally British, eaten on Twelfth Night (6 January).

TWIST
A length of thinly pared citrus peel used to flavour and/or decorate a hot or cold drink (alcoholic or non-alcoholic).

TYBO
A Danish cows' milk cheese, very similar to Elbo but with more holes throughout the paste.

à la TYROLIENNE
French term meaning in the style of the Tyrol in northern Italy and Austria, referring to a garnish of tomatoes and fried onions.

TZIMMES
A Jewish New Year dish made from brisket simmered very gently with sliced carrots, potatoes and onions, sweetened with sugar or honey and thickened with flour.

UDDER
The milk gland or sac of cows, sheep, goats and pigs. The udder from young calves can be used in the same way as tripe.

UDON NOODLES
Thick, wide Japanese wheat flour noodles, available as flat sticks and almost white in colour.

UGALI
A type of East African cornmeal 'porridge' eaten with stew.

UGLI
A fruit which is a hybrid of the grapefruit and the tangerine and is about the size of a large grapefruit. The skin is rough and lumpy, fitting loosely round the flesh within. The colour may be greeny-yellow to greeny-orange. The juicy flesh is generally yellowy-pink when ripe and tastes sweeter than a grapefruit but sharper than a tangerine. Ugli may be eaten by itself or used in any dishes suitable for the orange or grapefruit. The fruit is one variety of the North American tangelo.

UITSMIJTER
A popular Dutch all-day snack which consists of an open sandwich made from white or brown bread, slices of ham or underdone beef and two fried eggs, garnished with tomato, slices of gherkin and small lettuce leaves.

UKRAINE EGGS
Highly ornamented eggs, regarded as an art form in the Ukraine, dating back about 3000 years.

ULSTER ROLL
(Spencer)
A bacon joint used in Northern Ireland. It is boned and rubbed with a mixture of saltpetre, salt and sodium nitrate. It is then laid in a bed of salt, cured for a specific length of time (approximately one day per 450 g/ 1 lb) and subsequently soaked in water for a day. Finally it is dried and smoked.

ULTRA-HEAT TREATED CREAM
(UHT/Long Life/Extended Life Cream)
The following creams can all be ultra-heat treated to prolong their natural life: half, single, whipping and double. Aseptically packed into foil-lined containers, the creams will keep for several months if unopened and are a useful store cupboard standby. The whipping and double creams tend to whip to a softer consistency than their fresh equivalents.

ULTRA-HEAT TREATED MILK
(UHT/Long-Life Milk)
Homogenized milk, heated for an extended time at lower temperatures to stabilize the protein, then subjected to ultra-high temperature treatment: not less than 132°C/270°F for 1–2 seconds. It is cooled quickly and aseptically packed into containers. Ultra-heat treated milk, if left unopened, will keep fresh for almost 6 months but, once opened, must be treated as fresh milk.

UMBRELLA MUSHROOM
See *Parasol Mushroom*.

UNBLEACHED WHITE FLOUR
White flour which has not been subjected to chemical treatment.

UNDERDONE
Not thoroughly cooked; rare.

UNLEAVENED
Bread or biscuits containing no raising agent in the form of baking powder or yeast. See Leaven.

UNTREATED MILK
Labelled 'raw unpasteurized milk', this must be bottled on the farm where it is produced and sold only by licensed distributors. The milk must come from *brucellosis*-accredited herds. It is sold in Britain in green-capped bottles, unless it is from Channel Islands herds when the bottles have green caps with golden stripes.

UPSIDE-DOWN CAKE
A cake mixture baked in a fairly shallow tin on top of an arrangement of fruit such as peaches or pineapple. When turned out, the fruit is uppermost.

Utensils

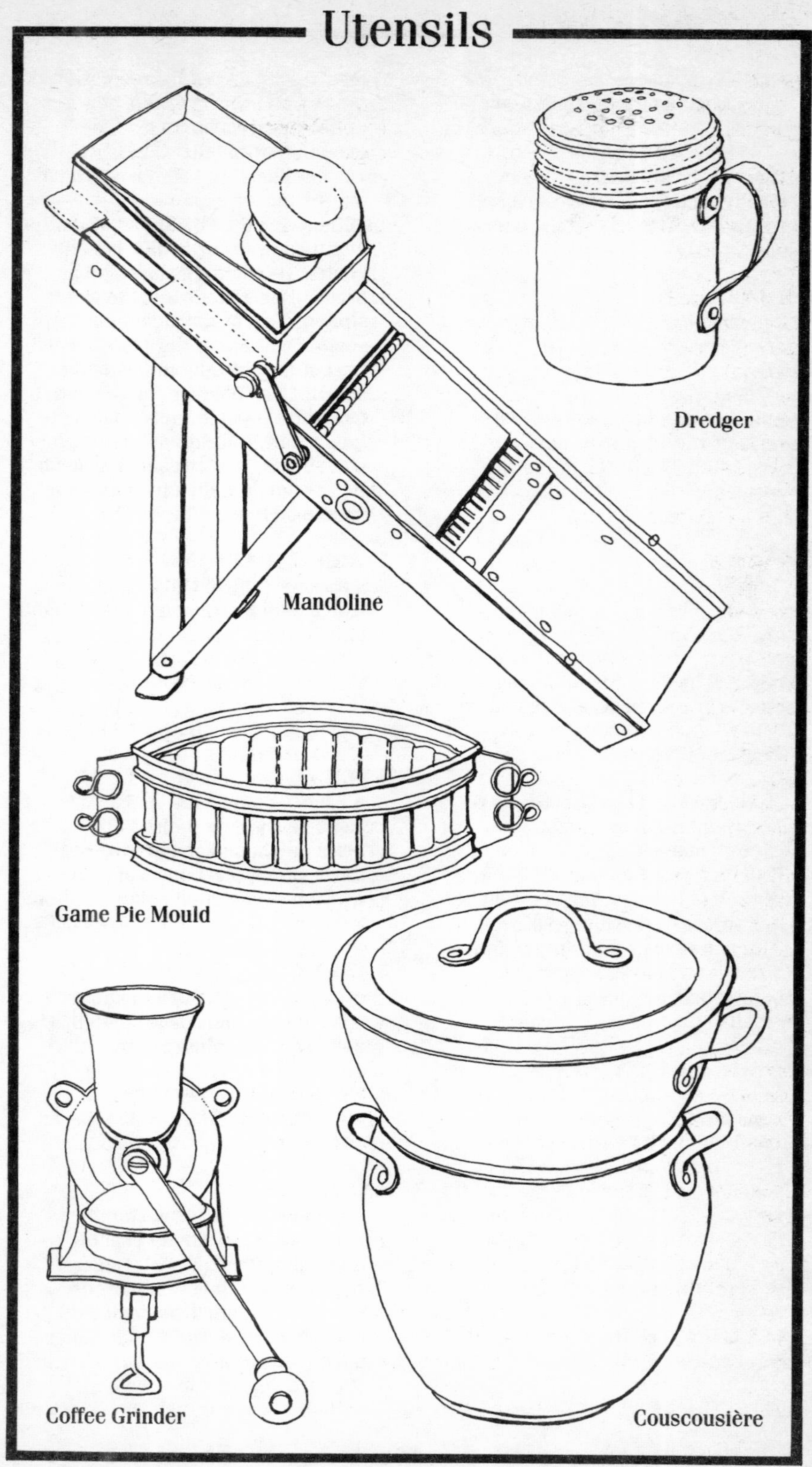
Dredger
Mandoline
Game Pie Mould
Coffee Grinder
Couscousière

UPSIDE-DOWN PUDDING
This pudding originated in North America and is made in a dish or tin, base-lined with melted fat, brown sugar and fruit such as canned pineapple or peach halves, topped with a Victoria sandwich mixture and baked.

URBASA
See *Idiazábal*.

URDÂ
(Urda)
A Balkan and Czechoslovakian version of Italian Ricotta.

VACHERIN
Layers or a shell of meringue filled with whipped cream. It is served as a cake or dessert.

VACHERIN FRIBOURGEOIS
A 15th-century Swiss mountain cheese, made in the canton of Fribourg from cows' milk. A softer version of Gruyère and also smaller, it is golden-yellow, interspersed with holes of varying shapes and sizes. It used to be served at state banquets in honour of visiting royalty.

VACHERIN MONT D'OR
A Swiss cheese made from unpasteurized cows' milk. Traditionally it is a winter cheese, bound in the bark of fir trees and sold in boxes made of thin wood. It is very rich, soft and creamy with a rust-coloured crust. It is either spooned out on to plates for serving or carefully cut into wedges.

VACUUM FLASK
See *Thermos*.

VACUUM-METHOD COFFEE
(Cona Coffee)
Coffee prepared in a two-compartment pot, usually made in clear glass. The coffee — which may be fine or medium ground — is put into the upper section and water into the lower one, which is then heated. As the water boils, steam pressure is built up and the water siphons its way through to the upper section of the pot. Here it mixes with the coffee, aided by some gentle stirring. The pot is removed from the heat after 2–3 minutes. A vacuum then forms in the lower part of the pot, sucking the made coffee down. Before serving, the upper section should be removed.

VACUUM-PACKING
A form of 'long life' packaging in which food is heat-sealed in airtight, plastic vacuumpacks.

VAL
(Valor)
The Indian name for hyacinth bean.

VALENÇAY
A French goats' milk cheese which is a speciality of the Loire Valley. It is pyramid-shaped and gets its full flavour from the wood ash with which it is coated. It is fairly soft and left to mature for 4–5 weeks.

VALENCIA
A sweet orange with an almost spherical shape, a thin smooth skin and very juicy flesh.

VANASPATI
A hydrogenated vegetable fat used as a butter substitute in India.

VANILLA
A member of the orchid family, a tropical climbing plant (*Vanilla planifolia*) which produces green blossom and long, thin pods or beans. The liquid from inside the pods has a powerful flavour and is used to make vanilla essence, which is characteristically brown in colour. The dark brown pods, after

drying, are often put into jars of sugar so that the flavour permeates through the grains, producing vanilla sugar, widely used in Europe in the making of cakes, confectionery and desserts. Due to demand, artificial essence is more readily available in Britain than pure vanilla essence. Vanilla was first discovered in the early part of the 16th century by the Spanish explorer Cortez, who noticed that the Aztecs were using it to flavour chocolate drinks. It was introduced to the rest of Europe via Spain and, because of its unique flavour and fragrance, soon became one of the most appreciated flavourings for all manner of sweet foods ranging from ice creams to chocolate and baked goods.

VANILLA BEAN
See *Vanilla Pod*.

VANILLA POD
(Vanilla Bean)
The fruit of the vanilla plant.

VANILLA SUGAR
Widely used in northern Europe for baking, this is made by putting one or two vanilla pods into an airtight container of sugar so that the grains absorb the distinctive taste and aroma.

VARAK
Indian silver leaf which is used for decorative purposes.

VARIETY MEATS
North American term for offal.

VÄSTERBOTTEN
(Västergota)
A Swedish cows' milk cheese with a strong flavour and pliable texture. It dates back to the 19th century.

VÄSTKUSTSALLAD
This is one of Sweden's finest dishes and its name means 'west coast salad'. It is made from prawns, lobster meat, cooked and shelled mussels, cooked peas, sliced raw mushrooms, tomato wedges and asparagus tossed in French dressing flavoured with dill. The salad is transferred to individual glasses and garnished with mayonnaise and dill.

VAT
(Tub)
Container in which the milk is poured for cheesemaking; also used in distilleries.

VEAL
Meat from the calf.

VEAL AND HAM PIE
A British raised pie filled with equal quantities of diced pork and veal.

VEAL CHOPS
Cut from the loin of the animal, situated between the rump and shoulder, and containing pieces of bone. They are suitable for frying or grilling.

VEAL CORDON BLEU
A French-Swiss dish, consisting of a veal 'sandwich' containing Emmental cheese and ham which is coated in egg and breadcrumbs, then fried. It is garnished with lemon and parsley and accompanied by fried potatoes and salad.

VEAL PARMIGIANA
A North American speciality based on an Italian concept, consisting of veal chops coated with egg, breadcrumbs and Parmesan cheese which are then baked or fried. They are sometimes served with tomato sauce.

VEAL RIBLETS
Breast of veal separated into riblets by cutting in between the ribs. The riblets are then divided into lengths of equal size and stewed, braised or casseroled.

VEGAN
A strict vegetarian who will not eat any animal products at all and lives exclusively on vegetables, fruit, cereals, nuts and pulses.

VEGETABLE EXTRACT
A dark brown, concentrated extract made from vegetables and sometimes yeast. It is used to flavour soups, stews and casseroles and also eaten as a savoury spread. It can be diluted with hot water and turned into a drink.

VEGETABLE MARROW
(Marrow)
A vegetable which is the fruit of a trailing plant (*Cucurbita pepo*) and is grown both commercially and in gardens in Britain where it is the best-known edible gourd. It is probably native to tropical North America although the origin is obscure and the details of its introduction to Britain are uncertain. The most common kind of vegetable marrow is tubular in shape, its smooth skin coloured with light and dark green lengthwise stripes. The flesh is tender and watery and there is a central core of inedible seeds. Although a marrow may be allowed to grow very large for exhibitions and competitions, for culinary purposes it is best when relatively immature, 15–30 cm/7–12 inches in length. The marrow has comparatively little taste but may be cooked as a vegetable or used in savoury dishes as it readily absorbs flavours from other foods. Large, mature marrows may be used in jam- or chutney-making.

VEGETABLE PARER
See *Corer*.

VEGETABLE PEAR
See *Chayote*.

VEGETABLE PICKLES
A mixture of vegetables which have been brined and then pickled in spiced vinegar. The vegetables can include pieces of cauliflower, pickling onions, shallots, sliced cucumber and gherkins.

VEGETARIAN
Someone who will not eat flesh foods and whose diet consists primarily of vegetables, fruit, nuts, grains and cereals. Some vegetarians will also not eat eggs in case they contain the embryo of a living creature, or drink milk.

VEIN OF BEEF
Term used in north-west England for clod of beef.

VELOUTÉ SAUCE
A classic French sauce, similar to béchamel, the main difference being that stock is used instead of milk. The stock can be from meat, poultry, fish or vegetables (depending on the dish); other additions include lemon juice and sometimes cream. It can be served with meat, poultry, fish or vegetables.

VENDACE
A small freshwater fish (*Coregonus albula*) which is a member of the same family as the lake whitefish. It is found in Britain and in a number of other countries under a variety of different local names. The flesh is moderately oily and the fish may be baked or fried.

VENDACE ROE
A delicacy from Finland, the orange roe from the tiny vendace fish which is found in local lakes. Very highly prized, the roe has the same exclusivity as caviar and is served in a bowl resting on ice. It is generally eaten with chopped onion, smetana and blinis.

VENISON
The meat of deer, of which there are three kinds: red deer, which is the largest; fallow deer, the middle weight; and roe deer, the smallest. The male deer, known as buck venison, is in season in Britain from June to September; the female deer, known as doe venison, is in season from October to December. The flesh of both is close-textured, lean and distinctively flavoured and may

be braised, stewed, casseroled or roasted. The accompaniments for roast venison are gravy and either cranberry sauce or redcurrant jelly.

VERDI
The Italian word for 'green', used to describe pasta containing spinach purée such as *lasagne verdi*.

VERMICELLI
A thin pasta, resembling fine *spaghetti*.

VERMICELLINI
See *Angel's Hair*.

VERMONT
A cows' milk Cheddar-type cheese, produced in Vermont in the USA. It is full-flavoured and firm.

VERMOUTH
Wine-based aperitif flavoured with spice, herbs, fruit peels and so on. It is sometimes strengthened with brandy to bring it to the desired strength of around 38–40° proof (22–23° GL). Vermouth dates back to biblical times when it was made from wine and wormwood.

VÉRONIQUE
French term for any savoury dish containing or garnished with grapes, especially poultry and white fish. *Sole Véronique* is a classic example.

VIANDS
(Victuals)
Old-fashioned formal term for provisions and food.

VICHY WATER
See *Seltzer* and *Mineral Waters*.

VICHYSSOISE
A North American chilled soup, made from a purée of leeks and potatoes, enriched with cream. Chopped chives are sprinkled over each portion before serving. It is based on a recipe created by the renowned French chef, Louis Diat, when he was at the Ritz-Carlton Hotel, New York. He was born in Vichy, France, hence the name.

à la VICTORIA
French term meaning in the style of Victoria, referring to a garnish of tomatoes, macaroni, lettuce, potatoes and sometimes artichokes.

VICTORIA SANDWICH
The best-known, two-layer sandwich cake. It is made from a creamed cake mixture and is baked in two shallow sandwich tins. When turned out and cold, it is usually filled with whipped cream and/or jam and the top is dusted with icing sugar. Victoria sandwich cakes are often the basis of gâteaux and *torten*.

VICTUALS
See *Viands*.

VIENNA BREAD
(Vienna Loaf, Vienna Stick)
A basic white dough which is formed into a fairly short, oval-shaped stick before baking. A Vienna loaf rarely exceeds more than 30 cm/12 inches in length.

VIENNA SAUSAGE
(Wiener)
A small frankfurter; also, the North American term for frankfurter.

VIENNESE COFFEE
A ground coffee with the addition of dried figs which provide a particular and distinctive flavour. The term may also be used as an alternative to the name mocha for a drink made from a mixture of coffee and chocolate.

à la VIENNOISE
French term meaning in the style of Vienna, referring, for example, to an egg-and-crumbed escalope of veal garnished with lemon, anchovy, hard-boiled egg and sometimes capers; also a garnish for roasts composed of noodles, spinach, celery and potatoes.

VILLALÓN
(Pata de Mulo)
A Spanish cream cheese made from ewes' milk which is fresh-tasting, mild, young, white and a little similar to Burgos cheese. It is produced in Valladolid and is often shaped like an animal's foot, hence the name Pata de Mulo.

VILLI
A Finnish soured milk which is not exported.

au VIN
French term for food cooked in wine.

VIN ORDINAIRE
French term literally meaning ordinary wine and usually referring to a non-vintage red or white restaurant wine, brought to the table in an open carafe.

VIN-AIGRE
Old French term for vinegar, meaning sour wine.

VINAIGRETTE DRESSING
Similar to French dressing but flavoured with mustard and a little Worcestershire sauce. It is suitable for all salads.

VINDALOO CURRY
A hot curry from the south and west of India which is eaten with rice. The term *vindaloo* comes from the words vinegar and *aloo*, meaning potatoes; thus an authentic *vindaloo* curry should be made from vinegar-marinated meat and also contain potatoes. Other pungent herbs and spices are also included, together with a preponderance of chillies or chilli powder.

VINE LEAVES
Suitably shaped grapevine leaves are particularly useful for stuffing and are available fresh, salted in packets or canned. The flavour is mild but distinctive and vine leaves are the basis for many Greek and Middle Eastern dishes.

VINEGAR
A sharp, sour liquid, containing varying amounts of acetic acid, produced by fermentation of wine, cider or malt. Cider and wine vinegar have an acetic acid content of 50–60%; malt contains a little less, about 50%. Vinegar is used for pickling, in various sauces and salad dressings, and as a condiment.

VINTAGE COLOMBIAN
The finest kind of Colombian coffee bean.

VIRGIN OIL
Oil which remains untreated after pressing. Due to their vitamin E content, such oils last longer than those which have been refined; they also have a more distinctive flavour.

VIRGINIA HAM
North American ham, originally from Virginia. It is produced, traditionally, from pigs fed on peanuts and chestnuts, and is salted and smoked over fires made from hickory and apple wood.

VIRGINIA-STYLE HAM
A term used to describe commercially produced ham, which owes its individual character and flavour to the special curing and smoking techniques employed by the manufacturer.

à la VIROFLAY
French term meaning in the style of Viroflay near Paris, referring to a garnish of spinach, artichokes, potatoes, parsley and sometimes Mornay sauce.

VISCERA
The internal organs of an animal.

VISPI PUURO
A Finnish speciality, meaning whipped porridge in English. It is made by cooking sweetened fruit juice, from summer berries, with semolina and then whipping the

mixture off the heat until it becomes very light and frothy in consistency. It is served sprinkled with sugar and accompanied by milk.

VITAMIN A

(Retinol, β Carotene)
A fat-soluble vitamin, particularly important in protecting the mucous membranes lining the nose, mouth and throat against such conditions as catarrh and bronchitis. It is vital for healthy skin and hair, and is also necessary for good vision. Vitamin A is one of the recognized treatments for night blindness. Growing children must have an adequate supply of the vitamin as it helps in the formation of strong bones and teeth. It is found in fish liver oils, oily fish, dairy products, liver, eggs, leafy green vegetables, carrots and fortified margarines. Canning, frying or exposing to light can destroy the vitamin A in food. Laxatives containing liquid paraffin, and certain medications can cause a deficiency. Cooking in water does not harm the vitamin.

VITAMIN B COMPLEX

Term used to describe the group of water-soluble B vitamins: B_1, B_2, B_3, B_5, B_6, B_{12}, biotin and folic acid. These are all relatively unstable when heated and liable to be damaged by ultra-violet light. Although not chemically related, these vitamins are often found together in the same types of food, for instance, milk, cereals, liver.

VITAMIN B_1

(Aneurin, Aneurine, Thiamine)
A water-soluble vitamin, unstable at high temperatures and destroyed by the action of any alkali. Vitamin B_1 ensures that a continuous release of energy is obtained from carbohydrates taken in by the body and is important for normal growth and development in children. It also prevents nervous conditions, such as neuritis, irritability and depression, and helps to ward off a Far-Eastern disease known as beri-beri, the result of eating a diet based on processed white rice which contains almost no vitamin B_1. Most well-balanced diets should provide the daily requirement of the vitamin (which cannot be stored in the body), but the richest sources are whole grain cereals, wheatgerm, yeast extracts, pork, bacon, oatmeal, pulses, fish and eggs. Deficiency of Vitamin B_1 may be caused by heavy smoking and an excess of alcohol.

VITAMIN B_2

(Riboflavin)
A water-soluble vitamin which, although not readily destroyed by heat unless excessive, is destroyed by the action of heat combined with ultra-violet rays; for this reason, milk should not be left standing in the sun. Basically, vitamin B_2 helps the body obtain energy from the foods it takes in, especially fats and proteins. An adequate daily intake of this vitamin is necessary for the normal and healthy development of children. A deficiency of Vitamin B_2 can cause inflammatory conditions of the mouth and tongue, chapped lips, nervousness, depression, poor skin and digestive disorders. Good sources of the vitamin are dairy products, soy beans, yeast extract, wholemeal bread, wheatgerm, offal, lean meat, fish, nuts, pulses and oatmeal. Women who take the contraceptive pill may suffer from a deficiency of this vitamin.

VITAMIN B_3

(Niacin, Nicotinic Acid)
A water-soluble vitamin which is often destroyed when foods are cooked. It is essential for healthy growth and development, a good skin, the efficient functioning of the nervous system and the digestion of carbohydrates. Vitamin B_3 is found in peanuts, yeast extract, brewer's yeast, wheatgerm, bran, pork liver, meat, fish, cheese, wholemeal bread, eggs and pulses. A diet based on fast-foods and 'junk' foods can result in a deficiency, the result

being digestive problems, insomnia, skin rashes, nervousness and depression.

VITAMIN B_5

(Pantothenic Acid)

A heat-sensitive vitamin which is destroyed by boiling. Its function is to ensure that hair, nails, skin and body tissue in general remain in a healthy condition. It is found in eggs, wheatgerm, liver, wholemeal bread, brown rice, wholemeal pasta, yeast, and foods and drinks containing yeast. A deficiency of vitamin B_5 is often the result of a diet containing too many processed foods or foods which have been over-cooked.

VITAMIN B_6

(Pyridoxine, Pyridoxal, Pyridoxal)

A water-soluble vitamin which is often destroyed in cooking. It is very important for the successful metabolism of protein and helps to protect nerves, muscles and skin. It is also believed that the vitamin has a role to play in the control of nervous tension, pre-menstrual tension, morning sickness in pregnancy, menopausal problems, muscle cramp and insomnia. Vitamin B_6 is found in lean meat, fish, wheatgerm, wholemeal bread, yeasted goods, oatmeal and leafy green vegetables. A deficiency of the vitamin may occur as a result of heavy smoking; an excess of alcohol and the contraceptive pill.

VITAMIN B_{12}

(Cyanocobalamin)

A water-soluble vitamin which is often destroyed when foods are cooked. It is the only vitamin which contains a metal, namely cobalt, from which the name cyanocobalamin is derived. It is essential for normal growth and development, is also instrumental in preventing certain forms of anaemia and nervous disorders and has a part to play in the metabolism of protein. Vitamin B_{12} is found in liver, kidney, meat, fish, yeast products and eggs. A deficiency of the vitamin may be caused by heavy smoking or insufficient protein foods in the diet; certain types of antibiotics, the contraceptive pill and some other forms of medication may also occasionally lead to a deficiency. (Vegetarians need to take especial care, and vegans may require supplements.)

VITAMIN C

(Ascorbic Acid, Ascorbate)

The most sensitive vitamin, which can easily be lost in cooking and through prolonged soaking of foods in water. It is also quickly destroyed by heat and exposure to oxygen, daylight and sunshine. When fresh foods are stored for a long time, the vitamin C content will be adversely affected. Because foods containing this vitamin are so vulnerable, cooking should be as swift as possible and only the minimum amount of water or other liquid used. Vitamin C is essential for the normal and healthy development of babies and children. For adults it is important in helping the body to absorb 'non haem' iron found in pulses and wholegrain cereals, to ward off viral and bacterial infections and to keep teeth, gums and skin in good condition. It also acts as a natural diuretic, antihistamine and healer; wounds, fractures and cuts heal more quickly when there is an adequate supply of vitamin C in the diet. The vitamin used to be known as a preventative for scurvy, a skin disease which affected seamen who were deprived of fresh fruit and vegetables on long sea voyages. Some of the best sources of Vitamin C are rose hips, kiwi fruits, blackcurrants, guavas, green vegetables, parsley, green peppers and citrus fruits. Because the body is unable to store vitamin C, a regular daily intake is necessary to prevent muscular pains, aching joints, fatigue, mouth disorders and irritability. The vitamin also assists in preventing illnesses caused by viruses and bacteria. A deficiency of the vitamin may be brought about by heavy smoking, an excess of alcohol, antibiotics, and the contraceptive pill.

VITAMIN D

(Cholecalciferol D3, Ergocalciferol D2)
A fat-soluble vitamin which is almost unaffected by cooking. It helps the body to absorb calcium and phosphorus (essential in pregnancy, for growing children and the elderly) and is also thought to help sufferers of rheumatoid arthritis. It is found chiefly in cod liver oil, oily fish, dairy products, eggs, evaporated milk, margarine and fortified breakfast cereals. Lack of vitamin D is known to be one of the prime causes of the disease rickets, which in young children results in deformed legs, muscle weakness, poor teeth and impaired growth and development. Canning foods and exposing them to light can destroy the vitamin D content. A deficiency may result from a shortage of dairy products in the diet and the taking of excessive amounts of laxatives which contain liquid paraffin. A lack of sunshine or daylight can also lead to a deficiency of this vitamin which is synthesized under the skin via the chemical reaction of ultra-violet light on the epidermis.

VITAMIN E

(Tocopherol, Tocotrienols)
The exact functions of this fat-soluble vitamin are still being scientifically investigated but it is thought to be necessary for fertility, to prevent the formation of blood clots and to keep the muscles healthy. As a powerful and natural antioxidant, it is known to 'mop up' certain harmful chemicals in the body. It is found in wheatgerm, vegetable oils (especially olive oil), peanuts, cold pressed oils and lettuce. Lack of the vitamin is said to aggravate muscle disorders and infertility. Exposure to light and air can sometimes affect the vitamin E content of foods. A deficiency may arise when taking laxatives containing liquid paraffin and the contraceptive pill; people suffering from diabetes may also be at risk.

VITAMIN K

(Phytomenadione, Menaquione)
A fat-soluble vitamin which helps blood to clot. A lack of vitamin K causes cuts and wounds to bleed for a longer time and more profusely than normal, and those on anti-coagulant therapy (Warfarin, for instance) are treated with vitamin K if their blood has thinned down too much. It is found in cauliflower, most green vegetables and pork liver. The vitamin K content of foods may be affected by the action of light, acids and alkalis, and deep-freezing.

VITAMINS

Discovered during the early part of the 20th century by Dr Casmir Funk, vitamins have an important role to play in the maintenance of sound health and essential body processes. They are known to prevent a number of illnesses which, at one time, were thought to be caused by bacteria. Some vitamins, such as A and D, are measured in international units, abbreviated to IU; others are measured in milligrams. They can be generally classified as either water soluble (required daily in small amounts) or as fat soluble (which may be stored in certain organs of the body).

VITELLO TONNATO

An Italian speciality made from slices of cold roast veal coated with a sauce made from finely mashed canned tuna, mayonnaise and lemon juice and garnished with wedges of lemon.

VODKA

A strong spirit made from grain or potato, especially popular as an accompaniment to meals in Eastern Europe and parts of Scandinavia. Vodka may sometimes be flavoured with, for example, cherry or honey.

VOL-AU-VENTS
Puff pastry cases containing hot or cold fillings which may be sweet or savoury, usually capped with their own lids, which have been cut out of the centres of the cases before or after baking. Small *vol-au-vents* are often served hot as a cocktail savoury; medium-sized ones make a popular *hors d'oeuvre* or main course.

VOLEIPÄPÖYTÄ
Finland's open table, similar to Sweden's *smörgåsbord*, Russia's *zakuski*, Denmark's *koldebord* and Norway's *koldtbord*.

WAFER BISCUITS
Unsweetened biscuits made with flour and water.

WAFERS
Speciality biscuits, frequently cone-shaped for holding ice cream. Other shapes, such as fans and oblongs, are used to decorate ice cream desserts in bowls or glasses.

WAFFLE IRON
Two oblong or circular metal trays, about 2.5 cm/1 inch thick, joined by a hinge with handles on the opposite side. The grooved surfaces of the trays give the waffles their characteristic square pattern. A waffle iron may be used on hobs of gas, electric or solid fuel cookers but maker's directions must be closely followed to ensure success.

WAFFLES
Light, crisp batter cakes cooked in a greased waffle iron, which forms a pattern, usually squares.

WAITER (WAITRESS)
Someone who waits at table in a restaurant or at formal functions.

WAKAME
A sea vegetable (*Undaria pinnatifida*) of the brown algae group of plants, found mainly in the coastal waters of Japan. It is a leafy vegetable which is blanched and dried before being sold in whole-leaf form. *Wakame* is also sold in Japan as a fresh vegetable, blanched but undried. It has a mild flavour and may be eaten with land vegetables or used in Japanese dishes.

WALDORF SALAD
Of North American origin, a salad comprising celery, apples, walnuts and mayonnaise.

à la WALESKA
French term meaning in the style of the Comtesse Waleska, mistress of Napoleon, denoting a garnish for fish, generally sole, composed of Mornay sauce, lobster and truffles.

WALLEYE POLLOCK
(Alaska Pollock)
A member (*Theragra chalcogramma*) of the cod family with an average weight of under 1 kg/2¼ lb and a length of about 45 cm/18 inches. The back is olive-green to brown and the underside is silvery. It is caught in the Pacific off the North American coast all year round, with a specific February catch for the roe which has a ready market in Japan when salted. The flesh is lean and white and the fish may be poached, steamed, baked, fried or grilled. Commercially it is used for fish sticks and other products.

WALNUT OIL
A fine-quality, expensive oil made from walnuts, and containing polyunsaturated fatty acids. It has a delicate, nutty flavour and is used primarily for salad dressings.

WALNUTS
The stones of fruits of walnut trees (*Juglans regia* and *J. nigra*), native to the Middle East but now grown throughout Europe and the USA. Enclosed in a hard beige shell, the nuts have a crinkly, wrinkled appearance and distinctive flavour. European varieties are milder than American and the shells are also lighter in colour.

WARA EINAB
(Waraq Ainab)
A Middle Eastern appetizer made from salted vine leaves stuffed with cooked rice, pine nuts and raisins.

WARM (TO)
To heat slowly to below boiling point.

WARSZAWSKI
A Polish version of Balkan Kashkaval cheese, made from ewes' milk.

WASEBI
Very strong and potent Japanese horseradish (*Wasabia japonica*) which should be used sparingly. Its English name is mountain hollyhock.

WASHED-RIND CHEESES
These are soft paste cheeses which initially have white *penicillium* coats. However, with some types such as Pont-l'Evêque and Limburger, the growth of the coats is deliberately interrupted by salt water 'baths' to encourage the development of yellowy-orange to light brown skins.

WATER CHESTNUTS
See *Chinese Water Chestnuts*.

WATER ICE
See *Sorbet*.

WATER ICING
See *Glacé Icing*.

WATERCRESS
A member of the nasturtium family, watercress (genus *Rorippa*) is an aquatic plant which fares best in moist meadows and shallow streams. It has dark green, peppery-tasting leaves and is used in salads, soups and for garnishing. It is a good source of vitamin C and iron.

WATERMELON
The fruit of a plant (*Citrillus vulgaris*) of the same family as other melons but in a class of its own. The origins of this melon are obscure but it is now cultivated in many parts of the world with suitable climates. It is spherical or elongated in shape and different varieties are of different sizes but even the smallest are larger than any other genus of melon. The thick skin is dark green or yellow, sometimes patterned and usually smooth and shiny. The flesh is made up of two concentric layers; just under the skin there is a light-coloured, thinnish, inedible layer and inside is a much thicker layer of the true red or pink-coloured pulp in which the seeds are embedded. The centre of the melon is a continuation of the pink pulp, but is seedless. Some completely seedless watermelons have been developed, but in many countries the seeds are valued as food. The watermelon does not have the intensity of fragrance or flavour of other melons but its high water content (over 90%) makes it a very refreshing fruit when eaten ice-cold. The light-coloured outer layer, or rind, may be used as a pumpkin-like vegetable or in preserves. The pink flesh may be eaten on its own, added to fruit salads or used in any dish requiring melons.

WATERZOOI
A Belgian speciality, a stew of fish or chicken containing leek, onion, celery, carrot, parsley and stock or water, thickened and enriched with egg yolks, cream and cornflour. *Waterzooi* originated in Flanders.

WAX BEAN
(Waxpod Bean)
Term for any of several types of French bean with creamy yellow to bright yellow waxy pods.

WAX PALM
See *Carnauba*.

WEBB'S WONDERFUL LETTUCE
(Webb's Wonder)
One of the main types of commercially grown lettuce, this is ball-shaped and the green leaves are firm and slightly crinkly. It is one of the more substantial varieties of lettuce.

WEDDING BREAKFAST
A celebratory meal following a marriage which has taken place fairly early in the day.

WEDDING CAKE
A multi-tiered rich fruit cake divided by pillars. It is generally coated with almond paste and royal or fondant icing. Appropriate decorations and ornaments are added.

WEINSCHAUM SAUCE
A foamy German sauce, served warm, made by whipping wine, eggs and sugar in a similar manner to *zabaglione* sauce. It can be served over cooked or canned fruit, baked or steamed puddings or, German fashion, over vanilla-flavoured blancmange.

WEISSLACKER
(Bierkäse, Weisslacker Bierkäse)
A German cows' milk cheese with a name meaning 'white lacquer'. Its varnished appearance is the result of the way it is treated during production (with salt, humidity, etc.). It is a strong and forceful cheese which is very much an acquired taste. It was first produced about a hundred years ago and is a Bavarian speciality. It is rindless and completely smooth in texture.

WEISSWURST
Firm and creamy-coloured sausage from Bavaria in Germany, made principally from light meat such as pork and veal. Mildly flavoured and sometimes containing chopped parsley, the *weisswurst* is generally heated through in water and/or crisped in a frying pan or under the grill. The traditional accompaniments are mustard and bread.

WELL-DONE
British term to describe steak or roast beef which is cooked through.

WELL-HUNG
Term to describe game or meat which has been hung for a sufficient length of time to allow flavour and tenderness to develop.

WELSH CAKES
Fried round cakes, similar to dropped scones, made from a flour mixture containing fat, eggs, sugar, currants and milk.

WELSH RAREBIT
A well-seasoned cheese mixture spread on to freshly made toast and browned under a hot grill.

WENSLEYDALE
An English cows' milk cheese which matures in only 3–4 weeks, Wensleydale is a flaky white cheese with a refreshing and mildly tangy taste. It is very slightly salty and is enjoyed in the North Country with apple pie.

WEST COAST HALIBUT ROYAL
A speciality of British Columbia in Canada, consisting of halibut steaks marinated in salt, paprika and lemon juice, then topped with fried onions, pepper strips and melted fat. They are then baked.

WEST COAST SALAD
See *Västkustsallad*.

WESTFÄLISCHE BOHENSUPPE
A German vegetable soup from Westphalia which contains haricot beans.

WESTPHALIAN HAM
German speciality meat, made from boneless ham treated naturally with both salt and brine and left to mature for 3–4 weeks in a cool cellar, then smoked over resin-free ash and beech wood with the addition of juniper berries for up to 5 weeks. The ham is dark in colour with a characteristic smoky flavour and is either left in an irregular piece or rolled before processing. It is served in thin slices as an *hors d'oeuvre*, often wrapped round pieces of melon.

WET FISH
Term used in Britain for fresh, uncooked fish sold in fishmongers or supermarkets.

WETHA SEE PYAN
A mild Burmese pork curry, flavoured with lemon, turmeric, garlic and ginger, and served with rice.

WEXFORD
An Irish version of Cheshire cheese.

WHALE
A large family of fish-like mammals (order Cetacea), including the largest mammal in the world, the meat from which may be stewed, braised or casseroled like beef. It requires a good deal of flavouring to offset the fishy and oily flavour of the flesh.

WHALE BLUBBER
See *Blubber*.

WHALE OIL
Comes from the whale and is used by food manufacturing industries.

WHEAT
A grass-like grain of the genus *Triticum*, widely grown for use as a food since prehistoric times. It is now cultivated worldwide, providing a very important cereal food. Its basic use is in all forms of bread-making.

WHEAT FLAKES
Produced from kibbled or cracked wheat, first hulled and parboiled, then roller-crushed until flat. The flakes are lightly toasted and used in breakfast cereal mixes such as muesli.

WHEAT FLOUR
Flour milled from wheat.

WHEATEN
A term used to describe anything made of wheat, wheatmeal or wheat flour.

WHEATGERM
(Germ)
The embyro or kernel of wheat which is rich in nutrients including vitamins of the B and E groups, protein, iron and trace elements. It constitutes about 2% of the whole wheat grain. As it contains oil, it is classed as perishable and therefore should be stored in airtight containers, preferably in the refrigerator. As a dietary supplement, it can be sprinkled over breakfast cereals, cooked or canned fruits and salads. It can also be stirred into yogurt and added to other dishes such as stews, casseroles, bread dough and cake mixtures. Additionally, it makes an unusual coating for fish and poultry prior to frying or baking.

WHEATMEAL FLOUR
Also described as 81% or 85% brown, depending on the kind of grain used, this is nutritious flour from which 15–19% of coarse particles (mostly bran and wheatgerm) have been removed. The residual flour is more nourishing than white and less coarse than wholemeal.

WHELK
(Waved Whelk)
A carnivorous marine snail (*Buccinum undatum*) whose shell can be 10–15 cm/4–6 inches in length. The colour of the shell varies with habitat and the finest specimens are found in the open seas off north-west Europe. The main season is from February to August when the flesh is white and the shells are full. The muscular foot is the part most often eaten and may be poached, baked or grilled. Relatives of the whelk are found on both sides of the North Atlantic and can reach up to 30 cm/12 inches in length. Whelks are normally boiled at the place of landing and it is best to buy them commercially prepared as at certain times they may be toxic due to their diet.

WHEY
The serum or watery part of soured or cultured milk which separates from the curds. It occurs in cheese-making and is a good source of lactose, minerals and vitamins. In Iceland, whey is used as a pickling solution for blubber and other foods.

WHEY CREAM
After some cheeses have been made, the residual whey liquid is further separated to make butter and whey cream.

WHIM WHAM
An 18th-century version of trifle, comprising sponge fingers soaked in muscatel wine and then topped with whipped cream.

WHIP (TO)
To whisk ingredients to incorporate air and/or thicken. This technique can be carried out with electric beaters, a balloon whisk or rotary beater.

WHIPPED CREAM
Whipping cream sold already whipped.

WHIPPING CREAM
A pasteurized cream which has a legal minimum butterfat content of 35%. When whipped, it doubles in volume, but must be used straight from the refrigerator and not left to stand at room temperature.

WHISK
An implement for beating, mixing and aerating. There are many kinds but they are all based on the principle of wire loops on a handle.

WHISK (TO)
To aerate and combine mixtures by beating with a hand-held or electric mixer.

WHISKED CAKES
Usually sponges, made from a base of whisked eggs and sugar into which sifted flour is folded. It is essential that the eggs and sugar are well-whisked: one egg with 25 g/1 oz caster sugar should bulk up to 175 ml/6 fl oz. The mixture should be pale cream in colour and the consistency of softly whipped cream.

WHISKY
(Whiskey)
A grain spirit (barley, maize, rye and wheat) which is widely produced in Scotland, Ireland (whiskey), North America (rye and bourbon) and Canada (rye). It is honey-coloured and strong; 70–75° proof (40–43° GL). The drink is becoming more prevalent in regional Scottish dishes and is also sometimes used in Christmas puddings and cake.

WHITE BEER
(Berliner 'Weisse', German White Beer)
Its German name means 'Berlin White'. It is a pale beer which is served in a huge, bulbous glass with a shot of raspberry syrup.

WHITE BREAD
Made from a dough containing only white flour.

WHITE BUTTER SAUCE
English term for *Beurre Blanc*.

WHITE CABBAGE
(Dutch White Cabbage)
See *Cabbage*.

WHITE CHESHIRE
An uncoloured version of Britain's oldest cheese.

WHITE COFFEE
Black coffee to which milk or cream, or powdered milk-substitute, is added.

WHITE DISTILLED VINEGAR
A colourless vinegar which, with an acetic acid content of 40%, is particularly useful for pickling foods which should remain pale in colour such as silver-skin cocktail onions, pepper or pimiento strips, assorted vegetables, cucumbers and baby sweetcorn. It is a little milder than other varieties and can be used in salad dressings, mayonnaise or any dish where a mild acid is required.

WHITE FLOUR
Flour from which the wheatgerm and bran have been removed.

WHITE LYMESWOLD CHEESE
A fairly new British cheese, made from cows' milk with the addition of fresh cream. It is soft, supple, rich and mild, dotted here and there with small holes. The rind is velvety white and the cheese is sold in wedge-shaped pieces, wrapped in foil.

WHITE MEAT
A term which usually refers to the flesh of veal and poultry.

WHITE MUSTARD
See *Mustard*.

WHITE PEPPER
The berries are left on vines (*Piper nigrum*) until they are completely ripe, when the outer hulls split and partly separate. The berries are soaked in water and the hulls removed. The white peppercorns are then thoroughly washed, dried and ready for use. Because the outer brown hulls have been removed, ground white pepper has a pale and even colour without dark speckles.

WHITE PUDDING
Britain's version of *boudin blanc*, now something of a rarity, consisting of a sausage made from light meat, cereal, suet, oats or barley groats, herbs, seasoning and milk. The mixture is put into a casing, then gently simmered until cooked.

WHITE RADISH
See *Daikon*.

WHITE SAUCE
A creamy, pale-coloured sauce, usually made from a roux of equal quantities of melted fat and flour with the addition of milk or other liquids to achieve the required consistency. It should be flavoured to suit the dish with which it is being served.

WHITE STEW
A stew made from poultry or veal plus onions, milk, stock and seasonings.

WHITE STILTON
A white, fresh-tasting Stilton without blue-green marbling. It is sold young, at about 6–8 weeks, and is made in the same way as Blue Stilton but without culture; thus the cheese stays white.

WHITE SUGAR
Refined sugar, including granulated, caster and icing sugars.

WHITECURRANT
An albino strain of redcurrant (*Ribes* species).

WHITING
A round-bodied fish (*Merlangius merlangus*) of the cod family which is caught all year round in the North Atlantic from Iceland to Spain, and

also the North Sea, but is at its best from December to February. Average length of the whole fish in the shops is 25–40 cm/10–16 inches. The colour of the upper side ranges from a greyish-yellow to a darker green or blue, but becomes paler on the underside. The flesh is white, lean, delicate and bony and the fish may be poached, steamed, baked, fried or grilled.

WHOLE GAMMON
Comprising the leg and thigh. It could be described as a party-sized joint; weighing about 7 kg/15 lb, it will serve 30 people generously.

WHOLE GRAIN WHEAT
Complete wheat grain with nothing added or removed. Flour produced from the whole wheat grain is known as wholemeal flour.

WHOLEFOODS
Unrefined pulses, grains, nuts, sugars and so on which are in their natural form and less deficient in nutrients than manufactured refined foods. With the exception of sugar, they are fairly rich in fibre.

WHOLEMEAL FLOUR
(Wholewheat Flour)
'Complete' brown flour which includes, by law, the whole of the wheat grain; it is generally described as 100% wholemeal. It is coarser than white flour, more nutritious and flavoursome, and has a high bran content which is approximately double that of white flour.

WHOLEWHEAT FLOUR
See *Wholemeal Flour*.

WHOLEWHEAT LASAGNE
Lasagne made with wholewheat flour.

WHOLEWHEAT PASTA
Pasta made with wholewheat flour.

WHORTLEBERRY
See *Blueberry*.

WIENER
North American term for frankfurter.

WIENER SCHNITZEL
An Austrian speciality, consisting of a veal escalope which is beaten until very thin and then coated in flour, beaten egg and fine white crumbs before being fried in hot oil or lard. Its origins are obscure and though it is said to have come from Vienna, the *Schnitzel* may have its roots in Milan in Italy (where it is called *scallope milanese*), or Turkey when a Turkish cook, held prisoner after the siege of Vienna in the latter part of the 17th century, showed his captors how to coat the veal in traditional style.

WIENER SCHNITZEL HOLSTEIN
A *Wiener Schnitzel* topped with a fried egg.

WIGEON
(Widgeon)
A type of small, wild duck which is often served with orange and sherry-flavoured gravy.

WILD BOAR
A Eurasian wild pig, from which most domestic pigs have been derived. It is now extinct in Britain but still eaten in many other European countries.

WILD DUCK
Smaller than the domestic duck, this variety comes under the category of water game and is in season from the beginning of September to the end of February. Although the flesh has a natural saltiness, it can be prepared and cooked in exactly the same way as domestic duck and one bird per person should be allowed. It is recommended that wild duck be hung for 2–3 days before cooking.

WILD MARJORAM
See *Oregano*.

WILD RICE
Classed as a cereal, wild rice is the seed of wild grass (*Zizania aquatica*) which grows in shallow lake areas of North America, the Great Lakes and eastern coastal areas of North America. Wild rice for home consumption is also grown in certain areas of China, where it is known as *kawsun*. It is a relative of rice but much rarer and its long and slender seeds are dark brown, turning purple when cooked. Fairly expensive, wild rice is often combined with white or brown rice to make it go further and is sometimes added to turkey stuffing, especially for Thanksgiving. Wild rice is a relatively high-protein food, rich in the B vitamins and trace elements. It is low in calories.

WILD STRAWBERRY
(Wood Strawberry)
The native wild strawberry (*Fragaria vesca*) of Europe, producing small, delicious fruit. It is readily cultivated but always retains its two main characteristics: small size and distinctive flavour.

WILTSHIRE CURE (OF BACON)
A British method of curing bacon which originated in Wiltshire about 200 years ago. About 60% of all bacon eaten in Great Britain is cured by this method and the technique is also used in other countries. The curing process involves injecting brine or pickle, under pressure, into whole sides of pigs to ensure the even distribution of curing salts throughout the carcass. The sides are then stacked in large vats, steeped in brine and left for 2–3 days. After draining, they are left to mature in cool cellars for about 7 days and then sold as green bacon. If the bacon is subsequently smoked, this is done by suspending the sides over slow-burning oak sawdust which produces a golden rind, deep pink flesh and a distinctive smoky flavour, closely associated with British bacon.

WIMPY
British trade name of a meat hamburger, served inside a plain bread bun with or without fried onions.

WINDERMERE CHAR
See *Arctic Char*.

WINE
Produced internationally for drinking and use in cooking, wine is the fermented juice of fresh grapes. It can be dry, medium or sweet, and either white, rosé (pink) or red.

WINE VINEGAR
A superior type of vinegar made from both red and white wines which has an acetic acid content of around 50%. It tends to be blander in taste than the other vinegars and is useful in cooked dishes, salad dressings and some sauces. As a general rule, it is not as suitable for pickling as cider, malt or white distilled vinegar.

WINEBERRY
(Japanese Wineberry)
The fruit of a prickly, deciduous shrub (*Rubus phoenicolasius*) of the rose family, native to northern China and Japan and related to the blackberry and raspberry. The shape is basically conical and the fruit consists of a cluster of bright red, tiny-seeded globules on a fleshy stem from which it separates easily when ripe. The wineberry is sweet and juicy and may be eaten on its own or used in place of blackberries or raspberries in dessert dishes.

WING
Wing bone of a chicken, duck, turkey or other bird and the flesh and skin covering it.

WING KELP
North American name for alaria.

WING RIB OF BEEF
A triangular cut of beef from the top of the animal, between the sirloin and fore ribs. It is a tender joint and

suitable for roasting. Sometimes it is boned and sliced into steaks for grilling or frying.

WINKLE
(Periwinkle)
An edible sea snail (*Littorina littorea*) found in coastal waters round the world. The shell colours vary from habitat to habitat and they are about 2.5 cm/1 inch long. They are boiled, the flesh is removed from the shells and either eaten suitably seasoned or used in made-up dishes.

WINTER FLOUNDER
(Common Flounder, George's Bank Flounder)
A flatfish (*Pseudopleuronectes americanus*) of the plaice family with an average length of 45 cm/18 inches and weight of 2–3 kg/ 4½–6½ lb. It is reddish-brown in colour with some mottling on the upper side; the paler underside may be tinged with yellow. It is caught from February to October, with the main catches in the summer months, in the waters of eastern Canada and the New England coast. It has lean, white, firm flesh and the fish may be poached, steamed, baked, fried or grilled. It is called the winter flounder because it tends to seek shallow, warmer waters during the cold season.

WINTER MELON
A type of thick-skinned melon with good keeping qualities, such as the honeydew. Winter melons have been developed from a variety called cassaba. Also, a huge Chinese watermelon with mild, creamy-coloured flesh, sold in slices and used to make winter melon soup.

WINTER RADISH
Term used for certain kinds of radish which can be left to mature in the ground and then lifted and stored for later use.

WINTER SAVORY
See *Savory*.

WISHBONE
A forked bone in front of the breastbone in a bird consisting chiefly of the two collarbones joined at their middle or lower end.

WISHY-WASHY
A British colloquial term to describe food and drink which are lacking in flavour.

WITCH SOLE
See *Lemon Sole*.

WITLOOF
The Belgian name for the country's national vegetable, otherwise known as chicory or Belgian endive.

WOK
A metal, bowl-shaped cooking utensil used for stir-frying food in the Chinese style. Some versions are made with a built-in electric element.

WOLF-FISH
See *Catfish*.

WONTON WRAPPERS
Squares of very thin noodle pastry used for making Chinese specialities such as wontons and spring rolls. Packets of the pastry are available from Oriental food shops.

WONTONS
Chinese appetizers, very similar to Italian *ravioli*, which are either deep-fried and served hot or served in soup. The fillings are generally composed of minced fish, meat, vegetables and seasonings.

WOOD BLEWIT
See *Blewit*.

WOOD EAR
A Chinese fungus (*Auricularia polytricha*) which is related to Jew's ear. It is dark and gelatinous, and is available dried.

WOOD GROUSE
See *Capercailzie*.

WOOD PIGEON
See *Pigeon*.

WOOD STRAWBERRY
See *Wild Strawberry*.

WOODCOCK
A pigeon-sized, wading game bird (*Scolopax rusticola*) in season in Britain from the beginning of October to the end of January. It is usually roasted and served on fried bread or toast, accompanied by melted butter, cranberry sauce and gravy. One bird per person should be allowed.

WOODRUFF
An important and interesting herb (*Asperula odorata*) with a scent resembling freshly mown hay which only becomes noticeable after the herb has partially dried. At one time, woodruff was used like lavender and packed into small sachets for use in the linen cupboard, drawers and wardrobe. Its prime uses now are for flavouring continental wine, apple juice, some liqueurs and German white beer. Woodruff is a wild perennial plant belonging to the Rubiaceae family and grows in the shade, usually in woods and similar sheltered spots. It has star-shaped white blossoms.

WORCESTERBERRY
A fruit which is a hybrid of the North American gooseberry and a blackcurrant. It has the blue-black skin of the blackcurrant but is several times larger. The worcesterberry may be substituted for the blackcurrant or blueberry in cooked dishes or eaten raw when fully ripe.

WORCESTERSHIRE SAUCE
(Worcester Sauce, Lea and Perrins)
A strongly flavoured, proprietary brown sauce/condiment made from vinegar, molasses, sugar, salt, anchovies, tamarinds, shallots, garlic, spices and other flavourings. It can be served with roast and grilled meat and poultry and added to salad dressings, tomato juice and to dark-coloured sauces (Espagnole, for example) to heighten the flavour.

WORK (TO)
To draw a crumbly mixture together and form it into a smooth pastry or dough with the finger-tips; to mould a soft mixture into shapes.

WORMWOOD
A bitter herb and member of the daisy family, wormwood (*Artemisia absinthium*) is a perennial bush with silvery leaves and yellow flowers. Native to Europe, wormwood grows in North America and the USSR and its prime use is to flavour absinthe and vermouth. At one time it replaced hops in the brewing of beer.

WURST
German term for sausage.

XYLITOL
A modern sugar substitute used in Britain.

YAKIMONO
The Japanese term to cover all grilled foods.

YAKITORI
Japanese chicken kebabs which are grilled and served with a soy sauce mixture containing *mirin*, sake and sugar.

YAM
A vegetable tuber (*Dioscorea* species) of a climbing vine. There are hundreds of species in this family, mostly native to Africa and now grown worldwide in tropical and sub-tropical regions. A typical yam available in Britain is an elongated potato shape sometimes with slightly hairy skin; the colour is either reddish-brown, red or brownish-pink. The size varies with the species and smaller ones are preferable. Some very large kinds may weigh as much as a whole sack of potatoes and these are sold in sections. The flesh is fairly bland in flavour and can be white, yellow or occasionally red. The texture of yam is soft or firm (like potatoes) and it is either treated as a vegetable in its own right or used in ethnic dishes. As some species contain harmful chemicals, yam should never be eaten raw. A few varieties of yam resemble the sweet potato and are sold as such, but the two vegetables are not of the same botanical genus.

YAM
The Thai term for the highly decorative and skilfully prepared salads of the country.

YANG-BAECHU GIMCHI
Korean pickled cabbage, stuffed with white radish and spring onion and flavoured with ginger, garlic, chillies, anchovies and salt.

YANG-HOE
The Korean version of steak tartare, in which the raw minced beef is mixed with sesame oil, sesame seeds, ginger, garlic, onions and sugar. Mounds of the mixture are served topped with an egg yolk and sprinkled with chopped pine nuts. The garnish is thin strips of peeled, fresh pear.

YAOUT
The name used in Bulgaria and Russia for yogurt.

YAPREK DOLMASI
A Turkish speciality of stuffed vine leaves. The filling is a mixture of rice, raisins, onions, pine nuts, seasonings and chopped parsley or dill. They are baked in the oven, then served lightly chilled.

YARD-LONG BEAN
(Asparagus Bean, Long Bean, Yard Bean)
A vegetable (*Vigna sesquipedalis*) native to Asia and grown in the Far East and the Caribbean region. It is a legume which grows as a long, thin and flexible green-coloured rod and is mainly available in shops specializing in Asian foods. It is eaten both as a fresh vegetable and dried pulse.

YARROW
A wild perennial herb (*Achillea millefolium*) which was said to have been used by Achilles to ease the wounds of his soldiers, yarrow grows in Europe, Asia and North America. With a distinctive, strong scent, deep green leaves which look like feathers and pink or white blossom, yarrow is an antiseptic and healing herb, used in tisanes and herbal medicine.

YASSA AU POULET
A West African marinated chicken dish in which the bird is fried with onions, then simmered in the marinade.

YAUTIA
See *Tannia*.

YEAST
A living organism which reproduces itself under the right conditions (including gentle warmth, liquid and carbohydrate food) and, through various enzymes in the yeast itself and the ingredients with which it is mixed, is converted into alcohol and carbon dioxide. When yeasted goods, such as bread and buns, are baked, the alcohol is expelled and the carbon dioxide expands in the heat of the oven, causing the dough

to rise. The action of the yeast ceases when the middle of the loaf reaches a temperature of 60°C/40°F. Yeast is quickly destroyed by heat and should never be blended with boiling water.

YEASTED GOODS
Flour and liquid-based doughs raised with yeast.

YEASTY
Of or resembling yeast; tasting of yeast.

YELLOW BEAN PASTE
A Chinese flavouring made from soy bean paste. It is strongly flavoured and should be used sparingly.

YELLOW PASSION FRUIT
(Golden Passion Fruit)
The fruit of a plant (*Passiflora edulis flavicarpa*) of the passion flower family with golden-yellow skin. It is slightly larger and has a more pulpy flesh than the closely related purple passion fruit.

YELLOW SPLIT PEA
(Green Split Pea)
See *Pea*.

YELLOW SQUASH
See *Crookneck Squash*.

YELLOWTAIL FLOUNDER
(Yellowtail Dab)
A flatfish (*Limanda ferruginea*) caught off the north-east coast of North America. It is olive-brown with rusty spots on the upper side and is distinguished from its near relatives in the flounder family by the yellowish tail. It grows up to 40 cm/16 inches long and weighs about 500 g/18 oz. It is a close relative of the European dab. The fish can be poached, steamed, baked, fried or grilled.

YIAOURTI
The name used in Greece for yogurt.

YIOUVETSI
A Greek speciality consisting of lamb braised in tomato sauce or soup and served with a topping of cheese and macaroni.

YOGURT
(Natural Yogurt, Plain Yogurt, Unsweetened Yogurt, Yahourt, Yaourti, Yiaourti, Yoghourt, Yoghurt, Yogur, Yourt, Yourti)
A viscous product, dating back many centuries, which is the traditional cultured milk of western Asia and the Balkans. Yogurt can be made from the milk of cows, ewes, buffaloes and goats but, in Britain, the tendency is to concentrate on cows' milk for commercial yogurt production. This milk may be whole, partially skimmed, skimmed, evaporated or dried, or any combination of these blended together to achieve the correct mixture for a specific type of yogurt. Yogurt has always been held in the highest possible esteem, especially in Bulgaria where it is said to be responsible for the remarkable longevity of some of the native people. *Lactobacillus bulgaricus*, the organism which gives yogurt its distinctive flavour, was first isolated and named by Metchnikoff at the Pasteur Institute at the beginning of the 20th century; fairly late, considering that yogurt and cultured milks had already been produced for hundreds of years in the Balkans. Yogurt is produced according to the taste of individual countries and, while Britain prefers a firm consistency coupled with a mild acidic flavour, much of the rest of Europe chooses yogurt which is fairly fluid and relatively acidic in taste. British yogurt is made from the types of milk listed above and is pasteurized at between 70–95°C/158–203°F for between 5 minutes and 1 hour. It is then homogenized. The pasteurization which the mixture undergoes destroys any harmful bacteria which may be present and makes it a better medium for growth of the

yogurt organisms. This process, together with homogenization, helps to improve the consistency and firmness of the yogurt and also ensures a creamy flavour and smoother, velvety texture. When the milk has cooled, it is mixed with a culture made from equal amounts of *Lactobacillus bulgaricus* and *Streptococcus thermophilus*. The yogurt, be it natural or fruit-flavoured, is incubated in the containers in which it is sold. The cartons are filled, capped, heat-sealed and incubated in an oven at 37–44°C/99–111°F for 4–6 hours. After incubation, the product is cooled gradually to 4.5°C/40°F. If possible, the yogurt should be kept at this temperature until consumed. When labelled low-fat, the yogurt yields approximately 52 kilocalories per 100 g/4 oz and has a refrigerator life of about 10 days. It has the same nutritional value as milk and is a high-protein food, containing vitamins A and D. Yogurt should be kept cool and eaten fresh, especially the unpasteurized variety where the bacteria remain 'live'. When it is stale, the yogurt develops an acid taste and separates.

YORK

(Cambridge Cheese)
A soft, English cheese made from raw or pasteurized cows' milk. It has a rich, fine flavour and is very creamy in texture.

YORK HAM

Superior English ham from York which is cured with dry salt, sugar, saltpetre and spices, left to mature for a minimum of 3 months and then usually smoked over oak chips. It is mild, pink, firm, tender and boiled before serving. York ham has now become a general term to describe any variety of cooked ham.

YORKSHIRE CHEESECAKE

(Yorkshire Curd Tart)
A typically British open tart, made from shortcrust pastry filled with a mixture of curd cheese, butter or margarine, currants, eggs, sugar, grated lemon peel and nutmeg. Sometimes sieved cottage cheese is substituted for the curd cheese.

YORKSHIRE PARKIN

Similar to gingerbread but containing fine or medium oatmeal. It originated in Leeds in Yorkshire.

YORKSHIRE PUDDING

A savoury baked pudding made from a pouring batter. In the North of England it precedes the main course; in other parts of the country it is an accompaniment to roast beef.

YORKSHIRE SPICE BREAD

(Spice Bread)
A heavily-spiced fruit cake from the North of England which is raised with either yeast or baking powder. In texture, it is a cross between bread and cake.

YOUNGBERRY

A fruit which is a hybrid of the loganberry and the dewberry and was developed in the southern United States by a man called Young. It looks like a rather large, dark red loganberry and may be eaten raw or used in recipes instead of the blackberry or raspberry.

YUCA

See *Cassava*.

YULE LOG

An Anglicized version of France's *bûche de Noël*, also served traditionally at Christmas.

YUNNAN

Produced in the mountainous Yunnan province of south-west China, a traditional cheese which is hand-made from goats' milk.

Z

ZABADY
(Zabade, Roba, Rob)
The name used in Egypt, the Sudan and Iraq for yogurt.

ZABAGLIONE
(Zabaione)
A light-textured, foamy dessert made from Marsala, egg yolks and sugar. It is an Italian speciality and is always served warm.

ZABAGLIONE SAUCE
A foamy Italian sauce made from whipped eggs, sugar and Marsala. It should be served warm over canned fruit, steamed or baked puddings, fruit flans and baked apples.

ZAKOUSSOTCHNYÏ
A cheese from the USSR, made from pasteurized cows' milk. It is the Russian version of Camembert.

ZAKUSKI
The open table of old Russia, similar to those provided in Scandinavia; also, the Russian word for *hors d'oeuvre*.

ZAMPONE
An Italian speciality from Emilia-Romagna, made from a well-spiced pork sausage mixture which is packed into a boned pig's trotter. It is gently boiled and served with potatoes and sometimes a sweet sauce resembling *zabaglione*.

ZANDER
The name given to the freshwater pike-perch caught in European rivers and lakes, particularly in Germany, and considered a great delicacy.

ZARZUELA
A Spanish stew of assorted seafood, primarily shellfish. The word *zarzuela* is given to light, comic Spanish operettas, a reflection on the stew which is, in itself, bright and cheerful in flavour and appearance.

ZATZIKI
(Talattouri, Tsatsiki, Tzajiki)
A Greek dip made from grated cucumber, yogurt, garlic, oil, vinegar, mint and seasonings. It is served as an appetizer.

ZESTER
A small implement, comprising a wooden handle and metal blade. The square-ended blade is tipped with fine cutting perforations which remove the peel or zest from citrus fruits in thin, narrow strips.

ZEYTINYĂGLI SEBZETER
A Turkish speciality consisting of mixed vegetables, garlic and seasonings which are simmered slowly until tender. The mixture is sprinkled with chopped parsley and served lightly chilled.

ZIEGEN
The German term for goats' milk cheese.

à la ZINGARA
French term for food cooked in gypsy style with a garnish of ham, tongue, mushrooms and tomatoes.

ZITI
(Zita)
Fairly thick macaroni in long lengths, which can be broken into smaller pieces as desired.

ZITI MEZZE
(Zita Mezze)
A slightly thinner version of *ziti*.

ZITONI
Macaroni-type pasta, double the thickness of *ziti*.

ZSENDICE
A rich ewes' milk cheese from Hungary which is like a fairly smooth curd cheese.

ZUCCHINI
See *Courgette*.

ZUNGENWURST
A German blood sausage interspersed with pieces of tongue and fat.

ZUPPA INGLESE
An Italian version of trifle made with a base of macaroons moistened with Marsala and a topping of custard, decorated with whipped cream and glacé fruits.

ZUPPA PAVESE
An Italian dish based on a clear soup and a speciality of Venice and Liguria. Slices of toast topped with poached eggs are floated on bowls of clear beef broth and each serving is sprinkled with grated Parmesan cheese.

ZWIEBACK
French term for rusk, also used in German.

ZWIEBELROSTBRATEN
A Viennese version of fried steak and onions with gravy. The traditional accompaniments are fried potatoes and gherkins.

Index of Cross-References

This index enables you to trace those words for foods, ingredients, etc. which have an interesting part to play in more than one dictionary definition. After each word in the index there follows a list of the main dictionary entries in which the cross-referred term is mentioned.